A Library
of Literary
Criticism

Leonard S. Klein

General Editor

A Library
of Literary
Criticism

Frederick Ungar Publishing Co.

New York

MODERN BLACK WRITERS

Compiled and edited by

MICHAEL POPKIN

*Selections in these volumes
are quoted with the approval of copyright owners
and may not be reprinted elsewhere without their consent.
The exact source is given at the end of each selection.
For acknowledgments see p. 489.*

Library of Congress Cataloging in Publication Data

Main entry under title:

Modern black writers.

   (A Library of literary criticism)
   Includes index.
   1. Literature—Black authors—History and criticism—
Addresses, essays, lectures.   I. Popkin, Michael.
II. Series.
PN841.M58   809'.889'6   76–15656
ISBN 0–8044–3258–9

Third Printing, 1983

INTRODUCTION

The past ten years have seen the phenomenal growth of Black Studies in colleges and universities throughout the United States. The courses and special programs that were instituted in the late 1960s, usually in response to student demand, have prospered and led, in turn, to a large number of anthologies, reprintings, and scholarly studies. To some degree this expanded interest in black writers reflects the significance of many younger writers who had barely begun their careers ten years ago. To a larger extent, however, literary works by Africans and Afro-Americans are simply beginning to assume the importance that should have been theirs all along.

More and more critics are looking at the work of black writers as a totality, and searching for what Margaret Walker Alexander calls the "common system that we share whether we are Afro-Americans, Afro-Caribbeans, or native Black Africans." Many college courses, such as the surveys taught by Ezekiel Mphahlele at the University of Pennsylvania, "The Novel of the Black World" and "The Poetry of the Black World," deal with the similarities and contrasts among African, Afro-American, and Afro-Caribbean writers. This effort to make connections between black writers from seemingly quite different backgrounds has been intensified by the renewed interest of black Americans in their not-so-distant African roots.

"What is Africa to me?" asked Countee Cullen, who responded with a magical dreamscape. In general, Africa is conceived by black American writers as something of a lost paradise, an idyllic land in which oppression did not exist and life was made meaningful by a complex system of inherited values. The way in which the best African writers portray their land before the coming of colonialism is often remarkably similar to that American vision of a vanished Eden, but presents enough illuminating variations to make a close study of such works as Chinua Achebe's *Things Fall Apart* and Thomas Mofolo's *Chaka* rewarding. The theme of the tragic and horrifying passage between African freedom and American bondage is treated not only by the Americans Robert Hayden (in "Middle Passage") and Amiri Baraka (in *Slave Ship*) but by the Barbadians George Lamming (in *Natives of My Person*) and Edward Brathwaite (in his poetic trilogy *Rights of Passage*). The experience of oppression in America is not entirely without analogies to the demeaning experience of living as a third-class citizen in contemporary South Africa; it is therefore not surprising to find striking similarities between the autobiography of Richard Wright and that of Peter Abrahams.

The new American awareness of Africa was given recent thrust by the publication in 1976 of *Roots*, followed closely by its television dramatization. Alex Haley's discovery of his African ancestors has had an incalculable impact on the imagination of black Americans, who no longer see their individual and collective past as inaccessible. One can easily understand why what Addison Gayle, Jr., called the Black Aesthetic and applied to Afro-American writers has been further expanded to encompass black writers from Africa and the Caribbean as well. Margaret Walker Alexander states the case very forcefully:

> Just as there are Anglo-Saxon and white American standards by virtue of our segregated systems of education, religious institutions and separated ethnic and national cultures there are, of necessity, a black standard, a set of black value-judgments and what is more, a history of traditions of black idioms, and black conceptualizations that determine this ethos and this philosophic system of aesthetics.

Evidence both for and against the existence of a world-wide Black Aesthetic will be found in the selections in this volume, which brings together the essential critical background for a consideration of the best creative work by the black writers of this century. Readers will be directed by these excerpts to the most important writers and critics not only in the English language but in French and in some African languages as well. There are other contexts in which to consider any of the eighty writers in this volume, but the fact that they are gathered together here may enable the reader to draw unexpected and meaningful parallels among novelists, poets, and dramatists who were previously considered to be more than an ocean apart.

The "mainstream" of world literature, as it is usually traced, flows inexorably from its origins in Greece and Rome through the Middle Ages and Renaissance in Western Europe, ultimately to wind its way around what Edmund Wilson called *Axel's Castle*, an imposing edifice created by the contributions of a handful of prominent writers, all from Western Europe and the United States. Traditional introductions to literature deal rather summarily with the largest part of the world; what college students read in survey courses is what John A. Williams has called the "literature of the winners." There is little use in urging a broadening of the standard classical curriculum when that curriculum now seems threatened with abandonment in favor of popularized psychology and sociology. Nevertheless, any effort to communicate the "best that is known and thought" has to deal with some of the writers in this volume, if the true scope of twentieth-century literature is not to be totally falsified. *Modern Black Writers* is thus meant as a means of calling attention to worthwhile literary works, not as another attempt to define the nature and purpose of black writing.

The assertion of an entity called Negritude, first made by the African Léopold Sédar Senghor, was at least partly based on the study of American writers, and was certainly meant to link all the black peoples of the world in a more than fraternal unity. Senghor made a distinction between the analytical reason that he called characteristically European and the intuitive, spontaneous emotions that enabled blacks to participate fully in objects instead of evaluating them coldly from afar. Senghor's definitions of Negritude have shifted with the years, but their effect is to make literary productions by Africans and Afro-Americans categorically different from all other works of world literature. This difference is seen as the inevitable result of the African experience, however, not as an aesthetic formula for black writers to follow. To achieve Negritude, a black writer needed only to cast off the inappropriate lessons taught by Europe.

For many black American writers and critics, however, who have been thinking more of their own situation than that of Black Africa, the Black Aesthetic is a conscious goal which all black writers must set for themselves; otherwise they risk being totally useless to their race or, worse, serving the interests of the white oppressors. Senghor wished to validate Negritude as a cultural force worthy of being set alongside the European tradition. A black American writer like Baraka, however, who once drew on that European tradition in *The System of Dante's Hell*, now wants no part of it; for writers like Baraka the Black Aesthetic is not *another* cultural system but a radical alternative.

It then follows that the only ones who should properly be writing about black literature are black writers and critics. As Addison Gayle, Jr., has written, "To evaluate the life and culture of black people, it is necessary that one live the black experience." This notion sounds bizarre if not repugnant to those thinking in traditional humanistic terms. Cannot a Swedish critic, for example, write lucidly about Italian literature? The difference, of course, is that Sweden has not been oppressing Italy for hundreds of years, and the critic cannot stand accused of simply continuing that oppression in another form, of using culture as a weapon when all other weapons have failed. While Africans like Chinua Achebe are simply irritated at the way European outsiders set themselves up as experts on Ibo village life, many black Americans could more properly be described as furious that their literature has been seized upon by white critics, misrepresented by them, and usually denigrated by them.

By the very nature of Ungar's Library of Literary Criticism, which sets out to present as wide a range of critical viewpoints as possible, any critical doctrine that would drastically narrow that range cannot be a determining factor in the selection of excerpts to be included here. As it happens, well over half of these excerpts are by blacks, but the uninformed reader would be hard-pressed to determine the racial origin of many of these critics on the basis of their analyses and judgments. For one thing, this literary arena has been the scene of more intense infighting than most others, and more incisive attacks have come from fellow black writers than from the white critics outside the arena. For another thing, not all the black writers and critics represented here share all or even part of the Black Aesthetic; Charles W. Chesnutt or Jean Toomer would probably have been highly offended by it. Finally, any critical dogma is only as good as its ability to provoke thought when practiced by a good critic. The excellence of Addison Gayle, Jr.'s *The Way of the New World* is the best justification for the Black Aesthetic, just as the excellence of such French critics as Jean Wagner and Michel Fabre is the best reason for opening the doors of criticism of black writers as widely as possible.

The eighty writers discussed in this volume are all noted primarily for their work in either fiction, poetry, or drama. The emphasis of this series has meant not including some remarkable black authors best known for essayistic writings, a list ranging from W. E. B. Du Bois to Alex Haley. Similarly, blacks writing in Spanish or Portuguese, and usually considered primarily in the context of Latin American literature, have not been included. It has been necessary to omit many interesting younger writers, for lack of enough substantial criticism dealing with their work. A critical consensus is sometimes slow in forming, and even Ishmael Reed and Ayi Kwei Armah, perhaps the most important new writers of the past ten years, remain highly controversial figures, as the selections dealing with their work illustrate. In short, this volume attempts to reflect the current state of writers' reputations, not to create it.

Few of these eighty writers are the objects of adequate full-length studies. Fortunately, however, a number of outstanding surveys have been published quite recently, chief among them O. R. Dathorne's *The Black Mind* and Arthur P. Davis's *From the Dark Tower*. It is to these surveys, all of them represented in this volume, that interested readers should first turn for additional information.

The criticism reprinted here has been selected not only from books, of course, but also from a large number of periodicals, many of them available now only in a handful of specialized collections. In the field of black literature, as in so many other fields, periodicals spring into existence, flower, and disappear instantly when the money runs out or the founder moves on. At the moment a record number of specialized journals seems to be flourishing, and more are announced almost weekly. Those interested in keeping abreast of new publications would be well advised to read such periodicals as *The Black Scholar*, *The Journal of Commonwealth Literature*, *CLA Journal*, and a host of others.

The writers included in this volume are arranged alphabetically. The critical excerpts dealing with each writer's work are arranged chronologically, almost always beginning with a very early review and concluding with a very recent summary. Not only are all the leading critics represented many times each, but as often as possible writers whose work is discussed in this volume also appear as critics, discussing the work of their colleagues. The listing of Authors as Critics should be used in conjunction with the Index to Critics to find all the passages in which Langston Hughes, for example, writes about his contemporaries. The list of Works Mentioned includes every work in the text, followed by the year that work was first published. In the case of works originally written in a language other than English, a literal translation is used in the text, and the title of the published translation, if any, is given in the Works Mentioned section. A dagger at the end of the credit line indicates translations made by the editor, in collaboration with Debra Popkin.

The editor wishes to express his appreciation to the Schomburg Collection of the New York Public Library, whose preservation is so crucial to the study of black writing; and to Leonard S. Klein, the General Editor of A Library of Literary Criticism, for his continuing advice and encouragement.

M. P.

AUTHORS INCLUDED

Abrahams, Peter
Achebe, Chinua
   (Albert Chinualumogu)
Aidoo, Ama Ata
   (Christina Ama Ata Aidoo)
Alexis, Jacques-Stéphen
Aluko, T. M.
Amadi, Elechi
Anthony, Michael
Armah, Ayi Kwei
Attaway, William
Awoonor, Kofi
   (George Awoonor-Williams)
Baldwin, James
Baraka, Amiri
   (LeRoi Jones)
Beti, Mongo
   (Alexandre Biyidi)
Bhêly-Quénum, Olympe
Bontemps, Arna
Brathwaite, Edward
Brooks, Gwendolyn
Brown, Sterling A.
Brutus, Dennis
Bullins, Ed
Camara, Laye
Césaire, Aimé
Chesnutt, Charles W.
Clark, John Pepper
Cullen, Countee
Dadié, Bernard Binlin
Damas, Léon-Gontran
Demby, William
Diop, Birago
Diop, David

Dunbar, Paul Laurence
Ekwensi, Cyprian
Ellison, Ralph
Gaines, Ernest J.
Hansberry, Lorraine
Harris, Wilson
Hayden, Robert
Himes, Chester
Hughes, Langston
Hurston, Zora Neale
Johnson, James Weldon
Jordan, A. C.
Kane, Cheikh Hamidou
Kelley, William Melvin
Killens, John Oliver
Kunene, Mazisi
   (Raymond Mazisi Kunene)
La Guma, Alex
Lamming, George
Laye, Camara
   (*See* Camara, Laye)
Maran, René
Marcelin, Pierre
   (*See* Thoby-Marcelin, Philippe)
McKay, Claude
Mittelholzer, Edgar
Mofolo, Thomas
Morrison, Toni
Mphahlele, Ezekiel
Mqhayi, S. E. K.
Ngugi wa Thiong'o
   (James Ngugi)
Nzekwu, Onuora
Okara, Gabriel
Okigbo, Christopher

AUTHORS BY COUNTRY

BARBADOS

Brathwaite, Edward
Lamming, George

BENIN

Bhêly-Quénum, Olympe

CAMEROON

Beti, Mongo
Oyono, Ferdinand

CONGO

U Tam'si, Tchicaya

FRENCH GUIANA

Damas, Léon-Gontran

GAMBIA

Peters, Lenrie

GHANA

Aidoo, Ama Ata
Armah, Ayi Kwei
Awoonor, Kofi

GUINEA

Camara, Laye

GUYANA

Harris, Wilson
Mittelholzer, Edgar

HAITI

Alexis, Jacques-Stéphen
Marcelin, Pierre
Roumain, Jacques
Thoby-Marcelin, Philippe

IVORY COAST

Dadié, Bernard Binlin

JAMAICA

McKay, Claude

KENYA

Ngugi wa Thiong'o

LESOTHO

Mofolo, Thomas

MARTINIQUE

Césaire, Aimé
Maran, René

NIGERIA

Achebe, Chinua
Aluko, Timothy
Amadi, Elechi
Clark, John Pepper
Ekwensi, Cyprian
Nzekwu, Onuora
Okara, Gabriel
Okigbo, Christopher
Soyinka, Wole
Tutuola, Amos

RHODESIA

Brutus, Dennis

SENEGAL

Diop, Birago
Diop, David
Kane, Cheikh Hamidou
Sembène, Ousmane
Senghor, Léopold Sédar

SOUTH AFRICA

Abrahams, Peter
Jordan, A. C.
Kunene, Mazisi
La Guma, Alex
Mphahlele, Ezekiel
Mqhayi, S. E. K.
Plaatje, Sol T.
Vilakazi, B. W.

ST. LUCIA

Walcott, Derek

TRINIDAD AND TOBAGO

Anthony, Michael

UGANDA

p'Bitek, Okot

UNITED STATES

Attaway, William
Baldwin, James
Baraka, Amiri
Bontemps, Arna
Brooks, Gwendolyn
Brown, Sterling A.
Bullins, Ed
Chesnutt, Charles W.
Cullen, Countee
Demby, William
Dunbar, Paul Laurence
Ellison, Ralph
Gaines, Ernest J.
Hansberry, Lorraine
Hayden, Robert
Himes, Chester
Hughes, Langston
Hurston, Zora Neale
Johnson, James Weldon
Kelley, William Melvin
Killens, John Oliver
Morrison, Toni
Reed, Ishmael
Thurman, Wallace
Tolson, Melvin B.
Toomer, Jean
Walker, Alice
Walker, Margaret
Williams, John A.
Wright, Richard

AUTHORS AS CRITICS

The following is a listing of authors included in this book who are also quoted as critics on their colleagues. See the Index to Critics, which begins on p. 509, for complete details.

Abrahams, Peter
Achebe, Chinua
Aidoo, Ama Ata
Alexis, Jacques-Stéphen
Awoonor, Kofi
Baldwin, James
Baraka, Amiri
Beti, Mongo
Bhêly-Quénum, Olympe
Bontemps, Arna
Brathwaite, Edward
Brooks, Gwendolyn
Brown, Sterling A.
Bullins, Ed
Clark, John Pepper
Cullen, Countee
Diop, David
Ekwensi, Cyprian
Ellison, Ralph
Harris, Wilson
Himes, Chester

Hughes, Langston
Hurston, Zora Neale
Johnson, James Weldon
Jordan, A. C.
Kelley, William Melvin
Kunene, Mazisi
Lamming, George
Maran, René
McKay, Claude
Mphahlele, Ezekiel
Ngugi wa Thiong'o
Reed, Ishmael
Senghor, Léopold Sédar
Soyinka, Wole
Thoby-Marcelin, Philippe
Thurman, Wallace
Tolson, Melvin B.
Walker, Alice
Walker, Margaret
Williams, John A.
Wright, Richard

PERIODICALS USED

Where no abbreviation is indicated, the periodical references are used in full.

	Africa (London)
AfricaR	Africa Report (New York)
AT	Africa Today (Denver)
AA	African Affairs (London)
AfrA	African Arts (Los Angeles)
AfrC	The African Communist (London)
AfrF	African Forum (New York)
ALT	African Literature Today (Canterbury)
AfrS	African Studies (Johannesburg)
AfrSR	African Studies Review (East Lansing, Mich.)
	L'Afrique actuelle (Poissy, France)
	America (New York)
ASch	The American Scholar (Washington, D.C.)
Atlantic	The Atlantic Monthly (Boston)
BantuS	Bantu Studies (Johannesburg)
	Bim (Christ Church, Barbados)
BO	Black Orpheus (Ibadan, Nigeria)
BlackS	The Black Scholar (Sausalito, Cal.)
BlackW	Black World (Chicago)
	The Book Buyer (New York)
BkWd	Book World (Chicago)
Bkm	The Bookman (New York)
BA	Books Abroad (Norman, Okla.)
BAALE	The Bulletin of the Association for African Literature in English (Freetown, Sierra Leone)
CS	Cahiers du Sud (Marseille)
CarQ	Caribbean Quarterly (Mona, Jamaica)
CarS	Caribbean Studies (Río Pedras, Puerto Rico)
	Choice (Middletown, Conn.)
CSM	The Christian Science Monitor (Boston)
CLAJ	CLA Journal (Baltimore)
Cmty	Commentary (New York)

Com	Commonweal (New York)
	Congo-Afrique (later Zaïre-Afrique, Kinshasa)
	Congressional Record—Senate (Washington, D.C.)
CL	Contemporary Literature (Madison, Wisc.)
Crisis	The Crisis (New York)
CA	Cuadernos americanos (Mexico City)
EAJ	East Africa Journal (Nairobi)
	Ebony (Chicago)
ECr	L'esprit créateur (Lawrence, Kan.)
	Esquire (New York)
	Europe (Paris)
FilmQ	Film Quarterly (Berkeley, Cal.)
	Freedomways (New York)
FR	The French Review (Chapel Hill, N.C.)
	The Guardian (Cape Town)
	Haïti-Journal (Port-au-Prince)
Harper	Harper's Magazine (New York)
	Hémisphères (Brooklyn)
	Holiday (Indianapolis)
HdR	The Hudson Review (New York)
	Ibadan (Ibadan, Nigeria)
IowaR	The Iowa Review (Iowa City, Ia.)
	Joliso (Nairobi)
JCL	The Journal of Commonwealth Literature (London, later Leeds)
JNALA	Journal of the New African Literature and the Arts (New York)
LO	The Legon Observer (Legon, Ghana)
LetF	Les lettres françaises (Paris)
List	The Listener (London)
LHY	The Literary Half-Yearly (Mysore, India)
LitI	Literature & Ideology (Toronto)
London	The London Magazine (London)
MakJ	Makerere Journal (Kampala, Uganda)
MR	The Massachusetts Review (Amherst, Mass.)
	Mawazo (Kampala, Uganda)
MQR	The Michigan Quarterly Review (Ann Arbor, Mich.)
ModQ	The Modern Quarterly (New York)
	Le monde (Paris)
	Ms. (New York)
Nation	The Nation (New York)
NALF	Negro American Literature Forum (later Black American Literature Forum; Terre Haute, Ind.)
NegroD	Negro Digest (Chicago)
NQ	The Negro Quarterly (New York)
NewA	The New African (London)
NLr	The New Leader (New York)

NewL	New Letters (Kansas City, Mo.)
NR	The New Republic (Washington, D.C.)
NS	New Statesman (London)
NSN	The New Statesman and Nation (London)
NYHT	New York Herald Tribune Book Section (New York)
NYP	The New York Post (New York)
NYR	The New York Review of Books (New York)
NYT	The New York Times Book Review (New York)
NYTts	The New York Times, Sunday theater section (New York)
Nwk	Newsweek (New York)
NigM	Nigeria Magazine (Lagos)
NRF	La nouvelle revue française (Paris)
Obs	The Observer (London)
	Okike (Amherst, Mass., later Nsukka, Nigeria)
	Opportunity (New York)
PR	Partisan Review (New Brunswick, N.J.)
PRA	Partisan Review and Anvil (New York)
PP	Philologica Pragensia (Prague)
	Phylon (Atlanta)
	Players (DeKalb, Ill.)
	PM (New York)
	Poetry (Chicago)
PoetryA	Poetry Australia (Five Dock, N.S.W.)
PA	Présence africaine (Paris)
	Punch (London)
Reporter	The Reporter (New York)
REL	A Review of English Literature (London)
RdP	La revue de Paris (Paris)
SR	Saturday Review (New York)
SAO	South African Outlook (Mowbray, South Africa)
SoR	The Southern Review (Baton Rouge, La.)
SWR	Southwest Review (Dallas, Tex.)
Spec	The Spectator (London)
	Standpunte (Stellenbosch, South Africa)
SBL	Studies in Black Literature (Fredericksburg, Va.)
	The Sunday Times (London)
TamR	The Tamarack Review (Toronto)
TDR	TDR: The Drama Review (New York)
TM	Les temps modernes (Paris)
TP	Temps présent (Paris)
	Tendances (Paris)
TLS	TLS: The Times Literary Supplement (London)
TSW	Toronto Star Weekly (Toronto)
	Transition (Kampala, Uganda; later Accra, Ghana; later Ife, Nigeria)
TCL	Twentieth Century Literature (Hempstead, N.Y.)
UCM	The University of Chicago Magazine (Chicago)

VV	The Village Voice (New York)
VQR	The Virginia Quarterly Review (Charlottesville, Va.)
	Voices (Portland, Me.)
WA	West Africa (London)
WAR	West African Review (Liverpool)
WLB	Wilson Library Bulletin (Bronx, N.Y.)
	World (New York)
WLWE	World Literature Written in English (Arlington, Tex.)
YR	The Yale Review (New Haven, Conn.)
YULG	The Yale University Library Gazette (New Haven, Conn.)

Modern
Black
Writers

ABRAHAMS, PETER (1919–   )

SOUTH AFRICA

Mr. Peter Abrahams is a South African native. This fact dominates whatever he writes. In South Africa, as you travel by train, you look out of the window and see, in that large, empty land, a solitary native walking delicately, in his ochre-coloured blanket, across the red earth dotted with scrubby trees of an incredible apple-green. It makes a fine picture, and then you forget it. Or if you have a house you have also a native "boy," or, in the Cape, a coloured maid. Then it is a case of the servant question, which, from the master's point of view, is the same everywhere. And sometimes, in very liberal company, you discuss the native problem, generally with the feeling it is our problem, not his. Altogether it is high time Mr. Abrahams came along to remind us that ultimately it is not a matter of pictures or servants or political embarrassments but of a backward society that must eventually be educated and given generous opportunity.

Dark Testament is a miscellany—scenes from the author's life and two or three short stories, also largely from life though much influenced by the writing of Mr. William Saroyan. Naturally it is an emotional book, but it is first of all a book—in spite of alien influences and the author's melancholy cast of mind the most honest piece of literature that has come out of Africa for years. The reader will find that familiar scenes have taken on strange shapes. This is not the polite Cape Town (for instance) of Malay flowerwomen still sitting in the urban principal street or of parties at Kelvin Grove: this is District Six and the region round Roeland Street as seen by those who must live in them. This is the outlook of those whose life is squalor and poverty and nothing whatever to look forward to. On the spot it is as easy to see things too large as it is, with laziness or lack of conscience, to ignore them. But if Mr. Abrahams can presently add humour, to forestall the charge that he has no sense of proportion, he will have provided exactly the loud, deep, moving voice his nation sorely needs.

TLS. Jan. 16, 1943, p. 34

1

Wild Conquest, which is a story of the Great Trek, has a special interest, for its author, Mr. Peter Abrahams, is a South African Negro. He writes with vividness and great dignity. He is just to the Boers, and his picture of the Matabele, about to be crushed, moves one with its restraint and suppressed emotion. This is a good novel in its own right, and it may be the forerunner of an entire school of African literary art.

C. P. Snow. *The Sunday Times*. May 20, 1951, p. 3

Undoubtedly *Black Boy* is only one daguerreotype of the South as it was in Richard Wright's youth. There are other, fairer pictures just as true. No one book, no one individual, has ever told all there is to tell about our home. But *Black Boy* is not, therefore, to be waved airily aside. It reveals too much about an effect, the effect of a system upon a person sensitive enough to produce some of the most valuable writing in this our time.

Now, from one of South Africa's Coloured people comes a book which it is hard not to compare with *Black Boy*. Like Richard Wright, Peter Abrahams is a foremost voice of a distressed group. Like *Black Boy*, Abrahams' *Tell Freedom* covers the years of boyhood and youth its author spent in an environment that galled him to the quick. Like *Black Boy*, *Tell Freedom* ends with its author on his way to what he hopes will be a freer life.

But *Tell Freedom* is a tenderer record than *Black Boy*. That is, however, only because Peter Abrahams is a gentler spirit than Richard Wright. It has nothing to do with the picture of South Africa he paints or with its racial tensions between whites, Coloured, natives and Orientals. Much of this recital is played out against the background of Johannesburg, in a racial slum—named Vrededorp—in which Peter Abrahams spent his youth. It shifts in brief episodes to the country, to the missionary college he attended, and finally, first, to Cape Town and at last to Durban, whence he embarks at the book's end for England. And yet, in a sense, the scene never shifts. Wherever it takes us, the great, unforgettable features are the virulence and the obduracy of South African color caste.

Blyden Jackson. *Phylon*. 15, 4, 1954, pp. 410–11

Had [*Mine Boy*] not been about a South African Negro, I dare say no one would pay it much attention, for it clearly lacks distinction of any sort, though the subject leads one to expect vastly more of the sociological and the melodramatic than actually emerges. The story of Xuma, the young Negro who comes to work in the mines and runs up against the racial problem, has possibilities that we who have had our proletarian novel could face with equanimity.

Mr. Abrahams has not focused his lens. He does not decide, at any point, whether he is writing a picaresque novel, a tract, a love story, or a kind of *Bildungsroman*. Nor does Mr. Abrahams have the novelist's eye, the eye for detail which reveals a way of life and a society. His people drink beer, dance, fight, and love rather in the style of Catfish Row, and although the author tells us how warmly human everybody is, and how deeply everyone feels for everyone else, there doesn't seem to be any particular reason why they should. As for the characters themselves, they are shadows. We have no sense of their blackness as a race nor of their essence as individuals, and again I suggest that this lack derives from the author's uncertainty as to his own intention: neither he nor the reader is ever sure of just how to take the story. Is this a call to arms? to empathy? to esthetic appreciation?

The ending of the book provides the gauge of the extent of Mr. Abrahams' confusion: Xuma goes rigorously off to jail in support of his white friend, for a reason surely, but not, as it works out in this story, for a reason cogent enough to move us to full sympathy. One simply says to oneself, Life is not, cannot be, like that. Xuma learns that the black man must not lust after the goods of the white man, that white and black must love one another or die, but we see only in the haziest, most sentimental way that this is true. Who on earth would quarrel with the notion? I think I would, when it gets mixed up with art, and in the inevitable confusion, art and life vitiate one another.

All this seems to me as much as to say that Mr. Abrahams has not mastered the two most telling techniques of the novelist: dramatization and expression.

Louis O. Coxe. *YR*. Sept., 1955, pp. 154–55

The first half of [*A Wreath for Udomo*] slowly meanders, its water touching every nook, so that we intimately know the minutest details about the actors involved. . . .

When the reality comes—when Udomo has to go out to Panafrica for the cause—sacrificing his English girl whom he loves and who has helped to make him—romantic dalliance gives way to ruthless action. The contrast in mood is so striking that the writing could have been done by a different Peter Abrahams, the same one who wrote *Mine Boy* and *Wild Conquest*. Tension mounts all the time. The Africans, not fully realised in the first part of the book, suddenly come into their own. The white men on the coast are handled with a touch of ironic humour.

One feels a genuine involvement in the fates of the actors of this fevered drama and each one comes to an end at once unexpected and dramatic but thoroughly in character. The climax of the story, achieved by a kind of poetic montage, is grand and leaves a lasting impression on the mind.

If only the same man had written both parts of the book, charging even the dream with a suggestion of the tension to come, the effect would have been better sustained and the book would have lost nothing either artistically or in political intention.

Cyprian Ekwensi. *WAR*. June, 1956, p. 603

Peter Abrahams's *Wild Conquest* is one of the few novels that try to go back to the beginning of the great moral dilemma of black and white. In his story Peter Abrahams (who is himself a black South African) shows how a double burden of savagery and guilt on the part of both black and white bred hatred, and he takes as his starting point the day when the British decreed the freeing of slaves. Out of fear, the Boer masters of a band of black men who have been their slaves precipitate a killing of both black and white. The slaves had intended to leave peaceably the land they had tilled and the homestead that they had built for their masters. But the Boers fear that their ex-slaves will try to take the farm and homestead, as has happened elsewhere, and they kill one of the slaves as a gesture; there is a fight and the Boer family leaves to join the Great Trek to the hinterland, away from the jurisdiction and adminis-tration of the British. They set the homestead on fire behind them.

This novel gives us, too, an idea of what the trek meant to the forebears of those who make up the great majority of the nation—the Africans themselves. The wise man of the Matabele says that the coming of the white man deep into the interior meant "the end of living by the spear and the beginning of living by the head." The book ends at the great clash between black and white, when the Matabele were defeated. It is "the point between yesterday and tomorrow. The old ends here; the new starts here. This is the end of a lifetime. The beginning of a life-time." . . .

A Wreath for Udomo . . . is about the sort of problems ex-victims have to face when they are freed of an imposed system, and have to work out a discipline and morality of their own.

Nadine Gordimer. *TLS*. Aug. 11, 1961, p. 522

[Abrahams] is a classicist who takes less from Europe than from Africa. In Black Africa ancient tales are striking in their *concision*; contemporary tales, in their verbosity. The modern ones can get lost in details and commentaries; the ancient ones are firmly based on *facts*. The fact is an image, which has symbolic value; reasoning cuts off the roots of facts, of *life*. Abrahams has rediscovered the *style* of the ancient tales, thus confirming that there is no truth—or art—but the general.

Let us only compare him to the other South African novelists and story-tellers, who live their stories by presenting them to us under a magnifying-glass, which prevents these writers from *bringing their stories to life*. It is true that *A Wreath for Udomo* was written after a trip to South Africa, but from a distance, with a degree of physical and moral perspective. . . .

The lesson I learn from *A Wreath for Udomo* is the following. Negritude, to express itself, must go beyond itself by going beyond folklore and exoticism. It will do so by returning to the very sources of Negritude: to our ancient art, which is *art* because its subject is *Man* and because its rhythm is marked not by *abundance* but by *restraint*, the very restraint that gives everything its proper place. This is why I say that Peter Abrahams is the *classicist of Negritude*. [1963]

Léopold Sédar Senghor. Liberté I: Négritude et
humanisme (Paris, Éditions du Seuil, 1964),
pp. 427–28, 430†

On the African side in South Africa Peter Abrahams stands high on the list. His early novels, *Dark Testament, Song of the City, Mine Boy*, are all in the Richard Wright tradition. One of his most successful novels though is *Wild Conquest*, a novel based on the story of the Great Trek. The urgency in this novel at times makes the style erratic and patchy, but he gives us introspection and characters who have lives of their own, capable of expansion. But even Abrahams does bother us in some of his passages . . . [when he writes the] kind of protest which limits the emotional and intellectual range of characterization. The total framework of the novel has been chalked out for us; the situations are familiar. We know we are in a country which considers it a crime for two people with different pigmentation to fall in love with each other. The temptations to overplay the situation somehow detract from the impact of the characters.

Abrahams overplays in this novel the ready-made group attitudes and responses. There is an excessive play of fate in the lives of the characters and, as a result, their experience becomes a minute fraction of life. On the other hand, however, Fieta, the coloured woman who emerges from a dissipated life and grows to know and accept the importance of her love for crippled Mad Sam whose own life is perpetual pain, is interesting as a character. The image of Fieta is not limited by any impending disaster from outside herself or from Mad Sam, although these impending disasters loom large and engulf the total lives of these two people. Their image is capable of development. Here again we know that they are underdogs and this makes them vulnerable. There is a wide area of self-response open to them and to the reader. Their conception has no bounds.

David Rubadiri. *Transition*. No. 15, 1964, p. 40

In this autobiographical statement, *Tell Freedom*, where colors and races collide and clash, where social circumstances are fat with poverty and suffering, [Abrahams] moves from the dream within a drop of rain through an ever-increasing, darkening awareness to the point of departure, where the "long night" comes to an end.

From the very beginning of the book, Abrahams sets its basic tonality—the contrapuntal interplay between illusion and reality, between fantasy and actuality—the juxtaposition of the warm security of the author's inner being with the threatening harshness of the outer world. . . .

Christianity had failed him; his love-making had gone awry. He was moving away from his family. He realized that to many whites he seemed as filth, when he was physically flung onto the floor by a shopkeeper who was "near the point of nausea through touching human waste," while another customer boomed something about his being a "black baboon." Even though he was becoming increasingly conscious that many international ideologies and credoes did not extend to the black and Colored man's situation, yet he still attempted to grasp at one of these, Communism. But there, too, the equation did not work; the egalitarian illusion proved fraudulent. To Abrahams, it was ideology without humanity.

And so Peter Abrahams, like so many black writers, has no recourse but to flee from a land which is both tender and austere, for he could not bridge the distance between the open landscape and the closed social reality. In the claustrophobic actuality of South Africa he could not feed the fantasy imagination so necessary to him as a writer.

But any flight by black writers creates another paradox since it is their intelligence and vision which must be called upon to carve freedom for their people, to lead to the justice and dignity which the land itself breathes.

Wilfred Cartey. Introduction to Peter Abrahams, *Tell Freedom* (New York, Macmillan, 1970), pp. vii, xiv

[In *The Path of Thunder*] Abrahams made a bold venture into the complex racial patterns of his early experience. This novel is a tale of melodramatic violence set in the northern Cape Province, the Karroo. In form it is not unlike novels such as [Dickens's] *Little Dorrit*, [Hardy's] *The Return of the Native* and [Faulkner's] *Light in*

August. A mystery about paternity is solved across the colour line (also the line of social class) and the pattern of a dangerous society is exposed by a near blind old woman. . . .

The strong central hero gives cohesion to the work. We are never far from the circle of Lanny's thoughts, which give a focus to the action rather like those of other radical heroes in novels of the 1950s such as [Kingsley Amis's] *Lucky Jim* and [John Wain's] *Hurry on Down.* Like the heroes of Lawrence and Thomas Hardy, Lanny feels with his blood and sees the landscape as an extension of personal experience. . . .

From the widening horizons of London, and doubtless stimulated by his acquaintance with [the Caribbean intellectual and activist] George Padmore and others of his circle, Abrahams attempted increasingly ambitious themes in his next four novels. *Wild Conquest* is a South African's view of the Great Trek without the conventional northwards slant. Abrahams looks southwards as well and shows the process of expansion and invasion from both sides. *A Night of Their Own* is a fragment, again showing both sides, from the modern politics of subversion and mass imprisonment in South Africa. *A Wreath for Udomo* shows the rise to power and betrayal of his aides and a South African confederate by a modern African political leader. *This Island Now* sketches the rise to power and the enfeebled tyranny of a black nationalist party in a Caribbean island. Despite their flaws these are works which provided a new impetus in writing about African subjects.

Christopher Heywood. In Christopher Heywood, ed.,
Perspectives on African Literature (New York,
Africana, 1971), pp. 165, 167–68

The most prolific novelist from South Africa is Peter Abrahams; and his early novel, *Mine Boy*, which was published in 1946 . . . is representative of the South African novel as a whole. The story itself is relatively uncomplicated—an account of a young man's exposure to life in Johannesburg and his work as leader of one of the work crews in a gold mine. The concentration, however, is on life in Johannesburg itself; thus *Mine Boy* is a novel with urbanization as its theme. . . .

There is little plot in *Mine Boy*. Rather, Abrahams' story is one of character and atmosphere, for, like Cyprian Ekwensi's Lagos, Abrahams' picture of Johannesburg's Malay Camp is in many ways the prime concern of his novel. Blacks, Coloureds, and whites are all in the novel but it is only the sections of the story that are set in the Malay Camp among the African characters that are truly alive. The brief sojourns that Xuma makes in the segregated white areas of the city are flat and considerably less realistically drawn; Abrahams' white characters are often given to mouthing ideas of racial equality—rather than living these ideas as the African characters do. . . .

If Xuma is lonely and isolated because of his unfulfilled love and the debilitating life in Johannesburg, there is still companionship. Again and again Abrahams illustrates the growing friendship Xuma shares with Leah, Ma Plank, and Marsy. This is of crucial importance since *Mine Boy* differs so greatly from other African fiction where the family still plays a significant part. In *Mine Boy* the family has been completely destroyed, there is no sense of the communal consciousness. People band together out of a common need. There is no sense of the basic filial unit which plays such an important function in tropical African fiction. Nor are there any children to give the novel warmth and humor and the happiness we have seen in other African novels. Abrahams has created an adult world instead—in a city which eventually destroys its inhabitants. The strong characters, other than Xuma, are all women, and in spite of the optimistic and overly didactic ending, one cannot foresee much of a future for Xuma. He is still young; the city will eventually count him in its toll.

Charles R. Larson. *The Emergence of African Fiction*
(Bloomington, Indiana University Press, 1971),
pp. 162–63, 165–66

Peter Abrahams is a novelist of ideas. He writes about the machinery of politics and power, but he uses his considerable grasp of this area of activity to serve his central interest, which is the problem of individual freedom in contemporary human affairs. . . .

It should be stated at the outset that Abrahams' ability as a writer of fiction is in the middle range, and the grandiose claims made for his work from time to time by propagandists of African literary culture have been misguided. He is a skilful, if flawed, writer, and there is evidence that he finds the writing of fiction arduous. What is most apparent about his fiction is the complete sincerity and honesty of the author. He has not chosen an easy path; he feels every word he writes and seems incapable of writing conscious pot-boilers. The subjects he returns to again and again in his fiction are the problems which have most exercised—and come near to paralysing in the process—the liberal mind in the West since the end of the second world war. They are the problems of how to reconcile the liberal conscience to the unpleasant consequences of necessary action; how to resist inroads made into the integrity of the individual, especially where these inroads are the results of justified attempts to set others free, to put them on the road to the liberal goal of individual fulfilment. Abrahams invokes and even to some extent typifies the liberal dilemma of the twentieth century.

Michael Wade. *Peter Abrahams* (London, Evans Brothers, 1972), pp. 4–5

ACHEBE, CHINUA (1930–   )

NIGERIA

In powerfully realistic prose [Achebe] sets out [in *Things Fall Apart*] to write a fictional but almost documentary account of the day to day happenings in a small Nigerian village without evasion, sophistry or apology. Fascinated one reads about the customs, the culture, and the strange rituals, the fearful hazards of the yam harvest, and the bewildered downfall of our hero Okonkwo, the great wrestler and successful farmer. There is horror in some of the ritual and the superstition, but somehow they are less fearful when simply and naturally described by a writer who clearly has some recollection of them himself. In the same way the Spanish Inquisition is not as horrifying to Roman Catholic zealots as it is to Protestants or even Pagans. There is plenty of humour too, especially in the description of the first two missionaries on the scene, one liberal and gentle and understanding, and the next attacking his problems with fundamentalist rage and zeal. Even a Christian reader must surely compare this last unfavourably with the simple and human medicine man, although the author makes no effort to force any such conclusion.

Altogether the African villagers appear as happy, self-contained people, who like most men, blame or praise the Gods for their sorrows and pleasures. Village discipline was stern, even harsh, but its very inescapability makes nonsense of some of the early descriptions of these villages by explorers and missionaries. Many books and anthropological treatises have told about the power of religious superstition, but here is one which forcefully but impartially gives us the reasons for both.

Mercedes Mackay. *AA*. July, 1958, p. 243

It is a credit to Mr. Achebe's judgement that he has constructed his first novel [*Things Fall Apart*] along very simple lines but I think it possible to find it too simple. Art is, of course, all selection, yet one cannot help remarking that the subject which he tackles in a short novel cannot be exhausted in a twenty-volume anthropological treatise. And although as novel readers we may be interested in anthropological data, we are even more interested in the shifting relations between these data and the adventures of the individual, the modes of thought which produce them and are produced by them. It also seems to me that for the implicit assertion that West Africa has a culture of its own to have its fullest effect, the form of the novel ought to have shown some awareness of the art of this culture. We do not have the novel form, of course, but there are implications in our music, sculpture and folklore which the West African novelist cannot neglect if he wishes to do more than merely imitate a European fashion. (Civilisation is, after all, an integration of diverse regional elements, and we shall not be justified to make use of its resources unless we are prepared to add to them.)

I am in particular disappointed that there is in *Things Fall Apart* so little of the lyricism which marks our village life. So pronounced is this quality that Joyce Cary, an acute observer quite incapable, unfortunately, of interpreting his observations, repeatedly portrayed Nigerian life as a musical farce, and the typical Nigerian as a lyrical half-wit. Mr. Achebe was probably inhibited by the difficulty he experiences in writing passable verse. All the same, I suspect that his sensitivity to "dark" Africa (of the late nineteenth century) is insufficient—and not surprisingly, because his generation did not know the life he is out to present.

Ben Obumselu. *Ibadan*. Feb., 1959, p. 38

Mr. Chinua Achebe is the young Nigerian writer who made something of a name for himself with a first novel called *Things Fall Apart*, which portrayed the collapse of tribal life through the story of one Okonkwo of the Obi tribe. The hero of Mr. Achebe's new novel [*No Longer at Ease*] is the grandson of Okonkwo: Obi Okonkwo who leaves his village to be educated in England. He returns after four years and takes a job as a civil servant in Lagos. He acquires a girl friend. He buys a car. He pays his mother's hospital bills and his brother's school bills. He lends small amounts of money to uneducated Africans. He has trouble repaying the money which the Umuofia Progressive Union raised to send him to London. He has to pay for an abortion. He accepts a bribe. He is arrested. And that is all. His white boss, Mr. Green, says, "I'm all for equality and all that. I for one would hate to live in South Africa. But equality won't alter facts." Another breath of the wind of change has been charted.

It is usual, almost traditional, to pay tribute to the simplicity of style of novels such as this. We tend to harp on about it, as if short words were something new in fiction. I suppose the fact of the matter is that simplicity is all we ask for in the African novel. We want a lucid, uncluttered account of the way life is changing in these territories. We want sound, competent craftsmen to put up the framework; later, when the chronicles of change are more or less complete, some very fortunate writers indeed will be able to fill the framework in, wallowing in the new luxuries of characterisation, motivation, depth, psychology and all the rest of it. Meanwhile we are grateful to such as Mr. Achebe for such unadorned tales as *No Longer at Ease*.

Keith Waterhouse. NS. Sept. 17, 1960, p. 398

No Longer at Ease is bound to create a certain sense of diffuseness and slackness after the austere tragic dignity of *Things Fall Apart*, a dignity which recalls Conrad, who is in fact one of Chinua Achebe's mentors. The fluid world of Obi Okonkwo is simply not susceptible of the same classic treatment, and to have captured it at all is an achievement of sympathy and imagination. Achebe measures the decline in the simple contrast of Obi and his grandfather; the grandson has more humanity, more gentleness, a wider awareness, but he lacks the force and integrity of his ancestor. . . .

If *No Longer at Ease* is something less than a tragedy, it is because Achebe does not see Obi Okonkwo as a tragic hero. The pressures that pull and mould him are all pressures making for compromise and accommodation; these are not the stuff of tragedy but of failure and decline. The alien forces that destroyed old Okonkwo were mysterious and inexorable, but still largely external and dramatic. He could see his enemies and die fighting them, even without comprehending them. But Obi is destroyed by "doing what everyone does"; by running away from scandal, living above his income, taking bribes. The enemies of his integrity are all-pervasive and do not dramatize themselves.

Gerald Moore. Seven African Writers (London,
Oxford University Press, 1962), pp. 68–71

Chinua Achebe chose to bring out his back cloth in relief at the areas of tension. In a sense—not a pejorative one—he is a chronicler, content to follow creases and stress lines, not to impose his own rearrangement on them. That this can be a creative process is demonstrated by the inexorable fate that overtakes his hero, Okonkwo, in *Things Fall Apart*. The demand we make of an expressed way of life is, first and foremost, reality. The writer must impress an acceptance. Enactments of tribal peculiarities must emerge from characters in that society, not interfere with our recognition of basic humanity, not be just a concession to quaintness-mongers. Why, for instance, do we accept so easily and unreservedly the accident of the hero's exploded gun especially as a prelude to the final downfall of one of the village elite? Dissected coldly, events that are not part of the dramatic progression of character or other events are instantly suspect. But Achebe has established another pattern, a rhythm compounded not merely of motives but of understated mysteries —mysteries as much to the characters as to their remote observer—of psychical influences on daily routine, of a man's personal *chi*, of initiations, of guilt and purifications whose ethics are not those of a court of law but of the forces of Nature cycle, of the living and the dead. It is a subtle process, and its first principle, faithfully observed by the author, is the philosophy of acceptance. Not blind, slavish acceptance but a positive faith, an acceptance of forces that begin where the physical leaves off. . . .

Language lends nobility to the life and downfall of Okonkwo; the same language in *No Longer at Ease* merely rebukes the author, as if he has taken his main character too seriously. It is doubtful if Achebe's forte lies in the ability to spit occasionally, or to laugh from the belly when the situation demands it, but he must learn at least to be less prodigal with his stance of a lofty equipoise. For this has bred the greatest objection to his work, this feeling of unrelieved competence, of a lack of the active spark, inspiration.

Wole Soyinka. *ASch.* Summer, 1963, pp. 392–94

Upon reading Chinua Achebe's two novels, *Things Fall Apart*, and its sequel, *No Longer at Ease*, one encounters an interesting structure of tragic characters in the Okonkwo family, intriguing one to seek a means of explaining the situation. . . .

What precisely accounts for the fact that each of these characters in the lineage depicted in the novels was a failure? Achebe himself is probably inclined to think that the *ndi-ocha* (white men) caused it all, and in some respects he could be partially correct. Others might find that the causes of the several failures are ascertainable only because each particular character has such and such a temperament and was faced with certain difficulties which would "naturally" bring about his downfall. I believe that the explanation, if one exists, lies in the fact that Okonkwo severely antagonized the *ndichie* (ancestors) and *Chukwu* (Chineke, Eze Chitoke, Eze-Binigwe, etc.—the High God, Creator, and Giver of all life and power) by killing Ikemefuna, the boy who called Okonkwo "father." Okonkwo thus alienated his *chi* (*God Within*, not "personal god" as Achebe blasphemously refers to *chi*, reflecting possibly a jaundiced attitude toward his own people's religion). . . .

Achebe makes a vainglorious attempt in these two books—and I suspect he will continue so in *Arrow of God*—to ascribe all the evils which occurred in Ibo society to the coming of the white men. But he stacks the cards in the novels, hinting here and there at the truth, yet not explaining fully the substratum of divine forces working to influence the characters. His own motives perhaps are linked with his patent desire to indicate that outsiders can never understand the works of Igbo-speaking writers (whose novels are in English), although one must properly leave the subject of authors' motivations to psychiatrists. Whatever the case may be, however, what caused "things" to "fall apart" and what made the Ibo man "no longer at ease" in the case of Achebe's works were the evil actions of Okonkwo, who brought the wrath of Chukwu, the *alusi* [spirits], and the *ndichie* upon his own lineage.

Austin J. Shelton. *Transition*. March–April, 1964,
pp. 36–37

In a recent interview, Achebe said that having "learned a lot more about these particular people, you know, my ancestors," he had himself come to think of his first book as no longer adequate. Such a writer as he does not have to do research. As he himself admits, when he was born in 1930 things had not changed that much, and as he grew up he was able to talk freely with those whom he now remotely refers to as "ancestors"; ceremonies were still celebrated, with less intensity perhaps than in the old days, but their original meaning could be inferred by a mind mature enough to grasp the significance of their forms. But this is the point: As the author's own imaginative life has thickened with awareness, so the society he writes about—Umuofia in another guise—has also become more complicated, the forces and characters surrounding the central consciousness of the hero standing out in sharper, more radical relief.

Ezeulu, the hero of Achebe's *Arrow of God*, bears a certain resemblance to Okonkwo of *Things Fall Apart*. Again we are confronted with an old man's personal struggle with the undeniable facts of Christianity and colonialism, a struggle exacerbated by tensions and loyalties within the self, and within the clan as related to the self. But here we have the further complication of a god, Ulu, whose agent, or "arrow," this grand old Ezeulu effectively is. And in making Ezeulu the vehicle of a god, Achebe begins to ask a series of psychological and moral questions, questions which we Westerners usually discuss in connection with the exceptional, the fanatical (like Luther or Joan of Arc), but which in the Nigerian context are associated with the deepest common proprieties. What is it like being in a society where *all* men act in the company of the unseen as a real presence, as a plurality of presences whose influences are immediately felt, exploited, and perhaps misinterpreted or dangerously gainsaid?

Judith Illsley Gleason. *This Africa* (Evanston, Ill.,
Northwestern University Press, 1965), pp. 86–87

In two previous novels, *Things Fall Apart* and *No Longer at Ease*, the young Nigerian writer Chinua Achebe performed a difficult task with skill and ease. In each, he played one theme against another to produce a work of fiction that, while striking in the simplicity of both style and story, projects a sense of the complex realities—the passion and the tragedy of change and adjustment, of cultural death and revival, of social disorganization and rebuilding—that only an African who stands astride the two worlds of present-day Africa can truly know. In *Arrow of God*, Achebe has done it again. The new novel is not without faults, but it is a tribute to Achebe's growth as an artist and a man to say that he now commands even greater skill and a deeper compassion than he did before. . . .

As moving as the story itself is, *Arrow of God* is perhaps more remarkable for its vividly pictorial descriptions of tribal village life in eastern Nigeria, and for its insights into the workings of the African mind. The rituals and ceremonies, the logic and passion behind them, all come clear, and we know more of humanity, which has nothing to do with time and place and states imposed upon the soul by the artifices of a social order. *Arrow of God* combines imaginative power with literary gifts that much older and more sophisticated (Western) writers might well envy.

Saunders Redding. *AfrF.* Summer, 1965, pp. 142–43

At first it would seem as though in *Arrow of God*, Achebe is giving us the mixture as before, in *Things Fall Apart*. Several images, proverbs and devices from the old novel reappear. The python is once again a symbol of the Igbo-Christian conflict. The bird *Eneke-nti-Oba* who wrestled with his *chi* appears again to underline a philosophical idea which by its persistence seems central to Achebe's writing. Winterbottom's complete failure to understand the thinking of his subjects or to treat them as human beings instead of administrative pawns, reminds us of the earlier D.O. *Arrow of God* is nevertheless essentially different in conception. While the central conflict in *Things Fall Apart* has been between traditional Igbo civilization and Christian imperialism, the conflict in *Arrow of God* is really within Igbo society itself. . . .

[*Arrow of God*] is more substantial than either of Achebe's two earlier works—more complex than *Things Fall Apart* and hence lacking the endearing simplicity of that novel. Its great contribution is its shift of emphasis from the clash of Africa with the outside world to the internal tensions of Africa itself, a clash which seems to be absent in much African writing. We had this in the urban setting of *No Longer at Ease*, here we have it in an unidealized rural setting.

Achebe neither idealizes nor patronizes the Africa of yesterday. His villages are not paradises. They are the scenes of love as well as hatred, goodwill and envy, peace and war. Thus his novel is a human novel. His success in bringing out the general humanity above the Africanness of his themes is what gives him a high place among African writers.

Eldred Jones. JCL. Sept., 1965, pp. 176, 178

[*A Man of the People*] is doubly significant, for apart from confirming the author's mastery of technique and his succinct use of language (this time it has a relaxed warm flow), it marks a break with his earlier attitude. He has turned his back on the European presence. He no longer feels the need to explain, or point out mistakes, by merely re-creating. The process, I believe, started with *Arrow of God*. But even there (though the teacher is not reacting to the colonizer's view of Africa he is in fact more interested in problems of power and responsibility) the teacher took his time, was patient with his pupils. What has happened in *A Man of the People*—the change in attitude to his audience—is something which can only be felt by following, through the earlier novels, Achebe's creative response to a rapidly changing society.

Now, in the new novel, the teacher talks to his pupils, directly. He has lost patience. He retains self-control in that he does not let anger drive him into incoherent rage and wild lashing. Instead he takes his satirical whip and raps his pupils—with anger, of course, sometimes with pathos verging on tears, but often with bitterness, though this is hardly discernible because below it flow compassion and a zest for life. His pupils are—or ought to be—disturbed. For in *A Man of the People* the teacher accuses them all of complicity in the corruption that has beset our society. *Your* indifference and cynicism has given birth to and nurtured Chief Nanga, he says. . . .

What Achebe has done in *A Man of the People* is to make it impossible or inexcusable for other African writers to do other than address themselves directly to their audiences in Africa—not in a comforting spirit—and tell them that such problems are their concern. The teacher no longer stands apart to contemplate. He has moved with a whip among the pupils, flagellating himself as well as them. He is now the true man of the people. [1966]

Ngugi wa Thiong'o. Homecoming (New York,
Lawrence Hill, 1973), pp. 52, 54

Chinua Achebe is well known as a writer throughout Africa and even beyond. His fame rests on solid personal achievements. As a young man of twenty-eight he brought honour to his native Nigeria by writing

Things Fall Apart, the first novel of unquestioned literary merit from English-speaking West Africa. Critics tend to agree that no African novelist writing in English has yet surpassed Achebe's achievement in *Things Fall Apart*, except perhaps Achebe himself. It was written nine years ago, and since then Achebe has written three novels and won several literary prizes. During this time his reputation has grown like a bush-fire in the harmattan. Today he is regarded by many as Africa's finest novelist.

If ever a man of letters deserved his success, that man is Achebe. He is a careful and fastidious artist in full control of his art, a serious craftsman who disciplines himself not only to write regularly but to write well. He has that sense of decorum, proportion and design lacked by many contemporary novelists, African and non-African alike. He is also a committed writer who believes that it is his duty to serve his society. . . .

What gives each of Achebe's novels an air of historical authenticity is his use of the English language. He has developed not one prose style but several, and in each novel he is careful to select the style or styles that will best suit his subject. In dialogue, for example, a westernized African character will never speak exactly like a European character nor will he speak like an illiterate village elder. Achebe, a gifted ventriloquist, is able to individualize his characters by differentiating their speech. . . . Achebe has devised an African vernacular style which simulates the idiom of Ibo, his native tongue.

Bernth Lindfors. *ALT*. No. 1, 1968, pp. 3–4

To interpret Achebe's work as mere explication of the Nigerian scene, either that of his grandfather's or his own generation, is to mistake his intention and his achievement. In kind with most writers of his generation, he has shown in his published novels and short stories a pre-occupation with certain basic themes, of which the legacy of colonial rule is the central core. It is true that the novels reveal the destructive consequences of the rule of the colonial period. But these are not displayed for their own sake. They are there because they arise out of and reflect to a sensitive mind a manifest indifference and caprice which mirrors life itself. This pre-occupation is found in each of the novels as Achebe explores its meaning and seeks to accommodate himself to it. The heroes of the first three novels have their origins in this. These heroes, conceived in tragic terms, are men in varying degrees conscious of the fact that life turns out to be less manageable and less perfect than they had expected, they react to life in various ways—with courage, honesty and generosity, with pessimism and cynicism—in their attempts to get through life with honour and reward.

It can be argued that for Achebe the principal virtue is to accept stoically what life serves up. But his pre-occupation is more than this: it is the plight of the individual in a world characterized by uncertainty, pain and violence. Achebe is essentially a moralist, concerned with considerations of right and wrong as they are revealed by the individual's responses to the circumstances which surround him.

G. D. Killam. The Novels of Chinua Achebe
(New York, Africana, 1969), p. 11

No Longer at Ease seems to be too socially satirical to be able to carry off convincingly the tragic effect Achebe gives us reason to think he is striving for. What one misses is the artistically cohesive tension between chief character and setting that occurs in *Things Fall Apart*. The setting is as economically and convincingly created, but is felt to be almost incidental to the story of Obi. Like one of the magi, Obi returns from abroad, having caught the flavour of a different—an efficient, rational—dispensation. His mind is packed full of elevated notions of public service, and he is determined to play his full part in reinvigorating the Nigerian civil service and stamping out all the old corruption that so ill befits a new nation. The story records his failure. It is an attempt at a tale of muted tragedy, told laconically rather than with detachment.

Achebe's method is clearly hinted at in the account of Obi's interview for his job. During a discussion of Graham Greene's *The Heart of the Matter*, Obi says that life is "like a bowl of wormwood which one sips a little at a time world without end." "A real tragedy," he asserts, "takes place in a corner, in an untidy spot." It would seem that Achebe intends Obi's story to be tragic in this sort of Audenesque way, a view confirmed by the very banal level at which Obi's defeat takes place. He succumbs because loans have to be repaid, money sent home, expenses accounted for. For this effect to be produced Obi has to be made so naïve and self-deluded that he comes close to appearing merely childish. While his story can also be read partly as a paradigm of a man caught between the irreconcilable values of different ways of life, his enmeshment happens too easily to win our sympathetic involvement. As the catalogue of debts and expenditure mounts, one becomes too aware of the cards being stacked against him. It is a very simple-minded young man indeed who does not expect to receive a demand for income tax or an electricity bill.

Arthur Ravenscroft. Chinua Achebe (London,
Longmans, Green, 1969), pp. 20–21

Although every piece tells its story, the stories [in *Girls at War, and Other Stories*] are slight and, except for one or two imponderably

African twists, more or less predictable. The book is chiefly memorable for its vivid sketches of African life, especially where new ideas of religion and social custom or new political upheavals infringe upon the settled life of the village.

More scholarly hands than mine will one day attempt a critical assessment of the extent to which the extreme differences of cultural background between, for instance, a Yoruba writer like Soyinka and an Ibo writer like Achebe have influenced their art. My own feeling is that the village community of Ibo tradition provides the ideal setting for almost any sort of novel, and I should be surprised if the literary world is not soon assailed by a great flood of Ibo writings now that the surviving Ibos are shut up in the tiny enclave prepared for them, with nothing else to do.

But the overwhelming impression one receives from Achebe's writing—more strongly, I think, than from any other African writer—is one of anger against those who speak of tribalism as something to be disparaged, something impeding Africa's advancement to the delights of Coventry, Slough, and Detroit.

Auberon Waugh. *Spec.* March 11, 1972, p. 397

A Man of the People is very likely a slighter thing than the sturdy, plodding, much better-known *Things Fall Apart*; but what it lacks in massive solidity of structure, *A Man of the People* more than makes up in technical refinement: in flexibility of characterization and subtlety and delicate assurance of tone. The nature of Achebe's achievement might be made clearer if one imagined a new generic name for such a work as *Things Fall Apart*: an historical/cultural fiction, perhaps, or a sociological presentation, or a ritual, anthropological drama. (This novel, for good reason, is most popular with ethnologists and anthropologists, with social scientists in general, and with "African studies" experts.) *A Man of the People*, on the other hand, is pre-eminently a "novel," with all the dramatized complexity of human relations implied by the tradition of the novel.

While the satire of *A Man of the People* rejects, there is a parallel movement, focussing on Odili and his moral growth, that makes discoveries and accepts, that integrates experience around a new personal center and asserts this individual personality as a replacement for the village code of conduct that has been violated and destroyed. *A Man of the People* takes place in a world much worse off, much more corrupt and cynical and generally nasty, than the world of *Things Fall Apart*, yet Achebe, or at least his hero, finds in this wretched world a life that is both meaningful and possible. *A Man of the People* does not merely show that a certain world of grace is lost forever—of course it is—but takes that loss for granted and attempts to say what there may be of value in this world without innocence that lies about us.

James Olney. Tell Me Africa (Princeton, N.J., Princeton University Press, 1973), pp. 202–3

Arrow of God is decidedly Achebe's most balanced and finished novel. The theme of conflict between two cultures is not here exploited per se. Around this theme, however, and operating at a more dramatic level is the theme of man and god. This theme, as indicated, is borrowed entirely from the African theological thinking. The Europeans are also instruments in the hands of the gods; each moment of Ezeulu's confrontation with his enemies, his friends, and his god breathes the authenticity of that history and that past whose dignity Achebe has promised to restore. But as an artist, he goes beyond the mere restoration, creating a story of tragic grandeur, based firmly in a culture and owing its strength to the re-creation of the very idiom and language of that culture.

Achebe's latest novel, A Man of the People, owes very little to any theme or principle derived wholly or in part from his African world. It is the story of African decline, the collapse of those dreams raised by the dawn of independence. What marks it is its satirical quality, its journalistic accuracy, and its peculiarly restless inability or refusal to confront the heart of the political malaise by creating an almost hopeless political situation and a group of naïve leftists who mistake their own self-interest for political motivation. A Man of the People is a modern novel that points to the larger questions of the future, especially as it deals with the theme of political growth and direction. It points to the future both in theme and style more than any of the earlier novels, with the exception of No Longer at Ease with which it shares a common ground. More realistic, it ushers the reader into the contemporary African predicament.

Kofi Awoonor. The Breast of the Earth (Garden City, N.Y., Doubleday, 1975), p. 279

Named by Christianized parents after Queen Victoria's beloved; master of the colonial master's tongue, splendidly appropriating it to interpret his country's and people's past; bold user of freedom won by Africa against white domination; Albert Chinualumogu become Chinua Achebe is himself the definitive African experience. It is not a linear one. The importance of his book of essays, Morning Yet on Creation Day, is that in an unpretentious hundred-odd pages it establishes this so impressively. . . .

Achebe writes of having lived, as an Igbo child born in 1930 in

Eastern Nigeria, at the crossroads of cultures. He adds of Africa: "We still do today." But unlike most contemporary black writers and thinkers, he does not see this circumstance as fission and refraction. He regards the inheritance of many cultures as his risk and right. To him the criss-cross of Africa and Euroamerica is a place of a "certain dangerous potency; dangerous because a man might perish there wrestling with multiple-headed spirits, but also he might be lucky and return to his people with the boon of prophetic vision." Achebe himself has done so with—to borrow an irresistible Achebean phrase from elsewhere in the book—"unfair insights." This book brings us the benefit. In his sanity and shrewd sagacity he is like the market town in his essay "Onitsha, Gift of the Niger," to which the great river brings the people and produce of the 2,600-mile journey it makes from its source: "Because Onitsha sees everything it has come to distrust single-mindedness."

Nadine Gordimer. *TLS*. Oct. 17, 1975, p. 1227

AIDOO, AMA ATA (1942–   )

GHANA

Miss Christina Ama Aidoo's play, *The Dilemma of a Ghost* . . . was performed by Theatre Workshop of Lagos from January 26th to 28th. This play takes off where Lorraine Hansberry's *Raisin in the Sun* left off, with Assegai the African on the brink of marrying an American Negro girl. That play has given a glimpse of the extraordinary vision of their "homeland" prevalent among less informed American Negroes. This vision was the result of little knowledge and much romance.

Miss Aidoo's play explores the situation in which an American Negro bride returns "home" with her Ghanaian husband, to find herself a complete stranger, colour not withstanding. The agonising situation is portrayed with the kind of humour that is next door to tears. The crux of the play is the differing attitudes to childbearing. . . .

Miss Aidoo displays a gift—very useful to a social dramatist—of showing both sides of the coin at the same time. She shows the reverence of African village society towards motherhood while at the same time exposing the inherent cruelty of a system which makes the childless woman utterly miserable.

The play has a hopeful end. Not the rather doubtful hope that black people, whatever their background, can always understand each other, but the more universal one that there is common underlying essential humanity, which, given certain conditions, can come to the surface. In this play, motherhood, suppressed in one person, gratefully welcomed by another, and agonisingly unavailable to a third, is the unifying link.

Eldred Jones. *BAALE*. No. 2, 1965, p. 33

Since she has only one play and two short stories so far published, it is perhaps too early to herald [Aidoo] as a pathfinder; but she clearly represents a movement that is gathering force among the younger writers. In her story "No Sweetness Here," published in the *Black Orpheus Anthology*, she describes with tenderness and compassion a woman's love for her child. To an American or European reader, this story might seem charming if not particularly unusual in form. In African writing, however, the story is quite unique, for it explores with convincing legitimacy the intensity of individual emotional experience. Now, to show that she can turn to wider issues, Miss Aidoo has given us *The Dilemma of a Ghost*, a play that has already been performed in Accra, Lagos, and Ibadan. . . .

The Dilemma of a Ghost is a delightful piece of writing, simple, delicate, and containing much wisdom. The dialog has authenticity, as well as sparkle and wit, though there are occasional failures in the use of American slang. It is less successful as a play, because Miss Aidoo lacked an experienced stage director to help her work out a final version before publication. In this she suffers the same lack as all dramatists in West Africa, where there is no professional English-language theater group. . . .

Since Miss Aidoo wrote *The Dilemma of a Ghost* when she was still an undergraduate at the University of Ghana, it may seem churlish to draw attention to weaknesses in the dramatic construction. On the other hand, she is an artist exploring new realities with skill and distinction, and a patronizing accolade would be out of place. We look forward to seeing developments in Miss Aidoo's dialectic skill and personal insight, for she is among the first of a growing literary line of Africans unburdened, at least in part, by the problem of the color line, beneath which has always lain the problem of the culture line. And there are many more ghosts needing this kind of exorcism.

C. J. Rea. *AfrF*. Summer, 1965, pp. 112–13

The play *Anowa* cries out to be performed. The story is simple enough, of the life of a girl in "the state of Abura" in the 1870s, a strange girl, too advanced for her time, whose father felt should perhaps have been a priestess. Instead, being a progressive woman, Anowa chooses her own husband, Kofi Ako, and they go to the coast where the husband grows rich on the palm oil trade. But Anowa is barren, and slowly becomes ghost-like, trying to persuade her husband to take another wife. The climax is a great quarrel between the two, following which they both commit suicide. Although there is a certain Greek starkness about it, the language switches easily from the folksy-conversational to the apocalyptic. . . .

The short stories [in *No Sweetness Here*], like the play, are simple and direct, being concerned with the real problems of ordinary people. There is a certain social consciousness, in some of them, a burning desire to point a lesson, such as in the tale of the woman who worries that her sister is the mistress of a politician. With the coup she hopes the situation will change, but then her sister comes home with a highly-placed army captain. Ama Ata writes with transparent honesty: behind it there is the feeling, the same as in the novels of Ayi Kwei Armah, of being near to tears. She and Armah are in the front rank of the literary talents that have come to the fore in recent years in Ghana.

K. W. *WA*. Jan. 30–Feb. 5, 1971, p. 133

[In *No Sweetness Here*] Ama Ata Aidoo celebrates womanhood in general and motherhood in particular. She stands up for the woman who must go and protect her own; who must go through "pregnancy and birth and death and pain, and death again." There will always be a fresh corpse and she will weep all over again. The woman who, even while she is nursing an infant, must lose her husband to the south, where there will be better money for one's work. And it will still be the woman—the mother—who must receive the news first that her son is going to leave his wife and child. . . . The woman who watches over a sick child. . . . The mother who waits for the man who never returns—son or lover or husband. . . . The mother who knows that she is giving birth for the second time when she launches her son on the road to higher education. . . .

The men in Miss Aidoo's fiction are mere shadows or voices or just "fillers." Somewhere, quietly, they seem to be manipulating the woman's life or negatively controlling it or simply having a good time, knowing that they are assured of something like a divine top-dog position in life. Given this premise the woman, without worrying about her traditional place, simply gets up on her feet and asserts not her importance in relation to the male, but her motherhood.

Ezekiel Mphahlele. Introduction to Ama Ata Aidoo,
No Sweetness Here (Garden City, N.Y., Doubleday,
1972), pp. xix–xx

Various African writers have depicted the conditions and quality of life of traditional and modern African womanhood. . . . Still, it seems to me that the Ghanaian writer Ama Ata Aidoo is unique for she almost exclusively rivets attention on black African womanhood of the village and the city. And because she is a woman, Miss Aidoo is able to view the plight of African women from a natural and familiar vantage point.

In *No Sweetness Here*, a collection of eleven short stories, the male characters generally play a peripheral role. They are frequently in the background, usually managing directly or indirectly to bring about the suffering of women. In those allusions to life in Accra and other urban centers of Ghana Miss Aidoo depicts the moral failings of young women who become prostitutes or mistresses of wealthy men in order to enjoy the material opportunities offered in a city. On the other hand, the stories set in villages do not offer a particularly pleasant alternative for the African woman, especially if she is the least respected wife in a polygamous household. In such a case the wife asserts her identity as a woman through her love of her children. A tragic situation occurs if she can have no children or her single child dies. Such is the case in the title story "No Sweetness Here." . . .

Does Miss Aidoo offer a solution to the dilemma of the modern urban African woman? Not directly. However, she does suggest that education offers a chance for a woman to develop herself independently of the pressures placed upon her by men. Otherwise she must be content to exploit her body and be exploited.

Donald Bayer Burness. *SBL*. Summer, 1973,
pp. 21, 23

ALEXIS, JACQUES-STÉPHEN (1922–1961)

HAITI

[In *Comrade General Sun*] Alexis tells the story of Hilarion and Claire-Heureuse, who are poor blacks in Haiti in the prewar years. The novel is primarily a love story, for Hilarion and Claire-Heureuse love each other, love the joy of the sun and the peacefulness of conversations and the beach; they love life. But the novel is also a story of poverty and hatred, for the protagonists are hungry; Hilarion has stolen in order to eat. He has been locked up, beaten, and humiliated, and he has come out of prison a communist. . . .

This long, sumptuously colored romantic chronicle, which combines evocations of Caribbean family life and political demands, and which uses the resources of the art of the popular tale and the richness, preciosity, and naïveté of the Creole dialect, reveals the power of a literature that is nourished by the folklore, the language, and the passions of a country that is still innocent of "western" literature. In this respect, Alexis's novel seems much more promising than, for example, Aimé Césaire's poetry, which is all too full of surrealist memories and is too Europeanized. . . .

Throughout *Comrade General Sun* there run a force and a lyric freedom that unify the love story, the exoticism, and the political message. The message thus appears as a necessary metamorphosis of the storyteller's sensibility, not as the result of a deliberate choice among several ways of telling the story. Alexis's achievement is that he does not in any way give the impression of having written the novel out of his convictions as a Haitian communist; instead, his work suggests that there is no other way to speak about the Caribbean people today. Passages as different as Paco's death and his immediate assumption of a symbolic function, scenes of labor in the sugar-cane fields, and the love of the young couple all become simultaneous moments—the colorful, violent, and tender scenes of a single painting illuminated by the rays of "Comrade Sun," who is the great joyful source of strength for the men tied to poverty and to hope for their land.

François Nourissier. *NRF*. Oct., 1955, pp. 787–88†

In the Blink of an Eye revives the sentimental theme, made fashionable by Hugo and Alexandre Dumas *fils*, of the fallen woman who is redeemed by love. But the story of the woman's fall is very long in Alexis's novel. The details about La Nina Estrellita's "profession" and her vices recall the climate of crudeness that reigns in Zola's *Nana*. And yet, despite the evidence of La Nina's moral debasement, she is the woman whom El Caucho has chosen. Around this couple there is an indefinable halo which indicates the similarity of their souls and which is the sign of the eternal promises inscribed in their flesh. . . .

Is *In the Blink of an Eye* Jacques Alexis's best novel? Perhaps so, if one shares the novelist's own conviction. In any case, this novel is the book in which he accomplished his mission. The characterization of El Caucho is indeed the culmination of an undertaking begun with Hilarion. . . . El Caucho is a true proletarian. He does not have to be trained: his training has been completed. He is the worker who is conscious of his role in society and of his importance in the struggle that is being waged. . . .

Yet the character of El Caucho does not entirely account for Alexis's preference for this novel. In *In the Blink of an Eye* he not only accomplished his mission but he also liberated himself [from his obsession with the bourgeoisie]. *Comrade General Sun* is overloaded with criticism of society. It is the story of a revolt against God and against the capitalistic organization of man's work. The description of the strikes that stand out in the narrative and the murders that are committed has the appearance of protest writing. And the moral of *The Musical Trees*, whereby the earth takes revenge and triumphs over the greed of the authorities, has no other meaning than its protest.

In the Blink of an Eye, on the other hand, calmly asserts refusal by creating a universe outside the bounds of bourgeois virtue and the demands of conventional morality. The milieu in which the novel takes place, the atmosphere of vice, perversion, and obscenity in which it is clothed, is itself a defiance of the bourgeoisie. But that is not all. La Nina's rehabilitation is a symbol, as is El Caucho's natural chivalry. This book is a vision that contrasts with the portrait drawn elsewhere by the novelist of a bourgeois society in which everything is borrowed, falsely enlightening, and obscurely corrupt.

Ghislain Gouraige. *Histoire de la littérature haïtienne*
(Port-au-Prince, Imprimerie H. A. Théodore, 1960),
pp. 293–97†

As a novelist Alexis is similar to the unanimist Jules Romains. Like the author of *Men of Good Will*, Alexis wished to express life in all its multiplicity and movement during an era of his country's history. A panorama of Haitian life from 1934 to 1942 is presented in *Comrade General Sun* and *The Musical Trees*.

Alexis does not construct his works around a single plot. . . . The life of Hilarion and that of Gonaïbo [the hero of *The Musical Trees*] are only secondary to an immense documentary fresco composed of descriptions, portraits, various peasant scenes, and psychological analyses. The danger of this style is quite evident: it diffuses the reader's interest.

Like Voltaire and Anatole France, Alexis has made his ideas explicit in his various works. It is easy to discover his political and social thoughts and his religious ideas in his writing.

In politics he leans toward communism. His liking for Pierre Roumel and Doctor Jean-Michel and for his hero Hilarion, who has been indoctrinated by these two militants, is clear. The message left by the dying Hilarion leaves no doubt about this point.

It must be added that Alexis is profoundly nationalist. The narrative of *The Musical Trees* is in itself enough proof of Alexis's nationalism. He also seems anti-bourgeois—which is explained by his socialism. His depictions of Port-au-Prince society are often satirical. On the other hand, Alexis loves the common people: he commiserates with their poverty and defends their customs and traditions.

It cannot be said that Alexis is indifferent to religion. He favors a national Catholic clergy and also the Catholic Church. But he would like Haitian priests to be more attentive to the voices of the native land and to the voices of the ancestors. Thus, people came to believe that he was urging the Haitian clergy to practice an impossible "mixture" [of Christianity and voodooism]. . . .

He chooses images that are sometimes realistic, sometimes ethereal, sometimes grandiose, and sometimes pretty. It is evident that Alexis possesses an extraordinary, marvelous imagination, a gift that had never been granted to a Haitian novelist before him.

Manuel illustré d'histoire de la littérature haïtienne
(Port-au-Prince, Éditions Henri Deschamps, 1961),
pp. 487–88†

Jacques Alexis was born on April 22, 1922, in the city of Gonaives. He studied medicine in Paris. His admiration for Jacques Roumain is well known. A writer and a political militant, Alexis was the cofounder in 1959 of a Haitian communist party, the Entente Populaire. To carry out a secret mission, he landed surreptitiously on the northwest coast of Haiti. There he was spotted, seized, and executed. That was in April, 1961.

Direct political activity was not the only field on which Jacques Alexis struggled. He also fought on the literary battlefield for the development of his country. A struggle for development was indeed the way in which he conceived of his mission as a novelist. . . .

The novel *The Musical Trees* is an analysis of the situation in Haiti in 1941–42. At that time the rural world of the Haitian peasants was under attack on two fronts, economic and religious: an American rubber company was setting up a plantation on land stolen from the peasants, and the Catholics were campaigning against the voodoo religion. This intertwining, this overlapping, this intersecting of events, provides the author with an opportunity to develop his views on the role of the Catholic religion in the development of rural Haiti. What, in Jacques Alexis's opinion, is the role played by the Catholic religion? His negative attitude toward the Church is very close to that of Jacques Roumain. Indeed, Roumain himself is present in the novel under the name Pierre Roumel, a journalist defending the peasants' cause. When Alexis attacks the Church, he uses almost the same arguments Roumain used.

Claude Souffrant. *Europe*. Jan., 1971, pp. 34–35†

Alexis took advantage of his exile in France to continue his medical studies. He specialized in neurology. His innate restlessness led him to frequent the numerous intellectual circles that blossomed in Paris right after the war. He got to know Césaire, Senghor, and all the exponents of

Negritude. He was drawn to existentialism. He became friendly with Aragon and the most advanced of the progressive intellectuals. He immersed himself in social realism, which dates back to Zola and Anatole France; he discovered socialist realism, Gorki and Ehrenburg. A need, an impulse, a new passion then arose, and took form through these new aesthetic prisms. Between his busy hours at the hospital, Alexis the neurologist wanted to write, to re-create the distant image of his fatherland by harmonizing the flow of images that besieged his mind despite the years of exile and separation. . . .

Alexis's first two novels, as well as his collection of stories [*Romancero in the Stars*], explored the unlimited field of traditions, legends, and beliefs of rural life in Haiti. "If the zombi stories are legends," insists Alexis, "happy are those whose legends are so great and alive!" Thus, the artist's imagination and the multicolored marvels of social reality intertwine to the point at which it is difficult to distinguish one from the other. Then a new dimension of realism is born: "magic realism," which suffuses Alexis's literary works. His characters seem to spring from the most authentic tableaux in Haitian primitive painting. They arise from real life as well. Their lives are shaped by the lush tropical vegetation, the tribulations of peasant life, the mysteries and rites of voodoo, and the serene desire for improvement characteristic of the Haitian people.

Gérard Pierre-Charles. *Europe*. Jan., 1971,
pp. 67–68†

ALUKO, T. M. (1918–   )

NIGERIA

[Aluko] has attempted to do for Yorubaland what [Achebe] has done for Iboland, namely to present an image of the past at that point where the civilisation of the Western world came into contact with it. But whereas Mr. Achebe assesses the two civilisations objectively, writing from the inside at the same time, Mr. Aluko attitudinises and, what is more, does on the whole lack that empathy which is so necessary if a historical novel is to rise above the level of bald observation. The result is that [*One Man, One Wife*] convinces only in patches, and that his interpretation of the past appears to suffer from bias and preconceptions. His is almost a total rejection of the past.

He imposes a sort of Manichaean division. It is acceptable that the pastor should regard his mission as bringing light into the darkness of the Yoruba religion; but from cover to cover the impression is given that this is also the author's standpoint. Thus the indigenous religion means for him as it does for the pastor nothing more than "the worship of streams and trees." He fails to see it as a philosophy of life or as a social system; and so, looking back, he sees only its inadequacies. For children it is only the fear of evil spirits in the dark; for adults the fear of a god of smallpox, and so on. One is tempted to say that if the author's comprehension and interpretation of Yoruba life did not exceed that of the Rev. David, the latter should have been the mouthpiece of the story. To put it differently, one expects of a novelist that his view of things be larger and more comprehensive than the sum total of the views of his characters.

One is not here concerned with whether this interpretation of the past is right or wrong. The point is that it is too limited and biased to serve as a basis for the imaginative truth which we demand of fiction. Polygamy emerges as an institution without a single creditable feature. Indeed, the clash between it and Christian monogamy hardly appears to be a clash between two approaches to life; even for the author it is simply a clash between light and darkness.

Arthur D. Drayton. Ibadan. Nov., 1960, p. 29

The main strength of *One Man, One Matchet* lies not so much in the plot as in the magnificent characterisation. There is a fascinating interplay of character and motivation. The characters are drawn with warmth and sympathy and at no point does the author try to manipulate them for his own ends. Mr. Aluko has a sharp eye for human foibles and even the most dignified of his people are not above ridiculousness. The characters are memorable: flamboyant Benjamin Benjamin; irascible old Chief Momo; rich, vain and gullible Olowekere, jockeying for a chieftaincy; meek and mild Reverend Josiah Olaiya, anxious to divert some of the streams of campaign money into his church. But they are lovable people—even the unworthiest of them. And in the unhurried, rural tempo of the book they play out their individual dramas under the author's kindly but ever-watchful eye. Life is charmingly inconclusive and here and there Mr. Aluko gracefully squanders an incident which promised possibilities. But the sure touch is always there, evoking the smell of life.

In an age of axe-grinding it is remarkable that Mr. Aluko does not seem to have an axe of his own to grind. There is an absence of posturing: that is left to his characters. Mr. Aluko, too, never passes judgment: that is left to his readers. And neither does he explain his characters to potential foreign readers: there is no need because his characters are universal. The writing is clear, with many a sudden comic turn. Perhaps the book could have done without the last chapter which is explanatory, for by then the drama has been well and truly played out. *One Man, One Matchet* is a significant contribution not only to African writing but to the world's writing and one looks forward to this talented Nigerian writer's next book.

Alfred Hutchinson. NewA. July, 1965, p. 114

There is not much difference between the situation in [*Kinsman and Foreman*] and the situation in Aluko's second novel, *One Man, One Matchet*; an honest man and a rogue are in conflict, and the rogue eventually loses out. What gives *Kinsman and Foreman* an interesting twist is the family connection between the honest man and the rogue. . . .

Taken as it is, the novel has several good points. Amusing incidents are skillfully strung together and knotted at the end into a hilarious climax. The narrative moves along unfettered by the distracting irrelevancies and digressions that crippled Aluko's earlier novels. Aluko's characterization has improved too. Major figures are well-defined and minor figures sketched in a variety of gay colors. Each character has a particular role to play in the parade of comic events. Also, Aluko's satirical thrusts are sharper and more widely distributed than in his previous novels. He slashes with vigor at church, state, family and individual. Even the follies of British justice and American philanthropy receive a few pertinent jabs. If one compares *Kinsman and Foreman* with Aluko's formless first novel, *One Man, One Wife*, one can see quite clearly that Aluko has come a long way in seven years. He still has a good distance to go before he will be close to front-runners like Achebe, but at least he is moving in the right direction and making better progress than Ekwensi. . . .

Bernth Lindfors. AT. Oct., 1967, p. 29

One Man, One Matchet is a more ambitious novel than *One Man, One Wife*. The clash of concepts is once again the theme. This novel should be required reading for every European or American technician and teacher involved in aid schemes in Africa, as well as for every African government official dealing with development projects, for Aluko sees clearly the heartbreaking difficulties which such projects inevitably entail, and he manages to make comprehensible the genuinely held and diametrically opposed views of the old chiefs and the new young men of government. . . .

Aluko displays great talent in catching the individuals' voices and the general tone of village meetings—the Yoruba love of words, the lengthy speeches and interminable preliminary greetings, the unhurried way in which everyone is allowed his say and yet the way in which this age-old tribal method now impedes action. . . .

The ending, with Udo's resignation and his discussion of the country's problems with his successor, is flat and too theoretical. Nevertheless, for its incisive irony, perceptive social analysis and convincing character portrayals, *One Man, One Matchet* will remain worth reading for a long time to come.

Margaret Laurence. *Long Drums and Cannons*
(London, Macmillan, 1968), pp. 171–72, 175–76

Chief the Honourable Minister is a bad, a very bad, piece of writing. Indeed, Mr. Aluko cannot be serious. Life is just too short to spend on either writing or reading such nonsense. This light pile of numbered pages reminds me of the "plot" cards I discovered as a freshman in college: the penurious yet budding writer could arrange and rearrange them in geometric manner for plot, subplot, counterplot, and so forth. He would then send the fleshed-out result to the Western and detective pulp story publishers. Mr. Aluko's listless tale is reminiscent of just this. His heroes, villains, mistresses, expatriate midget brains in the imaginary African state of Afromacoland have absolutely no pretense at depth or dimension. The story—of governmental corruption and incompetence—reads like an editorial from the *Daily Times* of Lagos, Nigeria, in the worst days of that nation's strife. . . .

The author of this tale should tell us why Moses is a good guy, why Dauda is a bad guy, why bribery, corruption, incompetence exist. These things do not happen from nowhere, just as men are not born good guys, bad guys, or even bumbling guys. At the outset of this book all the characters, undimensional, are, as it were, poised at the starting line. They have no substance; they are just *faits accomplis*. The book then goes on as if the characters and events were wound up and let go in some elementary good-bad-bumbling dialectic.

J. Dennis Delaney. *AfrSR*. Sept., 1971, p. 329

Chief the Honourable Minister is a satire of the national "democratic" government, the "Freedom for All Party," which is established at the end of British colonial rule. The story is set in an imaginary state called Afromacoland. Throughout the novel, attention is directed not at the people of the state, but at the government officials. Hardly any mention is made of there even being people over which the officials rule. Each official is titled a minister in charge of a department, but it is never established what the function or purpose of each department is in regard to the people. The people of Afromacoland are not served by the government; they are only used by the government officials to support their selfish gains.

Aluko's failure to portray each minister in detail does not weaken the book's impact; rather it highlights the meaninglessness of the government and contributes to the general satirical nature of the novel. Actually, the ministers are not individuals; they are stereotyped as selfish, ridiculous, fat men. Their actions, judgments, and minds are all one. Their lengthy, meaningless titles are the only identity they possess; never do they identify with the country or people they control.

Aluko was always a social satirist, but his early novels were in a light vein. Now as an outsider, he is able to treat seriously the plight of the ordinary man, surrounded by self-seeking politicians. The laughter in the last two novels is not merely laughter for its own sake but laughter directed at reforming society. This was the function of masquerade verse in traditional Yoruba society, and, as has been seen, Aluko has moved strongly in this direction.

O. R. Dathorne. The Black Mind (Minneapolis, University of Minnesota Press, 1974), pp. 168–69

Aluko is now one of the most prolific novelists in West Africa, yet his fifth novel is not essentially very different from his first. In *His Worshipful Majesty* we find the same type of thin plot, the same weakly developed characters and the same bombastic language juxtaposed with the same kind of overbearingly moralistic theme that runs through all his work. In his early novels of culture conflict, as well as in his more recent one about a political coup, we find much that has been derived from Achebe; in this novel with its attempts to incorporate Yoruba festivals and Yoruba praise poetry, we hear echoes of Soyinka. Such derivation is legitimate, but Aluko never seems to go beyond, or even come up to, his models. In short, one is tempted to dismiss him as a second rate novlist.

However, despite his lack of originality there are both literary and extra-literary reasons that make Aluko's novels, and in particular *His Worshipful Majesty*, worthwhile reading. . . . Though the work as a whole may not be a finely wrought novel, Aluko has again shown himself to be a master of hyperbole and an important chronicler of the cultural changes in West Africa that were brought about by European colonialism.

Richard Priebe. BA. Spring, 1974, p. 412

AMADI, ELECHI (1934–   )

NIGERIA

Novels about daily life in Eastern Nigerian villages by past or present inhabitants of them now appear almost weekly. [*The Concubine*], the latest, is particularly interesting for two reasons. First, Elechi Amadi, whose first published work this is, was educated at Government College, Umuahia, and the former University College, Ibadan, and is now a captain in the Nigerian army, attached to the Military School in Zaria. He took a degree in mathematics and physics and did not take his commission until he had spent some time land surveying and teaching. One knew that Nigerian army officers were versatile, in view of their role in running their country now: but Captain Amadi is probably the only novelist among them.

The other point of interest in the book is that this is not a novel of conflict. No Europeans, or even European influences, disturb the village scene. The writing is clear, simple and economical although some of the dialogue is rather stilted—not because it uses traditional Ibo forms of address, but because it is not always all in "key." . . .

One is tempted to speak of a "classical tragedy," with the gods ever at hand to demand allegiance and to punish remorselessly human offences and frailties. But the figures are not of the stature demanded by classical tragedy.

The pace is slow, one is spared few details. But this is a story told for its own sake and is not a substitute for an anthropological treatise or a political manifesto. Captain Amadi's people still lack sufficient depth. If they acquired that his work would acquire a new dimension.

D. B. *WA*. June 11, 1966, p. 657

Amadi goes even further than Chinua Achebe in portraying traditional religious concepts, for the Ibo society about which Achebe is writing was already affected and altered by life-views dissimilar to its own. Amadi's Ibo villages in *The Concubine* represent a society which had not yet fallen prey to self-doubts. Its gods could be cruel, but they were real, and they affected the lives of mortals in real and inexplicable ways. Strangely, what at first appears to be a limitation of the novel—the single viewpoint, as contrasted with Achebe's ability to grasp and convey a multiplicity of viewpoints—turns out to be a type of strength, for Amadi's effect ultimately depends upon the extent to which he can convey the gods as actual and potent. He is not writing primarily about people's relationships with one another, although these provide much of the novel's substance. The underlying theme is always man's fate, to what extent he can change it, and how he chooses to face the inevitable. In this respect, Amadi's writing has something in common with that of John Pepper Clark, who is also concerned with destiny in very similar ways. . . .

The Concubine expresses in admirably simple poetic prose the age-old conflict of man with his gods, his awe of them and at the same time his proud attempts to bind them, to make them do his will. Although Amadi differs sharply from Wole Soyinka in that *The Concubine* does not offer alternative and contemporary interpretations to the struggle between men and gods, he resembles Soyinka in another way, for most definitely neither writer is a liberal humanist. Amadi, like Soyinka, does not ever suggest that man is improving and will ultimately be able to direct wisely and knowingly every facet of his life. On the contrary, *The Concubine* expresses the mystery at the centre of being. Amadi's is an essentially sombre view of life, and his novel contains an acute awareness of fate's ironies, for at the exact moment when we think the prize is within our grasp, the gods cut the thread. This outlook is reminiscent of the references Achebe makes to Chukwu, the supreme God, who severs a man's life when it is sweetest to him.

Margaret Laurence. *Long Drums and Cannons*
(London, Macmillan, 1968), pp. 182–84

It would . . . be very naïve to think that [*The Great Ponds*] is simply the account, powerful as it might be, of a feud between two tribes, and of their ultimate destruction. . . . The second level of the story is implied in the final laconic sentence: "Wonjo, as the villagers called the Great Influenza of 1918, was to claim a grand total of some twenty million lives all over the world." Thus is explained the death of the inhabitants of both Chiolu and Aliakoro, wrongly attributed to the blind rage of Ogbunabali "executing judgment, killing off both parties to a dispute. . . ." Thus is made clear the weakness of Man. Limited as he is in his comprehension and knowledge, he does not understand how derisive are his quarrels and vain his victories. He pitiably tries to give a meaning to things far above his reach and opposes events which cannot be opposed. He passes away without ever realizing that he is a mere dot in the intricate pattern of mankind.

The Great Ponds is a lesson in humility. The simplicity of the style and the minute selection of detail further enhance the dramatic aspect. Amadi is a master at rendering the innermost feelings of his characters. Olumba, the great warrior from Chiolu, is the anti-hero *par excellence*, because of the multiplicity of questions he asks himself and the gulf of doubt he vainly attempts to conceal in his soul. But at the same time and owing to his very ambiguity, he is one of the finest portraits ever drawn by an African writer. Critics will not fail to draw a parallel between the story which is told here and recent events in Africa. Amadi might well have been inspired by the bloody Civil War in Nigeria; however, to explain the book in this light will not do justice to its power and tragic value. It is a tale of human fragility, stubbornness and despair. The characters are not so much Nigerians, or Africans, but Men, victims of their own limitations, unable to grasp the tragedy of the world.

Elechi Amadi opens new roads to the African novelist. He leaves aside the purely grand essays in homage to the past; he is not concerned with the satire of modern Africa; he forces the reader to search for the very meaning of life.

Maryse Conde. *PA*. No. 80, 1971, pp. 164–65

Although many readers applaud Elechi Amadi's *The Concubine*, quite a few have grave reservations about the novel. While praising the novelist's presentation of his society and his powers of characterization, they are unable to accept his portrayal of the supernatural. They compare him with Hardy, and deplore his attempt to attribute responsibility to the gods, when their experience shows that the motivations of conduct and the agents of destiny are strictly sociological. On the other hand, I have met many students who frankly admitted that of all the African novels they have read, *The Concubine* was the only one they could respond to fully, because it presented an almost exact copy of village life as they knew it. This conflict of opinion presents a very interesting problem. On the one hand, the strictures against the novel are honest and serious, and have to be seriously considered; but on the other hand, one has to be careful about denigrating a work which elicits such a powerful response, precisely because of its especial relevance to people's lives. I rather suspect that some people condemn the novel as a reflex action, simply because they do not believe in the supernatural at all, and not because of any stylistic defect. . . .

Amadi is not conducting a rational argument to prove the existence of supernatural forces. He may not even believe in the supernatural himself; there is no evidence in the novel that he does. He merely presents to us a group of people for whom the supernatural is important, and he tries to make their way of life as realistic as possible.

Eustace Palmer. *An Introduction to the African
Novel* (New York, Africana, 1972), pp. 117, 128

The Great Ponds, by Elechi Amadi, not only gives a Homeric nobility to the tiny war between Nigerian villages but recovers, in its acceptance of magic as a fact, the power the Greek dramatists had—of making mental acts seem momentous. . . .

At a symposium in Lagos a year ago, I heard a dazzling variety of literary tactics enunciated by a dozen Nigerian writers and critics. Elechi Amadi (addressed as "Captain Amadi," in deference to the Army years of his varied career) put forward with an arresting earnestness the opinion that supernatural reality should play its part in a narrative whose characters believe in magic. The first question from the audience challenged this notion, or, rather, asked that it be clarified to mean that such belief should be shown to be *subjectively* influencing the characters. Captain Amadi, a slender, gracious, and handsome figure in a white robe, appeared to consent to the modification, there in the juju-proof setting of the university auditorium, amid the steel chairs and the flex-necked microphones and the beaming pink faces of U.S.I.S. officials, with the metropolis of Lagos clattering beyond the windows. But it seemed to me that Captain Amadi did not in fact mean anything quite so reasonable as the proposition that believers believe, but something more supernatural, and his novel confirms my impression. . . .

The suspense of Olumba's struggle not to die is frightful. The motions of his morale feel immense. We see life as pre-scientific man saw it—as a spiritual liquid easily spilled. The invisible forces pressing upon Olumba are totally plausible. The novel treats magic respectfully, as something that usually works. The recipes of witchery are matter-of-factly detailed, as are the fevers and divinations they inarguably produce. But Olumba's heroic battle is against a force deeper than magic— the death wish itself, the urge toward osmotic reabsorption into the encircling ocean of darkness wherein life is a precarious, thin-walled epiphenomenon. [Jan. 21, 1974]

John Updike. *Picked-Up Pieces* (New York, Alfred
A. Knopf, 1975), pp. 327–29, 331–32

ANTHONY, MICHAEL (1932–   )

TRINIDAD AND TOBAGO

The Games Were Coming suffers from a heavy dose of Hemingway, so much so that it is sometimes difficult to tell whether Mr. Anthony intends a parody. The centre of the story is the fifteen-mile bicycle race of the Trinidad Southern Games. Leon has given up everything, including his girl, to fulfil his dream of winning the race, and when the girl seeks distraction elsewhere she goes a little too far and becomes pregnant by her employer. Leon, all unknowing, has promised to marry her if he wins, and his victory therefore takes on a double meaning, for it will keep her from shame and the streets. This is a plain tale simply told, and it should have been more complicated; Mr. Anthony is quite good on Carnival, and on the actual running of the race. But too much stylistic understatement does not hold up the rather unsubstantial narrative.

Peter Cohen. Spec. Nov. 22, 1963, p. 674

For his second novel Mr. Anthony, a West Indian writer, has set himself the difficult task of presenting adult relationships as seen through the eyes of a sensitive and reflective twelve-year-old boy. It is to his credit that *The Year in San Fernando* is a thoroughly convincing and pleasing book. The boy, Francis, is sent from his village in Trinidad to the town of San Fernando to act as the servant-companion of old Mrs. Chandles. Coming from the limited environment of his small village, he is at first overwhelmed by everything, by the town itself, and by the complexity of the relationships existing between the adults he meets—between Mrs. Chandles and her two sons, Linden and Edwin, and between Linden Chandles and the two women, Marva and Julia. The reader shares the transformation with Francis, as significant patterns gradually emerge from a kaleidoscope of general impressions, and as his awareness and understanding of these relationships grow.

In carefully maintaining the physical and social perspectives as they would be apprehended by a young boy, Mr. Anthony shows that he has an instinct for telling detail, seen to particular effect in the descriptions of the daily scene in San Fernando and in the development of Francis's friendship with Julia.

M. Macmillan. JCL. Sept., 1965, p. 175

[Anthony] is no literary tyro awaiting discovery. On the contrary, he has already chalked up three novels of more than usual merit and one can only despair that they have not won him wider recognition. Possibly this is because the particular virtues of his work, a scrupulous regard for truth at the expense of false drama and a lucid unflamboyant style, no longer appeal to a reading public almost exclusively hooked on a diet of sex, fantasy and hokum. Even so, as a West Indian writing of his native Trinidad, he might well have expected more attention from those critics who once embraced the Caribbean cult as feverishly as they now swallow tales of proletarian lust and squalor. It was not to be, however, and in the face of their continued neglect, it seemed that at least one immigrant novelist had missed the boat, if not to England itself where he has now settled, certainly to the sort of critical acclaim scored by a number of his fellow expatriates. But this, I fancy, may have had less to do with a shift in fashion than with the fact that the books themselves, although touching on the most inflammatory issues, allowed little scope for the airing of those social and political shibboleths so beloved by progressive writers.

The truth is that Mr. Anthony seems blissfully unaware that the accepted role of the Negro writer in our society is to propagandize, scarify and aggravate that burden of guilt in which—or so it often appears—the truly dedicated White liberal takes such masochistic pleasure. Consequently it would seem that his work is not so much inspired by any deep sense of racial injustice as by the desire to celebrate the beauty of his country, illuminate its social and cultural features, and portray its people as they really are, not as so many symbols of colonial exploitation, but as ordinary human beings who, pigmentation aside, might also be the less privileged natives of Brixton or Huddersfield. The pity is that such a persuasive and enlightened approach will be largely ignored by a society weaned on the notion that anger is the only effective weapon against ignorance and prejudice.

Frank McGuiness. *London.* April, 1967, pp. 117–18

[Like George Lamming] Michael Anthony is another novelist in exile whose sustenance is back in the West Indies. Indeed, this is even truer of him than it is of George Lamming. For, whereas the latter's dialectical concern leads him to the *roman à thèse*, for which the highly conceptualised situation suffices, Anthony has been drawing on his childhood in South Trinidad. The differences between their work stem directly from this: Lamming's novels are involved in design and style, Anthony's are delicate and straightforward, written as it were for the finely attuned ear; Lamming's appeal is to the intellect, Anthony's to a discriminating sensibility. And in his delicate recall of West Indian rural childhood, Michael Anthony recaptures its innocence and its fragility, thus exploring a vital area of experience through which exploration the Trinidadian, and I believe the West Indian, is better able to understand the nature of his sensibility.

To the imaginative fund out of which he writes, his sojourn in England could add nothing new—save that it could make more compelling and etch into sharper focus those values which, in the author's view, informed that childhood. Nor, indeed, can such a fund be inexhaustible. One can only hazard guesses, but my own feeling is that as the moment of that exhaustion draws nearer Michael Anthony's peculiar genius would be better served if he were in the West Indies rather than outside. He has recently taken up residence in Brazil, and if it is true that that country still retains a quality of innocence, then it is sure to sustain the freshness of his imagination and keep him along congenial paths.

A. D. Drayton. *LHY*. Jan., 1970, pp. 77–78

The New World intellectual, according to the Argentinian writer, Ezequiel Martínez Estrada, lives even more divorced from the small sufferings and daily lives of the people than his European counterpart. He understands this suffering with his intellect. . . . In this sense, Michael Anthony, like Samuel Selvon, is of all the West Indian writers, the least "intellectual." As ethnically "negro" as Selvon is "East Indian," Anthony in his novels, as Selvon in his short stories, fulfils the potential of that *cultural* fusion which is the unique imperative of being a Trinidadian, a West Indian, a New World man, i.e. the inevitable prototype of man in the future; if that future survives. . . .

Green Days by the River portrays consciously this unconscious and unaware *creole* fusion. The book is a long short story rather than a novel. It is simple in style and at times its simplicity palls—people laugh too much, are amused too often. But these are irrelevant faults compared to the fact that the book is accessible to the people whom he writes about. Made into a film, *Green Days by the River* would draw the interest and involvement of the young generation of West Indians. One can envisage the camera evoking what Anthony calls the "strange world of forest and shade." The book is penetrated with sun, the river Ortoire, sluggish with alligators—real? or imagined?—the cashew trees under which the young boys gather; their rivalry as they pelt at the thick stems or circle Rosalie Gidharee at the dance.

Sylvia Wynter. *CarS*. Jan., 1970, pp. 111–14

The boy's vision [in *The Year in San Fernando*] suffuses elements of experience which we are habituated to seeing as disparate or indeed as belonging to opposed categories, like nostalgia-anticipation,. town-country, pure-sordid. . . . Anthony is committed in *The Year in San Fernando* to involving us in the feel of a peculiarly open state of consciousness; and this is achieved by a scrupulous adherence to the boy's point of view, in a deceptively easy style that carries the necessary sensuous burden as well as sustaining the illusion of adolescent reportage. . . .

We might say that *The Year in San Fernando* continuously leads us away from a settled notion of the person to a more liberal view of latent and only sporadically realized possibilities. As on the level of character, so with respect to object and event: one of the effects of

Anthony's narrative technique in *The Year in San Fernando* is to promote a vision for the reader in which each "known" factor in experience
is restored to a more primordial condition of latency.

It is here I think that the astonishing originality of *The Year in San
Fernando* lies. The image of Francis, deprived, and tethered to the
Chandles house (even to having a lair below the house), in a circumscribed world of which he is trying to make sense, is an image of the
condition of the modern West Indian. But out of this distress, Anthony
has created an archetypal situation. On the one hand, there is the pattern of growth and natural progression suggested by the spontaneous
metaphorical activity of the novel's language. On the other, there is the
narrator's extreme openness to the possibilities of experience, marked by
Francis's capacity for shock. Through the boy's consciousness Anthony
induces us to make the confession of weakness, of unknowing, by which
an unstable world is transformed into the flux of re-creation.

> Kenneth Ramchand. *The West Indian Novel and Its*
> *Background* (New York, Barnes & Noble, 1970),
> pp. 212, 221–22

Michael Anthony's stories [in *Cricket in the Road*] are rich in tropical
atmosphere and most of them explore, with an "innocent eye," the
world as seen by the child. They are short and lyrical and are more
concerned with pin-pointing perceptions and emotions than with developing character or a strong story-line. Feelings are described with great
simplicity—sometimes, it seems, with deliberate naivety—and the
storms of childhood rage gently within a rather frail, bone china cup.
But this shouldn't lead one to underestimate them: frequently, in stories
like "The Valley of Cocoa" and "Cricket in the Road," the simplicity is
both delicate and convincing.

> Chris Waters. *NS*. Nov. 9, 1973, pp. 696–97

ARMAH, AYI KWEI (1939–   )

GHANA

The Beautyful Ones Are Not Yet Born turns on the purgatory of a
railway clerk (we never learn his name) who will end his days as
a railway clerk because he carries the terrible burden of principle in a
climate of ethics that permits advancement only under the table. . . .

Armah's handling of the clerk's ordeal is, to put it mildly, unusual.
In fact, quite a few readers are going to find it revolting. For his message

almost seems to be that power corrupts while absolute power defecates. The extent to which Armah relies on human waste to symbolize the decay of personal integrity is all but breathtaking—and this can, if you wish, refer to holding the nose. In brief, it really hits the fan.

This is literary talent? You bet it is. And I say that as one who finds most scatalogical prose not only disgusting but bady written. It calls for no small gift to expound on excreta and neither offend nor bore, even greater ability if this unlovely topic is to be made valid within the context of a novel. Armah brings it off, his objective being, of course, to convey a moral lesson—by highlighting his protagonist's un-compromising ethical rectitude through personal fastidiousness. To the clerk, going to the toilet is a nightmare, not only because the public lavatories which he uses happen to violate every rule of hygiene but because they also represent, in a very physical sense, the moral contam-ination which surrounds him—sometimes even tempts him in its foul way—and against which he must always be on guard. Armah has treated a most indelicate function with remarkable skill—and force.

Charles Miller. *SR*. Aug. 31, 1968, p. 24

One could say that perhaps Mr. Armah has allowed his revulsion [in *The Beautyful Ones Are Not Yet Born*] to influence his use of visible symbols to describe the less visible but general decay of the people and the country. Even a "bad" Ghanaian (one who does not believe in the national uniqueness in all things) could find it difficult to accept in physical terms the necessity for hammering on every page the shit and stink from people and the environment. One has encountered similar and even worse physical decay in other parts of the world. Though again, like the fate of the workers, this does not make it any easier to put up with. But somehow one feels a slight unease that the ordinary people should be subjected to the rather hyperbolical exposure which this book makes. There are quite a few angles from which one can judge cleanliness, including the emotional and clinical. For instance, quite a few people might prefer to live any day in the city or town which forms the background to the book than in Santa Monica, near Los Angeles, with its cold, sterilized cleanliness. The choice may be between a pigsty and an expensive mortuary, of course.

What is clear, then, is that whatever is beautiful and genuinely pleasing in Ghana or about Ghanaians seems to have gone unmentioned in *The Beautyful Ones Are Not Yet Born*. Yet, what kind of beauty is that which is represented by a human being like that avaricious tinsel of an Estella? Or what could be pleasing in the heartless betrayal of a people's hopes? And can there be anything at all beautiful about the generation which does this betraying? Is it not true also that, when an atmosphere is polluted anyway, nothing escapes the general foulness? Besides, one has to grant Mr. Armah that there is a nightmarish possibility that a full awareness of all this can become so crippling, that its effect on even a potentially active individual might be to make him want to withdraw completely into himself—a tendency the Teacher already betrays and which this rather obscure and almost redundant figure in the book imparts to "the man."

Christina Ama Ata Aidoo. Introduction to
Ayi Kwei Armah, The Beautyful Ones Are Not Yet
Born (New York, Macmillan, 1969), pp. xi–xii

[The protagonist in *The Beautyful Ones Are Not Yet Born*] is an epitome of the pathos and despair of the African who is caught up in the situation that Franz Fanon has brilliantly dealt with in *The Wretched of the Earth*: the African revolution has been betrayed at every turn. The only thing that has changed is the internal composition of the class of political masters. The underdog still suffers because national resources have yet to be harnessed and redistributed in a way that would meaningfully improve the lot of the man in the street.

The translation of such a dialectic into imaginative literature is not easy, especially when one's hero is so shadowy that when he engages in dialogue with other nameless characters (for instance with the naked man in Chapter Five) the reader is exposed to a lot of potential confusion. But there is enough evidence of Ayi Kwei Armah's competence as a writer to make one believe that he could have made satisfactory literature out of this material. The atmosphere of gloom is quite convincing, as is the fundamental pessimism and cynicism. . . .

In the end, the reader joins the unheroic hero in pondering (Chapters Nine and Ten) over what the African Revolution has done to its promises. This is a question all right-thinking Africans should ask themselves. They should seriously examine Ayi Kwei Armah's attempt at an artistic appraisal of this theme and should on no account be put off merely by the superabundance of filth in it. For it is important to condemn the book solely on artistic grounds and to protest only where one finds some elements that have not been effectively pressed into the service of art.

Jawa Apronti. LO. Mar. 14, 1969, p. 24.

The hero of *Fragments* is a passive man. He is a "been-to," an African who has been abroad. He is returning from America, where he has studied, and where he decided to become a writer. He also has had a nervous breakdown in the States, and needs a special drug to counter any attack. Baako is a symbolic African figure, the educated young man torn between the values of the old and new. But the distinction that Armah brilliantly shows is that even the new values have turned. In early African novels of colonialist Africa when the educated hero returned to his country he was adrift. He belonged neither to his tribesmen nor the British who acknowledged his education but never accepted him socially and personally. Such heroes, in African novels, usually ended in despair and often self-inflicted violence. Now the "been-to" returns to his own country but finds the corrupt bureaucracy has changed from a white British to a black Ghanaian skin. . . .

The novel, while a powerful moral indictment of the present state of his country, makes its force felt through symbolism, not direct propagandistic means. This use of symbology is both Armah's weakness and virtue. The killing of a dog, the capture of gulls, the unfinished house in the hills—all these take on added layers of sense, as in a tone poem or painting—and sometimes the result is a wonderfully sensuous appreciation of the dissociation of life, the inward nature of each individual, the ultimate unknowingness of things. Yet the technique is so richly used that it becomes a drug. The pictorials, the moments are resonant phrases tossing suggestively in a dream.

I think the novel fails of its promise—for [The Beautyful Ones Are Not Yet Born] promised more than fragments. It still succeeds as a tone poem of powerful allegorical force.

Martin Tucker. NR. Jan. 31, 1970, p. 26

A careful reading of [The Beautyful Ones Are Not Yet Born] will not sustain [Christina Ama Ata Aidoo's] generalization that there is Ghanaian excrement, filth, and stink on every page, not even if we expand the disgusting objects to include other kinds of painful and ugly sights and unpleasantnesses of various sorts. And it is not clear that "whatever is beautiful and genuinely pleasing in Ghana or about Ghanaians seems to go unmentioned." . . .

What keeps this novel, with its rather sad action and its multitude of images of excrement and nastiness, from giving an overall impression of disgust, or depression, or even from seeming ridiculous or incredible? Well, there are a number of qualifying elements in the novel, elements which make a chord with the sad events and the more repugnant images, which help to make much beauty out of the ugliness. First, there is the gentleness, the kindness, the self-critical lovingness of the man, at once the main character of the novel, and its central intelligence and reflector, in whose mind we stay continually throughout the novel. His kindly thoughts for his wife, his children, his Teacher, and the poor and wretched of Ghana permeate the novel. . . .

Another qualifier of the harshness of the events and the repugnant images is the style of the novel. It is not a colloquial style, as might seem appropriate for the low-colloquial level of much of the vocabulary. Neither is it a harsh, staccato style, which would perhaps seem to fit some of the excremental and nasty language. It is a style of high rhetoric, fairly formal, a distinctly literary style, with a rhythm that swells and soars a bit. It is a style with language generally elevated, with allusions and referents of considerable portentousness. . . .

Another qualification: the images of excrement and filth always cluster around the corrupt Ghanaians, the bribers and the crooks, the party men and the white men's apes, the calloused and the brutal. . . .

Every reader must decide for himself about the total effect of Armah's *The Beautyful Ones Are Not Yet Born* in accordance with his literary intuition, his taste, his reading experience. For one reader at least the novel is splendid, one of the two or three best to come out of Africa, one worthy of a place of honor among the novels of its time in the whole world. And the images of excrement and nastiness, which are so conspicuous in the novel, find their justification in the mode of fiction Armah has chosen to write in and in the fact that they are skillfully qualified by other elements. . . . Even if "the beautyful ones" are *never* born in his country, Armah has made from the dirt and the despair, from the corruption and the foulness of all sorts, a beautiful work of art.

Harold R. Collins. WLWE. Nov., 1971, pp. 45–47, 49

The Beautyful Ones Are Not Yet Born is a symbolic moral fable. What strikes one most forcefully, is the strength of the author's moral earnestness. On almost every page, in unusually vigorous and realistic language, Armah expresses his nausea at the corruption he sees everywhere. The symbolic nature of the characters and the vagueness of the setting reinforce the impression of a moral fable. Indeed, the temptation to compare this work with *Everyman* or Bunyan's *Pilgrim's Progress* is very strong. The characters are important not for what they are in themselves, but for what they represent. Most of them are very vaguely particularized and indicated by generalized names. The hero himself is known only as "the man," and is referred to variously as "the watcher," "the giver" and "the silent one." His immediate dependants are called "the loved ones," and one of the most important characters is called "the teacher." Although Maanan, Oyo, and Koomson have names, it is clear that their function is mainly symbolic. Ghana is itself symbolically presented, one of the consequences being that Accra is much less vividly described than the Lagos of Achebe or Ekwensi. But this deliberate vagueness makes it similar to *Everyman*'s "Field Full of Folk" or Tutuola's "Land of the Deads." . . .

At the centre of the novel is the hero—the man—whose anonymity represents everyman, the ordinary Ghanaian citizen. He is a man of unquestioned integrity. . . . Nevertheless, Armah, far from idealizing his hero, demonstrates his passive impotence, and weakness. . . .

Although there can be little doubt that Armah makes his point about corruption in Ghana, the novel is not without its weaknesses. *The Beautyful Ones Are Not Yet Born* consists largely of the man's reflections, and the various impressions which impinge on his senses. But these impressions and reflections are about one thing and one thing alone—corruption and the rottenness that goes with it. Consequently, the novel seems to have a peculiarly theoretical and didactic quality, with the doctrine about corruption being persistently hammered into the reader's brain.

> Eustace Palmer. *An Introduction to the African Novel* (New York, Africana, 1972), pp. 129, 131, 141

Why Are We So Blest?, by Ayi Kwei Armah, is more of an inspired travelogue than a novel. The real journey that the author deals with, however, is an uneasy one taken by Modin, a young African intellectual, in and out of the peripheries of revolutionary involvement. Modin is a young man inspired not by hope but by a death wish. One of the revolutionary bureaucrats declares in his Algiers office after Modin's first visit with his white American mistress: "He is one of those intellectuals who wants to die. He should have the courage to do it himself."

There is an obsessive preoccupation with black-white sexual relations throughout the book and the author offers far too many unnecessary and repetitive clinical details, which in the end produce yawns instead of fresh insights. This novel, unlike the other two by Armah, is one bereft of genuine emotions. Somehow in dissecting characters, situations, settings, there is an absence of tension. It demonstrates the sterility of a purely intellectual involvement in revolution, sex or life itself.

> Jan Carew. *NYT*. April 2, 1972, p. 14

Armah has already established himself through his first two novels as one of the leading West African novelists. *Why Are We So Blest?* not only confirms that evaluation, but caps his earlier achievements with an even more brilliant work. He is still working with the same counters, his own very personal experiences and a resultant sense of almost overwhelming despair, but he continuously pushes these counters into a larger public arena. He is like one of his characters, looking for "the kind of truth which merges all things and reveals the day's solid rock as only the pliable clay in the larger changing patterns of ages."

Written as a journal, the novel is built around the lives of three central characters, Solo, Modin and Aimée. Solo, a disillusioned revolutionary, is living in the country of Afrasia (read Algeria) supporting himself as a translator and doing occasional work for a group concerned with the liberation of the African Portuguese colonies from which he himself has come. Alternating with sections from his journal are journals of Modin, an African educated in the United States at Harvard, and his white American girl friend, Aimée. Modin and Aimée come to Afrasia to work for the liberation group, meet Solo and are put off by his cynicism. As the novel progresses we see all three being trapped in the cages of racism they strove to avoid. . . .

Many will read anti-white sentiments into [Armah's] treatment of Aimée. But neither the individual characters nor the book as a whole should be seen in terms of a simple black-white dichotomy. On an ethical level we can in fact see it as a carefully planned attack on all racism, but esthetically we can also apprehend it as a sensitive exploration into the minds of three alienated individuals and the web of relationships which created their respective sensibilities.

Richard Priebe. *BA*. Autumn, 1972, p. 724

[*The Beautyful Ones Are Not Yet Born*] is a well-written book. Armah's command of language and imagery is of a very high order indeed. But it is a sick book. Sick, not with the sickness of Ghana, but with the sickness of the *human condition*. The hero, pale and passive and nameless—a creation in the best manner of existentialist writing—wanders through the story in an anguished half-sleep, neck-deep in despair and human excrement of which we see rather a lot in the book. Did I say he *refused* to be corrupted? He did not do anything as positive as refusing. He reminded me very strongly of that man and woman in a Jean-Paul Sartre novel who sit in anguished gloom in a restaurant and then in a sudden access of nihilistic energy seize table knives and stab their hands right through to the wood—to prove some very obscure point to each other. Except that Armah's hero would be quite incapable of suffering any seizure.

Ultimately the novel failed to convince me. And this was because Armah insists that this story is happening in Ghana and not in some modern, existentialist no man's land. . . . But his Ghana is unrecognizable. This aura of cosmic sorrow and despair is as foreign and unusable as those monstrous machines Nkrumah was said to have imported from Eastern European countries. Said, that is, by critics like Armah.

True, Ghana was sick. And what country is not? But everybody has his own brand of ailment. Ayi Kwei Armah imposes so much foreign metaphor on the sickness of Ghana that it ceases to be true. And finally, the suggestion (albeit existentially tentative) of the hero's personal justification without faith nor works is grossly inadequate in a society where even a lunatic walking stark naked through the highways of Accra has an extended family somewhere suffering vicarious shame.

Armah is clearly an alienated writer, a modern writer complete with all the symptoms. Unfortunately Ghana is not a modern existentialist country. It is just a Western African state struggling to become a nation. So there is enormous distance between Armah and Ghana. [1973]

Chinua Achebe. *Morning Yet on Creation Day*
(Garden City, N.Y., Doubleday, 1975), pp. 39–40

Since the publication of his first novel, *The Beautyful Ones Are Not Yet Born*, in 1968, there has been little dispute that of all the younger African novelists, Ayi Kwei Armah is one of the most talented. Now six years later, with the publication of a fourth novel, *Two Thousand Seasons*, it is clear that Armah is not only one of the most prolific contemporary African novelists, but also one of the most highly original —certainly the major prose stylist from Anglophone Africa. . . .

Two Thousand Seasons is an unfinished chronicle of Africa's servitude—two thousand seasons (wet and dry), one thousand years of struggle—against the invaders from the north, first the Arabs and then the Europeans: "a thousand seasons wasted wandering amazed along alien roads, another thousand spent finding paths to the living way." It is also a parable of epic proportions—in many ways more like an oral tale told by a griot, a song of life and death, than a realistic story as Armah's earlier works have been. Or, to put it still another way, *Two Thousand Seasons* is the first African novel—the first novel an African would have written several hundred years ago if Africans were writing novels then, the African version of the initial meeting with the West. . . .

His temporal thrust is intentionally confusing. One thing is clear, however. The two thousand seasons are far from being completed. They didn't end with the 1960s when so many African nations became independent. They won't end in the 1970s or the 1980s. And that is another reason why *Two Thousand Seasons* is such a fascinating novel. I have called it the first African novel because, historically, it describes the initial African reaction to the West, but it is also a novel about Africa today. And tomorrow, regrettably.

For Armah himself this is all quite a change from his earlier works —a continuous evidence of his growth as a writer, his ability to strike into new areas and not to write the same novel over and over again as so many writers (not just African writers) do throughout their careers. Instead, Armah has written a totally original work, the most significant book of his career—a complete break from his earlier works.

Charles R. Larson. *AT*. Spring, 1974, pp. 117, 119

ATTAWAY, WILLIAM (1912–   )

UNITED STATES

[*Blood on the Forge*] is a story of transition and contrasting values. In the first part of the novel we are shown the naïve, almost formless personalities of the farm workers in their "natural" sharecropper setting. While the main portion of the narrative centers in the mill town, where we see the quicksilver personalities caught within the hot, hard forge of industry. The boys' names—through which Attaway symbolizes three basic attitudes to the world of steel—now become meaningful: Melody embodies the artistic principle; Big Mat, the religious; and Chinatown, the pagan. We see the new routine of toil (product of a way of life technologically years ahead of that from which they've come), grinding down upon these boys. Under it Big Mat's vague religion and mythology become inadequate; Melody, whose relationship to his world has always been expressed through his guitar, gives musical utterance to a new attitude, the blues; and the "blow-top" Chinatown's life becomes a mad ritual of "whiskey, whores, and wheel-barrows." Thus in this world of changing values all the old rules of living are melted away. . . .

Conceptionally, Attaway grasped the destruction of the folk, but missed its rebirth on a higher level. The writer did not see that while the folk individual was being liquidated in the crucible of steel, he was also undergoing fusion with new elements. Nor did Attaway see that the individual which emerged, blended of old and new, was better fitted for the problems of the industrial environment. As a result the author is so struck by the despair in his material that he fails to see any ground for hope for his characters. . . .

Some [Negroes] found in unionism a large part of the answer to their suffering. It was these, at the beginning only a few, who by pursuing their vision despite the antipathy of some white unionists and bosses alike, established those values embraced by a growing number of Negroes today. Serious writing about the Negro must spread this hard won consciousness.

Ralph Ellison. *NQ*. Spring, 1942, pp. 88–91

The thesis in *Blood on the Forge* is that Negroes are objects of discrimination and injustice on the labor market, especially when they offer "competition to white men." Attaway develops this thesis around economic conditions in the steel mills of Pennsylvania after World War I when Negroes were brought from the South for scab labor purposes. . . .

Big Mat and his brothers are the victims of unsatisfactory labor union strategy, for they are employed to break a strike rather than to become members of the union. Big Mat is given the official role of strikebreaker deputy. In the labor battle which follows, Big Mat loses his life, and Chinatown and Melody are left blind and mutilated. . . .

Attaway follows the conventional approach which is essentially documentation of evils inherent in the social order with particular reference to the Negro. Usually, flagrant injustices, discriminatory practices, and oppression compose the framework of such a novel. The danger that a Negro writer has to avoid is being too reportorial and documentary. There is, of course, no room for sentimentality because this is the grim business of projecting incidents of real life truthfully yet with narrative skill. Again, the Negro author has to prevent himself from becoming tractish in his fervor for advocating change rather than remaining purely objective. Attaway achieves success in *Blood on the Forge*.

Carl Milton Hughes. The Negro Novelist (New
York, Citadel, 1953), pp. 79–82

Ellison's comment notwithstanding, *Blood on the Forge* is more than a novel of dissolution. Counterposed to the Moss brothers is the figure of Zanski, an old Ukrainian steelworker who represents a superior adjustment to the new industrial environment. Confronted with similar problems of acculturation, the transplanted Ukrainian peasants have been quicker to put their roots down than the Negro migrants. Zanski, knowing instinctively that no peasant can be happy unless he is growing things, insists at least upon having kids growing in his yard. In addition to realizing the importance of family life, the Slavs are overwhelmingly pro-union. Since Attaway will eventually part company with the Moss brothers on ideological grounds, Zanski helps to prepare the ground for this decisive shift in tone. . . .

The Moss brothers see the strike strictly from a racial point of view; there is nothing in their experience which would cause them to do otherwise. . . . It is clear from Attaway's tone, however, that he is playing devil's advocate; his aim is to discredit Negro nationalism, from a somewhat broader point of view. Ideologically speaking, *Blood on the Forge* represents the shift from race consciousness to class consciousness which so many Negro intellectuals experienced during the Red Decade.

Robert A. Bone. *The Negro Novel in America* (New Haven, Conn., Yale University Press, 1958), pp. 138–39

[*Let Me Breathe Thunder*, Attaway's first novel] celebrates the loyalty and decency of men on the move, and the essential virtues of the life of the soil. Attaway's Negro themes . . . are muted and disguised, which allows him to speak the language of protest without using its rhetoric. In shying away from making his main characters Negroes, Attaway was perhaps fearful of having his novel labeled protest fiction. The two Negro characters who do appear in the novel have no especial "Negro" traits, and although one of them is nearly lynched for the supposed attempted rape of a white girl, scarcely any allusion is made to his race. It appears as if Attaway were bending over backwards to assure his readers that he is not writing "sociology." Such a position is absurd, since any reader would naturally associate lynchings and imaginary sex crimes with race. The novel falters on other counts: the characters rarely spring to life, and their situations vaguely suggest those Steinbeck described two years earlier in *Of Mice and Men*. Yet for all that, the narrative does possess a certain verve, and the prose is economical and clean in the Hemingway manner—objective but replete with undertones of irony and sadness. . . .

His first novel . . . was promising; his second, a classic of its kind. Why then did Attaway stop writing fiction? He was only twenty-nine when *Blood on the Forge* appeared. . . . It is perhaps in the realm of ideas that we may look for the source of Attaway's arrested artistic development. Basically Attaway is a romantic. *Let Me Breathe Thunder*, for all its praise of stable family life and the virtues of farming, ultimately celebrates the free-wheeling bohemianism of hoboes—and Attaway, by manipulating his plot this way and that, manages to free his protagonists from any social and moral obligations. In another romantic vein, *Blood on the Forge* projects the myth of the "good" soil corrupted by man's greed, whose logical absurdity manifests itself in the manufacture of steel. While no one would deny that the excesses of American capitalism have produced cruel and dehumanizing injustices, it is hard, after Darwin, to ascribe moral virtues to nature. And since it is scarcely possible any longer to look to nature as something apart and holy, Attaway may well have written himself out of subject matter.

Edward Margolies. *Native Sons* (Philadelphia, J. B. Lippincott, 1968), pp. 52, 63–64

Blood on the Forge is a well-written novel. It deserved the plaudits of critics past and present. It is a structurally sounder novel than *Native Son*, and the inner mechanics—symbols and images of life, death, and destruction—work as effectively for Attaway as they do for Wright. Yet, Attaway, unlike Wright, has accepted the argument that themes of universal import take preference over those of more parochial import; that is, the conflict between man and the machine is more universal than that between black man and a racist society. . . .

This despite the fact that Attaway lives in a universe marred by turmoil and dissension. The depression, as he knows so well, has brought men to the brink of revolution, the migration made it impossible for people to survive by the patterns of old. In such a new world, Melody and Chinatown, of course, are doomed; hedonism and paganism, twin evils for black men, are useless in a world in which the race war is an eternal given. This is not so for Big Mat; in a world of violence and turmoil, violence is the norm, and the man who tempers it with the proper humanism has come close to constructing a new ethic. Attaway could not accept this idea. There is too much of the naturalist in him, too much of the sociologist; he adheres to a code that preaches universal brotherhood, yet one that refuses to acknowledge the historical fact that such has been achieved only when one man possessed guns as powerful as the other. When Big Mat exchanges the Bible for the sheriff's cudgel, he has leaped across centuries of black history into the modern world. Attaway, however, cannot accept him, recoils in horror from his own creation, attempts to convince the reader that excessive rage and compulsive anger have driven Mat to become more insane than other men, that violence represents not redemption for him, but vengeance, and that the race war, unlike other wars, must be fought out on the high plane of moral niceties and meaningless epithets. . . .

Attaway backs away from Armageddon at sight of the flames. What might have become a novel representing man's courage and strength, becomes one instead which consigns him to doom and damnation.

Addison Gayle, Jr. *The Way of the New World*
(Garden City, N.Y., Doubleday, 1975), pp. 164–66

AWOONOR, KOFI (1935–   )

GHANA

Christophe Okigbo . . . passes through a succession of Heavensgates. [In *Rediscovery*] George Awoonor-Williams waits at "hellgate," not to pass through but to be "delivered" from his place of waiting to a pleasanter spot. The fascination that Awoonor-Williams has with things basic, mysterious, such as death or the ritual acts of love or worship leads him to the temporary rediscovery and fleeting recognitions that he desires. He reminds one of Okigbo because he goes on and on with the purifications and is as dissatisfied with the "purified" state as Okigbo. But, unlike Okigbo's poetic litanies, Awoonor-Williams' poems are single moments selected out of a pattern of rediscovery. The points of crystallisation are recorded—both low and high, the moments of inglorious desire, the moments of discovering the strengths that his own soul possesses. Okigbo presents the notes and feelings of the entire journey; Awoonor-Williams selects the moments of greatest importance, ones which have a significance beyond themselves. Awoonor-Williams' great achievement is his use of "extended rhythms" and, in this, he is as skilful as Ezra Pound or the William Carlos Williams of *Paterson*. . . .

Awoonor-Williams extends his rhythms by extending the lines into other poems. . . . He is not "writing the same thing" as the similar lines might lead one to believe, but enlarging his theme by repetition in depth. Anyone who has read the Bible knows that Awoonor-Williams was not the first to sit "by the rivers of Babylon," but he puts this theft to work for him. And this also adds to the symphonic effect of the body of poems.

Paul Theroux. BO. Aug., 1966, pp. 47–49

Awoonor's first volume of poetry, *Rediscovery*, was published by Mbari Publications (of Mbari Writers and Artists Club in Ibadan). Since then he has grown from strength to strength. Throughout, his poetry is characterized by the aura of a sage's words: now pleading, now cautioning, now ruminating over the African's position in relation to the ancestors or his father's gods, now asserting his need to go out in search of a stabilizing agent. The sage's voice often seems to ramble, strike out in some direction and return to reassert what it said before. Consequently, Awoonor's poems supplement one another, and a continuity of theme is maintained. The lyricism seldom flags, however. . . .

Awoonor speaks with a quiet voice always. No ranting, no squirming. The voice comes through in the beat of his lines—a beat which, coupled with the simplicity of the diction, captures the mood and slow pace of African contemplative speech. . . .

Kofi Awoonor has a keen ear for verbal music. I do not know of any African poet who can, like Awoonor, compose a line of verse in English that rolls off the tongue with exquisite music and do it again and again. The late Christopher Okigbo also had a sharp ear for verbal music, but he exploited the music that is inherent in the English language which he had mastered so remarkably. Awoonor, on the other hand, seems to bring another element from outside of the English language. Ewe, his mother tongue, is a highly musical language, but the music of an African language cannot be translated into that of a European one. It is an unnameable element he brings to the music he replays. . . .

· The elegiac mood that pervades Kofi Awoonor's poetry reaches its high water mark in his "Lament of the Silent Sister." The cry for what Africa has lost in her traditional values with the accompanying exhortation for us to take a grip of ourselves, to ask our fathers to "sew the old days" for us, finds in "Lament of the Silent Sister" a concrete and still elevating subject—that of Christopher Okigbo, who died in the Nigerian war in 1967. I consider this elegy to be the finest in African writing, one of the finest in the English-speaking world. It is truly African, taking us on a wave that rises and falls, rises and falls to the deep tones of a funeral drum. And from deep down there the voice of the mourner rides on a diction that comes straight to the heart. . . .

Although Kofi Awoonor's poetry is packed with ideas, his gentle diction carries us there with its emotional drive, its traditional speech patterns. For all that, the poetry stays on the ground, avoiding any intellectual horseplay.

Ezekiel Mphahlele. Introduction to Kofi Awoonor,
Night of My Blood (Garden City, N.Y., Doubleday,
1971), pp. 9–10, 15, 17–18

[As] Wole Soyinka did in his novel *The Interpreters*, Awoonor [in *This Earth, My Brother...*] uses the most advanced literary techniques of Western fiction to present the whole scale of an African society, from the most "primitive" to the most "advanced." His story takes a man from his birth in a back-country Ewe village through his education and his successful career at the bar in Accra to his mental and emotional breakdown and death.

The story is given to us in a series of scenes at crucial or at casual moments, interspersed with internal dreamlike monologues. Every one of these episodes or reveries is presented in such a brilliant light that at first the reader may have an impression of a glowing but disordered kaleidoscope. Actually, as the reader soon realizes, this is a very economical means of giving us, in a little over two hundred pages, a knowledge of the inner life of a man and of the society that drives such a man to his final despair.

The reveries, we soon see, are those of a man in a madhouse. They are wild and in the vein of poetry that we know often represents the eruption of the unconscious. . . .

We have now a few books like *This Earth, My Brother...* which are bound to stand, it seems to me, not only as chronicles of the first tragic era of African independence but as noble contributions to the art of the world.

John Thompson. NYR. Sept. 23, 1971, p. 4

The jacket and title page insist that *This Earth, My Brother...* be called "An Allegorical Tale of Africa," though it seems no more allegorical than any novel is; i.e., its hero represents many men and his plight illustrates an aspect of the human condition. The hero, Amamu, is a young Ghanian lawyer, who, through the alternation of objective and introspective chapters (set, I think too fussily, in different sizes of type), proceeds to nervous breakdown and death. The stress he suffers is presumably the inordinate gap (and here the typographic device may have a point) between his primitive, hopeful, partially idyllic past and the mediocre, nagging, disappointed present of his life in an African metropolis no better able to cope with corruption and pollution and poverty than any other modern city. . . . Awoonor's Ghana is familiarly dismal, except that all the faces are black and the problems of over-development experienced in America are matched by the not dissimilar embarrassments of underdevelopment. Amamu is a thorough bourgeois male—uneasy in his work, a witness to injustice yet a professional participant in it, a citizen perpetually testifying, inwardly, to his own puzzling incrimination in the venal, weary workings of a mercenary society. . . .

Viewed externally, Amamu is not very impressive or dynamic, and his fate is less tragic than damply sad, a shadow melting back into shadows. Yet the novel's strength is its refusal to be spectacular, to feign anger it doesn't feel, or to present Ghanian life as anything much more than a fumbling, disheartened extension of colonial rule, a blurred carbon. Humanity is not . . . locked out; there are pages of faithful, inconsequential dialogue, with a lilt never heard in the West, and perhaps it is this sense of voice and voices that makes *This Earth, My Brother...* aimiable, despite its allegorical grimace. [Nov. 13, 1971]

John Updike. Picked-Up Pieces (New York,
Alfred A. Knopf, 1975), pp. 321, 323

Kofi Awoonor was known until now for his poetry—a strong, muscular, controlled poetry. With [*This Earth, My Brother...*] he makes a dramatic new appearance in the role of prose-writer—again strong in his accents and in full confidence.

He calls the book "an allegorical tale of Africa." An allegory is as good a name as one can call this rather unusual and highly personal form. It is in fact a medley of forms—intense and tight sequences of poetic prose alternating with more open stretches of realistic narrative and now and again broken by shots of running commentary, all moving sometimes forwards in time sometimes backwards or in circles and at yet another time completely flung outside our accustomed historical time-scale. . . .

Despite those laughing people, laughing with all their white teeth, Africa is a place of torment and ugliness. Being Ghanaian and Ghana being so central to modern Africa, Awoonor can sometimes particularise his Africa into his Ghana—a "revolting malevolence" he calls it, reminding us of that other Ghanaian writer, Ayi Kwei Armah, author of the novel, *The Beautyful Ones Are Not Yet Born*.

Awoonor's allegory teems with people, places, incidents, thoughts, emotions, actions, evasions. It follows (pursues may be more apt) the hero from the very orgasm of his conception through his feverish life. It takes off without warning to any part of the world and makes unscheduled stops where it pleases. Yet despite such wide ranging techniques Awoonor never falls into superficialities. What he unfolds before us may be fleeting but it is always sharp and never, one is convinced, unimportant. And it is not a succession of haphazard impressions either despite the seeming arbitrariness of its sequences. There is a cumulativeness, indeed an organic, albeit bizarre, development towards the ultimate failure. But here is no existential futility; at every stage there is a misty hint of a viable alternative, of a road that is not taken, of a possibility that fails to develop. The central failure is African independence whose early promise is like the butterfly that the child Amamu caught in the fields of yellow sunflower as the moon, and it flew away again. He searched for it for days and found others that looked like it; but no, it was gone. . . .

So the death of [British] Empire was not to be seriously lamented. Senile and absurd it no longer had the will to stand by and protect its very own. But at least it had its heyday, its years of honour. Its successor, Independence, did not even wait to grow old before turning betrayer.

Chinua Achebe. Transition. No. 41, 1972, p. 69

Even the title [*This Earth, My Brother...*] is an exhalation of frustration and despair. To the lament "This Earth, my brother..." I can almost hear the "boh, na wah!" of the listener. Because we are warned by the author that this is an allegory I do not waste effort trying to read it straight like a thriller. But then, by what code shall I decipher the encoded commentary on Africa? Taking my cue from the title I first read it as a disillusioned portrait of the times as observed through the eyes of a suffering innocent. I followed the milieu-painting to its end;

went along on a guided tour of the stations of dislocation and the marshes of corruption; went along on this tour of the ruins till I came to the final ruin—Amamu's madness. But this device of insanity? Having paddled down the river of his consciousness, having shared his inner musings, I found myself asking: Did Amamu have to go mad? Are his experiences and visions far out of the ordinary? What is there in them to justify his going mad? Yaro's troubles, Ibrahim's death, the disastrous party the night before, all being really peripheral to the core of Amamu's being, do not seem to be sufficient forces to finally shove him over the brink into insanity. And so I am led to a reconsideration. . . .

But whatever the case, let us remember that to ask for more and for better is not to belittle what we have been already given. As a novel which unearths issues of fictional craft, *This Earth, My Brother...* is certainly worthy of critical note. As a work which tackles problems of African reality today, it is also worthy of general note. And of course, passages of poetic delight run through the realistic and stream-of-consciousness sequences of which the work is composed. Whatever its failings, however much it portrays surfaces without revealing shadows from the depths, this book is certainly not a soporific.

Chinweizu. Okike. Dec., 1974, pp. 88, 95–96

Primarily through his poetry, Awoonor has established himself as one of the most significant contemporary African writers. His first two books of poetry, *Rediscovery* and *Night of My Blood*, show a powerful progression from a fascination with his roots, through an uncertain poetic and cultural synthesis with the west, to a voice that is confidently his own. More than any other western-African poet, with the possible exceptions of Christopher Okigbo and Wole Soyinka, Awoonor has succeeded in transcending the raw tensions of culture conflict. His poetry should be read as a series of attempts to find in the history and poetry of his people correlatives to his own personal anguish as a modern African. Poems that serve to accentuate the anguish and give definition to the progression may appear to be difficult, or simply uneven and rough, when removed from this context.

In both form and imagery Awoonor's poetry has been heavily influenced by the Ewe dirge. According to traditional Ewe beliefs, those who have just died and are entering another existence represent potential danger to those left behind, for the physical loss interrupts the continuity of society and threatens it with dissolution. Yet, good may also come out of a death, for a successful transition ends with the dead individual becoming an ancestral being who can be a beneficial force in the community. The purpose of the Ewe dirge is to aid the individual in making this transition.

For Awoonor the dirge becomes symbolic not only of an individual and societal process but also of the poet's passage from insufficiency to fulfillment, from chaos to order, from alienation to integration. Death and anguish pervade his poetry as mediating agents that force the continual restructuring, refocusing, and revitalizing of individual and communal order. In effect, Awoonor explores the relationship between contemporary society and traditional myth and ritual.

Richard Priebe. In *Encyclopedia of World Literature*
in the 20th Century (New York, Frederick Ungar,
1975), Vol. IV, pp. 28–29

BALDWIN, JAMES (1924–   )

UNITED STATES

In his first novel [*Go Tell It on the Mountain*] James Baldwin has used the familiar story-within-a-story device to produce good enter-tainment—and something more: even the most insensitive of readers will put the book down with a troubled feeling of having "looked on beauty bare."

It is not, however, the kind of beauty to which lazy senses respond —no honeysuckle and moonlight, no pastoral charm or urban elegance, no pure young love, no soft, sweet lostness of the brave and the damned. Its beauty is the beauty of sincerity and of the courageous facing of hard subjective truth. This is not to say that there is nothing derivative—of what first novel can this be said?—but James Baldwin's critical judg-ments are perspicacious and his esthetic instincts sound, and he has read Faulkner and Richard Wright and, very notably, Dostoevski to advan-tage. A little of each is here—Faulkner in the style, Wright in the narrative, and the Russian in the theme. And yet style, story and theme are Baldwin's own, made so by the operation of the strange chemistry of talent which no one fully understands.

Baldwin's style is lucid and free-running but involved. It is a style that shows the man to be keenly sensitive to words. The frame story of *Go Tell It on the Mountain* is relatively slight. It is a simple account of what frustration does to an adolescent boy named John Grimes. The fact of his being a Negro has little significance other than as description. John could have been any susceptible fifteen-year-old, illegitimate boy, hated by his stepfather, estranged by younger children from his mother, and forced to live within himself. But living within oneself is unnatural for a physically healthy boy in Harlem, and John, in a violent burst of seeking for he knows not what, finds another world.

J. Saunders Redding. NYHT. May 17, 1953, p. 5

[In *Go Tell It on the Mountain*] John succumbs to his guilt and to his longings for reconciliation with his family, with his Negro-ness, and with

God, and is seized by a religious convulsion. In submitting to it he chooses one of the two fates allowed the Negro. If he were to revolt, as so many in his family had done, the world would strike him down. If, on the other hand, he accepts the literal nothingness of what the world offers, and forfeits his hopes for a better life on earth, he will be accepting the burden of religion and of being a Negro. . . .

There are two "mountains" in this book. When, at the end, John is "saved" and has begun his tortured ascent of the mountain of Holiness, we feel that the injustice of his condition is subsumed for the moment in the larger, impersonal justice of the novel—the strange justice of tragedy. This is his doom, and there is a rightness about it if only because it is inevitable. But we recall that other "mountain," the hill in Central Park from which John, at the beginning of the book, looked down beneath "the brilliant sky, and beyond it, cloudy and far away, he saw the skyline of New York." It is the same kind of elevation from which, I am sure Mr. Baldwin wants us to remember, Eugène de Rastignac, at the close of [Balzac's] *Père Goriot*, surveys Paris. It is the prominence from which all the "young men from the provinces" catch their glimpse of the worlds they are to love and win. But for John Grimes there can be no winning; and when we realize this, that he can stand only on the mountain of Holiness, an otherworldly mountain made of bitterness and renunciation, a mountain where he finds his real identity, the poignancy of his earlier vision comes upon us with great force.

Steven Marcus. *Cmty.* Nov., 1953, pp. 460–61

James Baldwin writes down to nobody, and he is trying very hard to write up to himself. As an essayist he is thought-provoking, tantalizing, irritating, abusing and amusing. And he uses words as the sea uses waves, to flow and beat, advance and retreat, rise and take a bow in disappearing.

In *Notes of a Native Son*, James Baldwin surveys in pungent commentary certain phases of the contemporary scene as they relate to the citizenry of the United States, particularly Negroes. Harlem, the protest novel, bigoted religion, the Negro press and the student milieu of Paris are all examined in black and white, with alternate shutters clicking, for hours of reading interest. When the young man who wrote this book comes to a point where he can look at life purely as himself, and for himself, the color of his skin mattering not at all, when, as in his own words, he finds "his birthright as a man no less than his birthright as a black man," America and the world might well have a major contemporary commentator.

Few American writers handle words more effectively in the essay form than James Baldwin. To my way of thinking, he is much better at provoking thought in the essay than he is in arousing emotion in fiction. I much prefer *Notes of a Native Son* to his novel, *Go Tell It on the Mountain*, where the surface excellence and poetry of his writing did not seem to me to suit the earthiness of his subject-matter. In his essays, words and material suit each other. The thought becomes poetry, and the poetry illuminates the thought.

Langston Hughes. *NYT*. Feb. 26, 1956, p. 26

Giovanni's Room is the best American novel dealing with homosexuality I have read. . . .

No one who has read any of James Baldwin's highly intelligent, clear-eyed essays—most recently, his quietly pitched reply in *Partisan Review* to William Faulkner's views on the desegregation problem—would expect him to treat so tangled a subject as homosexual relationships cheaply or too simply. He successfully avoids the cliché literary attitudes: overemphasis on the grotesque, and the use of homosexuality as a facile symbol for the estrangement which makes possible otherwise unavailable insights into the workings of "normal" society and "normal" people; in short, the Homosexual as Artist.

Not that *Giovanni's Room* is without faults. The novel's ending . . . is somewhat lame, his descriptions of the hero's emotions run too heavily to beating hearts, trembling, bright lights, overwhelming stirrings, falling, drowning, the bottom of the sea. Also, Baldwin's blond-athlete-type hero, like Norman Mailer's in *The Deer Park*, never wholly emerges from dimness.

Nevertheless, these shortcomings only slightly detract from the book's impact. If David, the American, remains even more lumpish than he is supposed to be, Giovanni, the experienced European more vulnerable than a child, is beautifully and economically realized. Baldwin insists on the painful, baffling complexity of things.

William Esty. *NR*. Dec. 17, 1956, p. 26

When I read Baldwin's first collection of essays, *Notes of a Native Son*, I realized that the tortured intellectual consciousness I felt behind his fiction could be turned into the self-representation of an absolutely first-class essayist, reporter, and social critic. *Notes of a Native Son* is one of the two or three best books ever written about the Negro in America, and it is the work of an original literary talent who operates with as much power in the essay form as I've ever seen. I'm sure that Baldwin doesn't like to hear his essays praised at the expense (seemingly) of his fiction. And I'm equally sure that if Baldwin were not so talented a novelist he would not be so remarkable an essayist. But the great thing about his essays is that the form allows him to work out from all the conflicts raging in *him*, so that finally the "I," the "James Baldwin" who is so sassy and despairing and bright, manages, without losing his authority as the central speaker, to show us all the different people hidden in him, all the voices for whom the "I" alone can speak.

Each of his essays in this new book [*Nobody Knows My Name*] is a facet of this different experience, each is a report from the battlefield that is himself, that he sometimes feels may be *only* himself. . . . No doubt other writers could have done all these pieces coolly, as correspondents from another shore to us; for Baldwin, each of his subjects represents a violent conflict in himself. . . .

What ultimately makes these essays so impressive and moving is not merely the *use* Baldwin makes of his conflicts but the fact that this personal form is an urgent necessity. This is the book of a deeply troubled man, the spiritual autobiography of someone who hopes, by confronting more than one beast on his way, to see whether his fear is entirely necessary. [1961]

Alfred Kazin. Contemporaries (Boston,
Little, Brown, 1962), pp. 255–57

A lot of people would like to believe that [James Baldwin's writing is limited to his experience as a Negro] I suppose, because it makes it unnecessary to confront the reality of which Baldwin writes. Be that as it may, race is one of the major facts of our time and perhaps one reason it has become so explosive is precisely because it has been consciously ignored in literature. Besides, it is at least as important a theme as sex or dope, and if it moves Baldwin to expression, to eloquence, then our proper concern is with what he makes of it artistically. Undoubtedly he brings enough passion to it to indicate that the impact of race upon personality is a very important matter for him and he gives voice to it with impressive skill. On the other hand my own concerns with race are a bit muted and perhaps I am really more impatient, more concerned with putting race in a wider perspective. Perhaps matters which I work out in the silence of my room, Baldwin works out on the printed page; perhaps I have less hope, I don't know.

Ralph Ellison. UCM. April, 1962, p. 8

Baldwin's intention [in *Another Country*] is to deny any moral significance whatever to the categories white and Negro, heterosexual and homosexual. He is saying that the terms white and Negro refer to two different conditions under which individuals live, but they are still individuals and their lives are still governed by the same fundamental laws of being. And he is saying, similarly, that the terms homosexuality and heterosexuality refer to two different conditions under which individuals pursue love, but they are still individuals and their pursuit of love is still governed by the same fundamental laws of being. Putting the two propositions together, he is saying, finally, that the only significant realities are individuals and love, and that anything which is permitted to interfere with the free operation of this fact is evil and should be done away with.

Now, one might suppose that there is nothing particularly startling in this view of the world; it is, after all, only a form of the standard liberal attitude toward life. And indeed, stated as I have just stated it, and held with the mild attachment by which most liberal and enlightened Americans hold it, it is scarcely more shocking than the usual speech made at every convention of the American Society of Social Workers. But that is not the way James Baldwin holds it, and it is not the way he states it. He holds these attitudes with a puritanical ferocity, and he spells them out in such brutal and naked detail that one scarcely recognizes them any longer—and one is frightened by them, almost as though they implied a totally new, totally revolutionary, conception of the universe. And in a sense, of course, they do. For by taking these liberal pieties literally and by translating them into simple English, he puts the voltage back into them and they burn to the touch. [Oct., 1962]

Norman Podhoretz. *Doings and Undoings* (New York, Farrar, Straus, 1964), pp. 247–48

James Baldwin has quite literally been raising hell since he returned from a long European exile in the middle 1950's. . . .

From the Paris of Sartre, Beauvoir and Camus, from the expatriate Paris of Richard Wright, of the progenitors of the concept of "Negritude," Senghor, Diop and Césaire, came Baldwin, cutting, slashing and stabbing his way onto the American literary scene. Just over thirty years old, he had a solid first novel under his belt, *Go Tell It on the Mountain*, a second one, *Giovanni's Room* (a little strong on homosexuality for most American stomachs), and a remarkable book of penetrating essays, *Notes of a Native Son*. In Europe he had certainly heard of Marx and Engels, imperialism and colonialism, but in his exile he had missed the day-to-day struggles (the Rosenbergs, Willie McGee, the Martinsville Seven) that had helped to shape his Afro-American contemporaries. Perhaps as a consequence, he was remarkably free of clichés, the bane of the creative writer, clichés not only of expression but of ideas. He had absolutely no gods, either of the Left or the Right. He seemed free, as dice-shooters say of the houseman, to call the shots the way he saw them. Naturally he was possessed of an outsized ego. One felt from the intensely personal nature of his work that he believed the earth had been created on the day he was born, and that the entire white power structure of the United States had been mobilized with the single purpose of oppressing *him*. . . .

Can one say precisely what has been Baldwin's achievement? I think it has been his ability to capture, in beautiful, passionate, and persuasive prose the essence of Negro determination to live in the American house as a free man or, failing that, to burn the American house down. I don't think Baldwin is himself yet willing to set the torch to the house. Other militant black intellectuals have, for the most part, broken off their dialogue with white America. As far as possible they address themselves only to their own people urging them to more aggressive levels of struggle. Baldwin, almost alone, still talks to the whites, in love and compassion, offering them a way out, if only they will listen.

Julian Mayfield. *Freedomways.* Spring, 1963,
pp. 148–50, 155

It is on the whole encouraging that James Baldwin should have become the voice of American Negroes, because he is also the voice of an American consciousness (conscience) which is not Negro. The word "home" occurs frequently in his writings, sometimes bitterly, sometimes quite ordinarily: and by it he means America, in spite of his being acutely aware that the white men of his country have never shared their home with the Negroes. James Baldwin is an American writer, regarded and criticized as such, one of the outstanding living writers in the English language. His very faults as a writer and a person—given the fact of his immense distinction as both—strengthen his position, because he can be criticized and argued with as a man who is neither black nor white, but who uses, and exists, within the English language.

As a writer, he has no color, but only mind and feelings as they are realized in words. One can quarrel, for example, with his misuse of words like "precisely" and "strictly" (usually introduced at a place where his argument is most blurred). James Baldwin is neither the golden-voiced god who sometimes descends on us from a black cloud— like those Negro athletes or Paul Robeson in his prime—nor is he a poet from another race and sphere of life—like Langston Hughes—for whom allowances have to be made. He is simply a writer in English who has had imposed on him by circumstances a point of view made tragic by those very circumstances. All his writings are speeches out of the play which is the tragedy of his race.

Stephen Spender. *PR.* Summer, 1963, p. 256

Another Country is a shocker. For the most part it is an abominably written book. It is sluggish in its prose, lifeless for its first hundred pages, stilted to despair in its dialogue. There are roles in plays called actor-proof. They are so conceived that even the worst actor will do fairly well. So *Another Country* is writer-proof. Its peculiar virtue is that Baldwin commits every *gaffe* in the art of novel writing and yet has a powerful book. . . .

It is at least a novel about matters which are important, but one can't let up on Baldwin for the way he wrote it. Years ago I termed him "minor" as a writer; I thought he was too smooth and too small. Now on his essays alone, on the long continuing line of poetic fire in his essays, one knows he has become one of the few writers of our time. But as a Negro novelist he could take lessons from a good journeyman like John Killens. Because *Another Country* is almost a major novel and yet it is far and away the weakest and worst near-major novel one has finished. It goes like the first draft of a first novelist who has such obvious stuff that one is ready, if an editor, to spend years guiding him into how to write, even as one winces at the sloppy company which must be kept.

Nobody has more elegance than Baldwin as an essayist, not one of us hasn't learned something about the art of the essay from him, and yet he can't even find a good prose for his novel. Maybe the form is not for him. He knows what he wants to say, and that is not the best condition for writing a novel. Novels go happiest when you discover something you did not know you knew. Baldwin's experience has shaped his tongue toward directness, for urgency—the honorable defense may be that he has not time nor patience to create characters, milieu, and mood for the revelation of important complexities he has already classified in his mind. [July, 1963]

Norman Mailer. Cannibals and Christians (New
York, Dial, 1966), pp. 114–15

In the brief note James Baldwin has written as an introduction to the published version of *Blues for Mr. Charlie*, the only character he mentions at any length is the man appearing in the play as Lyle Britten, a white store-owner in a Southern town who murders a young Negro. Baldwin says of the killer, "We have the duty to try to understand this wretched man." But in the play that follows, the writer's sense of this particular duty seems to me to fail him. . . . I don't intend to hold a play deficient for failing an intention whose execution may properly have been thwarted in the act of writing, and is perhaps only recalled here in nostalgia for some purity of purpose. The deficiency is in the failure to be true not to the particular intention announced in the Introduction, but to those numerous intentions apparent in the first act, all most worthy, but none able to survive the unhealthy competition. . . .

In the remaining two acts of the play all the purposes of the first act collapse: indeed, everything collapses, sense, craft, and feeling. The duty to understand is replaced with a duty to do what is practically its opposite, to propagandize, or (reversing Blake's dictum) "to put off intellect and put on holiness." Hardly anything anyone has said or done to anyone else in Act One seems to have taken hold, and the not taking hold isn't what is made to seem the point, either. The point is that the writer has pronouncements to make which stand in the way of the play he began to write. . . .

If there is ever a Black Muslim nation, and if there is television in that nation, then something like Acts Two and Three of *Blues for Mr. Charlie* will probably be the kind of thing the housewives will watch on afternoon TV. It is soap opera designed to illustrate the superiority of blacks over whites.

Philip Roth. *NYR*. May 28, 1964, pp. 10–11

To a certain extent, Baldwin's work is the logical culmination of a literature that is conscious of its immersion in the absurd, rejecting any retreat even to an illuminated cellar, insisting upon the integrity of its characters, eager for human contacts, and determined, despite every-thing, to explore the world. The fervor shown by this young black writer to explain the condition of his brothers in his sparkling essays (*The Fire Next Time*) is the natural extension—or rather the concretization of the intentions—of the novelists of the possible. But Baldwin sometimes becomes so impassioned that his tone is reminiscent of that of the courtroom. Then the domain of literature is abandoned for that of the prosecution and the defense.

In his novels Baldwin attempts to be just as free from racial pre-occupations as he is immersed in them in his essays. The themes of his novels are independent of skin color: the difficulty of loving, of penetrat-ing another's universe (in *Another Country*), and the search for contact —even only physical contact—between two men who do not succeed in sharing "Giovanni's room." The style of his novels is pallid, just as the novels themselves are colorless. The contradiction in Baldwin is that he writes "white" novels (by their style and subject), while his essays are "black," profoundly committed, and written in flamboyant language.

Pierre Dommergues. *Les écrivains américains d'aujourd'hui* (Paris, Presses Universitaires de France, 1965), pp. 109–10†

James Baldwin now belongs to The Establishment he continues to pro-fane. Rich, famous, sometimes snarling, sometimes beguiling, with a flat in Istanbul, a new apartment in Paris ("behind the Bastille, naturally") and a newer house in New York, he is an essayist, novelist and playwright esteemed on at least four continents, an American relatively secure in the literary firmament (yet sweating to stay there), the Negro author younger Negro authors must measure themselves against and—yes—occasionally try to put down.

He is a distillation of the nation's experience as well as his own. Talking of whites and Negroes, writing about them, he wavers between the first person plural and the third. But his duality reflects his country's. Growing up in a culture that is neither all white nor all black, he assimilated both parts. . . .

Inevitably, as the penalty of his success, he is castigated by many white Americans as an extremist and flailed by more radical Negroes as a moderate. A pamphlet published by a black nationalist satirized him with such viciousness that it made him weep. Yet at that very moment shoplifting drug addicts, desperate for a quick sale to finance their next fix, were hawking his books in Harlem's bars, perhaps the ultimate tribute to his popularity.

Fern Marja Eckman. *The Furious Passage of
James Baldwin* (New York, M. Evans, 1966),
pp. 239–41

I, as I imagine many others did and still do, lusted for anything that Baldwin had written. It would have been a gas for me to sit on a pillow beneath the womb of Baldwin's typewriter and catch each newborn page as it entered this world of ours. I was delighted that Baldwin, with those great big eyes of his, which one thought to be fixedly focused on the macrocosm, could also pierce the microcosm. And although he was so full of sound, he was not a noisy writer like Ralph Ellison. He placed so much of my own experience, which I thought I had understood, into new perspective.

Gradually, however, I began to feel uncomfortable about something in Baldwin. I was disturbed upon becoming aware of an aversion in my heart to part of the song he sang. Why this was so, I was unable at first to say. Then I read *Another Country*, and I knew why my love for Baldwin's vision had become ambivalent. . . .

There is a decisive quirk in Baldwin's vision which corresponds to his relationship to black people and to masculinity. It was this same quirk, in my opinion, that compelled Baldwin to slander Rufus Scott in *Another Country*, venerate André Gide, repudiate [Norman Mailer's] *The White Negro*, and drive the blade of Brutus into the corpse of Richard Wright. As Baldwin has said in *Nobody Knows My Name*, "I think that I know something about the American masculinity which most men of my generation do not know because they have not been menaced by it in the way I have been." O.K., Sugar, but isn't it true that Rufus Scott, the weak, craven-hearted ghost of *Another Country*, bears the same relation to Bigger Thomas of *Native Son*, the black rebel of the ghetto and a man, as you yourself bore to the fallen giant, Richard Wright, a rebel and a man?

Eldridge Cleaver. Soul on Ice (New York,
McGraw-Hill, 1968), pp. 97–98, 105–6

Tell Me How Long the Train's Been Gone is a remarkably bad novel, signaling the collapse of a writer of some distinction. . . .

Language rarely lies. It can reveal the insincerity of a writer's claims simply through a grating adjective or an inflated phrase. We come upon a frenzy of words and suspect it hides a paucity of feeling. In his new book Baldwin rarely settles into that controlled exactness of diction which shows the writer to have focused on the matter he wishes to describe or evoke; for Baldwin is now a writer systematically deceiving himself through rhetorical inflation and hysteria, whipping himself into postures of militancy and declarations of racial metaphysics which—for him, in *this* book—seem utterly inauthentic. One sign, a minor sign, of these troubles is Baldwin's compulsive obscenity. . . .

A much more important sign of difficulty is the abandon with which Baldwin opens wide the spigot of his rhetoric, that astonishing flow of high eloquence which served him so well in his later essays but is a style almost certain to entrap a novelist. For if you sound like the voice of doom, an avenging god proclaiming the fire next time, then you don't really have to bother yourself with the small business of the novelist, which is to convey how other, if imaginary, people talk and act. Baldwin seems to have lost respect for the novel as a form, and his great facility with language serves only to ease his violations of literary strictness.

There is still a third way in which Baldwin's language betrays him, perhaps most fundamentally of all. When he writes about Proudhammer's rise to fame and the adulation he receives from friends and public, Baldwin slips into the clichés of soap opera, for which he had already shown an alarming fondness in the past when dealing with homosexual love. Buried deep within this seemingly iconoclastic writer is a very conventional sensibility, perfectly attuned to the daydream of success. Now, if you add all these styles together, you get a weird mixture: the prose of *Redbook* (the magazine for young mamas) and the prose of *Evergreen Review* (the magazine for all them mothers).

Irving Howe. Harper. Sept., 1968, pp. 95–97

The significance of *Another Country*'s being a *regional* novel cannot be over-emphasized. The experience it describes is in many respects peculiarly New York, the conditions which operate are not to be found in quite the same way anywhere else in the country. This is the anxiety-ridden, abrasive, neurotic and merciless world of the artistic underground. What the characters seek is not simply love, and an end to loneliness, but to "make it." They are seeking to force the society to come to terms with their own existence, that is to say, seeking their public identity. So the natural insecurity of the modern human situation is for them heightened by the competitive and spiritually destructive hustle of New York's talent jungle. There are among the major characters, two writers, one actor, a singer and a T.V. producer. And as Truman Capote put it, "a boy's got to hustle." Their common enemy and the source of much of their neurosis, is anonymity and obscurity. They are all past the first flush of youth and some have begun to establish the basis of their fame and success. It is significant that the one character that seems to have established working terms on which to confront his own identity is Eric, the actor, who is "making it" on pretty much his own terms and without having done visible violence to his creative integrity. That he is also unrepentantly bi-sexual and appears to have made his personal peace with that reality also, is undoubtedly the cause of much of the heterosexual indignation that greeted the book. . . .

What this character represents is more subtle than simply an attack on the virility of the conventional American he-man. His ability to discover what and who he is, to accept this, and to be honest to his emotional impulses, however socially unacceptable they may be, is an expression of one of Baldwin's major insights.

Mike Thelwell. In C. W. E. Bigsby, ed., *The Black American Writer* (De Land, Fla., Everett/Edwards, 1969), Vol. I, pp. 189, 194

[One night in Paris in 1953] we hurried to the [Café des] Deux Magots and found Baldwin waiting for us at a table on the terrace across from the Église Saint-Germain. I was somewhat surprised to find Baldwin a small, intense young man of great excitability. Dick [Richard Wright] sat down in lordly fashion and started right off needling Baldwin, who defended himself with such intensity that he stammered, his body trembled, and his face quivered. I sat and looked from one to the other, Dick playing the fat cat and forcing Baldwin into the role of the quivering mouse. It wasn't particularly funny, but then Dick wasn't a funny man. I never found it easy to laugh with Dick; it was far easier to laugh at him on occasion. Dick accused Baldwin of showing his gratitude for all he had done for him by his scurrilous attacks. Baldwin defended himself by saying that Dick had written his story and hadn't left him, or any other American black writer, anything to write about. . . .

In the course of time [the others] left us to go to dinner, and still Baldwin and Dick carried on while I sat and watched the people come and go. Later we went down the boulevard to a Martiniquan café. It had grown later, close to midnight, and we had not eaten, but still the discussion went on. It seemed that Baldwin was wearing Dick down and I was getting quite drunk. The last I remember before I left them at it was Baldwin saying, "The sons must slay their fathers." . . . He was right. On the American literary scene, the powers that be have never admitted but one black at a time into the arena of fame, and to gain this coveted admission, the young writer must unseat the reigning deity. It's a pity but a reality as well.

Chester Himes. *The Quality of Hurt* (Garden City, N.Y., Doubleday, 1972), pp. 200–201

In his previous two novels [*Another Country* and *Tell Me How Long the Train's Been Gone*] Baldwin produced fantasies of black-white relationships in which various characters loved and lusted after one another seemingly *just because* they belonged to different races. In the process, he took very large liberties with the truth about such relationships as they normally exist in our society and, by so doing, may unwittingly have confirmed an impression which certain whites would be eager to embrace: that actually there is no race problem in America which cannot be solved by the application of a little tenderness and the recognition that what we all really want is to enjoy splendid sex together.

In *If Beale Street Could Talk* Baldwin has produced another fantasy of rather larger social implications, this time one in which the characters of black people living in contemporary Harlem are shown to be so noble and courageous that one is constrained to wonder how we ever imagined that conditions in the black urban ghettos are anything other than idyllic. If to be black is to be beautiful, to be poor and black is to be positively saintly. Yet another fiction of great attractiveness to the white mind is thus perpetrated: Ghetto blacks are very happy with their lot. In fact, they are just as simple and fun-loving as the grinning old darkies of southern legend.

To be sure, there is a good deal of adversity in Baldwin's story, but it is there just to demonstrate how well his characters can cope with it and come through with courage undaunted and hopes unsullied. . . .

It is extremely sad to see a writer of Baldwin's large gifts producing, in all seriousness, such junk. Yet it has been evident for some time that he is deteriorating as a novelist and becoming increasingly a victim of the vice of sentimentality. This seems a particular pity because Baldwin may have one great novel left within him which it would take the most radical courage to write, the story of a talented black writer who achieves worldwide success on the strength of his anger and, in succeeding, gradually loses his anger and comes to be loved by everybody. Clearly, such acceptance can be considered a triumph for a black man in America, but it can be death for a black writer in whom anger and talent are indivisible.

John W. Aldridge. *SR*. June 15, 1974, pp. 24–25

BARAKA, AMIRI (1934–   )

UNITED STATES

In this first book [*Preface to a Twenty Volume Suicide Note*], where the poems are arranged chronologically, one can see even as the chaff flies that the grain is good. [LeRoi Jones's] special gift is an emotive music that might have made him predominantly a "lyric poet," but his deeply felt preoccupation with more than personal issues enlarges the scope of his poems beyond what the term is often taken to mean. . . .

I feel that sometimes his work is muddled, and that after the event he convinces himself that it had to be that way; in other words, his conception of when a poem is ready to be printed differs from mine. But . . . he is developing swiftly and has a rich potential. Certain poems— especially "The Clearing," "The Turncoat," "Notes for a Speech"— show what he can do. They are beautiful poems, and others that are less complete have passages of equal beauty.

Denise Levertov. *Nation*. Oct. 14, 1961, p. 252

Blues People, like much that is written by Negro Americans at the present moment, takes on an inevitable resonance from the Freedom Movement, but it is in itself characterized by a straining for a note of militancy which is, to say the least, distracting. Its introductory mood of scholarly analysis frequently shatters into a dissonance of accusation, and one gets the impression that while Jones wants to perform a crucial task which he feels *someone* should take on—as indeed someone should —he is frustrated by the restraint demanded of the critical pen and would like to pick up a club. . . .

Read as a record of an earnest young man's attempt to come to grips with his predicament as Negro American during a most turbulent period of our history, *Blues People* may be worth the reader's time.

Taken as a theory of American Negro culture, it can only contribute more confusion than clarity. For Jones has stumbled over that ironic obstacle which lies in the path of any who would fashion a theory of American Negro culture while ignoring the intricate network of connections which binds Negroes to the larger society. To do so is to attempt a delicate brain surgery with a switch-blade. And it is possible that any viable theory of Negro American culture obligates us to fashion a more adequate theory of American culture as a whole.

Ralph Ellison. *Shadow and Act* (New York, Random House, 1964), pp. 248–253

I am not too happy to see Mr. Jones being hailed in the papers and on television for his anger; for it is not an anger of literary value, and he is a writer. Rather it is rage, it is blind, and, artistic considerations aside, it may well have made it nearly impossible for him to write an important play. The sad and depressing fact about *Dutchman* is that the writer so hates Lula, and so wants us to hate and detest her too, that he has not patience or strength enough to reveal the true nature of what it is she does.

I hesitate to make the chilling observation that perhaps Jones has not really interest enough at this point, and that like certain policemen or professional soldiers, he has come to hate the criminal more than he hates the crime. If only the playwright could have admitted not only to Negro anger, but to Negro dread and Negro lust. But instead of identifying the fear in the hero, he cleanses him of it by projecting the fear as a reality which is not even feared, and the lust is the lust of any healthy man. Jones seems unwilling, or unable, to believe that a crime more horrible than a crazy white woman killing an innocent Negro man with a knife is the crime committed against the spirit which causes it to imagine knives. To symbolize the attempt to murder a man's sexuality by having him actually murdered is to indulge a literary pretension at the expense of a human truth, to substitute false profundity for real sorrow.

The truth that *Dutchman* might have forced through our baffled sense of the racial nightmare is that the Negro humiliation has been so profound and so deep that a man as intelligent and educated and disciplined as Clay is supposed to be, living in a moment so full of possibility for Negroes as this one, cannot but be burdened with the most primal fears for his flesh. Ironically, in making Clay so badly innocent of his condition, and Lula so madly and viciously secret in her intention, Jones finally lets the white audience off much too easily. They may leave the theater saying, as in their genial and useless masochism they are more than willing to say, "Yes, yes, we are guilty," but of what and why they cannot have much knowledge. And refusing them such knowledge, Mr.

Jones, for all his anger, will never force their well-intentioned liberal ideas to be converted into feelings of compassionate suffering.

Philip Roth. *NYR*. May 28, 1964, p. 13

Mr. Jones is currently the white-haired black boy of American poetry. Talented in other forms of writing as well, particularly theater, Mr. Jones might become America's new Eugene O'Neill—provided he does not knock himself out with pure manure. His current offering, *The Toilet*, is full of verbal excrement. . . . So realistic is both acting and direction in this play that the leading white boy, beaten to his knees by a gang of Negroes, drools spittle upon the stage as he tries to rise. The triumphant black boys end up sticking the white student's head into a urinal. What all this does for race relations (as if it mattered at this late date) I do not know. . . .

For the sake of today's sensitive Negroes and battered white liberals, I would like to offer the producers at St. Mark's Playhouse a suggestion—double cast both [*The Toilet* and *The Slave*], and alternate performances racially. Every other night let all the present Negro characters be played by white actors, and vice versa. Four times a week I would like to see *white* school boys in *The Toilet* beating up a *colored* boy and sticking his head into a urinal. In *The Slave* let a bullying *white* man kick, curse, browbeat and shoot a nice liberal *black* professor and his wife in their suburban living room. To reverse the complexions on stage every other night by alternating casts would make for a very intriguing theatrical evening. Black would then be white—and white, black—which alternately would cancel out each other—since some critics (like the able Michael Smith in *The Village Voice*) claim that LeRoi Jones may not really be writing about color at all, but instead is concerned with no group "smaller than mankind." God help us all!

Langston Hughes. *NYP*. Jan. 15, 1965, p. 38

The war-cry [in *Dutchman*] does not really differ from those that whites hurl at one another. Just as Aimé Césaire's *The Tragedy of King Christophe* and, *a fortiori*, [Jean] Genet's *The Blacks* borrow European forms of art and thought to plead the cause of the blacks, so LeRoi Jones's Negritude seems to assert itself (especially as we see it from Paris) in the same forms the theme of bastardy takes in the white American writer Edward Albee. Lula's hysteria recalls Martha's in *Who's Afraid of Virginia Woolf?*, and Clay's demands those of the outcast in *The Zoo Story*.

The difference is that Albee feels a concern for his female characters approximating that of a son for his mother, even if she is only an adopted one, and a vague respect for the established order like that of a ward of the state who has difficulty becoming integrated into society; whereas LeRoi Jones spares nothing and no one. He has burned all his bridges, whence, from the same stylized naturalism, there arises an excess of crudeness, aggressiveness, and provocation. Because the notion of human solidarity itself is being contested, the white woman Lula is described with no more sense of decency or pity for her real disorder than if she were a dog; and Clay, once he has discovered his true feelings, ceases to place any limit on his scorn.

The result is a woman's being given a portrait marked by an indecorousness rarely encountered in the theater, and a spouting of invectives whose violence is no less unusual. But the play as a whole has more to it than the interest of a strange paroxysm. There is an obvious dramatic strength, and there are truths to meditate upon, in Clay's speech, which combines Bessie Smith's singing or Charlie Parker's music with cries of revulsion and racial hatred; and Lula's provocations have beauty in their mad obscenity.

Bertrand Poirot-Delpech. Le monde. Nov. 6,
1965, p. 16†

If *The System of Dante's Hell* is a novel, then the *Divina Commedia* is a newspaper feature article in three installments. As eclectic as the novel is in both structure and content, it is not so indiscriminately inclusive as to accommodate a *collection* of impressionistic (and clearly) autobiographical sketches—particularly if the sketches do not add up to a story, nor to the development and revelation of character, nor to a consistent illusion of reality and an intimation of truth. LeRoi Jones' assemblage of pieces does none of these. Excepting a short essay, disingenuously spun out of black nationalist platitudes, at the very end, *The System of Dante's Hell* closes with a section called "The Heretics," which could have been a narration had it not been strained into an anagoge. And this piece about a Negro soldier's drunken weekend is as close to that succession of consequential events that we call a story—dramatic conflict, exposition, characterization, etc.—as Jones gets. In this piece, he tries to tell (say, show) something.

As for the rest, nothing. From the dust jacket you learn that the book is supposed to be "an account of childhood and adolescence in the Negro slums of Newark," and you struggle with its unclosed parentheses, abrupt shifts in form and technique, sportive spellings and fragmented sentences. . . . The unexpected details, the far-fetched metaphors, the fantastic imagery lack integration and logic, and the result is a confirmation of the impression of pretentiousness—of fakery indeed!—that first strikes you in the symbolism of the title.

Saunders Redding. Crisis. Jan., 1966, p. 56

I went to see *The Toilet* and *Dutchman,* and a whole new world opened up to me. Until I saw *The Toilet,* I didn't realize how right I was in what I had done in *Clara's Ole Man.* I knew *Clara's Ole Man* was a radical departure from the work of those Black playwrights I had read. It was radical in its depiction of Black people, but I didn't realize how right it was in a deep and profoundly revolutionary sense, until I saw *The Toilet. . . .*

LeRoi has greatly influenced many young Black artists. I say without reservation that LeRoi is one of the most important, most significant figures in American theatre. Hardly anybody realizes this now except Black playwrights and artists. We know that the Man (LeRoi) has changed theatre in this country. His contribution to Black theatre will have a great effect on all theatre in this country. If people say that I'm the greatest American playwright, then they must also admit and acknowledge that LeRoi Jones is one of the most significant figures in American, world, and Black theatre.

Ed Bullins. In Ed Bullins, ed., *New Plays from the*
Black Theatre (New York, Bantam, 1969),
pp. xiv–xv

LeRoi Jones's *The System of Dante's Hell* . . . ostensibly consists of disconnected scenes and random thoughts or observations. Some early reviewers asserted that Jones used a pretentious title as an appeal to intellectuals. Yet, with meticulous precision, with broken but somehow poetic sentences, Jones does expose a Hell, a black ghetto thriving on incontinence, violence, and fraud, surrounded by "white monsters" who add to the torment of the Inferno and prevent escape. As his own protagonist, Jones . . . has penetrated the very depths of Hell—Newark Street: "This is the center I mean. Where it all, came on. The rest is suburb. The rest is outside this hole. Snakes die past this block. Flames subside."

Yet in a very real sense Jones believes that he belongs in the Inferno which he himself has helped to build. He has witnessed and participated in the basest evil. . . . In this urban Inferno the victims are not only tormented by their environment and their monsters but by each other, thereby removing the last trace of humanity. It is a city dominated by the Gorgon of Despair.

Olga W. Vickery. In Melvin J. Friedman and
John B. Vickery, eds., *The Shaken Realist* (Baton
Rouge, Louisiana State University Press, 1970),
p. 157

Brooks: I personally feel that [Jones] is one of the very good poets of today, and people hearing this who have no real knowledge of his work, but have seen merely a couple of "inflammatory" passages in the newspapers, might say, "Well, what in the world do you mean? That's no poet." But he is a most talented person. His work *works*.

Stavros: What do you feel makes Jones' the voice of his generation?

Brooks: Well, first of all he speaks to black people. They appreciate that. And he's uncompromising in his belief that the black people must subscribe to black solidarity and black self-consciousness.

Stavros: Is it his message or a poetic method that makes his poetry appeal particularly to blacks?

Brooks: If it is a "method," it comes just from the sincere interest in his own people and in his desire to reach them, to speak to them of what he believes is right.

Stavros: Is he employing any traditional forms, would you say, that may be associated with blacks, say, jazz rhythms?

Brooks: Yes, he and a number of the other black poets such as Larry Neal are interested in supplying black poetry with some strains of black music which they feel is the authentic art of the black people. They worship [John] Coltrane and Ornette Coleman, and whenever they can they try to push such music into their work. Sometimes the poetry seems to grow out of black music. [Winter, 1970]

Gwendolyn Brooks. Interviewed by George Stavros
in Gwendolyn Brooks, *Report from Part One*
(Detroit, Broadside, 1972), pp. 150–51

The characters in Baraka's early plays, particularly Clay [in *Dutchman*] and Walker [in *The Slave*], have all the fury of Bigger [in Richard Wright's *Native Son*] but it is their awareness, their ability to analyze and articulate their situation which is so terrible and shocking. Their fury and pain have been internalized to such an extent that even outward action, as in *The Slave*, brings no release and they, like Bigger, choke on their own rage. It is not without significance that *The Slave* and *Dutchman* take the physical form of dialogues or conversations between a Black man and white people, for just as Wright abstracts the message of *Native Son* by putting into the mouth of Bigger's white lawyer a long analysis of the social context of Bigger's crimes and the subsequent appeal to the white jury (white society), Baraka seeks to educate white society to the feelings and situations of the collective Black man. All three works are addressed to the collective might and power of the white man. . . .

Walker and Clay are latter-day Bigger Thomases. They are viewed, it is true, from a different perspective, but Baraka's sights are trained on the same object as Wright's. And, while there is overstatement in Charles Gordone's view that "[Baraka] has said everything there is to be said in terms of Black and white relationships," it is certain that he has exhausted by thorough exploration in these and other plays Black/white conflict as a literary theme, leaving other artists the room to explore the Black heart.

Sherley Anne Williams. Give Birth to Brightness
(New York, Dial, 1972), pp. 103–4

The strongest piece of theatre I have seen in the past few years is <i>Slave Ship</i> by LeRoi Jones, as produced in 1969 at the Chelsea Theatre Center. Where [Richard] Wesley merely falls backward into racism [in his play <i>The Black Terror</i>] Jones leaps delightedly into it, face-forward. What is the white theatregoer to do? Stay away from Jones's play? Play at being black? That surely is an effort at identification with the victim which soon becomes ludicrous. Enjoy being put down by such a fanatic down-putter? That surely is an exercise in white masochism that only black sadists can contemplate with satisfaction. White middle-class liberals can be counted on for a goodly amount of breast beating, it is true, but not for this much.

As for myself, though I'm as guilt-ridden as the next man, I didn't really feel guiltier for seeing Jones's play, for, rightly or wrongly, I just didn't identify myself with the whites in it. How could one? They were monsters. Then I identified myself—sentimentally—with the blacks? Not that either. Not that <i>exactly</i>. Feeling detached from both groups, I found myself instinctively taking the play as an image of all such struggles. Finally, I did identify myself with the blacks but for me they weren't necessarily black. They were yellow, and from Vietnam. They were red, and from Manhattan. They were white-skinned and black with coal dust like the miners of Lancashire, where I come from. As a Socialist, I read LeRoi Jones's play as a series of extremely vivid images of capitalist exploitation, and this is not something I thought of later, it is only my later formulation of what I was actually feeling during the performance. So, as a Socialist, I got my consciousness raised by a writer who (I must assume) wants me liquidated as a carrier of the white plague; and whom I disapprove of as a racist.

Eric Bentley. Theatre of War (New York, Viking,
1972), pp. 404–5

LeRoi Jones's early poetry is difficult. It even found its way into white American anthologies as a token Negro might be found in a white club. And after I have been struggling to decode his knotted language that darts in so many directions, the parentheses that run wild in much of the poetry—all in vain—I have no capacity for an emotional response for even the little I can understand. I feel as if I had been wading through a swamp the extent and shape of which I could not and cannot comprehend. What is often so exasperating about such poetry is that one suspects, and perhaps even *feels*, from the ring of the words that there is a coherent meaning here. . . .

But I know, from reading those poems I *do* understand and which therefore move me, I am prepared to take my chances with Jones and read him several times over. It is not a matter of allusions with him: it is another kind of intellectual complexity. He knows too that he is taking his chances when he writes a kind of poetry that several others besides me will not take the trouble to reread. If I were not teaching poetry, and were not also interested in black poetry in America, I do not think I should take so much trouble. Maybe he will say that's the people he writes for—those who are interested desperately enough. That is still taking a chance. Every so often I am happy to understand a poem of his. Because I find it is rich, it says a hell of a lot, it penetrates the blood. But I don't want to feel, as the old Browning Society used to feel, I belong to a coterie—the chosen ones who can enter LeRoi Jones's mental and spiritual workshop. I want to be able to shout and slap the back of a friend, shake him up and scream, "This is poetry, man!" and get a similar reaction from him.

Ezekiel Mphahlele. *Voices in the Whirlwind* (New York, Hill and Wang, 1972), pp. 33, 38

[Baraka] uses the theatre mainly as a political weapon, an extension of Black Power. To him, the theatre is not a medium of "protest," which Blacks see as a concession to the White world; it is rather an expression of Black culture, a mode of self-consciousness as well as of assault. Baraka's Revolutionary Theatre has only superficial resemblances to the Theatre of Cruelty of [Antonin] Artaud or Genet, which still adheres to formal art. Direct in its hatred, impatient with the obliqueness of drama, abusive and at times hysterical, the Revolutionary Theatre tends to draw energy from the passion of its audience rather than the imagination of its author. At its best, however, it draws also on the poetry, music, dance, on all the iconographies of Black culture. . . .

In *Slave Ship* Baraka resorts to a series of tableaux, a historical pageant of the Negro, a kind of "total theatre" that, although partial in its ideology, deploys in its "metalanguage" an experience larger than any of its verbal parts.

Ihab Hassan. *Contemporary American Literature* (New York, Frederick Ungar, 1973), pp. 166–68

In a general way, Jones is a romantic in the sense that many literary historians and scholars consider the post-Romantic Period symbolists, imagists, realists, naturalists, dadaists, impressionists, and other modern writers as latter day romantics or as part of a romantic continuum. He is a romantic in more specific ways as well. Like Emerson and certain other romantic writers, in a transcendentalistic way Jones places great faith in intuition, in feelings. As he applies this faith in an ethnocentric way, he would have blacks place faith in what he assumes to be their singular mystical impulses. He is antirational in the way that romantics of Western European literature were opposed to the "cold" rationality of neoclassicism. Moreover, in connection with this reliance upon innate urgings and promptings, Jones inescapably asserts, as Blake and other romantic mystics contended, that man is divine, although, as Baraka, Jones would argue that the white man has perverted his, the white man's, divinity. Also, Jones is, like those romantics who would not conform to neoclassical religious dogma and traditions, romantic in that he is disdainful of the organized and orthodox religion of the majority and in that he has been himself a religious speculator and seeker. Next, Jones is romantic in his concern for the well-being, freedom, and dignity of the economically and politically weak, the dispossessed, the oppressed, and the downtrodden, as were the past century's romantic political and social libertarians and romantic champions of "humble" people. Further, Rousseau-like in his concern for the full development of man's potential, Jones sees his contemporary social, cultural, and political institutions as destructive of (black) man, so he would have man destroy, change, or control these institutions so that they, in his opinion, serve man rather than have man serve them. Further, Jones, like the Shelleys of the Romantic Period, is a visionary who sees creative artists as providers of philosophical and ideological bases for change. Next, in regard to technique, Jones, like many romantics of the past, will have little to do with conventional and prescribed forms and techniques, insists upon using the "language of the people," and constantly strives for new ways of writing, searching for what he calls a "post-American form." And it is obvious that Jones, as have countless romantics, uses his creative imagination to inform and shape his literary work.

> Theodore R. Hudson. *From LeRoi Jones to Amiri Baraka: The Literary Works* (Durham, N.C., Duke University Press, 1973), pp. 179–80

A good many poets and critics don't like what's happened to the old LeRoi Jones, promising young Negro poet of *Preface to a Twenty Volume Suicide Note*. Baraka, obviously, is not interested in their opinions. Nevertheless, it is a mistake to dismiss him as an angry propagandist, as so many have done, because he appears to run against the literary grain. The old art of LeRoi Jones was written to be read. The new writing of Baraka is calculated to be heard—*how we sound*, he would say now—and his audience must have some sense of the Afro-American perspective from which his new writing issues.

The black aesthetic which shapes his writing is neither lacking in artistic taste (strident, anti-poetic, uncontrolled, say the critics) nor in itself startlingly new. It only appears that way from a literary point of view, one that is in many respects incongruous to the cultural context upon which his stylistic rationale is based. What is remarkable, from a literary standpoint, is the range of innovation his political ideology and altered cultural consciousness have required of him as a writer. For Baraka, though, it is not remarkable at all, but only the result of an inevitable artistic transformation, the sure spelling out of his specific placement in the world as a black writer. LeRoi Jones' *Preface to a Twenty Volume Suicide Note, Blues People*, and *The Dead Lecturer*, for all their apparent difficulties, lead comprehensively to the revolutionary identity of Imamu Amiri Baraka. And the transformation is not significant simply as a painful individual struggle, but more importantly represents the reintegration of the poet and his art into the stream of Afro-American culture.

William C. Fischer. MR. Spring, 1973, p. 305

The final rite [in *Slave Ship*], with its mimed cannibalistic aspect, is apocalyptic in both a mythical and a religious sense. In its mythical dimension, the ending completes the absorption of the natural, historical cycle into mythology. Its mythical movement is one of comic resurrection and integration, completed by the marriage of the spectator into community and the birth of the "old-new" black nation. This fertility ritual clearly has a religious dimension that has been prepared for by the continuous prayers to Obatala and Jesus, curses of the "Godless, white devil," and litanies such as "Rise, Rise, Rise, etc." Indeed, by creating basic images of resurrection with accompanying sensations of magic, charm, and incantation, Baraka returns the black audience to the most fundamental religious ground of tribal ceremony from which sprung the two greatest epochs of Western theatre (Greek and Christian), and which gave life to the archetypical African spirit. The spectators are as integral a part of the work as the congregation of a black Baptist church is of its service, and they function in much the same way. The nationalist myth of African-inspired renewal and Afro-American triumph is taken up by the audience because Baraka has called upon the community's shared aesthetic—the genius for musical improvisation. . . .

By claiming African roots in their totality, the black community controls its destiny as Clay, the middle-class greyboy [in *Dutchman*] could not. Now, Baraka's black heroes, not the witch-devil Lula, dance in triumph. The tragedy-burdened slave ship of *Dutchman* has become the dance-filled celebration of *Slave Ship*; musical transcendence has risen from the spirit of tragedy. . . .

Baraka's theatre, from *Dutchman* to *Slave Ship*, has clearly evolved from a concern with the individual cut loose from society to the community itself as victim, rebel, and, finally, triumphant hero.

Kimberly W. Benston. Baraka: The Renegade and
the Mask (New Haven, Conn., Yale University
Press, 1976), pp. 254–55

BETI, MONGO (1932–   )

CAMEROON

In his novel [*The Poor Christ of Bomba*] Mongo Beti's central focus is the problem of the Christianization of the blacks. Father Drumont, a rough, determined missionary, thinks that after twenty years of work he has succeeded in driving Christ's message into Negro skulls. He is particularly proud of his *sixa*, which, as the author explains in a note, is a "house that as a rule shelters young girls engaged to be married. Any native woman who wants to get married according to orthodox law has to stay in the *sixa* from two to four months." But one tour through the Catholic villages is all Father Drumont needs to measure his failure. The teachings he had bestowed upon the Negroes according to seemingly infallible methods turn out to have been useless. Baptism was only a means, thought the Africans, of taking over the power of the whites and avoiding colonialist extortions. The girls in the *sixa*, who were supposed to be governed by a strict premarital control, were in fact taking great liberties with Christian morality. Indeed, the whole edifice that had been patiently constructed by the missionary crumbles within a few days. He leaves Africa, discouraged and gnawed at by doubt.

Through this personal failure, the failure of colonization itself becomes apparent. This priest, who thinks he knows the Africans and wants at all cost to impose upon them a behavior that conflicts with their habits and their conception of the world, is the administrator who, starting from prejudices set up as principles for action, persists in forcing the colonized people to enter a preestablished framework. He is the ethnologist who, after an "educational" trip to Africa, comes back with scholarly notes that would make an African villager laugh if he knew how to read French.

Like Ferdinand Oyono, Beti employs a humorous tone, and his racy conversations preclude any boredom. Perhaps this book, which is too full of facts for my taste, would have been improved by being more compressed and less loaded down with details. Nevertheless, Beti has given us incontestable proof of his talent as a novelist, and we can confidently await his next novel.

David Diop. PA. Dec., 1956, pp. 126–27†

At the age of twenty-two, while still a student at Aix, Mongo Beti offered his first novel to Présence africaine. After publishing a key chapter in the review, they decided to issue the whole book, though Beti himself already had doubts about it. Cruel Town was duly published by Éditions Africaines in 1954, under the name of Eza Boto. The author has since indicated his opinion of the novel by jettisoning this nom de plume and taking that of Mongo Beti for all his subsequent books.

Cruel Town is a bad novel; but it is manifestly not the work of a bad writer. Rather is it the trying out of a young talent, as yet loose and uncontrolled, but open and rich. If the book is sentimental, its very naïveté is often disarming; if its action is melodramatic, it bears everywhere the marks of feeling and experience.

The book begins rather well. The first chapter, in which the young hero Banda casually throws off his mistress and declares his intention of marrying a girl more acceptable to his dying mother, does not fully prepare us for the orgies of filial sentiment which are to follow. The next chapter, devoted to the cruel town itself, is certainly the best thing in the book. This, one of the few pieces of extended impersonal description in the novel, is beautifully built up and displays a gift of compassionate irony which is seldom apparent in the later pages. . . .

If [the] brilliance of observation [in this chapter] were maintained, Cruel Town would be a novel indeed. However, we are soon plunged into the raw and often tiresome emotions of young Banda, who now arrives in the town to sell his seasonal crop of cocoa. . . . All through [a] string of improbabilities runs the interior monologue of Banda. Often the naïve exclamations, repetitions and self-questionings of the hero are happily natural and unforced, but gradually they become tedious and, finally, infuriating. We have had enough of Banda. . . .

Strangely enough, it was precisely by the more controlled and skilful use of this exclamatory, naïve monologue that Mongo Beti developed some of the most effective passages in his second novel, The Poor Christ of Bomba. With this book, published only two years after Cruel Town,

the writer emerged as a formidable satirist and one of the most percipi-
ent critics of European colonialism.

Gerald Moore. *Seven African Writers* (London,
Oxford University Press, 1962), pp. 74–77

Compassion is the twin brother of Mongo Beti's grand iconoclasm (or
perhaps what we are looking for is a word that combines the two).
Mission Accomplished, bawdy, riotous, bursting on every page with
sheer animal vitality, reads like that rare piece of studied artistry, an
unpremeditated novel. In the literary effort to establish the African as,
first before all else, a human being, Mongo Beti with this novel has
leaped to the fore as the archpriest of the African's humanity. Mongo
Beti takes the back cloth as he finds it, asserting simply that tradition is
upheld not by one-dimensional innocents, but by cunning old codgers on
chieftaincy stools, polygamous elders, watching hawklike the approach
of young blood around their harem, by the eternal troublemaking fe-
males who plunge innocents, unaware, into memorable odysseys. Hos-
pitality is not, as we are constantly romantically informed that it is,
nearly so spontaneous. There is a mercenary edge, and this, alas, is not
always traceable to that alien corrupt civilization! . . .

He has translated the slight alienation of his hero into village
terms, with no condescension, no stances; the magnificent candor of the
hero, Jean-Marie Medza, stranger to Kala, creates a vigorous clarity in
characters, a precision of edges that Chinua Achebe, with no such uninhibited agent to hand, achieved in neither of his [first two] books.
Sex is restored to its natural proportions, not a startling discovery made
by the European every publishing day, nor a neo-Africanist venture sung
by the apostles of Negritude and sanctified in shrines to puberty. Beti
makes sex an unquestioned attitude; the result is that he demonstrates a
truly idyllic love dignified by humor, by pathos, and crucial to the novel
as a major factor in the development of a young, sensitive personality.

Wole Soyinka. *ASch.* Summer, 1963, pp. 394–96

Mission Accomplished was published in Paris in 1957. It is the first
novel by Mongo Beti to have been translated into English. . . . Because
of a need to mystify the reader, which is characteristic of Beti's way of
thinking, he took a title from detective and spy novels, a title pompous
in its brevity, in order to point up everything grotesque about the celebrated "mission," while describing it in a falsely smooth-spoken tone.

What is the book really about? A wife who fled (with her lover) in
an attempt to free herself from her husband's rule must be brought back
to her legal husband. Jean-Marie Medza, a high school student who has

just failed the second part of his *baccalauréat* examination, is entrusted with this delicate mission, because he is a distant cousin of the husband. . . .

In this bush symphony, Jean-Marie Medza plays the solo part of the "naïve" boy, surrounded by a chorus of happy villagers. From beginning to end, Jean-Marie is the comic butt of the farce while acting as an accomplice. He accepts this adventure in Kala because he enjoys playing a country knight, but the ridiculous aspects of the situation at no time escape him. He enjoys telling us about them and stirring up a continuous flow of unrepressed laughter. He is not as foolish as he tries to appear, and the unexpected nature of the farce delights him all the more since it protects him for a while from his father's anger. . . .

[Beti's] "rebel's voice" (as Gerald Moore called it) is fond of obscenity, which he claims is persuasive, and indecency, true or false. One can admire or criticize him for these penchants. At any rate, he can always take shelter behind his characters, who never attended any Academy, Parisian or Bantu.

Roger Mercier and M. and S. Battestini. Mongo Beti
(Paris, Fernand Nathan, 1964), pp. 35–37†

Beti is an experimenter, creating various situations and examining their evolution and the results. All the various side issues have equally to be analysed and occasionally—as with Kris in *The King Miraculously Healed*—a foreign element is added to give a little more spice to the brew. His novels are much more rambling than Oyono's. Many more aspects of colonial life among Africans are dealt with and the novels' effect, from the point of view of social criticism, is less direct, less forceful than those of Oyono. On the other hand, Beti's Europeans are not only the colonial "type" but also, and more especially, the kind who want to do good for the Africans but, unfortunately for them, start from the premise that all Africans are unable to organize their lives unless helped by Europeans. His favourite butts are, for this reason, missionaries and dedicated colonial administrators. . . . He shows how superficial Catholic influence is and how, if tribal customs and Catholicism exert conflicting pressures on the Africans in the backwoods, the former is the stronger. . . .

The characters of this novel have in fact much more importance in the novel and greater independence of action than those in [*The Poor Christ of Bomba* and *Mission Accomplished*]. Here, instead of being presented through the descriptions of a narrator, they are developed through their own words and acts, without a third person to interpret them. They are important because it is the interaction of their desires and interests which forms the basis of the comedy and satire of the novel. Because their motivations are an important factor in the novel Beti makes these characters much more definite as individuals. Their own personal interests are shown influencing every gesture and, in one case at least, the result is tragically grotesque rather than farcical. . . .

This novel is the last published by Beti. Like his others and those of Oyono it is, behind the humour, totally negative. The satirical attack on colonial Africa is totally destructive. This novel, with its emphasis on self-interest is, in this respect, Beti's most pessimistic.

A. C. Brench. *The Novelists' Inheritance in French Africa* (London, Oxford University Press, 1967), pp. 64, 68, 73–74

After *The King Miraculously Healed* Mongo Beti turned from literature to politics as Cameroon prepared for its independence. He returned from France to Cameroon in 1959, shortly before independence, as a sympathizer if not a partisan of the radical Union des Populations du Cameroun. He briefly landed in jail as a political suspect and after his release made his way back to France where he wrote a lively report on his experiences entitled "Tumultuous Cameroon." In this satirical attack on the cooperation between the French colonial authorities and the future government of Cameroon he places his faith in the youth of Africa, without the doubts he had expressed in his novels, and confidently claims the leadership role for the young educated Africans. . . . But this revolution of youth has not yet materialized in Cameroon, the government he attacked so scathingly is still in power, and Mongo Beti has since 1959 lived in exile in France where he no longer writes but teaches French literature.

Mongo Beti's fiction is a record of failure, the failure to discern either the "intellectual direction" of the new Africa or the type of leader who can initiate the African into the mysteries of the modern world. But it is a successful record of failure. The author's ability to assume a multiplicity of frequently contradictory points of view, his capacity to bring out the humor in the contradictions and incongruities of modern Africa, as well as his realistic appraisal of African village society, indicate a critical detachment, an intellectual stance, which are rare in contemporary African literature. Mongo Beti has characterized himself as a "free traveler" whose writings are a running commentary on his native Cameroon. It is a pity that exile put such an early end to his journey.

Thomas Cassirer. *ECr*. Fall, 1970, pp. 232–33

A careful reading of Mongo Beti's works reveals the writer's constant concern, his systematic desire, to dissociate himself from his fictional universe, to keep his distance from the characters and events that have sprung from his imagination. . . . Even when what happens in his novels is confirmed and strongly corroborated by real life, his subject is always the life of others and never his own. His own ideas are expressed only indirectly, only if another takes the responsibility for them and thus guarantees his safety.

This desire for camouflage and obvious distancing is immediately noticeable in his way of signing his works and taking legal responsibility for them. Alexandre Biyidi [his real name] never appears as such under his writings, except for his short story "Without Hate, Without Love" in which, by claiming to be disinterested, he offends nobody or irritates everybody, which actually amounts to the same thing. His rather personal diatribe against Laye Camara is signed "A. B.," and the initials are not immediately identifiable as his. His novels are always signed with a pseudonym. And for his explosive article "African Unity," he takes refuge behind the editorial board of the *Revue camerounaise*. This need of distancing does not mean only that Mongo Beti seeks to protect himself in public, to escape possible prosecution; it also reflects the very character of an ideologically repressive postcolonial police state, with its omnipresent censorship and its treacherous attacks on protesters who are isolated but too brazenly visible. And who could be more isolated and more visible in such circumstances than a distinctive artist?

Thomas Melone. *Mongo Béti: L'homme et le destin*
(Paris, Présence Africaine, 1971), pp. 252–53†

It has been rumored that Mongo Beti's *Plunder of Cameroun*, a searing criticism of government and politics in Cameroon published by F. Maspéro in Paris not long ago, has been banned in his country which in turn has succeeded in getting France to ban it also. And, so far, this writer has not been able to obtain a copy of the book in the United States. Nevertheless his most recent novel *Perpétue and the Habit of Unhappiness* is nonetheless a dramatic indictment of the ill-fated independence in his native land dominated by corrupt dictatorial power, as well as a forceful denunciation of the disgraceful status of African women in such regimes. With this novel Mongo Beti proves once again that he is one of the best of the contemporary Black African novelists, who seek to promote true liberty in Africa and to insure a lasting dignity for her.

With *Perpétue and the Habit of Unhappiness* the author's outstanding literary talent is again confirmed. The picturesque art of the storyteller is still there. Because of the seriousness of purpose and manner which the themes of politics and status of women demand of the author, one does not find an abundance of Mongo Beti's usual humor here and laughter does not dominate completely the various situations presented. Except for the doomed but sincere affection exchanged between Perpétue and Zeyang, tender love has no chance of survival in this novel. True friendship and camaraderie, as portrayed in the relationship between Perpétue and Anna-Marie her trusted and faithful companion, occupy great space in the book. The jealousy and treachery which Édouard unbridles against Perpétue never seem to be justified, but serve the author's purpose in dramatizing the status of African women.

Robert P. Smith, Jr. *CLAJ*. March, 1976, pp. 310–11

BHÊLY-QUÉNUM, OLYMPE (1928–   )

BENIN

[*An Endless Trap*] is fiction, but one feels the reality of each detail so strongly that one has the impression of having lived the story—at first so beautiful, afterwards so tragic.

Ahouna lives with his parents, who are well-off peasants from the North of Dahomey. He tills the fields with his family and friends and this affords us very lively and beautiful descriptions. . . . Ahouna is also a poet. While tending his herds, his soul sings and the book often contains passages of tender and rustic poetry. His sensitive heart explodes with joy and happiness when he is loved by Anatou and the countryside echoes with sweet or passionate, nostalgic or animated music which he improvises. . . .

I think that [the] subtleties [in this novel] will be appreciated. In fact, the author is rarely violent, even in the second part of the book where Ahouna is in prison. I prefer not to tell how it came out in order to leave the full shock and horror of discovery to the reader. There are descriptions of "quarries" where the prisoners climbed down countless steps every day to find death under falling granite blocks, or madness under the implacable sun. I thought that I was reading a description of Mathausen concentration camp.

The author is an excellent painter of patriarchal scenes, and is just as good with tragic descriptions. A phrase or only single words recall how the Negroes see and feel and live under oppression and colonization. My ears can still hear their cries of rage. . . .

To sum up, this novel is a fresco from Dahomey, full of reality and lyricism. There are some delightful love-stories written in a very beautiful language which have the merit of "being seen from the inside" and described by a Dahomeian.

Andrée Clair. *PA* (English ed.). 8, 1, 1961,
pp. 170–71

Ahouna [the hero of *An Endless Trap*] combines within himself the values of life and death. The black Orpheus of the beginning of the novel becomes a black Orestes. . . . His is a drama of fate: a pastoral hero destined for happiness, he suddenly falls under the yoke of fetishes eager to destroy him: the *obas* [spirits that inhabit objects] stir up the vindictive hatred of the parents of the victim [who was murdered by Ahouna] in order to assure that Ahouna will disappear forever.

Born for simple happiness, Ahouna reaches the point of madness, horror, and panic. He does not understand why his destiny has abruptly changed course; he experiences the anger of the gods, of humans, and of objects, and when faced with the imminence of his own death, he will not utter one cry of hatred or make one move to rebel. Nor even, we should note, will he experience a feeling of Christian charity, an impulse that makes us forgive those who have injured us.

Ahouna's attitude is that of the fetishist (although he claims not to be one); despite the frequent references to Allah, the hero's attitude is related neither to Islam nor to Christianity (which is the religion practiced by Olympe Bhêly-Quénum himself). Ahouna's attitude is an unconditional surrender to the sovereign hidden powers, if that is their will. Although he does not recognize himself as completely guilty, he knows that he has unleashed the gods' anger and that only his immolation can appease them.

Roger Mercier and M. and S. Battestini. *Olympe
Bhêly-Quénum* (Paris, Fernand Nathan, 1964), p. 8†

As a youth, Ahouna [in *An Endless Trap*] lived the dreamy life of a herd boy with his flute, by means of which he called up visions of plenitude. But this northern harmony was destroyed by his wife's ill will, which triggered the spring, released what Ahouna calls "the monster within." Once freed, this spirit of destructiveness ravages him from within and without. From his home on the high plains of Baribaland, he is compulsively driven south, down the length of Dahomey to the lowlands of the Fon.

As the viciousness around and about him increases, the more despised he becomes, the closer he comes to the littoral. For the men of the south are subtle, he says, sullen and superstitious, corrupt products of a crossplay of influences from the sophisticated Yoruba and the wily traders from overseas. Everything is denser. The clenched fist thuds dully upon the earth's anvil, raging impotently over and over again. Exhausted, Ahouna finally falls victim to a clandestine ceremony of blood revenge. Thus the literature of the south, from the lower Niger to the lower Volta, seems inevitably linked to "the earth and dreams of the will" and that of the north, from the Senegal to the Upper Niger, to "the earth and dreams of repose."

Judith Gleason. AfrF. Spring, 1966, pp. 82–83

The Song of the Lake . . . bears the message that traditional Africa, far from having to be rescued from oblivion, is very much alive and may have a more crucial role to play in the future of the continent than "modern" Africa. In Olympe Bhêly-Quénum's novels, the common themes of modern African literature—the impact of colonialism, the problem of acculturation, the social and political effects of modernization—usually appear as peripheral to the powerful influence of irrational supernatural forces. His first novel, *An Endless Trap*, tells the story of one individual destroyed by an inexplicable fate; *The Song of the Lake*, set like the earlier novel in the author's native Dahomey, portrays an African community held in the grip of animism. The village of Wêsé, situated on the shore of a lake, is the focus of a tale in which political issues, the impact of Western rationalism, and the villagers' traditional fear of the man-eating gods of the lake are woven into a symbolic portrait of Africa as the battleground between the forces of enlightenment and those of fear. Using a narrative technique that seems alternatively inspired by the palaver and the adventure story, Bhêly-Quénum recounts a day of crisis on which this struggle reaches a climax in the village. . . .

The Song of the Lake is too short a novel to do full justice to the complexity of Olympe Bhêly-Quénum's conception. Themes and characters are at times outlined rather than fully developed, and the author is not entirely successful in weaving the many strands of his plot into a coherent whole. Yet this does not detract from the interest and value of the book. Bhêly-Quénum combines humor and psychological penetration with a talent for evocative description; and the extraordinary richness of levels in this novel—its blending of folk legend, social criticism, symbolism, and allegory—makes it stand out among modern African fiction.

Thomas Cassirer. AfrF. Spring, 1967, pp. 135–36

The idea of the absurd is an obsession of the hero of Bhêly-Quénum's [*An Endless Trap*]. He assumes an attitude toward life that is both negative and pessimistic. . . .

The interest of *An Endless Trap* lies neither in its narrative, which is diffuse, nor in its formal unity, since there isn't any—in fact, some of the episodes and characters are incoherent and very poorly integrated into the work's thematic universe. The interest in Bhêly-Quénum's novel lies primarily in the vision . . . of the absurd as incarnated by its hero, Ahouna, a vision that imparts allegorical strength to the hero's situation.

The feeling of absurdity is first presented as a fundamental idea in the hero's consciousness. Ahouna's mind is shown to be particularly sensitive to the slightest disturbance in his inner life. Any phenomenon, even an atmospheric one, increases his feeling of ontological unbalance. . . . This feeling is accompanied by the awareness that life is completely devoid of meaning. . . .

For Ahouna, human existence is nothing but an "enormous trap set for man by Allah." . . . This causal reference to Allah, an absolute transcendental being, shows the extent to which the problematic individual's spirit tries to rationalize or to justify his downfall. . . . Is not the truly absurd or problematic man the one who, from the depths of his being, considers himself an absurdity, a meaningless being, yet who nevertheless clings to life with an unheard-of tenacity? In other words, however rational some of Ahouna's words may seem, they are less the result of a sober reflection on the overt world than the self-criticism of a psychological state mutilated by existential anxiety. It is in this anxiety that the real meaning and the motive of the hero's crime must be sought. And this crime, the murder of an innocent woman, can be considered here a gratuitous act. It has no other motivation than what can be furnished by a pathological neurosis. . . .

Sunday O. Anozie. *Sociologie du roman africain*
(Paris, Éditions Aubier-Montaigne, 1970),
pp. 161–62, 164–65†

BONTEMPS, ARNA (1902–1973)

UNITED STATES

Arna Bontemps' first venture in fiction [*God Sends Sunday*] is to me a profound disappointment. It is of the school of [Carl Van Vechten's] *Nigger Heaven* and [Claude McKay's] *Home to Harlem*. There is a certain pathetic touch to the painting of his poor little jockey hero, but nearly all else is sordid crime, drinking, gambling, whore-mongering, and murder. There is not a decent intelligent woman; not a single man with the slightest ambition or real education, scarcely more than one human child in the whole book. Even the horses are drab. In the "Blues" alone Bontemps sees beauty. But in brown skins, frizzled hair and full contoured faces, there are to him nothing but ugly, tawdry, hateful things, which he describes with evident caricature.

One reads hurriedly on, waiting for a gleam of light, waiting for the Sunday that some poor ugly black God may send; but somehow it never comes; and if God appears at all it is in the form of a little drunken murderer riding South to Tia Juana on his back. . . .

Well—as I know I have said several times before—if you like this sort of thing, then this will be exactly the sort of thing you will especially like, and in that case you ought to run and read it.

W. E. B. Du Bois. Crisis. Sept., 1931, p. 304

In that limited and almost barren field known as the Negro novel, Arna Bontemps's *Black Thunder* fills a yawning gap and fills it competently. Covering all those skimpy reaches of Negro letters I know, this is the only novel dealing forthrightly with the historical and revolutionary traditions of the Negro people.

Black Thunder is the true story of a slave insurrection that failed. But in his telling of the story of that failure Bontemps manages to reveal and dramatize through the character of his protagonist, Gabriel, a quality of folk courage unparalleled in the proletarian literature of this country. . . .

When considering Gabriel solely as an isolated individual, he seems sustained by an extremely foolish belief in himself; but when one remembers his slave state, when one realizes the extent to which he has made the wrongs of his people his wrongs, and the degree in which he has submerged his hopes in their hopes—when one remembers this, he appears logically and gloriously invincible.

The plan for the uprising is so simple and daring that when it is disclosed and tracked to its source, the fear-ridden whites can scarcely believe it. But Gabriel believes, he believes even when he is caught; even when the black cowl is capped about his head, even when the ax swings, he believes. Why?

For me the cardinal value of Bontemps's book, besides the fact that it is a thumping story well told, lies in the answer to that question. Perhaps I am straying further afield than the author did in search for an answer. If I do, it is because I believe we have in *Black Thunder* a revelation of the very origin and source of folk values in literature.

Even though Gabriel's character is revealed in terms of personal action and dialogue, I feel there is in him much more than mere personal dignity and personal courage. There is in his attitude something which transcends the limits of immediate consciousness. He is buoyed in his hope and courage by an optimism which takes no account of the appalling difficulties confronting him. He hopes when there are no objective reasons or grounds for hope; he fights when his fellow-slaves scamper for their lives. In doing so, he takes his place in that gallery of fictitious characters who exist on the plane of the ridiculous and the sublime. Bontemps endows Gabriel with a myth-like and deathless quality. And it is in this sense, I believe, that *Black Thunder* sounds a new note in Negro fiction, thereby definitely extending the boundaries and ideology of the Negro novel.

Richard Wright. *PRA*. April, 1936, p. 31

Black Thunder is written with restraint and detachment. Bontemps portrays slaves, freedmen, planters, and French radicals with impartiality, showing no disposition to glorify pro-Negro nor to traduce anti-Negro characters in the book. Miscegenation on the Southern scene is not blinked. Furthermore, Bontemps succeeds in weaving Gabriel's uprising into the web of state and national life. We observe the Virginia legislature considering the sectional segregation of Negroes as an approach to the solution of racial difficulties and note the Federalist press, while championing a second term for John Quincy Adams, citing Gabriel's insurrection as an offshoot of the radicalism of Thomas Jefferson and his adherents. Although *Black Thunder* is not without blemish, A. B. Spingarn is quite correct in his observation that the book is "the best historical novel written by an American Negro." . . .

Drums at Dusk, a worthy successor to *Black Thunder*, is another vivid illustration of the richness of the Negro's past as a source for historical fiction.

Hugh Gloster. *Negro Voices in American Fiction*
(Chapel Hill, University of North Carolina Press,
1948), pp. 214–16

Arna Bontemps is a transitional figure whose novels bear the mark both of the Negro Renaissance and of the Depression years which follow. Born in Louisiana of Creole parentage, he moved to Los Angeles at an early age. He was educated at Pacific Union College and the University of Chicago; at present he is head librarian of Fisk University. A minor poet during the 1920's, Bontemps turned later to fiction, history, and books for children. He has written three novels, of which the first, *God Sends Sunday*, is an unadulterated product of the Negro Renaissance. The setting of the novel is the sporting world of racetrack men and gamblers, of jazz and the shimmy, of fights and razor carvings. His historical novels, however, which deal with slavery times, reflect the mood of the Depression era. By choosing slave insurrections as a basis for his plots, Bontemps stresses an aspect of slavery which was emotionally appealing to the rebellious thirties. . . .

It is Bontemps' intention in *Black Thunder* to credit the Negro slave with an obsessive love of freedom. The extent to which this interpretation is historically valid is a moot point. That some slaves felt an overwhelming desire to "go free" and acted upon it is certainly beyond dispute. In any case, complexity of characterization, together with a tone of restraint and a tendency to underwrite, combine to save *Black Thunder* from the worst features of a propaganda novel. What remains of protest and of race pride limits the book but does not destroy it.

Arna Bontemps' second historical novel, *Drums at Dusk*, is in every respect a retreat from the standards of *Black Thunder*. Deriving its plot from the Haitian slave rebellion which brought Toussaint l'Ouverture to power, the novel is unworthy of its subject. In writing of a successful rebellion, Bontemps is deprived of the dramatic power of tragedy, and he discovers no appropriate attitude to take its place. Upon a highly romantic plot he grafts a class analysis of society which is post-Marxian and flagrantly unhistorical. Frequently lapsing into crude melodrama, he embroiders his narrative with all of the sword-play, sex, and sadism of a Hollywood extravaganza.

Robert A. Bone. *The Negro Novel in America* (New Haven, Conn., Yale University Press, 1958), pp. 120, 122–23

My ex-student and friend, Robert A. Bone, is at his critical poorest with Arna Bontemps' fiction. "*God Sends Sunday*," he writes, "is an unadulterated product of the Renaissance." This is an unadulterated lie. . . .

Arna Bontemps was not of the "Harlem Renaissance" . . . for seven good reasons. This is especially ironic, for at the close of his busy life he should have been tending to more important business than plaintively, nostalgically wailing them good old days (which Langston [Hughes], Wallace Thurman and Zora Neale Hurston later said never existed). Again, thanks to whatever gods may be, Arna, bless his aesthetic sensibility and his Christian heart was *not* a member of that motley crew. If he had tried to join that Mystic Order of the Sons of —— Harlem, he would have been blackballed for the following cogent reasons:

1. He was born in Alexandria, La., or leastways "above Aleck" in the local parlance.

2. He was a painstaking writer, respecting the English language. He certainly did not write "Black," if there is such a monstrosity.

3. He knew a great deal about literature, foreign and domestic.

4. His first novel and his poems are all that he wrote during this nebulous period, and they all appeared just when the such-and-such hit the fan, and the Renaissance flopped.

5. His major accomplishment before 1930 was a good novel which later became a bad play (good only because it introduced us to that immortal Pearl Bailey). Well, this novel never mentions or touches upon Harlem or even New York life. The title of the play was *St. Louis Woman* (*Harlem* Renaissance?).

6. He was a sober, austere, melancholy, meditative, meticulous Christian gentleman, who was far from the hedonism blatant in the "Harlem Renaissance" credo. How far the lust for life credo went in actuality is an intriguing idea, later to be pursued.

7. He was a decent artist.

Sterling A. Brown. *BlackW.* Sept., 1973, pp. 94–95

The poetry of Arna Bontemps has appeared in every major anthology of Negro writing since the Renaissance, but it was not until 1963 that he brought out a collection of his verse, *Personals*, a thin volume of only twenty-three poems published by Paul Bremen in London. . . .

Bontemps' poems make use of several recurring themes: the alien-and-exile allusions so often found in New Negro poetry; strong racial suggestiveness and applications; religious themes and imagery subtly used; and the theme of return to a former time, a former love, or a remembered place. On occasion he combines in a way common to lyrical writing the personal with the racial or the general. Many of these poems are protest poems; but the protest is oblique and suggestive rather than frontal. Over all of Bontemps' poetry there is a sad, brooding quality, a sombre "Il Penseroso" meditative cast. In *Personals* there are no obviously joyous or humorous pieces. . . .

The poems of Arna Bontemps lack the clear, unambiguous statement of those of his contemporaries: McKay, Cullen, Hughes. There is modern obscurity in these verses, and the so-called meaning often eludes the reader. Their craftsmanship, however, is impressive. The reader somehow feels a certain rightness in Bontemps' lines, that what he has said could not be expressed otherwise. There is a quiet authority in these poems.

Arthur P. Davis. *From the Dark Tower* (Washington, D.C., Howard University Press, 1974), pp. 84–86

BRATHWAITE, EDWARD (1930–   )

BARBADOS

West Indian poetry has suffered in locally-edited anthologies from a total absence of critical standards. In fact, apart from the Martinique-based Césaire, who still awaits a good translation, there has up till now been virtually only Walcott. In the circumstances, perhaps, it is scarcely surprising, though set against West Indian prose and the liveliness of the best Calypso performers like Lord Beginner and Mighty Sparrow, disappointing. Neither the rich raciness of Caribbean idioms nor the spectacular conjunctions of visual images seem to have got into West Indian poetry, which as a genre exudes a technical timidity and general atmosphere of piety totally at odds with its political and social character.

Edward Brathwaite, in his *Rights of Passage*, makes an ambitious attempt to redress the balance. Eighty-six pages long, and the first part of a trilogy, it describes, in a variety of styles, a kind of double pilgrimage, personal and evolutionary; in private terms, the poet's travels from his birthplace to England and America before his final return home, in historical terms the long climb from slavery to independence.

It is altogether an impressive effort. . . . Making use of work-songs and blues, and alternating dense descriptive passages with short-lined and sharp résumés of local incident, Brathwaite builds up a coherent picture of contemporary Caribbean life. A Barbadian, he manages to achieve a balanced perspective without losing any of the historic thrust or sacrificing the native melancholy and nostalgia that underlie all West Indian exuberance. His poetic drive cannot always prevent drops into flatness but usually the sheer evocative power of place-names, and the sense of communities sustained by the shared rhythms of poverty, work and racial memory, keep the poem afloat.

Alan Ross. *London*. March, 1967, pp. 96–97

[*Masks*] is the second in what is planned to be a trilogy. The first one was *Rights of Passage*. *Masks* deals with [Brathwaite's] eight-year sojourn in Ghana. By theme, idiom and rhythm he shows what excellence can emerge from an honest awareness and utilisation of one's inheritance. Even where the inheritance is on hand, Africa. He has done what other black writers have done, or tried, or should try, to do but never succeeded so well. This includes everyone from Césaire and Senghor to the contemporary young crop. I refer to, first, acceptance of Africa—our shame, our glories, past and present—not in defense or aggression, but quietly, as being us and all that is us: and that it is out of this that anything meaningful can come, including our "contribution to a universal culture." This is the awareness of the reality contained in his lines. . . .

There is a touching reverence in Edward Brathwaite for African usages, and this is quite obvious in his lines on libations and the sacrifice. However, what is really overwhelming about his poetic genius is what he makes English do for him. His language is sensitive to his awareness and his moods. . . .

His totally skilful use of the one African language he understands, Akan, in combination with English, makes some of us ashamedly envious and jealous. Naturally, non-Akan speakers, African and otherwise, would find the sections in the collection which are almost written entirely in Akan slightly irritating. But the book contains nothing but that which is alive and breathing, and anyone who cares would on second and third reading (which is only when it's possible to enjoy any poetry) find that the Akan bits, even when not understood literally, add to the beauty of the whole.

Ama Ata Aidoo. *WA*. Sept. 21, 1968, p. 1099

Whereas Walcott is centrally concerned with Caribbean man, with his present and his island world, Brathwaite is haunted by a vision of the historic destiny of the negro race, not only in the Caribbean but everywhere. His poem [*Rights of Passage*] begins in the Sahara, all images of drought and sharp glitter, then moves into the damp silence of the forests, the savage encounter with the armed intruders, the enslavement and the passage to the New World—the last a literal image of hell. Later it picks up the cyclical rhythm which seems to dominate the literature of the islands, the cycle of Discovery, Departure and Return upon which Book One of the present work is based. But Brathwaite's discovery of the new island home lacks the joy which Walcott imparts to it. The negro islander soon finds himself facing a new exile, to the urban slums and savage discrimination of America and England. Finally he returns to the islands, only to confront once more their poverty, hopelessness and squalor. The long shadow of the U.S. Marines now lies over the whole archipelago, inhibiting the process of revolution which can alone redeem them.

In his later poem *Masks*, Brathwaite does chronicle a kind of African homecoming, a personal exploration of what Africa was and is. But that poem . . . also ends upon a note of departure. The historical severance from Africa was, he implies, a final one. The West Indian can revisit it, draw strength and inspiration from it, but cannot, in the fullest sense, return.

Where Walcott, poet of seascape, rock and sunlight, cries "home is here!", Brathwaite, poet of voyages, train-whistles and quaysides, replies, "home is nowhere!" . . . If Walcott shows us how Caribbean man may learn to know and love his island, Brathwaite reminds us why he so often has to leave it. [1969]

Gerald Moore. The Chosen Tongue (New York,
Harper & Row, 1970), pp. 28–29

Much of [Brathwaite's] poetry, especially in Islands and Masks, is an attempt to document in verse the historical experience of tribal Africa and of the deracinated African in the New World. When Brathwaite is successful a peculiar thing happens; not only is history compressed into poetry, but poetry finds its fulfilment in history. By this I mean that the poetry is so much an abstract of racial and historical experience, that significant events from contemporary history seem daily to reinforce and fulfil the poetry which then derives extra value from the hard clear light which it casts not only on the colonial past, but on our present historical moment. . . .

Brathwaite illustrates that the Black West Indian like his American counterpart does have an exceedingly rich, or at least a potentially rich, identity, but it is buried under centuries of slavery, colonialism and the self-contempt which goes with these. This is perhaps why Islands is saturated with the idea of death and rebirth. Brathwaite sees us as celebrating these two things in our every action. Death and rebirth are of course analogous to slavery and rebellion, or slavery and the independence which comes only when the slave consciously acts to free himself. Independence, like identity, cannot be given, it can only be asserted. So Brathwaite uses everything, Limbo, Cricket, politics, pocomania, steelband, carnival, the wake, to explore these related themes of death and rebirth, slavery and rebellion. He seems to see us as perpetually wavering between the two states, always in danger of being sucked back into the womb-grave of the slave ship's hold.

G. Rohlehr. LHY. July, 1970, pp. 171–72, 175

Brathwaite, who is the foremost poet of the English-speaking Caribbean and at least in some sense a revolutionary, is never shrill, is always keen to the pathos of his people's plight, yet the basic exuberance of his feeling cannot be doubted. In part it is revolutionary optimism, in part a closeness to his sources in folk culture. Brathwaite has said that the chief literary influence on his work has been the poetry of T. S. Eliot, but if this is so it has been an influence almost entirely limited to matters of organization and structure, and perhaps to Eliot's manner of rhyming, though this could have come from anywhere. In texture, in verbal technique, in almost everything, nothing could be further from Eliot's poetry than Brathwaite's.

Brathwaite has made his reputation on three long poems, *Rights of Passage, Masks*, and *Islands*. Now they have been published in one volume, *The Arrivants: A New World Trilogy*, and it is a book everyone should read. Brathwaite uses many voices, ranging from standard English to dialects of several kinds, and in many rhythms, from subdued free cadence to calypso. Not all passages are equally successful; sometimes his jazz tempos remind us too much of [Vachel] Lindsay's "Congo" or his dialect slips too far toward the type of Auden's ballads. But in general he has been remarkably successful in reproducing black speech patterns, both African and Caribbean, in English syntax, using the standard techniques of contemporary poetry, and he has been equally successful in suggesting to an international audience the cultural identities and attitudes of his own people.

Hayden Carruth. *HdR*. Summer, 1974, p. 318

BROOKS, GWENDOLYN (1917–   )

UNITED STATES

Two sections of [*A Street in Bronzeville*], including the one that gives it its title, represent rather unexciting vignettes of sentiment and character. They have, however, something of the spice and movement which many of the better Negro poets commonly lend to their work. No doubt a great bulk of the proficient and marketable poems written by poets of whatever color deal with such sure-fire or easy-mark situations as those in these groups. The good child envies the bad. Dreams are hard to sustain amid onion fumes or where red fat roaches stroll up one's wall. God must be lonely. The hunchback speculates on heaven. Yet even these sketches are somewhat safeguarded in the present case by some actuality of detail, freshness of image, dryness of angle or flexibility of tempo. . . .

All in all, despite the fact that this first book has its share of unexciting verse, there are considerable resources evidenced for future work. Miss Brooks, to use one of her own phrases, "scrapes life with a fine-tooth comb." And she shows a capacity to marry the special quality of her racial experience with the best attainments of our contemporary poetry tradition. Such compounding of resources out of varied stocks and traditions is the great hope of American art as it is of American life generally.

Amos N. Wilder. Poetry. Dec., 1945, pp. 164, 166

Miss Brooks is a very accomplished poet indeed, often boiling her lines down to the sparsest expression of the greatest meaning, sometimes almost to a kind of word-shorthand that defies immediate grasp. Less simple and direct than the poems in her initial volume [*A Street in Bronzeville*], those in *Annie Allen* give, upon careful reading, as much interest and emotional impact. The book is a mood story in varying poetic forms of a girl's growth from childhood to the age of love, marriage, and motherhood.

There are sharp pictures of neighborhoods, relatives, friends, illnesses and deaths; of big city slums, cafes, and beauty shops. To me the third section, containing about half the poems in the book, "The Womanhood," is its most effective. The qualms, the longings, the love of a poor mother for her child is here most movingly expressed. . . .

The people and the poems in Gwendolyn Brooks' book are alive, reaching, and very much of today.

Langston Hughes. Voices. Winter, 1950, pp. 55–56

[Brooks] tends to use conventional forms with tightly locking rhymes that constrict her unduly, to fit an inappropriate vocabulary to a loose ballad rhythm, or to write poems of statement that would be more effective as poems of understatement. [*Annie Allen*] has the adventitious interest that attaches to relatively fresh subject matter, for Miss Brooks takes her themes chiefly from the world of the urban Negro. But she fails to make the most of her material. The intrinsic value of her work is the poet's prevailing attitude; here vitality and compassion are mingled in a manner not unique with Negroes but exhibited by them with remarkable frequency.

Babette Deutsch. YR. Winter, 1950, pp. 362–63

The fact that Miss Brooks displays an excellent knowledge of form, whether in the versatile handling of types of forms of poetry included in *Annie Allen* or in the metrical variations in the volume, can be readily seen as proof of [the] new emphasis upon conventional form. She skillfully handles a number of stanzaic forms including couplets, quatrains, the Italian Terza Rima, and even in "The Anniad," the difficult rime-royal or the seven line stanza named for Chaucer. . . . In addition to these conventional forms she includes several poems written in free verse as well as occasional lines of blank verse. In regard to types she includes short lyrics, ballads, and sonnets written with veteran aplomb.

As a whole, *Annie Allen* is a fine delineation of the character of a young Negro woman from childhood through adolescence to complete maturity, but with slight racial exceptions it could apply to any female of a certain class and society. The entire volume is tinged with an highly sophisticated humor and is not only technically sure but also vindicates the promise of *A Street in Bronzeville*. Coming after the long hue and cry of white writers that Negroes as poets lack form and intellectual acumen, Miss Brooks' careful craftsmanship and sensitive understanding reflected in *Annie Allen* are not only personal triumphs but a racial vindication.

Margaret Walker. Phylon. 11, 4, 1950, pp. 351–52

There is every indication in *Maud Martha* that poetess Gwendolyn Brooks is capable of well rounded characterizations of which her heroine Maud is a finespun, fractional specimen. For what Miss Brooks presents in this slender volume are bright glimpses of a world turning upon Maud's soft meditations. Writing with the quiet charm and sparkling delicacy of tone which brought Emily Dickinson's bird down the walk to drink a dew, Miss Brooks has begat a kind of beauty upon ugliness by lighting up the humanity of her creation against the background of a Chicago slum area. . . .

Maud has not accepted herself with that unconscious assurance which makes her male counterpart, [Langston Hughes's] Jesse Simple, so articulate in his easy living with hard conditions. She finds herself too often wishing to be what her husband Paul, absorbed as he is in surface values, believes he wants her to be. For all practical purposes, this is as it should be, for what the author is dealing with from the inside of her creation are those very human hopes which grasp straw values in reaching very hungrily for real ones. In all this, Miss Brooks maintains a kind of subtle, close-lipped control over her style which so heightens its rich suggestiveness that one is led to believe he understands more for being told less.

Henry F. Winslow. Crisis. Feb., 1954, p. 114

[In *The Bean Eaters* the] poems, generous and full of humanity, rattle with verbs and jangle with action. Their images are everyday; their subjects are poor people (often Negroes), the dreams of the downtrodden, the frustrations of the meek.

Yet, for all the worthiness of their themes and their aims, you will probably find them incomplete as poems. Miss Brooks appears more concerned to condemn social injustice and to draw sympathetic character portraits than to write poems that echo on every level, and as a result she repeats the same kind of statement too often for poetic truth.

The best poem in her book is a ballad of racial segregation ["The Ballad of Rudolph Reed"] with the stark rhythms and devices of the traditional ballad adapted to a theme that suits it perfectly. Most of this book, however, has the same virtues and faults as the title poem, which for the sake of journalistic realism ends in a catalogue that reminds the reader of nothing so much as Ogden Nash and destroys the poem's serious intent.

Peter Davison. Atlantic. Sept., 1960, p. 93

When many of us think of protest poetry we tend to recall the fiery lines of "If We Must Die," written by McKay during those exciting days of the New Negro Movement. Moreover, we have somehow come to expect the same kind of bitterness and defiance in all poetry of this kind. But Miss Brooks's protest poems, written in an integration age, are usually quite different in spirit and approach from those of the New Negro generation. She has subtle irony, a quiet humor, and oftentimes a sense of pity, not only for the black victims of prejudice but also for the whites who are guilty. But her works as a rule are not fiery or defiant, and they are seldom bitter. . . .

When one compares Miss Brooks's racial problems with those of an earlier generation of Negro writers, he finds this significant difference. In most of the earlier poems, regardless of the bitterness expressed, there is an implied faith in a better day which will come either through the fulfillment of the American Dream or through the workings of a Just God. In these earlier works, there was also on occasion the kind of self-abasement one finds in [James David] Corrother's lines: "To be a Negro in a day like this—/Alas! Lord God, what evil have we done?" There is no self-pity in Gwendolyn Brooks's racial poems and precious little optimism. She doesn't seem to have much faith in either the American Dream or a Just God. Expressing neither hope nor fear, she is content to describe conditions as they are in Bronzeville. She seems to be saying: these things are so, and they are bad; but modern men, white or black, are not heroic. One can't expect too much.

Arthur P. Davis. CLAJ. Dec., 1963, pp. 120, 125

It's too soon to say anything definitive about the work of Gwendolyn Brooks. Perhaps she hasn't yet written the poems that will stand out a hundred years from now as her major ones. But she has already written some that will undoubtedly be read so long as man cares about language and his fellows.

There have been no drastic changes in the tactics and subjects she has dealt with over the years. It's doubtful if future critics will talk about the early and the late Brooks, not unless she strikes out into much different territory after 1969. What one observes is a steady development of themes and types.

Her poetry is marked by a number of central concerns: black experience; the nature of greatness; the way in which man expresses his needs, makes do, or lashes out. Ordinarily the view is one of delicate balance, that of a passionate observer. The poems strike one as distinctly those of a woman but always muscled and precise, written from the pelvis rather than the biceps.

Dan Jaffe. In C. W. E. Bigsby, ed., *The Black American Writer* (De Land, Fla., Everett/Edwards, 1969), Vol. II, p. 93

When you view Gwendolyn Brooks's work in the pre-1967 period, you see a poet, a black poet in the actual (though still actively searching for her own definitions of blackness), on the roadway to becoming a conscious African poet or better yet a conscious African woman in America who chose poetry as her major craft. However, Gwendolyn Brooks describes her poetry prior to 1967 as "work that was conditioned to the times and the people." In other words, poetry that leaped from the pages bringing forth ideas, definitions, images, reflections, forms, colors, etc., that were molded over a distance of many years—her poetry notebook started at the age of eleven—as a result of and as a reaction to the American reality. And for black people, regardless of the level of their perception of the world, the American reality has always been a battle, a real alley fight. . . .

Gwendolyn Brooks's post 1967 poetry is fat-less. Her new work resembles a man getting off meat, turning to a vegetarian diet. What one immediately notices is that all the excess weight is quickly lost. Her work becomes extremely streamlined and to the point. . . .

We can see in the work of Gwendolyn Brooks of 1972 positive movement from that of the sayer to the doer, where she recognizes that *writing is not enough* for a people in a life and death struggle. For so few black writers to reflect the aspirations and needs of so many (there are about three hundred black writers who are published with any kind of regularity) is a responsibility that should not be taken lightly. Every word has to be considered and worked with so as to use it to its fullest potential.

Don L. Lee. Preface to Gwendolyn Brooks, *Report from Part One* (Detroit, Broadside, 1972), pp. 13–14, 22, 29

The world of white arts and letters has pointed to [Gwendolyn Brooks] with pride; it has bestowed kudos and a Pulitzer Prize [for *Annie Allen*]. The world of black arts and letters has looked on with mixed emotion, and pride has been only one part of the admixture. There have also been troubling questions about the poet's essential "blackness," her dedication to the melioration of the black American's social conditions. The real duality appears when we realize that Gwendolyn Brooks—though praised and awarded—does not appear on the syllabuses of most American literature courses, and her name seldom appears in the annual scholarly bibliographies of the academic world. She, it would seem, is a black writer after all, *not* an American writer. Yet when one listens to the voice of today's black revolutionary consciousness, one often hears that Miss Brooks' poetry fits the white, middle-class patterns that LeRoi Jones has seen as characteristic of "Negro literature." . . .

Gwendolyn Brooks represents a singular achievement. Beset by a double-consciousness, she has kept herself from being torn asunder by speaking the truth in poems that equal the best work in the black and the white American literary traditions. Her characters are believable; her themes are manifold; and her technique is superb. The critic (whether white or black) who comes to her writing seeking only support for his ideology will be disappointed, for as Etheridge Knight has pointed out, she has ever spoken the truth. And truth, one likes to feel, always lies beyond the boundaries of any one ideology. Perhaps Miss Brooks' most significant achievement is her endorsement of this point of view, for from her hand and fertile imagination have come volumes of verse that transcend the dogma on either side of the American veil.

Houston A. Baker, Jr. *CLAJ*. Sept., 1972, pp. 24, 31

Report from Part One is a seemingly chunk and hunk assemblage of photographs, interviews, letters—backward glances on growing up in Chicago and coming of age in the Black Arts Movement. It is not a sustained dramatic narrative for the nosey, being neither the confessions of a private woman/poet or the usual sort of mahogany-desk memoir public personages inflict upon the populace at the first sign of a cardiac. It is simply an extremely valuable book that is all of a piece and readable and memorable in unexpected ways. It documents the growth of Gwen Brooks. Documents that essentially lonely (no matter how close and numerous the friends who support, sustain and encourage you to stretch out and explore) process of opening the eyes, wrenching the self away from played-out modes, and finding new directions. It shows her reaching toward a perspective that reflects the recognition that the black artist is obliged to fashion an esthetic linked to the political dynamics of the community she serves. . . .

Like the younger black poets, Gwen Brooks since the late Sixties has been struggling for a cadence, style, idiom and content that will politicize and mobilize. Like the young black poets, her recent work is moving more toward gesture, sound, intonation, attitude and other characteristics that depend on oral presentation rather than private eye-balling. It is important to have the poet herself assess these moves in her own way so as to establish the ground for future critical biographies. But "change" and "shift" may be too heavy-handed, somewhat misleading; for in rereading the bulk of her work, which *Report from Part One* does prompt one to do, we see a continuum.

Toni Cade Bambara. *NYT*. Jan. 7, 1973, p. 1

[Gwendolyn Brooks's] *A Street in Bronzeville* and her *In the Mecca*, in all seriousness, could be used as reference works in sociology. Her *Annie Allen* quietly demonstrates the wealth of her observation of normal, not abnormal, psychology. She is at home with fact. Her alert mentality gathers in the evidence presented to the senses. But she is at home, also, with reflective thought. She sees not only the bare circumstance. She sees also its place in a rich context of fine relationships. Her craftsmanship is careful. Miss Brooks belongs to the school of writers who do not believe in wasting a single word. Selection and significance —one can divine in her diction how she has brooded over them, how every word has been chosen with due regard for the several functions it may be called upon to perform in the dispensation of a poem. But the brooding goes deep and it affects not only words. The words must be put together. And the principle of dire economy which governs her choice of diction disciplines severely all of her poetic maneuvers. Terseness, a judicious understatement combined with pregnant ellipses, often guides the reader into an adventure which permits a revelation of Miss Brooks's capacity for sensitive interpretations of the human comedy.

She never writes on "big" subjects. One finds on her agenda no librettos for Liberia [like Tolson's], no grand excursus into history like [Hayden's] "Middle Passage." *Annie Allen* typifies her method, the study, as it were, of the flower in the crannied wall. In such a method her genius operates within its area of greatest strength, the close inspection of a limited domain, to reap from that inspection, perhaps paradoxically, but still powerfully, a view of life in which one may see a microscopic portion of the universe intensely and yet, through that microscopic portion, see all truth for the human condition wherever it exists.

Blyden Jackson. In Blyden Jackson and Louis D. Rubin, Jr., *Black Poetry in America* (Baton Rouge, Louisiana State University Press, 1974), pp. 84–85

Beckonings exemplifies Brooks' movement toward her new style, which is characterized by a struggle between her normal tendency to make each word bear its full measure of weight and suggestion and an insistence upon directness and simplicity of diction. Actually, despite her reputation for complexity, there are already many poems across the body of her work which are simple and direct. *A Street in Bronzeville* contains a large number of simple poems, some of which become favorites with readers. I would suppose the main difficulties for the uninitiated readers in some earlier poems would be the presence of irony and understatement. *Beckonings* reduces the element of irony and often goes into direct statement. . . .

"Five Men against the Theme 'My Name Is Red Hot. Yo Name Ain Doodley Squat' " and "Sammy Chester Leaves 'Godspell' and Visits *Upward Bound* on a Lake Forest Lawn, Bringing West Afrika" use older techniques in a new way; that is, the unusual junction of words, the coinages, the sudden contrasts, and repetitions, remain within the bounds of a simplicity which is accessible to the pause for thought. There are other poems which make such combinations, and still others which move close to direct statement. "A Black Wedding Song" is a good example of this group.

The poems are evidence that the newer techniques will not sacrifice the complex rhythms of existence in their attempts to reach a wider audience.

George E. Kent. *Phylon*. Spring, 1976, pp. 110–11

BROWN, STERLING A. (1901–   )

UNITED STATES

Mr. Brown's work is not only fine, it is also unique. He began writing just after the Negro poets had generally discarded conventionalized dialect, with its minstrel traditions of Negro life (traditions that had but slight relation, often no relation at all, to *actual* Negro life) with its artificial and false sentiment, its exaggerated geniality and optimism. He infused his poetry with genuine characteristic flavor by adopting as his medium the common, racy, living speech of the Negro in certain phases of *real* life. For his raw material he dug down into the deep mine of Negro folk poetry. He found the unfailing sources from which sprang the Negro folk epics and ballads such as "Stagolee," "John Henry," "Casey Jones," "Long Gone John" and others.

But, as I said in commenting on his work in *The Book of American Negro Poetry*: he has made more than mere transcriptions of folk poetry, and he has done more than bring to it mere artistry; he has deepened its meanings and multiplied its implications. He has actually absorbed the spirit of his material, made it his own; and without diluting its primitive frankness and raciness, truly re-expressed it with artistry and magnified power. In a word, he has taken this raw material and worked it into original and authentic poetry.

> James Weldon Johnson. Introduction to Sterling A.
> Brown, *Southern Road* (New York, Harcourt, Brace,
> 1932), pp. xiv–xv

Many critics, writing in praise of Sterling Brown's first volume of verse, have seen fit to hail him as a significant new Negro poet. The discriminating few go further; they hail a new era in Negro poetry, for such is the deeper significance of this volume (*Southern Road*). Gauging the main objective of Negro poetry as the poetic portrayal of Negro folk-life true in both letter and spirit to the idiom of the folk's own way of feeling and thinking, we may say that here for the first time is that much-desired and long-awaited acme attained or brought within actual reach. . . .

I do not mean to imply that Sterling Brown's art is perfect, or even completely mature. It is all the more promising that this volume represents the work of a young man just in his early thirties. But a Negro poet with almost complete detachment, yet with a tone of persuasive sincerity, whose muse neither clowns nor shouts, is indeed a promising and a grateful phenomenon. . . .

If we stop to inquire—as unfortunately the critic must—into the magic of [his] effects, we find the secret, I think, in this fact more than in any other: Sterling Brown has listened long and carefully to the folk in their intimate hours, when they were talking to themselves, not, so to speak, as in Dunbar, but actually as they do when the masks of protective mimicry fall. Not only has he dared to give quiet but bold expression to this private thought and speech, but he has dared to give the Negro peasant credit for thinking. In this way he has recaptured the shrewd Aesopian quality of the Negro folk-thought, which is more profoundly characteristic than their types of metaphors or their mannerisms of speech. They are, as he himself says, "Illiterate, and somehow very wise," and it is this wisdom, bitter fruit of their suffering, combined with their characteristic fatalism and irony, which in this book gives a truer soul picture of the Negro than has ever yet been given poetically. [1934]

Alain Locke. In Nancy Cunard, ed., *Negro:
An Anthology* (New York, Frederick Ungar,
1970), pp. 88–90

Sterling Brown has penetrated the essence of Negro song, of folk song, and has utilized the expressiveness of dialect. But, the racial distinctiveness of his poetry does not depend exclusively on dialect; it also arises from the subtlest nuances of the ironic life of black men, from Brown's ability to plumb the depths of their feelings and pinpoint their psychology. . . .

Alain Locke, who has an admirable knowledge of the psychology of his race, tells us that the stereotyped black man is a clown, a buffoon, an easy smiler, a foolish weeper, and a credulous Christian, but that the real Black man is frequently a cynical fatalist, a sly pretender, and an impudent, whimsical pagan. Sterling Brown should be considered a rectifier of the false presentation of the black man, an excellent interpreter of the soul of his race who, in his songs, makes us familiar with all the subtleties of racial feelings. In the poem "Children of the Mississippi" he reaches the heights of poetic expression, in an orchestral harmony that arouses many deep feelings. The muddy, black flood waters of the Mississippi, with their hunger for death, overflow in the poem to sublime language, equal to that of the best poetry of any age.

Ildefonso Pereda Valdés. In Ildefonso Pereda Valdés,
ed., *Antología de la poesía negra americana* (Santiago,
Chile, Ediciones Ercilla, 1936), pp. 12–13†

Through the Thirties and into the Forties there were three critics whose ideas on literature were dominant. These were Benjamin Brawley, Alain Locke, and Sterling Brown. . . .

Sterling Brown, the third and youngest of the formative critics of the Thirties, had barely begun his public career as critic when the Renaissance in its original form died away. Himself a poet, whose *Southern Road* appeared at the beginning of the Great Depression, he shared few of the urban delusions of the central figures of the Renaissance though he followed and understood them fully. Like Brawley, he was physically located away from the great Harlem metropolis during most of the Twenties but, unlike Brawley, he found the time and followed the urge to investigate more fully the Negro folk cultures of semirural Virginia, Missouri, and Tennessee while on teaching assignments in those regions. In both his poetry and in his criticism he therefore employed in greater depth a knowledge of the folk sources of literary expression. This knowledge was greater than that of prior and most contemporary interpreters of Negro expression; in addition it was buttressed by what most of his contemporaries also lacked: a thorough grounding in past and contemporary literatures. The newer traditions of realism and naturalism were not uncongenial to him and his studies in the Irish literary movement had convinced him that the major worth for the Negro literary movement lay in the life and expression of the people themselves. . . .

[His] credo is, essentially, that valid literary expression, in whatever form, must be true to its subject matter. The author must therefore forego all literary and social traditions which, either by softening sentimentally or exaggerating for effect, distort the substance for the sake of form, sales, conformity, or anything else which is properly extraneous to the subject matter at hand.

Ulysses Lee. Phylon. 11, 4, 1950, pp. 330, 334–35

Southern Road depicts the Negro as the victim not of the white man alone, but of all that surrounds him. He is enslaved by the land he cultivates, victimized by the lawless natural elements whose predilection it is to fall on him, as he is victimized by his own fear and that of others, and by his own ignorance and credulity. In short he is exposed to a terrible fate whose whole pitiless cruelty is sung in the blues and whose effects the people had always sought to ward off by means of superstitious precepts passed from generation to generation. . . .

The Negro's destiny, as presented in Brown's work, is ultimately a depressing one. But his outlook strikes us as significantly more pessimistic than that of his predecessors because he practically excludes the spiritual forces from his universe. In some obscure way, a vital bond still subsisted between the black man and God in the writings of James Weldon Johnson and Langston Hughes. Sterling Brown, on the contrary, makes the situation entirely clear: the black man suddenly finds himself isolated and must derive his whole strength from the people, who thus become the sole source of all true value. . . .

As for the poet himself, does he differ from them to any great extent? It would have been easy to understand, had the disillusioning portrait of the black man that he has painted for us ended in despair. The reason this does not occur is that he too has hit upon a way of escaping from an appalling reality. For it is an art of living that he has discovered in the humorous philosophy in which his race is steeped, and it may be more than a coincidence that Brown, the poet of the Negro Renaissance who most pitilessly excludes from his universe the whole range of religious forces, is at the same time the only truly humorous poet in the group. [1963]

Jean Wagner. *Black Poets of the United States* (Urbana, University of Illinois Press, 1973), pp. 483, 496–98

Southern Road, the first collection of poems by Sterling A. Brown, was published in 1932, at the end of the New Negro Renaissance and the beginning of the Great Depression. Some time after the appearance of this small volume, which was generally favorably reviewed, Brown prepared for publication a second collection with the intriguing title *No Hiding Place*. This collection, however and regrettably, was never published. Meanwhile Brown's rising status as a poet was evidenced by occasional appearances of new poems of his in national periodicals and scholarly anthologies. No second collection of Brown's poems appeared, withal, until the recent publication of *The Last Ride of Wild Bill, and Eleven Narrative Poems*. The title poem in this collection is an excellent example of modern narrative folk poetry at its best. . . .

Contrary to Wagner's view, Brown's collections of poems can hardly be said to furnish proof that the dialect movement Johnson referred to has gone forward. Neither of them abounds in the mutilated English commonly called Negro dialect. Nor does it appear from them that Brown ever intended to indulge in—or perpetrate—that kind of writing. Rather he seems to have had his several characters employ only such illiterate and semiliterate usage as was expressive of their individuality. The substandard grammar and the comparatively few dialect spellings to which he resorted give the impression that he endeavored to represent without exaggeration illiterate and semiliterate usage as he had attentively heard it in his native Washington, D.C., in Lynchburg, Virginia; Jefferson City, Missouri; and Nashville, Tennessee, where he spent several years teaching college English; and in his travels elsewhere in the United States. Accordingly the usage in his poetry is at once radically different from what has been conventionally called Negro dialect and remarkably close to actual folk speech, as one would expect to find it in folk poetry.

W. Edward Farrison. *CLAJ*. Dec., 1975, pp. 286, 289

BRUTUS, DENNIS (1924–   )

RHODESIA

Brutus's intellect is distinguished by its skill and intensity, certainly not . . . by depth. . . .

If Brutus is not a rare genius, he surely boasts a skillful, forceful, trained intelligence. The way he exercises his sure intellectual grip on his subjects calls to mind the method of John Donne and the Metaphysicals. A typical Dennis Brutus poem opens with a line or a couple of lines which holds in embryo the central motif of the piece. . . . Brutus then builds up his poem by developing this stated motif, arguing, describing, expounding, analysing, illustrating with vivid and living imagery, occasionally bolstering the argument with conceits, all the while echoing the opening lines either directly or through new images and descriptive details which embody the *idea* of the opening lines, and finally concluding in a dialectical and emotional point of rest in which the opening lines resound again.

Daniel Abasiekong. *Transition*. No. 23, 1965, p. 46

J. P. Clark, who has criticised Brutus, is right in saying that Nigerian poets do not write lines like "obscene albinos"; but Nigerians are not murdered or imprisoned because they are black; they are not considered the black stinking lubrication that helps the huge cogs of the economy to run smoothly. Brutus is whipped and he lashes back furiously. It is true that sometimes his punches are wild, sometimes he misses, but he swings enough times for us to see what he is aiming at. Brutus, speaking for the millions of black South Africans, has been frustrated and turned away and confined and shot at and still nothing has changed. And so he continues to rage. . . .

There is horror in these poems [in *Sirens, Knuckles, Boots*], but it is not the horror of a man skittering in a high wind away from white ghosts stalking him with Sten-guns. It is rather the horror of a man seeing love nourished in bad soil, in a country made ugly by hatred. Perhaps Brutus likes to picture himself in flight, but I read these poems differently. He is not moving (living furiously does not mean bobbing around); he is staying, suffering the phantasms, and he is recording them faithfully. This takes great strength and dedication; he has escaped the decayed language of revolt, the clichés of the man oppressed. If the poems are depressive in their raging tenderness it is because Brutus is being hammered from within his soul and from without: the sirens in his ears, the knuckles and boots against his body.

Paul Theroux. *BO*. Aug., 1966, p. 43–45

Dennis Brutus is now living in exile in London. Were it not for the tragedy the last years have brought him and his family, one might think his situation part of some nightmarish Kafka farce. Yet its horror is only a bitter reflection of the edicts by which a "coloured" such as Brutus is forced to live in the Republic of South Africa. His poetry is denied publication in his country and only a slender volume published by the Mbari Writers and Artists Club of Nigeria [*Sirens, Knuckles, Boots*] is available to indicate the quality of both the spirit and poetry of this man. . . .

Throughout Brutus' poetry runs an infinite and continuous love for his sad yet beautiful country. Brutus never denies this affection. Replying to the newsman's inevitable question, he explained how he could feel affection for a country that treated him so viciously: "It's a suffering people and a suffering land, assaulted, violated, raped, whatever you will, tremendously beautiful and I feel a great tenderness for it." This emotion shows in everything Brutus writes. . . .

Brutus affirms the hope that love and poetry, in mutual combination, can simultaneously reinforce the spirit. His lines take on an evocative lilt in their repetition:

> Somehow we survive
> and tenderness frustrated, does not wither . . .
> But somehow we survive
> Severance deprivation loss . . .
> but somehow tenderness survives.

His assertion is vague. It is inexplicable but sure. How tenderness can survive, how even the very man can survive under such a dispensation we can hardly say. But Brutus affirms his own certainties. His attitude plays no heroics, though in avoiding that pose he is the more heroic. He answers oppression by the humane strength by which he lives—survives. Such strength is full enough; it even permits a little flamboyance in its confidence. . . .

Brutus once wrote "under jackboots our bones and spirits crunch." The rest of his poetry contradicts this for it asserts the eventual triumph of spirits over jackboots. He rearticulates Orwell's view of the future of the jackboot stamping on the human face forever. But Brutus concludes with a courageous optimism that Orwell could not accept. His poetry convinces us that such optimism is not delusive. It is the source, not only of Brutus' capacity for survival, but of all hopes for equity in South Africa.

John Povey. *JNALA*. Spring, 1967, pp. 95–96, 99–100

Dennis Brutus's first published poetry, *Sirens, Knuckles, Boots*, which came out in the early 1960's in Ibadan, displays the usual features of a beginner's work: brash, raw anger wielding the long thundering line and harsh sounds. In *Letters to Martha*, the long thundering lines and awkward phraseology have given way to a subdued diction. And yet so much of the collection lapses into talkative verse which sounds like tired prose: like a guitar string that has lost its tension. One tends to condone this lapse because of the singleness of emotion and mood *Letters to Martha* represents. The impact is cumulative.

The promise one senses in *Letters to Martha* is certainly not anywhere near fulfillment in Brutus's later work. *Poems from Algiers . . .* is disappointing. There is nothing important the poems say, no specific emotion they can be said to be conveying. Only observational fragments. Two closely connected factors must account for this poverty: the poignant condition of exile that does not even have a base around which one's creative energies can regroup and rediscover their language; Brutus's ambivalence about the value of poetry or any other kind of creative writing in the present struggle against South African fascism. He has for ten years and more been at the head of a movement that is campaigning against racism in South African and international sport. . . . He feels the inner compulsion to write poetry, but he does not concede that it is important enough to warrant time off to organize his energies, to collect himself, and to hammer out a language that will match his sincerity of passion. And yet that impulse to communicate through the means of verse will not let him be. He feels guilty about not writing and yet will feel equally guilty for spending that much time writing.

Ezekiel Mphahlele. *Voices in the Whirlwind* (New York, Hill and Wang, 1972), pp. 91–92

The core of *Sirens, Knuckles, Boots* had been the love poems: each, while generally complete and satisfying, acquires additional force from its place in a closely linked sequence. A remarkable thoroughness is achieved mainly through a close application of imaginative and technical means; Brutus benefited from his reading of John Donne. Love inspires man's finest, most complete expression. And that expression, bred out of intense needs, assembles a language equal to the demands of feeling inspired by other experiences. Donne used it to chart his love for God: Brutus, his love for country. The language of love, by a semantic shift, is also the language of patriotism. . . .

His love for his wife is the base upon which [Brutus's] double-vision rests. And the double-vision, diffused throughout the poetry, adds a measure of variety and compensates for the relative narrowness of his subject-matter. Brutus must have seen the poetic advantages in such a move. By describing one, he describes the other. It is a double cropping of experience, compressing them to a point where they come to reside in a common vocabulary. . . .

How to restore love and loveliness, how to heal the rift in the feelings are recurring themes in Brutus's poetry. *Sirens, Knuckles, Boots* contains some of the most poignant pieces to come from Africa, contradicting those who allege that the "situation of protest" cannot yield

vital, comprehensive poetry. They would be right if the protest sub-
merges the poetry. Brutus's work, while narrow in range on account of
its antecedents, is skilful and intelligent. The nature of his material lent
itself to treatment in short lyrical poems, for which he developed a
sharp, pungent style. The way he sets about a poem shows relentless
logic. A quick glance at the first lines confirms that almost all those
poems in *Sirens, Knuckles, Boots* start from specific moods and events,
stated simply and concisely. He seems to know the limits, the emotional
and mental area, within which the poem will find itself, and this enables
him to maintain a firm grip as well as to construct his poem. While
Letters to Martha adopts a loose, rambling discursive style, his first
volume is reminiscent of metaphysical poetry, in the introspection, the
combination of thought and feeling, tone, conceits, images and dialectical thrust.

Edwin Thumboo. Joliso. 2, 2, 1974, pp. 36–38

Brutus's earlier verse explored the finest nuances of grammar, image and
association; these poems [*China Poems*] achieve daring leaps of logic.
They are exquisite and brief. Although inspired by haiku and *chüeh-chü*,
they lack even the structural features of those forms which can be
represented in English. Furthermore, their greatest success is in exactly
the opposite effect of those genres: Brutus dictates the reader's response,
both conceptual and affective. . . .

   Thoughts Abroad displays Brutus's characteristic technique
whereby involuted grammar and sound-play combine to accent each
separate image, paradox and subtlety. Almost metrical, the rhythm creates an aura of Olympian remove while underscoring emotional and
intellectual discords. Several poems maintain independent levels of
meaning wherein, for example, a love lyric is addressed simultaneously
to a woman and to his homeland. But the importance of the poems lies
in the lucid, passionate reflections of a political exile in ironically greater
comfort and distress, greater successes in vain, greater alienation in
communing and commuting worldwide as he fights mankind's most vicious tyranny today.

David Dorsey. BA. Spring, 1976, pp. 459, 463

BULLINS, ED (1935–   )

UNITED STATES

Unlike the general run of young playwrights, Bullins does not spend
most of his time showing what a whiz he is at creating monologists who

gab endlessly in back rooms about their cranky existences. He gives his attention to the impact of one character on another, the blood of drama, not its gristle. . . .

Clara's Ole Man . . . is one of the best short American plays I have come across: realistic in manner yet throbbing with weirdness and driven by bursts of extravagant invention that make a definition by genre seem impertinent. Clara, a winsome young woman, invites an innocent fellow named Jack to her apartment. She shares the place with Big Girl, a huge rubbery male woman, and with Big Girl's sister, Baby Girl, a teenaged spastic who repeats any obscenity she hears in a croaking distortion.

The suspense grows out of the intimidation of Jack, who takes a long time to realize that he has landed in a lesbian nest and has unwittingly challenged Big Girl's ownership of Clara. All the characters are Negro, but I suspect the play would (and probably will) function almost as well with a German, Japanese or Turkish cast. . . .

Albert Bermel. NLr. April 22, 1968, p. 28

The white problem in America is at the core of all Bullins's work. He denies being a working-class playwright: he is from the criminal class. All the other men in his family have been in prison. He is the only one who went to high school, who went to college; but he claims that working people in Harlem like his surrealist, intellectual plays.

The Electronic Nigger is not straight propaganda. An evening class in literary expression is being gently conducted by Mr. Jones, a novelist: the session is interrupted by a penologist, Mr. Carpentier, who spouts large generalisations in technical language—not unlike Marshall McLuhan's—and takes over the class, until Jones's head is full of noise and Carpentier is leading pupils in a mechanical goose-step, bawling abstract inanities. (All this is well staged, in-the-round, with life-like acting shifting slowly to an expressionist style, with a climax of disciplined noise and nightmare.) Neither Jones nor Carpentier is white. During the clash, Jones at one point appeals to Carpentier as his "black brother," but the latter denies being black. A white pupil calls him "Uncle Tom" and a black pupil says: "No. It's for me to say that."

D. A. N. Jones. List. Aug. 22, 1968, p. 253

In the Wine Time by Ed Bullins, author of *The Electronic Nigger*, unskins the exhaustion and hopelessness of the ghetto without any references to whites or to white racism—which are unnecessary. A simmering August night: on a worn wooden porch, a family marinates in cheap port, while a strolling cop swats his club against a wire fence, neighborhood voices yell down the block, their words entangling many lives, and people mutter through screen doors. A husband bickers with his pregnant wife. She berates him for being jobless while *she* goes out to work: again and again, she says that he's not a man. . . . It's the recurrent theme of poverty: that women have the authority (which they also resent) because more jobs are open to them, and because whites have crippled the black male. At the same time, more and more black women are rebelling against this role casting—and against the accusations made against them by black men. . . .

Neighbors join the querulous porch life. People swear at each other for swearing, fight without meaning to, remark grimly on the numbing repetitions in their lives. Ed Bullins has distilled the language and the experience of the ghetto so magnificently that we learn more from this one mood play than from scores of sociological studies about growing up in the black slums, where the fatigue that oozes out of the suppression seems even stronger than despair. [Jan., 1969]

Nora Sayre. Sixties Going on Seventies (New York,
Arbor House, 1973), pp. 345–46

The Gentleman Caller is a farce with a theme that recalls [Jean] Genet's *The Maids*. All the characters are symbolic. Madame, with a painted face, large pearl necklaces, and a blonde wig, is the white race. A black intellectual comes to read silently in her living room, and refuses her advances. Mamie, the huge black servant, who looks like a peasant, embodies the primitive wisdom of the masses. She kills the Gentleman, a ridiculously insignificant character dominated by his wife. She kills Madame, and, in the heat of the action, shoots the intellectual, who is doubtless guilty of preferring his books to guerrilla warfare. Mamie then dons a long African gown and answers the telephone with a revolutionary speech that greatly excited the young people in the audience at the Chelsea Theater, when the play was performed there on April 25, 1969: "Teach!" they shouted, laughing. . . .

Punch and Judy show, myth of Orpheus, minstrel show, electronic farce, humor, poetry, drama—Ed Bullins invents and masters different forms of action. His language, whether it is that of muggers or whether it parodies the whites, whether it speaks of electronics or of secret passions, is always theatrical. He is probably one of the best playwrights, white or black, of the new American theater.

Franck Jotterand. Le nouveau théâtre américain
(Paris, Éditions du Seuil, 1970), pp. 206–7†

By saying that the oppressed are destroyed and debased by their experience, writers like Jones, Bullins, Franz Fanon, James Baldwin and [Eldridge] Cleaver expose themselves as apologists for imperialism. . . .

Ed Bullins' drama is one of despair and self-destruction. For him the enemy is other black men who are rapacious and irrational. His is a world of pimps and whores, criminals and junkies. In his *Goin' a Buffalo*, Bullins has a grim picture of these family and criminal relationships. Art who had supposedly saved Curt's life in a prison riot in *Goin' a Buffalo* insinuates himself into Curt's home and family and betrays him to the police in order to get his wife and money. In *Clara's Ole Man* nothing is possible for the people but parasitism; they live off each other's misfortune. Black people inflict violence, infidelity and betrayal on each other. In this psychological and social view of the blacks there is only self-destruction and soulfulness with which blacks can console themselves. . . .

The political line in dramatists like Jones, Bullins, Baldwin, [Douglas Turner] Ward and many others is the line of class collaboration and not struggle. This endears them to the monopoly capitalist class and wins them publicity and other forms of recognition from the class they serve. These dramatists are trying to mobilize political support for the decadent imperialists by saying that possibilities for change do not exist. The progressive dramatists create public opinion in favour of revolutionary change and present the black struggles as part of the worldwide united front against U.S. imperialism.

Mary Ellen Brooks. *LitI*. No. 10, 1971, pp. 43–46

The Duplex is part of a cycle of twenty plays. I can only hope that future installments, or such past ones as I have missed, achieve more. For this is mere commercial theater, rather slow and faltering in the first two acts, quite slick in the second two, and brought to a sudden end without much of a resolution. It is, to be sure, *black* commercial theater, which in these confused times easily passes for art in both black and white circles. To me, it looks like second-rate William Inge, with the significant difference that Inge would not have required two acts for the kind of exposition that two scenes could have taken care of. . . .

There is nothing embarrassingly bad or unendurable about the play —with the possible exception of some of the old woman's maunderings; but neither its insight nor its language, neither its dramaturgy nor its perspective, is in any sustained way compelling. Its laughter is routine, and its poignancies, with one or two exceptions, are perfunctory. Yet there is a smooth functionalism about its better parts. . . . The chief virtue of Bullins' work is that black audiences can doubtless identify themselves with it wholeheartedly—as the black part of the opening-night audience noisily did—but here hides a danger. Recognition of yourself up there on the boards is not the end-all of art, at best the beginning. It is understandably satisfying for the audience of an emergent theater to see itself raised to the heights of the stage, with the social and cultural importance this implies. But for the work to become art, it must take the audience beyond mere self-recognition, identification with mirror images. It must do, say, envision things that in some profound sense have never been done, said, envisioned before, and this *The Duplex*, in terms other than its Negritude, fails to do. It is all basic minimums. [March 27, 1972]

John Simon. Uneasy Stages (New York, Random
House, 1975), pp. 376–78

Beyond the political activism and the racial consciousness of his plays (which are, of course, what Bullins most values in them), there is another side. *In the Wine Time, In New England Winter, Goin' a Buffalo,* and other Bullins plays create a mood of lost innocence, purity and beauty that is universally meaningful. In fact, the dramatist creates in most of his work a counter-mood to that which dominates the actual dialogue—there is a sense of once-glimpsed loyalty, sensitivity, and romance which the ghetto reality of the setting makes impossible to attain. This obbligato of tenderness is so overpowered by the brutality of the ghetto that it exists in the plays as something once envisioned, but almost forgotten, by one or two main characters. . . .

That the reality of Black life in America perverts and destroys human dreams—whether of pure romance or of economic independence—and makes personal loyalty all but obsolete is Bullins' message. His technique is, through brutal dialogue and incident, to emphasize the grim reality of the ghetto; the better life his characters desire can be glimpsed in his plays as an increasingly remote ideal and finally only in the thwarted generosity of a few characters.

James R. Giles. Players. Oct.–Nov., 1972, pp. 32–33

Bullins' plays can generally be divided into two categories: satire and serious. But the line that divides them is sometimes very thin. Plays such as *The Electronic Nigger* and *The Pig Pen* are obviously satire. *The Electronic Nigger* is a scathing condemnation of the would-be black intellectual, and *The Pig Pen* is a laughing look at the world of so-called "revolutionary" integration (about eight black men and one white woman). This kind of satire is very explicit and the playwright's position is very clear on these subjects.

The serious plays, however, like *The Duplex, Clara's Ole Man,* and . . . *The Fabulous Miss Marie* . . . do not lend themselves to easy interpretations. *The Duplex* ends, for example, with the older woman, the landlady, going back downstairs in resignation to get her head-whipping from her man because of what she's done. And nobody moves to help her because supposedly anything her man does is within his right. But, we ask, will that help ease her loneliness? Will that prevent her from seeking out some other young man when things come down on her too hard again? Bullins doesn't say.

Clara is a young black girl living in a stifling tenement and her ole man turns out to be an older woman, the only one who seems to have cared enough, for whatever reason, to take her in and care for her. Is it wrong? Should Clara have tried to do something else? Bullins leaves it up to us to decide.

Perhaps it's only in *The Fabulous Miss Marie* that we see an exact blending of Bullins the satirist and Bullins the serious, for in "Miss Marie" we have a very skillfully drawn portrait of the Los Angeles bourgeoisie, with all its flaking superficialities and differing forms of greed. Near the end of the play a member of Miss Marie's clique remarks that none of them, the aging playboy teacher, his pill-popping wife, parasitic Miss Marie and her young boyfriends, or her castrated, overworked husband, have any children. They will not be perpetuated. Bullins is not elusive here. He shows a group of people that the audience clearly feels shouldn't be perpetuated. Here the lines are sharply drawn.

Lisbeth Gant. *TDR*. Dec., 1972, p. 52

[*The Reluctant Rapist*] has the tone and the content of the 19th-century *Bildungsroman*, in which the youthful protagonist—in this case Steve Benson—is educated from innocence to experience. In the classic tradition, Steve is a loner, an outsider, and finally an outlaw. He rapes, dimly off in the background to the main action, but is "reluctant" to rape a woman he cannot love. Indeed, the reader is asked to believe that a mystical union is effected by that violation of another person's will, and that some of the women are bound to him for life. . . .

The Reluctant Rapist is a handbook to [Bullins's] plays. As a playwright, Bullins rips, tears, rapes; he blows apart black life. As a novelist, he explains what the ripping, tearing and raping are all about. They are the acts of a lover in deep need of blasting away the conventional laws and customs, the traditional faiths and beliefs to expose the truthful, irreducible center so that he and his beloved may at last be free. Steve Benson the rapist is a metaphor of Ed Bullins the playwright. And Steve's story is a reassembling of the bits from the exploded bombs and tearing beak. It is done through a reconstitution of time and a renewal of sex. Time unrolls and unwinds in this novel, opens out and folds back on itself, stops and starts. Pieces of Steve's life loom up before us as if cut loose from chronology. But the conventional order of events is one of those beliefs that has to be destroyed. And Bullins is successful in destroying it, in fusing the past with the present, in giving us the feeling of living the past again from the standpoint of the present and seeing the future infuse the past.

Jerry H. Bryant. *Nation*. Nov. 12, 1973, p. 504

For the critic, the value of this collection [of stories, *The Hungered One*] lies in its revelations about the early intellectual career of Bullins. For those familiar only with his later writings, and more particularly, the plays, this volume will remind them of the uncommon diversity of his early work. Yet, within this diversity and within this mixture of experimentation, the germ of the work that is later transformed into Bullins' realistic plays and stories can be discovered. Here, in this collection, we can find the early lineaments of some of his later characters waiting to be fleshed out. A few of the macabre themes that Bullins exploits later can be detected here, gradually merging. Testing narrative vehicles, for their limitations and merits, is present too. On the other hand, it is possible, through comparing Bullins' later work with this earlier material, to trace the shifts in his work—away from the symbolist mode and the metaphorical narrative. For all these reasons, it is valuable to have these stories.

However, these works raise a disquieting intellectual issue, one that relates to Bullins' later writing as well. Perhaps, only a very few Afro-American writers at work presently can equal the trained eye of Bullins. Seeing plainly and correctly is his great skill. Deploying these observations in economical, exceedingly lucid writing makes his work extremely accessible. Years from now, when his reputation is not so artificially inflated, his reports on Afro-American life will still constitute a major historical record of black society. It will be the fictional equivalent of an Afro-American *cinéma verité*. This is no ordinary achievement. And yet, it must be said that Bullins' eye is an extremely neutral one: he appears excessively timid about moving beyond mere observation, to insert himself in the record; he seems wary of structuring his perceptions into a definite intellectual format. Always, there is a hint that Bullins is verging on a political or ideological or strangely personal statement, but just as often, this energy is dissipated in verbal pyrotechnics, easy lampooning, or is reduced to a bare record of events and personalities. He proceeds along the smoothest course.

Kennell Jackson, Jr. *CLAJ*. Dec., 1974, pp. 297–98

In his dramas about Black life, Bullins generally suggests a vision by picturing the absence of vision. Love is a ruse for stealing a wife from a benefactor; it is adultery and lesbianism; it is abuse and betrayal. Manhood is the practice of Walter Younger's false dream [in *A Raisin in the Sun*]—to exploit others before they exploit you. And there is no good life. Bullins' vision is at best a dream which will never materialize, a nostalgia for what might have been. I have said that Black Arts drama assumes the responsibility of educating Black People to awareness of their needs for liberation. Bullins' dramas are educational primarily in the sense that they depict the sordid realities which must be transformed if Black life is to improve. . . .

Bullins' characters live in an all-Black world in which survival requires one to assume everyone else to be his enemy. Education is judged desirable, but crime provides more money. Whites who flutter through this world are not villains but alcoholics, dope addicts, prostitutes—as easily deceived as are the Blacks. Like Baldwin [in *The Amen Corner*], Bullins offers no problem to be solved by a White audience. If there is any significant difference between Baldwin and Bullins, it is that, whereas Baldwin rationalizes the behavior of a wandering musician who drinks liquor excessively, Bullins spares no feelings in portraying his protagonists as alcoholics, murderers, hypocrites, exploiters, bullies, and criminals who betray one another and even themselves. Pathetically, they succeed neither in self-improvement nor even in the crimes they attempt. The very multiplicity of examples of lack or loss of vision, I believe, suggests the need for vision and, thus, implies Bullins' educational thesis—that such a world is salvageable only if it is supplied with visions of love, manhood, and a good life.

Darwin T. Turner. IowaR. Spring, 1975, pp. 93–95

[*The Taking of Miss Janie*] devotes itself principally to black-white relations in the 1960's ("This tale is about the spirit of those times"), symbolized—or at least given some sort of framing device—by the ultimate rape of a naïve white girl by the black poet she wants simply as a "friend."

The rape opens the evening, with the toweled girl sobbing over the destruction of her dream, the cool and confident stripped male pointing out that it always had to come to this. The '60s, we gradually learn if we pay extremely close attention, were years of self-delusion: while blacks and whites, in the time of Kennedy and King, thought, through a marijuana haze, that they were "getting it all together," they were doing no such thing. Blacks, in the words of a cliché-spouting revolutionary who marches marionette-style to a drum in his head, were "still in love with their slave masters," were stupidly fighting a war "while loving the enemy." Whites were simply kidding themselves—pretending to understand black poetry, inventing Platonic social harmonies that didn't, couldn't, exist.

If I say that it takes extremely close attention to pick up this thread of meaning—provided I have myself got it straight—it's because author

Bullins is so prodigal, not to say wandering, in his recall. . . . Most of the evening is flashback, the lion's share of it taken up by a black-white party in which sex and hostility give off approximately equal "vibes." Mr. Bullins, as a writer, has a thing about parties. Play after play has made use of them—not so much dramatic as nearly stenographic use, as though the faithful recording of all that might be said and done in a casual, then hyped-up, personal and/or ethnic mix would surely end in some kind of intelligible patterning. A cat's-cradle formed of all those comings and goings must, in the end, convey *something*, mustn't it? . . .

Almost all of the best things [in the play] pull us away from Janie and her problem. The play's frame doesn't really contain or explain the things that shimmer inside it, and, quite apart from our losing the two principals for long stretches of time, we are left wondering why Janie's "taking" should be made to serve as summary of a decade's mishaps and misapprehensions. Is physical conquest the only answer to the thousand questions raised; was "rape" the resolution the '60's *ought* to have been seeking? Or is Janie no more than a nitwit, making impossibly childish demands in a situation too grave for children? The play's *structure* doesn't say, and we are forced to weave spider-webs of meaning for ourselves out of random snatches of biography, period echoes, interpolated monologues close to harangues.

Walter Kerr. *NYTts*. May 11, 1975, p. 5

CAMARA, LAYE (1928-   )

GUINEA

I am afraid that those who would open [*The Black Child*] with the thought of satisfying a hunger for the picturesque or escaping for a moment from the enervating condition of "civilized" man will be left unappeased. Unless they absolutely insist upon it, prejudice being stubborn, they will not find the classic "darkest Africa" nor the "prelogical mentality" so dear to the heart of the armchair traveler.

Of course, the book deals with animistic beliefs and practices, spirits intervene in the day-to-day life and a whole chapter is devoted to the rites of circumcision, but obviously the basis of the story is not to be found here. It is primarily universal man, man unqualified, with whom we are concerned. As a matter of fact, Camara was born at Kouroussa in French Guinea, a country with an old civilization. He is descended from the black Sudanese who in the Middle Ages founded the fabulously rich Mali Empire which was ruled for six centuries by the Moslem dynasty of the Keytas. . . .

Yet Camara does not speak to us of his people's past. He makes neither direct reference nor the slightest allusion to it, and he is content to evoke for us with emotional restraint the simple life of a dark child of the great plain of Guinea—a story told at first hand, since it is his own; but an awareness of this past helps us better to understand the psychology of the author and his characters. For me, this past—veiled as in a watermark—is always associated with the story.

Philippe Thoby-Marcelin. Introduction to Camara
Laye, *The Dark Child* (New York, Farrar, Straus,
1954), pp. 8, 11

All the poetry of [*The Black Child*] has flown away like feathers in the wind [from *The Gaze of the King*]. Therefore, the inadequacies of Camara as a novelist now stand out sharply: haphazard construction, uninteresting dialogue, none of the density fiction can have, no notion of how to present a climactic scene. Camara has not assimilated the technique of the novel! I could go on listing other defects.

After the black child, thoughtful and sensitive, we are presented a young king, slender and completely loaded down with gold. I am sure that Camara creates his characters in his own image. Perhaps he resembles this young king more than he thinks, this king who submits to the role he must play, who is elusive, and who has a rather limited capacity for judgment, since he seems hardly interested in worldly affairs. Like this king, under the cheap finery of elegant style, held by heavy conventional clasps, Camara allows us to perceive his skinny body. Like this king, he walks around like a somnambulist in a world which is "such stuff as dreams are made on" and which is carefully maintained by a "judicious unconsciousness." Lastly, like his king he is an illusionist: he plays with mirages of hollow symbols and pretended richness. . . .

Sartre said somewhere that new ideas, since they are disconcerting and even shocking, necessarily displease. If Camara pleases people so easily, it is because he is reassuring; consequently, he offers us nothing really new. . . .

A. B. [Mongo Beti]. *PA*. April–July, 1955, pp. 143–44†

What first strikes the reader about *The Gaze of the King* is the ease and purity of the style. I am not speaking of grammar or punctuation; editors in publishing houses are paid for those things. I am speaking of the innate sense of the language, which is a gift; of the loving choice of the appropriate word, especially the manner of seizing words, of charging them with meaning and retaining their simplicity at the same time.

But Camara is more than a stylist; he is a novelist. In *The Gaze of the King*, the writer's imagination lies essentially in his ability to create characters and bring them to life. I am well aware that the subject of the novel was supplied by a dream. It could have been supplied by a news item. That Camara may have, as a starting point, borrowed some of Kafka's techniques does not bother me. Camara's symbolism is of the black-African variety. What makes it particularly black is that it opens the door to hope and that it is mystical. . . .

The African intelligentsia should not rush to condemn Camara once again, using the claim that his novel is not "anti-colonialist." There are several ways of fighting colonialism. The writer could not follow the same route of commitment as the politician. French critics were right in being shocked (although they tried to hide it) at seeing Clarence, a fallen white man, try to find redemption through the Black King, who symbolizes the radiance of purity. [April 22, 1955]

Léopold Sédar Senghor. *Liberté I: Négritude et humanisme* (Paris, Éditions du Seuil, 1964), pp. 173–74†

Camara, though being a school child, shared most of the experiences of the common village children, participating in their work and play and undergoing the traditional initiation rites. But as he grew older he was sent to a secondary school in Conakry and later he came to France to study engineering. When his money ran out he had to find work in a car factory. Lonely and depressed he sat down and wrote [*The Black Child*], this nostalgic book about his childhood. With great sensitivity the author describes his earliest memories and with infinite affection he builds up before our eyes the picture of his parents. . . .

Comparison springs to mind between Camara's *The Black Child* and the famous autobiography of an American Negro: Richard Wright's *Black Boy*. What a contrast between this gentle, nostalgic book and Richard Wright's bitter account of his stubborn childhood.

Camara's youth was happy, he was surrounded with love and affection and grew up in comparative security. Richard Wright's youth was all poverty and hunger and hatred. Camara describes his childhood with a touch of romanticism and he leaves the world of his parents with sadness and regret. Richard Wright describes his own youth with brutal realism and his whole effort is to cast off his past. Camara emerges from these experiences a deeply religious person. . . . Richard Wright emerges as a strict rationalist. . . . The immense difference in background and upbringing between these two writers symbolises the gulf that has arisen between the African and the American Negro and it may help us to understand the failure of Richard Wright to understand the people and the problems of Ghana about which he writes in his book *Black Power*.

Akanji. BO. Sept., 1957, pp. 47–48

Encountering Camara's *The Gaze of the King*, will the [European] critic not say, Why has this man not stuck to the simple, straightforward narrative of his *The Black Child*? For presumably the Western critic knows his Kafka. The cultivated naïveté of *The Black Child* charmed even the African reader. Even if it often grew precious, it carried an air of magic, of nostalgia, which worked through the transforming act of language. If the author was selective to the point of wish fulfillment, it was unimportant. That a reader could be so gracefully seduced into a village idyll is a tribute to the author.

But most intelligent readers like their Kafka straight, not geographically transposed. Even the character structure of Kafka's *The Castle* has been most blatantly retained—Clarence for Mr. K.; Kafka's Barnabas the Messenger becomes the Beggar Intermediary; Arthur and Jeremiah, the unpredictable assistants, are turned into Nagoa and Noaga. We are not even spared the role of the landlord—or innkeeper—take your choice! It is truly amazing that foreign critics have contented themselves with merely dropping an occasional "Kafkaesque"— a feeble sop to integrity—since they cannot altogether ignore the more obvious imitativeness of Camara's technique. (I think we can tell when the line of mere "influence" has been crossed.) Even within the primeval pit of collective allegory-consciousness, it is self-delusive to imagine that the Progresses of these black and white pilgrims have sprung from independent creative stresses.

Wole Soyinka. ASch. Summer, 1963, pp. 387–88

The beauty of [*The Black Child*] is to be found in Camara's form and style, his deep understanding of people and, especially, of the mind of a growing child. He re-creates his childhood because he needs to understand why he has become the man he is, why so much that was precious had been irrevocably lost. His nostalgia, therefore, gives the novel meaning and continuity.

The Black Child is divided into twelve chapters. Each one of them is devoted to one particular event. Together, these represent the most important aspects of his childhood. Some events are unique, such as his circumcision, the conversation with his father about the little black snake, his first journey to Conakry. After this first separation from his family and Kouroussa such events predominate. Before it, however, they are deliberately balanced by descriptions of episodes which were repeated time and again during his early childhood; his father fashioning the gold ornament, holidays with his grandmother at Tindican, school-days. . . .

[Camara] uses words to summon the meaning which lies behind his thoughts and emotions as a child, to evoke nostalgia. The descriptions are simple and unpretentious. At the same time they are complex, through the memories invoked by the re-creation of ordinary, day to day actions or the special events which changed his childhood. The deep meaning behind these simple descriptions is brought out by his use of repetition. A word is repeated, savoured almost, until its every implication, joyful and sad, has been extracted. . . .

A. C. Brench. The Novelists' Inheritance in French
Africa (London, Oxford University Press, 1967),
pp. 38–41

Dramouss leads us directly into the politics of Guinea, as seen and experienced by Fatoman, a native Guinean who has returned from Paris, where he completed his technical studies and worked at the Simca factory and even in Les Halles. . . .

Dramouss is primarily a political novel, directed at Sékou Touré, at a regime that had "immolated democracy after the advent of the

'Defferre Law' and had begun to muzzle the naïve people of Guinea."
To struggle against this state of affairs, one must first know what one
wants for oneself before acting on behalf of the country. Fatoman, more
a sentimentalist than a Muslim, says: "What I do for my neighbor, I am
also doing for myself and for God." But "Dramouss," the female-
symbol of Guinea, seen in a profoundly poetic dream, replies with
common sense: "Rather than serving others, you should tend to serving
yourself."

Fatoman flees his country after escaping from a Kafkaesque prison
into which men are thrown without knowing why, then are judged and
executed as in Kafka's *The Trial*. When he returns to his country, none
of his friends are still alive: they have all been executed because they
were against the regime.

Camara has painted a picture of Guinea under its present regime,
where he himself has lived. The description of dreams and real events
helps convey the authenticity of a situation that does not do credit to
Africa. "The Black Child" has grown up: he has learned to become
aware of his milieu, and he speaks about it simply, even when rebellion
seems to be crying out within him. He is a true writer.

Olympe Bhêly-Quénum. L'Afrique actuelle.
Nov., 1966, pp. 49–50†

Dramouss is a sequel to *The Black Child*. The earlier book ends with the
author's departure for Europe. Six years later Camara returns to
Conakry and to his hometown of Kouroussa. He finds Guinea in the full
effervescence of national liberation. There are, naturally, problems
created by colonization and those concerning human relations as well as
social and religious development. . . .

Dramouss is a woman, a divinity who reveals Guinea's future to
the hero in a dream. First the present, with its cruel abominations; then
the future, illuminated by the leadership of the "black lion." . . .

[Camara] chooses to see human problems—both political and
social—through [his parents'] religious concept of the world. The
"Black Lion," the symbol in the novel of the liberator Guinea is waiting
for, is a religious animal: he is powerful yet pious, strong yet gentle. He
is the ideal counterpart of the goddess Dramouss, the female savior.
Camara dares to endure the life of his country because he is a believer.

But while it heartens him to place his hopes in the revelations of
Dramouss, his contemplation of a brilliant world-to-come seems to make
few demands on him. He does not show us the actual steps leading to
the realization of that world in harsh everyday terms. His goal is that the
"incommunicable be communicated, and that African thought, thus

reintegrated and totally restored, be a nonaggressive but productive force." But to achieve this goal, to make our life of tomorrow more humane, is it necessary or is it enough for us to have a lovely poetic-religious flight of oratory?

Christophe Gudijiga. Congo-Afrique. May, 1967,
pp. 257–59†

An important notion suggested throughout [*The Gaze of the King*] is that the cultural superiority of the European depends upon the European's being in a control situation in which others must adapt to his culture; but that when the situation is reversed, the individual European is as much at a loss as the African when forced to adjust himself to European culture. Consequently, notions of cultural superiority and inferiority are invalid and at best superiority is relative to one's situation.

[A. C.] Brench has argued that Camara "alone has described the positive effect Africa can have on a white man in terms of assimilation, generally considered a problem to be faced exclusively by Africans in their contact with Europe." But this . . . misses the point. The problem does not concern *assimilation*, for Clarence—like Africans caught in European culture—doesn't *become* something else, but by ridding himself of evils makes himself worthy of *charitable acceptance* by the African king. The whole affair, by turning the tables, is a protest against such concepts as that of assimilation, in which one must give up one's own culture and blindly accept an alien culture. Camara is suggesting, rather, that although giving up error may be good, giving up one's culture for the sake of another is not.

Nor is it true, as [Gerald] Moore has said, that "quite as much as a search for God, Clarence's pilgrimage seems to be a search for identification." Clarence knows who he is, so there is no real problem of identification, but of his relationship with others, of his *relative worth*. As the African cannot be assimilated into European society, so the European cannot be assimilated into African society, although either can be accepted by performing certain approved actions. . . . To be assimilated by the alien society, Clarence must lose his original culture. This is the problem facing the African who succumbs to the hope of assimilation into French society: he will never become European at all. But Clarence is not destroyed: he is cleansed of evil; it is demonstrated that his worth is only relative to the culture in which he finds himself, so his notions of racial and cultural superiority were wrong and led to evil.

Austin J. Shelton. ECr. Fall, 1970, pp. 216–17

In everything he has written—a more or less pure autobiography (*The Black Child*), a more or less pure novel (*The Gaze of the King*), and a book that is half-and-half (*Dramouss*)—different as the books may be formally, Camara develops a single theme that he works out in two opposed, complementary, and joined movements, movements that are the mirror opposites and the reversed images of one another. Separation and return, disunion and reunion—they are like the two sides of a single coin, or like an event and an image of that event reflected in the artist's eye. When Camara's father, in *The Black Child*, murmurs distractedly of "those far-off lands," he is thinking of the imminent separation that will take his son away to France, to Europe, to the non-African world; spiritually as well as physically the boy is about to depart, as his father recognizes, for a country that is distant in all ways from the country of his own being.

But when the young man sits down (as Camara has described himself doing) in a cold and cheerless hotel room in Paris to try to recapture his past experiences, a complete transformation has been effected: it is now Kouroussa, the African world of his father and mother and the town of his own childhood, that is "a far-off land." Through ambition he was separated, in nostalgia he returns. In *The Black Child* the two-fold theme revolves about the unified community on the one hand and the separated individual on the other; paradoxically it is the separated individual who recreates, in an act of memory and artistry, that world that in fact no longer exists—if it ever did exist in fact. . . .

This disunion and reunion, this separation and return, and the mystery wherein they are made one and the same, has been the theme of all of Camara's writing. In *The Black Child* the return is achieved through the artist's imagination; in *Dramouss* the return is literal (and disappointing); and in *The Gaze of the King* the return is symbolic and vicarious, the white man Clarence discovering in Africa the world of simplicity that Camara had lost through experience and had refound through art.

> James Olney. *Tell Me Africa* (Princeton, N.J., Princeton University Press, 1973), pp. 126–27

CÉSAIRE, AIMÉ (1913–   )

MARTINIQUE

[In 1942] Aimé Césaire gave me a copy of his *Notebook on a Return to My Native Land*, which had been published in a limited edition by a

Paris magazine in 1939. The poem, which must have gone unnoticed then, is nothing less than the greatest lyrical monument of our time. It brought me the richest certainty, the kind that one can never arrive at on one's own. Its author had gambled on everything I had ever believed was right, and he had incontestably won. What was at stake, with all due credit to Césaire's own genius, was our common conception of life.

Now that a bilingual edition in the United States has given this work wider circulation, people will see in it first its exceptionally rich movement, its exuberant flow, and a faculty of ceaselessly scanning the emotional world from top to bottom, to the point of turning it upside down. All these characteristics distinguish authentic poetry from the false, simulated poetry, of a venomous sort, that constantly proliferates around authentic poetry. "To sing or not to sing": that is the question, and there could be no salvation in poetry for anyone who does not "sing," although the poet must be asked to do *more* than sing. And I do not need to say that for those who do not sing, any recourse to rhyme, fixed meter, and other shoddy baggage could never deceive anyone's ears but those of Midas. Césaire is, before anything else, one who sings. . . .

Césaire's poetry, like all great poetry and all great art, has as its highest merit its power to transform what it uses; he begins with the most unlovely material, among which we have to include ugliness and servitude, and ends up producing the philosopher's stone, which we well know is no longer gold but freedom.

It would be useless to try to reduce Césaire's gift of song, his ability to reject what he does not need, and his power of magical transmutation . . . to a specific number of technical secrets. All one can validly say about these qualities is that all three contain a greater common denominator, which is an exceptional intensity of emotion in the face of the spectacle of life (leading to an impulse to act on life so as to change it) and, as such, this intensity will retain its full force until some new order comes into being.

André Breton. *Hémisphères*. Fall–Winter, 1943–44,
pp. 8–9†

A poem of Césaire . . . bursts and turns on itself as a fuse, as bursting suns which turn and explode in new suns, in a perpetual surpassing. It is not a question of meeting in a calm unity of opposites but rather a forced coupling, into a single sex, of black in its opposition to white. This dense mass of words, hurled into the air like rocks by a volcano is the Negritude which arrays itself against Europe and colonization. That which Césaire destroys is not all culture, it is the white culture; that which he conjures forth is not the desire of all, it is the revolutionary aspirations of the oppressed Negro; that which he touches in the depths of his being is not the soul, it is a certain form of humanity concrete and well determined. One can speak here of an automatic writing which is at the same time engaged and even directed; not that there is the intervention of reflection, but because the words and the images continually express the same torrid obsession. At the bottom of his soul, the white surrealist finds release; at the bottom of his soul, Césaire finds the fixed inflexibility of vindication and of resentment. . . .

In Césaire the great surrealist tradition is achieved, takes its definite sense, and destroys itself. Surrealism, European poetic movement, is stolen from the Europeans by a black who turns it against them and assigns it a rigorously prescribed function. . . . In Europe, surrealism, rejected by those who could have transfused it into their blood, languishes and expires. But at the moment it loses contact with the Revolution, here in the West Indies, it is grafted to another branch of the universal Revolution; here it unfolds itself into an enormous and sombre flower. The originality of Césaire is to have cast his direct and powerful concern for the Negro, for the oppressed and for the militant into the world of the most destructive, the freest and the most metaphysical poetry at a time when [Paul] Éluard and [Louis] Aragon were failing to give political content to their verse. And finally, that which tears itself from Césaire as a cry of grief, of love and of hate, is the *Negritude-object*. Here further, he follows the surrealist tradition which desires that the poem *objectivize*. The words of Césaire do not describe Negritude, they do not designate it, they do not copy it from outside as a painter does of a model; they *make* it; they compose it under our eyes. [1948]

Jean-Paul Sartre. Black Orpheus (Paris,
Présence Africaine, 1963), pp. 36–39

This passage by Césaire ["those who have invented neither gunpowder nor the compass," in *Notebook on a Return to My Native Land*] is of crucial importance: it contrasts the spirit of Negro-African Civilization with that of the European world, the *farmer* with the *engineer*, to use Sartre's terms. We know that man's attitude toward nature is the essential problem, whose solution conditions man's destiny. "Man's attitude toward nature" contains both the essential *subject* and the essential *object*. The European, *homo faber*, has to get to know nature so as to make it the instrument of his will for power: to *use* it. The European will give nature a fixed place through analysis, will make it a *dead* thing in order to dissect it. But how can one create life from a dead thing?

The Negro, on the contrary, subjective, "impervious to all the winds of the world," discovers the object in its reality, in its *rhythm*.

And he yields to it, following its living movement, going from the subject to the object, "playing the game of the world." What does this mean except that, for the Negro, to know is to live—the life of the Other—by identifying with the object? To know [con-naître] means to be born to the Other by dying to the self: it is making love with the Other, it is dancing the Other. "I feel, therefore I exist." Césaire writes: "By thinking of the Congo/I became a Congo rustling with/forests and rivers." [1952]

Léopold Sédar Senghor. *Liberté I: Négritude et humanisme* (Paris, Éditions du Seuil, 1964), p. 141†

The voice of Aimé Césaire, the black poet, which reached us right after the Liberation, was like a fresh breath; we heard tones that had never been sounded in French poetry. His first work, *Notebook on a Return to My Native Land*, a book woven of a single poem, seemed to obey no rule other than haste, as if it were appropriate to say everything at once, not omitting anything, as if it were necessary, here and now, to echo the most extreme urgency. This poem rose to the heights of French poetry like a meteor. What! A black voice finally refused to conform to our rhythms, to the rituals of our style, to the form we had imposed on the world—a form based on our landscape, our bearing, and our customs.

It seemed to me that this poem had been too quickly labeled as orthodoxy, surrealist orthodoxy, a literary preciosity of the same order as [André Breton's] *The White-Haired Revolver*. Césaire's poetry was quite a different matter: his revolt had a real basis; it was not related to any sort of ill humor or directed against a denigrated tradition. His revolt had its own sources . . . and its own mission [political freedom]. . . . It was marked by more haste, more determination, and more seriousness than the exercises of surrealism. Although we could become comfortable with surrealism—and we all got used to the *manifestos* of that school—we could not become comfortable with these cries, this long cry that was beginning to form its principles, to establish itself, and finally to bring in its wake things that were clearly going to threaten us. . . .

Hubert Juin. *Aimé Césaire, poète noir* (Paris, Présence Africaine, 1956), pp. 19–20†

In Paris, at the Lycée Louis-le-Grand, Césaire met Léopold Sédar Senghor. This meeting led to a great friendship almost at once and to Césaire's discovery of Africa, the land of his heart, which he adopted immediately: "When I got to know Senghor [wrote Césaire], I called myself an African." . . .

In 1932 a little magazine called *Légitime défense* appeared; in it, communist and surrealist Caribbean students a few years older than Césaire violently denounced the corrupt society of Martinique, the misery of its people, and the ridiculous literary parrotry of its native writers. These were just the words that Césaire needed! For Césaire, Senghor, and Damas, that magazine was a true catalyst. The elders had their problems; they had to keep silent. That was not very important; a breach had been opened, and the three friends would make the roaring river of Negritude rush into that breach. . . .

Césaire, Senghor, and Damas began by founding a little newspaper, *L'étudiant noir*, which brought together the black students in Paris on the basis of color rather than country of origin. This new grouping meant a recognition of two obvious and essential facts: that a black man is not a white man, and that all blacks have certain problems in common. This was a healthy reaction against the attitude of those Caribbean students who had rejected their origins, had tried to act like whites and like Frenchmen, even more so in Paris than at home, and had tried to forget their color! This first stage of Negritude, this recognition of oneself, was followed, for Césaire and his companions, by an assumption of responsibility for their destiny as Negroes, for their history, and for their own culture. . . .

Instead of the classical French writers, *L'étudiant noir* set forth as models the spontaneity of black American writers, like Claude McKay and Langston Hughes, as well as the style of African sculpture, and the naturalness and humor of local tales, all of which were examples of a freedom of expression accordant with the original Negro temperament. . . .

For the first time, blacks spoke out to tell their fellow blacks "that instead of doing everything like a white man," they should, on the contrary, stay completely black, that their truth lay in their blackness and that it was beautiful. . . . Negritude was an enterprise undertaken to end the alienation of a whole race, and this movement laid the foundation on which the ideology of the decolonization of Africa would be built.

Lilyan Kesteloot. Aimé Césaire (Paris,
Pierre Seghers, 1962), pp. 20–23†

The Tragedy of King Christophe was published in 1963, two years after the death of Patrice Lumumba. Therefore, Césaire was aware of the circumstances of Lumumba's death when he wrote that play. But it was not until 1966, five years after Lumumba's murder, that Césaire finally decided, it seems, to deal directly with the African leader who was murdered in such a cowardly way.

Once again Césaire created a play about an African chief offered by destiny as a sacrifice to the Negro cause. *A Season in the Congo*, however, shows a development in Césaire's thesis about the Black Leader. In Christophe the portrait of the Leader was generally but not entirely clear. In Lumumba, who is closer to us, the portrait of the Black hero is made more precise. Césaire is able to repeat himself while renewing himself at the same time. *A Season in the Congo* presents the same theme as *And the Dogs Were Silent* and *The Tragedy of King Christophe*, yet the play is not the same. Even if the theme is the same, its presentation has evolved toward realism and precision. *A Season in the Congo* is also closer to historical truth than *The Tragedy of King Christophe* or *And the Dogs Were Silent*, whose stories are essentially invented.

The scenes of *A Season in the Congo* are short, quick, and, so to speak, choppy. The play is a kaleidoscope in which all of Patrice Lumumba's political life passes by. . . . Except for Lumumba and a very few others, the characters in *A Season in the Congo* are fragmented. This is as it should be, for, whether he is present or not, all the scenes center and converge on Lumumba.

Hénock Trouillot. L'itinéraire d'Aimé Césaire
(Port-au-Prince, Imprimerie des Antilles, 1968),
pp. 156, 158†

In 1942 André Breton, the leader of the French surrealist movement, in flight from the Nazis came to Martinique and there met Aimé Césaire. These two poets developed a strong friendship. It was an important event in Césaire's life. André Breton brought Césaire to the notice of important literary circles in France. By 1944 Aimé Césaire was back in Paris and received with great fanfare. In 1956, *Présence africaine*, a literary magazine founded in 1947 by Alioune Diop, reissued the *Notebook on a Return to My Native Land*. *Présence africaine* served as a forum for some of the most outstanding African and West Indian writers and intellectuals like Alioune Diop, Léopold Senghor, Césaire, Damas and many others who later played an important role in the African Independence movement.

In 1946 Césaire fought and won the election as Deputy to the French National Assembly for Martinique. He also became Mayor of Fort-de-France, a position he has occupied to this day. Martinique is a constituency of the French National Assembly and is represented by three deputies. Most of the deputies have always advocated association with France as the cornerstone of their politics. Césaire's election meant that for the first time a man who identified with the economic and political realities of Martinique was to become a voice in the French National Assembly. For Césaire, the scope for expressing his intense hostility against French domination and assimilation was widened. He was now not only the ideologist of the oppressed but their representative. Indeed he could rightly claim that he understood their needs and their demands because he was one of them. In spite of his educational achievements, he had refused to be assimilated. His position as Deputy demonstrated the extent to which Césaire had embraced his beliefs in active participation. He had realized that only by the exercise of power could what he considered better political and cultural values be implemented. He saw the position he occupied as Deputy as a power base from which he could effect the desired change.

Mazisi Kunene. Introduction to Aimé Césaire, *Return to My Native Land* (Baltimore, Penguin, 1969), pp. 25–26

The memory of having been torn from the maternal breast, from a culture and spirituality of the soil that were deeply rooted in the Negro soul, is present throughout Aimé Césaire's works. He cannot forget the extent of the looting of Africa, and the poet grieves for this violated Africa as much as he grieves for his native Martinique. . . .

The first European plunderers and exploiters were sure of their superiority over the inhabitants of the countries "liberated" from the darkness of ignorance. [In his *Discourse on Colonialism*] Césaire is persuaded that the "main responsibility in this area lies with Christian pedantry for having set forth dishonest equations: Christianity = civilization; paganism = savagery. These equations could lead only to abominable colonialist and racist consequences, whose victims were to be the Indians, the yellow-skinned peoples, and the Negroes." . . .

Basilio [the Belgian King in *A Season in the Congo*] recognizes that once Belgian domination will have ended in the Congo, the spirit of the Negroes, their own personality, will be reborn. What he calls the "barbarous root" is the vital essence of the Congolese. It is the negation of colonialist omnipotence and is the most dangerous threat to the Church, guardian of the established order. . . .

Africa hungers for itself because it has gone through the traumatic experience of having its own negation forced on it. For Césaire, this experience extends all the way to Martinique, for the experience is not rooted in the obscure mysticism of a place or continent, which has been humiliated, but in the spiritual condition of a whole people. The African and the Martinican share the same fate. The torture they suffer makes time and place relatively unimportant. Only details differentiate the Rebel [in *And the Dogs Were Silent*] and Lumumba [in *A Season in the Congo*], King Christophe [in *The Tragedy of King Christophe*] and Césaire. . . .

The Negro hero, aware of the role assigned to him by Western society, mocks the vain attempts to enslave him by force and to make him deny his brothers.

Frederick Ivor Case. *ECr. Fall*, 1970, pp. 242–44†

Against the backdrop of the magical, enchanting world of Shakespeare's *The Tempest*, Aimé Césaire [in his play *A Tempest*] re-creates his vision of the black man's struggle against white tyranny. Original levels of metaphoric and thematic complexity recede to focus on the stark drama between oppressor and oppressed, between the desire for domination and the will to freedom. The setting is no longer a realm suspended in time and space where art and magic resolve the disorders and inequities of the temporal, political world. No longer can the play be considered in terms of spiritual and moral rebirth, as the movement from sin or crime through ordeal to contrition and forgiveness symbolized by the progression from tempest to the harmony of music. From the conflict between "civilization" and "primitive society," between colonizer and colonized, from the view of Caliban as "natural man"—all aspects of the play traditionally pointed out by critics—Césaire fashions a spectacle of racial conflict whose roots plunge deep into his own experience in colonial Martinique and whose chant echoes his early *Notebook on a Return to My Native Land*.

Césaire compresses the action into three acts and resolves the conflicts of Shakespeare's *Tempest* by the end of the second act: Ariel announces Prospero's forgiveness and the marriage of Ferdinand and Miranda. . . . The tension which has been building between Prospero and Caliban then intensifies freely. From Shakespeare to Césaire, Prospero evolves from the Renaissance symbol of Reason and what is best in man to the white colonizer whose very existence derives from power. Deposed not for his interest in the liberal arts but in a coup over his discovery of valuable new lands, Prospero rules over Caliban and Ariel as the colonial governor over native slaves. Usurping legitimate authority, as his brother did before him, he attempts to "teach" his values to the ignorant and resistant black indigene. But Caliban refuses the white culture as he rejects the white world's image of him as incorrigibly dirty and sexually obsessed. He will not deny his past and as a constant reminder of his disinheritance he will take the name X—as the Black Muslims do—to be "the man whose name has been stolen." Unlike Ariel, the non-violent mulatto integrationist who submits and seeks to stir Prospero's conscience, Caliban has become the black militant revolutionary whose cry, in English, "freedom now," links him to the universal struggle of his oppressed brothers. He prefers death with dignity: "death is better than humiliation and injustice."

Richard Regosin. FR. April, 1971, pp. 952–53

It has been noted that there is a fundamental unity among Césaire's heroes and that this unity arises from the author's presence in each of them. His presence is very apparent in the Rebel in *And the Dogs Were Silent*, who expresses Césaire's state of mind. He is doubly present in *The Tragedy of King Christophe*, speaking directly through the character of Metellus and showing his sympathy for one aspect of Christophe —his dream of grandeur for his people. In *A Season in the Congo* Patrice Lumumba's personality is too well known and his story is too recent for Césaire to transform them. The writer's voice, nevertheless, is often heard in the poetic and visionary remarks of his protagonist.

In his theater political questions have a central place, focusing on his greatest concern—the position of the black man in our era. But his theater is also "intentionally poetic." . . . Césaire's theater gives the spoken word, the dialogue, a special importance that stems from the lofty idea the author himself has about the power of language.

Rodney E. Harris. L'humanisme dans le théâtre
d'Aimé Césaire (Sherbrooke, Quebec, Éditions
Naaman, 1973), p. 161†

CHESNUTT, CHARLES W. (1858–1932)

UNITED STATES

The critical reader of the story called "The Wife of His Youth," which appeared in these pages two years ago, must have noticed uncommon traits in what was altogether a remarkable piece of work. The first was the novelty of the material; for the writer dealt not only with people who were not white, but with people who were not black enough to contrast grotesquely with white people—who in fact were of that near approach to the ordinary American in race and color which leaves, at the last degree, every one but the connoisseur in doubt whether they are Anglo-Saxon or Anglo-African. Quite as striking as this novelty of the material was the author's thorough mastery of it, and his unerring knowledge of the life he had chosen in its peculiar racial characteristics. But above all, the story was notable for the passionless handling of a phase of our common life which is tense with potential tragedy; for the attitude, almost ironical, in which the artist observes the play of contesting emotions in the drama under his eyes; and for his apparently reluctant, apparently helpless consent to let the spectator know his real feeling in the matter. Any one accustomed to study methods in fiction, to distinguish between good and bad art, to feel the joy which the delicate skill possible only from a love of truth can give, must have known a high pleasure in the quiet self-restraint of the performance; and such a reader would probably have decided that the social situation in the piece was studied wholly from the outside, by an observer with special opportunities for knowing it, who was, as it were, surprised into final sympathy.

Now, however, it is known that the author of this story is of negro blood—diluted, indeed, in such measure that if he did not admit this descent few would imagine it, but still quite of that middle world which lies next, though wholly outside, our own. Since his first story appeared he has contributed several others to these pages, and he now makes a showing palpable to criticism in a volume called *The Wife of His Youth, and Other Stories of the Color Line.* . . .

He has sounded a fresh note, boldly, not blatantly, and he has won the ear of the more intelligent public.

W. D. Howells. *Atlantic.* May, 1900, pp. 699–701

Nothing could exceed the tenderness with which the old and faithful figure of the wife is brought before us [in "The Wife of His Youth"], the soft dialect reproduced with indescribable art and charm. It is interesting to observe also that in this masterpiece of [Chesnutt's] accomplishment, as in much of his other work, we get the recurring note of comedy, suggesting that the farcical side of life is never wholly concealed from the writer's mental vision. At the most unexpected moments this capricious humor darts out at us, not always potent to amuse us, but always spontaneous and simple like the playfulness of a child. . . .

Closely allied to this purely humorous tendency is an inclination toward a more ironical banter, the subject of it always the idiosyncrasies of the negro race. We see their delight in posing, their easy irresponsibility in matters of veracity, their pompous snobbishness, their swift alternations of gayety and gloom, their thousand and one indications of imperfect development, as clearly as we see their gentleness and kindness, their luxuriant imagination, their amazing possibilities. In a word, we have in Mr. Chesnutt's three books [*The Wife of His Youth, The Conjure Woman, The House behind the Cedars*] . . . an ethnological study of extreme importance, such as only a peculiar union of two races and two historic periods could have made possible. Like Janus, the author turns his face toward the past, his vision embracing a drama that is over and never to be revived, and a still more mysterious drama that is hardly yet begun.

Elisabeth L. Cary. *The Book Buyer.* Aug., 1901,
pp. 27–28

Of [Chesnutt's] novels, *The House behind the Cedars* is commonly given first place. In the story of the heroine, Rena Walden, are treated some of the most subtle and searching questions raised by the color-line. Rena is sought in love by three men, George Tryon, a white man, whose love fails when put to the test; Jeff Wain, a coarse and brutal mulatto; and Frank Fowler, a devoted young Negro, who makes every sacrifice demanded by love. The novel, especially in its last pages, moves with an intensity that is an unmistakable sign of power. It is Mr. Chesnutt's most sustained treatment of the subject for which he has become best known, that is, the delicate and tragic situation of those who live on the border-line of the races; and it is the best work of fiction yet written by a member of the race in America.

In *The Marrow of Tradition* the main theme is the relations of two women, one white and one colored, whose father, the same white man, had in time been married to the mother of each. The novel touches upon most every phase of the Negro Problem. It is a powerful plea, but perhaps too much a novel of purpose to satisfy the highest standards of art.

Benjamin Brawley. *The Negro in Literature and Art*
(New York, Duffield, 1918), pp. 47–48

The struggle between Chesnutt the artist and Chesnutt the man (not immediately resolved) is evident in *The Wife of His Youth.* In these stories Chesnutt discards folk material to deal with the lives of a certain Negro type in Cleveland, the "Groveland" of his stories. These people represent the special and important group of Negroes with a large admixture of white blood. Because the peculiar situation of the near-whites was (and is) considered ideal for the purposes of propaganda, their lives had been used by nearly all the Negro novelists prior to Dunbar. This put upon such characters a certain stamp, and in that stamp lay danger for Chesnutt the artist.

The moods in which Chesnutt approaches his material are puzzling. In only a few of these stories is the reader sure of the author's point of view, his convictions. In "A Matter of Principle," for instance, a story of the color line in which the daughter of a well-to-do quadroon family loses a brilliant marriage because her father mistakes a stout, black gentleman for the lover whom he has never seen—what is the author's point of view? Based on the tragic absurdity of colorphobia, the story is a comedy of manners in the Molière sense. But what is Chesnutt's conviction as an artist? Does he sympathize with the existence of a color caste within the race? Is he holding his characters up to ridicule? Of what is he trying to convince us? In this and other stories one seems always at the point of making a discovery about the author, but the discovery never matures. The truth seems to be that in 1899, more than ten years after his return to Cleveland, Chesnutt's struggle was still in progress. He still was not sure what his attitude should be.

> J. Saunders Redding. *To Make a Poet Black* (Chapel
> Hill, University of North Carolina Press, 1939),
> pp. 70–71

After *The Colonel's Dream* [in 1905] Chesnutt did not publish another book. A news article in *The Pittsburgh Courier* for June 30, 1928, announced a novel by Chesnutt which was to be published during the following winter, but this book did not appear. Chesnutt was quoted as having made the following statement concerning the volume: "The book is a novel dealing with Negro life of the present day, just as my former novels dealt with the same subject twenty-five years ago." Perhaps his silence was due, partly at least, to disappointment in the results of his campaign for the betterment of social conditions in the South.

Whether disappointed in his campaign or not, Chesnutt was an important trail-blazer in American Negro fiction. In his early stories of plantation life he not only made the folk tale a more faithful transcript of actual conditions but also became the first colored writer of fiction whose work was generally criticized without consideration of race. In *The Wife of His Youth, and Other Stories of the Color Line* he experimented with racial subject matter which he subsequently handled at greater length in *The House behind the Cedars, The Marrow of Tradition*, and *The Colonel's Dream*. All four of these books are favorably disposed toward the mulatto, who ostensibly represented for Chesnutt the most accomplished character in the Negro group. In treating the complexities of caste and color during the Reconstruction period, Chesnutt sometimes seems to accept the racial myths of his time; but he had a keen eye for social injustice and, before laying down his pen, he had either used or suggested many of the themes of the fiction of Negro life as we know it today.

> Hugh Gloster. *Negro Voices in American Fiction*
> (Chapel Hill, University of North Carolina Press,
> 1948), pp. 45–46

The tales of *The Conjure Woman* are all narrated by a white Northerner [John] who has gone South after the War in search of a suitable place of business for himself and a hospitable climate for his ailing wife. He settles on a plantation in North Carolina, where he hopes to develop a grape-growing industry. At the heart of each tale is a story within the story told by Uncle Julius, a shrewd old ex-slave who recalls pre-War incidents of conjuration. The white narrator retells these stories, always making clear to the reader that he is aware that Uncle Julius usually has a lurking personal interest in his entertaining tales. Julius probably profits from his employer's purchase of a worthless horse—a purchase prompted by Julius' conjure tale about a mule. Or Julius' church gains the use of a building which he has discouraged his employer from tearing down by a tale about the lumber from which it is made. The narrator, however, is paternalistically indulgent and good humored about Uncle Julius' motives. . . .

[But] as John patronizes Julius, he testifies to his own limitations and to the white world's fumbling inability to appreciate the wisdom, humor, and heart of a black man's experience, rooted in the cruelties of the slave experience. John's limited sympathy, his inability to fathom Julius' experience, is a hauntingly familiar projection of the white response to America's racial problem. Julius' various efforts to engage his employer's imagination, to arouse his sympathy, and to focus his indignation reflect Charles Chesnutt's own many-sided efforts to reach the imagination and the heart of his largely white audience.

Robert M. Farnsworth. Introduction to Charles W.
Chestnutt, *The Conjure Woman* (Ann Arbor,
University of Michigan Press, 1969), pp. viii–ix, xvii

The Conjure Woman puts Joel Chandler Harris and Stephen Foster and all those dudes up to and including [William] Styron in their places. Uncle Julius is out to win. And he does. He convinces the cracker that the grapes have a spell on them and are therefore better left alone. He shows what would happen if the white man had to live in the Black man's shoes in "Mars Jeems's Nightmare." And he keeps his nephew's job for him. He uses the white woman's natural curiosity about Black men to his advantage. She always sympathizes with him while her husband is prone to back off. He is a good Black politician. The cracker gives the lumber that is "Po' Sandy" to the Black church. Uncle Julius is one of Black literature's most exciting characters precisely because he is so definite about his aims. He intends to see his people come out on top. John, the white voice, thought he could use Julius while it was the other way around. And Chesnutt drops a few gems on us dispelling the romantic theory about slavery's charms.

Nikki Giovanni. *Gemini* (Indianapolis, Bobbs-Merrill,
1971), pp. 100–101

Dr. Miller [in *The Marrow of Tradition*] is Wellington's most success-ful Negro in the sense that he is as close to white as the town's written and unwritten laws will allow any black to be. His "white" appearance, his superior education, deportment, speech, wealth and social standing seem to place Miller in a class by himself, making him the classic "middle man," neither fish nor fowl, whose existence both dramatizes the arbitrariness of distinctions based on race and simultaneously rein-forces the absolute force of such distinctions.

The wealth of incidents and details contained in Helen Chesnutt's biography of her father indicates that much of Miller's personality was a projection of Charles Waddell Chesnutt. Chesnutt was a man who seemed extraordinarily in control of himself, stable, disciplined, capable of enormous sustained effort, a self-taught intellectual whose strivings for knowledge, culture and a career brought him into line with the Anglo-Saxon success model of his age. Like Miller, Chesnutt had learned to compartmentalize; the roles of professional man, father of a family, member of an oppressed minority, could be separated so that success in one area would not be undercut by insult or frustration in another. Chesnutt could view his writing as a business and give up a full-time commitment to it because the income from his books did not support his family in the style they were accustomed to. On one hand such com-partmentalization is admirable and healthy, but taken to the extreme sanctioned by Western industrialized culture at the turn of the century, such an aptitude allowed Christian gentlemen to butcher and rob the nonwhite peoples of the earth. By forestalling an honest appraisal of the whole man, by resisting that long, hard look at the stresses and contra-dictions inherent in the multiplicity of "faces" he presented to Welling-ton, Miller was committing a perilous blunder. Chesnutt was serious enough, insightful enough, to realize that the individual will someday, somehow, be called upon to account for the arbitrary divisions by which he has shaped his life. . . .

The truth of the riot forces Wellington to recognize in itself *The Marrow of Tradition*, the bone-deep knowledge that men are either black or white and that nothing can occur between them that does not first take into account that dichotomy. This truth has stripped away the margin that Miller had believed supported his special kind of life.

John Wideman. *ASch.* Winter, 1972–73, pp. 130, 133

Perhaps the most impressive embodiment of Chesnutt's technical artistry was his last novel, *The Colonel's Dream*. The book's financial and popu-lar failure at the hands of a biased, prejudiced readership should not blind us to its obvious artistic success when viewed by readers no longer caught up in the political and social narrowness of the early 1900s. . . .

The skeletal structure of *The Colonel's Dream* is a kind of missionary travel novel, which operates on the framework of a national allegory, as Colonel French travels South with Northern ideas and attempts an economic conversion. French himself is a national American hero "type": a figure of military bearing who is also a successful businessman. He is also a man who represents the "whole country," coupling a Southern past with a Northern present and attempting to unite the two under the banner of his industrial Northern way of life. The geographic movement and semiallegorical characterization are essential elements of the plot structure: both are important, not only for the traditional elements contained, but also for the innovations which Chesnutt added. . . .

French is a man with a tragic flaw stemming from his personality, and not just an allegorical hero who is defeated by a hostile, looming society. While he is partially the storybook hero of wealth, charm, money, ideals, and leisure, he is also the realistic product of his own past. Thus he brings to his crusade to the heathen South the same traits that made him successful in New York, and for that reason he is defeated. . . . The persistence and drive which have made French successful in the North now greatly harm him in Clarendon; and he is too insensitive to realize this fact. As Chesnutt realistically portrays him, the Colonel is not only too weak to be victorious everywhere, but he is even blind at times.

J. Noel Heermance. Charles W. Chesnutt (Hamden,
Conn., Shoe String, 1974), pp. 184–86

CLARK, JOHN PEPPER (1935–   )

NIGERIA

What Ezra Pound is to Okigbo, Eliot and Hopkins are to Clark. As in the case of Okigbo one finds it occasionally disturbing to recognise the "ready made" language. But again we have to accept the fact that Eliot and Hopkins form a legitimate starting point for a young poet and that again we feel that the poet has often enough succeeded to burst out of the limitations set by the adopted language. Clark's *Poems* like Okigbo's *Heavensgate* gives us the immediate feeling that we are in the presence of a sincere, genuine poet. But that is where the similarity ends.

I have not observed either of them at work, but I am almost certain that they employ opposite techniques. I visualise Okigbo as a poet who gradually chisels away all the superfluous detail from a large chunk of experience. I see him filing away, balancing, reconstructing, until his verse has the hard edge and the transparency of a crystal. Clark on the other hand appears to me a more spontaneous poet. His writing is immediate. There is a feeling of urgency. He has so much to say, that he tries to cram more and more into the fragile form of his poem. His verse is packed with meaning; overloaded, bursting at the seams. One critic has said his poems are over-written. I should prefer to call them over-charged or over-powered. . . .

Clark's writing is extremely visual. One cannot fail to see that enormous rock on the sacred hill in Abeokuta boiling in the sun. But the visual experience leads the poet on to other thoughts basically quite unconnected. Yet this is no idle, aesthetic type of reflective poetry. In Clark's work we always feel that the poet is hard pressed, that he is writing under a form of compulsion, that he is himself like a "pot all night on the boil," or a "cauldron that cracks for heat."

I cannot see Clark working for a long time on a poem. I imagine him writing in a kind of explosion, under the extreme pressure of experience, writing only if cornered by life, as it were, and then having got the thing off his chest losing interest and turning to the next thing.

The result is poetry that makes heavy reading, but which is moving, because it is always nourished by immediate experience and because the author's harassed, tormented and irrepressible personality is present in every line.

Ulli Beier. BO. No. 12, 1963, pp. 47–48

John Pepper Clark, in the few poems he has in the [Langston] Hughes anthology [*Poems from Black Africa*], but more so because of his verse play *Song of a Goat*, convinces me that he is one of the most interesting Africans writing, English or French. Mr. Clark is a Nigerian, born in 1935, though I understand he is now in the graduate school at Princeton. For sure, nothing he could ever learn at Princeton would help him write so beautiful a work as *Song of a Goat*. It is English, but it is not. The tone, the references (immediate and accreted) belong to what I must consider an African experience. The English is pushed, as Senghor wished all Africans to do with European languages, past the immaculate boredom of the recent Victorians to a quality of experience that is non-European, though it is the European tongue which seems to shape it, externally. But Clark is after a specific emotional texture nowhere available in European literature or life. . . .

The play is about a traditional West African family split and destroyed by adultery. And the writing moves easily through the myth heart of African life, building a kind of ritual drama that depends as much on the writer's insides for its exactness and strength as it does on the narrating of formal ritualistic acts. The language is gentle and lyrical most of the time, but Clark's images and metaphors are strikingly and, I think, indigenously vivid. . . .

LeRoi Jones. Poetry. March, 1964, p. 399

I confess readily that like everyone else (except perhaps the American) I had enjoyed the crude vigour of *America, Their America*. Stronger even than the feeling of antagonism which the American generates by his overt actions is the contempt which he arouses by his lack of self-knowledge, his blind displacement of a true image of himself. Any work which goes towards the destruction of the American self-image must enjoy an immediate validity and give a vindictive pleasure to all non-Americans, and even praise from what we hope will be a new generation of Americans.

So much for America, and so much for why *America, Their America* hit the easy chord of transferred enjoyment. Would that the appreciation of this book had been left purely on this level! But Nigeria would not be Nigeria and literary critics semi-literate if an attempt was not made to raise this book to some level of literary achievement to which even the author never aspired. Beginning with what could be shrugged off as the natural overspill of enthusiasm it has now reached the absurd proportions where a critic in the *Nigeria Magazine Literary Supplement* actually compares *America, Their America* to James Baldwin's *The Fire Next Time*.

On what level? Mr. Clark donned a pair of oversized gloves, shut his eyes tightly and delivered a wild-swinging, two-fisted clobbering attack with head for a battering ram and knees up in his opponent's crutch, relying on the principle that with so many random and energetic blows, the law of averages must ensure a hit. Each page of *America, Their America* reads exactly like that picture we see often in the Nigerian street, of a child fighting a man ten times his size who stands very still while the child's arms flail wildly over his head, crying all the time in frustration and self-pity.

Even this accompanying whine is not missing from Mr. Clark's book. His final interview with the Colonel which degenerates most strangely into a plea for human sympathy is the last act of the troublesome child who is now faced with his punishment, but hopes to avoid it.

To compare the adult, perceptive analysis and the studied prose of James Baldwin with the catalogue of "maverick" reactions in *America, Their America* is not doing the author any good as it brings his work up for the kind of criticism which would normally be applied to a work of greater pretensions.

Wole Soyinka. *Ibadan*. June, 1966, pp. 59–60

[Clark] has three plays to his credit—*Song of a Goat, The Masquerade* and *The Raft*. But it is as the author of *Song of a Goat* that he has made his reputation as a playwright. Clark's three plays are tragedies and critics have attempted to show how close to Greek tragedies they are. In each of these plays an individual is faced with some inexorable law of nature or unchangeable law of society. He tries his best to escape an impending woe. Perhaps in this sense the comparison with Greek tragedy is not irrelevant.

However, it should at once be stated that Clark's declared aim is to portray life in the Rivers as he knows and has observed it. Each of his plays deals with an aspect of life important to his people. Their social practices and beliefs, their shortcomings and difficulties are dramatised on the stage. This is why these plays have been so popular. That they all end in tragedy is not meant to be a reflection on their lives. This is the type of ending dictated by both the content of the plays and the approach of the playwright. . . .

J. P. Clark writes plays which depict a confrontation between an individual and forces much greater than himself. He has set a high standard for himself and it is a measure of his brilliance and literary competence that his plays are successful and well received by Nigerians and non-Nigerians alike. *Song of a Goat* is particularly widely acclaimed and has been staged many times in Nigeria, Africa and Europe. It was applauded at the Commonwealth Festival of the Arts not only for its dramatic excellence but also for the poetic language used to portray the overwhelmingly tragic atmosphere of the play.

Oladele Taiwo. *An Introduction to West African Literature* (London, Thomas Nelson, 1967),
pp. 76–77

As a playwright Clark has seemed to suffer from a lack of familiarity with the demands of the theatre, and his plays have never fitted as comfortably on to the stage as have Soyinka's. The latter's craftsmanship stems from a close practical knowledge of the theatre as a director and actor, whereas Clark has no comparable experience. One result of this is that Clark's characters tend to talk where they might act, to recite where they should converse, and to remain static where they should move. Reported action has always been preponderant in his plays and the demands made upon his actors, directors and designers have tended to be unrealistic. A case in point, in *Song of a Goat*, is the decapitation of a goat, on stage, in order that its head can be thrust into a pot as a symbol of cuckoldry. The opening performance of a production of this play at Mbari, Ibadan (directed by Soyinka) tried to execute this instruction (without, for obvious reasons, adequate rehearsal), and the chastening experience upon actors and audience caused a symbolic gesture to be substituted on later nights. Similar appalling difficulties face the director in *The Raft*. To draw attention to this is not to ridicule Clark's dramatic aims, but rather to pinpoint what prevents the realization of his full potential as a playwright. For with *Ozidi* Clark has written a major piece for the theatre, of epic span and scope, and yet, once again, almost impossible to stage. . . .

On the modern stage and away from an Ijaw audience *Ozidi* will work effectively *only* if the director can return to the conditions in which the myth is at home, and make extensive use of dance and music (much of which is indicated in the text). *Ozidi* can become a most exciting dance-drama where the communication of mime and movement can overcome the limits of realism. It is in this form that one would like to see *Ozidi* tackled, for J. P. Clark has offered the theatre one of the most fascinating works to have been created in Nigeria in recent years.

Martin Banham. JCL. July, 1969, pp. 132–33, 135

Neither Clark nor Okigbo is detained by [English] influences for very long. In fact Clark himself acquired the assurance and lyric power of his mature style rapidly, as a cursory glance through *Poems* and *A Reed in the Tide* would confirm.

Clark assumes—an assumption shared by Wole Soyinka, Lenrie Peters, Gabriel Okara, and Okigbo—that what he has to say is important. The change is not in the material out of which the poems are forged. It is demonstrably more fundamental, part of a new intellectual outlook based on a belief in the poet as a pioneer of a different kind. Poetry no longer catered for popular causes. The poet's sensibility is free and uncompromised, and functions as the focal point of his work, the still center of the turning world. . . .

As we should expect, Clark is conscious of the demands of his craft, aware that poetry is not a matter of popular sentiment alone; that the act of creation is critical in the best sense of the word. His own formal criticism is impressive for its perception and depth and the degree to which it supports and clarifies his practice as a poet and dramatist. . . . Taken in an African context, or the context of emerging nations where art is frequently tempted into propaganda, [his] priorities are eminently sensible. Clark's interests being what they should be, there is no tendency to classify experiences as suitable or unsuitable for poetry, or, what is more objectionable, to advocate set themes such as the "African personality." By saying that there is nothing special in the kind of experience a poet has, he places the impact and meaning, the *value* of a poem, squarely on the performance, not on the intrinsic attraction of the theme.

Edwin Thumboo. BA. Summer, 1970, p. 388

Clark's success [as a poet] was due not only to [his] gift for recreating the local environment but also his genuine interest in the oral traditions which formed the only extant tradition. Clark was to complain later that Nigerians did not know as much about their oral traditions as they did about European mythologies. Apart from the absence of a written tradition which made the creation of a genuine national verse tradition a difficulty, the Nigerian poet also had to contend with the prejudice that the writer in a developing country is free from those sophisticated inhibitions which stifle the creative mind. Apparently he had only to look in his heart and write. Because of the spontaneous nature of his own verse Clark has had to contend with this prejudice in a greater measure than other writers. . . .

For the modern Nigerian poet writing in English, as for any other poet, a spontaneous outburst of emotion is inadequate, for the poet must not merely translate emotions or ideas from the life of one culture into the language of another, he must create a product that is a new whole in itself. He must not merely write as if so "hard pressed" that he is "writing in a kind of explosion, under the extreme pressure of experience" [Ulli Beier], but he must also ensure the quality of the expression. Mere reproduction of the experience could easily become sociological. So Clark attempts to escape from this through technique, first by experimenting with the techniques of other poets, then moving away from this pastiche making.

Dan Izevbaye. In Bruce King, ed., Introduction to
Nigerian Literature (London, Evans Brothers,
1971), pp. 152–53, 157

The predicament [in *The Raft*] of the four men on the raft—Olotu, Kengide, Ogro, and Ibobo—drifting helplessly in the night, is meant to be taken as the predicament of the Nigerian nation as a whole as it looks for directions, searches for a teleology while floating about in the dangerous waters of the modern world. The raft is adrift, its moorings gone. Who or what cut it loose? Will anyone tell the four men where they are? Can anyone tell them where they are going? Without stars or moon to guide them (where Clark presumably means the certainties of the old order), they are lost. . . .

The raft floats helplessly on, until a big steamer passes. Ogro confidently swims to it for help; but he is beaten back into the water and drowns. Clearly this is a foreign vessel, a representation of the outside world, and the West in particular. The point of the incident is clear. Ogro, his friends, and their broken raft are not wanted by the crew of the passing ship; they receive no help in their calamitous situation. They are alone. They are powerless. Their situation, to use a happy phrase of Clark's that occurs here and as the title of his book of verse, is that of "a reed in the tide," moving at the mercy of forces beyond its control. There seems to be no hope. Even when, near the end of the play, the raft approaches Burutu, its destination, a brief eruption of hope is smothered by a blanket of fog. The two survivors can see nothing; they are drifting helplessly past Burutu towards the open sea. . . .

There is something approaching great art about the close of this play: two men, holding hands, shouting hopelessly in the night. They have no control over their situation; they drift on to an unknown fate. Even on land, at Burutu, the destination they had been happily anticipating, all is confusion and alarm, with the noise *of men crying and calling out to one another in fear.* A fact stressed at the close is the aloneness of Ibobo and Kengide now, an aloneness which stands out starkly as a modern feature against a traditional African background of family and tribal togetherness.

Adrian A. Roscoe. *Mother Is Gold* (Cambridge,
Cambridge University Press, 1971), pp. 209–11

A vision of war. Four such words can only mock any attempt to describe J. P. Clark's latest book of poems (*Casualties: Poems 1966–68*]. Not content merely to elegize both the dead and living casualties of the Nigerian tragedy, Clark sets out to force the reader to actively participate in the human act of suffering. That he is remarkably successful in this despotic enforcement of the rites of Death is largely due to his decision to write in a style which, while closely paralleling the parable, often moves into an enigmatic tunnel vision. Clark watches the mindless destruction of both sides, "the roar of leopards amok from the forest," and manages to focus on individual acts of terror as well as the general state of fratricide; he does this by sculpturing *each* word as if it alone had to carry some two or three times its normal weight. . . .

Such a technique of arbitrarily holding us at arm's length, only to unexpectedly jerk us face to face with the realization that these symbols of death and chaos are no longer symbols but actual pain, demands our passage into Clark's world of frustrated despair. Even the second portion of the collection, "Incidental Songs for Several Persons," while not dealing with the horror of the Nigerian poems, is nevertheless dominated by a vision of ironic social decay.

R. Langenkamp. *WLWE*. Nov., 1971, pp. 106–7

CULLEN, COUNTEE (1903–1946)

UNITED STATES

This first volume of musical verses [*Color*] offers promise of distinction for its author, shows him to be a young poet of uncommon earnestness and diligence. Serious purpose and careful work are apparent in all of his poems. One feels that he will cultivate his fine talent with intelligence, and reap its full harvest. He has already developed a lyric idiom which is not, perhaps, very unusual or striking in itself, but which he has learned to employ with considerable virtuosity. To be sure, the many elements which have entered that reservoir below the threshold of his consciousness have undergone as yet no thorough chemistry. But although some of the poems are flagrantly reminiscent, not only in detail but in outline, one never catches him resting idly on his fulcrums. Indeed, he accepts them with such dignity and appreciation, and often uses them to such telling advantage, that one is inclined to call attention to them only by remarking that he "has taken his own where he has found it."

Perhaps the only protest to Mr. Cullen that one cares to insist on is against his frequent use of a rhetorical style, which is surely neither instinctive in origin nor agreeable in effect. "Yet do I marvel," he writes, instead of, "And yet I marvel," the natural and fitting phrase; and many of his poems are marred by similar distortions. Lofty diction in poetry, when it is unwarranted by feeling (and therefore, intermediately, by rhythm) is liable to seem only stilted and prosy. Neither can personal emotion survive conventional expression. It is because of this, I think, that I find Mr. Cullen's longest poem, "The Shroud of Color," the least moving of any he has written.

George H. Dillon. *Poetry*. April, 1926, pp. 50–51

For two generations Negro poets have been trying to do what Mr. Cullen has succeeded in doing. First, trying to translate into lyric form the highly poetic urge to escape from the blatant realities of life in America into a vivid past, and, second, fleeing from the stigma of being called a *Negro* poet, by, as Dunbar so desired to do, ignoring folk-material and writing of such abstractions as love and death.

There is hardly anyone writing poetry in America today who can make the banal sound as beautiful as does Mr. Cullen. He has an extraordinary ear for music, a most extensive and dexterous knowledge of words and their values, and an enviable understanding of conventional poetic forms. Technically, he is almost precocious, and never, it may be added, far from the academic; but he is also too steeped in tradition, too influenced mentally by certain conventions and taboos. When he does forget these things, as in his greatest poem, "Heritage" . . . he reaches heights no other Negro poet has ever reached, placing himself high among his contemporaries, both black or white. But he has not gone far enough. His second volume [*Copper Sun*] is not as lush with promise or as spontaneously moving as his first. There has been a marking time or side-stepping rather than a marching forward. If it seems we expect too much from this poet, we can only defend ourselves by saying that we expect no more than the poet's earlier work promises.

Mr. Cullen's love poems are too much made to order. His race poems, when he attempts to paint a moral, are inclined to be sentimental and stereotyped. It is when he gives vent to the pagan spirit and lets it inspire and dominate a poem's form and context that he does his most impressive work. His cleverly turned rebellious poems are also above the ordinary. But there are not enough of these in comparison to those poems which are banal, though beautiful.

Wallace Thurman. *Bkm*. July, 1928, pp. 559–60

The danger of falling below expectations is especially great in the case of the poet who turns novelist. Mr. Cullen, whose poetry is admired by so many, and whose danger therefore is the greater, has nevertheless challenged fate successfully. His first novel [*One Way to Heaven*] goes over. . . .

Be not misled by the announcement that "this is a mad and witty modern picture of high life in Harlem." That part of it which portrays the "high life" of Harlem is not important and seems even less important than it might, because the effect is completely submerged in the larger and simpler realities of the rest of the book. This is because Mr. Cullen has chosen to change his method and his viewpoint in dealing with the upper level. Here he becomes a caricaturist, suppressing all his sympathies, sketching with a sharp and ungracious pen. But the less pretentious folk he has treated gently and delicately, in color. This juxtaposition of two so different subjects so differently handled is somehow like exhibiting a lovely pastel and a cartoon in the same frame.

Rudolph Fisher. *NYHT*. Feb. 28, 1932, p. 3

Mr. Cullen has rendered Euripides's best-known tragedy [*The Medea*] into living and utterable English. He has made little attempt to convey the poetry of the original, preferring to concentrate on dramatic situation and realistic portrayal of character. The result is a very forceful and poignant re-creation of the story of the barbarian sorceress whose fury against a faithless lover wins the tragic conflict with her love for her children. Only a few of the choruses have been put into lyrical form: the rest of the play has been cast in prose that is simple often to the point of baldness and, except for two or three incongruous lapses into slang, both colloquial and dignified. . . .

Perhaps fifty persons today read the classics in translation to one who reads them in the original; if there is to be a popular revival of interest in the Greek drama, it appears that this is more likely to originate in Harlem than in the universities.

Philip Blair Rice. Nation. Sept. 18, 1935, p. 336

One important writer among the new Negroes stands out as having contributed nothing or little to this conglomeration [of vivid Negro characters]. That writer is the poet Countee Cullen. He for himself (as well as others for him) has written numerous disclaimers of an attitude narrowed by racial influence. He may be right. Certainly *Caroling Dusk*, his anthology of "verse by Negro poets," represents a careful culling of the less distinctive, that is to say, the less Negroid poetry of his most defiantly Negro contemporaries. Nevertheless it remains that when writing on race material Mr. Cullen is at his best. His is an unfortunate attitude, for it has been deliberately acquired and in that sense is artificial, tending to create a kind of effete and bloodless poetry in the manner of [William Stanley] Braithwaite. The essential quality of good poetry is utmost sincerity and earnestness of purpose. A poet untouched by his times, by his conditions, by his environment is only half a poet, for earnestness and sincerity grow in direct proportion as one feels intelligently the pressure of immediate life. One may not like the pressure and the necessities under which it forces one to labor, but one does not deny it. . . .

Now undoubtedly the biggest, single unalterable circumstance in the life of Mr. Cullen is his color. Most of the life he has lived has been influenced by it. And when he writes by it, he *writes*; but when this does not guide him, his pen trails faded ink across his pages.

J. Saunders Redding. To Make a Poet Black (Chapel
Hill, University of North Carolina Press, 1939),
pp. 108–9

About half of [Cullen's] "best poems" were written while he was a student of New York University, and it was during these years that he first came up for consideration as an authentic American writer, the goal to which he aspired. Up at "The Dark Tower," a gathering place of awakened Harlem, the very name of which was taken from one of Cullen's sonnets, there was never any doubt that he would make it. At the *Opportunity* banquets, where prizes were awarded by that once-influential magazine in order to encourage the efforts of new Negro writers, it was taken for granted that Cullen was in. Before he finished college, his poems had been published in a dozen or more magazines, including *The Nation, Poetry, The American Mercury*, and *Harper's*. *Color*, the first collection of these lyrics, made a solid impression in 1925, the year in which Cullen celebrated his twenty-second birthday.

Copper Sun and *The Ballad of the Brown Girl*, both presenting more of his undergraduate output, followed. . . . Meanwhile, the young poet went abroad on a Guggenheim Fellowship, perhaps, as much as anything else, to take stock. His stay in France was extended a year beyond his original plans, but even that wasn't long enough. His spring-time leaves had fallen, and he was still waiting for a new season to bring another yield. He kept writing as a matter of habit, and the little shelf of his books increased steadily, but that wasn't the real thing; that wasn't what he was waiting for. A decade later he wrote to a friend, "My muse is either dead or taking a twenty-year sleep." . . .

Cullen did not live to see another springtime resurgence of his own creative powers comparable with the impulse that produced his first three books of poetry, the books which give his selected poems most of their lilt and brightness.

Arna Bontemps. SR. March 22, 1947, pp. 13, 44

Why did Countee Cullen drop racial poetry so suddenly and completely? What happened after the publication of *The Black Christ* to dry up the springs of racial verse? It has been argued that Cullen turned from racial themes because he came to feel too keenly the inner conflict which his status as poet and Negro imposed upon him. . . . Undeniably, Cullen the poet was disturbed by the added burden of race, but I am inclined to believe that he turned from racial themes for a much more realistic and down-to-earth cause; namely, a consciousness of waning powers in this particular area of poetry. He had worked the racial lode to depletion, and he realized it. . . .

Cullen's heart had had its say on the matter of race, and he preferred a "stony silence" to futile sound. We can easily understand his position. After all, there are only so many things that one can say on the race problem. The alien-and-exile theme with its glorification of Africa had become discredited even while Cullen was using it. Protest, like religion, is a very narrow subject for poetry. Cullen, a highly sensitive and intelligent artist, came to realize this and turned to greener pastures in children's literature.

Arthur P. Davis. *Phylon.* 14, 4, 1953, pp. 399–400

It is easy to understand why this long poem of 963 lines ["The Black Christ"] finally lost Cullen the sympathies of the black public. For the poem, with its mystical character, and despite the title and the theme of the narrative, is not essentially Negro in any way. Its very mysticism was condemned as childish [by J. Saunders Redding], and one critic [Benjamin Brawley] actually reproached the author for having dated the poem from Paris.

There may be more meaning in this reproof than might be thought, for "The Black Christ" has affinities with a type of literature that could scarcely arouse any echoes in an American reading public. It is, as we see it, something like the transposition into another setting of a French medieval miracle play with, at the same time, the character of a votive offering, on the lines of a well-known Passion play [that performed in Oberammergau, Bavaria] which was expressly composed to give thanks to heaven for having spared a whole population the horrors of the plague.

"The Black Christ" must be read as a poem of thanksgiving for the bestowal of the light of faith, as well as the translation into words of a contemplative experience. The religious exaltation that dictates the poem's entire structure bears the marks of the neophyte's sense of wonderment and his whole touching naïveté. With such characteristics, however, "The Black Christ" was inevitably inaccessible to all but a handful of readers. [1963]

Jean Wagner. *Black Poets of the United States* (Urbana, University of Illinois Press, 1973), pp. 345–46

Cullen's satire [in *One Way to Heaven*] is friendly; Mrs. Brandon is never malicious and is a most likeable character. But it was satire directed towards Negroes, and doubtless some of Cullen's own patrons, and such satire stands practically alone in the Harlem Renaissance. Perhaps most important is the relationship of the satire to Cullen's own career. From Harlem newspapers and from the portrayal of Mrs. Brandon and her friends, we can infer that the middle class Harlem reading public often bought Harlem Renaissance books without reading them, and were more concerned with the fact of a Negro literary renaissance than with the quality of the writings. Much of Cullen's own poetry, with its chauvinism and cloistered romanticism, seems to have been directed towards this group. And Cullen himself indulged almost as much as Mrs. Brandon in using high-sounding language where simple Anglo-Saxon words would suffice.

By 1932, judging from *One Way to Heaven*, Cullen was disillusioned, detached, and a little quizzical towards the Harlem Renaissance. Here he was breaking his own dictum that Negro writers should present only the appealing sides of Negro life to the white public. And he was ridiculing a main source of his own reputation, along with the excesses of chauvinism the Harlem Renaissance produced.

Stephen H. Bronz. Roots of Negro Racial
Consciousness (New York, Libra, 1964), pp. 63–64

[Cullen] often tried out his verses [for children] by reading them to his cousin's little girls. Their greatest enjoyment came from the stories in verse about the strange animals he invented, such as the Wakeupworld with twelve eyes arranged clockwise in his head, the Lapalake that could never get enough to drink, and the proud Snakethatwalkeduponhistail. When the children demanded to know the origin of these amusing creatures, he had a ready answer. With a straight face he told them that Christopher, his cat (whom the youngsters knew and loved), had told him a long story about these unusual beasts. They were animals whose species are lost to us because they failed to get into Noah's Ark when the world was destroyed by the great flood. Each one had missed the boat because of a particular flaw in his character. Christopher had learned the story from his father through a long line of ancestors descended from the first Christopher, who had sailed on the Ark.

These stories in verse with prose interludes were later published as *The Lost Zoo*. . . . The love for his pets and his deep feeling for all animals gave this book a special place in Countee's affection.

Blanche E. Ferguson. Countee Cullen and the Negro
Renaissance (New York, Dodd, Mead, 1966),
pp. 155, 165

[Cullen] was, and probably still is, considered the least race-conscious of the Negro poets. . . . Nevertheless, it was because of the color of his skin that Countee Cullen was more aware of the racial poetry and could not be at all times "sheer poet." This was clearly a problem for Cullen —wanting to write lyrics on love, death, and beauty—always so consciously aware of his race. This can be seen, for instance, in his poem "Uncle Jim," where the struggle is neatly portrayed through the young boy, thinking of Keats, and his uncle, bitter with thoughts of the difference between being a black man or a white man in our society. . . .

For Cullen, then, the racial problem was always there, even when one was thinking of odes by Keats, and he was impelled—*in spite of everything I can do*—to write about this subject. This was the cause of much weakness in his writing, as well as some strength; for there are poems about race which have an emotional intensity that most of his white peers could not have matched.

Margaret Perry. *A Bio-Bibliography of Countee P. Cullen* (Westport, Conn., Greenwood, 1971), pp. 26–28

A significant writer—even a lyric poet—must perceive some truth, some reality which he wishes to reveal. It is the quality of this vision which elevates his song from the transitory to the memorable. In his earliest poems, Cullen sought such truth in a presumed affinity with Africa. He wanted to believe that impulses of his African heritage surged past his censoring consciousness and forced him to repudiate the white gods of Western Civilization. Cullen's Africa, however, was a utopia in which to escape from the harsh actualities of America, and the heritage a myth on which he hoped to erect a new faith to comfort himself in a world seemingly dedicated to furthering the interests of white men. . . .

As the African impulse waned, Cullen knelt before the altar of love, but there also false gods demanded sacrifices he would not offer. Like a wanderer disconsolate after a worldwide search, Cullen turned back to Christ. But he still could not rely upon the white god who governed the Methodist Church in which he had been reared; he could not believe a white god capable of comprehending the depths of a black man's suffering. Therefore, he fashioned for himself a black Christ with "dark, despairing features." This image, however, furnished scant comfort; Cullen knew that his own creation could not correct mankind's transgressions. Without faith, without vision, Cullen, whom Saunders Redding has compared with Shakespeare's ethereal Ariel, lost his power to sing and soar above the fleshly Calibans.

Darwin T. Turner. *In a Minor Chord: Three Afro-American Writers and Their Search for Identity* (Carbondale, Southern Illinois University Press, 1971), pp. 60–61

Most Anglo-American poetry tends to employ an iambic beat. In "Heritage" Cullen resorts to the use of a trochaic measure. It seems valid to assume that his choice of the descending line was no accident. Under such an assumption, it also seems highly possible that in the rhythms of "Heritage" Cullen hoped to suggest the throb of African drums, for certainly the percussive movement of a trochaic line may fall upon the ear like the big and small booms of tom-toms in the African bush. Moreover, if the trochees of "Heritage" are tom-toms, and especially if they are consciously so, they might be further proof of how un-African Cullen really was. They might tell us again that Cullen's Africa existed only when Cullen was able to put his mind on what he was doing, as he could put his mind on the *selection* of a beat. So it may be that his Africa was contrived and synthetic, not integral within him as it must have been to justify the claims he makes in "Heritage" of the presence of his forefathers' continent in his "blood." How significant, then, might be Cullen's allusion in "Heritage" to rain: "I can never rest at all when the rain begins to fall." The rain brings back, that is, so Cullen is implying, the drums and Africa. And very probably it did, at the literary level, the same level at which Eugene O'Neill could put his drums into *The Emperor Jones* or Somerset Maugham his rain into the play of the same name, with which almost surely Cullen was better acquainted than with Africa.

Blyden Jackson. In Blyden Jackson and Louis D. Rubin, Jr., *Black Poetry in America* (Baton Rouge, Louisiana State University Press, 1974), p. 49

DADIÉ, BERNARD BINLIN (1916–   )

IVORY COAST

In *The Circle of Days* the lyrical movement is different [from that of David Diop's poetry]. Humor, tenderness, and harmony with life have a different density. *The Circle of Days* is more like a Negro spiritual than a message bearing vindictive fire. It expresses a more secretive consciousness and inner life. But Africa is equally present, and as sometimes in the works of Langston Hughes, it is colored with an evangelical humor: "I thank you, God, for having created me Black,/for having made me/the sum of all sorrows. . . ."

Dadié's lyricism remains intimate and casual even when he makes accusations; he never appeals to the powers of hatred. . . . Besides a tender humor, a joy in living seems to me to best define Dadié's originality. It is a joy that defies death: "Never a sad goodbye . . . Carry me/as if we were going to a celebration/hand in hand. . . ."

It is natural for the poet from the Ivory Coast to be sensitive to the magic of love. On this plane, Dadié attains the Dionysian fervor of David Diop. For Dadié, too, love is a participation in the elementary pulsations of life. . . .

The African charm that characterizes Dadié's stories also pervades his poetry, and leaves within us, as on his native sand, imprints of bare, agile feet!

René Depestre. *PA*. Dec., 1956, pp. 112–13†

Dadié belongs to the early post-First World War generation and for this reason his work reflects rather well the period of the true beginnings of the African evolution. Thus, he is a part of that group of intellectuals composed of doctors and teachers trained in Dakar who are commonly known as the "educated persons" of Negro Africa and who, to a large extent, make up our present-day governments. Consequently, he was caught up in the mesh of the movement, especially in politics, which shows us the constructive character of his book called *A Negro in Paris*. He thus follows the development of present-day Africa. . . .

His work is diverse and contrary and consists of legends, poems and novels, including [*A Negro in Paris*]. This book is splendid for its diversity of form: in some passages we find real poetic inspiration; in others, we have the impression that we are reading Voltaire or Montesquieu. It is well constructed and coherent, though in certain places the spirit of the work is somewhat lost.

I do not think this book seeks to transplant Western development —a part of whose culture we have acquired—into Africa. The issue is one involving her individual evolution confronted with Western culture, because it must be said that she can only evolve in terms of what she has received. This does not mean a mere copying but a synthesizing of her own in order to acquire her own individuality.

Joseph Miezan Bognini. PA (English ed.). 8, 1, 1961,
p. 156

As a counterpart of *Tales of Renart the Fox*, which belongs to the French Middle Ages, and the Cycle of Leuk the Hare, which belongs to the Senegalese soil, the Ivory Coast (together with [southern Togo and southern Dahomey]) offers us the Tales of the Spider.

Kacou Ananzè [in Dadié's *The Black Skirt*] personifies trickery, cleverness, and above all dishonesty and treachery, without the likeable and joyous traits that make Leuk and Renart so intensely vibrant. Kacou Ananzè incarnates the malicious spirit lying in wait for animals and men. Although surrounded by numerous other creatures, this character . . . creates the unifying element in this Book of Animals. Of the sixteen stories collected in *The Black Skirt*, ten are devoted to the spider. . . .

If Renart, Leuk, and their feathered and furry friends correspond approximately to their equivalents in nature, Kacou Ananzè, on the contrary, in no way shows the zoological features of the spider; he can reach the size of a man, bow down, stand up straight, and walk on two legs. His behavior is in every way reminiscent of that of the Ivory Coast peasant: he lives in a hut, cultivates his land, goes fishing, and does his shopping. Kacou Ananzè's anthropomorphism therefore precludes our classifying him as a zoological or mythical beast.

Roger Mercier and M. and S. Battestini. Bernard
Dadié (Paris, Fernand Nathan, 1964), p. 7†

[In *Boss of New York*] Dadié looks in an unusual way at "surprising America," and this "old west" about which "I thought everything had been said but which yielded things never revealed to anyone else." Dadié turns his gaze upon this land in which beauty and ugliness mingle without colliding. With a subtle knowledge of human psychology, he depicts this nation torn from a peaceful life by an infernal quest for supremacy. He explicitly describes this nation's shifting profile, letting America's whole ridiculous pretension be reflected through his naïveté.

Paris and New York do not make Dadié feel disillusioned, strangely uprooted, or sadly nostalgic. On the contrary, his trips allow him to observe minutely the "immense absurdity" surrounding him. From his deliberations there arises a grain of humor sufficient to set up that liberating distance which makes the "Negro," formerly condemned to being observed and kept at a distance, into a human being who observes and judges in turn. Dadié is a remarkable manifestation in literature of the movement toward awareness as a prelude to liberation.

Boss of New York, for some readers a simple "chronicle" of a trip, is actually an amusing satire revealing the unknown, fragile underbelly of Yankee power.

C. Quillateau. Bernard Binlin Dadié: L'homme et
l'œuvre (Paris, Présence Africaine, 1967), pp. 25–26†

[*A Negro in Paris*] is cast in the form of a traveler's book in which a foreign visitor writes a detailed and presumably "objective" description of the interesting customs and manners of his hosts. *A Negro in Paris* is extended irony, Dadié placing his main character, a West African, in the reverse role of many a rather smug European traveler to West Africa. Whereas the European would describe the quaint behavior of Africans for home consumption so that others might "understand" them, the narrator of this work describes Parisian mores with the same critical eye for relationships among minute, often ridiculous details. . . .

Dadié's basic theme seems to be that the Parisian is really a human being after all, and worthy of study, having a history and traditions which he reveres, gods whom he worships. And by drawing comparisons between the West African and the Parisian, the author suggests that Africans are as good as Europeans, or that Europeans are as bad as Africans, however the case might appear. The core problem is the understanding of persons of one culture by those of another.

Austin J. Shelton. ECr. Fall, 1970, pp. 217, 219

Like so many other French-speaking Africans, Dadié is continuously asserting the beauty of African life as a constant reminder that colonialism cheated the black man out of his heritage. . . . *Climbié*, like the other prose works of its family, portrays the quality of African childhood experiences. The general outlines of the pattern are common: tough elementary education, dogged by poverty, sadistic schoolmastership, and so on; life among the many relatives in the African extended family; childhood ambitions; secondary education which is perpetually haunted by the fear of failure; the day one sets out in pursuit of one's vision; new experiences in the encounter with white authority that invariably suspects and fears the "educated native."

Nothing spectacular happens to Climbié until he has finished secondary school and is working—towards the end of the book.

His development is like the muted process of plant growth in which the seed germinates, pushes through, always in an upward thrust, until it blossoms and lays bare its foliage, now exposed to wind, sun, rain, insects that lie in wait for its juices, in a way it never happened before. As with the plant, things happen to Climbié; he never "happens" to them, until he reacts to white domination once he is back home from Senegal. His development is fully rendered by the marvellously subtle shift in Dadié's style, especially in Part II; the style "grows up" with Climbié. And yet, again, like a plant, he is part of the landscape which we view through him. Dadié has portrayed for us, often in a volatile idiom that reflects his mercurial personality, a human and physical landscape that is alive, at once friendly and hostile, and indifferent.

> Ezekiel Mphahlele. Introduction to Bernard Dadié,
> *Climbié* (London, Heinemann Educational Books,
> 1971), pp. viii–ix

DAMAS, LÉON-GONTRAN (1912–   )

FRENCH GUIANA

For a long time I have hesitated to write about *Pigments*—not because its merits as poetry are negligible, but because it is primarily a testimony: a Negro poet tells us his reactions to White Society. . . . This point of view explains the tenseness of Damas's tone, the violence of an inspiration that makes the poet defend himself against others' curiosity and suffer the scars of his condition. These scars are also the reasons for his pride, since he feels he is a Negro and asserts himself as a Negro. Because of this self-assertion, Damas's lyricism coincides with his analysis of what it means to be a poet, a central theme in contemporary poetry. Damas—who has, so to speak, more enemies than anyone else because of his race—also nourishes a more forceful hatred of all forms of oppression. . . .

The Negro has been exploited and is no longer sure of having his own consciousness. What black intellectual has not been corrupted by a certain desire for "assimilation," an attitude that disgusts Damas and makes him reject his childhood. . . . But the poet's very tragedy leads him to make protests that often go beyond his intentions: "I always feel ready to foam with rage/against everything that surrounds me/against everything that prevents me from ever being/a man." Certainly I understand this language only too clearly. But listen, Damas, what prevents you from being a man is also what prevents me from being one, and the color of my skin or of yours is not really important! Your poems are ours, as is your sense of lost grandeur, a feeling that can be experienced by anyone, man or nation, who is sensitive enough. Is not the knowledge that we share the same enemies the most beautiful reason for us to like one another?

Léon Gabriel Gros. CS. Sept., 1937, pp. 511–12†

For the most part, the French Negro poetry with which we are most familiar now (e.g., the recent work of Léopold Sédar Senghor and Aimé Césaire) is *engagée* [committed] in a European sense, supporting the Negro cause everywhere while often criticizing "white" civilization, and it owes a great debt to French culture and language; but it has its own idiom and standard of excellence that have developed from a new sense of Negritude bursting free. This poetry looks, at last, to Africa and speaks from an African heritage over the corpse, the still warm corpse, of colonialism.

However, *Pigments* is largely another thing, a little classic from another time. It is the poetry of a bitter Negro citizen of pre-war France —Damas, by the way, was among the first of the militant French Negro poets: Aimé Césaire, for instance, did not begin writing until the Forties. The result is often that kind of passionate social protest characteristic of the Thirties. . . . One is reminded more of Langston Hughes than of Senghor. But that is not necessarily bad, and besides, not all of the poems in [the present edition of *Pigments*] are products of the Thirties or a Thirties mind-set. Moreover, less subject to dating is the poet's art; it, like the whole idea of French Negro poetry or American jazz, is a product of a cultural blend; and the best analogy for Damas's art (and one that he insists on) is to jazz. That is, Damas's technique, whether his goal is direct social utterance or, just as characteristic, disinterested poetic utterance, or is a combination of the two, is best described as a jazz technique—endless theme and variation, incremental repetition, improvisation, and a kind of verbal counterpoint that adds up to a most impressive expression of a trapped man's Negritude. . . .

C. E. Nelson. BA. Autumn, 1963, p. 476

Co-founder with Senghor and Césaire of the Negritude school, Léon-Gontran Damas was born in Cayenne, Guyane (French Guiana), South America. After completing his secondary studies at the Lycée Schoelcher in Fort-de-France, Martinique, he went on to Paris, where he studied law and met Césaire and Senghor. In Paris, Damas was an habitué of all the places frequented by blacks from many countries of the world who had been attracted to this intellectual "Mecca" and bastion of individual freedom. . . . Being a poor student, M. Damas lived intensely the intellectual and moral tragedy of his race, undergoing the identity crisis common to all his fellow blacks. His poetic sensitivity made him all the more vulnerable to that tragedy.

Damas's poetic works include *Pigments, Graffiti*, and *Black Label*. His poetry, in contrast to that of Césaire and Senghor, is unsophisticated. It finds expression through everyday words, common or noble, most often those words and expressions of the common people, colored at times by an outmoded gracefulness and the use of certain Creole terms, and all of it subjected to the rhythm of the *tam tam*, for with Damas, rhythm takes precedence over melody. Being unsophisticated, Damas's poetry is direct, brutish, and at times brutal; and not infrequently it is charged with an emotion disguised as humor, a characteristically Negro humor that has been the black man's saving grace in a harsh and cruel world in which he has had, for years, no other defense or technique of survival.

Edward A. Jones. In Edward A. Jones, ed., *Voices of Négritude* (Valley Forge, Pa., Judson, 1971), pp. 63–64

When *Pigments* appeared in 1937, it caused a sensation. Claude McKay's lines, "Am I not Africa's son, Black of that black land where black deeds are done," which Damas used as an epigraph, and the title's unmistakable allusion to color, were underlined in Robert Desnos' introduction. . . . "With Damas, there is no question of his subject matter nor how he treats it, of the sharpness of his blade nor the status of his soul. Damas is Negro and insists on his Negro-ness and on his condition as a Negro. . . . These poems are . . . also a song of friendship offered in the name of his whole race by my friend, Damas the Negro, to all his white brothers." . . .

As for Desnos' characterizing *Pigments* as Damas' "song of friendship . . . to his white brothers," this is true only by the most generous extrapolation. Why sweeten the pill? The short poems of *Pigments* are a bitter testimony, variations on themes of *pain*. They do reveal compassion for fellow-sufferers other than the Black man (the Jews under

Hitler, for example). But nowhere in these pages does this reader find, nor does she ask for, "a song of friendship." If anger, tenacity and a certain despair are the impact of this first book of poems, this first major work of the Negritude group, they are valid, sufficient and important in and by themselves. . . .

"Et Cetera," which ends the book *Pigments* . . . reflects its historical moment. Senegalese soldiers were long known as among the best in the French Army. Here the poet exhorts them to fight for their *own* independence, "to invade Senegal," rather than defend their colonial masters against the Germans. Doubtless this was among the Damas poems recited in Baoulé translation by rioting African draft resisters in the Ivory Coast in 1939. As a result, *Pigments* was quickly banned throughout French West Africa, an early indication of the revolutionary proclivities that the later poetry of Negritude, particularly Césaire's and David Diop's, would demonstrate even more.

Ellen Conroy Kennedy. BlackW. Jan., 1972, pp. 8–11

Damas's early poems struck a note of mockery, muffled laughter, irony. But in the three volumes following his first, one notices the intensity of violence that was found in Césaire. In them, however, we see more and more what becomes less and less apparent in Césaire—a definite rejection of the props of the white world and a turning toward the African continent which was to become *all* of him. . . .

The past in Césaire's poetry is one long, grim night and when he refers to the glory of Africa, he does so almost with the modesty of the stranger. Damas, on the other hand, recognizes a past within the disturbed environment, for he feels that the efforts of misdirected currents of history were responsible for his dilemma. With anguish therefore he exclaims in "Limbed" that he wishes to be given back the black dolls so that he could play games that would restore his world of instinct. . . .

Damas's anger is quieter, more reflective than Césaire's; he can look back on the centuries and forgive. Another interesting point of comparison between Damas and Césaire is that although they share in common the same subject matter, there is a different expression of tone. Whereas Damas laments in "Reality" that he is almost a negative person because he has accomplished nothing, Césaire ironically celebrates those who do not invent anything. In Damas's poetry little attempt is made to vaunt racial superiority by stating negative virtues. When he does attempt this kind of writing, he does not succeed. . . .

Damas is at his best when, as a participant in the culture, he can nevertheless strongly denounce it. When he goes completely over to the other side and writes semi-songs of mourning or praise, he does not succeed. He is too much the poet and person; the African oral tradition had spokesmen, never individualists.

O. R. Dathorne. *The Black Mind* (Minneapolis,
University of Minnesota Press, 1974),
pp. 315, 317–18

DEMBY, WILLIAM (1922–   )

UNITED STATES

Except that it is not deliberately complex and probing, *Beetlecreek* brings to mind Carson McCullers's *The Heart Is a Lonely Hunter*; for it is about the barriers—only temporarily surmountable—which separate human beings. The immediate foreground is the Negro quarter of a small town in West Virginia. The central figures are an old and half-crazed white man, a hermit tempted to give himself "the right and power to reach out and touch people, to love," and a sensitive and imaginative adolescent Negro boy, the immediate cause of the temptation. The action the hermit takes, after a propitious beginning, is disastrous. The innocence of his feeling for the boy—he seeks a son as the boy a father—is beautifully conveyed. But to the Negro suburb he rapidly becomes a "sex-fiend." Ultimately, in a fit of hysteria, the boy kills him, demonstrating Mr. Demby's gloomy views on the racial problem and the universal impossibility of any lasting communication between two human beings.

I like this novel very much, though it has an entirely predictable and banal ending. Unlike Langston Hughes and Richard Wright and William Gardiner Smith, Mr. Demby has avoided the inevitable pitfalls which beset the American Negro who writes out of his own experience. His book is only in a secondary sense about "the Negro problem"; it is no *roman à thèse*, except for the general gloomy view about *all* human relationships. To put it very tritely, he is interested in his characters first as human beings and then as black or white. For all his painful awareness of what it means to be a Negro in a small Southern town, he never merely exploits his subject.

Ernest Jones. *Nation*. Feb. 11, 1950, pp. 138–39

Thematically [*Beetlecreek* moves] toward an existentialist definition of evil: if no other confirmation of his existence is possible, man will attempt to assert himself in negative and destructive ways. It is so with Bill Trapp, who even as a child preferred to be tormented than ignored;

it is true of the townspeople, who find in their malicious persecution of Bill Trapp relief from their empty lives. It is true above all of David and Johnny, who suffer their creative powers to be perverted, rather than endure a spiritual vacuum. . . .

Recurrent images assume symbolic value and are used extensively to buttress the theme. The frantic, swooping birds, for example, provide an objective correlative to David's and Johnny's feelings of restlessness and dissatisfaction. The mirrors (each of the main characters studies himself in a mirror) underscore the problem of identity, while the swinging bridge suggests the social separation between colored and white in Beetlecreek. The season in which the action takes place (Indian summer) is converted into a particularly rich symbol. On one level, it helps to dramatize the necessity of choice, of decision: "The birds swooped and swooped, all the time screaming, undecided what to do. The freak summer fooled everybody and everything." On another, it suggests that the crucial decisions faced by Bill Trapp, David, and Johnny represent their last chance for life.

Robert A. Bone. The Negro Novel in America (New Haven, Conn., Yale University Press, 1958), pp. 195–96

The Catacombs, by William Demby, is in many ways an unusual novel. It purports to tell a story about a young Negro girl, Doris, but it is equally involved in telling the story of the writer, as well as recording snatches of news about the members of the bohemian circle in Rome to which the writer belongs. In addition, it details the major world news topics covered by the Italian press, events beside which the little personal dramas of the characters shrink into insignificance. The writer, a film script-writer and translator, makes use of the film technique of quick cuts and no continuity, a bold and frontal attack on narrative continuity. The action, if action it can be called, extends from 1961 to 1964, from the time Demby began to write the novel to the time he left Rome (where he had lived many years) to return to the United States. The focus of the novel is Doris's life in Rome as the dominant partner in a liaison with a weak-willed Italian count. Why Demby should decide to write a novel about Doris is not exactly clear. What is clear, however, is that she is a mere pretext.

The novelist, whose occupation and travels have no doubt made a cosmopolite of his psyche, succeeds very well in showing how insignificant the modern individual has become in the face of the larger issues that stir the world to its foundations. It is no wonder that the exploration of character in this novel comes flat and just short of the ridiculous. Doris is a mere representative of the rootless American adolescent found floating all over the world, especially in the exciting cities and bohemian centers of Europe. She patters philosophy, makes a show of cynicism and sophistication; but she is at bottom pathetically ignorant, completely confused, and given to outbursts of neurotic self-rejection. When the curtain falls, she is understandably lost in the dark maze of the Roman catacombs, while her Italian count prepares to follow his fortune to Hong Kong and his biographer to return with his wife and son to the United States.

Emmanuel Obiechina. AfrF. Winter, 1966, pp. 108–9

[*The Catacombs*] achieves something of a collage effect in which at odd moments the newspaper accounts Demby reads and quotes super-impose themselves, however precariously, on the narrative—the effect is a hovering sense of world and time on even the most private situations. But the various strands of the novel crisscross in other places as well. Demby may intrude on his story with seemingly vagrant thoughts of his own, with a letter someone is writing, with a street scene being played far outside the main arena of the drama by persons whom the reader does not know—or more frequently he may break into any dramatic action of his principals by projecting what some of the other major or minor characters may be doing or thinking at the precise moment.

This simultaneity of presentation is presumably what Demby means when he speaks somewhere of "cubistic time." It is something almost animate—"time, always time, listening always listening, billions of years of imprisoned memory undistilled, electric-pointed stylus, plastic ballpoint pen." Actually, although the narrative generally unfolds in chronological order, Demby will, on occasion, shuttle back and forth in time in personal recollection or fantasy, or in a kind of Jungian race memory in which some odd newspaper item or disparate event suddenly assumes symbolic or archetypal importance. And yet the fragments do piece together. The novel begins and ends at the Easter season, the themes of death and resurrection become everywhere apparent like spirals within spirals.

If Demby's technique makes *The Catacombs* sound like something of a jigsaw, it is surprising to discover what intensely good reading the novel is.

Edward Margolies. Native Sons (Philadelphia,
J. B. Lippincott, 1968), pp. 182–83

Bill Trapp, Johnny, and David are the only ones [in *Beetlecreek*] in the swirl and mire of what is called life in Beetlecreek who have a chance to pull themselves out. The others have long since succumbed to the disease of decay. But Trapp, the old "carny," and his two new friends clearly see the options available to them. Trapp can give up his solitary exile and, through Johnny, can allow his trust in people and life to be restored. Johnny can accept the old man's friendship and thus repudiate the demands of the barber shop crowd and the Nightriders that he stay away from the "queer" hermit. And David, by abandoning his lifeless wife, Mary (whom he married because she was pregnant and he wanted to "do the right thing," and with whom he shares no love whatsoever), could return to the city for which both his education and his temperament make him better suited.

Demby sustains the drama of his plot with fine precision: Trapp moves closer to accepting people; Johnny moves closer to accepting the friendship of the recluse which will give them both life; and David seriously contemplates leaving Beetlecreek. But decay wins out. . . .

Demby's characters, like Ellison's protagonist in *Invisible Man*, are only incidentally black. While the black section of the town of Beetle-creek is the setting of Demby's novel, there is little significance in the author's focus on black life except, as Demby suggests, that the inanity of this black community simply reflects the corresponding inanity of the whole human community. It is this human community that Demby is probing, with its death-sustaining charade of organizations, rituals, and pettiness—a charade that an individual, given the capacity and courage to make personal moral choice, *can* repudiate, thereby redeeming himself for the *art* of living.

Roger Whitlow. Black American Literature (Chicago,
Nelson-Hall, 1973), pp. 123–25

DIOP, BIRAGO (1906–   )

SENEGAL

Birago Diop is indeed an enchanter, because he is a storyteller, a real one, a member of the race that is on the road to extinction in European countries, one of those people who grab hold of you, whether you like it or not, to make you see miracles through their eyes and listen to secrets through their ears. . . .

On some evenings—"for in the black country, tales are not to be told until nightfall"—the old storyteller Amadou Koumba told Diop tales he had already heard as a child; but Amadou also taught him others and embellished them with maxims and proverbs. Diop absorbed them, around the fire, while the tom-tom rolled, and the crowd beat on inverted calabashes in time to the chants. And the stories and legends bore fruit [in *Tales of Amadou Koumba*].

That is how we—the deaf, blind, busy, and gloomy—get to know Fari the She-Ass, Golo the Monkey, Kakatar the Chameleon, Koupou-Kala the Crab, Bouki the Hyena, Leuk the Hare. . . .

There is a whole universe in which human beings play an almost exclusively subordinate role. It is a whole world—a world that is very young and very old. It is old because it has wisdom and humor, but young because of its new ways of looking at things, and that extra-keen, dazzling faculty of perception which you only have at the dawn of life but which you retain if you are a poet.

Magdeleine Paz. *PA*. No. 5, 1948, pp. 890–91†

The first virtue of the Negro-African storyteller, as of any true artist, is to cling to reality, to *make things live* . . . Birago Diop, following the model of Amadou Koumba, depicts the men and animals of Africa such as we perceive them. Not only men and animals, but also the "bush" with its poor villages and immense sandy spaces. . . . But, beyond the silhouettes of the living, the storyteller reveals their *essences*, those inner realities that are their miseries and their dreams, their work and their worries, their passions. He shows us the role played by food in these villages that are periodically threatened by drought and famine.

Because nothing that *exists* is foreign to him, the Negro-African storyteller integrates into the traditional subjects those of today, especially those of "colonial" life: the Commandant de Cercle, the School, the Hospital, the Machine, the Marabout and the Missionary, trading and money. . . .

As a faithful disciple of Amadou Koumba, Diop renews his links with tradition and revives ancient fables and stories—in the original spirit and the original style. He renews them, however, by translating them into French, with an art that, while respectful of the genius of the French language—this "language of graciousness and courtesy"—at the same time preserves all the qualities of the Negro-African languages.

Léopold Sédar Senghor. Preface to Birago Diop,
Les nouveaux contes d'Amadou Koumba (Paris,
Présence Africaine, 1958), pp. 14–15, 22†

There is as much cunning and malice in [Diop's stories] as there is in Aesop and La Fontaine. One must hardly ever allow oneself to deviate from Nature and realism in order to please Man, even when confronting him with hard truths. With Diop's latest book [*New Tales of Amadou Koumba*] we have to deal with a three-fold moral criticism.

This is proved by his story called "The Bone." The central character is Mor Lame; his gluttony is not explained but is *dissected and exposed* with a skill which the reader should be allowed to unravel for himself. But will one say that the author does not mean to do the same for Moussa? Moussa is "the more-than-brother," the "Bok-m' bar" and incarnates parasitism which is the cancer of African families. . . .

The third complex criticism concerns the authority of Serigne-le-Marabout (a witch-doctor), against which nobody seems to have the right to rebel. This authority incarnates a shocking tradition which, alas, still exists. . . . Serigne is a cad, an evil-doer whose many negligences are castigated in the story "The Excuse." . . .

Must it be repeated for the benefit of those who have not yet understood, that the significance of Negro-African literature lies in the disinterment of abolished Negro cultural values? Birago Diop, certainly as wise as his master, Amadou Koumba, sets into his stories more than one jewel of Negro-African speech. . . . The author is equally a poet, and he proves that in his latest work he has mastered the secret of writing, which is perhaps the most difficult of all diagnoses.

Olympe Bhêly-Quénum. PA (English ed.). 8, 1, 1961, pp. 160–61

The *griot*'s [storyteller's] function in the community was as much to instruct as to entertain, and many of [the *Tales of Amadou Koumba*] are fables, pointing a clear moral, particularly those in which the characters are humans. This moral is often as direct as in traditional folk-tales. . . . In "The Inheritance," we have the most elaborate allegory of all the tales—a sort of multiple fable, with several layers of meaning. All man's existence and its many possible vicissitudes are illustrated symbolically by the fantastic adventures of the three sons in their pilgrimage. At the same time their father's mysterious bequests contain a message about community living, just sharing and a wise assessment of the value of worldly goods.

Sometimes Birago Diop's tales seem to have a more doubtful moral. Are we to believe that loyalty and diligence in a lifetime of service are always repaid by neglect and cruelty in old age? Is a good turn always repaid by evil? Is it so that we should rely on Falsehood if we are to get on in this life, as obviously Truth is a bad guide? And what of the more tragic element of "Little-Husband," where we see a love that dare not declare itself hound its object to death? In these tales, and particularly in those where conventional ethics are cynically reversed, Birago Diop adds the more sophisticated element of irony to the straightforward morality of the traditional fable, and proves himself more than the mere mouth-piece of his household *griot*. Just as he showed up many of the foibles of human nature in his portraits of man and animals, so here too there is satire, sometimes more subtle and deep-seated, of human and social weaknesses.

Dorothy S. Blair. Foreword to Birago Diop, Tales of
Amadou Koumba (London, Oxford University
Press, 1966), pp. xiii–xiv

Birago Diop, Master Griot, was born in 1906 at Ouakam, a suburb of Dakar. After completing his education at Toulouse and writing most of the poetry published later as *Lures and Lights,* he was a qualified veterinary doctor and, returning to Africa, he met Amadou Koumba N'Gom, the old griot, whose stories became the inspiration for almost all Diop's future work. . . .

His work as a veterinary officer, requiring an objective approach to men and animals, tempers the passion which he might feel through his involvement in the movement for African freedom. It also gives him the sense of dispassionate commitment to the problems, needs and weaknesses of men and animals which is expressed in his stories. In return, his involvement and feeling for animals and men must surely temper the clinical attitude of the practician. This, too, is seen in his stories; everything, good or evil, is approached with the same equable humility and humour.

Like La Fontaine, Diop has spent his life in close contact with men and animals, and in observing them. The "tales," so he tells us in the introduction to *Tales of Amadou Koumba,* were written to fulfil his own need to re-establish contact with his own country while he was in exile in France and then, later, when he was traveling through the Sudan, Upper Volta and Mauretania as veterinary officer and in Tunis as ambassador. Apart from the similarity of the vagabond life, there are many other comparisons to be made between the seventeenth century fabulist and Diop. In the first place, they share the same interest in popular, traditional tales. They have, too, the same capacity for objective but charitable assessment of human behaviour. Finally, and the point at which they meet as artists, both have a profound understanding and feeling for the rhythm and vocabulary of the French language; Diop, too, introduces African dialects and onomatopoeia into the stories to give greater effect, using them to establish links with the popular, oral tradition which is the source of his inspiration.

A. C. Brench. The Novelists' Inheritance in French
Africa (London, Oxford University Press, 1967),
pp. 14–15

[In *Tales of Amadou Koumba*] the woman is placed under guardianship, first that of her father, then that of her husband. Many tales illustrate the unlimited powers of the father. The father disposes of his daughter as he pleases; he can marry her off to anyone he likes. He does not have to answer to anyone. He does not take the trouble, in any of the tales in the book, to consult his daughter on the choice of her future husband. Tradition makes it the daughter's duty to bow to her father's will, as she later will have to submit to her husband's wishes when he gets the notion to take other wives. In "An Errand" Mor, Penda's father, decides to find an intelligent husband for his daughter; yet he does not choose the best way to reach this goal. Nowhere is Penda's consent to this marriage ever brought up. She seems rather like a kind of trophy, since she will belong to the man who will send Mor dried beef in return, by means of Bouki the Hyena, the intermediary. . . .

The marriage guardianship is maintained with equal strictness; but the clever wife can turn things to her advantage. Generally, she is not recognized as having any particular rights in marriage. She has only duties; at least, she can only assert her rights insofar as she carries out her duties perfectly, duties that exceed her rights to the point of practically canceling them out. This situation comes from a combination of traditional African and Islamic attitudes toward women. . . .

In Birago Diop's tales, humor and satire triumph; he leaves no room for sentimentality. . . . Since he does not have any intention of producing an ethnological document, Diop does not make the effort to define precisely woman's place in society. His indictment of women should not be taken literally. . . . These delightfully sketched portraits of women are too suffused with the author's humor to have originated from any motive other than the desire for healthy amusement.

Mohamadou Kane. Les contes d'Amadou Coumba
(Dakar, Université de Dakar, 1968),
pp. 75–76, 78–79†

Africans believe that although man's body decomposes after death to mingle eventually with the earth, the spirits of the dead continue to live an intense life, especially if the descendants strive to maintain the invisible existence of their ancestors through offerings, prayers, and sacrifices. After establishing this fact, specialists in African civilizations debated it at such lengths that they finally exhausted the topic. Nobody, however, aside from these experts, has described this concept better than Birago Diop, and he has succeeded by enhancing his descriptions with all the charms of poetry.

Diop accomplished this remarkable feat in "Breaths," his most beautiful poem, which is a living synthesis. "Breaths" contains at least three concepts: the superiority of objects over living beings; the presence of the dead in nature; and the idea of a vital universal force. . . .

Between the African storyteller and the poet of Negritude, between *Tales of Amadou Koumba* and *Lures and Lights*, there is a definite relationship, one combining profane and religious wisdom within the framework of a traditional Africa. . . . *Lures and Lights* shows reality in general and African reality in particular, through a double perspective that justifies its title.

René Piquion. *Ébène* (Port-au-Prince, Imprimerie
Henri Deschamps, 1976), pp. 179–81†

DIOP, DAVID (1927–1960)

SENEGAL

The works of this twenty-nine-year-old Senegalese writer display a lyricism directed toward practical goals. The poems he writes are militant, but . . . he bears essentially poetic arms. David Diop celebrates our African riches with humor and sensuality. His voice is always sober and concise. Yet his concern for exactness never stifles the final object of the poem. A spirit of healthy rebellion—sometimes underlying the poem, sometimes right on the surface—dominates his lyricism. His poems are a "hymn to the taut muscles," in which the lyrical vitality is never locked in a "coffin of words." . . .

In *Hammer Blows* "the heart and the brain are joined in the straight line of battle," and their union is a lesson in morality that we should remember as we see around us so many intellects who discredit the power of the heart in the name of a colorless and frozen intelligence. Through the culture of his people the poet finds the universal meaning of humanity. It is therefore not surprising that he brings us hope. . . .

Diop also knows how to write about the dizziness of physical love. To his eyes, the act of love is not a biological or recreational act but one of the most dazzling forms of participation in the world, in life. Love is a glorious dance in the sun by the senses, a dance during which the partners, who become equals through the incandescent virtues of blood, discover the riches they have in common. . . .

René Depestre. *PA*. Dec., 1956, pp. 110–11†

Hammer Blows is a thin booklet, but there is more in this short work which is disturbing in its compactness than in many modern *complete works*. Before qualifying this poetry—which is always a means of curtailing it or justifying what is foreign to it—let us recognise its fundamental merit, which is of being *poetry* above everything else. The closer a work comes to the *intrinsic poetic phenomenon*, the more it defies analysis. . . . This is true of David Diop's poetry. It is difficult to analyse by reason of its singular poetic compactness and its high content of poetry. The work is complete in itself and perfectly impervious. It is like those works of art whose beauty is beyond question but defies explanation.

On reflection, it may perhaps be suggested that this verbal achievement cannot be accounted for solely by talent and that unexplainable spontaneity causes a poet to write poems in the same manner as apple-trees yield apples. Indeed, on closer examination, one finds that the great impulse that underlies, illuminates and sanctifies David Diop's lyricism is beautiful as the daylight and life itself—Love. Love with a capital "L," in all its forms with all its subtleties and climes. Filial love . . . passionate love with that irresistible breath which comes from deeper than the heart . . . the love of the fighter who exorcises the subtle devils and unmystifies . . . the man who claims the penalty and assumes the crimes of others . . . and lastly outright love: love of life, rhythm, and grace. . . .

Hammer Blows is a work of profound faith in Man. The poet's African temperament breathes through these verses which are written in a generous, fiery vein.

PA (English ed.). June–Sept., 1960, pp. 244–45

In September 1960 the young poet David Diop died in a plane crash off Dakar. With him went his wife and all his manuscripts. At the age of thirty-three the most promising of West Africa's younger French poets was thus snatched from the scene, leaving only a single pamphlet of seventeen short poems behind him. That little pamphlet, *Hammer Blows*, was enough to establish David Diop as the most interesting and talented African poet of the fifties. Its appearance in 1956 aroused hopes of a career which never happened, but the unifying passion and fire of these few poems earn Diop a place here as the spokesman of a new age, the age for whom Senghor must appear a figure too deeply committed to the idea of a French Community uniting many peoples under the umbrella of a single civilization; the age, in short, of the Guinean Revolution.

David Diop was born in Bordeaux in 1927, the son of a Senegalese father and a Camerounian mother. His youth was spent partly in France, partly in West Africa. This background might superficially suggest the "cultural mulatto" far more strongly than Senghor's. In fact, we are now in a new political atmosphere. Diop uses his French culture, not to seek a reconciliation, a synthesis, or even a polarity of tensions, but to unleash an unrelenting hatred of Europe and all that it stands for.

Across centuries of bitterness and hate, he proclaims the dawn. It is a dawn to which Europe has contributed nothing but the prelude of darkness. But if the extremity of his position may repel in cold prose, the urgency and fervour of his verse give it the quality of a "Marseillaise." . . .

Gerald Moore. Seven African Writers (London, Oxford University Press, 1962), p. 18

David Diop's literary career began while he was still a student at the Lycée Marcelin Berthelot near Paris, in the late 1940's. His teacher, Léopold Sédar Senghor, was impressed with the youngster's "original inner life" and selected several early poems for inclusion in the history-making *Anthology of New Negro and Malagasy Poetry* (1948), which Jean-Paul Sartre prefaced with the famous essay "Black Orpheus." Later, David Diop contributed to *Présence africaine*, the cultural review of the Negro world edited in Paris, and participated in the Negro Writers and Artists Conference in Paris (1956) and Rome (1960). . . .

Until his untimely death, David Diop was emerging as a leader of the younger generation of "negritude" writers, those who reached their twenties in the postwar years. Many of his poems take up images, themes and accents already introduced by such older French-speaking West Indians in the negritude school as Jacques Roumain and Léon Damas. The influence of Aimé Césaire on David Diop's work is especially strong. While the younger poet's gifts cannot be compared with Césaire's, his work has a distinct personal stamp that stems from its directness, simplicity, and raw emotional power. The impact of every line, every word, is intentional. The angry young man meant his poems to "burst the eardrums of those who do not wish to hear them." . . .

The incident that inspired the poem ["To a Black Child"] is the 1955 lynching in Mississippi of a Chicago youngster named Emmet Till. David Diop had not been to America, but like nearly all Africans and West Indians in the negritude movement, he identified closely with the American Negro. He was deeply shocked by the Till affair, and by the fact that the murderers, though known, were acquitted in a trial that made a mockery of justice. . . .

Léopold Sédar Senghor had hoped to see his young countryman's talent mature, his bitterness and anger soften with understanding and compassion. It was President Senghor who pronounced the funeral oration in Dakar, recalling David's courage during the "long calvary" of his youth, the months and years of sickness [in sanatoriums with a recurrent illness that plagued him from childhood]. These, and the more purely psychic anguishes, David Diop has recorded in a series of lucid images: "ragged days with a narcotic taste," "anxious hangings on the edge of cliffs," and "sleep inhabited by alcohol," together with a love that brought "necklaces of laughter," his second marriage. "Through your long hospital nights," said President Senghor, "you identified with your crucified people. Your sufferings became their sufferings; your anguish, their anguish; your hope, their hope." Senghor's words were a generous tribute to a voice he found "hard and black as basalt," a voice destined never to reach maturity, but which sang ardently and unforgettably of "Africa my Africa."

Paulette J. Trout and Ellen Conroy Kennedy.
JNALA. Spring–Fall, 1968, pp. 76–78

According to Gerald Moore, David Diop "uses his French culture . . . to unleash an unrelenting hatred of Europe and all that it stands for." Considering the poet from another viewpoint, the editors of *Présence africaine* interpret Diop's "fundamental drive" as "Love." A more comprehensive description of Diop's inspiration might define him as a poet of passion. *Passion*, derived from the Latin *patior, pati, passus sum*, which means *suffer*, is not limited to erotic experience. Rather, it is violent and intense emotion which may run the gamut of feelings from hatred to love, and from the limits of pain to those of pleasure. . . .

"Negro Tramp" reveals several of the fundamental elements of Diop's passion: abomination of the whites ("their big mouths full of principles"); compassion for others who suffer; a belief in the fertility of revolt ("I excite the hurricane for future fields"); and an almost paradisiacal dream of what will come. In this way, Diop's fury against the oppressor provides the ferment for his dreams of revolution. . . .

But Diop's poetry goes beyond his hate. Often his poems fall into two-part structures. After his tirade against what oppresses him, he soars upward to hope. . . . Mediating between his hatred and his vision are the poet's compassion and faith in creative revolt. . . . As Diop treats it, rebellion is not an act of hatred; rather, it is a process of creative violence which includes notions of fertility, hope and even love. Through revolt he seeks to overcome his suffering and his subjection. Storms, symbolic of the forces of destruction, are for him images of reconstruction. He calls them "virile tempests." Often erotic imagery describes the passion of his re-creation since he regards revolt as fertile when nourished by love. In "The Vultures," for example, his hands, "profound like revolt," will "impregnate the belly of the earth." Hope, in the figure of spring, will be born in the flesh beneath his steps imbued with light. . . . Revolt merges with the erotic impulse in the passion of Diop's re-creation.

Enid H. Rhodes [Peschel]. ECr. Fall, 1970,
pp. 234–35, 237

DUNBAR, PAUL LAURENCE (1872–1906)

UNITED STATES

A month or two ago, while in Dayton, O., I attended a meeting of the Western authors. About half way down the informal programme the presiding officer announced the reading of a poem by Paul Dunbar. Just the name for a poet, thought I. Great was the surprise of the audience to see stepping lightly down the aisle between the rows of fluttering fans and the assembled beauty and wit of Dayton, a slender Negro lad, as black as the core of Cheops's pyramid. He ascended the rostrum with the coolness and dignity of a cultured entertainer and delivered a poem in a tone "as musical as is Apollo's lute." He was applauded to the echo between the stanzas, and heartily encored at the conclusion. He then disappeared from the hall as suddenly as he had entered it, and many were the whispered conjectures as to the personality of the man, and the originality of his verses, none believing it possible that one of his age and color could produce a thing of such evident merit.

After repeated inquiries I succeeded in locating the rising laureate of the colored race, and called upon him. He was an elevator boy in one of the down-town business blocks. I found him seated in a chair on the lower landing, hastily glancing at the July *Century*, and jotting down notes on a handy pencil tablet. . . .

Poor Dunbar! He deserves a better fate. Dayton, the terminus of the old underground railway, should be proud of him, and yet, with all his natural brilliancy and capability for better things, he is chained like a galley slave to the ropes of a dingy elevator at starvation wages. [Summer, 1892]

James Newton Matthews. Quoted in Jay Martin, ed.,
A Singer in the Dawn: Reinterpretations of Paul Laurence Dunbar (New York, Dodd, Mead, 1975),
pp. 14–15

It appeared to me [when I first read *Majors and Minors*], and it appears to me now, that there is a precious difference of temperament between the races which it would be a great pity ever to lose, and that this is best preserved and most charmingly suggested by Mr. Dunbar in those pieces of his where he studies the moods and traits of his race in its own accent of our English. We call such pieces dialect pieces for want of some closer phrase, but they are really not dialect so much as delightful personal attempts and failures for the written and spoken language. In nothing is his essentially refined and delicate art so well shown as in these pieces, which, as I ventured to say, described the range between appetite and emotion, with certain lifts far beyond and above it, which is the range of the race. He reveals in these a finely ironical perception of the negro's limitations, with a tenderness for them which I think so very rare as to be almost quite new. I should say, perhaps, that it was this humorous quality which Mr. Dunbar had added to our literature, and it would be this which would most distinguish him, now and hereafter. [1896]

> W. D. Howells. Introduction to *The Complete Poems*
> *of Paul Laurence Dunbar* (New York, Dodd, Mead,
> 1948), pp. ix–x

Folks from Dixie consists of distinct and brilliant little sketches of the various negro types of the South, most of them extremely amusing, a few of them pathetic, all of them cheerfully impersonal, as if written from the standpoint of an interested but not deeply sympathetic observer, with an eye for all picturesque accidents and an intuitive knowledge of the temperaments he has to portray. Of the imagination and profound sentiment pervading Mr. Chesnutt's writing, making itself most felt where least stress is laid upon it, there is barely a hint. . . .

Mr. Dunbar's other books of prose are novels in which the negro race plays no part. They have neither conspicuous merits nor conspicuous defects. Like Mr. Chesnutt's novels, both [*The Uncalled* and *The Love of Landry*] are free from any elaboration or complexity of plot, following a single thread of interest from the beginning to the end. Mr. Chesnutt and Mr. Dunbar have, indeed, despite their unlikeness, what we may call a marked family resemblance in this extreme simplicity, and in a certain homeliness of metaphor relieved at times by the quaintness of phraseology characteristic of the race that gives them their great distinction among writers. We feel that much of what they have written could not have been written in just the same way by anyone less than kin to the people whose individuality they bring before us with such remarkable truth. They have added to our complex literature an element entirely new and greatly to be prized.

> Elisabeth L. Cary. *The Book Buyer*. Aug, 1901, p. 28

[Dunbar] was a child of the city, a small city, true, where Nature was not so ruthlessly crushed away from the lives of men. There were trees and flowers near home, and a never-to-be-forgotten mill-race, which swirled through all his dreams of boyhood and manhood. Like the true poet that he was, he reached out and groped for the bigness of out-of-doors, divining all that he was afterwards to see, and in his earlier verse expressing his intuitions, rather than his observations.

Love of nature was there, but the power to express this love was not. Instead, he harked back to the feeling of the race, and intuitively put their aspirations into song. Tennyson and Lowell meant much to him, because they had expressed his yearnings for the natural world, and his soul yearned toward their verse. . . . The poet loved Tennyson, he walked with him in his earlier years, he confessed his indebtedness to him in his later days; he always praised him, and defended him hotly against the accusation of too much mere academic phrasing.

In the poem "Preparation" we see more of this groping toward the light; the urban child trying to throw off the meretriciousness of city life. Say what you will, or what Mr. Howells wills, about the "feeling the Negro life esthetically, and expressing it lyrically," it was in the pure English poems that the poet expressed *himself*. He may have expressed his race in the dialect poems; they were to him the side issues of his work, the overflowing of a life apart from his dearest dreams.

> Mrs. Paul Laurence Dunbar. In Mrs. Paul Laurence
> Dunbar, Prof. W. S. Scarborough, and Reverdy C.
> Ransom, *Paul Laurence Dunbar* (Philadelphia,
> Reverdy C. Ransom, 1914), pp. 6–7

As a man, Dunbar was kind and tender. In conversation he was brilliant and polished. His voice was his chief charm, and was a great element in his success as a reader of his own works. In his actions he was impulsive as a child, sometimes even erratic; indeed, his intimate friends almost looked upon him as a spoiled boy. He was always delicate in health. Temperamentally, he belonged to that class of poets who Taine says are vessels too weak to contain the spirit of poetry, the poets whom poetry kills, the Byrons, the Burnses, the De Mussets, the Poes.

To whom may he be compared, this boy who scribbled his early verses while he ran an elevator, whose youth was a battle against poverty, and who, in spite of almost insurmountable obstacles, rose to success? A comparison between him and Burns is not unfitting. The similarity between many phases of their lives is remarkable, and their works are not incommensurable. Burns took the strong dialect of his people and made it classic; Dunbar took the humble speech of his people and in it wrought music.

> James Weldon Johnson. Preface to James Weldon
> Johnson, ed., *The Book of American Negro Poetry*
> (New York, Harcourt, Brace, 1922), p. xxxv

Among the American writers who have been unable to judge what they could and could not do Dunbar is conspicuous. In 1898, the year of *Folks from Dixie*, he published his first novel, *The Uncalled*. It was to a certain extent autobiographical, an exposition of Dunbar's own ordeal in deciding whether he ought to enter the ministry. Since he was really writing about a personal experience, one cannot help wondering why he did not put himself into the story as a colored man. The action deals with the conflict in the mind of a white youth living in a small Ohio town who feels that he should not become a preacher but who is forced by circumstances into a seminary and then into the pulpit. There is not a single Negro character in the book.

As a story about whites written by a Negro it introduces us to the second type of fiction which the Negro of the period attempted. Such a type Dunbar should have painstakingly avoided. All of the bubbling spontaneity which he showed in his tales on blacks is replaced in *The Uncalled* by cheap conventional story-telling, with echoes of Dickens and the popular magazine, and with an English which is often downright faulty.

The book came as a great disappointment to Dunbar's admirers. Despite its weakness, it seems to have had some commercial success, and in 1900 Dunbar published a second novel in which all of the characters are whites, *The Love of Landry*. It is a story of Easterners, all treacly sentimentalists, who think that they find the sublime beauty of reality on a Colorado ranch. It was, if that is possible, even a poorer performance than *The Uncalled*.

Vernon Loggins. *The Negro Author* (New York,
Columbia University Press, 1931), pp. 316–17

Dunbar's conception of his art was based on his theory of life. He felt that he was first of all a man, then an American, and incidentally a Negro. To a world that looked upon him primarily as a Negro and wanted to hear from him simply in his capacity as a Negro, he was thus a little difficult to understand. He never regarded the dialect poems as his best work, and, as he said in the eight lines entitled "The Poet," when one tried to sing of the greatest themes in life, it was hard to have the world praise only "a jingle in a broken tongue." His position was debatable, of course, but that was the way he felt. . . .

To a later school of Negro writers, one more definitely conscious of race, Dunbar thus appears as somewhat artificial. The difference is that wrought by the World War. About the close of that conflict Marcus Garvey, by a positively radical program, made black a fashionable color. It was something not to be apologized for, but exploited. Thenceforth one heard much about "the new Negro," and for a while Harlem was a literary capital. In Dunbar's time, however, black was not fashionable. The burden still rested upon the Negro to prove that he could do what any other man could do, and in America that meant to use the white man's technique and meet the white man's standard of excellence. It was to this task that Dunbar addressed himself. This was the test that he felt he had to satisfy, and not many will doubt that he met it admirably.

Benjamin Brawley. *Paul Laurence Dunbar* (Chapel
Hill, University of North Carolina Press, 1936),
pp. 76–77

When propaganda enters into prose fiction it acquires necessarily some of the broad solidity of the prosaic medium, and this firm quality immediately puts the reader on the defensive. The reader's reaction is as of one being gulled, being shown a thing for the good of his soul. These are the things one comes to feel in too many of the stories of Dunbar. Like a leaden ghost, Purpose treads the print of "Silas Jackson," "The Ingrate," "One Man's Fortunes," and "At Shaft 11." Not only is the technique of the stories faulty, but plausible, character-derived motivation and convincing situation are lacking. The story that brushes aside esthetic ends must be faultless in construction and style in order to succeed. It must captivate by sheer perfection of form. Dunbar was not aware of this. He brought to this difficult art only a zest in the message of his serious tales, and an instinctive sense of the humor inherent in certain situations in his burlesque stories. The latter are saved from failure; but a story representative of the former, "The Strength of Gideon," with its powerful theme and well-defined plot, boils off in the end to a watery pottage.

The gem of Dunbar's stories is "Trustfulness of Polly." In it Dunbar did not seek to express the Negro, but to re-create him. It was written in 1899, five years before his writing career ended, but he never again found such perfect focus of characterization, motivation, theme, plot, and style. It is a story of the low-life school, a type that was not to become popular until twenty years after Dunbar's death. It deals with that insidious evil (then as now) in the life of the New York Negro, the policy game. "The Trustfulness of Polly" is the first story of Negro low-life in New York written by a Negro. Not only is it significant as the forerunner of the long list of low-life stories from [Claude McKay's] *Home to Harlem* to [George Washington Lee's] *Beale Street*, but it presaged the courageous, if misled, objectivity with which the post-war Negro artist was to see the life of his people.

J. Saunders Redding. *To Make a Poet Black* (Chapel
Hill, University of North Carolina Press, 1939),
pp. 60–61

Catering to the demands of publishers and readers of his time, Dunbar generally evaded themes such as those presented in Chesnutt's novels and usually specialized either in the treatment of white American life or in the perpetuation of the plantation tradition. Three of his novels—*The Uncalled, The Love of Landry*, and *The Fanatics*—deal almost entirely with white characters; and the fourth, *The Sport of the Gods*, though a promising naturalistic study, illustrates the plantation-school concept that the Negro becomes homesick and demoralized in the urban North. . . .

Though amateurish in execution, *The Sport of the Gods* is Dunbar's worthiest effort in fiction and suggests abilities which possibly did not achieve fruition because of the author's early death. Written under the influence of naturalism, which [Vernon L.] Parrington defines as "pessimistic realism," *The Sport of the Gods* follows Émile Zola's *Nana* (1880), Stephen Crane's *Maggie: A Girl of the Streets* (1893), Frank Norris' *McTeague* (1899), and other novels in which man is conceived as a powerless figure in an amoral and careless world. Showing race prejudice as an all-destructive virus, the book reveals social corruption in the South as well as in the North. In the Southern small town, interracial distrust is exposed, and the vaunted chivalry of Dixie gentlemen is debunked through the characterization of Francis and Maurice Oakley. In the New York setting, inexperienced Negro youth are pictured in a treacherous environment which deterministically produces degeneration and disaster. By treating the challenging and comparatively unworked Harlem low-life scene, Dunbar analyzed a background that was later to intrigue Claude McKay, Carl Van Vechten, and other writers of the 1920's.

Hugh Gloster. *Negro Voices in American Fiction*
(Chapel Hill, University of North Carolina
Press, 1948), pp. 46, 50–51

During the years between the Civil War and World War I, Negro poetry produced no personality that can be set beside Dunbar's. His inadequacies may be deplored, yet one must admit that none of his contemporaries had the same delicate sensibility, the variety of inspiration, or the extraordinary feeling for rhythm and musicality that served him equally well in his English verses and in his dialect poetry. Nor did anyone else suffer as he did from the sense of his own weaknesses. In short, throughout this long period he remained the only genuine lyric poet. . . .

Dunbar's death marked the end of an era. Although he survived by a few years the century of his birth, the attitude he embodied to the very end was that of a bygone age. It was the ambivalent attitude of the Negro during Reconstruction—uncertain of himself, subservient, and still a quasi-prisoner within the mentality that two hundred and fifty years of slavery had transformed into second nature. In addition to that, the flaccid, falsely distinguished poetry of the late nineteenth century, which constitutes so large a part of Dunbar's work, was also headed for extinction as a result of the renewal which, beginning in 1912, would so significantly alter the appearance of American poetry. Thus the first prominent poet of the black race was at the same time the last representative of a world doomed to disappear. [1963]

Jean Wagner. *Black Poets of the United States*
(Urbana, University of Illinois Press, 1973),
pp. 127, 149

Dunbar is probably still the best-known Negro poet among Negroes. For many years he was a race hero in the company of Joe Louis and Booker T. Washington, and his disfavor (like theirs) among the intelligentsia may take a while to spread to the lower orders. He was a successful magazine poet of the turn of the century (he died at thirty-four), sponsored by William Dean Howells; a master sentimentalist who wrung the heart of a simpler America. Today, reading his collected poems—three hundred pages of Golden Book moralism, purple poesy, and dialect pastorals in the James Whitcomb Riley vein, of hometown nostalgia and barbershop wisdom ("Keep a-Pluggin' Away") is like eating jars of peanut butter. He was lionized for his "plantation nigger" narratives ("When de Co'n Pone's Hot," "When Malindy Sings"), which even uncritical Negroes might find hard to take today. Only two or three poems—"We Wear the Mask," "Sympathy"—appear to hide genuine, adult, and still honorable emotions. . . .

Dunbar wrote a number of his harmless "plantation nigger" folk stories in a manner less aggressively sentimental than that of his poems, stories told half in dialect, half in an orotund, authorial-declamatory voice. Two or three make what is, for Dunbar, strong anti-slavery or anti-lynching protests; but they are outbalanced by a far greater number of reactionary pieces or worse, depicting plantation darkies as jolly children all, whose best friend—even after Emancipation—was always Ol' White Massa.

David Littlejohn. *Black on White* (New York,
Grossman, 1966), pp. 23–25

Paul Laurence Dunbar is a natural resource of our people. He, like all our old prophets and preachers, has been preserved by our little people. Those who could command words and images, those whose pens thundered across the pages, those whose voices boomed from lecterns, those who set policy for our great publications then, as now, were quite silent. Not ever quite knowing what to do about one of America's most famous poets, when they spoke his name it was generally to condemn his dialect poetry—as if black people aren't supposed to laugh, or more as if Dunbar's poems were not the best examples of our plantation speech. One gets recitation after explanation of Dunbar's poetry, his love of his "white poems," his hatred of his need to please the white critics, but something rings quite hollow to me. I refuse to believe Paul Dunbar was ashamed of "Little Brown Baby." The poem has brought too much happiness to me. I categorically reject a standard that says "A Negro Love Song" should not make me feel warm inside. . . .

Dunbar preserved a part of our history. And accurately. It would be as foolish to say all blacks struggled against slavery as it would to say all acquiesced to it. The truth lies somewhere in the blending. Perhaps Dunbar's greatest triumph is that he has survived all those who would use his gift for their own dead-end purposes.

Nikki Giovanni. Afterword to Jay Martin, ed.,
*A Singer in the Dawn: Reinterpretations of Paul
Laurence Dunbar* (New York, Dodd, Mead, 1975),
pp. 243–44

EKWENSI, CYPRIAN (1921–   )

NIGERIA

The hero of *People of the City* is Amusa Sango, crime reporter for the *West African Sensation* by day and dance-band leader by night. He has only recently arrived in the big city (Lagos, I imagine) and finds the mixture of new experiences a bit too rich and indigestible. So do most of the younger generation, among them Miss Dupeh Martins, aged sixteen, who is content to "hang about the city hotels and ice-cream bars with not a penny in her handbag, rather than marry a farmer with a thousand pounds a year." She, and her boy friends in their 25*s*. ties, and the petty racketeers who peddle penicillin injections, seem almost indistinguishable from European or American delinquents, but primitive Bush influences, though less strong than you might have expected, are plainly felt.

There is not much story but plenty of action. Sango witnesses a mining riot and a *crime passionnel*, has some love-affairs, and leaves for the Gold Coast (reputed land of freedom and enterprise) with a lost girl named Beatrice. The picture may be incomplete but you feel it is true so far as it goes. Mr. Ekwensi writes with a curiously impressive artlessness. Some of his dialogue is excellent.

Maurice Richardson. NSN. Nov. 27, 1954, p. 718

[*People of the City*] is a simple tale, and yet a genuine one, for . . . Ekwensi is a journalist, and he notices and records accurately and honestly, the result being that this novel probably portrays Lagos life more accurately than any other piece of serious writing in Nigeria. It is a sympathic portrayal, and one that captures the charm, humor and pathos that is at the heart of this section of Lagos society. Therefore, while Ekwensi does not create he does record. But his language is journalese, and the influence of America is found equally in his vocabulary and his female characters. Nevertheless even here he is probably reflecting the pseudo-American behaviour of the Lagos younger set today, striving to be part of the modern world with all its relaxations and moral sophistications, and breaking away from any suggestion of association with the strict rules of tribal behaviour.

Jagua Nana, Ekwensi's second major novel, is an amusing and well-written story about a Lagos prostitute, who, fearing her advancing years (though confident of her charm and beauty), tries to marry a man "on the way up." Her great desire is respectability, which she interprets to mean "class." Her pursuit of the young school-teacher, Freddy, and eventual disillusionment form the basis of the novel. Again Ekwensi's journalistic outlook has given this book an authenticity that is appealing and there is also a developing sympathy for the simpler and less fortunate members of society. As a satire of certain aspects of Lagos life, political campaigns, the secret habits of "big men," life in crowded tenements, and even the activities of the British Council, *Jagua Nana* has considerable merit, though it tends towards sentimentality in the closing stages.

Martin Banham. *REL*. April, 1962, pp. 91–92

Those who know Ekwensi's *When Love Whispers* and the reasons for its popularity when it appeared several years ago will not be surprised at either *People of the City* or *Jagua Nana*. Ekwensi began his writing career as a pamphleteer. Writing, it is true, was to him then, as now, a way of expressing himself. But he wrote to a formula (it would be interesting to know how he inherited it) for a public that could neither endure the full-length novel nor appreciate the taut and delicate balance of the short story. Because he was the greater artist than the other pamphleteers of the time, and also because perhaps he sought recognition of a greater order than he could have realised from these publications, Ekwensi turned away from pamphleteering, as such, to write the first modern Nigerian novel.

Even so, the background out of which Ekwensi's *People of the City* emerged is not difficult to trace. The episodic nature of the plot, its lack of organic development, its very "innocence" can be traced to the formula of the pamphlet. The story itself may be engaging, but the incidents, as they pile up, appear to have no further motivation than the good fortune that some principal characters are involved. Hence, too, though several episodes are powerfully narrated, the total performance is somewhere short of being impressive. This failure some have seen as a "masterly blend of ingenuousness and sophistication"! Of course it is no such thing. The fact is that Ekwensi has not grown clear of the world of the newspapers and of pamphleteering. . . .

The peculiar favour which *People of the City* received was in no small measure connected with the fact that Ekwensi was tackling rather seriously the problem of the African city. Indeed the image of Ekwensi now current is that of the sophisticated and blunt man of the 20th century, not of the folklorist and the primitivist. I am therefore inclined to see the publication of *Burning Grass* as an important event, and in a way, a happy one. It represents, in germ, an awareness (I hope) on the part of Ekwensi that fiction is not always the story of prostitutes and bandleaders.

M. J. C. Echeruo. NigM. Dec., 1962, pp. 63, 65

Ekwensi's *People of the City* is a novel of urban manners in what one might call the analytic, as opposed to the synthetic, sense. Like Balzac or Dickens, Ekwensi is intrigued by the relentless potential honesty of "the facts." But he does not at the same time weave a coherent veil of illusion, he does not organize the appearances into a coherent expression of current social values beneath which the realities starkly lie. *People of the City*, in its form, is a novel of bad manners, a rogue's tale, really, despite its superimposed plot which is designed to show to a susceptible popular audience the moral evolution of the hero, "exemplary" in the Onitsha market sense. . . .

People of the City gives a tantalizing sense of the extraordinary possibilities of hybrid city life in West Africa as material for fabrication and scrutiny in the novel. Those two basic and complementary drives, the hectic pursuit of pleasure and the equally hectic flight from poverty and fear, which lie right at the social foundations of all modern city life, are here and there disclosed and in all of the complexity of their new-old African setting. But Ekwensi cannot sustain and develop these insights, and it is too bad that, so far, his first is also his most exciting book.

Judith Illsley Gleason. This Africa (Evanston, Ill.,
Northwestern University Press, 1965), pp. 126, 130

Ekwensi's writing may be described as superior yellow journalism. It was no less than this twenty years ago and is no more than this today. Ekwensi has always had an eye for the lurid, an ear for the strident, a taste for the spicy, and a stomach for everything. As a consequence, his novels have been racy, action-packed melodramas, full of sound and fury but empty of substance and significance. His latest novel, *Iska*, is no exception.

Iska records the ups and downs of a beautiful Ibo girl, Filia Enu, who secretly marries a Hausa civil servant in Kaduna, capital of Northern Nigeria. When he is killed in an Ibo-Hausa barroom brawl, she moves to Lagos, capital of Western Nigeria, and begins to associate with prostitutes, politicians, and pot-smoking neer-do-wells. . . .

Filia Enu is a Nigerian Moll Flanders but Ekwensi, alas, is not a Nigerian Defoe. He lacks not only the genius which enabled Defoe to build a lasting monument out of the rubble of his heroine's life, but also the art and craft which a novelist needs to cement such fragments into a coherent, harmonious structure. Filia herself cannot pose as a model of neat construction. Her fall into sin and later regeneration are entirely unconvincing because Ekwensi seems unable to decide whether to blame her or Lagos for her plight. She is allowed to waver too freely between good and bad. Above all, she lacks the flesh, blood, sweat and perfume that make Jagua Nana, the happy harlot heroine of one of Ekwensi's earlier novels, so appealing.

But even with these defects, *Iska* is not an entirely unsatisfactory reading experience. Ekwensi's writing, though flecked with clichés, always has some bounce and sparkle. *Iska* has the merit of being topical as well.

Bernth Lindfors. AT. June, 1966, p. 29

Each of Ekwensi's books forms a complete unit in itself, and they are all different; only perhaps *Jagua Nana* and *People of the City* resemble each other. Ekwensi applies his versatile mind to any type of topic. The range is from politics, as in *Beautiful Feathers*, to a book of purely anthropological interest like *Burning Grass*; and the author adopts a style appropriate to his subject. He is sometimes criticised for writing in styles that are too sophisticated for West Africa and that seem to have been adopted primarily for the foreign market. It is also said that the style and content of his books are such that they could equally well have been written by a foreigner who knew Nigeria well. This is only partly true. It is true that Ekwensi adopts a more catholic approach to writing than most West African writers. Present events seem more important to him than the obscure glories of the past. What he holds dear is literary efficiency and the ability of the creative artist to reflect the lives and aspirations of his society; and indicate the way the future may go. . . .

Cyprian Ekwensi's realism is deliberate. His aim is not to make city life look more romantic or attractive than it is, but to present it as he knows and sees it. It is no secret that his attitude has offended many in high places. Man at times lives in ignorance of himself and does not always like to be told his failings. Ekwensi deserves our applause for having the courage to open the eyes of city dwellers to the evils which they are perpetrating and to bring to their notice the possible undesirable effects of a social life which is morally lax and decadent.

Odalele Taiwo. An Introduction to West African
Literature (London, Thomas Nelson, 1967,)
pp. 61, 162

The political question posed [in *Beautiful Feathers*] is this: how should an African nation-state attempt to implement the concept of continental unity? Achebe had failed to portray fully the vast political forces in motion in a nation-state; in *Beautiful Feathers* Ekwensi is no more successful in presenting the complex subject of Pan-Africanism with all its multilayered possibilities. . . .

But *Beautiful Feathers* is concerned with more than Pan-Africanism. Ekwensi emphasizes the social immorality at work in society not only by presenting many scenes of infidelity but by making the wife of a young, idealistic, and highly respected Pan-African leader, Wilson Iyari, unfaithful to him. Thus, the second problem posed in the novel is this: how is it possible that a man who is working for and stands as a symbol of African solidarity cannot achieve the same solidarity in a much smaller unit, that of his family? . . .

Beautiful Feathers is a slight novel where minor incidents are related in language more suited to a weightier, denser treatment of the subject of Pan-Africanism.

Wilfred Cartey. *Whispers from a Continent: The
Literature of Contemporary Black Africa* (New York,
Random House, 1969), pp. 193, 195

Ekwensi's limitations as a novelist are many and it is as well to mention them at the outset. He has often declared that he considers himself a writer of popular fiction, and if we define popular fiction to be that which pleases or is read by a class of reader commonly indifferent to literature, we understand that Ekwensi directs his work to a wider audience than, say, Achebe, Clark or Soyinka, and suggests, as well, the limitations that work may possess. His novels do not possess the unique qualities which are inherent in works of literature—a formal beauty of design and execution which lead the reader on to a new awareness of the greater potentialities of self. Rather, Ekwensi's work is concerned with the external features of modern Nigerian life, especially the life in and of the city. His heroes seek for but never make profound discoveries about themselves. Perhaps this accounts for the fact that in each of the full-length novels we find the same kind of hero—almost a stereotype—who, progressively lacking energy, becomes unconvincing as a character.

His plots suffer in the same way: just as we find the same kind of hero in each of the novels, so we find him (or her) in more or less the same circumstances. Moreover, Ekwensi pays little attention to his plots and his novels are full of inconsistencies and contradictions. . . .

Yet despite these limitations—which are considerable—Ekwensi is a serious novelist whose writing reflects his serious concern with some of the most pressing problems facing modern Nigeria. Ekwensi's fiction represents, almost exclusively, an attempt to come to terms with the

chaotic formlessness and persistent flux of the modern Nigerian city—
that is, with Lagos.

Douglas Killam. In Bruce King, ed.,
Introduction to Nigerian Literature
(London, Evans Brothers, 1971), pp. 79–80

Unlike Achebe, Ekwensi usually describes individualities, not literary
types, and is more successful in his psychological analyses of women
than Achebe is. His novels are less abstracted from reality and represent
more immediate accounts of real events. They are more journalistic,
more in line with the orientation of Nigerian descriptive realism. Their
true-to-life nature is strictly preserved and the characters' way of speaking is carefully presented as authentically as possible. . . .

Special attention should be paid to Ekwensi's long efforts to convey
his ideas in English as effectively as possible. Being a pioneer of Nigerian fiction, he naturally set examples for his West African anglophone followers, but he was handicapped by the fact that the English
language was foreign both to him and to his surroundings. The . . .
introduction of pidgin into dialogues in *Jagua Nana* and some other
books was an attempt to "Africanize" Nigerian fiction in English to a
generally acceptable extent. It was a compromise in practice and hardly
any theoretical conclusions can be drawn from it, because pidgin is not
standardized. It is definitely less understandable than Standard English
to readers overseas and, after all, its application will always depend on
the writer's desires and tastes. . . .

While a certain compromise can be found in Ekwensi's language,
none exists in the content of his novels. He was asked, of course, why he
was so critical of his compatriots living in Lagos and why he wrote so
little criticism of the colonialists. This question is answered by his fiction, which shows little interest in the problem of racial oppression in
Africa—a problem so intensely discussed in multi-racial communities
and countries still dominated by the whites. But the situation in Nigeria
is different and Ekwensi deals with other issues. Unlike most of his
Nigerian colleagues, he rarely portrays the disintegration of the old
tribal society in a direct way (*Burning Grass* pursues a different purpose
and constitutes an exception among his novels). While many other
Nigeran writers describe villagers in the countryside, Ekwensi is interested chiefly in the fates of these villagers after their arrival in the city
and during the process of their urbanization.

Vladimír Klíma. In Vladimír Klíma, Karel František
Růžička, and Petr Zima, *Black Africa: Literature and
Language* (Dordrecht, Netherlands, D. Reidel,
1976), pp. 106–7

ELLISON, RALPH (1914–   )

UNITED STATES

Fleeing toward Hell, Dante beheld a man whose voice seemed weak from a long silence, and he cried to him, saying, "Have pity on me, whoever thou art, shade or real man!" Shade or real man? Visible or invisible? The Invisible Man [in *Invisible Man*] would have smiled in recognition if hailed like that. He lives, he tells us, in an underground hole. To fill this dark hole with light, he burns 1,369 bulbs. He burns them free. A fine Dostoevskyan touch. In his "Notes from the Underground" Dostoevsky says: "We are discussing things seriously: but if you won't deign to give me your attention, I will drop your acquaintance. I can retreat into my underground hole."

The Invisible Man is also discussing things seriously. His report in this novel might be subtitled, "Notes from Underground America," or "The Invisible Black Man in the Visible White Man's World." That is part of his story, but the deeper layer, revealed, perhaps, in spite of himself, is the invisible man becoming visible. The word, against all of the odds, becoming the flesh. Neither black nor white flesh, however, for where the color line is drawn with profundity, as it is here, it also vanishes. There is not much to choose, under the skin, between being black and invisible, and being white, currently fashionable and opaque. . . .

Perhaps it is the nature of the pilgrim in hell to see the visible world and its inhabitants in allegorical terms. They do not exist, so much as they represent. They appear to be forces, figures of good and evil, in a large symbolical frame, which makes for order, but diminishes our interest in their predicament as people. This may well be the price of living underground. We are deprived of uniqueness, no light illuminates our individuality.

The reader who is familiar with the traumatic phase of the black man's rage in America, will find something more in Mr. Ellison's report. He will find the long anguished step toward its mastery. The author sells no phony forgiveness. He asks none himself. It is a resolutely honest, tormented, profoundly American book.

Wright Morris. *NYT*. April 13, 1952, p. 5

My hat is off to the author [of *Invisible Man*], his overall skill and—with some reservations—to his most original conception, as also to his guts and integrity. But alas, did I say it was interesting after, say, page 245. I wouldn't quarrel with its necessary complexity, but in my opinion

the book itself—with a few miraculous cloudbursts of recovery—begins
to fail and become arider and arider, even fall to pieces (pardon my
mixed metaphors) approximately from this point on. I more or less
dissent too from the opinions expressed by certain reviewers of the book
in this regard. However noble the multiple intention, the book itself
begins to fail as a work of art, in my opinion, though fragmentarily still
it can still show itself a hell of a sight better than many or most novels.
Possibly this is because the beginning, likewise the enclosing theme, is so
good. Either that or he leads you to expect too much of himself. But the
irony utterly ceases to be out of the top drawer, becomes somewhat
derivative finally. The reporting of the communist brotherhood is as
boring very often as their dialectics probably were in real life. One has
been invited so often to these cocktail parties of well-heeled communists
before and the essential and important points are too often clouded as a
result of the technical out-of-touchness of the writing. . . .

The race riot, so highly praised by others, strikes me as at worse
resembling one of those very early Soviet futuristic films such as *Ar-
senal*, where symbol and the thing symbolized, man and meaning and
photographic virtuosity are so confused that it is only your respect for
the ingenuity of the director and the hope of what he may do at the next
moment that keeps you from leaving the theatre out of exasperation
with the sheer inertia and muddle he imposes: but above all this I had
the feeling that here Ellison was not writing what he wanted to and
knew it. My final feeling is, though, that his final remark is universally
justified and that in the main he does, like Kafka, strike at the soul of
man himself. At least he strikes at mine, and I shall certainly prize the
book as the work of someone I feel may be important indeed. [May,
1952]

Malcolm Lowry. In Harvey Breit and
Margerie Bonner Lowry, eds., *Selected
Letters of Malcolm Lowry* (Philadelphia,
J. B. Lippincott, 1965,) pp. 316–18

It is commonly felt that there is no strength to match the strength of
those powers which attack and cripple modern mankind. And this feeling is, for the reader of modern fiction, all too often confirmed when he
approaches a new book. . . . But what a great thing it is when a brilliant
individual victory occurs, like Mr. Ellison's [in *Invisible Man*] proving
that a truly heroic quality can exist among our contemporaries. People
too thoroughly determined—and our institutions by their size and force
too thoroughly determine—can't approach this quality. That can only be
done by those who resist the heavy influences and make their own
synthesis out of the vast mass of phenomena, the seething, swarming

body of appearances, facts, and details. From this harassment and threatened dissolution by details, a writer tries to rescue what is important. Even when he is most bitter, he makes by his tone a declaration of values and he says, in effect: "There is something nevertheless that a man may hope to be." This tone, in the best pages of *Invisible Man*, those pages, for instance, in which an incestuous Negro farmer tells his tale to a white New England philanthropist, comes through very powerfully; it is tragicomic, poetic, the tone of the very strongest sort of creative intelligence. . . .

In our society Man—Himself—is idolized and publicly worshipped, but the single individual must hide himself underground and try to save his desires, his thoughts, his soul, in invisibility. He must return to himself, learning self-acceptance and rejecting all that threatens to deprive him of his manhood.

This is what I make of *Invisible Man*. It is not by any means faultless; I don't think the hero's experiences in the Communist party are as original in conception as other parts of the book, and his love affair with a white woman is all too brief, but it is an immensely moving novel and it has greatness.

Saul Bellow. *Cmty.* June, 1952, pp. 608–9

In the thirty years' span of my active reviewing experience, there have been in my judgment three points of peak development in Negro fiction by Negro writers. In 1923 from a relatively low plateau of previous problem fiction, Jean Toomer's *Cane* rose to unprecedented artistic heights. . . . In 1940, Richard Wright's skillful sociological realism [in *Native Son*] turned a hard but brilliant searchlight on Negro urban life in Chicago and outlined the somber tragedy of Bigger Thomas in a well-studied setting of Northside wealth and Southside poverty. . . .

But 1952 is the significant year of Ellison's *Invisible Man*, a great novel, although also not without its artistic flaws, sad to say. Ralph Ellison is a protege of Wright, who predicted for him a bright literary future. Written in a style of great force and originality, although its talent is literally smothered with verbosity and hyperbole, *Invisible Man* is both in style and conception a new height of literary achievement. . . . Stylistically [it] unrolls in a volcanic flow of vivid, sometimes livid imagery, a tour de force of psychological realism. A double symbolic meaning piled on top of this realism gives the book its distinctive and most original tone and flavor: *Invisible Man* is actually a surrealistic novel because of this, and but for its lack of restraint would rank among the very best of the genre. But the unrestrained bravado of treatment, riding loose rein at full gallop most of the time and the overprecious bravura of phrase and diction weight it down where otherwise it would soar in well-controlled virtuosity. Many readers will be shocked at Ellison's daring franknesses and dazed by his emotional intensity but these are an integral part of the book's great merit. For once, too, here is a Negro writer capable of real and sustained irony. *Invisible Man*, evidently years in the making, must not be Ralph Ellison's last novel.

Alain Locke. *Phylon*. 14, 1, 1953, pp. 34–35

[In *Invisible Man*] elements of farce, tragedy, pity, hatred, and love are mixed with a vivid exhilaration for which I really cannot find a parallel. An American critic quoted on the wrapper compares Ellison to "Kafka or Joyce," and there are certainly pages of writing here which justify the mention of such names. All the same, Ellison's strength lies in his being the opposite of writers who through a limited contemporary experience have created an intellectual picture of modern civilisation. He has had an immense experience of what it is like to be an *object* acted upon by modern conditions, which have had the result of beating him into a white-hot rage of sensibility and thought. His great achievement is that he is not content to be a "social realist" learning the lesson of oppression and building up a solid case against social evil. He becomes a humanist who sees the farcical side of the most tragically cruel social situations, who caricatures suffering until it becomes a warmly rich part of the human comedy, and who realises that rebels are as mean and power-seeking and greedy as the people or forces they are rebelling against. . . .

Mr. Ellison is as much a born American writer as, say, Thomas Wolfe; and perhaps he has Wolfe's weaknesses of a certain disorderliness and lack of control, and of being too attracted by violence. But the vivid ease with which his large scenes of movement are handled is truly remarkable.

Stephen Spender. *List*. Jan. 15, 1953, p. 115

Ellison's protagonist [in *Invisible Man*] is invisible not through his own desire but through the force of circumstances; not because he passes by unnoticed but because nobody manages to understand his true spiritual identity.

This incomprehension arises from the fact that everyone sees the protagonist through a screen whose existence they are unaware of, just as they are unaware of the attempts they make to make the protagonist fit into the pattern on that screen (actually, a preconceived psychological pattern), which the character in his humanity does not fit into at all. . . .

The protagonist does not have a name. In this way, I believe Ellison suggests that he is viewed by the many other characters with whom he comes into contact, not as a distinct individual but as an anonymous (because undifferentiated) member of a certain race, in this case, the black race. This undifferentiated anonymity is complemented by the vastness of the panorama presented in the novel. Unlike the majority of contemporary American novelists, who tend to concentrate on a limited number of characters or on a particular class of society and to condense into a few events the writer's feelings and conception of life (in this tendency Hemingway's influence can be recognized), Ellison uses a technique that seems closer to the nineteenth century: he creates a vast tableau in which the protagonist moves through incidents too numerous to be summarized. [Oct. 27, 1953]

Salvatore Rosati. L'ombra dei padri (Rome, Edizioni
di Storia e Letteratura, 1958), pp. 136–38†

That Ralph Ellison is very good is dull to say. He is essentially a hateful writer: when the line of his satire is pure, he writes so perfectly that one can never forget the experience of reading him—it is like holding a live electric wire in one's hand. But Ellison's mind, fine and icy, tuned to the pitch of a major novelist's madness, is not always adequate to mastering the forms of rage, horror, and disgust which his eyes have presented to his experience, and so he is forever tumbling from the heights of pure satire into the nets of a murderously depressed clown, and *Invisible Man* insists on a thesis which could not be more absurd, for the Negro is the least invisible of all people in America. (That the white does not see each Negro as an individual is not so significant as Ellison makes it—most whites can no longer see each other at all. Their experience is not as real as the experience of the Negro, and their faces have been deadened in the torture chamber of the overburdened American conscience. They have lost all quick sense of the difficulty of life and its danger, and so they do not have faces the way Negroes have faces—it is rare for a Negro who lives it out to reach the age of twenty without having a face which is a work of art.)

Where Ellison can go, I have no idea. His talent is too exceptional to allow for casual predictions, and if one says that the way for Ellison may be to adventure out into the white world he knows so well by now, and create the more difficult and conceivably more awful invisibility of the white man—well, it is a mistake to write prescriptions for a novelist as gifted as Ellison.

Norman Mailer. Advertisements for Myself (New
York, G. P. Putnam's Sons, 1959), p. 471

Invisible Man is a novel of salvation, a salvation won with difficulty through a series of ordeals. The hero is at first docile, allowing himself to be soothed by the double illusion of submissiveness and "social re-sponsibility." Then the harsh lesson of reality shows him the need for struggle and rebellion. But the rebel may be deceived by illusory utopias. It is only when he has rejected yet another of mankind's deceptions or distortions—political action—that he acquires a kind of clear-sighted-ness. This clarity of vision could lead to crime (the character of Rine-hart, the nocturnal charlatan of Harlem, tempts him at one point), but the narrator comes out of his cellar with an identity and a philosophy which have been paid for dearly but which are truly his own and not imposed from the outside. . . .

Invisible Man is a very powerful book, one that gives the reader the feeling of having been thrown up in the air by a bulldozer. It is also a work of art, admirably written and constructed, a work which, a dozen years after its publication, remains profoundly contemporary. Closer to us than Richard Wright, a better novelist than James Baldwin, Ellison occupies a unique place in contemporary American literature.

Pierre Brodin. *Présences contemporaines: Écrivains*
américains d'aujourd'hui (Paris, Nouvelles Éditions
Debresse, 1964), pp. 55–57†

Even if Ralph Ellison were not the author of *Invisible Man*, his recent collection of essays, *Shadow and Act*, would be a very significant work. There are astute commentaries on literature, music, and society, and the commentaries are enriched and validated by an underlying sense of a life being lived with energy, sympathy, and joy. But Ralph Ellison is the author of *Invisible Man* and of an impending novel which, if we are to judge from excerpts, promises to illustrate new powers and to extend his fame; and this fact inevitably imputes a further significance to the es-says. Here we can see how, over more than a score of years, in another dimension, the mind and sensibility of Ellison have been working, and we can hope to see some enlightening relations between that dimension and the dimension of his fiction. . . .

The basic unity of human experience—that is what Ellison asserts; and he sets the richness of his own experience and that of many Negroes he has known, and his own early capacity to absorb the general values of Western culture, over against what Wright called "the essential bleakness of black life in America." What he is saying here is not that "bleakness" does not exist, and exist for many, but that it has not been the key fact of his own experience, and that his own experience is part of the story. It must be reckoned with, too. . . .

To be an artist partakes, in its special way, of the moral force of being a man. And with this we come again, in a new perspective, to Ellison's view of the "basic unity of experience." If there is anguish, there is also the possibility of the transmutation of anguish, "the occasional joy of a complex double vision."

Robert Penn Warren. *Cmty.*
May, 1965, pp. 91, 94–95

If the most damaging criticism one can make of *Invisible Man* is that its characters and situations are too abstractly conceived and executed, it is also true that perhaps its greatest strength is its capacity to show in action the power that ideas and ideologies can exert. One of the ways this is done is through bravura set-pieces of rhetoric, which Mr. Ellison uses brilliantly for his dramatic and ironic purposes. So it comes as a disappointment, in reading this collection of essays [*Shadow and Act*] to find Mr. Ellison occasionally serving up his rhetoric straight, with little apparent awareness of its dangers. . . .

The most moving passages in the book I found to be those of direct autobiography: the glimpses we are offered of the author's parents, of his boyhood in Oklahoma City (where he and a group of his friends formulated the ambition to become "Renaissance Men"), of his adventures riding freight trains during the Depression, of the period when he earned his living by hunting birds, of his entanglement with the Communist Party. It is a tribute to his agility of mind that all these unexpected, convincing details should be used to illustrate his literary and cultural arguments; but they also make me rather sorry we don't have more of them simply for their own sake.

Dan Jacobson. *NS.* Jan. 20, 1967, p. 82

Both Baldwin and Wright seem to have overlooked the rich possibilities available to them in the blues tradition. Both profess great pride in Negroes, but in practice seem to rate the theories and abstract formulations of French existentialism over the infinitely richer wisdom of the blues. Both, like most other intellectuals (and/or most of the social scientists), seem to have missed what should be one of the most obvious implications of the blues tradition: *It is the product of the most complicated culture, and therefore the most complicated sensibility in the modern world.* . . .

Somehow or other James Baldwin and Richard Wright seem to have missed the literary possibilities suggested by this. Ralph Ellison has not. . . .

Invisible Man was *par excellence* the literary extension of the blues. It was as if Ellison had taken an everyday twelve bar blues tune (by a man from down South sitting in a manhole up North in New York singing and signifying about how he got there) and scored it for full orchestra. This was indeed something different and something more than

run of the mill U.S. fiction. It had new dimensions of rhetorical resonance (based on lying and signifying). It employed a startlingly effective fusion of narrative realism and surrealism; and it achieved a unique
but compelling combination of the naturalistic, the ridiculous, and the
downright hallucinatory. . . .

And like the blues, and echoing the irrepressibility of America
itself, it ended on a note of promise, ironic and ambiguous perhaps, but
a note of promise still. The blues with no aid from existentialism have
always known that there were no clear-cut solutions for the human
situation.

Albert Murray. *The Omni-Americans* (New York,
Outerbridge & Dienstfrey, 1970), pp. 166–67

It is now 1970—which means that 23 years have passed since Ellison
has given us his first and so far, only novel [parts of it were first
published in 1947]. This is a matter of great discussion among writers
younger than he. Just why have 23 years been allowed to pass with just
one other book (but several articles), *Shadow and Act*, nonfiction, left
to stand as the slim wedge between Ellison and oblivion? (Writing is a
craft or profession or rite of stupidity that can bring oblivion swifter
than anything else I know about.)

I wish I could answer that. It is known that on his lecture swings
Ellison does read parts of his new novel. I draw the comparison between
him and Katherine Anne Porter, whose *Ship of Fools*, dealing with the
mentality from which sprang German fascism, was 20 years in coming
and turned out to be a dud, despite all the fanfare and the inept film of
the novel.

I do not with this for Ellison. I don't wish it for anyone. But many
things transpire during the course of a couple of decades; one can lose
touch with them, and it is suspected that this may be the case with
Ellison. I do not know this for a fact. I *do* know that his contacts with
the young writers I know have been absent, or very unsatisfying. . . .

We urgently need older writers to help mold anew the tradition of
Black communication, whether it be written or oral. And we are running
out of senior Black writers. Wright talked to people; so did Langston
Hughes; Himes is eager to talk to people, should they make the long trek
to Spain. And John O. Killens, who must rank near the top in this
endeavor, is still running writing workshops. We need Ellison and Baldwin to give us a hand. We've got a Black wave of writing and writers
sweeping over the land who would be so much more enriched through
contacts with them.

John A. Williams. *BlackW.* Dec., 1970, pp. 10–11

The task of that ironic picaresque, the nameless hero of *Invisible Man*, is exactly this: to move from invisiblity to vision. Through the dangers, corruptions, and temptations awaiting him, he recapitulates the history of his own race, conducting a ceaseless "psychological scrimmage" with everyone, himself included. Exploited by all—white Communists and African nationalists, Southern bigots and Northern liberals, women and men alike—he proceeds, less in the manner of an arrow than a boomerang, from innocence to disillusionment to the edge of a new wisdom, a dialectic sense of himself. In the surreal cool cellar lit by 1,369 light bulbs where he ends, he perceives the essential chaos of the mind, and finds freedom in a form that can "condemn and affirm, say no and say yes, say yes and say no."

Invisible Man is a profound and brilliant work, which engages issues of History, Soul, and Art still alive in our midst. It may be criticized for being too prolix, too diffuse, in specific parts; yet the novel is resourceful in its syncopation of reality, musical in its organization of themes, its screams and grotesque laughter issuing from a heroic consciousness willing to surrender nothing to its own ease. Ellison's novel is more than an example of Black fiction; it stands as an early landmark in all of postwar literature.

Ihab Hassan. *Contemporary American Literature*
(New York, Frederick Ungar, 1973), pp. 74–75

Invisible Man invades the comfortable universe of detached literary analysis with a reading experience which, in the tradition of all authentic art, could involve us in profound personal change ("things as they are/ Are changed upon the blue guitar"). As everyone knows, the reader is asked to come to terms with overwhelming sets of contraries—black and whiteness as interdependent aspects of each other, racism and American democracy, responsibility within anarchy, the one and the many, naturalism and fairy tale, sociology and myth, chaos and order. This is paradox of a vastly different order from the arid device we learn to cherish and chatter about in discussing modernist literature; we cannot cope with it meaningfully without the *agon* of remaking ourselves so as to accommodate its way of responding to the world.

Hence a basic irony in the career of this very successful book, a "classic" to educated readers in America and Europe, almost smothered in commentary, and yet largely ignored on its most demanding and meaningful levels. Since its 1952 publication in America, one or another dimension of its readers' makeup has consistently interposed itself to short-circuit the book's total vision: first it was the white self-image, later the black; most recently it is the renewed assault of sociology upon art which sets the balance askew. To be sure, any book, especially one like *Invisible Man*, must assert its worth within the context of our chaotic everyday lives. But the pressure of social and racial upheavals has created so much uncertainty that the tolerance for broad reflection and inner change has all but disappeared in the frenzied search of all parties for immediate, tangible panaceas. One misreads a novel if one seeks to extract from it short-range social panaceas, and *Invisible Man* has certainly been a dramatic casualty of such misreading.

Jacqueline Covo. *The Blinking Eye: Ralph Waldo Ellison and His American, French, German and Italian Critics, 1952–1971* (Metuchen, N.J., Scarecrow, 1974), pp. 124–25

GAINES, ERNEST J. (1933–   )

UNITED STATES

Ernest J. Gaines' novel, *Catherine Carmier*, was not reviewed in any of the popular national book reviewing media. Yet, it is a well-written story about a young man's return to his rural hometown community in Louisiana. Jackson Guerin returns home armed with a college degree to find that things have not changed too much among the Creole, black and Cajun families, most of whom are farmers. One exception is that during the previous summer a few outsiders from the big cities had tried to get Negroes to vote. . . .

Catherine, the heroine, is of a Creole family and is a sensitive and intelligent young woman who is controlled by and unbelievably dependent on her father, Raoul. There is a touching and warm love affair between Catherine and Jackson that carries the story. The Carmier family traditionally looks down on their black brethren, as is historically true of many families in many sections of Louisiana. Raoul, the proud patriarch with only a drop of Negro blood, clings tenaciously to the silly notions of skin color. He hates the Cajuns because they are white and control the best land, and the Negroes because they represent to him everything inferior. Catherine, torn between a desire to please Raoul and her feelings for Jackson, never reconciles the ambivalence of her life. Although she professes her love for Jackson, Catherine cannot leave her father. Therein lies the essence of the book. On the surface this might not seem to be much meat for a plot, yet the conflicts of values and of family traditions are, in the main, well presented.

The striking part of this work is that there is no bitterness nor clarion call for racial equality in it. While there are divisions among people because of differences in skin color and education, *Catherine Carmier* is outstanding for its simplicity and the universality of its people.

Miles M. Jackson. Phylon. Fall, 1965, pp. 216–17

As a subjective, emotive and often-treated theme, the colour problem bristles with traps. No one could be detached in either writing or reading

198

about this subject. For the author there are the dangers of hysteria and over simplification. Worst of all, he may, with the best motives in the world, produce a book that is first-rate pleading, second-rate art.

Of Love and Dust avoids these traps. The theme—that a white man may love a negro woman but a southern negro may not love a white woman and live to tell the tale—is ominously familiar. But treated by Ernest Gaines with objective quietness, a familiar situation has made, if not a major novel, an impressive one. The Louisiana plantation talk, which can make this kind of novel almost unreadable, is never obtrusive. It is a steady, dense, unshowy book in which passion is cumulative rather than explosive, but no less powerful for being so. The drama, between Marcus, the young, rebellious negro, and the baby-doll wife of his overseer, is worked out with a steady, almost balletic certainty of step before the watchers, paralysed by heat, weariness and fear. We are drawn in, forced to observe, by the narrator, the negro tractor-driver Jim Kelly. He is a good, intelligent man, torn in his attitude to Marcus between anxiety and admiration. The anxiety is touching and understandable, but I could not share his ultimate respect for a character whose mindless rebellion seems petty and petulant beside Jim's wiser, more experienced grief.

This is my only reservation. Otherwise, Mr. Gaines's ear and eye cannot be faulted. He neither pleads nor passes judgment. There is no black and white moralising about the colour problem. The effect is all the stronger for this restraint.

Janice Elliot. *NS*. June 7, 1968, p. 769

Gaines somehow manages to show that there is more even to a redneck than his racism. Racists are dangerous, unstable, vicious individuals, but never that alone. They are people, fully realized in Gaines's fiction, and have a haggard futility, a pale and shrieking dullness, a pained unsatisfiedness that makes them appear wounded and deficient and far less complete than the blacks they attempt to intimidate.

Gaines's people are never completely wiped out by whites, even when they are killed by them. They are too large and the whites around them too small. His heroes would fight to walk upright through a hurricane. They do no less when confronted with a white world intent on grinding them down. They fight to maintain small human pleasures and large human principles in a hostile and morally degenerate world. They have seen the level to which humankind can sink and have managed to remain standing all these many years.

Gaines is much closer to Charles Dickens, W. E. B. DuBois, Jean Toomer and Langston Hughes than he is to Richard Wright or Ralph Ellison. There is nothing in Gaines that is not open—to love or to interpretation. He also claims and revels in the rich heritage of Southern black people and their customs; the community he feels with them is unmistakable and goes deeper even than pride. Like the beautifully vivid, sturdy and serviceable language of the black, white and Creole people of Louisiana, Gaines is mellow with historical reflection, supple with wit, relaxed and expansive because he does not equate his people with failure.

Alice Walker. *NYT*. May 23, 1971, p. 12

Ernest Gaines' *The Autobiography of Miss Jane Pittman* covers a period of struggle for life and dignity extending beyond the Civil War to the 1950's. Miss Jane Pittman, the novel's chief character, reveals the tough spirit within herself and others and provides an interpretation of people and events that accord with the more forceful slave narratives found in such a work as B. A. Botkin's *Lay My Burden Down*. It provides an insight lacking in Faulkner, who naturally inclined to a concern with the Southern past which explained more about whites than blacks. Gaines' stark tones are more like those of Margaret Walker's *Jubilee*, although it differs from *Jubilee* in being told as first person narrative and does not repeat *Jubilee*'s concerns. *The Autobiography of Miss Jane Pittman* also has something of the folk spirit of the little noticed novel *All God's Children* by Alston Anderson (1965), but surpasses it in sweep and density.

Through the novel, the reader gets a sense of the continuity of a black spiritual assertion both in everyday life and in its struggles against oppression. The most interesting section of the novel deals directly with Miss Jane's experiences during Reconstruction, her marriage, and the hopes she directly pursues. There is a loss of intensity where she is not directly the center of the action, but *The Autobiography of Miss Jane Pittman* is a fine remaking and regrasping of the dense past deriving from secure grasp of black culture and its mixtures.

George E. Kent. *Phylon*. Winter, 1972, pp. 307–8

Gaines uses the rural Louisiana countryside as the setting for most of his stories. The countryside and most particularly the quarters, those ancient structures which have served as homes for generations of Black people back to the times of slavery, are captured in a purposely ill-defined time between the Second World War and the present, a time not quite yesterday, not quite today. The struggle for ascendency in the small Southern backwater Gaines has created is not between white and Black. The racial order, with the Blacks who are on the bottom, rich white people who are on the top and the Cajuns (the descendents of the white Arcadians who were resettled in Louisiana by the British after the close of the French and Indian Wars in the late eighteenth century), who, no matter how high their income, are not quite as good, at least in the eyes of Blacks, as the Anglican whites, but no matter how poor, are at least one step above the Blacks, is slowly changing. But change, in an overtly racial manner, seldom moves beyond the periphery of Gaines's attention. His concern is for the ways in which people attempt to hold on to or break from the past, adjust to the present or influence the future. Thus, his major theme, in its broadest sense, is the clash between the old and the new, the past and the future. The old is violated by the new, not out of wanton destruction; rather it is attacked in an attempt to wrench new definitions, new images of manhood and dignity, new realities out of the old.

Sherley Anne Williams. Give Birth to Brightness
(New York, Dial, 1972), pp. 170–71

Pessimism does indeed seem to be foreign to Gaines's interpretation of his world, and this is indicated by a piece of external evidence involving the composition of <i>Of Love and Dust</i>. It is plausible that Marcus dies at the hands of Sidney Bonbon. The system depicted in the novel encourages such an outcome. But it is not the ending Gaines originally chose. In the first version he sent to the publisher, Marcus and Louise escape the plantation and, like two errant and fun-loving children, go off to the city on a spree, thumbing their noses at the code. Gaines's publisher asked for another conclusion; Gaines supplied it, and did no irreparable damage to the integrity of the novel. But the great difference between conclusions is instructive. Gaines's first inclination was not toward making Marcus a martyred revolutionary. It was toward creating a joyful and ironic triumph over a stifling system, which would have harmonized perfectly well with Marcus as a swaggerer and a dandy.

Gaines's best work roughly follows the course of that first version of <i>Of Love and Dust</i>. It has a general tone of comic irony and it shows inertia being overcome by new and more vital forces, though not without pain and some sense of loss. It is the tone and the theme we get in the short story collection <i>Bloodline</i>, and his third novel, <i>The Autobiography of Miss Jane Pittman</i>. In them, Gaines still writes about his fictional city of Bayonne and the area around Baton Rouge, about the old resisting the young, the whites murdering and cheating. But the time and the power have shifted to the side of rebirth and virility, the energy now flows toward illumination and successful change, not darkness and failure. They contain no political or psychological rationalizations because their content and form grow out of convictions and observations with which Gaines is more consistently comfortable. And we are burdened with no gratuitous assertions about an optimistic future because the stories themselves embody that optimism.

Jerry H. Bryant. *SoR.* Autumn, 1974, pp. 855–56

The greatest difference between the historian and the novelist is this: The historian simply demands a recognition of history; seldom does he encourage men to alter it; the novelist demands recognition of history only as a prelude toward changing it. The Jane Pittmans, Ned Douglasses, and Jimmy Arrons are able to assault the patterns of the past, only when they understand the matrix of the society in which they live; only through such understanding can they move to alter reality. Gaines demands such understanding from his people as evidenced in his novels from *Catherine Carmier* to *The Autobiography of Miss Jane Pittman,* and the formula for his historical novels is easy to discern: Realization precedes action; recognition of the truth of history is a prelude for rebellion and revolution.

This is the final theme, arrived at by the author, after three novels. If *Catherine Carmier* suffered from an intricate, not well-developed plot structure, and if *Of Love and Dust* loses strength and power through flaws in the makeup of the major protagonist, *The Autobiography of Miss Jane Pittman* reaches near perfection because of the unity of form and content, because the themes are interwoven into the fabric of the novel in such a way as to complement the form. The autobiographical novel which takes history as its material must be so well structured that events proceed in chronological order—if not on the printed page, then in the eyes of the reader. If clarity is to prevail, smooth transition from episode to episode is demanded. Through limiting the use of flashbacks and stream of consciousness, and depending upon the central narrator to move the story along, Gaines avoids a chaotic novel.

The result is a people's novel, one revealing unwritten history and depicting the examples of those who, in refusing to accept reality without question, rebelled against it.

Addison Gayle, Jr. *The Way of the New World*
(Garden City, N.Y., Doubleday, 1975), pp. 364–65

HANSBERRY, LORRAINE (1930–1965)

UNITED STATES

If *A Raisin in the Sun* had been written by a white instead of a colored woman and if it had been written about a white family, it would have done well to recover its investment. As it is, it has received praises from all sides and the public is flocking to see it. As a piece of dramatic writing it is old-fashioned. As something near to the conscience of a nation troubled by injustice to Negroes, it is emotionally powerful. Much of its success is due to our sentimentality over the "Negro question."

Miss Hansberry has had the good sense to write about a Negro family with vices as well as virtues, and has spared us one of those well-scrubbed, light-skinned families who often appear in propaganda pieces about discrimination. If she avoids the over-worked formulas of the "Negro" play, however, she does not avoid those of the "domestic" play. . . .

It may have been Miss Hansberry's objective to show that the stage stereotypes will fit Negroes as well as white people, to which my own reply must be that I never doubted it. They will fit anybody. Rather, anybody can be made to fit them. The play is moving as a theatrical experience, but the emotions it engenders are not relevant to the social and political realities.

Tom F. Driver. *NR*. April 13, 1959, p. 21

Although *A Raisin in the Sun* occasionally slips over into triteness, it makes an extraordinarily compelling evening's theatre—which shows once again, I suppose, the degree to which drama is an extra-literary activity. As a play it may be patchy, but as a vehicle for the actors it is superb. One reason is that a powerful rhetoric comes naturally to Miss Hansberry. This puts her in a rather small club of writers, most of the other members of which are Celts. But with a difference: the rhetoric of a talented Negro writer always gives you the impression that it is about something, which is certainly not true of the Irish or the Welsh.

Miss Hansberry has more than a gift of the gab; she also has a great deal to say on questions that deeply concern her. So her rhetoric is not just colourful; it has a natural dignity, which presumably has something to do with the fact that the rhythms and diction of passionate Negro speech come straight from the Bible. The language is felt and meant to a degree where it can afford to be simple. Finally, Miss Hansberry's characters continually talk about the subjects which concern all Negroes: the jobs they can get, the areas they can live in, the strategies by which their pride is preserved or undermined, the problem of assimilation and racial independence. This means that the otherwise nice, rather sentimental family life, with its humdrum quarrels, ambitions and pieties, is continually strengthened by outside loyalties and outside hatreds.

A. Alvarez. *NS.* Aug. 15, 1959, p. 190

There is a sort of inverted miracle in the way Miss Hansberry [in *The Sign in Sidney Brustein's Window*] manages to distort so many things —taste, intelligence, craft—and be simultaneously perverse as dramatist, social commentator, political oracle, and moral visionary. A further miracle is her union of bitchiness with sentimentality. But it is borrowed bitchery, for in her incredibly awkward drama, in which scene stolidly follows scene like a row of packing cases and character talks to character like droning telephone poles, Miss Hansberry plunders from every playwright around, most thoroughly, Edward Albee.

The play can be said to be about the editor of a weekly New York newspaper who joins a local political crusade, is disillusioned, then revived by the knowledge that "love is sweet, flowers smell good, and people want to be better." But Miss Hansberry is a master of changing the subject, so that there is a plethora of entirely separate plots: a domestic drama; an interracial one; the tragedies, respectively, of a good-hearted whore, a fainthearted queer, and a lily-livered liberal; the melodrama of a blackhearted dope pusher, and the tragi-comedy of a cheated-on wife.

Yet none of this suggests the uses to which Miss Hansberry puts her dragooned themes. They serve exclusively as containers for her venomous anger: she hates homosexuals, liberals, abstract artists, nonrealistic playwrights, white people unwilling to commit suicide, Albert Camus, Jean-Paul Sartre, Samuel Beckett, William Golding, and, especially, poor, plundered Edward Albee. Miss Hansberry ostensibly wants to attack sham and hypocrisy, but her lack of charity chokes the play and becomes itself an intellectual vice which, ironically, stings her with its backlash. Her attack on "success" name-drops furiously, and her savage assault on intellectuality brandishes every intellectual catch-word that can be snatched from the *Zeitgeist*.

[Richard Gilman.] *Nwk.* Oct. 26, 1964, p. 101

One of the biggest selling points about *A Raisin in the Sun*—filling the grapevine, riding the word-of-mouth, laying the foundation for its wide, wide acceptance—was how much the Younger family was just like any other American family. Some people were ecstatic to find that "it didn't really have to be about Negroes at all!" It was, rather, a walking, talking, living demonstration of our mythic conviction that, underneath, all of us Americans, *color-ain't-got-nothing-to-do-with-it*, are pretty much alike. People are just people whoever they are; and all they want is a chance to be like other people. This uncritical assumption, senti-mentally held by the audience, powerfully fixed in the character of the powerful mother with whom everybody could identify immediately and completely, made any other questions about the Youngers, and what living in the slums of Southside Chicago had done to them, not only irrelevant and impertinent, but also disloyal: *A Raisin in the Sun* was a great American play, and Lorraine was a great American playwright because everybody who walked into the theatre saw in Lena Younger—especially as she was portrayed by Claudia McNeil, his own great Amer-ican Mama. And that was decisive. . . .

It was good that people of all color, strata, faiths and persuasions could identify so completely with Lena Younger, and her family, and their desire to better themselves in the American way. But that's not what the play was about! The play was about Walter Lee, Lena's son, and what happened to him as a result of having his dream, his life's ambition, endlessly frustrated by poverty, and its attendant social and personal degradation. Walter Lee's dreams of "being somebody," of "making it," like everybody else, were not respectable to Mama, and not very important to us. He wanted a liquor store which would enable him to exploit the misery of his fellow slum dwellers like they were exploited by everybody else. Walter Lee is corrupted by the materialistic aspira-tions at the heart of Western civilization, and his corruption is bodied forth in his petty, little dream. But it was his dream, *and it was all he had*! And that made it a matter of life or death to him, revolutionary, dangerous in its implications. For it could explode if frustrated; it could destroy people, it could kill, if frustrated! That's what Lorraine was warning us about. But we would only listen to Mama, and Mama did not ever fully understand Walter Lee!

Ossie Davis. *Freedomways.*
Summer, 1965, pp. 399–400

The Sign in Sidney Brustein's Window is a good play. It just misses being great. Miss Hansberry tried to sum up in the personality structure and the private conflicts of a single character all the social anxieties, the cultural confusion and the emotional debris that litter and torment our days. The remarkable thing is that Miss Hansberry nearly succeeded.

Sidney Brustein is modern man in confrontation with a world he never made and which he must remake to conform to the definition of himself. But this definition of himself is buried under layers of casual, cynical collaboration with expediency and the code of the disengaged, the uncommitted, and it begins to come clear to him only as these layers are stripped away by successive encounters with aspects of stone-hard truth. His wife, Iris, represents one aspect of it, her sister, Mavis, another, and her sister, Gloria, a third. Then there are the men: Alton, the Negro; David, the homosexual playwright; and Wally, the negotiator, who strips away the last layer, and Sidney discovers himself to be one ". . . who believes that death is waste and love is sweet and that the earth turns and men change every day and that rivers run and that people wanna be better than they are and that . . . tomorrow, we shall make something strong of this sorrow." Given all the characters and all the situations, and given especially the character of Sidney Brustein, this hymn of affirmation is the right ending for the play.

Saunders Redding. *Crisis*. March, 1966, p. 175

When *A Raisin in the Sun* burst on the scene with a Negro star, a Negro director plus a young Negro woman playwright everybody on Broadway was startled and very apprehensive about what this play might say. What obviously elated the drama critics was the very relieving discovery that, what the publicity buildup actually heralded was not the arrival of belligerent forces from across the color line to settle some long-standing racial accounts on stage, but a good old-fashioned, home-spun saga of some good working-class folk in pursuit of the American Dream—in their fashion. And what could possibly be thematically objectionable about that? And very well written also. We shall give it an award (A for effort), and so they did, amidst a patronizing critical exuberance I would have thought impossible in the crassly commercial institution of Broadway. Not a dissenting critical note was to be heard from Broadway critics, and thus the Negro made theater history with the most cleverly written piece of glorified soap opera I, personally, have ever seen on a stage. Only because it was about *Negroes* was this play acceptable, and this is the sobering fact that the aspiring Negro playwright *must* live with. If this play—which is so "American" that many whites did *not* consider it a "Negro play"—had ever been staged by *white actors* it would be judged second-rate—which was what the British called it, and what the French said of the film version.

Harold Cruse. *The Crisis of the Negro Intellectual*
(New York, William Morrow, 1967), p. 278

Black people ignored the theatre because the theatre had always ignored them. But, in *A Raisin in the Sun*, black people recognized that house and all the people in it—the mother, the son, the daughter and the daughter-in-law—and supplied the play with an interpretative element which could not be present in the minds of white people: a kind of claustrophobic terror, created not only by their knowledge of the house but by their knowledge of the streets. And when the curtain came down [after one of the early performances], Lorraine and I found ourselves in the backstage alley, where she was immediately mobbed. I produced a pen and Lorraine handed me her handbag and began signing autographs. "It only happens once," she said. I stood there and watched. I watched the people, who loved Lorraine for what she had brought to them; and watched Lorraine, who loved the people for what they brought to *her*. It was not, for her, a matter of being admired. She was being corroborated and confirmed. . . .

She was a very young woman, with an overpowering vision, and fame had come to her early—she must certainly have wished, often enough, that fame had seen fit to drag its feet a little. For fame and recognition are not synonyms, especially not here, and her fame was to cause her to be criticized very harshly, very loudly, and very often by both black and white people who were unable to believe, apparently, that a really serious intention could be contained in so glamorous a frame. She took it all with a kind of astringent good humor, refusing, for example, even to consider defending herself when she was being accused of being a "slum lord" because of her family's real-estate holdings in Chicago. I called her during that time, and all she said—with a wry laugh—was, "My God, Jimmy, do you realize you're only the second person who's called me today? And you know how my phone kept ringing *before*!" She was not surprised. She was devoted to the human race, but she was not romantic about it.

James Baldwin. Preface to Lorraine Hansberry,
To Be Young, Gifted and Black (Englewood
Cliffs, N.J., Prentice-Hall, 1969), pp. x–xi

Structurally, Lorraine Hansberry remains essentially within the bounds of the conventional realistic well-made play, something almost anachronistic amidst the styles of the 1960s. The term "well-made" can

be misleading because of its unfortunate connotations with the emptiness of nineteenth century tradition, but we need only look at the plays
of a modern dramatist such as Lillian Hellman to recognize that orderly
development of plot and a neatly planned series of expository scenes,
complications, and climaxes can greatly assist in thematic and character
development of a superior nature. Plot in Miss Hansberry's plays is of
secondary importance, for it is not her main dramatic purpose. Nonetheless, because the audience has considerable interest in *what* is happening
as well as *to whom*, both *A Raisin in the Sun* and *The Sign in Sidney
Brustein's Window* are thoroughly enhanced by well-ordered revelation
of the events which are so important in the lives of the characters. The
straightforward telling of a story remains a thoroughly honorable literary accomplishment, and Miss Hansberry has practiced this ancient
dramatic art with eminent respectability. Moreover, the scene, incident,
and dialogue are almost Ibsenesque, avoiding overt stylization for its
own sake and performed within the standard "box" set that progressively becomes more rare.

Jordan Y. Miller. In C. W. E. Bigsby, ed., *The Black
American Writer* (De Land, Fla., Everett/Edwards,
1969), Vol. II, p. 161

Despite [Lorraine Hansberry's] need to *say* something, to make a
social point, she did not want to sacrifice art to argument, to go agitprop
as a few of the young black playwrights have recently done. She was
forced, then, to embrace the traditional American realism, to do as
serious American playwrights from James A. Herne to Arthur Miller
have done, to use plot to make her points and character to express her
sense that it is all more complicated than it seems. There are traps in the
form, the temptation of easy devices (the lost insurance money in *A
Raisin in the Sun*) and pat character reversals (Mavis's revelations in
Act II of *The Sign in Sidney Brustein's Window*). There are virtues,
however—characters, like Sidney Brustein and Walter Lee in *A Raisin
in the Sun*, which transcend stereotype, become so rich and suggestive
that the message itself is always about to be swallowed in human complexity. In *The Sign in Sidney Brustein's Window*, Miss Hansberry
attempted to go beyond the simplicity of *A Raisin in the Sun*, to introduce non-realistic elements, but they were systematically cut away in the
Broadway production.

It is impossible to guess how she might have grown as a writer, but
her two plays indicate that she had wit and intelligence, a strong sense of
social and political possibility and a respect for the contradictions in all
men; that she could create a milieu (the family in *A Raisin in the Sun*,
the Greenwich Village circle in *The Sign in Sidney Brustein's Window*)

with both bite and affection; that she was a playwright—like Odets, like Miller—with easily definable flaws but an inescapable talent that one cannot help admiring.

Gerald Weales. Com. Sept. 5, 1969, pp. 542–43

I commend *Les Blancs* to your immediate attention, not so much as a great piece of theater (which it may or may not be) but, more significantly, as an incredibly moving experience. Or, perhaps, as an extended moment in one's life not easily forgotten or regularly discovered in a commercial theater that takes such pains to protect us from knowing who and what and where we are in 20th-century America. . . .

The play divides people into sectors inhabited on the one hand by those who recognize clearly that a struggle exists in the world today that is about the liberation of oppressed peoples, a struggle to be supported at all costs. In the other camp live those who still accept as real the soothing mythology that oppression can be dealt with reasonably— particularly by Black people—if Blacks will just bear in mind the value of polite, calm and continuing use of the democratic process. . . .

The play is flawed—what play not completed by its original author would not be? Yet, beyond the imperfection of its ragged perimeters, or its frequently awkward transitional sections and fitfully episodic construction, there is a persistent glow, an illumination. Somewhere, past performance, staging and written speech, resides that brilliant, anguished consciousness of Lorraine Hansberry, at work in the long nights of troubled times, struggling to make sense out of an insane situation, aware—way ahead of the rest of us—that there is no compromise with evil, there is only the fight for decency. If even Uncle Sam must die toward that end, *Les Blancs* implies, then send *him* to the wall.

Clayton Riley. NYTts. Nov. 19, 1970, p. 3

The Drinking Gourd, a three-act drama well suited for television presentation, is what may be called in television jargon a documentary of American plantation slavery. It is a compact yet comprehensive, authentic, and vivid portrayal of the "peculiar institution," correctly called the sum of all villainies, as it was especially in the cotton kingdom on the eve of the Civil War. The action in the drama is framed between a long prologue and a brief epilogue both of which are spoken by a soldier "perhaps Lincolnesque" in appearance. The prologue kaleidoscopically reviews the history of American slavery from its beginning to the middle of the nineteenth century. The epilogue avows that by that time the Civil War had become necessary to keep slavery from destroying the United States. . . .

Imaginative, unified, easily documentable, and intensely interesting

story that it is, and being good theater as well as good dramatic literature, *The Drinking Gourd* is in the best tradition of historical dramas—
much more so than *Les Blancs*, which is also an historical drama. In
both of these works, nevertheless, as in the drama which first won her
acclaim as a playwright, Miss Hansberry skillfully used original and
vivid dialogue to reveal character and develop action. In *Les Blancs* she
wrote all of the dialogue in standard informal spoken English, having no
reason to use any other kind. In *The Drinking Gourd* she used the same
kind of English to represent the speech of semiliterate and illiterate
people. This she did convincingly without resorting to mutilated English,
which has so often been perpetrated as "dialect," whereas it represents
nobody's actual speech.

W. Edward Farrison. *CLAJ*. Dec., 1972, pp. 193, 196

The untimely death in 1965 of Lorraine Hansberry, one of the most
poetic voices in the American theatre today, deprived us of one of our
most gifted dramatists and of one of our best authors, but she left a
legacy for the newer Black dramatists in that she pointed the way to a
new direction, a newness in content and attitude, and a purpose for
Black theatre. "Positive and unflinching, deadly serious" [Loften
Mitchell], she won the 1959 New York Drama Critics Circle Award
for her first play, *A Raisin in the Sun*, which was monumental in commitment.

The anger of the play is somewhat tempered when compared with
the anger of later, more notably "Black" dramatists, such as Baraka and
Baldwin. But her play is a well-crafted one, reflecting the world of
Blacks on two levels of awareness. One is the daily struggle for existence
shown in Mama's relentless desire to endure in the face of her son's and
daughter's "modern" objections to their lot in life, and the other is the
illusionary world of dreams. The dreams center on the money Mama is
to receive from her husband's life insurance, which creates new hopes in
a family almost without hope. . . .

The play indeed strikes an awareness of the changing attitudes of
the Black man. As the play ends, Mama's world seems to be a thing of
the past, while the family, it is hoped, is on its way. They all agree to
move into a house in a white neighborhood, against the whites' judgment, and we notice how Mama's dormant fear of equality has been
replaced with a new-found optimism and self reliance. . . .

Miss Hansberry's *A Raisin in the Sun* brought something new and
honest to the New York stage, but it also brought with it a warning. The
Chicago of the Negro, with all its frustrations, anger, and small hope of
the late 40's and early 50's, was recreated for New York and the American theater. The Black theater of protest had its inception. Others would

take up, with more anger and less sentimentality, what Lorraine Hansberry had begun.

Robert J. Willis. *NALF*. Summer, 1974, pp. 213–14

HARRIS, WILSON (1921–   )

GUYANA

If Mittelholzer the novelist uses the trees and the jungle to produce the goons and goblins of his fantasy, Wilson Harris, the poet, takes a more serious view of it. His metaphors [in *Eternity to Season*] are based and nourished on the plurality of the forest. For him, the jungle is "the world-creating jungle." . . . Wilson Harris' world is in a unique sense created by the jungle, and his metaphors of the "world-creating jungle" which travels "eternity to season," touch and explore and express limits of experience and perception on a dimension reflected elsewhere perhaps only by Rainer Maria Rilke. . . . These images are valuable realizations, arising as they do out of Harris' profound imaginative experience of the forests of British Guiana. His statement and projection of this world is one of the significant achievements of West Indian writing, and it is more than unfortunate that his poetry should be considered by many to be so "difficult." . . .

The same sense of the restriction of the individual to external pressures and conditions can also be found in the work of the Nigerian "forest" writer, Amos Tutuola. But whereas in the work of Mittelholzer and Tutuola, despite all the fantasy, the attention and concern is fixed on the individual and on his position within the context of human society; in Harris', human society (*domesticity and lights*) is itself an aberration; something to be abhorred. Human society is *artificial*. . . .

Edward Brathwaite. *Bim*. Jan.–June,
1960, pp. 105–6, 110

I admire Wilson Harris's novels greatly; he is one of the very few living novelists whose works are too brief for my taste. On the other hand, think of him as an author picking away at a theme from different angles in book after book, as Eliot picked away in *Four Quartets*, and he turns into a writer creating, in instalments, one of the major fictional statements of our time.

The Eye of the Scarecrow is a novel about confrontations and tensions in a Guyanese setting. The narrator's childhood past meets the present and generates current; the jungle has one voice and civilisation another. Mr. Harris's fine tetralogy had this potent theme—the modern man's thrust against the wild, the wild's counterthrust—as well as a poetry not usually associated with the novel-form. *The Eye of the Scarecrow* has, if anything, a deeper poetry. It also has a power like the blow of the Guyanese heat.

Anthony Burgess. Spec. Dec. 3, 1965, p. 745

It is from Yeats's great phrase about "the unity from a mythology that marries us to rock and hill" that we may, justifiably, begin an examination of Wilson Harris's singular exploration of his corner of the West Indian experience. To Harris, this sacramental union of man and landscape remains the lost, or never established, factor in our lives. We enjoy, we exploit, we are coarsely nourished by our respective Caribbean territories—but illegitimately. We have yet to put our signatures to that great contract of the imagination by which a people and a place enter into a domestic relationship rather than drift into the uncertainties of liaison. No other British Caribbean novelist has made quite such an explicit and conscious effort as Harris to reduce the material reckonings of everyday life to the significance of myth. . . .

It is important to remember this element of the dream, and of the dream's sister, death, if we are to come to any understanding of these four Wilson Harris novels—*Palace of the Peacock, The Far Journey of Oudin, The Whole Armour* and *The Secret Ladder. F*or the quartet opens with one dream of death, and closes with another dream of creation. Between these two dreams lies an evocation of being not accessible to any reviewer's summary. If we are to share the writer's experience, we must accept possession of the living by the dead; we must accept the resurrected man and the fact that "the end precedes the beginning" and that "the end and beginning were always there." Harris's world is not only one of prosaic action, but one of rite and mythical formation. "The first condition for understanding the Greek myth," said [André] Gide, "is to believe in it." And it is not improper that Harris makes belief the condition for entry into his Guyanese world.

John Hearne. In Louis James, ed., The Islands in
Between (London, Oxford University Press, 1968),
pp. 140–41, 145

Wilson Harris's long sojourn in the Guyanese interior has made him an equal participant in the worlds of forest and savannah, the first expressing eternity and the perpetual flux of life, while the second speaks of season and the limited mortality of individual plant or tree. His poetry shows how long he has brooded upon the power of this contrast, which embraces the dual fate of man, who must die in season and seek freedom in eternity. The great uniting river of time flows through all things, stemming from eternal sources and seeking an oceanic repose, it rolls the bodies of the dead over and over till they are rounded like pebbles. This is the imaginative geography of Harris's *Palace of the Peacock*, as it is of Africa. Indeed, the African parallels to much of Harris's thought and imagery are remarkable. The River Congo plays in the poetry of Tchicaya U Tam'si the very role allotted to the Mazaruni or the Canje in the work of this Guyanese novelist whose veins mingle the blood of many races. . . .

In the years since it appeared Harris's novel has gradually made its way to a commanding place in the sensibility of the modern Caribbean. Artists, poets, historians and novelists have alike been haunted by its imagery. Despite obscurities of language that are occasionally impenetrable, despite the overworking of words like "musing" and "dreaming" in the interests of casting the reader adrift, *Palace of the Peacock* abounds in those insights and unifying flashes of illumination which Wilson Harris uniquely offers to the persevering reader. Every fresh reading of the book is a pilgrimage in which we relive Harris's vision of Guyana's history, his intimate interpretation of landscape and his longing to liberate man from the dialectics of hatred imposed on him by time and circumstance. Savannah and forest, mountain and waterfall, have interacted with a profoundly reflective temperament and a passion for spiritual truth to produce a masterpiece. [1969]

Gerald Moore. *The Chosen Tongue* (New York,
Harper & Row, 1970), pp. 75–76, 82

Anyone interested in gaining insight into the nature and potentialities of imagination should look deeply into Wilson Harris's *Tumatumari*. This eighth of Harris's extraordinary novels reveals his unusually original imagination at its present high state of development—a height to which it has evolved in the practice of the creative process he describes theoretically in his lectures and essays.

It is a process in which the imagination plays a role that is "passive" as well as active, not imposing itself upon the material under scrutiny but immersing itself in it, freeing itself as completely as possible from its own preconceptions and limitations, and being itself continuously transformed in the experiment. The imagination is encouraged to respond readily to all that the material suggests, to engage in the freest association of ideas, words and images, until the underlying relationships and processes (and the necessary ways to express them) emerge to be more actively observed and organized. . . .

In spite of the almost indescribable difficulty of *Tumatumari* as a whole, large sections of it read along smoothly enough, and many passages can be enjoyed for their sheer sensuous beauty (while others read like the output of a computer). The novel can be read simply as "experience"; in fact this novel, like all of Harris's novels, should be read for the first time in just this way and not primarily for the intellectual pleasure of it. What will happen with this kind of relaxed approach to it is that some of the underlying philosophical significance will gradually come through to provide illumination for subsequent readings in which intellectual perceptions and sense perceptions will be united. . . .

But even if this point is valid, that an additional view of history is needed to supplement Harris's view in which mankind is assumed to have a representative consciousness and experience before the unity of man, in this sense, is achieved, yet the question is of minor importance in relation to *Tumatumari* with its stimulating wealth of ideas and the contact it makes possible with Harris's rare mind and imagination and his commitment to Man.

Joyce Adler. JCL. July, 1969, pp. 20, 30–31

In *The Waiting Room*, a blind woman, convalescing after a series of operations, sits like a statue in a room full of antiques and relics of her past. There is little authorial direction, the language is dense and involuted, and the narrative yields itself fragmentarily. But it is apparent that through a process of memory of which she is not in full control, Susan Forrestal is reliving her unfinished affair with a rapacious lover she had dismissed in the past. As the disjointed memories of her absent lover float into the woman's consciousness, the reader becomes aware that the statuesque person, the inanimate relics in the room and the absent lover are bound together in the waiting room, in the way that the enthralled Ulysses was bound to the saving mast while his crew moved free on the deck below, their ears, however, deafened to the Sirens. Such a distribution of strengths and weaknesses between animate and inanimate objects in the room allows for a relayed digestion of the whole catastrophe while offering mutual protection from its annihilating powers.

So the ground of loss or deprivation with which most West Indian writers and historians engage is not for Harris simply a ground for protest, recrimination and satire; it is visualized through the agents in his works as an ambivalent condition of helplessness and self-discovery, the starting-point for new social structures. By the time that *The Waiting Room* comes to be written, Harris's exploration of this condition in the person has gone so far that the personal relationship—violent rape, irresponsible lover, involuntarily responsive mistress learning to digest catastrophe—absorbs the burden of an equally rapacious imperial relationship. Susan Forrestal, blind, helpless, and deprived, involved in the waiting room in the development of new resources and capacities for relationships with people and things, becomes the exciting ambivalent emblem of a so-called "hopeless," "historyless" West Indian condition.

Kenneth Ramchand. *The West Indian Novel and
Its Background* (New York, Barnes & Noble,
1970), pp. 11–12

As one ventures deeper into the novel [*Ascent to Omai*] images proliferate in an astonishing way to produce reverberations of meaning. Victor is an everyman figure who, early in the novel, comes to represent the people of an "Old" as well as "New" world: post- as well as pre-Columbian Man. Like Prudence of *Tumatumari*, he seems to be the soul of Man seeking in the "well of the past" the means of a new birth. "Omai" is an American root-word with multiple meaning used to suggest the "peak experience" of the mystics—the unpredictable flash of spiritual illumination. "Omai" is also the mythical El Dorado, the "lost worlds" of Roraima and Atlantis: a place which exists and does not exist—a "hill of cloud." Victor's ascent of the hill has an archetypal significance: one thinks of Moses' ascent of Sinai, the "eight-fold path" of the mystics, Dante's hill of purgatory. There are echoes of a symbolic retracing of the Middle Passage. . . .

Victor's quest is symbolic not only of Caribbean Man's search for ancestral origins, but also of Mankind's longing for a pre-lapsarian world, and there are deeper echoes, such as the suggestion, in the appearance of the spectral pork-knocker as a "tabula rasa," a doppelganger with a "faceless face," of a "regressus ad uterum"—a return to formlessness—from which, as in mythology, the hero is reborn. The use of memory as a means of acquiring the necessary self-knowledge for this painful regeneration (here one thinks of the section in *Palace of the Peacock* called "The Straits of Memory" where the characters all gain self-knowledge in extremity) is a vital process of the inner alchemy which helps Victor to come to a new understanding of himself. By going beyond History and its "crass realities," by achieving a "new dimension" of *feeling*, Victor gains insight and so breaks out of the prison of History. A new direction is now possible.

Michael Gilkes. *LHY*. Jan., 1974, pp. 124–25

The novels of Wilson Harris ([*Companions of the Day and Night*] is his thirteenth) form one ongoing whole. Each work is individual; yet the whole sequence can be seen as a continuous, ever-widening exploration of civilization and creative art. *Ascent to Omai*, for instance, took subjective consciousness to a point beyond which further communication seemed impossible. This was answered, after two excursions into the realm of folklore, with *Black Marsden,* in which the creative imagination is Marsden, a trickster/illusionist whom the artist hero finally throws into the street. In *Companions of the Day and Night* the hero of *Black Marsden* is sent manuscripts by Marsden himself which he orders into an assertion of the creative interpenetration of history and imagination.

At a recent conference at Stirling [Scotland], Wilson Harris explained his present preoccupation with moments in which a suppressed cultural pattern erupts through a decaying later one. In *Black Marsden,* it was Scottish history in Edinburgh. In this novel, it is Mexico City, where Christian and Western patterns overlie traditional cultures going back to pre-Conquest Toltec times. Recurrent archetypes are the focus for conflicting cultural strata; and the naked, creative, suffering human spirit is embodied in the Fool, Nameless, or Christ, with his answering image of spiritual love, Mary or Beatrice. In the ancient Mexican religion he was a human sacrifice; in the Catholic conquest, the figure of Christ; in the modern world, a political martyr. . . .

Companions of the Day and Night is not Wilson Harris's finest novel. It does not have the architectonic strength of *Tumatumari* or the better known *Palace of the Peacock.* The surrealist fantasy weakens the texture of the sacrificial drama. But never has the wily magician Black Marsden created more startling effects, or Mr. Harris's extraordinary use of language been more assured.

Louis James. TLS. Oct. 10, 1975, p. 1217

HAYDEN, ROBERT (1913–   )

UNITED STATES

This first volume of poetry [*Heart-Shape in the Dust*] represents the emergence of a new and vigorous talent in American letters, with an obviously encouraging prospect of attaining an even higher level of achievement in the future. The reason for this promise—"promising" is often a patronizing term on the lips of a critic, a Pharisaic "assent with civil leer"—is that Mr. Hayden has something to say, and he knows how to say it. There is a true marriage of form and content, a happy fusion of mastery of technique with the rough and raw material of life-experience. Among Negro American poets only two challengers to Mr. Hayden come readily to mind: Sterling Brown and Langston Hughes. . . .

It is always invidious to quote poetry in truncated form, and some of Mr. Hayden's best poems are longish; "These Are My People," a mass chant, is a case in point. Varied are his moods and language. Like Sterling Brown, he has the exceptional faculty of investing a poem in dialect with tragic dignity, as, for example, "Ole Jim Crow." He has a spontaneity and an originality of expression which impart to his verses an accent all their own. Whatever he has learned from British or American literary tradition he has succeeded in integrating in his style, and so while the reader may discover faint echoes of past and contemporary masters, he will find it difficult to identify them with the accuracy which imitation always guarantees.

William Harrison. *Opportunity*. March, 1941, p. 91

yes really [*the lion and the archer*] is like that and like this so you can see it is original and l'art and worth a dollar because whenever something is printed in 12 point without capitals you know because it has been known for forty years that it is original and full of dazzleclustered trees and jokes of nacre and ormolu and poltergeists in imperials and of course worth a dollar for a swooney evening on the leopard skin exploring the navel with candybar joy

indeed all for a dollar you can join robert hayden's heart when it escapes from the mended ferris wheel and the clawfoot sarabande in its dance . . .

yes really it is like that and more like that than like this and maybe just maybe someday somewhen mr hayden will get right into selden rodman's anthology instead of *the negro caravan* (dear mr editor dont worry because you can minuscule the word when it's art) which will prove the oneness of mankind and the vision of being "violently opposed" to the wickedness of thinking that while there is sociology and politics the poet is the first sociologist and the vanguard politician

Cedric Dover. *Crisis*. Aug., 1948, p. 252

Seriously dedicated to his work, Hayden is a conscious artist rather than a spontaneous one, a deliberate worker, a careful polisher. While he does not scorn Negro themes and has used them in his most successful poems to date, he would like his work to stand or fall by objective poetic standards. As was the case with Countee Cullen, one gets the impression that Hayden is bothered by this Negro thing. He would like to be considered simply as a poet.

Arna Bontemps. *Phylon*. 11, 4, 1950, pp. 356–57

If war presents a growing problem for poetry, being an American Negro presents a worse one. The subject matter is inescapable—and if one is a

Negro, he will not wish to escape it. The subject matter is explosive and elemental; hard stuff for poets, it provides a discouraging paradox: the more you face it, the more you are driven to one of two extremes— sentimentality or hyper-erudition. Hughes or McKay would illustrate the former; Tolson, the latter. [In *Selected Poems*] Hayden is saddled with both. He oscillates from semi-dialect blues and corrupted ballads to Poundian notation; predictably, he resorts to the former for portraits of his childhood, family, and friends, and to the latter for "historical evidence" poems describing the white man's burden. Predictably, too, with a subject so fearfully basic and seemingly insoluble, Hayden is capable of high eclecticism when dealing with salvation (on the theological plane); witness his poems concerned with the Baha'i faith, a prominent nineteenth-century Persian sect whose leader was martyred. Might not the example of Jesus have sufficed? For the white man, probably.

Hayden is as gifted a poet as most we have; his problem is not one of talent but frame of reference. It is fascinating, moving, and finally devastating that the finest verse in this book [a speech in "Middle Passage"] is spoken by a Spanish sailor, a witness of the *Amistad* mutiny, who describes the slaughter of their captors by "murderous Africans." . . . Hayden is a superb ironist in this passage. The crime of it is he has not chosen his forte; it has chosen him.

David Galler. Poetry. July, 1967, pp. 268–69

The section of [Stephen Vincent Benét's] *John Brown's Body* which is closest to Hayden's "Middle Passage" is the one that appears immediately after the "invocation," "Prelude—the Slaver." Benét presents here the captain of a slave ship who is moved to comment on a profession in which he is skilled, while actually transporting a cargo of black ivory from Africa to America. The impulse toward self-revelation is aroused by the questions, often not stated but implied, posed by a young mate, who is inexperienced and innocent. . . .

Hayden takes over the problem of reconciling Christianity and slavetrading in "Middle Passage," though the machinery of his narrative is much more complicated. The first of three parts offers the log entries, the prayers, and the ruminations of a pious member of the crew of a slaver. The conflict, however, is internal rather than external. The spur toward self-revelation is not an innocent youth on a maiden voyage, but the consciousness of the speaker, as he feels the threat to body and soul in the hazards and the emotional excesses that come from participation in the slave trade. . . .

His narration is not simple because it is made complex by the fact of his piety. On the one hand, there is the sailor's prosaic voice, instructing us in entries in ship's logs and, finally, in a legal deposition, of the hazards of a rebellious cargo, disease, and lust. On the other hand, there is the voice praying for "safe passage" to bring "heathen souls" to God's "chastening." What the sailor tells has so much cruelty and depravity that it seems finally to overwhelm the teller of the tale. The secure sense of accomplishing God's design departs, and there is only the cry, despairing now, rather than confident: "Pilot Oh Pilot Me."

Charles T. Davis. In Donald B. Gibson, ed.,
Modern Black Poets (Englewood Cliffs, N.J.,
Prentice-Hall, 1973), pp. 99–101

In "We Wear the Mask," probably the most widely reprinted of all Afro-American poems, Dunbar defines a tactical masquerade consciously assumed as a pragmatic defense in a hostile world. . . .

For Hayden's diver [in "The Diver"] the temptation to "fling aside the mask" is overcome in his ambiguously motivated ascent. What he rises towards, however, remains as vague as the reasons for his rising; he faces, in fact, much the same kind of indeterminate, existential future as Ralph Ellison's invisible man who resolves to emerge from the cave of his self-imposed meditation and seek a "socially responsible" form of salvation on the streets of America. Like the invisible man, the diver must return to a world which he cannot control from a temptation which he has, if not defeated, at least neutralized, although a temptation, it must be noted, which differs from that of Ellison's protagonist in springing from the emotions rather than the intellect, in residing in the wet and ill-defined phantasms of the unconscious rather than the dry and well-illuminated categories of the understanding, and in luring him to eternal activity rather than eternal memory or contemplation; unlike the invisible man, his ascent is not the result of a conscious act of the will and he has for protection not a private cloak of invisibility but a life-supporting mask of cultural awareness developed through generations of introspection. Hayden offers a modern audience the period Dunbar had implicitly promised, a time when the grinning, lying, laughing mask of anguish and forbearance has metamorphosed into the tactically expressionless mask of the emerging diver.

Maurice J. O'Sullivan, Jr. CLAJ.
Sept., 1973, pp. 91–92

Hayden's poetic career spans the years from the period of the late-Harlem Renaissance down to the current Black Arts Revolution. His first publication shows the influence of the Renaissance, but as that influence diminished, Hayden, unlike Gwendolyn Brooks and others of his generation, did not adopt the militant, nationalist, anti-Western-tradition stance of contemporary Black Arts writers. On the contrary, he has tried in every way to make even his so-called Negro poetry conform to and measure up to the best that Western civilization has produced. A superb craftsman, and a perfectionist, Hayden has consistently written for a "fit audience, though few." . . .

Always a skillful craftsman in verse, Hayden has grown and improved with the years. When he decided to abandon the kind of racial protest verse that he wrote in his first work, he seemingly decided to give up most of the conventional verse forms used in the early volume. In *Heart-Shape in the Dust*, for example, one finds quatrains (with varying line-lengths and rhyme-schemes), Shakespearian sonnets, mass chants, and other conventional forms. In his *Selected Poems*, one finds practically no rhyme (even his sonnet, "Frederick Douglass" is not rhymed). In this later volume, he employs a number of varied, unshackled, free-flowing verse forms, and he handles them effectively and on occasion brilliantly. . . . Perhaps Hayden's most impressive poetic techniques are those found in "Middle Passage." In this long poem, Hayden subtly and musically blends several kinds of writing—prose statement, refrains, excerpts from other poems, and lines from an old hymn—to produce a symphonic whole. To achieve his effects, the poet depends on the well-chosen, suggestive word *and* a cadence that reflects the varying moods of the poem.

Arthur P. Davis. *From the Dark Tower*
(Washington, D.C., Howard University Press,
1974), pp. 175, 179–80

Too much fame too soon has been the ruin of many poets. Until recently, black poets have not had to suffer this dubious blessing. Poets like Robert Hayden won recognition abroad but were ignored by our own literary king-makers. Hayden's collection of new and selected poems [*Angle of Ascent*] in a climate that is more openly aware should bring him the fame his talent deserves, and, luckily, it comes too late to harm that gift. . . .

Hayden keeps his eyes and ears open to the magic of the moment, to the moose in the wood ("tall ungainly creatures/in their battle crowns") to the "Creole babies,/Dixie odalisques,/speeding through cutglass/dark." A window washer, a religious confidence man, hunters or country dancers play their momentary part in his parody of freak and minstrel shows. Anger and love move these images into being, and, as in all true poetry, language gives them life. Robert Hayden will survive in his poems, long after current fashions of literature fade.

James Finn Cotter. *America*. Feb. 7, 1976, p. 103

HIMES, CHESTER (1909–   )

UNITED STATES

[In *If He Hollers Let Him Go*] Himes pits an educated, Northern Negro against poor Southern whites in a West Coast shipyard, and the results are violent and shocking. The author's stripped and functional prose style, developed in the slick magazines, takes on a new quality when it describes, in psychological terms, the contrast between a Negro believing in democracy and the brutal realities of our industrial system. In the end, Robert Jones, the hero, is crucified on a cross of chromium and steel. . . .

Jerky in pace, *If He Hollers Let Him Go* has been compared with the novels of James M. Cain, but there is more honest passion in 20 pages of Himes than in the whole of Cain. Tough-minded Himes has no illusions: I doubt if he has ever had any. He sees too clearly to be fooled by the symbolic guises in which Negro behavior tries to hide, and he traces the transformations by which sex is expressed in equations of race pride, murder in the language of personal redemption and love in terms of hate.

To read Himes conventionally is to miss the significance of the (to coin a phrase) bio-social level of his writing. Bob Jones is so charged with elementary passion that he ceases to be a personality and becomes a man reacting only with nerves, blood and motor responses.

Ironically, the several dreams that head each chapter do not really come off. Indeed, Himes's brutal prose is more authentically dreamlike than his consciously contrived dreams. And that is as it should be.

In this, his first, novel, Himes establishes himself not as what has been quaintly called a New Negro, but as a new kind of writing man.

Richard Wright. *PM*. Nov. 25, 1945, pp. m7–m8

In *If He Hollers Let Him Go*, published in 1945, Chester Himes studied, with rage and sometimes with disturbing perception, the struggle and defeat of one Negro war-worker on the West Coast, our native tensions intensified by war and the protagonist's relationships with his upper-class mulatto girl and the sexual tensions between himself and a female white war-worker. It was one of those books for which it is difficult to find any satisfactory classification: not a good novel but more than a tract, relentlessly honest, and carried by the fury and the pain of the man who wrote it. It seemed to me then one of the few books written by either whites or Negroes about Negroes which considered the enormous role which white guilt and tension play in what has been most accurately called the American dilemma.

Lonely Crusade can almost be considered an expansion of the earlier novel. Much of the rage is gone and with it the impact, and the book is written in what is probably the most uninteresting and awkward prose I have read in recent years. Yet the book is not entirely without an effect and is likely to have an importance out of all proportion to its intrinsic merit. For, just as the earlier book was carried by rage, this book is carried by what seems to be a desperate, implacable determination to find out the truth, please God, or die.

In less than four hundred pages Mr. Himes undertakes to consider the ever-present subjective and subconscious terror of a Negro, a dislocation which borders on paranoia; the political morality of American Communists; the psychology of union politics; Uncle Tomism; Jews and Negroes; the vast sexual implications of our racial heritage; the difficulty faced by any Negro in his relationships with both light people and dark; and the position of the American white female in the whole unlovely structure. This is a tall order and if we give Mr. Himes an A for ambition—and a rather awe-stricken gasp for effort—we are forced also to realize that the book's considerable burden never really gets shoulder high. It is written almost as though the author were determined within one book, regardless of style or ultimate effect, to say all of the things he wanted to say about the American republic and the position of the Negro in it. Part of the failure of the book certainly lies in this fact, that far too much is attempted. . . .

The value of his book lies in its earnest effort to understand the psychology of oppressed and oppressor and their relationship to each other.

James Baldwin. *NLr.* Oct. 25, 1947, p. 11

This reviewer was impressed by the controlled force of Mr. Himes' earlier novel, *Cast the First Stone.* Now *The Third Generation* has been published, a far less skillfully modulated work which yet seizes the reader with a strong, if incoherent impact of its own. Much obviously autobiographical truth and a great deal of agonized sincerity has gone into the writing of it. . . .

Mr. Himes' difficulty stems from the fact that his novel is not one but two. *The Third Generation* starts as a basically robust saga of a family's search for a place in the sun. Its viewpoint is collective; it projects an acquisitive, restless and dynamic psyche. But suddenly the author changes focus. The narrative acquires an abrupt Oedipal undercurrent. Mr. Himes' camera focuses exclusively on Charles and his relationship to his mother. Thus the excesses at the end sometimes read like gratuitous melodrama.

Chalk it up to Mr. Himes' narrative talent, then, that his novel always lives and sometimes fascinates despite the bifurcation and despite a rather rough-hewn style. Count it as Mr. Himes' even greater merit that he has not written merely a protest novel. In this novel the suffering of the Negro is not for a propaganda end. It is rather a means of dramatizing all human fear and hatred of which prejudice is only a particularly shameful expression. It is this attitude on the author's part that lends his story much of its homely power.

Frederic Morton. *NYHT*. Jan. 10, 1954, p. 6

Chester Himes' *If He Hollers Let Him Go* is an impressive failure—with accent on the adjective. It takes the novel of pure race consciousness to its utmost limit, where it strangles to death in its own contradictions. The novel is Wrightian to the core, which is hardly surprising in view of the author's background and experience. . . .

In its denouement the novel reveals a fatal structural flaw. Here is a black nationalist, hypersensitive, neurotic, unable to mobilize his energies for anything but the race war, driven by his obsession to the brink of murder. The whole novel moves inexorably toward the opposing view that some kind of accommodation is the price of sanity. The protagonist chooses; he is born again; but suddenly we are confronted with a chain of events whose logic seems to justify his former view of reality.

Earlier in the novel, Himes has argued convincingly that in every human being there is an inner world which lies within his power to control. Is it now his thesis that in all crucial matters concerning a Negro's fate, the will of society is decisive? If so, we feel put upon, for we have been following Jones' inner conflict as if it mattered. Suddenly it is revealed as meaningless—no matter what Jones decides, society will dispose of his future. Such a thesis requires that the tensions of the novel be resolved on a sociological plane; the very basis of a psychological novel is destroyed.

At bottom the trouble is ideological: neither revenge nor accommodation is acceptable to Himes, and as a result, the novel flounders to an inconclusive finish.

Robert A. Bone. *The Negro Novel in America*
(New Haven, Conn., Yale University Press,
1958), pp. 173, 175–76

Himes's earlier novels were partly autobiographical, or at least based on the author's experiences. Using the methods of traditional novelistic psychology combined with the instantaneous imagery that has been the rule in American literature since Dos Passos, Himes has no trouble creating verisimilitude, and sometimes the sincerity of these novels is moving. Their shortcoming, as I have said, is that they support or illustrate a *thesis*, which is correct but which we think we already knew (our mistake). We quickly grow weary—or perhaps it is our guilty conscience, as when someone speaks to us about the Algerian war. The truth is, nevertheless, that an unhappy destiny, a destiny that contains nothing but misfortune, engages our interest only when it is enhanced by genius. . . . On the other hand, Himes's detective novels, or rather picaresque novels, aim at entertainment—and through the narrative alone. . . .

Himes submits to a genre, the mystery novel, and he observes its conventions. Novel after novel, we follow the incessant struggle of cops against crooks and crooks against one another. His plots owe little to mathematics, to the logic of a detective story; much to light opera and to shifts in point of view; he is closer to James Hadley Chase than to Agatha Christie. . . .

[In his mystery novels] Himes does not burden himself with a moral. He tells stories. It is up to us to laugh and, if we like, to think.

René Micha. *TM*. Feb., 1965, pp. 1512–13, 1522–23†

Chester Himes has mellowed, in the direction of humour, since his earlier effort, *If He Hollers Let Him Go*, a book violently black-versus-white, full of hot-tempered fistfights, bitterness, tragedy, and above all hatred. *Cotton Comes to Harlem* is a rollicking, funny book that begins with a Back-to-Africa movement launched in New York's Harlem. . . .

Chester Himes is an American Negro, born in Jefferson City, Missouri, and now living in France. One can understand why he chooses to live in France. Mr. Himes may be a funny writer, but he is also a novelist, and even in a book like this—with a laugh on nearly every page—it is evident he is concerned with the Negro's plight in Harlem, aware of every corruption from whores and dope-addiction to mere urine-stained walls, aware of the unkillable hope in the minds of many of these people and of the hopelessness of their situation as it is now. He can poke fun at white and black alike—as when a white policeman is slowly seduced by an undressing Negro beauty whom he's supposed to guard. It is his value as a writer, and it makes this book a novel, that he can jest at all of it, make stiletto social comments, and keep his story running at the speed of one of his Buick "Roadmasters" in the days of yore.

TLS. Jan. 20, 1966, p. 37

Chester Himes is one of the most prolific of all Negro novelists. At this writing, he is the author of six major novels and a number of lively potboilers about a couple of Harlem detectives. Although he enjoys a good reputation in France, where he now lives, for the most part the American critics have dismissed him as being of the Wright school of naturalism, whose "protest" is no longer fashionable. Such criticism is not altogether fair. Himes's interests are considerably different from Wright's, and his firsthand knowledge of certain areas of American life is more developed. His protagonists are generally middle-class, fairly well-educated, somewhat sophisticated in the ways of the world, and often intellectually oriented. They are concerned with ideas and the application of ideas to their experience; they are constantly searching out rational explanations for the irrationalities of their lives. They move with considerable aplomb among white liberals and radicals of both sexes, and engage them in dialectics on their own terms. Himes is also a more deliberate prose stylist than Wright. He seldom intrudes, moralizes, or explains. His characters are usually sufficiently articulate to say what they mean—and what they mean issues often enough from their character and intelligence. Himes does parallel Wright in his bitterness, fury, and frustration. He has given up on America, and rarely returns now on visits. . . .

[*The Primitive*] is Himes's most pessimistic work. He has lost faith in the human capacity to reason its way out of its dilemmas. Jesse and Kriss, two intelligent human beings, are as muddled and distressed about their own identities as the worst racists. But here lies the trouble. Himes has, in a curious way, written two books—one about Jesse and Kriss, and one about racist America—and the two do not quite mesh, because Jesse and Kriss are too atypical and too idiosyncratic. Himes's ideas require a novel with a wider scope than one shabby Harlem tenement, one Gramercy Park apartment, and a few decadent intellectuals. Whether or not he will succeed in writing such a novel remains to be seen.

Edward Margolies. *Native Sons* (Philadelphia, J. B. Lippincott, 1968), pp. 87–88, 99

Himes is perhaps the single greatest naturalistic American writer living today. Of course, no one in the literary establishment is going to admit that; they haven't and they won't. Reviews of his books generally wind up in the last half of the Sunday *New York Times Book Review*, if they are reviewed at all. Himes will tell you that he doesn't care; that all his career he has been shuffled under the table. Perhaps this is, after all, the smallest of hurts he has suffered. . . .

It gave me the greatest pleasure to be able to see Himes again, to see him at a time when a kind of physical comfort was coming his way at last; to see him still producing long, articulate and sensitive works. He let me read the first volume of his autobiography, *The Quality of Hurt* (394 pages, ending in 1955). It is a fantastic, masculine work whose pages are haunted by vistas of France and Spain, of family life in the United States, of his first marriage, of Richard Wright and Robert Graves and others. American male writers don't produce manly books. Himes' autobiography is that of a man.

John A. Williams. Flashbacks (Garden City, N.Y.,
Doubleday, 1973), pp. 294–95, 297

Himes chose his title, *The Quality of Hurt*, from Shakespeare's, "The quality of mercy is not strain'd/It droppeth as the gentle rain from heaven," and the chapters and Books are connected to each other by "hurts" Himes endured in a long History of Hurts. He was hurt by his mother, a strong-willed, highly-intelligent woman who could handle a pistol so well, she "beat anybody to the draw." She taught Himes and his brothers so expertly that when they entered school they were ahead of their classes, but she also "squeezed the bridges of our noses to keep them from becoming flat."

He was hurt by the reception to his writing, especially *Lonely Crusade*, the adverse criticism of which was one of the major factors leading to his exile. He was hurt by accidents so unbelievable as to lead one to compare the plight of the Himes family to the fictional Gothic ones, laboring under a curse. A chemistry accident almost totally blinded his brother, Joseph; the tormented relationship between his mother and father led to their divorce. He was hurt by a judge who sentenced him to 20-to-25 years for armed robbery, and he was hurt by his inability to support his Black wife, Jean. . . .

One of the remarkable things about *The Quality of Hurt* [is] the absence of rancor and self-pity. . . .

As for his capacity to calmly narrate these Hurts without cloying, Himes writes, "I hate exhibiting my wounds." . . .

Chester Himes is a great writer and a brave man. His life has shown that Black writers are as heroic as the athletes, entertainers, scientists, cowboys, pimps, gangsters, and politicians they might write about. Many Blacks have given Himes a bad time but his belief in the excellence and uniqueness of American Blacks continued unmitigated. . . .

The achievement of volume I is even more staggering when you realize that another volume is on the way. Surely, that will be an additional monster destined to mind slam the reader.

Ishmael Reed. *BlackW*. March, 1972, pp. 25, 35, 86

The five novels Himes wrote between 1958 and 1961 [*For Love of Imabelle, The Crazy Kill, The Real Cool Killers, All Shot Up*, and *The Big Gold Dream*] are classic detective stories. Each poses a problem, or a series of problems, usually expressed in hideous physical violence, which extends its corruption into personal and communal life, and threatens the always precarious balance by which individuals survive in Harlem. Each network of dangerous mysteries is explained by a single discovery of guilt, which restores that balance and redefines the worth of those characters with whom we sympathize. The discovery, of course, is made by Grave Digger and Coffin Ed, the heroic figures who embody all the attributes of the traditional literary detective. Opposed by violence and unreason, they struggle courageously to uncover truth; trapped in a hopelessly venal institution, they remain incorruptibly honest; burdened with a body of law ludicrously inappropriate to the conditions of Harlem life, they are lonely dispensers of justice. They implement most of their solutions outside the law; many of their methods defy it. The responsibilities and dangers involved in the search for decency rest upon them personally rather than upon the institutional apparatus which supposedly protects them.

But Grave Digger and Coffin Ed are more than familiar literary heroes; their cultural antecedents ultimately give them the moral authority they exercise. Simply enough, they are the "bad niggers" of Black Folklore. . . . Like all "bad niggers" they may seem at first glance improbable (or undesirable) models for humanity. But the "bad nigger" is an emotionally projected rather than a socially functional figure; he is valuable as a symbol of defiance, strength, and masculinity to a community that has been forced to learn, or at least to sham, weakness and compliance. As "bad niggers" Coffin Ed and Grave Digger are part of the continuing evolution of a black hero, and are thus studies in cultural lore rather than examples of individual character. In the Harlem series they lay all of their traditional qualifications on the line in a desperate fight against the crimes that endanger the integrity, even the collective sanity, of the black community.

Raymond Nelson. *VQR*. Spring, 1972, pp. 265–67

I know that Chester, whose friendship I value highly, is puzzled and annoyed by the comparative indifference of the American public to his books. At World and at Putnam's we paid him modest advances. We recovered our investment, not from hardback sales, but from the paper-back reprints. But the reprints, in turn, did not fare well. It is very hard to find any of Himes' paperbacks in the bookshops of America, although most of them are in print. Luckily, this is not true in Europe, especially France. The French readers love him. Gallimard, the foremost publishing house in France, publishes Himes' books with profit. Chester Himes is a VIP in Paris as anyone can see who visits the French bookshops. This is also true in Barcelona.

Himes has talent to burn: he has wit, a fine comic sense, an under-standing of scenic values; he's an inventive plotter; his characters are alive and easy to become involved with: his stories have action, animal heat, tension. He also usually has something vital to say. Added up, he should be popular in America. But he isn't. . . .

As an author his reward must come soon—I mean his American reward. Meanwhile, his *critical* reception continues good; the critics and the aficionados love and understand him and his worth. When his auto-biography is completed and published (possibly in 1976) some dra-matic changes may occur for him—for the better.

William Targ. Indecent Pleasures (New York,
Macmillan, 1975), pp. 291–92

To mention humor at all in discussing a novel that ends with a drunken murder scene seems macabre, but *The Primitive*, while tragic in outline, is filled with incidents and conversations that are handled with ironic Rabelaisian gusto. Gargantuan drinking and eating scenes are described in a style that effectively blends the high and the low, and the literary allusion and street language are combined in a manner that makes *The Primitive*, despite its gruesomeness, more engaging than any of Himes's earlier novels. It is also a work in which Himes pushes to conclusion, in a psychologically satisfying way, two themes of frustration that had haunted him since *If He Hollers Let Him Go*: his anger at being rejected as a writer, and the black man's obsession with the white woman and what she represents. For Himes, *The Primitive* represents a stopping point, an end to his confessional phase, and a settling of scores. . . .

It is the last of his confessional novels and ends the autobiographi-cal emphasis that occasionally interferes with the structure of his work. The novel was finished in Europe and coincides with Himes's rejection of the United States and his desire for a different kind of life in a different culture free from American "alchemy" and the pressures that drove Jesse Robinson to destroy himself in the process of becoming "equal."

James Lundquist. Chester Himes (New York,
Frederick Ungar, 1976), pp. 93, 105

HUGHES, LANGSTON (1902–1967)

UNITED STATES

[Hughes] represents a transcendently emancipated spirit among a class of young writers whose particular battle-cry is freedom. With the enthusiasm of a zealot, he pursues his way [in *The Weary Blues*], scornful, in subject matter, in photography, and rhythmical treatment, of whatever obstructions time and tradition have placed before him. To him it is essential that he be himself. Essential and commendable surely; yet the thought persists that some of these poems would have been better had Mr. Hughes held himself a bit in check. In his admirable introduction to the book, Carl Van Vechten says the poems have a "highly deceptive air of spontaneous improvisation." I do not feel that the air is deceptive.

If I have the least powers of prediction, the first section of this book, "The Weary Blues," will be most admired, even if less from intrinsic poetical worth than because of its dissociation from the traditionally poetic. Never having been one to think all subjects and forms proper for poetic consideration, I regard these jazz poems as interlopers in the company of the truly beautiful poems in other sections of the book. They move along with the frenzy and electric heat of a Methodist or Baptist revival meeting, and affect me in much the same manner. The revival meeting excites me, cooling and flushing me with alternate chills and fevers of emotion; so do these poems. But when the storm is over, I wonder if the quiet way of communing is not more spiritual for the God-seeking heart; and in the light of reflection I wonder if jazz poems really belong to that dignified company, that select and austere circle of high literary expression which we call poetry. . . .

Taken as a group the selections in this book seem one-sided to me. They tend to hurl this poet into the gaping pit that lies before all Negro writers, in the confines of which they become racial artists instead of artists pure and simple. There is too much emphasis here on strictly Negro themes; and this is probably an added reason for my coldness toward the jazz poems—they seem to set a too definite limit upon an already limited field.

Dull books cause no schisms, raise no dissensions, create no parties. Much will be said of *The Weary Blues* because it is a definite achievement, and because Mr. Hughes, in his own way, with a first book that cannot be dismissed as merely promising, has arrived.

Countee Cullen. Opportunity. Feb., 1926, pp. 73–74

Fine clothes may not make either the poet or the gentleman, but they certainly help; and it is a rare genius that can strip life to the buff and still poetize it. This, however, Langston Hughes has done, in a volume [*Fine Clothes to the Jew*] that is even more starkly realistic and colloquial than his first—*The Weary Blues*. It is a current ambition in American poetry to take the common clay of life and fashion it to living beauty, but very few have succeeded, even [Edgar Lee] Masters and [Carl] Sandburg not invariably. They get their effects, but often at the expense of poetry. Here, on the contrary, there is scarcely a prosaic note or a spiritual sag in spite of the fact that never has cruder colloquialism or more sordid life been put into the substance of poetry. The book is, therefore, notable as an achievement in poetic realism in addition to its particular value as a folk study in verse of Negro life.

The success of these poems owes much to the clever and apt device of taking folk-song forms and idioms as the mold into which the life of the plain people is descriptively poured. This gives not only an authentic background and the impression that it is the people themselves speaking, but the sordidness of common life is caught up in the lilt of its own poetry and without any sentimental propping attains something of the necessary elevation of art. Many of the poems are modelled in the exact metrical form of the Negro "Blues," now so suddenly popular, and in thought and style of expression are so close as scarcely to be distinguishable from the popular variety. But these poems are not transcriptions, every now and then one catches sight of the deft poetic touch that unostentatiously transforms them into folk portraits. In the rambling improvised stanzas of folk-song, there is invariably much that is inconsistent with the dominant mood; and seldom any dramatic coherence. Here we have these necessary art ingredients ingenuously added to material of real folk flavor and origin. . . .

After so much dead anatomy of a people's superstition and so much sentimental balladizing on dialect chromatics, such vivid, pulsing, creative, portraits of Negro folk foibles and moods are most welcome. The author apparently loves the plain people in every aspect of their lives, their gin-drinking carousals, their street brawls, their tenement publicity, and their slum matings and partings, and reveals this segment of Negro life as it has never been shown before. Its open frankness will be a shock and a snare for the critic and moralist who cannot distinguish clay from mire.

Alain Locke. SR. April 9, 1927, p. 712

Langston Hughes has often been compared to Dunbar. At first this comparison seems far-fetched and foolish, but on closer examination one finds that the two have much in common, only that where Dunbar failed, Langston Hughes succeeds. Both set out to interpret "the soul of his race"; one failed, the other, just at the beginning of his career, has in some measure already succeeded.

The younger man has not been content to assemble a supply of stock types who give expression to stock emotions which may be either slightly amusing or slightly tragic but which are never either movingly tragic or convincingly comic. When Langston Hughes writes of specific Negro types he manages to make them more than just ordinary Negro types. They are actually dark-skinned symbols of universal characters. One never feels this way about the people in Dunbar's poetry. For he never heightens them above their own particular sphere. There is never anything of the universal element in his poems that motivates Mr. Hughes's.

Moreover, Langston Hughes has gone much farther in another direction than any other Negro poet, much farther even than James Weldon Johnson went along the same road in *God's Trombones*. He has appropriated certain dialects and rhythms characteristically Negroid as his poetic properties. He has borrowed the lingo and locutions of migratory workers, chamber-maids, porters, boot-blacks, and others, and woven them into rhythmic schemes borrowed from the blues songs, spirituals and jazz and with them created a poetic diction and a poetic form all his own. . . .

But Mr. Hughes has also written some of the most banal poetry of the age, which has not, as in the case of Mr. Cullen, even sounded beautiful.

Wallace Thurman. Bkm. July, 1928, pp. 560–61

In *Not without Laughter* Langston Hughes has outlined almost every aspect of the racial problem in the United States. Poverty dominates everything else. Almost all the characters in *Not without Laughter* are engaged in a constant struggle against it, although their endurance and their good will cannot be questioned. In hotels, middle-class homes, or construction yards wages are ridiculously low. If a member of the black community manages by chance to acquire the outer signs of affluence, he immediately arouses the hostility of the whites. If, when provoked for one reason or another, he reacts, it will not take long before he and his innocent brothers experience the terrors of burning or lynching. . . .

Not without Laughter is unquestionably the result of the young novelist's personal experience. While traveling throughout the United States, Hughes gathered a great many facts. With his very personal art and his plain style, free from all vain literary contrivances, he has created a masterpiece which has been read with interest and excitement in the United States and which has been published in England, France, and Moscow.

René Piquion. *Langston Hughes: Un chant nouveau* (Port-au-Prince, Imprimerie de l'État, 1940), pp. 145–47†

The double role that Langston Hughes has played in the rise of a realistic literature among the Negro people resembles in one phase the role that Theodore Dreiser played in freeing American literary expression from the restrictions of Puritanism. Not that Negro literature was ever Puritanical, but it was timid and vaguely lyrical and folkish. Hughes's early [collections of] poems, *The Weary Blues* and *Fine Clothes to the Jew*, full of irony and urban imagery, were greeted by a large section of the Negro reading public with suspicion and shock when they first appeared in the middle twenties. Since then the realistic position assumed by Hughes has become the dominant outlook of all those Negro writers who have something to say.

The other phase of Hughes's role has been, for the lack of a better term, that of a cultural ambassador. Performing his task quietly and almost casually, he has represented the Negroes' case, in his poems, plays, short stories and novels, at the court of world opinion. On the other hand he has brought the experiences of other nations within the orbit of the Negro writer by his translations from the French, Russian and Spanish.

How Hughes became this forerunner and ambassador can best be understood in the cameo sequences of his own life that he gives us in his sixth and latest book, *The Big Sea*. Out of his experiences as a seaman, cook, laundry worker, farm helper, bus boy, doorman, unemployed worker, have come his writings dealing with black gals who wore red stockings and black men who sang the blues all night and slept like rocks all day.

Unlike the sons and daughters of Negro "society," Hughes was not ashamed of those of his race who had to scuffle for their bread. The jerky transitions of his own life did not admit of his remaining in one place long enough to become a slave of prevailing Negro middle-class prejudices. So beneficial does this ceaseless movement seem to Hughes that he has made it one of his life principles: six months in one place, he says, is long enough to make one's life complicated. The result has been a range of artistic interest and expression possessed by no other Negro writer of his time. . . .

Hughes is tough; he bends but he never breaks, and he has carried on a manly tradition in literary expression when many of his fellow writers have gone to sleep at their posts.

Richard Wright. *NR*. Oct. 28, 1940, pp. 600–601

Langston Hughes's poetry is what, in terms of the art of the motion picture, would be called documentary. His concern is to document the moods and problems of the American Negro, to set side by side in simple and lively form pictures and impressions which will add up to a presentation of the American Negro's present situation. This kind of writing is worlds apart from the subtle distillation of meaning aimed at by other contemporary poets. For Mr. Hughes, the idiom of poetry is valuable only to the degree that it pins down a situation and draws it to the attention of his readers. The ultimate meaning, the subtler vision of reality, the oblique insight into man's personality and man's fate are not for him; he has a more urgent and immediate problem, to project the living American Negro onto the page. And he does so, on the whole, with success.

David Daiches. *NYHT*. Jan. 9, 1949, p. 4

Few people have enjoyed being Negro as much as Langston Hughes. Despite the bitterness with which he has occasionally indicted those who mistreat him because of his color (and in this collection of sketches and stories [*Laughing to Keep from Crying*] he certainly does not let up), there has never been any question in this reader's mind about his basic attitude. He would not have missed the experience of being what he is for the world. . . .

Langston Hughes has practised the craft of the short story no more than he has practised the forms of poetry. His is a spontaneous art which stands or falls by the sureness of his intuition, his mother wit. His stories, like his poems, are for readers who will judge them with their hearts as well as their heads. By that standard he has always measured well. He still does.

Arna Bontemps. *SR*. April 5, 1952, p. 17

Unfortunately, Sandy disrupts the symbolic unity of [*Not without Laughter.*] Presumably torn by the conflicting forces which divide the family, his inner struggle fails to materialize. There is no laughter in his life, but only an altogether commendable determination to be a credit to the race. At this point, the novel bogs down in hopeless ideological confusion. . . .

Hughes tried to reject the Protestant ethic (joy is wrong), while retaining the success drive on which it is based. It is an untenable halfway house, which Claude McKay and Jessie Fauset would equally scorn to occupy. In any event, Hughes' ideological ambivalence has disastrous aesthetic consequences. The novel and its main character simply part company. Instead of supporting the defense-of-laughter theme, Sandy emerges as a symbol of racial advancement, which is hardly a laughing matter. Given his main theme of suffering and self-expression, Hughes might better have written the novel around Harriet, who emerges from a life of prostitution to become "Princess of the Blues."

Not without Laughter has been compared in some quarters to the first book of [James T. Farrell's] *Studs Lonigan* trilogy. No service is rendered either to American literature or to Hughes by this exaggerated claim. A mediocre novel, *Not without Laughter* was undertaken before its author was prepared to meet the rigorous requirements of the genre. Ideologically confused and structurally defective, the novel gives a final impression of sprawling formlessness. The author, to his credit, is fully aware of these shortcomings, if some of his friendly critics are not. In his autobiography, *The Big Sea*, Hughes makes a courageous apology to the characters of his early novel: "I went to Far Rockaway that summer and felt bad, because I had wanted their novel to be better than the published one I had given them. I hated to let them down."

Robert A. Bone. *The Negro Novel in America*
(New Haven, Conn., Yale University Press, 1958),
pp. 76–77

Hughes, in his sermons, blues and prayers, has working for him the power and the beat of Negro speech and Negro music. Negro speech is vivid largely because it is private. It is a kind of emotional shorthand—or sleight-of-hand—by means of which Negroes express, not only their relationship to each other, but their judgment of the white world. And, as the white world takes over this vocabulary—without the faintest notion of what it really means—the vocabulary is forced to change. The same thing is true of Negro music, which has had to become more and more complex in order to continue to express any of the private or collective experience.

Hughes knows the bitter truth behind these hieroglyphics: what they are designed to protect, what they are designed to convey. But he has not forced them into the realm of art where their meaning would become clear and overwhelming. "Hey, pop!/Re-bop!/Mop!" conveys much more on Lenox Avenue than it does in [Hughes's *Selected Poems*], which is not the way it ought to be.

Hughes is an American Negro poet and has no choice but to be acutely aware of it. He is not the first American Negro to find the war between his social and artistic responsibilities all but irreconcilable.

James Baldwin. NYT. March 29, 1959, p. 6

The conception of *Soul Gone Home* is that of fantasy, and it contains some ironically comic moments, but its impulse is far removed from comedy. In a vignette-like episode, Hughes creates with great economy the kind of play Zola called for in his preface to *Thérèse Raquin*. Although a fantasy in concept and structure, its atmosphere and effects are those of naturalism. Like one of Hughes' poems, *Soul Gone Home* bristles with implications and reverberates with connotations. That which is unsaid becomes almost more important than what is put into the dialogue. The repressive dominance of the white culture is suggested only by the arrival of ambulance attendants, who are white as the mother knew they would be. The tragedy is that of a people so repressed that they can no longer love, and the ironic implications build to a shocking climax. Its impact is stark and uncomplicated, and it is a difficult play to forget.

Hughes does not always write in a serious vein, as readers of his stories and poems well know. His folk plays of urban Negro life, at once humorous and revealing, are a true contribution to American folk drama. The three included [in the collection *Five Plays*]—*Little Ham, Simply Heavenly*, and *Tambourines to Glory*—are, if one must define them, comedies. But the triple specters of poverty, ignorance, and repression can be seen not far beneath the surface of the comedy. The "numbers racket," "dream books," and the "hot goods man" in *Little Ham*, Simple's wistful sadness that no Negro has seen a flying saucer, and Laura's attitude toward the "religion business" in *Tambourines to Glory*, all indicate the near poverty, the ignorance, and the superstition that prevail in the world of which Hughes writes. Nevertheless, it is a colorful, wonderful world he presents to us, and we cannot but admire the spirit and vigor of his characters. He gives us a dynamic view of a segment of life most of us will never know and can discover nowhere else. At times he may sacrifice dramatic action for the sake of portraying nothing more than the people of Harlem absorbed in living out their lives from day to day, but if the humor of the scene and Hughes' infectious interest in his characters carry us along with him, what more can we ask?

Webster Smalley. Introduction to Five Plays by
Langston Hughes (Bloomington, Indiana University
Press, 1963), pp. xi–xii

For many years Hughes, often hailed as "the poet laureate of the Negro people," has been recognized by white critics as an author-poet of the protest genre. Others, more conservative and denunciatory, have assailed Hughes as radical and leftist, to mention the more polite language. In both instances the critics referred to Hughes's treatment of imperfections in the American Dream that we, as a nation, hold so dear. . . .

Probably the greatest portion of Hughes's poetry does not refer specifically to the American Dream, despite the habit of many critics' labeling him a protest writer primarily. But in *Ask Your Mama: 12 Moods for Jazz* he returns to the Dream, in jazz tempo with barbs appropriate for a dream too long deferred. With an impish introduction of the melody "Dixie" in the background, the poet combines dreams and nightmares to produce a mural of black power in the South. . . .

But the grandiose dream sequence, itself reflecting how one-sided the American Dream has been in the South, is short-lived. The poet returns to the pessimistic here and now. The Negro can't keep from losing, even when he's winning, he moans in blues tempo. *Ask Your Mama* relates to the vest spectrum of the American Dream, as it affects Negroes. There are the hardships of blockbusting, or integrating a white residential area, the bitterness of Negro artists, the stereotyped attitudes of whites toward Negroes, the hope of a better material world for ambitious Negroes, and the eternal suspicions cast upon any Negro who does anything worthwhile or, often, anything that is ordinary for white folks to do.

James Presley. *SWR*. Autumn, 1963, pp. 380, 383–84

Ask Your Mama strikes me as something like the synthesis and the culmination of Langston Hughes's work. . . .

In this collection Hughes tries to attain his old dream of being a complete poet-musician. He has at least succeeded in breaking away from the approach of his early collections, which are primarily gatherings of poems at times quite incongruous, with the exception of *Montage of a Dream Deferred*, which anticipates *Ask Your Mama* in its elaborate structure and deliberate counterpoint. In short, *Ask Your Mama* does not simply contain poetry that is more or less sung; rather, it resembles a film's sound track improvised with great freedom by the imaginary or real musician, in the best tradition of jazz.

Despite the new form of *Ask Your Mama*, Hughes has in no way given up his favorite themes. Nor does he seek innovation in the manner of Joyce and the T. S. Eliot of *The Waste Land*, who were concerned mainly with form. As the jacket of the collection says, the poetry is "full of allusions to current events," and "current events" for Langston

Hughes can only be those that concern the economic and social conditions of the black man—primarily those of the black American, but also those of blacks throughout the world.

François Dodat. Langston Hughes (Paris,
Pierre Seghers, 1964), pp. 65–67†

Not without Laughter, the novel Hughes wrote in 1930, and *Tambourines to Glory*, written in 1958, contain the strong points of his best poetry, vigor, simplicity, and a sure sense of human relationships, but they lack a certain depth of characterization and unity. *Not without Laughter* is certainly the better work of the two, transcribing as it does a warmly human picture of Negro life. This novel is also important for its emphasis on life within the Negro group. Jimboy, Annjee, and Aunt Hager are certainly aware of racial discrimination, but they live their own lives not without laughter.

In the 1930's Hughes wrote a series of short stories on racial misunderstanding which appeared in leading literary magazines and afterwards received favorable attention in compiled form as *The Ways of White Folks*. They are dramatic and show penetrating insight, making the reader realize, as [Sterling Brown] put it, "that there is a greater depth in Negro-white relationships of the most casual sort than other writers have suggested." More recently Hughes has written stories on a variety of themes, race being but one. The collection entitled *Laughing to Keep from Crying*, published in 1952, shows Hughes's broadening interest in minority groups of all kinds, timid Negro leadership, and the curious workings of love and hate. Although both collections have strong and weak stories, *The Ways of White Folks*, with its subtle emphasis on Negro-white behavior, seems the superior book. [1967]

Donald C. Dickinson. A Bio-Bibliography of
Langston Hughes, 2nd ed. (Hamden, Conn.,
Shoe String, 1972), p. 114

Langston Hughes loved literature. He loved it not fearfully, not with awe. His respect for it was never stiff nor cold. His respect for it was gaily deferential. He considered literature not his private inch, but great acreage. The plantings of others he not only welcomed but busily enriched.

He had an affectionate interest in the young. He was intent, he was careful. The young manuscript-bearing applicant never felt himself an intruder, never went away with Oak turned ashes in the hand.

Mightily did he use the street. He found its multiple heart, its tastes, smells, alarms, formulas, flowers, garbage and convulsions. He brought them all to his table-top. He crushed them to a writing-paste. The pen that was himself went in.

Gwendolyn Brooks. *Nation.* July 3, 1967, p. 7

From his first book, *The Weary Blues*, published in 1926, through today—or rather, through yesterday, when he died—the entire oeuvre of this great poet has been marked by the tireless struggle for the freedom of black men in those "free" United States of America. Drama, biography, the novel, history, the short story, the humorous sketch, autobiography—Langston Hughes has used his talent in all these genres to reach this goal. . . .

He has been criticized—and he is not the only one—for treating the racial issue exclusively, and for ignoring everything else. Why should we forget, say such critics, that this is also the century of Proust and Joyce? Why should the black artist not take his place within the context of American and world culture, abandoning or reducing his dependence upon ethnic and folk art? I am not in disagreement with this line of reasoning. But it would have been very difficult—not only when Hughes began to write but even now—for a black artist to have written something like *Ulysses* or *In Search of Lost Time*, masterpieces of world literature that they are, at the same time that blacks were being burned alive in the South. I do not know whether they were immolated by readers of Proust and Joyce, but without a doubt their persecutors were savages of the worst kind that there were—that there are—savages who should have been—who should be—exterminated with bullets or with poetry.

Nicolás Guillén. *PA.* No. 64, 1967, pp. 36–37†

Langston Hughes's new poems [in *The Panther and the Lash*], written shortly before his death last summer, catch fire from the Negro American's changing face. To a degree I would never have expected from his earlier work, his sensibility has kept pace with the times, and the intensity of his new concerns—helping him to shake loose old crippling mannerisms, the trade marks of his art—comes to fruition in many of the best poems of his career: "Northern Liberal," "Dinner Guest: Me," "Crowns and Garlands," to name a few.

Regrettably, in different poems, he is fatally prone to sympathize with starkly antithetical politics of race. A reader can appreciate his catholicity, his tolerance of all the rival—and mutually hostile—views of his outspoken compatriots, from Martin Luther King to Stokely

Carmichael, but we are tempted to ask, what are Hughes's politics? And if he has none, why not? The age demands intellectual commitment from its spokesmen. A poetry whose chief claim on our attention is moral, rather than aesthetic, must take sides politically. . . .

"Justice," an early poem that teaches the aesthetic value of rage, exhibits Hughes's knack for investing metaphor with a fierce potency that is as satisfying poetically as it is politically tumultuous. . . . But this skill is all but asphyxiated in many of the new poems by an ungovernable weakness for essayistic polemicizing that distracts the poet from the more serious demands of his art, and frequently undermines his poetics. Another technique that Hughes often employs successfully in the new poems is the chanting of names of key figures in the Negro Revolution. This primitive device has often been employed as a staple ingredient in good political poetry, as in Yeats's "Easter 1920." But when the poem relies too exclusively on this heroic cataloguing—whether of persons or events—for its structural mainstay, as in "Final Call," it sinks under the freight of self-conscious historicity.

Laurence Lieberman. *Poetry*. Aug., 1968, p. 339–40

Langston Hughes had a view of art and the role of poetry different from both Countee Cullen and Claude McKay. The poets who influenced him were Carl Sandburg and, in a limited way, Vachel Lindsay. He, along with Sterling Brown, shared the American poetic vision that ran from Walt Whitman through Sandburg—its belief in the validity of the intuitive sense and the spontaneity of art. Hughes not only believed that art should be the immediate expression of the self, but he also shared with Whitman, Sandburg, and Lindsay a deep, open, optimistic faith in the common man. Hughes and Brown were democrats, accepting, without question, the rightness of the unadorned and unpretentious expression of ordinary people. . . .

In truth, Hughes was not writing to be approved as a literary poet (Brown sometimes did). While his poems appealed to an audience which included whites, Hughes created for himself a black audience, especially school children. And he expected his poems to be taken on the simple and unpretentious level on which they were written. One would be right in saying that Langston Hughes backed out of the Negro-artist dilemma by choosing not to deal with art as serious "high culture." His casual and almost anti-intellectual attitude about art permitted him a wide freedom of subject and a personal honesty. It allowed him to make the very important point that the people's language, and voice, and rhythms were legitimate stuff of poetry. But this same freedom deprived him of the control and mastery that might make each (or indeed any) of his poems really singular. Langston Hughes avoided the Scylla of formalism only to founder in the Charybdis of folk art.

Nathan Irvin Huggins. *Harlem Renaissance* (New York, Oxford University Press, 1971), pp. 221, 226–27

Everyone can see that [Hughes's Simple] stories are humorous because of the main character's posture and attitude about the truths of life presented in them. Few readers, however, recognize that Simple is completely a creation of his own words, his own rhetoric, and that all of the reader's impressions of what Simple is like—his moral nature, his hopes, dreams, and fears—are derived not with reference to an external universe but only with reference to the structured context in which Simple lives and moves and has his being. In the stories, there are few descriptions and few references to actions. As it works out in the context, the narrator, Boyd, sees Simple in a bar or on a street corner or sitting on the stoop in front of the place where Simple lives, and all of these encounters give rise to speeches by Simple. The reader hears and believes, laughs at, sympathizes with and trusts the things which Simple says. These effects are produced through Hughes's presentation of his character and by the series of rhetorical devices and types of embellishment that Hughes employs. . . .

Simple himself is a past master of language, as a rhetorician should be, and he can make words do anything he wants them to do. Yet in almost every instance in the stories where speech is structured to yield a comic effect, Boyd is involved. Part of this is due to the nature of rhetorical speech as addressed. Boyd serves in one respect as Simple's immediate audience, although in actuality he is consubstantial with Simple, that is, Simple and Boyd share the same value scheme, attitudes, hopes, and aspirations for the justice, truth, honesty, and racial equity which Simple promulgates over and over again. Boyd is the more moderate, less militant, Simple. In a larger sense, however, Boyd is representative of Simple's wider audience, and he reflects Hughes's assumptions that people of the United States and of the world subscribe to Simple's ideas about peace, freedom, and brotherhood; in a word, that the world constitutes an audience which is consubstantial with Simple, a world which is, therefore, able to appreciate Simple's essential humanity.

Harry L. Jones. In Therman B. O'Daniel, ed., *Langston Hughes: Black Genius* (New York, William Morrow, 1971), pp. 134, 138–39

Called the poet laureate of Harlem, Hughes retained all his life a deep love for that colorful city within a city, and he never tired of delineating the changing moods of that ghetto. Except for one, there are specific poems on Harlem in every major poetical work. To Hughes, Harlem was place, symbol, and on occasion protagonist. It is a city of rapid transformation: the Harlem of the first two works is a gay, joyous city of cabaret life, the Harlem that jaded downtown whites seeking the exotic and the primitive flocked uptown to see. This Harlem of "Jazzonia" was never the *real* Harlem; that begins to appear in *One Way Ticket* after a riot and a depression have made the ghetto into an "edge of hell" for its discouraged and frustrated inhabitants, though still a refuge from the white man's world.

The fullest and best treatment of Harlem (and Hughes's best volume of poetry) is found in *Montage of a Dream Deferred*. Actually one long poem of 75 pages, it employs a "jam-session technique" to give every possible shade and nuance of Harlem life. Very few cities have received such a swinging and comprehensive coverage.

Arthur P. Davis. *From the Dark Tower* (Washington, D.C., Howard University Press, 1974), p. 64

Perhaps it should be said, though not in scorn, that [Hughes] was limited. As he poetized at the beginning of his life, he poetized at its end, and vice versa. He never wrote an epic, large or small. Gravity of any kind was not his style. Nor was tediousness his bane. All of his poems, except a very few, are brief; and none are very long or ponderous from attempts at grandeur or sublimity. . . .

Hughes's touch may have been (for he was, of course, not perfect) in his art too much of precisely that, a touch. As he can be related to the ballad, he can also be related to Impressionism. Indeed, it is hardly too much to say that all his poetry ever does is collect impressions. It is highly probable that, in all of Negro literature, he must be accorded the title of the Great Impressionist. Thereto, of course, attaches a limitation. Impressions tend to lack depth, if not also concentrated power. Hughes's impressions do come from the right places. They are taken by an artist who does not stand in his own light. And they do witness to the reality of a group experience of American life. Yet they are still impressions. Hughes was not a genius at synthesizing big things. He could, and yet he could not, quite see the whole forest as some writers do. It may have been his greatest lack and probably the reason he has never seemed as "serious" as writers like Ellison and Wright, or Tolson at his best. Even so he saw enough of Negro America, whether in the particular or the general, to be the best of the triad of McKay, Cullen, and Hughes.

Through many years he saw enough to be a leading interpreter of the Negro in twentieth-century America and twentieth-century literature.

Blyden Jackson. In Blyden Jackson and Louis D.
Rubin, Jr., Black Poetry in America (Baton Rouge,
Louisiana State University Press, 1974), pp. 54, 57–58

HURSTON, ZORA NEALE (1903–1960)

UNITED STATES

One can readily see why Miss Hurston's first novel, *Jonah's Gourd Vine,* was received with small enthusiasm from certain quarters of the Negro race. With a grasp of her material that has seldom been equaled by a writer of her race, she had every opportunity of creating a masterpiece of the age. But she failed. She failed not from lack of skill but from lack of vision.

The hero, John Buddy, who rose from an outcast bastard of an Alabama tenant farm to a man of wealth and influence, could have been another Ben Hur, bursting the unjust shackles that had bound him to a rotten social order and winning the applause even of his enemies. But unfortunately, his rise to religious prominence and financial ease is but a millstone about his neck. He is held back by some unseen cord which seems to be tethered to his racial heritage. Life crushes him almost to death, but he comes out of the mills with no greater insight into the deep mysteries which surround him. Such a phenomenon, although not intended by Miss Hurston as a type of all Negro manhood, is seized upon by thoughtless readers of other races as a happy confirmation of what they already faintly believe: namely, that the Negro is incapable of profiting by experience or of understanding the deeper mysteries of life.

Nick Aaron Ford. The Contemporary Negro Novel
(Boston, Meador, 1936), pp. 99–100

Filling out Janie's story [in *Their Eyes Were Watching God*] are sketches of Eatonville and farming down "on the muck" in the Everglades. On the porch of the mayor's store "big old lies" and comic-serious debates, with the tallest of metaphors, while away the evenings. The dedication of the town's first lamp and the community burial of an old mule are rich in humor but they are not cartoons. Many incidents are unusual, and there are narrative gaps in need of building up. Miss Hurston's forte is the recording and the creation of folk-speech. Her devotion to these people has rewarded her; *Their Eyes Were Watching God* is chock-full of earthy and touching poetry. . . .

Though inclined to violence and not strictly conventional, her people are not naïve primitives. About human needs and frailties they have the unabashed shrewdness of the Blues. . . . Living in an all-colored town, these people escape the worst pressures of class and caste. There is little harshness; there is enough money and work to go around. The author does not dwell upon the "people ugly from ignorance and broken from being poor" who swarm upon the "muck" for short-time jobs. But there is bitterness, sometimes oblique, in the enforced folk manner, and sometimes forthright.

Sterling A. Brown. *Nation.* Oct. 16, 1937, pp. 409–10

Only to reach a wider audience, need [Zora Neale Hurston] ever write books—because she is a perfect book of entertainment in herself. In her youth she was always getting scholarships and things from wealthy white people, some of whom simply paid her just to sit around and represent the Negro race for them, she did it in such a racy fashion. She was full of side-splitting anecdotes, humorous tales, and tragicomic stories, remembered out of her life in the South as a daughter of a travelling minister of God. She could make you laugh one minute and cry the next. To many of her white friends, no doubt, she was a perfect "darkie," in the nice meaning they give the term—that is a naïve, childlike, sweet, humorous, and highly colored Negro.

But Miss Hurston was clever, too—a student who didn't let college give her a broad *a* and who had great scorn for all pretensions, academic or otherwise. That is why she was such a fine folk-lore collector, able to go among the people and never act as if she had been to school at all. Almost nobody else could stop the average Harlemite on Lenox Avenue and measure his head with a strange-looking, anthropological device and not get bawled out for the attempt, except Zora, who used to stop anyone whose head looked interesting, and measure it.

Langston Hughes. *The Big Sea* (New York,
Alfred A. Knopf, 1940), pp. 238–39

Out of her abundant stores of vitality Zora Hurston fashions an autobiography [*Dust Tracks on a Road*] which shoots off bright sparks of personality. . . . A woman of courage and action, she would scorn any academic retreat from the touch and feel of ordinary life. Not only is there nothing of the recluse in her nature, but there is, to state it positively, a preference for the jostling of the crowd. She feels a challenge to elbow her way along her traffic-jammed road with a roving eye for adventure. Tracks she leaves behind her in the dust, witnesses of her presence which only she among all those people can make. Mixing with others only enhances her individuality. . . .

Free of many routine moral obligations, Zora Hurston busies herself with unwrapping the happiness contained in each moment. She engenders an atmosphere of surprises both for herself and others who know her. Shrinking from the dullness of dogmatism, she blossoms out with an originality of thought and conduct. Although the author can hardly inform us that this originality is the secret of her charm, we can quickly detect it on each page of her autobiography. Even her literary style shows an out-of-the-ordinary quality, a concrete and earthy imagery, an uneven rhythm which reflect imagination, warmth, and impulsiveness. It is a safe guess that few people were bored in her presence. Angered sometimes, amused often, at least they must have responded positively to the unexpected course of her behavior. Sustained by her unflagging spirit, Zora Hurston is enabled to present a strong case for the doctrine of individuality in her own person.

Rebecca Chalmers Barton. *Witnesses for Freedom*
(New York, Harper, 1948), pp. 101, 114

The style of [*Jonah's Gourd Vine*] is impressive enough. Zora Neale Hurston, whom Langston Hughes has described as a rare *raconteuse*, draws freely on the verbal ingenuity of the folk. Her vivid, metaphorical style is based primarily on the Negro preacher's graphic ability to present abstractions to his flock. . . .

The genesis of a work of art may be of no moment to literary criticism but it is sometimes crucial in literary history. It may, for example, account for the rare occasion when an author outclasses himself. *Their Eyes Were Watching God* is a case in point. The novel was written in Haiti in just seven weeks, under the emotional pressure of a recent love affair. "The plot was far from the circumstances," Miss Hurston writes in her autobiography, "but I tried to embalm all the tenderness of my passion for him in *Their Eyes Were Watching God*." Ordinarily the prognosis for such a novel would be dismal enough. One might expect immediacy and intensity, but not distance, or control, or universality. Yet oddly, or perhaps not so oddly, it is Miss Hurston's best novel, and possibly the best novel of the period, excepting [Richard Wright's] *Native Son*.

Robert A. Bone. *The Negro Novel in America*
(New Haven, Yale University Press, 1958),
pp. 127–28

An effervescent companion of no great profundities but dancing perceptions, [Zora] possessed humor, sense of humor, and what a fund of folklore! Although she seemed to have very little indignation for the imposed status of her race, she knew her people. Probably this insensibility was due to the fact that her awakening powers and subsequent recognition tended to act as a soporific to her early sufferings and neglect. . . .

Her book of folk tales, *Moses, Man of the Mountain*, was written out of race memory, if such a thing there be; her autobiography, *Dust Tracks on a Road*, was the result of experiences conditioned by race. But she herself was a gift both to her race and the human race. That she died in poverty and obscurity was because for a decade at least she had deliberately removed herself from the large group of us who felt puzzlement and still do. Where lurked her ultimate defeat, ending in retreat? Why and how?

Despite her bright accomplishments, her books, including *Tell My Horse* (the result of her explorations into Haiti), *Their Eyes Were Watching God, Dust Tracks on a Road*, are Negro Americana, to the smell of fried chitterlings, which by the way she loved.

Yet the inescapable conclusion persists that Zora remains a figure in bas relief, only partially emerging from her potential into the whole woman.

Fannie Hurst. YULG. July, 1960, pp. 18–19

Miss Hurston's most accomplished achievement in fiction is *Moses, Man of the Mountain*, which provided a format in which she could best utilize her talents for writing satire, irony, and dialect. . . . If she had written nothing else, Miss Hurston would deserve recognition for this book. For once, her material and her talent fused perfectly. Her narrative deficiencies are insignificant, for the reader knows the story. Her ridicule, caricature, and farce are appropriate. The monstrous Hattie of *Jonah's Gourd Vine* and Mrs. Turner of *Their Eyes Were Watching God* reappear aptly in the jealous, accursed Miriam, who actually becomes a sympathetic figure after she has been cursed with leprosy. Finally, attuned to folk psychology, Miss Hurston gave the Hebrew slaves an authenticity that they lack in the solemn Biblical story. . . .

In her final novel, *Seraph on the Suwanee*, Miss Hurston for the first time focused upon white protagonists, in a work so stylistically different from her earlier efforts that it reveals her conscious adjustment to the tastes of a new generation of readers. Although *Seraph on the Suwanee* is Hurston's most ambitious novel and her most artistically competent, its prolonged somberness causes many readers to yearn for the alleviating farce and carefree gaiety of the earlier works.

Darwin T. Turner. In a Minor Chord: Three
Afro-American Writers and Their Search for
Identity (Carbondale, Southern Illinois University
Press, 1971), pp. 109–111

Miss Hurston's first, and perhaps best, novel, *Jonah's Gourd Vine*, is based loosely on the lives of her parents. Her intimate knowledge of the material gives the work an immediacy that the other works lack. Moreover, her skillful use of folk customs, folk superstitions, and above all else, folk speech helps make *Jonah's Gourd Vine* an unusual and fascinating work. Both Dunbar and Chesnutt had used folk material in their fiction, but neither had the knowledge of folk tales that Miss Hurston had (she was a trained anthropologist); and though both knew folk speech, neither gave it the poetic quality that Zora Neale Hurston gives it in this work; neither fused it as thoroughly as she does. . . .

The author's two folklore collections, *Mules and Men* and *Tell My Horse*, are fascinating works. Miss Hurston had a natural flair for collecting material from the folk. She had no difficulty in becoming one with the people from whom she sought songs or stories or customs, whether in the Deep South or in Haiti. She also had a great and natural gift as a raconteur of the stories she collected. Although the two works she published are impressive, one likes to think that with her undoubted ability as a collector and interpreter of folklore she would have made a far richer contribution to the field if she had continued to work in it.

Zora Neale Hurston has probably never received from Negro critics the credit she deserves, whereas white critics have occasionally overpraised her work. The reason for this, or at least part of it, is that she wrote counter to the prevailing attitude of protest and militancy which most Negro writers since 1925 have taken. Repelled by Zora Neale Hurston's unrealistic good-will stance, Negro critics have tended to dismiss her. This is unfortunate because, whatever one may think of her racial attitude, she had a real if uneven talent as a fiction writer and superb gifts as a collector and interpreter of folk materials.

Arthur P. Davis. *From the Dark Tower* (Washington, D.C., Howard University Press, 1974), pp. 115, 119–20

Despite structural and formal defects, *Jonah's Gourd Vine* is most important for its depiction of the character of the black woman. Lucy is far from being completely developed as a character. She does, however, contain elements seldom seen in fiction by men which feature black women. Moreover, Miss Hurston, in her portrayal of Lucy, has begun early to deal with the conflict between black men and women, which receives fuller explication in Chester Himes's *Lonely Crusade* and John Williams' *Sissie* later in the century. The conflict centers around two victims of the same oppressive society. Take John and Lucy as metaphors of black men and women. . . .

John, the metaphor of black men, remains, for Miss Hurston, essentially a creature of appetite, insatiable even though offered such a delectable morsel as Lucy Pearson. Her loyalty, perseverance, and love border upon the messianic. What her husband lacks in courage, strength, and initiative, she more than compensates for. The conflicts, therefore, given such personalities, can be resolved only when black men correct the defects in character. That this was the author's implicit commentary upon black men might be attributable to her distorted conception of them. The chances are, however, that she was less interested in John Pearson than in Lucy, less interested in the men of her novels than in the women, who receive more multidimensional treatment.

In *Jonah's Gourd Vine* and *Their Eyes Were Watching God,* she views them as modern women, patterned upon paradigms of the past, those of the courage and strength of Harriet Tubman and Sojourner Truth. Far from being the images of old, the willing copartners of white men in the castration of black men, her women are, instead, the foundations of a new order, the leavening rods of change, from whose loins will eventually come the new man. Past stereotypes aside, therefore, her women need only search for greater liberation, move even beyond the stoiclike devotion of a Lucy Pearson, move toward greater independence and freedom. Put another way, black liberation meant burying the old images and symbols that had circumscribed black women along with black men. What is needed, McKay had argued in *Banjo,* is "Women that can understand us as human beings and not as wild over-sexed savages." In the context of *Jonah's Gourd Vine* and *Their Eyes Were Watching God*, this meant that both sexes must move collectively outside of American history and definitions.

Addison Gayle, Jr. *The Way of the New World*
(Garden City, N.Y., Doubleday, 1975), pp. 143–44

JOHNSON, JAMES WELDON (1871-1938)

UNITED STATES

[*The Autobiography of an Ex-Colored Man*] is indeed an epitome of the race situation in the United States told in the form of an autobiography. The varied incidents, the numerous localities brought in, the setting forth in all its ramifications of our great and perplexing race problem, suggests a work of fiction founded on hard fact. The hero, a natural son of a Southerner of high station, begins his real life in a New England town to which his mother had migrated, runs the whole gamut of color-line experiences, and ends by going over on the other side.

The work gives a view of the race situation in New England, in New York City, in the far South, in city and country, in high and low society, with glimpses, too, of England, France and Germany. Practically every phase and complexity of the race question is presented at one time or another. The work is, as might be expected, anonymous.

Jessie Fauset. *Crisis*. Nov., 1912, p. 38

In [*Fifty Years, and Other Poems*] Mr. James Weldon Johnson . . . gathers together a group of lyrics, delicate in workmanship, fragrant with sentiment, and phrased in pure and unexceptionable English. Then he has another group of dialect verses, racy of the soil, pungent in flavor, swinging in rhythm and adroit in rhyme. But where he shows himself a pioneer is the half-dozen larger and bolder poems, of a loftier strain, in which he has been nobly successful in expressing the higher aspirations of his own people. It is in uttering this cry for recognition, for sympathy, for understanding, and above all, for justice, that Mr. Johnson is most original and most powerful.

In the superb and soaring stanzas of "Fifty Years" (published exactly half-a-century after the signing of the Emancipation Proclamation) he has given us one of the noblest commemorative poems yet written by any American—a poem sonorous in its diction, vigorous in its workmanship, elevated in its imagination and sincere in its emotion. In it speaks the voice of his race; and the race is fortunate in its spokesman. In it a fine theme has been finely treated. In it we are made to see something of the soul of the people who are our fellow citizens now and forever—even if we do not always so regard them. In it we are glad to acclaim a poem which any living poet might be proud to call his own.

Brander Matthews. Introduction to James Weldon
Johnson, *Fifty Years, and Other Poems* (Boston,
Cornhill, 1917), pp. xiii–xiv

The Autobiography of an Ex-Coloured Man, of course, in the matter of specific incident, has little enough to do with Mr. Johnson's own life, but it is imbued with his own personality and feeling, his *views* of the subjects discussed, so that to a person who has no previous knowledge of the author's own history, it reads like *real* autobiography. It would be truer, perhaps, to say that it reads like a composite autobiography of the Negro race in the United States in modern times. . . .

Mr. Johnson . . . chose an all-embracing scheme. His young hero, the ostensible author, either discusses (or lives) pretty nearly every phase of Negro life, North and South and even in Europe, available to him at that period. That he "passes" the title indicates. Miscegenation in its slave and also its more modern aspects, both casual and marital, is competently treated. The ability of the Negro to mask his real feelings with a joke or a laugh in the presence of the inimical white man is here noted, for the first time in print, I should imagine. Negro adaptability, touchiness, and jealousy are referred to in an unself-conscious manner, totally novel in Negro writing at the time this book originally appeared [1912]. . . . Jim Crow cars, crap-shooting, and the cake-walk are inimitably described. Colour snobbery within the race is freely spoken of, together with the economic pressure from without which creates this false condition. There is a fine passage devoted to the celebration of the Negro Spirituals and there is an excellent account of a Southern camp-meeting, together with a transcript of a typical oldtime Negro sermon. There is even a lynching. But it is chiefly remarkable to find James Weldon Johnson in 1912, five or six years before the rest of us began to shout about it, singing hosannas to rag-time (jazz was unknown then).

Carl Van Vechten. Introduction to James Weldon
Johnson, *The Autobiography of an Ex-Coloured
Man* (New York, Alfred A. Knopf, 1927), pp. v–ix

An experiment and an intention lie behind these poems [in *God's Trombones*]. It will be remembered that in *The Book of American Negro Poetry* Mr. Johnson spoke of the limitations of dialect, which he compared to an organ having but two stops, one of humor and one of pathos. He felt that the Negro poet needed to discover some medium of expression with a latitude capable of embracing the Negro experience. These poems were written with that purpose in view, as well as to guarantee a measure of permanence in man's most forgetful mind to that highly romantic and fast disappearing character, the old time Negro preacher.

The poet here has admirably risen to his intentions and his needs; entombed in this bright mausoleum the Negro preacher of an older day can never pass entirely deathward. Dialect could never have been synthesized into the rich mortar necessary for these sturdy unrhymed exhortations. Mr. Johnson has captured that peculiar flavor of speech by which the black sons of Zebedee, lacking academic education, but grounded through their religious intensity in the purest marshalling of the English language (the King James version of the Bible) must have astounded men more obviously letter-trained. This verse is simple and awful at once, the grand diapason of a musician playing on an organ with far more than two keys.

Countee Cullen. Bkm. Oct., 1927, pp. 221

In the familiar shaping of an epigrammatic idea, God makes James Weldon Johnson a creative artist, but he made himself a race-agitator. He had an intellectual motivation for the cause into which he threw the energies and devotions of his manhood's prime; and while the heat of debate, the tactics and strategies were pursued with ardour and often with consummate skill, there was none of the passion nor exalted moods of rationalization, which forged the spirit of [Frederick] Douglass or [Booker T.] Washington or [W. E. B.] Du Bois on the anvil of a diabolical oppression. If these race champions, Douglass, Washington, and Du Bois, flame across the pages of race and American history with a greater glory for stirring the hearts of their people with higher hopes and clearer visions, and a more determined effort to realize them, than James Johnson, that same history will record in its footnotes and appendices, that with Booker T. Washington he stands forth as one of the two best organizers of a racial program. . . .

James Weldon Johnson has lived a crowded life and he has recorded it minutely in this autobiography [*Along This Way*], which is incontestably the first work of its kind in American literature. Unlike any other autobiography, that of Frederick Douglass, Booker T. Washington, or even Dr. [Robert R.] Moton, it escapes from that category of racial recitals in the narrower sense, and remains the narrative of a man who for sixty years of his life has passed through an amazing series of social and intellectual adventures and events which lifted him steadily to a foremost place as an American citizen.

William Stanley Braithwaite. *Opportunity*.
Dec., 1933, pp. 376–78

A few of us tried to bring the Negro writers together in an organization with the late James Weldon Johnson as President. There are about twelve creative writers of some distinction in Harlem and an equal number of journalists. No one could accuse James Weldon Johnson of believing in any kind of Segregation. He was a member of numerous white cultural and artistic organizations, and his prestige then meant much in setting up a group, especially as he was a lecturer on Negro culture at New York University. He was the perfect person around whom we could organize—well balanced, a meliorist in his attitude toward race relations. . . .

However, Negro intellectuals among themselves, even more than the masses, are hard to organize. The Harlem Renaissance movement of the antic nineteen twenties was really inspired and kept alive by the interest and presence of white bohemians. It faded out when they became tired of the new plaything. And so even the prestige of James Weldon Johnson was of no avail. . . .

Suddenly, tragically, James Weldon Johnson was killed in the spring of 1938. And the group of Negro writers came together for the last time at his funeral.

Claude McKay. *Harlem: Negro Metropolis* (New
York, E. P. Dutton, 1940), pp. 247–49

Published anonymously in 1912 with a preface by Brander Matthews and reissued under the author's name in 1927 with an introduction by Carl Van Vechten, *The Autobiography of an Ex-Coloured Man* is noteworthy because of its restraint, its comprehensiveness, and its adumbration of the Negro Renascence of the 1920's. At a time when most Negro fictionists were giving blow for blow and painting extravagantly favorable pictures of members of the race, Johnson set out neither to glorify Negroes nor to malign whites but to interpret men and conditions as he knew them. . . .

Besides being more detached than any preceding novel of American Negro life, *The Autobiography of an Ex-Coloured Man* is groundbreaking in its introduction of a well-realized cosmopolitan milieu. Unlike most earlier Negro fiction, it is not localized in the South but moves out into the broader field of European and Northern urban life. . . .

In addition to being more impartial and more comprehensive than any earlier novel of American Negro life, *The Autobiography of an Ex-Coloured Man* is a milestone because of its forthright presentation of racial thought. Admitting the dual personality which some Negroes assume—one role among their own group and the other in the presence of whites—Johnson is himself not guilty of such a two-sided character. Not attempting to "wear the mask," he gives a calm, dispassionate treatment of people and situations as he sees them.

Hugh M. Gloster. *Negro Voices in American Fiction*
(Chapel Hill, University of North Carolina Press,
1948), pp. 79–80

In the language of *God's Trombones* Johnson found a much more flexible medium than Dunbar dialect for the interpretation of folk material. Traditional dialect attempts (sometimes unsuccessfully) a strict fidelity in metre and in rhyme scheme; Johnson adapted to an artistic form the rhythms of an actual sermon, the accents of actual speech and intonation. He freed himself from the necessity to rhyme, thus subordinating strict poetic form to the artistic interpretation of his subject matter. In *God's Trombones* Johnson approximated the vivid imagery of the folk, an imagery far superior to any he attained in the *Fifty Years* dialect poems and certainly an imagery which rivaled the best of Dunbar's. Johnson used all the tricks of the folk preacher's trade—hyperbole, repetition, juxtaposition, personal appeal to his listeners, the knack of making Biblical happenings have an intense meaning to current life. Johnson even used punctuation and capitalization to achieve his effect—dashes to indicate the frequent and dramatic pauses, capitalization to emphasize important words, such as "Old Earth" and "Great White Throne." The sensitive reader cannot fail to hear the ranting of the fire-and-brimstone preacher; the extremely sensitive reader may even hear the unwritten "Amens" of the congregation.

Eugenia W. Collier. *Phylon*. Winter, 1960,
pp. 358–59

If allowance is made for his borrowings from the Bible, from the spirituals, and from the Negro sermons he had heard, what then is the poet's share in *God's Trombones*? Johnson was certainly not the creator of these sermons but, as Synge remarked of his own indebtedness to the Irish people, every work of art results from a collaboration. In *God's Trombones*, the artist is clearly present on every page, and he gives even while he receives. The simplicity and clarity, so striking in these poems, are the fruits of his efforts. His musical sense is manifested in the choice of sonorities for the free-verse line which, in his hands, becomes docile and supple, and adjusts to the preacher's rhythm as well as to the rise and fall of his voice. Taking what were, after all, the heterogeneous elements of his raw materials, the poet has marked them with the unity and the stamp of his own genius, so that these sermons, as they come from his hands, have undeniably become his own to some degree.

If he deserves any reproach, it might be for his excessive zeal in idealizing and refining—or, in other words, for having thought it necessary to impose too much respectability on essentially popular material whose crudity is one of its charms, as it is also a voucher for its authenticity. His sermons are still folklore, perhaps, but stylized folklore. . . .

This work, furthermore, was the offspring of an outdated mentality. Like its author, the work set out to have a Negro soul, but one garbed in the distinction and respectability of whiteness. Despite appearances, its tendency was at odds with that total coming to awareness marked by the Negro Renaissance, and no more is needed to explain why *God's Trombones* remained an isolated venture. [1963]

Jean Wagner. Black Poets of the United States
(Urbana, University of Illinois Press, 1973),
pp. 383–84

For a reference point in Johnson's literary career, we must look to the year 1918. The year before he had published a respectable volume of poetry [*Fifty Years*], which, though it summed up his poetic efforts over the previous several decades, did not lay out a clear path to follow. In 1918 Johnson established that path with his poem "The Creation," published two years later. . . .

In "The Creation," as in the bulk of his literary activity in the 1920s, Johnson used a soft-sell tactic. He wished to impress both the black and the white middle-class with the overall contribution of black Americans to American culture. He came to feel during this period that the most effective way to do this, as well as to expose the basic nature of race prejudice, was indirectly through works of art. . . .

"The Creation" makes no mention of prejudice, discrimination, or the grinding poverty to be found in black communities of both rural and urban America. Nor did Johnson point out that the spontaneity of black poetic rhetoric often grew out of a desperate effort to survive in a social situation which seemed to breed endless oppression. He, of course, knew the situation, and he communicated it to the American public in his role as an official of the NAACP. In "The Creation," however, Johnson followed the path he had laid out in his song writing twenty years earlier. He chose not to emphasize the expressly tragic nature of the black experience, as he had done in "O Black and Unknown Bards";

rather he took a much ridiculed aspect of that experience and turned it into a work of art readily appreciated by his readers, both black and white.

Eugene Levy. *James Weldon Johnson: Black Leader,*
Black Voice (Chicago, University of Chicago Press,
1973), pp. 298, 301

Johnson had read and been greatly impressed by [W. E. B.] Du Bois's [*The Souls of Black Folk*], and it is not surprising that the mulatto status and the varying musical inclinations of his narrator [in *The Autobiography of an Ex-Colored Man*] act as symbolic projections of a double consciousness. The narrator modulates between the black world and the white (often with less than equanimity) and seems torn between the early melodies of his mother and the Chopinesque style that wins his white beloved. In a sense, *The Autobiography of an Ex-Colored Man* is a fictional rendering of *The Souls of Black Folk*, for Johnson's narrator not only stresses his bifurcated vision, but also his intellectual genius. He maintains an open, critical attitude toward the many sides of black American culture, condemns in unequivocal terms the limitations of the black situation, and assiduously records his movement from a naïve provincialism toward a broad cosmopolitanism. The narrator, in short, is a black man of culture recording the situations and attitudes that have succeeded in driving him underground, to a position the larger society might define as criminal. . . .

The Autobiography of an Ex-Colored Man* is both the history and the confession of one of the "talented tenth" (that class of college-bred black Americans in whom Du Bois placed so much faith); it offers the rehearsal of a "soul on ice" who draws substance from a world that could not recognize his true character nor sympathize with his longings. Each of its episodes is an effort at personal definition and a partial summing up of the black American past.

Houston A. Baker, Jr. *VQR.* Summer, 1973,
pp. 438–39

JORDAN, A. C. (1906–1968)

SOUTH AFRICA

[*The Wrath of the Ancestors*] is a grim tragedy of a young, educated but inexperienced chief of the Pondomise [a Xhosa tribe], who (along with his wife) sets out fully determined to educate his people—to lift them out of the pale of darkness, ignorance and superstition. Alas! the chief and his wife understand the customs and religious feelings of the people but imperfectly. In his zeal to eradicate superstition the chief cuts across the feelings of the "Reds," his educated wife does not *hlonipha* [follow traditional ways] and she kills the *inkwaklhwa*—a snake regarded by the Reds as the "guardian" of the tribe. By this thoughtless act she has incurred the wrath of the ancestral spirits and brought a curse upon the "Royal House." Things are brought to a point and the tribe is split into two camps—Reds versus the educated. The result is a delirious succession of treacheries, crimes, mental tortures and other atrocities, ending in a general funeral. The chief and his wife commit suicide by drowning themselves and their only child. The whole action becomes a nightmare. A tribal tragedy!

To justify such a tragic end reference must be made to the difference in religious outlook of the Red and the educated man. To an educated Christian man such a tragic end is a perversion of the accepted moral standards, that is, a triumph of evil over good. But to a Pondomise whose religious outlook is different the tragedy is the inevitable retribution of the *iminyanya* [ancestral spirits], whose wrath has been kindled by a wanton non-observance of the tribal customs on the part of the chief and his wife. Whatever the moral outlook, the author has deliberately chosen to make the end such as it is, strictly consistent with the title *The Wrath of the Ancestors*. Is not the way of freedom and salvation from the overwhelming evil and superstition of this world littered with the bones of martyrs?

I. Oldjohn. *SAO*. April, 1940, p. 77

No review of the vernacular novel can fail to mention the work of the African author, A. C. Jordan, who set a new standard by his *The Wrath of the Ancestors*. It was on a larger scale than former novels and was an attempt to reveal the workings of the African soul as it awakened to the claims of a higher type of life, while yet set in a primitive environment and fighting a grim fight with conservative and reactionary forces. . . .

The author did more than tell an enthralling story. He showed himself to have a conception of artistic values that was praiseworthy. At the close of the book . . . the forces of paganism and reaction win and there is a veritable blood-bath. Some who read the book in manuscript begged the author to give it a different and more happy ending. But he turned a deaf ear to their pleadings. "This is how it came to me," he declared, and declined to do violence to his own artistic conceptions.

R. H. W. Shepherd. *Standpunte*. June, 1953, p. 46

Jordan comes to grips with real life, his feet firmly set on the ground. In [*The Wrath of the Ancestors*] he makes a penetrating study of the central problems of a nation emerging from a tribal way of life. His mind, keen and sharp as an assegai, penetrates the turmoil of change and discerns two groups, those who advocate progress and those who cling to the past. He sees in their clash the central conflict and challenge of his people. Here is no facile evasion of the troublesome facts of life, but a very real effort to meet these challenges. This clash of the old and the new is ever with us, it is universal and eternal. It may and does assume various forms, having in each country an individual existence demanding an individual solution. But fundamentally it remains the same. The reader feels, no matter what his nationality, that here is a situation from real life, one in which he could easily be involved. Thus the novel assumes a universal interest and like a true work of art it transcends locality and age. . . .

The novel has proved to be equally popular with urbanized and tribal Africans. It is not difficult to see why. The book is steeped in tribal atmosphere so that even the urban African is caught up in that current. This, I think, is because he still feels in his bones the influence of the old tribal life. He instinctively loves it and respects it. His feeling must be akin to that which inspires the cry of an exile longing to see again his motherland. Even though the African be a Christian, his out-look is still largely coloured by the old tribal civilization. Generations of town life have not broken the links with a past which is instilled by song and story. Deep within the African, chords of sympathy with a golden age gone by are touched to music. Vilakazi exploits this sympathy to an extreme degree. The imagined glories of the past become an obsession and his cry a nostalgic utterance. Much the same is true of W. B. Yeats in his early poetry, when he dreamed his way through a world of mytho-logical creation, divorced from real life and so largely valueless. But Jordan gives these Africans aspirations, and the beauty and dignity of the tribal way of life, due recognition, without losing his balance or perspective.

John Riordan. AfrS. 20, 1, 1961, pp. 53–54

The final crisis in [*The Wrath of the Ancestors*] . . . focuses on Thembeka. From the beginning of her reign, the young queen antag-onizes the tribe because she goes about in short dresses and bareheaded. One day, she finds a serpent coiled near her child and kills it. Now, as anthropologists know, among the Pondos, "different clans regard a par-ticular species of snake as being a manifestation of their *ithongo* (ances-tral spirits), and treat it with respect, not killing it or driving it away when it comes to the *umzi* (compound, kraal), for it is *umninimizi* (the owner of the *umzi*). Whether the snake is poisonous or not makes no difference. Clearly, this is one of the points on which modern and traditional attitudes cannot be reconciled. It is perhaps the most important of such points, since devotion to the ancestral spirits is the cornerstone of many traditional societies, with the consequent belief—skillfully described by Jordan at the beginning of the book—that the ancestors inevitably take revenge on those who harm snakes.

To the Western mind, in killing the snake, the queen has courageously done her duty to save her child's life; in the traditional African view, she has committed the most grievous offense that can be conceived. This antinomy is the real core of the tragedy, and it is the source of further dilemmas and calamities. For the tribe is so outraged that Zwelinzima, in order to keep the throne, is compelled to renounce the queen to take another, more acceptable wife. Thembeka, in her turn, is frenzied by the wreck of her love and marriage; she drowns herself and her son, upon which the chief himself commits suicide. The whole process is of course a case of self-fulfilling prophecy: it is the tribe's belief in the wrath of the ancestors which is responsible for those catastrophic events, which in turn confirm and strengthen that very belief. This, however, is not how Jordan's tribesmen view it. . . .

The paradox defined by Oldjohn, or the response of Shepherd in *Bantu Literature and Life*—"At the close of the book, the forces of evil, of paganism, and reaction, win"—[is] enough to show that *The Wrath of the Ancestors* is a deeply disturbing novel, where the interplay of character and circumstance cannot be described in simple terms.

Albert S. Gérard. *Four African Literatures*
(Berkeley, University of California Press, 1971),
pp. 85–87

[*Tales from Southern Africa*] is a companion to Jordan's *Towards an African Literature*, though each volume is an independent work relating to the larger whole of African literature. Jordan's view, that of an Africanist born, bred and steeped in African culture and mores, is that concentration must be paid to the earlier, and oral, tradition before real awareness of African identity through the modern literature can be achieved. In this work he translates and "retells" *ntsomi* tales—Xhosa stories narrated, and performed, by a storyteller and passed traditionally down the generations by word of mouth. The difficulties of keeping the tone of the *ntsomi* are enormous, for they are an oral and dramatic and collective art (listeners contribute their reactions, comments and additions, and often these are incorporated into the next rendition). The narrator in the original tales described each character by *becoming* that character in dramatic performance. Consequently, these tales, even in the spare modern descriptive devices added by Jordan, are not really *ntsomi* but an approximation of the folk art.

The stories are frightening, funny, exciting, homey, exotic at turns —and always socially oriented. They are moral guides as well as entertainment. This book will interest specialized and general readers of all ages. The stories can be read easily for pleasure and insight. The two introductions [by Jordan], one on the political-social deprivations of the Xhosa artist and the other on the *ntsomi* tradition, are rewarding, stimulating studies.

Choice. Dec., 1973, p. 1557

KANE, CHEIKH HAMIDOU (1928–   )

SENEGAL

It is . . . as a philosopher of the absolute that Cheikh Hamidou Kane debates his own problem in *Ambiguous Adventure*. He writes about a problem connected to the history of our times, and more precisely to the dramas of African decolonization, for his novel concerns the moral crisis of a Senegalese intellectual torn between the spiritual traditions of his race and Western culture. . . .

[Samba Diallo, the protagonist] regards his Islamic blackness as a mystic wisdom that delivers to man the "interior heart of things," creating in him the happiness of contemplation, the fullness of life in which death itself ceases to be a trial since God's presence envelops everything. As for Western culture, Samba Diallo sees it as an objective philosophy that looks at the surface of the world in order to grasp it physically and to act upon it. Therefore, Africa will never conquer the West without becoming unfaithful to its soul, for it is not in the nature of things that the man who contemplates God should be powerful in history. But will not the victorious West lose the world? For it is not in the nature of things that the world, separated from God, should continue to exist. Samba Diallo's tragic death—he is killed by a fanatic from his country who considers him a traitor—undoubtedly means that the author does not perceive any solution.

Pierre-Henri Simon. Le monde. July 26, 1961, p. 9†

Strongly molded by a traditional Moslem education, Kane came to France to continue his studies in philosophy and colonial administration. Out of the rift between these two very different experiences, he created a novel, *Ambiguous Adventure*, which immediately won him a place among the best writers in Africa as well as among the most committed.

The "ambiguous adventure" in this "ambiguous Africa" is that of a society whose system of values is being attacked and eaten away by a foreign system of values. What attitude should the African adopt toward the European civilization that has already taken a foothold in his continent by force, troubled people's minds, and created new needs? Should he go to the white men's schools "to learn how to conquer without being right" and in this way acquire technical and scientific power, "because the hand is what defends the spirit"? But if one enters the whites' schools, he also courts disaster, for in addition to technology the European school also teaches its morality, religion, and philosophy, and separates one from his African civilization. It creates rootless people— the elite, yes, but unable to think for themselves, as Césaire would say.

This problem is set forth by Kane with an art and a depth that have not been achieved before now in world literature. The real problem of modern Negritude has finally been approached, and race no longer has anything to do with it; it is really a matter of cultural differences— irreducible differences. Kane's diagnosis does not leave any doubt about his position: either the African will succeed in synthesizing these two antagonistic cultures, or he will perish. This is the meaning of the death of the hero, Samba Diallo, at the end of the novel. According to the author's own interpretation, it is the "proof through absurdity that African civilization exists, and exists to such an extent that if an individual yields to the temptation to eradicate it or to abandon it, he inevitably destroys his soul and his personality."

Lilyan Kesteloot. In Lilyan Kesteloot, ed.,
Anthologie négro-africaine (Verviers, Belgium,
Gérard, 1967), p. 277†

The harmonious balance of form, the nobility of the characters and their sentiments, the predominance of reason over the emotions and yet the perpetual presence of the deep, mystical forces which lie behind men's actions, the sober language, simple but majestic images, all place *Ambiguous Adventure* in the classical tradition of French literature. In many ways it recalls Racine and Pascal. At the same time it must not be forgotten that the same clarity and mystery are to be found in the religious works of Islam. It is, possibly, because Kane has found this conjunction in form, style and thought between Islam and Europe that *Ambiguous Adventure* is able to stand between the two cultures and present the problem of assimilation with complete objectivity.

The language is, throughout, clear and simple. In the dialogue the sentences are short and straightforward. . . .

White and violet, together with red, silver, purple, the colours of nobility, of suffering, those of the sky and the desert, are the most frequent in the descriptions both of characters such as the Knight, the Chief, and "la Grande Royale" and of the settings of Samba's homeland. In contrast, the settings in Paris are dull, colourless, uninspiring. It is as if the contrast between European materialism and Islam exists even in their surrounding.

There is no excess in *Ambiguous Adventure*. Each word, each phrase has its meaning and adds to the whole meaning. The climax, in the final chapter, in which the ambiguity is resolved, recalls [Paul] Valéry's "The Graveyard by the Sea." Life and death, man and the universe, the finite and the infinite become one in the blinding, perpetual instant of complete understanding.

A. C. Brench. *The Novelists' Inheritance in French Africa* (London, Oxford University Press, 1967), pp. 107, 109

The importance of Cheikh Hamidou Kane, a great West African writer, comes from the fact that, in his novel *Ambiguous Adventure*, he treats two convergent problems: the European movement toward awareness and the African movement toward awareness. He treats these two problems as an existentialist philosopher and above all as a humanist of the absolute, and therein resides the profoundly universal interest of his work. . . .

The hero's conflict is that of an individual torn between the traditional view represented by Master Thierno and the reformist tendency represented by la Grande Royale. Samba Diallo incarnates the contradiction between the conservative values of Islam and progressive or reformist forces. . . .

In the center of each system, traditional or modern, African or Western, there lies a subtle negation of the individual as an absolute truth or autonomous liberty. . . . According to the Westerner [Lacroix, the spokesman for technological civilization], nature must be mastered so that the demands and needs of man will be better served; whereas the African [the Knight who is the hero's father] asserts that man should submit to the grandeur of nature—that is, seek the profound meaning of the world by contemplating the slightest movement in nature. . . . The tale simply presents two forms of tyranny or alienation of which man is the victim, namely, metaphysical tyranny or the tyranny of the absolute, and technological tyranny.

Sunday O. Anozie. *Sociologie du roman africain* (Paris, Éditions Aubier-Montaigne, 1970), pp. 148–49, 152–55†

KELLEY, WILLIAM MELVIN (1937–   )

UNITED STATES

A Different Drummer, a first novel by twenty-five-year-old William Melvin Kelley, born in New York and educated at Harvard, is in some ways a better book than [James Baldwin's] *Another Country*. For one thing, the major characters are more respectable and wholesome; and despite their weaknesses and failures, they never lose sight of the dignity and decency that might reasonably be expected of civilized human beings. For another thing, the experiences of the characters and the language by which they communicate their experiences are more acceptable to readers of normal sensibilities. Furthermore, racial overtones which are basic to both books are more subdued and indirectly expressed in *A Different Drummer*, really as if they are incidental explanations rather than central arguments. . . .

There are several weaknesses in this novel. First, the author fails to provide meaningful and convincing motivation for the major incidents in the story. The lynching of the Reverend Bradshaw, which is intended to be an emotionally charged climax, falls flat. It is a meaningless, unconvincing, ludicrous ending to a plot that is in other respects highly imaginative, largely original, and absorbing. In fact, the Negro cult leader is entirely extraneous to the basic development of the plot. Second, Tucker's motivation is obscure and far from compelling in terms of cause and effect. A writer who accepts the challenge of analyzing the hidden motives of his characters is obligated to produce reasonably believable results.

But, despite its shortcomings, this book is tremendously encouraging. It reveals a Negro novelist with unusual talents who can tell without bitterness a moving story with strong racial overtones.

Nick Aaron Ford. *Phylon*. Summer, 1963, pp. 128–30

For all the random virtues of the [stories constituting] the Bedlow cycle, the heart of *Dancers on the Shore* is in the linked stories about the Dunford family—the doctor father, the mother, elder son Chig, sister Connie and brother Peter. The milieu alone is arresting: they are well-to-do Negroes whose children attend private schools and Ivy League colleges, and the ambiguities of race touch them only obliquely. Their public existence as Negroes is only occasionally in evidence. . . .

Not one of these stories is unsatisfying; indeed, such is the consistent interest of the Dunfords that one reader, at least, looks forward to a fuller representation in a novel. Certainly the material is there.

As is customary with story collections, the quality of Kelley's work is variable, but the range of his imagination, combined with the evidence of his best work, offers impressive evidence of the continuing development of the talent that was also visible in his first novel, *A Different Drummer*.

Michele Murray. *Com.* July 3, 1964, p. 459

As a writer, Kelley is a long-distance runner. He intends to earn a living from his books, and at 30 has already published four. Moreover, the books are unified in over-all design. Each volume is part of a larger saga, so that what lies in store for his readers is a sort of [Faulknerian] Yoknapatawpha legend in reverse: an epic treatment of American history from a Negro point of view.

Kelley's novels are marked by a progressive mood of disaffiliation from the dominant values of his culture. The hero of *A Different Drummer*, for example, represents the earlier, nonviolent phase of the Negro revolution. Under the astonished gaze of his white neighbors he sows his fields with salt, slaughters his livestock and burns his home, thereby inspiring a vast migration from the rural South.

The hero of *A Drop of Patience* is a blind jazz musician. His blindness is an emblem of the Negro's vulnerability, so long as he accepts the values of the white middle class. Abandoned by his white mistress, he cracks up, spending several years in and out of mental institutions. Gradually he recovers, finding a sustaining vision in the folk values implicit in his craft.

Now, in *dem* ("lemme tellya how dem folks live"), Kelley turns to an overt satire of the ways of white people. His present mood is bitter, disillusioned, alienated to the point of secession from American society. The expatriate impulse, however, has found in satire a controlling form. Kelley's images are able to encompass his negative emotions. The result is a sharp increase in perception for the victims of his satire.

Robert A. Bone. *NYT.* Sept. 24, 1967, p. 5

William Melvin Kelley's ivy league tutelage along with his unassuming demeanor (for he is unperturbably cool), are totally disarming. He comes into town with no guns showing, with no loud booming agonies of black rage. His style is a quiet, easily readable, point by point, well-tempered, traditional form of writing. There is nothing about him to put one on guard. Before you know it though, even at the very instance when you are about to say, "Hey, man, com'ere and tell us what you learnt in that white school," he has stuffed your mouth full of cyanide.

Kelley's first novel, *A Different Drummer*, tells the story of what happens when all the black people vacate the South, as well as what has gone on during the years before. This book is not a "parable," no more than Howard Fast's *Freedom Road* is a parable. Kelley depicts the very incidents, the acts and thoughts of brutality and inhumanity that whites have historically inflicted upon blacks in the South. He depicts the rage set off in the whites when the blacks, whom the whites have repeatedly deemed unwanted, decide once and for all to leave. He depicts the very *atmosphere* in and by which blacks are victimized, but which has been created and enforced by whites alone. Kelley depicts reality. In fact, Kelley is often closer to reality as a novelist than was Howard Fast who, it would seem, was incapable of writing anything but masterpieces. But Kelley is often closer to reality because, unlike Fast who was a communist, Kelley's works are free of the restrictions of any kind of ideological feedback—Marxist, anti-Marxist, or otherwise. [1969]

Calvin C. Hernton. In John A. Williams and
Charles F. Harris, eds., *Amistad 1* (New York,
Random House, 1970), pp. 219–20

The title of W. M. Kelley's second novel, *A Drop of Patience*, is taken, significantly enough, from Shakespeare's *Othello* (IV, II). It is the story of Ludlow Washington, a Negro jazz musician. The irony in this book springs from the fact that the hero, forced to live in a coloured social pattern, does not and cannot recognize the difference between black and white, as he was born blind. . . .

He escapes to New York, where he meets Ragan, a white girl as lonely as he is; the two fall passionately in love, and this affair is a crucial point in Ludlow's life, in his career, and in the novel. It is an ordeal in the course of which his racial education is examined and the gaps in it filled in for him to "see" through his blindness. It is as if the Negro community, wiser now, wanted to remind the "blind" man of his wilful deafness to their warning, one stressed particularly by Norman Spencer, never to "depend on no white man for nothing," for "he ain't strong enough to keep his promises." If the message is not understood, Kelley clearly indicates, the knowledge can only come through suffering. . . .

In the preface to *Dancers on the Shore*, a collection of his short stories published in 1965, Kelley claimed that "a writer should ask questions" about man's life and the important topical issues of his day. The answers should come from "a sociologist or a politician or a spokesman." But in *A Drop of Patience* it looks as though he had lost "patience" with asking questions only and had decided to answer them himself. Not that an artist cannot assume the role of spokesman; James Baldwin is a good example of the ability of the two to coincide. But, as

Norman Mailer puts it, Baldwin's "affirmations are always full of little denials, his denials full of little reservations," while W. M. Kelley's statements and "answers" in his second novel possess a tone of finality from which the book suffers considerably. . . .

Of W. M. Kelley's two attempts at fictional actualization of the American Negro's search for his identity, the first one [*A Different Drummer*], executed in social, historical and political terms and in the form of a fantasy, was a brilliant success. . . . His second novel, dealing with the Negro's identity in terms of culture, can be accepted with reservations only.

Josef Jařab. PP. No. 12, 1969, pp. 167–70

Dunfords Travels Everywheres picks up the motto of *Finnegans Wake* in its title, points to Joyce in an epigraph, and even bravely attempts the late idiom, making a rumbling, punning amalgam of minstrel paper, journalese, advertising copy, and radio serial into a new language, an escape from "languish," from the "Langleash language," a descent into a racial collectivity of blacks, the tongue of New Afriquerque cropping up suddenly in the ordinary prose of the novel. . . .

There is an affinity with Joyce. Kelley, too, as a black American and a writer, is caught in the language and culture of an enemy country, and his use of *Finnegans Wake* reflects a legitimate distress: it is a mockery both of "good English" and of black manglings of it. The trouble is that the effort looks in the wrong direction. The experimental idiom is ingenious, but it is, also, thin and obscure. . . .

Kelley's real gift is for evoking an uncomplicated tenderness— there are remarkably drawn old men and children in his short stories— and for grand, improbable, epic exaggeration: the sudden sight of slaves in this book, or in his first novel, *A Different Drummer*, the exodus of the entire black population from a Southern state. From a man who can do these things, *Dunfords Travels Everywheres* seems gratuitous, an attempt to be new at all costs. Homage to Joyce? A book more clearly Kelley's own would have been better.

Michael Wood. NYR. Mar. 11, 1971, p. 43

[*Dunfords Travels Everywheres*] has three parallel story lines. One line is the story of Chig Dunford, a confused, impotent black male who seems to prefer the company of whites and who also seems incapable of offering a challenge to anybody. It is also the story, or rather a few episodes in the life of Carlyle Bedlow who secures grounds for divorce for a Harlem dentist and saves a buddy from a very sophisticated con- game. The third line, narrated in the distorted but highly symbolic language of the subconscious or the dream seems to contain another main character (called at times Mr. Charcarl, Mr. Chigyle, Mr. Chuggle and other names) whose adventures are similar to those of Chig Dunford but grounded on a different plane of reality. These sequences are alternated in ways that seem arbitrary but which may contain some pattern of meaning. . . .

Admittedly, *Dunfords Travels Everywheres* is a difficult novel. Its weakness, however, is not so much one of technique as of a certain confusion of meaning. If Kelley means to say that whole hearted and uncritical acceptance of the white world on the part of blacks is dangerous and castrating, he fails to provide us with much that is really positive and useful in Carlyle Bedlow's black world. The image of the con-man is one of the oldest and most honored of the black tradition. Bedlow's finesse in rescuing his buddy Hondo is certainly commendable and well executed. It is a decided contrast to Dunford's failure to do anything about the captive Africans. But Bedlow's approach bears no relation in the novel to issues outside the range of the Harlem underworld which is its setting and certainly cannot stand as the solution to the problems Kelley raises. The experiments in form and style in *Dunfords Travels Everywheres* are valuable in themselves as experiments but the ultimate message of the novel hardly justifies the difficulty of reading it.

Cynthia J. Smith. *Freedomways*. No. 2, 1971,

pp. 205–6

Cultural plurality is the key phrase necessary in any attempt to understand the over-all meaning of *Dunfords Travels Everywheres*. . . . For Dunford, salvation is possible because he has not forgotten elements of a language system which speaks to the question of diversity and non-conformity, is capable of retaining contact with his cultural past. Thus his travels, which take him through the cultural capitals of the Western world, lead inevitably back to Harlem, where cultural democracy, not cultural hegemony, is the prevailing factor.

In *A Different Drummer* and in *Dunfords Travels Everywheres*, Kelley is cognizant of a black cultural history which his characters either know or must discover. Caliban, intuitively, has always known that the cultural system which defined him was not that of the Euro-American imagists. Dunford, on the other hand, must discover his cultural heritage anew, and in so doing undertake the journey to a black identity. Eventually the journey will lead outside the definition of the West, away from images and symbols that represent Western man, and toward those, rich and enduring, in the African/Black heritage. At the end of the novel he has come to partial awareness, has made his break, tenuous though it may be, with the paraphernalia of imagistic language handed down from the West and gained a new perception of himself.

Addison Gayle, Jr. *The Way of the New World*
(Garden City, N.Y., Doubleday, 1975), pp. 374–75

[Kelley] turns the usual stereotypes on their heads by contending that the black race, traditionally associated with dark jungle evil, seems, from his experience and observation, to be the more passive and gentle of the two races. The white race, thinking itself just and fair, need not be so complacent in this belief, because Kelley constructs a credible argument that the white race is very aggressive and violent. The stereotypes of black sexuality and easy living are shown to have some validity and to be positive rather than negative traits.

Paradoxically, Kelley's fiction is both idealistic and pessimistic at the same time. In *A Different Drummer* and *A Drop of Patience*, he idealistically envisions deep wells of strength in black people, strength which they will need to deal with white man's violence, to carry them forward to a time when humanity will once again feel its common roots. However, the last two novels, *dem* and *Dunfords Travels Everywheres*, are quite cynical, depicting the black man trying to deal with whites, but being betrayed time and again by a white man he thought he could trust. The developing message seems to be that right now, no black person can trust any white person. But Kelley is not so idealistic as to think that the black people can win any open confrontation with whites, so each black man must use his imagination to wage his own figurative guerilla war for recognition of his humanity.

Jill Weyant. *CLAJ*. Dec., 1975, pp. 219–20

KILLENS, JOHN OLIVER (1916–   )

UNITED STATES

Early in [*Youngblood*], Joe Youngblood sums up the theme: "How do you live in a white man's world? Do you live on your knees—do you live with your shoulders bent and your hat in your hand? Or do you live like a man is supposed to live—with your head straight up?" This thematic question pervades the thinking, controls the action, dominates the conversation of all the characters—whether they be black or white.

The Youngbloods decided to live with their heads straight up. They paid dearly for the decision. Joe, the father, finally paid with his life. As a family, they were flogged, defrauded, victimized. Yet they found allies in unexpected places. One of them, Oscar Jefferson, was white. He allied himself with the Youngbloods, at first reluctantly, timidly, and finally forthrightly. Part of the richness and authenticity of *Youngblood* stems from the inclusion of the story of Oscar Jefferson.

This is a fine novel, vivid, readable. Even its minor characters, yellow haired Betty Jane Cross, Dr. Jamison, Reverend Ledbetter, Richard Myles, George Cross, Jr. are as arresting as its major ones.

Youngblood has one serious shortcoming. In order to dramatize the fear, the hate, the terror that accompanies what Hodding Carter called "this tragic predicament of race," Mr. Killens has used many scenes of hate-inspired violence, some of them worthy of the Grand Guignol. The repetition of these scenes tends to deaden the sensibilities of the reader.

Ann Petry. NYHT. July 11, 1954, p. 8

Among the contemporary American critics who attribute greatness to William Faulkner's depiction of Southern life, one—Irving Howe—has claimed that "No other American novelist has watched the Negroes so carefully and patiently" and that "none other has listened with such fidelity to the nuances of their speech and recorded them with such skill." John O. Killens' first novel, *Youngblood*, should be a revelation to both Faulkner and Howe, for here is a graphic portrait *of* people, not merely *about* them. It is of people because its characters are realized primarily in terms of natural, human inclinations. And what Mr. Killens measures out in bitter, dramatic doses—frequently interspersed with rollicking humor—is the cruel impact of the way of life in the South on a Negro family and community. . . .

It is Jefferson, however, who stands as the most memorable of Mr. Killens' characters, for through him Mr. Killens has illuminated one of the most misunderstood personalities in modern America: the tragic cracker. From his father, young Jefferson has learned to expect brutal thrashings; from his mother, a mixture of love and deception; from his friend Jim, the facts of life in race relations. The result is a serious-minded personality pondering the grave issues of right and wrong and finally realizing, in his slow, hesitant manner, that nearly all life as it is lived in the South is one huge, complicated lie.

Henry F. Winslow. Crisis. Oct., 1954, pp. 511–12, 515

In this big, polyphonic, violent novel about Negro soldiers in World War II [*And Then We Heard the Thunder*] John Oliver Killens drags the reader into the fullness of the Negro's desolating experience. The author, formerly a member of the National Labor Relations Board in Washington and now a movie and television writer, served in the Amphibian Forces in the South Pacific. His novel, therefore, has the depth and complexity of lived experience. It calls James Jones to mind, though Killens writes with less technical control and more poetically. But his battle scenes have the same hallucinatory power; his characters live and speak the raw language of the streets and the barracks.

This non-Negro reader who served in the Pacific alongside Negro troops recognizes the events and characters of this novel; but he sees them with a sort of brain-twisting transformation of insights. He never gave much thought, for example, to the hideous irony of asking the Negro to fight (in segregated units) and die in order to preserve the very freedoms which he could not enjoy at home. Few non-Negroes knew the Negro soldiers' common motto, the Double V for Victory: victory against Fascism overseas and victory against Fascism at home. Nor did it ruffle us to hear the band play "God Bless America" while we boarded troopships and then switch to "Darktown Strutters' Ball" when the Negro troops' turn came. But here, living it through the Negro's reaction, we cannot believe our ears. . . .

The reader, living all the indignities of the Negro soldier, sees clearly how it looked from the other side of the color line. Discrimination in the armed forces has been eliminated. But the deep wounds of Negro soldiers have not. This novel magnificently illumines the reasons why. Their second victory—against Fascism at home—is slow in coming.

John Howard Griffin. SR. Jan. 26, 1963, pp. 46–47

John Oliver Killens has written two long, detailed, humorless, artless, almost documentary race novels, *Youngblood* and *And Then We Heard the Thunder*. The first is a sort of Negro family epic, the expected tale of two generations of long-suffering blacks and their sadistic white masters in a Georgia town. The second tells the interminable story of Negroes (and whites) in wartime, where the ordeal of World War II seems less harrowing, in the long run, than the race war inside it. It runs through pages of somber "graphic realism," i.e., pages of vapidly obscene barracks chatter and hard-boiled crudeness of description: that's the way it was.

Both books are sincerely well intended, and packed to bursting with details of Negro (Southern, army) life, episode after episode, as retailed by a careful, intelligent, unimaginative Negro with absolutely no sense of the art of fiction. They represent the kind of novel most Americans with great stocks of experience would probably write, if they had the will and were Negroes. The books are useful, and, to readers who make no great demands on their novelists, mildly moving and exciting.

David Littlejohn. *Black on White* (New York, Grossman, 1966), pp. 143–44

Killens is not a cerebral novelist, but his intellect works well in his art. It does not betray him into pretentiousness and into a pseudo-sophisticated fooling around with ideas that might better be left to moral philosophers. His theme—so far there is only one, with variations—is simple, clear: the price of submission to unreasonable authority, economic or cultural, civil or military, social or sexual, intellectual or emotional. His treatment of this theme is as diverse as it is direct. No beating about the bush for Killens. No setting of "snares to catch woodcocks." And above all, none of the intellectual equivocations that some of his more "arty" and self-conscious contemporaries are inveigled into. His philosophy is plainly ethical: man has Man's soul to save. Sometimes the odds against man's saving his soul are terrific. It is the odds that make Killens's stories, that supply the dramatic action. The theme is pursued in the context of the American race situation.

And why not? It has always been *the* situation, and honesty demands, of the Negro artist especially, a frank acceptance of the fact. For the Negro writer to deny it, or even to gloss it, is to betray himself, and to lose the soul that he must save. And since both black men and (increasingly) white are caught up in the race situation, the creative writer is provided with a scope—in characterization, in incident, in setting, in atmosphere and mood—as broad as the scope of America itself (and as valid to his work as his imagination, his sensibilities, and his artistic genius can make it). Broader, indeed. *And Then We Heard the Thunder* ends in Australia, and the concluding episode in the book is just as right, true, and credible as the opening episode in Harlem.

Killens's art is naturally vivacious and robust. His style is not notable for its grace. His language is the earthy, literal, idiomatic language of his characters. His comedy—for he has a comic gift—is likely to be broad, meant only to evoke laughter; but he also uses it to other purposes. His sense of the comic flows from an ironic perception of the difference between appearance and reality, and from the equally ironic knowledge that neither appearance nor reality is always the same for black men and white. Killens uses comedy as an escape into pride and dignity and into a sense of that human equality the substance of which he strives for both as writer and man.

Saunders Redding. *AfrF*. Spring, 1966, pp. 25–26

Whenever Ronnie Gilbert, a Southern Negro college student in *'Sippi*, is deeply moved by someone or something he exclaims, "Baby I'm shook to my natural chittlins!" And that is just what this great novel will do to all who read it.

Beyond doubt we in the U.S. live in an age of tempestuous and twisting emotions, of brutal violence, of intrigue, of massive and mass produced ignorance and miniscule understanding, of heroism and cowardice. These are the ingredients used as Killens unfolds his story of how the Negroes in Wakefield County, Mississippi reacted after the Supreme Court outlawed school segregation in 1954. . . .

Killens is a master delineator of the deep meanings in the earthy ungrammatical language of the rural Negroes. For like them, he has used it not only as a medium of communication but as a weapon of struggle. The sermon on freedom by Rev. Purdy is a consummate exercise in word imagery, each pulsing with power, alive with motion and igniting the next sentence with an electric energy of its own.

Thus we have a poetic tapestry, richly woven with folkways, speech, movement, ideas, colors, smells, sounds and emotions. It is a fusing of the non-contemporary events like Malcolm X's death, persons like Martin Luther King, Lorraine Hansberry and others, into the living, breathing amalgam of black-white relations in the U.S. today.

John Henry Jones. Freedomways. Fall, 1967,
pp. 373–74

John Oliver Killens' satire *The Cotillion* brings humor and fun into both the hangups of black middleclassness and the often solemnly treated idea of moving into blackness. The easier of the two targets, of course, is the satire of the middle-class aspirations represented by Lady Daphne, etc., since the aspirations and aberrations of middleclassness have so often been outlined. His achievement with Daphne, mother of the heroine, is that she remains human and loveable, although narrow. The more difficult job is to deal with the main impulse of the story—to bring the beautiful Yoruba Eveylyn through a mad universe into real fulfillment—in popular terms, her blackness.

The book is good fun, although its humor is rather broad and seems to have excessive coping power as evidenced in the relations between mother and daughter. But the novel seems a refreshing change for a literature that so often seems to ignore the things boasted of in real life traditions: the humor, signifying, etc. What one would like to see is Killens' resources used for still more subtle analyses and in complex equations.

George E. Kent. Phylon. Winter, 1972, p. 308

In the works of John Oliver Killens, John Williams, Ernest Gaines, and William Melvin Kelley, a new tradition is begun, one which depends for its viability upon black perceptions based upon black definitions of reality. John Oliver Killens is the spiritual father of the new novelists. It is his direction—more so than that of Ellison—that the young writers have followed. He is the first of the modern period to begin anew, with conscious determination, the quest for new definitions, to attempt to give new meanings to old cultural artifacts. . . .

Differences in setting and plot are apparent in [*And Then We Heard the Thunder* and *The Cotillion*]; yet, on one level, the novels share similar themes and situations, deal with the same conflict—the attempt at self-education by each of its protagonists. Both Solly Saunders and Yoruba must move from a preoccupation with the self to embrace black people everywhere; from concern with their individual status as victims of the American society to an awareness of their own strengths and egos. Each must begin the study of history, must find there the artifacts which sustained their forefathers, and, having done so, manifest a love toward black people at home and abroad. More so than any novelist in black literary history, Killens is the novelist of love.

Addison Gayle, Jr. *The Way of the New World*
(Garden City, N.Y., Doubleday, 1975), p. 317

KUNENE, MAZISI (1930–   )

SOUTH AFRICA

Upon reading Mr. Kunene's poems, one immediately discovers that there is a poet, the secret of whose charming and touching verse is its simplicity, clarity and originality. To those who know him, the poet in question has never failed to win admiration because of his simplicity. He is not, like so many of us, mentally castrated in the Western tradition, a caricature of European culture. This is clearly demonstrated by the idiom and cadence of his poems which are steeped in the traditional Zulu oral poetry: apt lyrical associations interspersed with images from the sonorous world of the Zulu heroic epic. . . .

He invokes the familiar landscape of the land of Shaka, with word-pictures that are not mere structures superimposed over the overall piece of exotica. Rather they are associated with the deepest thoughts of the poet's people, with the sentiments of the land to which he is first and foremost addressing himself. They may be concrete place-names and proper names of historical significance; or some other phenomena that have come to be accepted as expressive of the best in human nature or the worst in life. But all these do undergo a complicated process in the creative mind of the poet, when they finally come out on paper they are closely and fittingly knit into the mosaic of words that transport ideas and aspirations and force a corresponding reaction on the part of the reader. . . .

Mr. Kunene has firmly established himself in the realist tradition. In doing so, he has not sacrificed the lively Zulu imagery at the altar of a fastidious demi-god of intellectualism.

Mofolo Bulane. NewA. June, 1966, pp. 111–12

Mazisi Kunene's Zulu Poems are all rich, rhetorical, full of emotional and intellectual over- and undertones that reverberate through all the musical variety of the chanting, singing, philosophising voice which he derives from an ancient and rich tradition. . . .

Away from home, out of his land—unfortunately, even unhappily, but of necessity—it is the pity of this that is crystallised in the simple, succinct expression of "Exile." . . . There are fullness and expressivity in this poem which speak not only in the rich metaphors of home but also of the loss entailed by conditions at home, expressing at the same time a condemnation of those conditions, and a resolution, bitter, present and active, to change, to improve, to revolutionise that situation in the place from which exile has driven one and in the places to which exile has forced one, may still send one. This awareness of the brutality and/or decadence of the world that chose "the bridegroom of steel" ("Europe"), this awareness of a trauma and an agony which needs revolutionary ardour, a revolutionary awareness of decadence and, more than anything, a revolutionary perception of goals to be attained, is another of the strands that this memorable volume weaves into the South African cultural pattern.

Langa Mokwena. AfrC. No. 2, 1971, pp. 119–21

Mazisi Kunene is a poet who speaks through a muted instrument. Very strange for a poet who is also full time in South African resistance politics based in London. There is no uptight posturing at all in his diction, which has a flow and beat peculiarly reminiscent of Kofi Awoonor. He writes his verse in Zulu and has rendered a translation of a significant portion of it, and he is head and shoulders above his predecessors in the area of Zulu poetry. What he says about Zulu poetry being a communal voice is true of all Bantu poetry in Southern Africa, indeed true of most African poetry we know of in indigenous languages.

There is a fascinating interplay in Kunene's [*Zulu Poems*] between the intense motivation peculiar to the political mood of today and the motivation that underlies oral poetry on the lips of an elder. This latter motivation is prophecy. Here is very little exploration.

Kunene speaks through a lyric that makes bold forthright statements which, taken together, have the effect of having taken the reader through some exploration of a kind. He admonishes the proud, the tyrants, those who worship steel and so on. In general he warns against self-deceit. As a prophet, the persona waxes more and more apocalyptic. The "widowed leopard," says the prophet, who is referring to the predatory white man, will retreat howling into the hill. She will walk about destitute, giving way to the young triumphant bulls of the earth who must take our place. The white people's guilt will pursue them, "driving them from wall to wall." Today's children must "burst forth with our tomorrows." No matter what the white man does, the one who is forever felling trees, the African is abundance itself. Always there will come a season of new fruit. Kunene sees the function of a poem as that of taking from people the "yearnings of their souls" and turning them into a huge fountain that will multiply into oceans.

Ezekiel Mphahlele. The African Image, rev. ed.
(New York, Praeger, 1974), pp. 239–40

Kunene's most ambitious poem, "Anthem of Decades," utilizes the style of the long Zulu epic poem which at times runs to five hundred or more lines. What appears in his collection *Zulu Poems* is only an extract of 186 lines. . . .

The epic characterizes the victory of one force over another; the victor, representing a higher morality and will, triumphs not because he is good and the other is evil; in his victory will be shown his humility dramatized in the act of cleaning the vanquished combatant's wounds. As Kunene points out, the characters are not gods, but personalized ideas, representing anthropomorphic conceptions of the universe as embedded in Zulu philosophy and thinking. Imprecise, the Zulu concept of the deity or Supreme Creator shares a pantheistic nature that is clouded in vagueness and mystery. . . .

It seems that in this poem Kunene attempts to unite the principles of creation and of the struggle between forces as contained in Zulu thought. The material is completely derived from Zulu cosmology. It is obvious also that the poem is suggested by *Paradise Lost*, even though its denouement presents a vision totally different from that of the Christian epic. Its predilection for abstractions seems obviously to be based upon an attempt to achieve for it a preciseness. But the language and style are based in Zulu imagery. The principles that inhabit the land-scape of the poem share of the Zulu conception of the world and express its creation myths.

Kofi Awoonor. *The Breast of the Earth* (Garden City, N.Y., Doubleday, 1975), pp. 199–201

LA GUMA, ALEX (1925–   )

SOUTH AFRICA

[*A Walk in the Night*] is Alex La Guma's first novel, though he is known for short stories in *Black Orpheus* and *Africa South*. La Guma, himself a colored South African, is writing of Cape Town's "District Six," a slum area populated by a mixture of people, but predominantly by coloreds. This is one of the most exciting books to emerge from Africa in recent years. La Guma writes in a most evocative manner, with a lovely style full of brilliant images. He refers to a man walking up a street "trailing his tattered raincoat behind him like a sword-slashed, bullet-ripped banner just rescued from a battle" and to a slum girl "wearing new, yellow leather, flat-heeled pumps that gave the impression of something expensive abandoned on a junk heap." He brings to life the characters of this squalid environment and writes of them with a sympathy that is almost poetic, yet with great objectivity. . . .

This is, of course, protest writing, but it is way above mere propaganda. As an indictment of a system it is powerful, but its unique quality is its full and tender humanity.

Martin Banham. BA. Autumn, 1962, p. 458

The immediate consequence of [the Sabotage Act in South Africa] was that [La Guma's] first novel, *A Walk in the Night*, published in 1962 by Mbari Publications in Nigeria, became forbidden reading for all South Africans. A few copies were smuggled into the country and passed from hand to hand. The book won instant recognition as a work of talent and imagination.

It is a short novel—barely ninety pages long. But within its covers teem the variegated types of Cape Town's District Six. Alex La Guma knows and loves District Six and its people, and has written of them with intimacy and care. . . .

During his period of house arrest he worked on his second novel, *And a Threefold Cord*, this time dealing with life in one of the shanty-towns sprawled on the periphery of Cape Town.

Few white South Africans can have any conception of what life in a shanty-town is like, for here are housed the tens of thousands of Non-whites for whom there is no "official" place to live, Coloureds and Africans clutching precariously to life on the outskirts of the cities which offer their only hope of sustenance. . . . These are areas where life is short and cheap, where violence flares out of hate and frustration, yet where humanity, love and hope sprout even from the dunghill of evil and decay.

And a Threefold Cord is drenched in the wet and misery of the Cape winter, whose grey and dreary tones Alex La Guma has captured in a series of graphic prose-etchings. Under a lesser pen, it could have been depressing, this picture of South Africa's lower depths, with its incidents of sordid brutality and infinite desolation. But Alex La Guma's compassion and fidelity to life have infused it with a basic optimism. His electric dialogue crackles with the lightning of the human spirit. His message is: "People can't stand up to the world alone, they got to be together."

Brian Bunting. Foreword to Alex La Guma, And a
Threefold Cord (Berlin, Seven Seas, 1964), pp. 14–15

Alex La Guma, the Cape coloured writer, most assuredly deserves wider notice abroad for his novella *A Walk in the Night*. Paradoxically, of all the black writers who have suffered the most at the hands of the South African Government, La Guma has been longest on the receiving end. He was one of the defendants in the protracted Treason Trial; he has been banned from attending gatherings of any kind and detained in prison several times. He is now under house arrest in Cape Town; his writings cannot, of course, be published or quoted in the country. This means he has been virtually denied the right to earn a living, as he has always done, through journalism.

Alex La Guma tills the same apartheid plot which the other writers have so exhaustively worked up, but what distinguishes him as a true novelist is his enthusiasm for life as it is lived. He has the artist's eye for the interesting detail; his stories and novels are sagging under the weight of real people waging a bloody contest with the forces of oppression; and credibly they celebrate their few moments of victory in sex, cheap Cape wine and stupid fights. The rooms they inhabit smell of decay, urine and sweat; they share them with "roaches, fleas, bugs, lice." Their only triumph is that they are human—superlatively human; and this is their sole claim upon our imagination. . . .

In *A Walk in the Night* La Guma follows the progress of Michael Adonis, a coloured boy thrown out of his factory job for talking back to the white foreman; and a supporting cast of thugs, derelicts, spivs, neurotic cops "doomed for a certain term to walk the night." By the end of this night Adonis has killed under an impulse a harmless old man; a neurotic policeman has shot a small-time thug; a penniless man has been "rolled" for money; but incontestably life has also been celebrated in the cheap bars, speakeasies and wretched slumhouses along the Harlem-like ghetto of Cape Town's District Six. This impressive short work has distinct Dostoevskian undertones, which, I hope, is not too large a claim to make for it.

Lewis Nkosi. BO. March, 1966, pp. 53–54

To hammer and hew a novel out of the monolithic social situation of South Africa is to apprehend a reality in which man is beset by fear, isolation, loneliness, is plagued by doubts and indecision. For South Africa is a society whose members live under the constant corrosion of dehumanization and the possibility of swift death. . . .

La Guma's view [in *And a Threefold Cord*] is gray, grim, hostile, humorless; and he expresses it through the physical atmosphere of the settlement where his novel is set. . . . The atmosphere is not only physical; it has a moral force which seeps into the very fiber of the characters and controls their total existence. The physical landscape, reinforced by a constant, hissing rain and an inimical sky, becomes a presence, indeed the main character of the novel. Description becomes novelistic action; background is foreground. . . .

The dialog of the novel is racy, shot through with local slang; the canvas, oversaturated with description and overdominated with detail, for the author seems bent on describing every physical characteristic of every phenomenon. Certain epithets and motifs recur, giving the sense of conflict and tension emanating from the canvas: fortress, battalion, garrison, driving wind and rain. As in all South African novels, the police play a role. When the police raids begin, the earlier generalized ambiance of poetry becomes specifically South African. As in his earlier novel, *A Walk in the Night*, La Guma shows the police as hard, harsh, brutal, applying to them the recurrent words "cinder" and "ash."

Wilfred Cartey. AfrF. Winter, 1966, pp. 115–17

[In *A Walk in the Night*] the debasement of life on the wrong side of the color bar hangs a pall of degradation over every human activity, so that every relationship is demeaned in the generalization of an overwhelming inhumanity: the color bar itself. Alex La Guma's protagonists in District Six do not talk about inequality; they bear its weals. In this novel, Michael Adonis is a colored boy who has just lost his job in a society where his ambitions are limited by job reservations and his security as a worker is not ensured by a trade union. He wanders the streets around his Cape Town tenement room, and in an atmosphere of cheap wine, sex, and the meaningless aggression of frustrated human beings, unintentionally kills a decrepit old white man who has sunk too low for acceptance among whites. Adonis's moral dissolution culminates when he lets his friend, Willieboy, be blamed for the crime, while Adonis himself joins a gang of thugs.

In his short stories, Alex La Guma shows the same ability to convey the sight, sound, and smell of poverty and misery, so that the flesh-and-blood meaning of the color bar becomes a shocking, sensuous impact. His stories are set in prisons, cheap cafés, backyards, yet eschew the cliché situations of apartheid—the confrontations of black and white in the context of the immorality act or liquor raids, which are done to death by lesser writers.

Nadine Gordimer. MQR. Fall, 1970, pp. 227–28

The moral action of La Guma's characters has been described as essentially defensive. There is evidence, however, that the author has found this method increasingly inadequate, and in the succession of his leading characters can be traced a development towards an outright political posture. Thus, while Mike Adonis [in *A Walk in the Night*] is shown in moral retreat, from the dignity of a factory worker to the questionable status of a petty criminal, Charlie Pauls, in *And a Threefold Cord*, is an occasional worker, in whom the roots of class consciousness have taken a precarious hold: ". . . if the poor people all got together and took everything in the whole blerry world, there wouldn't be poor any more." This statement is the novel's answer to the world which it portrays, a plausible articulation of the solidarity of the shanty-dwellers.

In *The Stone Country*, La Guma's main character is a fully-fledged political agitator. His role in the novel, however, is mainly as an onlooker, linking the various parts of a rather disjointed story. George Adams has a certain impact on the prison scene, by virtue of the personal courage he displays, and as a standard against which the other characters are measured. Used in this detached way, he does not, as representative of the author's point of view, interpose himself between the main substance of the novel and the reader's perception of it. The shortcomings of the "mouthpiece" character are thus largely avoided, though George Adams remains a little too good to ring true. In this train of development can be perceived the emergence of a technical obstacle derived from the author's hardening attitude to the reality which he confronts. It has become increasingly difficult for La Guma to allow to the fictional material itself the responsibility of political statement. In his most recent work [*In the Fog of the Season's End*] the problem has become acute. . . .

The book is about the play of pure forces. Since the vision of the principal characters is the vision of the author himself, no additional insight can be gained by refraction through their eyes. Thus the heuristic functions of the novel form become redundant. The technique of documentary will serve as well, indeed, better, since the artifices of fiction obscure where they do not further clarify.

David Rabkin. JCL. June, 1973, pp. 59–61

In the Fog of the Season's End, by the exiled South African Alex La Guma, delivers, through its portrait of a few hunted blacks attempting to subvert the brutal regime of apartheid, a social protest reminiscent, in its closely detailed texture and level indignation, of Dreiser and Zola. . . .

The writing [conveys] a jumbled, sweaty sensation not inappropriate to the subject—the human jungle the white man has imposed upon the South African black. And when La Guma's prose connects directly to outrage—as when Tekwane is tortured by two tweedy policemen, or when the maze of permits the police state has created is dramatized—the fuzz of overwriting burns away. As a thriller, *In the Fog of the Season's End* suffers not only from its chosen interweave of flashbacks but from a certain languid futility in its basic mission; the risk Beukes runs distributing the leaflets seems far greater than any possible effect they can have. As political description, the book is less strident than its metaphors. The black population Beukes moves through is represented, in what feel to be fair proportions, as amused, threatened, or inspired by him and his cause. Personal friendship among these oppressed counts for more than political commitment. . . .

In a modern state, strangers are the rule, and Beukes more than once reminds himself of the uncomfortable, comforting fact that he is anonymous while, with his carton of pamphlets addressed to the faceless masses, he dodges from one island of acquaintanceship to another. I have heard it observed that among black Africans South African exiles invariably stand out as the most dynamic. Perhaps "dynamic" should be read as "best able to deal with strangers." The people in La Guma's world are fighting for identity; Amadi's villagers have had theirs bestowed upon them—in their kinship, in their nicknames, in their hierarchical roles. Dragging its captive blacks in the ruck, the South African state has nevertheless dragged them into modernity, into the post-tribal impersonality that makes it necessary for the narrative artist to particularize every face. The need to describe, excessively felt in *In the Fog of the Season's End*, arises when teller and listener no longer share a common reality. [Jan. 21, 1974]

John Updike. Picked-Up Pieces (New York,
Alfred A. Knopf, 1975), pp. 328, 334–35

LAMMING, GEORGE (1927–   )

BARBADOS

The act of ripping the sensitive human personality from one culture and the planting of that personality in another culture is a tortured, convoluted process that must, before it can appeal to peoples' hearts, be projected either in terms of vivid drama or highly sensual poetry.

It has been through the medium of the latter—a charged and poetic prose—that George Lamming, a young West Indian Negro of Barbados, has presented his autobiographical summation of a tropical island childhood that, though steeped in the luminous images of sea, earth, sky, and wind, drifts slowly towards the edge of the realms of political and industrial strife. Notwithstanding the fact that Lamming's story, as such, is his own, it is, at the same time, a symbolic repetition of the story of millions of simple folk who, sprawled over half of the world's surface and involving more than half of the human race, are today being catapulted out of their peaceful, indigenously earthy lives and into the turbulence and anxiety of the twentieth century.

I, too, have been long crying these stern tidings; and, when I catch the echo of yet another voice declaiming in alien accents a description of this same reality, I react with pride and excitement, and I want to urge others to listen to that voice. One feels not so much alone when, from a distant witness, supporting evidence comes to buttress one's own testimony. And the voice that I now bid you hear is sounding in Lamming's *In the Castle of My Skin*.

> Richard Wright. Introduction to George Lamming, *In the Castle of My Skin* (New York, McGraw-Hill, 1953), pp. ix–x

It is easy to understand the incomprehension which has greeted Mr. George Lamming's third book. Mr. Lamming is a Barbadian Negro, and unless one understands the West Indian's search for identity, *Of Age and Innocence* is almost meaningless. It is not fully realised how completely the West Indian Negro identifies himself with England. Africa has been forgotten; films about African tribesmen excite derisive West Indian laughter. For the West Indian intellectual, speaking no language but English, educated in an English way, the experience of England is really traumatic. The foundations of his life are removed. He has to look for new loyalties. . . .

I thought this a better novel than *The Emigrants* [his second novel]. But Mr. Lamming creates difficulties for the reader. He has devised a story which is fundamentally as well-knit and exciting as one by Graham Greene. But you have to look hard for it. Mr. Lamming suppresses and mystifies; he shies away from the concrete, and grows garrulous over the insignificant. He is not a realistic writer. He deals in symbols and allegory. Experience has not been the basis of this novel. Every character, every incident is no more than a constituent idea in Mr. Lamming's thesis: the reader's sympathies are never touched. San Cristobal, the imaginary island which is the setting of Mr. Lamming's novel, could never exist.

I can understand Mr. Lamming's need for fantasy. His conception of the search for identity is highly personal; it has arisen from a deep emotion which he has chosen to suppress, turning it instead into an intellectual thing which is fine in its way, but would be made absurd by the comic realities of West Indian political life. Here is one West Indian writer who feels hindered rather than inspired by the West Indian scene.

Mr. Lamming is only thirty. He is one of the finest prose-writers of his generation. Purely as a work of fantasy *Of Age and Innocence* is really quite remarkable. It fails through its sheer unreadability. Mr. Lamming should be warned by this that his best subject, as in *In the Castle of My Skin* and the first 50 pages of this novel, is himself.

V. S. Naipaul. *NS.* Dec. 6, 1958, p. 827

[*Season of Adventure*] is about freedom—political freedom—in the West Indies; about the fact that if you were to release a diseased cat from a sack, it would still be diseased, although free; even more it is about the etiology of the disease, or diseases, as discerned in West Indians above the line of poverty or below it, falsified by an education or uneducated, with the echoes of respectability in their ears or the direct sound of the steel drum. It is about the ways in which a neglected, disconnected drift of humans does not "work," though its individuals live, think, feel, posture, whore, lie, cheat, murder and delude themselves, like everyone else. It is even about a universal revolution.

So much for abouts. It is, *per contra*, as a novel, extra-politically, extra-sociologically, a hot fuddle of sententious and sensational verbosity, unremitting, frequently ridiculous, which boils and boils and keeps moving a number of approximate dolls attached to names and explicatory functions. "Her sister had died of tetanus thirteen days after a wasp stung her on the left nipple of her tumoured breast." Dawn winds always break, drums have a "dark refrain." Peculiarities yes; but not that imaginative idiosyncratic extra "realness" one expects in novels above the average—a level this book does not reach.

Others think otherwise, I know, about the peculiarity of Mr. Lamming's fiction. I think they are being had in a dislike of drabness, much as one might be had by a mixture of grimacing and erotic sculpture in coloured plasticine slapped to a building which, after all, was only town councillors' asbestos. In *Season of Adventure* the peculiarity is upheld by very ordinary novel-making.

Geoffrey Grigson. Spec. Oct. 28, 1960, p. 663

One of the most interesting novelists out of the West Indies is George Lamming. Lamming was—and still is—regarded as a writer of considerable promise. What is the nature of his promise? Let us look at his novel *Of Age and Innocence.* This is a novel which somehow fails, I feel, but its failure tells us a great deal. The novel would have been remarkable if a certain tendency—a genuine tendency—for a tragic feeling of dispossession in reality had been achieved. This tendency is frustrated by a diffusion of energies within the entire work. The book seems to speak with a public voice, the voice of a peculiar orator, and the compulsions which inform the work appear to spring from a verbal sophistication rather than a visual, plastic and conceptual imagery. Lamming's verbal sophistication is conversational, highly wrought and spirited sometimes: at other times it lapses into merely clever utterance, rhetorical, as when he says of one of his characters: "He had been made Governor of an important colony which was then at war with England."

It takes some effort—not the effort of imaginative concentration which is always worthwhile but an effort to combat the author's self-indulgence. And this would not arise if the work could be kept true to its inherent design. There is no necessary difficulty or complexity in Lamming's novels—the necessary difficulty or complexity belonging to strange symbolisms—and I feel if the author concentrated on the sheer essentials of his experience a tragic disposition of feeling would gain a true ascendancy. This concentration is essential if the work is not to succumb to a uniform tone which gives each individual character the same public-speaking resonance of voice. . . .

In terms of the ruling framework he accepts, the individuality of character, the distinctions of status and privilege which mark one individual from another, must be maintained. This is the kind of realism, the realism of classes and classifications—however limited it may be in terms of a profound, poetic and scientific scale of values—the novel, in its orthodox mould, demands. Lamming may be restless within this framework (there are signs and shadows of this in his work) but mere extravagance of pattern and an inclination to frequent intellectual raids beyond his territory are not a genuine breakthrough and will only weaken the position of the central character in his work. [1964]

Wilson Harris. Tradition, the Writer and Society
(London, New Beacon, 1967), pp. 37–38

The problem facing George Lamming's work (and this is the burden of all true experiment and exploration) is one of form. His insights require poetry, and Lamming has been remarkably successful in deploying this within his novels' structure. But as he has moved from the childhood world of *In the Castle of My Skin*, he has become more and more concerned with the political and psychological ramifications of social living and consciousness (*The Emigrants, Of Age and Innocence, Season of Adventure*), and he has had to rely more and more on "prose" while still trying to retain the poetry. This tug of war has affected the shape of his work; preventing it from achieving a clear, coherent, over-all whole. Yet such is his power of realization, that any given section of his work reveals a hard, unwinking gleam that marks its authenticity. . . .

But the "shape" of Lamming's work is also conditioned by the kind of tradition he is working towards. He seems to be moving away from the European tradition of the "house" towards a different and more "Caribbean" form altogether. *Season of Adventure* opens with the experience of a voodoo ceremony and its effect, particularly, on a West Indian girl who, until she is faced with the Gods of the *tonelle* [voodoo ceremonial canopy], thinks that her sophistication renders her immune from the language of the drums. Within this alternative tradition, Lamming appears to be saying, lie the hidden and half-forgotten forces through which Caribbean society can be forged. . . .

Edward Brathwaite. Bim. July–Dec., 1968, pp. 162–63

In a sense, *Season of Adventure* is a celebration (the first literary one) of the steel band. Not only does the sound of the steel drums hang in the air throughout the novel: at the climax is a glorious parade of all the bands marching on to Freedom Square celebrating the coming of a new government. . . . But Lamming's nationalism is not the local-culture-waving [V. S.] Naipaul goes out of his way to snipe at. *Season of Adventure* is an analysis of the failure of nationalism in the newly independent San Cristobal. . . .

In the novel *Season of Adventure*, Lamming explores the problematic relation to Africa in terms proper to works of fiction. The middle-class West Indian's denial of the masses, and his shame of Africa are seen as obstacles to the fulfilment of the person, and the inauthentic existence of the unfulfilled person is a kind of death. Fola is imagined as such a dead person, and the creative task of the novel is to probe this condition and to feel for the problems and possibilities of re-birth. . . .

Season of Adventure is the most significant of the West Indian novels invoking Africa, and a major achievement, for several reasons: because it does not replace a denigrating excess by a romanticizing one;

because it embodies a corrective view without making this the novel's *raison d'être*; because it is so emphatically a West Indian novel—invoking the African heritage not to make statements about Africa but to explore the troubled components of West Indian culture and nationhood; and because it can do all this without preventing us from seeing that Fola's special circumstances, and by implication those of the West Indian, are only a manifestation, although a pressing one in the islands today, of every man's need to take the past into account with humility, fearlessness and receptivity if the future is to be free and alive.

Kenneth Ramchand. The West Indian Novel and Its
Background (New York, Barnes & Noble, 1970),
pp. 136, 143, 149

It will be our argument that although it is set in a village in a period well before any of the West Indian islands had achieved independence, *In the Castle of My Skin* is a study of a colonial revolt; that it shows the motive forces behind it and its development through three main stages: a static phase, then a phase of rebellion, ending in a phase of achievement and disillusionment with society poised on the edge of a new struggle; that it sharply delineates the opposition between the aspirations of the peasantry and those of the emergent native élite, an opposition which, masked in the second phase, becomes clear during the stage of apparent achievemnet.

The novel itself is built on a three-tier time structure corresponding broadly to our three stages: the first three chapters describe stable life, a village community whose social consciousness is limited to a struggle with immediate nature; the next six chapters deal with a village whose consciousness is awakened into a wider vision, involving challenge of and struggle against the accepted order of things; while the last chapters show the ironic denouement; a new class of native lawyers, merchants, teachers has further displaced the peasantry from the land. But underlying the story's progress in time is a general conception of human history as a movement from the state of nature to a "higher" consciousness; it is a movement from relative stability in a rural culture to a state of alienation, strife and uncertainty in the modern world. . . .

In light of what has happened to the peasant masses in Africa, the West Indies, and all over the former colonial world, *In the Castle of My Skin* acquires symbolic dimensions and new prophetic importance: it is one of the great political novels in modern "colonial" literature. [1972]

Ngugi wa Thiong'o. Homecoming (New York,
Lawrence Hill, 1973), pp. 110, 126

[Lamming's] first novel, *In the Castle of My Skin*, written in prose that was dazzlingly original, described a journey from childhood to adolescence; his second, *The Emigrants*, was the work of a brilliant but detached narrator accompanying a shipload of nomadic West Indians to Britain. *Of Age and Innocence* and *Season of Adventure*, his third and fourth books, almost defeat the reader with the sheer density of their prose, but they were occasionally seeded with ideas and illuminating insights that finally made the labor of reading them worthwhile. They took one back from Britain to the Caribbean, and it was as though Lamming was attempting to rediscover a history of himself by himself. His single nonfiction work, *The Pleasures of Exile*, was a neo-Gothic piece with ideas arching like flying buttresses; along with these ideas were varied and disparate existentialist happenings.

In all of Lamming's previous works he seemed to be balanced in an uneasy equipoise between the white colonizer and the black or brown colonized. But his most recent novel, *Natives of My Person*, the glittering product of 10 years of writing and rewriting, has finally released his spirit from its restive thralldom; he sheds the fear and the guilt of the colonized and makes an uninhibited journey to the heart of the colonizer. In order to accomplish this feat he abandons the slave—that ancestral archetype forever looming large in the West Indian psyche—to a limbo on the Guinea Coast. The slave ancestor in *Natives of My Person* is neither native nor person but a gigantic shadow forever lurking in troubled regions of the white imagination. The author gives us deliberately distorted glimpses of the slave coast where master and slave become phantoms moving in and out of primordial silences and where everything that lives is threatened with a sudden death. . . .

Natives of My Person is undoubtedly George Lamming's finest novel. It succeeds in illuminating new areas of darkness in the colonial past that the colonizer has so far not dealt with, and in this sense it is a profoundly revolutionary and original work.

Jan Carew. *NYT*. Feb. 27, 1972, pp. 4, 30

To help put across his points about disintegration of personality [in *Water with Berries*], especially in people who are products of a colonial past, Lamming makes elaborate use of a pattern with which by now his readers should be quite familiar. I refer to the Prospero-Miranda-Caliban triangular relationship of Shakespeare's *The Tempest*. Lamming is especially interested in the attitudes of the black man-Caliban toward the white woman-Miranda, and he explores a number of these relationships from various angles. Sometimes his use of this pattern is decidedly ironic. The frequent references in the novel to another of Shakespeare's plays, *Othello*, emphasizes this irony.

However, the *Tempest* pattern which might have been the strength of this novel proves its undoing. Lamming's persistent use of it comes to seem contrived. Even some of the names he has chosen—Myra for his Miranda figure and Fernando for his Ferdinand figure—seem too obvious. In his unrelenting faithfulness to this *Tempest* pattern Lamming loses touch with the characters he is creating; they cease to be credible, and the reader fails to be moved by their final catastrophe. The last impression that this novel leaves, unfortunately, is that the only real thing in it is its reliance on the *Tempest* theme, and that it has been severely overwritten.

By contrast, Lamming's style is admirably suited to the circumstances of his next novel, *Natives of My Person*. Its formality suggests the prose of the sixteenth-century travel account. Its richness, which is frequently Conradian, evokes well the complexity of the relationships between the characters on shipboard. The ship is used here, much as in a Conrad novel, to isolate a group of characters and to suggest a world in microcosm with its own social structure and system of order. . . .

By contrast to the pretentious complexity of the symbolical pattern of *Water with Berries*, the superficially simple allegory of *Natives of My Person* provides richly complex insights into human personality and the history of colonialism.

Both these novels deserve to be read carefully: *Natives of My Person* because it is a remarkable success, and *Water with Berries* because, despite its failure, it is a serious attempt to follow up on ideas which Lamming has raised in earlier books.

Anthony Boxill. WLWE. April, 1973,
pp. 112–13, 115–16

MARAN, RENÉ (1887–1960)

MARTINIQUE

Batouala, which has won the Prix Goncourt, is a rather weak book. . . .

Maran might respond that, as a novelist, he is exempt from presenting an overall view and that he has the right to choose the facts he describes. But he has given up his right to make this response by the tone of his preface, which is entirely political. He has given himself a mission and is trying to rally all French writers to his side. He may often be right. But he must submit to the rule of all criticism, without which there can be no honesty: to provide a complete account. Descartes established this rule at a time when Maran's ancestors were busy hunting wild animals. But Maran must get to know it. . . .

The antithesis between the noble savage and the conquering barbarian is a literary device that is not very new: Voltaire used it in *Alzire*. Civilization, to be sure, does not bring only benefits; it brought us Maran's book. Nevertheless, while Batouala laments the passing of the good old days, he is irritated because the railroad is not being built quickly enough. And he does not mention the hospitals, which, I believe, are of some service. I have seen regions in Guinea in which yellow fever and malaria were eliminated by the administration so denounced by Maran, who writes, "They are killing us slowly."

I have stressed the fundamental ideas of this book because they coincide, in what is most routinely literary about them, with the tendencies of the realist school of around 1880, which are still in part those of the Académie Goncourt. For them, literature was a shooting gallery, and the figures to be shot at were the judge, the bourgeois, the soldier, and the colonist. . . . This is probably one of the reasons why the Académie Goncourt chose to give its prize to this novel. I have trouble imagining any other reason. For the other elements of the novel are ordinary. The descriptions of customs are often entertaining but do not have any more merit than those found in so many accounts by travelers who never claimed to be men of letters. And as for the structure, it is worthless.

Henry Bidou. RdP. Jan. 15, 1922, pp. 400, 402–4†

Batouala, the novel by René Maran, a negro, winner of the Académie Goncourt prize of 5,000 francs for the best novel of the year by a young writer, is still the centre of a swirl of condemnation, indignation and praise.

Maran, who was born in Martinique and educated in France, was bitterly attacked in the chamber of deputies the other day as a defamer of France, and biter of the hand that fed him. He has been much censured by certain Frenchmen for his indictment of French imperialism in its effect on the natives of the French colonies. Others have rallied to him and asked the politicians to take the novel as a work of art, which it is; great art, except for the preface, which is the only bit of propaganda in the book. . . .

Launched into the novel itself, the reader gets a picture of African life in a native village seen by the big-whited eyes, felt by the pink palms, and the broad, flat, naked feet of the African native himself. You smell the smells of the village, you eat its food, you see the white man as the black man sees him, and after you have lived in the village you die there. That is all there is to the story, but when you have read it, you have been Batouala, and that means that it is a great novel.

Ernest M. Hemingway. *TSW*. March 25, 1922, p. 3

From the beginning [Maran's] literary career has been a succession of unexpected bombshells. The first of these came in 1921, when *Batouala* received the Goncourt award. A storm of protests greeted this decision. How could the Académie Goncourt have selected a book the preface of which bitterly denounced the French colonial system? And the story itself, did it not exaggerate the seamy side of life in French Equatorial Africa? Besides, who was René Maran? Gradually it became known that the author of *Batouala* was a thirty-four year old Negro born in Martinique in 1887. Natives of French Guiana, his parents were then stationed in Fort-de-France, where the father was an underclerk in the colonial service. In 1894, after the father had been transferred to a post in Gabon, it was decided to place the boy in a Bordeaux boarding school, where he developed mentally, physically—he became captain of the football team—and spiritually. . . .

In a reminiscent mood one Friday afternoon, M. Maran told me that when the news of the Goncourt award reached him in Africa, he was even more astonished than the French reading public. Hardly daring to believe the telegrams, he left his beloved bush for Paris where he was to encounter additional surprises. Despite his novel's success in France and elsewhere, publishing houses were refusing to handle his works. According to Maran, this refusal was dictated by politicians who feared his outspoken pronouncements on colonial matters. . . .

One should not infer, however, that Maran is merely a radical or a rabid racialist. In most of his books it is almost impossible to detect the author's racial identity. Nor has Maran played the political game; he prides himself on the fact that he has never voted. He loves France, which even in the preface to *Batouala*, he calls the "country that gave me everything," and he loves his art.

Mercer Cook. FR. Jan., 1944, pp. 157–59

Maran's vocabulary embraces the entire French-speaking world, in time and in space. His historical works, in particular, show him as a lover of the spicy, dense French language of the late Middle Ages. He takes pleasure in reviving archaic words, dialect, and technical terms. . . . Maran's writing embodies the very best qualities of French prose. As Charles Kunstler notes, his prose is "clear, firm, highly colored, and harmoniously rhythmical."

In these last two qualities, one perceives the black man, more precisely the *black writer*, who, when writing in French, can define himself only through his style. For the black writer, the French language is, as Brunetto Latini said, the "most delightful." And Maran is captivated by the "delights of good style." But what essentially characterizes Maran's style is the power of his images and the power of his rhythm—above all, the power of the images, which command attention: supple images in his poems, dynamic images in his "African" novels. In this way, Maran was the forerunner of the Negritude movement in the French-speaking world. One has only to reread *Batouala*. . . .

However, the black French writer is not merely a stylist. When he becomes a novelist, he is also a psychologist. All the black novels in French derive from Maran, whether their author is Ferdinand Oyono or André Demaison. After *Batouala*, one could no longer portray Negroes living, working, loving, crying, laughing, or speaking like whites. Nor would it do to have them speak pidgin French; rather, they would speak Wolof, Malinké, or Ewondo in French. For Maran was the first to express the "black soul," with a Negro style, in French.

Léopold Sédar Senghor. In Hommage à René Maran
(Paris, Présence Africaine, 1965), pp. 12–13†

Today's reader is less responsive to the [social criticism] in *Batouala* than to the realism in its depiction of collective life, to the skill with which ethnographic detail is joined to the plot. The main episode in *Batouala* is the great festival of circumcision. A clever progression has us move from the calm, serious religious ceremony to the explosion of the people's frenzy, provoked by the ritual dance in which two women simulate the sexual act. Couples are then formed at random, including

Batouala's wife and her lover. [Batouala], the chief, catches them, but he is prevented from taking his revenge by the unexpected arrival of the *commandant de cercle* [regional military administrator], who drives everybody away. The scene, far from being a digression, really contributes to the action of the novel and prepares the ending.

The Book of the Bush, Maran's masterpiece, does not contain any scenes that are as well developed as the central scene in *Batouala*, but it lets us enter intimately into African life, showing us the daily activities of the Bandas [a small river tribe of the Ubangi], the clearing of new land, the hunt, and races in the forest. It also depicts the animals of the bush, each with its own physiognomy. Therein lies Maran's true originality—his perception of life in equatorial nature: the sun, a source of health and joy; water, which sometimes brings fertility and sometimes devastation; and the vegetation, which is like a great cry of liberation rising from the earth toward heaven. The human actors [in the novel] merely participate in [nature's] drama of life and death; and the tragic story of Kossi and Yassi, happy at first and then pursued by fate and men's hatred, blends into the adventure of their people, torn by rivalries and victimized by the vengeance of the gods, who engulf all the land's riches under a flood.

Roger Mercier. Tendances. Oct., 1965, pp. 419/3†

When René Maran encountered French Equatorial Africa, he wanted to dip deep into his ancestral roots. He learned the Banda language and . . . his book *Batouala* was to challenge the colonial literature that made the Negro a caricature and denied him any culture. . . .

In his novels, especially *Batouala*, Maran shows the true face of Africa. He reveals the existence of Negro civilization, defends that civilization, and, in so doing, denounces those who try to undermine the Negro's humanity. In this novel we have our first defense and illustration of Negro culture, of the Negro "nation." . . . Sometimes the author informs us about old Africa and its customs; sometimes he presents this land, formerly virgin and peaceful, now in conflict with the conqueror who is trying to destroy it by every means of exploitation. . . .

Thus, Maran's work introduces us to the authentic Africa of our brothers. It laid the foundations for Negro-African literature, especially the literature that came to be called Negritude.

But René Maran the individual is somewhat disconcerting. Although he was a Negro, the writer remained primarily French in spirit and thought. Did he himself not admit, "I am a European with black skin"? This man, who was no better than anyone else, refused to accept his race totally. [As Frantz Fanon wrote,] he "is neither more nor less than a black deserter. He is a neurotic who needs to be freed from his infantile fantasies." His return to the roots therefore remained superficial. The struggle that he led for the rehabilitation of Negro values was like Montaigne's humanism. Like Montaigne, Maran could write that "every custom has its reason." It was, moreover, in the name of this humanism that Maran refused to be any forerunner of present-day Negritude.

Barthélemy Kotchy. PA. No. 76, 1970, pp. 147–49†

MCKAY, CLAUDE (1889–1948)

JAMAICA

Claude McKay, although still quite a young man, has already demonstrated his power, breadth and skill as a poet. Mr. McKay's breadth is as essential a part of his equipment as his power and skill. He demonstrates mastery of the three when as a Negro poet he pours out the bitterness and rebellion in his heart in those two sonnet-tragedies, "If We Must Die" and "To the White Fiends," in a manner that strikes terror; and when as a comic poet he creates the atmosphere and mood of poetic beauty in the absolute, as he does in "Spring in New Hampshire" and "The Harlem Dancer." Mr. McKay gives evidence that he has passed beyond the danger which threatens many of the new Negro poets—the danger of allowing the purely polemical phases of the race problem to choke their sense of artistry.

Mr. McKay's earliest work is unknown in this country. It consists of poems written and published in his native Jamaica. I was fortunate enough to run across this first volume. . . . However greater work McKay may do he can never do anything more touching and charming than these poems in the Jamaica dialect.

James Weldon Johnson. Preface to James Weldon
Johnson, ed., The Book of American Negro Poetry
(New York, Harcourt, Brace, 1922), pp. xliii–xliv

Claude McKay's [novel] *Home to Harlem* . . . for the most part nauseates me, and after the dirtier parts of its filth I feel distinctly like taking a bath. This does not mean that the book is wholly bad. McKay is too great a poet to make any complete failure in writing. There are bits of *Home to Harlem*, beautiful and fascinating: the continued changes upon the theme of the beauty of colored skins; the portrayal of the fascination of their new yearnings for each other which Negroes are developing. The chief character, Jake, has something appealing, and the glimpses of the Haitian, Ray, have all the materials of a great piece of fiction.

But it looks as though, despite this, McKay has set out to cater for that prurient demand on the part of white folk for a portrayal in Negroes of that utter licentiousness which conventional civilization holds white folk back from enjoying—if enjoyment it can be called. That which a certain decadent section of the white American world, centered particularly in New York, longs for with fierce and unrestrained passions, it wants to see written out in black and white, and saddled on black Harlem. This demand, as voiced by a number of New York publishers, McKay has certainly satisfied, and added much for good measure. He has used every art and emphasis to paint drunkenness, fighting, lascivious sexual promiscuity and utter absence of restraint in as bold and as bright colors as he can.

If this had been done in the course of a well-conceived plot or with any artistic unity, it might have been understood if not excused. But *Home to Harlem* is padded. Whole chapters here and there are inserted with no connection to the main plot, except that they are on the same dirty subject. As a picture of Harlem life or of Negro life anywhere, it is, of course, nonsense. Untrue, not so much as on account of its facts, but on account of its emphasis and glaring colors. I am sorry that the author of *Harlem Shadows* stooped to this. I sincerely hope that he will some day rise above it and give us in fiction the strong, well-knit as well as beautiful theme, that it seems to me he might do.

W. E. B. Du Bois. *Crisis.* June, 1928, p. 202

Home to Harlem is a book that has been a pleasure to the author to write. It is hard otherwise to explain the easy charm and assurance that glow upon every chapter. The author is coloured and describes a negro coming home to Harlem, the coloured quarter of New York, after the war. Once there, he has various adventures, and the book is a series of incidents strung together without much relation to each other. As a novel it is rather inadequate, as a study of coloured people it is fascinating and delightful, radiating enjoyment of life, and frank and promiscuous passion. One feels that the coloured people are a flabby crowd, but this moral reflection is entirely obscured by the simplicity of their relationships, the sweet distress of their hedonism and their equable view of life. So much art is created out of discontent with the world as it is, and is a minority report upon life, that it is a joy to come on all this frank glorification of existence in the rich dialect and naïve enthusiasm of this unpretentious story.

Cyril Connolly. *NS.* Aug. 18, 1928, pp. 591–92

In *Gingertown,* a book of short stories published last year, the sketches of Mr. McKay's native island were, to one reader at least, the most richly rewarding of the volume. Now Mr. McKay returns to Jamaican subject matter in his third and most successful novel. A quiet story, quietly told, *Banana Bottom* really approaches originality more than his Harlem fiction did. Mr. McKay seems really at home in this province; it is hardly likely that any novelist would be more so. . . .

This plot exists more as a framework for the characterization of many interesting folk figures than in its own right. . . . All of these are ably sketched. Mr. McKay insists that all of them are imaginary, but they all have the ring of real life.

The picture of the folkways of the people is similarly convincing. Life on this island seems a quiet pastoral. Occasionally sensational incidents break the easy tenor of life in *Banana Bottom*—Tack Tally's suicide, the obeah-man, and the fall from grace of Herald Newton being examples—but, for the most part, things seem to flow easily. Mr. McKay describes, with what seems remarkable memory since, according to reports, he has been away from Jamaica a long time, the dances, revivals, the marketing, the small town gossip, the school affairs, the color complications, the folkways such as the hawking of ballads, the ordinary life of the villagers and farmers. The dialect sounds true; in places it is rich in humor and shrewd wisdom. The flowers, fruits, and garden produce of the rich bottom-land are described frequently and with a great deal of charm.

But against this idyllic background, Mr. McKay does impose one problem: how far should the "missionary" attitude toward Negroes be allowed to go.

Sterling A. Brown. Opportunity. July, 1933,
pp. 217, 222

To turn from the poems of Claude McKay to the novels he has written is to be aware of something very close to a tragedy. For years he had been writing exquisite or dynamic verse, and the favor of the public, judged at least by commercial standards, was but luke-warm. Now there was a change of tone and emphasis. It is impossible for him to write incompetently; on everything he puts the stamp of virility. After the success of [Carl] Van Vechten's *Nigger Heaven,* however, he and some other authors seemed to realize that it was not the poem or story of fine touch that the public desired, but metal of a baser hue; and he decided to give what was wanted. The result was a novel, *Home to Harlem,* that sold thousands of copies but that with its emphasis on certain degraded aspects of life hardly did justice to the gifts of the writer. . . .

Gingertown is a collection of twelve stories, six of which are set in

Harlem and the others in the West Indies. The author shows that he is best when he is on his native hearth, but all of the stories are marked by robustness, though again and again the characters are wanton or gross. *Banana Bottom* goes back to Jamaica and in telling of the career of Bita Plant gives a fine satire on the ways of benevolent folk. An exceptional character is Squire Gensir, an Englishman interested in studying folk-ways but without any semblance of patronage. This book like the others has elements of strength, but one can not help thinking what Mr. McKay might do if he would take a little vacation from slums and water-fronts, see life somewhat more as a whole, and conceive the really great novel of which he is undoubtedly capable.

Benjamin Brawley. *The Negro Genius* (New York,
Dodd, Mead, 1937), pp. 244–46

Harlem Shadows [is McKay's] best known collection of poems. This book spoke the passionate language of a persecuted race, and its author did not make the least attempt to disguise his feelings. He did not attempt to please his white readers; his voice is a direct blast at them for their policy of discrimination. Many of the poems are saturated with protest. For example, in the octet of "Enslaved," McKay traces the ills and suffering of the race during its sojourn in various lands; then in the sestet he calls for the complete destruction of "the white man's world." One can easily find here the philosophy of a race expressed in the few lines of a poem. This is not the poetry of submission or acquiescence; this is not the voice of a gradualist; nor is this the naïve dialect of the jackass driver. It is one of scorching flame, a voice conscious of persecution, that dares to strike back with vehemence. . . .

In the title poem, "Harlem Shadows," one finds various shades of this protest, yet there is also some semblance of beautiful lyricism. There are some good interpretations of life in Harlem, the Negro section in upper Manhattan. The poem is mediocre, but reveals the author's bitterness toward the conditions which produce the Negro prostitutes of Harlem. I question the poet's choice of such as a title poem for his book. Certainly this is a sordid aspect of the race to thrust forward. In addition, it is not the best poem in the collection. The greatest justification that can be found for it is that it is realistic, and accurately describes a phase of existing life.

One must admit that the author's most powerful dudgeon lay in this protest poetry. Whether he wrote an epigram, a sonnet, or a longer poem, his thought is sustained. He expressed the deepest resentment, but even when doing so his feelings were lucid. He did not stumble as he attempted to express himself. This dynamic force within his poetry caused him to be constantly read and re-read by his admirers and critics.

They realized that here was a man of deepest emotions, as well as one who was a skilled craftsman.

Robert A. Smith. *Phylon.* 9, 3, 1948, pp. 271–72

Every now and then someone said he had heard that Claude had once been married, but he seemed bitter whenever any discussion of love or courtship arose and there was nobody who dared to ask about his past. In self-defense I had to acquaint myself with Claude's likes and dislikes of people and things. High up on the list of his many peeves were: "yellow Negroes," "people who spout religiosity," and "the Reds." He could say "you Catholics" with so much contempt it was useless to do anything but utter a silent prayer for him. That all of these prayers were answered is part of a later story. . . .

[A] member of the Negro Writers' Guild who had known Claude in Jamaica told me how the young poet acquired his dislike for fair complexions. According to his friend, Claude had once been a policeman. His immediate superior, a stern, uncompromising, sometimes unreasonable taskmaster, was a mulatto. The indignities—real and imaginary—which Claude suffered at this man's hands left their mark. I can also imagine that Claude, dressed up in a policeman's uniform, was not an obedient subordinate.

Ellen Tarry. *The Third Door* (New York, David McKay, 1955), pp. 129, 131

McKay depends upon atmosphere to carry [*Home to Harlem*]. The style is appropriately impressionistic, full of hyphenated adjectives aimed at vivid impressions of Harlem life. The beginnings of a dramatic structure may be seen, however, in the characters of Jake and Ray. Jake represents pure instinct. . . . Ray embodies the dilemma of the inhibited, overcivilized intellectual. . . . His is that profound disgust which modern life sometimes evokes in men of artistic sensibilities.

Through a faulty denouement, the symbolic import of Jake and Ray is imperfectly conveyed. Ray, disgusted with all that is sordid and ugly in the lives of the dining-car waiters, ships out on a freighter bound for Europe. Jake, in the closing pages of the novel, finds his lost Felice, whose name signifies joy. By contrasting Jake's happiness with Ray's restless wandering, McKay attempts to convey the superiority of instinct over reason. But at bottom, Jake and Ray represent different ways of rebelling against Western civilization. Jake rebels instinctively, while Ray's rebellion occurs on an intellectual plane. Both characters acquire a broader significance only through their negative relationship to contemporary society. McKay's failure to develop this relationship is the failure of the novel.

Jake is the typical McKay protagonist—the primitive Negro, untouched by the decay of Occidental civilization. The validity of this symbol, however, depends upon McKay's view of contemporary life. Since the author cannot take this view for granted, he introduces himself into the novel as Ray, in order to expound it. But Ray hardly helps matters; in *Home to Harlem* he does little more than state his prejudices. As a result, the novel is left without a suitable antagonist. Jake and Ray are vivid enough, but what they would deny is not always clear. The novel, unable to develop its primary conflict, bogs down in the secondary contrast between Jake and Ray.

Robert A. Bone. *The Negro Novel in America*
(New Haven, Conn., Yale University Press, 1958),
pp. 68–69

[McKay's] religious poetry is the expression of an inner growth, and his discovery of God the result of his individual search for truth. From a more general vantage-point, his poetic opus may be considered as the account of a vast attempt at a synthesis between the antagonistic elements of the black world and the Western world warring within him. There can be no denying that McKay, like every black exiled in a white milieu, was for a long time a divided man, so that it is possible to speak of his cultural dualism. But he never acquiesced in being torn apart by this dichotomy. His whole being urged him to find unity. The critique to which he subjected the antinomies deprived them, little by little, of their contingencies and laid bare their authentic values.

In Jamaica, he affirmed the primacy of the soil and contrasted it with the inanity of the dream, cherished by the mulattoes, of a heightened social status. He rejected the mirage of Africa as a source of racial pride, looking on it as merely pathetic. He shunned the nationalism of a [Marcus] Garvey, whom he regarded as a charlatan, and while he defended Negro folklore against whites, who would have denatured it, he nevertheless could not find spiritual sustenance in it. On the other hand, it was his natural instinct to evaluate the possibilities of spiritual advancement offered by Western, Christian culture, but there too he perceived the corroding evil that sowed hatred between men. In his dialogue with the West, conducted through the medium of his hatred, this emotion was slowly filtered of its dross as he came to grasp the necessity of raising himself above it. Unless the individual is engaged in a ceaseless effort to transcend himself, no victory over hatred will ever be possible. Neither rationalism nor Communism could provide the higher principle capable of reconciling the conflicting theses of his cultural eclecticism. At long last he discovered this principle within himself, and at the same time he discovered God. Thus his spiritual itinerary is an account of the internalization of his racial feeling. [1963]

Jean Wagner. *Black Poets of the United States* (Urbana, University of Illinois Press, 1973), pp. 248–49

McKay's position, so different from that of Countee Cullen and most other Harlem Renaissance writers, stemmed not only from his personality, but also from his various social situations. To whatever groups he allied himself, McKay remained always something of an outsider without deep and lasting commitments. Though he worked with the Negro lower classes in America and France, his interests and hopes extended beyond the next job, drink, or woman, for his writing provided a means of detachment from proletarian life. While on *The Liberator*, as the only Negro on the staff, McKay felt a special duty to represent the feelings of his race to his fellow staff members. Floyd Dell discoursed on art, and Michael Gold explored whatever socio-economic iniquities came to his attention, but McKay's *Liberator* work was almost wholly concerned with race. Furthermore, McKay felt apart from most Negro intellectuals because of his social radicalism and because of Negro intellectuals' criticisms of his own work. Finally McKay was a Jamaican. From personal experience he knew, as did returning Negro veterans, that American-style racial prejudice was not world-wide. Moreover, though most Negro veterans felt themselves to be Americans, McKay felt free both to praise and criticize America without a sense of identification with and commitment to America. . . .

Because McKay was not fully a member of any one group, and because of his radical education and outspoken personality, he set the outer limits of the Harlem Renaissance. No other important Negro writer in the 'twenties protested so fiercely and single-mindedly against prejudice as did McKay in his sonnets of 1919. And no other important Renaissance figure disregarded possible effects on the Negro public image so fearlessly as did McKay in his prose fiction. From his Jamaican days to his strange conversion to Catholicism, McKay forever spoke his mind, sometimes brilliantly, sometimes clumsily, but always forthrightly. In so doing he did much to make the Harlem Renaissance more than a polite attempt to show whites that Negroes, too, could be cultured.

Stephen H. Bronz. *Roots of Negro Racial Consciousness* (New York, Libra, 1964), pp. 85–86, 89

Home to Harlem and *Banjo* had ended with the departures of exiles. *Banana Bottom* begins with the return of a native. The characters of the first two novels extracted a living on the edges of society, the characters of the third are rooted in a landscape. The violent debates of the earlier works, in which there is only a thin line between author and character, are now succeeded by the controlled idyllic tone of a distanced narrator. The central character is not a figure of *malaise* like Ray of the preceding novels, nor does McKay find it necessary to externalize *malaise* in the form of a complementary but separated pair such as Jake and Ray or Banjo and Ray.

The polarized pair of heroes of the first two novels are replaced by a single heroine. Bita Plant, the daughter of a Jamaican peasant, is brought up by the Reverend Malcolm Craig and his wife Priscilla. After seven years abroad at an English University and on the Continent, Bita returns to her native land. *Banana Bottom* tells the story of how she gradually strips away what is irrelevant in her English upbringing, and how she marries Jubban the strong silent drayman in her father's employ. To put it in this way is to make it clear at once that McKay's theme is still cultural dualism. The differences between *Banana Bottom* and the other novels are differences in art. Bita Plant is the first achieved West Indian heroine and *Banana Bottom* is the first classic of West Indian prose.

Kenneth Ramchand. *The West Indian Novel and Its Background* (New York, Barnes & Noble, 1970), p. 259

[Harlem Shadows] not only swung the debate between the Black Ancients and the Black Moderns decisively in favor of the Moderns; but even more so, it served as the forerunner for the three most important literary movements among Black Writers: the Harlem Renaissance, Negritude, and the Cultural Nationalism of the present time. A poem such as "Outcast" bears more than accidental relationship to statements later made by Léopold Senghor and Aimé Césaire regarding Negritude. . . .

The theme of "Outcast" is the disharmony between body and spirit occasioned by the imprisonment of the body and the cultural plunder of the spirit. Slavery, in imprisoning the body, forced the spirit to dwell in a house of bondage where words were felt but never heard; and jungle songs which might have been sung were too soon forgotten in the face of cultural genocide. Thus, a silence was imposed upon the spirit, old cultural artifacts were destroyed, cultural ties were ripped asunder and truth and creativity distorted and stifled. . . .

Returning, then, with McKay to other times, when Western images and symbols were not so well solidified in the Black psyche, when Black men did not believe that their manifest destiny was to be changed into white men, when a people—from the jungles of Timbuctu to the streets of Harlem—were conscious of their beauty and self worth—returning to such times, Black poets have sought to make their impact throughout the world. The function of such poetry is, beyond a doubt, revolutionary, and it is in this sense that *Harlem Shadows* is a revolutionary document and Claude McKay is a revolutionary poet. He is the militant poet, the angry poet, the poet who calls for revolutionary action.

Addison Gayle, Jr. *Claude McKay: The Black Poet
at War* (Detroit, Broadside, 1972), pp. 37–39

By and large, [*A Long Way from Home*] is a pleasantly unpretentious account of [McKay's] experiences in New York, London, Russia, Europe, and North Africa. It contains interesting descriptions of the many individuals he had met during his travels, including such famous personalities as Frank Harris, Charlie Chaplin, George Bernard Shaw, H. G. Wells, Paul Robeson, and Henri Cartier-Bresson. Those chapters devoted to his work on *The Liberator* and his travels in England and Russia are detailed and especially valuable from a historical point of view.

McKay could not refrain, however, from occasionally bitter attacks upon his critics. These included several black journalists who had condemned his fiction, as well as those American Communists who considered his political independence a form of degenerate bourgeois adventurism. McKay also questions in *A Long Way from Home* the motives of many blacks whom he felt had merely used the Negro Renaissance to advance their social status among whites. In his final chapter McKay offers a general criticism of America's established Negro leaders. He maintains that their single-minded opposition to segregation was detrimental to any effective black community organization and to the development of a positive group spirit among blacks. . . .

McKay's criticisms in *A Long Way from Home* were only partially indicative of how completely involved he had become in the social and political controversies that dominated the American literature scene in the 1930s. By 1937 his best efforts were going into the occasional articles he managed to sell to such journals and newspapers as *The Nation, The New Leader,* and the New York *Amsterdam News.* In these articles he set forth more fully his position regarding the future of social change, both within and without the black community. Broadly speaking, McKay tried to maintain throughout the 1930s and 1940s the independent, left-wing stance he had first adopted as a *Liberator* editor after World War I. In this regard his position was similar to George Orwell's in England. Unlike the younger Orwell, however, his days as a creative writer were drawing to a close. The energy he had previously devoted to poetry and fiction went instead into his polemical articles.

> Wayne F. Cooper. Introduction to Wayne F. Cooper,
> ed., *The Passion of Claude McKay* (New York,
> Schocken, 1973), pp. 36–37

The poetry of Claude McKay is classic expression—clear, sculptured, restrained. Much of his early and best work is written in sonnet form. He seems to like the limitation which the sonnet placed on him, and he used those limitations superbly. Very few writers surpass him in economy of phrasing. It should be noted that his restraint in the use of racial tags and terms makes his poems more than Negro affirmations of defiance and protest. His poems—that is, his best poems—are, as Max Eastman has said, "characteristic of what is deep and universal in mankind."

Although he was much more prolific as a fiction writer than as a poet, McKay in all probability will be remembered for his verse far longer than for his prose. He seems to be a curiously ambivalent figure: though rigidly classic in his poetry, he was convinced that the primitive side of Negro life was more honest and more significant than the sophisticated side, the side that had adopted Western culture. . . .

Seen in perspective, McKay is not as impressive as he looked in the twenties and thirties. In all probability, very little of his fiction will survive, with the possible exception of *Banana Bottom*; it is too loosely constructed and too topical. His major thesis, the superiority of the primitive black to the middle-class Negro and to the white, was not tenable when he wrote it, and in spite of many foolish things now being said in the name of *blackness*, is not tenable now. The works of McKay which seem most likely to survive are those few poems of the "Flame-Heart" type and that group of racial sonnets of the "If We Must Die" attitude. McKay never bettered these early sonnets and lyrics. Excellent poetry in any language, they will survive their century.

> Arthur P. Davis. *From the Dark Tower* (Washington,
> D.C., Howard University Press, 1974), pp. 39, 44

MITTELHOLZER, EDGAR (1909–1965)

GUYANA

There is always a certain fascination in reading of primitive peoples, of their ways and customs and what seem to be their curiously restricted lives, but such accounts are usually to be met with in biographies or books of travel; it is seldom that the novelist succeeds in presenting these people in such a way as to hold the interest of the reader of fiction, who does not easily identify himself with the lives and thoughts of primitive society, but that is what Mr. Edgar Mittelholzer has, with this novel [*Corentyne Thunder*], succeeded in doing. He shows us an old East Indian commander living with his two daughters on the savannah in British Guiana. Their home was a one-roomed mud hut, their food rice and salt fish, with a curry feed once a month when the moon was full, and their relaxation when the day's work was done, singing to the beating of a goatskin tom-tom. . . .

There is an odd beauty in this book and a haunting pathos. The scenes, painted vividly and yet with an admirable restraint, live on in the mind, and the differing personalities that emerge, almost painfully, through the clouded mentalities of the principal characters, are instinct with life.

TLS. May 24, 1941, p. 249

[*A Morning at the Office*] is a story well worth a place on the book-shelf. The language flows with ease and grace, and the form of the novel is surprising and entertaining. The author maintains a clear unity by relating his frequent digressions to a particular morning in a Trinidad office. Though lightly held together, the threads of the story firmly weave the pattern of fourteen lives into an artistic tapestry depicting an authentic moment in West Indian life.

The authenticity never falters, and therein lies the power of the book. The writer is benignly objective and uses the morning as a convincing opportunity to describe the people of the West Indies whom he loves with fine understanding of human strength and weakness, and whom he knows in all their enchanting variety of race. . . .

Within the poetic licence of a theory of "Telescopic Objectivity," the author tells certain incidents in the past of a key, a desk, and a door in the office. These incidents influence the present and future of people in the office. I found this device intriguing and extremely well handled by the writer.

This novel is admittedly limited in scope, but within the limits that he has set himself the author shows that he is a serious craftsman of vivid imagination from whom, I hope, will come much, and more profound, writing. *A Morning at the Office* is a distinct indication of his ability.

Margery Foster-Davis. *CarQ.* 1, 4, 1951, pp. 43–44

I felt a great admiration for Mittelholzer for the simple reason that he refused to take any permanent employment in Trinidad. There was a reverse of the division of labour in the family. His wife went to an office; and he did the housework, shopping and the lot, leaving himself some seven or eight hours a day for writing. In Trinidad at the time (it's as late as 1946) a man who made Mittelholzer's commitment, and for the same reason, was regarded in much the same way I imagine that the French peasants came to regard Joan of Arc. They didn't call him a witch; but they said he wasn't altogether right in the head. This is always a way in the West Indies of warning that no-one will take you seriously. . . .

Why Mittelholzer is important is that he represents a different generation from [Samuel] Selvon and myself. He had suffered the active discouragement of his own community, and he had had their verdict sanctioned by the consistent rejection of his novels by publishers abroad. And in spite of this he made the decision, before anyone else, to get out. That is the phrase which we must remember in considering this question of why the writers are living in England. They simply wanted to get out of the place where they were born. They couldn't argue, you will see, pointing to similar examples of dejection in West Indian writers who were now regarded as great figures, because there were no such West Indians. They had to get out, and in the hope that a change of climate might bring a change of luck. One thing alone kept them going; and that was the literary review. *Bim*, which was published in Barbados by Frank Collymore, was a kind of oasis in that lonely desert of mass indifference and educated middle-class treachery.

George Lamming. TamR. Winter, 1960, pp. 48–49

[Mittelholzer's] novels abound in examples of the need for strength on the individual level, and he was consistent in the application of this philosophy even as regards himself, because we know that when he could no longer master the forces acting on his own life, he applied the principle so often expressed in his novels of victory or death, and with fortitude, sought a flaming end. This death-wish by fire was foreshadowed in his last novel, published posthumously, and looking back over the last books, we think we can discern the narrowing of horizons, the withering of faith and the crisis in belief in which he passionately identified himself with the deepening gloom on the international scene. . . .

The body of his work has a remarkable consistency and unity about it. There is a considerable complexity of elements and parts involved which he organized successfully into his stories. These stories, as a general rule, exhibit the inherent plausibility of poetic truth. We get the impression that in his stories we are kept above the humdrum of everyday living at a pitch of intense wakefulness, filling our imagination and stirring our emotion. Each novel, with its drums of suspense and magic compulsion creates a new world into which we are drawn and in which we seem to live with the illusion that we are seeing life steadily and whole.

I feel that this body of work represents a most remarkable achievement for any writer and I know that it has brought entertainment and enlightenment in many languages to thousands in many parts of the world, and bearing in mind the limitations of the society which produced him, and the pioneer nature of his tremendous single-mindedness and discipline, I feel Edgar Mittelholzer must take a high place indeed in the history of our young literature of Guyana and the Caribbean.

A. J. Seymour. *Edgar Mittelholzer: The Man and His Work* (Georgetown, Guyana, Ministry of Education, 1968), pp. 43, 53

[Mittelholzer's] work is interesting in many ways, especially for its pioneering quality; for it was his second novel, *A Morning at the Office*, which first won wide recognition for British Caribbean writing, stimulated critical interest in the region, and paved the way for the remarkable march of English-speaking Caribbean novelists who followed. Mittelholzer himself has received less critical acclaim than some of these later novelists, for example, Vidia Naipaul; but the popularity of his work has not been seriously rivalled by any other Caribbean novelist. Mittelholzer is too idiosyncratic a writer to be closely compared with any of his contemporaries, and if a parallel literary career is to be found, the closest is that of another pioneer, the early nineteenth-century American novelist Charles Brockden Brown. . . .

Since his moral aims are unfulfilled, Mittelholzer cannot be correctly called a moralist; nor can he be described as a pornographer in spite of his accounts of "the manifold perversions and vagaries of the sexual instinct," for these do not constitute his main theme or reflect his prevailing intention. He is, like the Marquis de Sade, a moralist manqué, and because he fails to achieve his moral aims, the purely artistic value of his work is inconsiderable. . . .

Only three of Mittelholzer's novels, those dealing with West Indian nationalism and colour-consciousness, fall into this category of the novel of manners; the remaining twenty-two deal mainly with psychological themes that are of both local and universal significance. Thus his greatest contribution to Caribbean literature in English is the treatment of themes not wholly limited by application to local conditions. And, in spite of the outrageous eroticism and trivial fantasy of his work, as Caribbean writing develops more universal themes, Mittelholzer will gradually come to be regarded as the true innovator of a literature that is finally free from parochialism.

Frank Birbalsingh. *JCL.* July, 1969, pp. 88, 98, 103

In the Kaywana trilogy [*Children of Kaywana, The Harrowing of Hubertus, Kaywana Blood*], the master's lashes on the body of the slave, the throbbing sexual energy temporarily sweeping away barriers of race and even those between a mother and son, and the fearful possibilities of in-breeding and heredity, are all played out against what [O. R.] Dathorne has called the "brooding landscape" of the Guyana jungle. The trilogy goes back to the seventeenth century; through the fortunes of one family, Mittelholzer recreates the violent history of Guyana to the dawn of the twentieth century. The Von Groenwegels believe in the preservation of the strong blood. Their motto is never to surrender even if the whole world is pitted against them, a doctrine which is passed from parents to children: their mission in life is to nurture the strong streak in the family even at the expense of inbreeding. Hendriekje, a second-generation Groenwegel, perfects this outlook into a Nazi-like obsession with the power and purity of a master race of which she is the great grandmother. She argues that the stronger always survive and the weaker get crushed. Life is brutal. This is not pleasant, but a Von Groenwegel must face it as the truth. With such an obsession, a clash across the colour-line (which is also the dividing line between the slave and the master) is inevitable. And when it comes, it is full of relentless cruelty as the slaves, temporarily free, attempt to assuage a century of terror by punishing the white oppressor. . . .

The subterranean corrosive effects of . . . what yet another West Indian writer [Elliot Boshen] has called "tint discrimination" are well examined and exposed in Mittelholzer's early novel, *A Morning at the Office*. With their different shades of colour and racial origins, people working for Essential Products Ltd. superficially make a harmonious cosmopolitan picture. But they are all trapped in their skins. . . .

In this novel, Mittelholzer has portrayed the secret, psychic forces that govern people's inner thoughts in a society which has made minute differences of the skin the basis of morality and human relationship. Such a society alienates its human individuals and makes them live as exiles from themselves and from a country to which they rightly belong. [1972]

Ngugi wa Thiong'o. *Homecoming* (New York, Lawrence Hill, 1973), pp. 102, 105, 107

MOFOLO, THOMAS (1877–1948)

LESOTHO

Those who believe that the negro races are incapable of great achievements should read *Chaka* . . . which paints a partly accurate and partly imaginary picture of the rise of the Zulu power in old South Africa, and combines it with a realistic study of a noble character consciously ruining itself by deliberately cultivating the quality of ferocity. . . .

The development and ruin of the central character are traced in a way that recalls the Nemesis of the Greeks. We watch with growing sympathy the cruel trials and extraordinary prowess of Chaka's boyhood, his first dealings with witch-doctors and his first romance. We watch his successive temptations by the supreme witch-doctor with alarm and soon with horror; for a trail of death and cruelty is the price of each advance towards Chaka's ultimate ambition—the lordship of all South Africa. When indeed the tempter offers him "such a chieftainship that if a man were to leave the place where thou now art, in his youth, on foot, and go to the bounds of thy territory, he would be an old man before he returned," at the price of murdering "the one thou dost love more than any other on earth," we first catch a real glimpse of the terrible path on which Chaka has entered. Gradually, as he grasps after greater and greater chieftainships and the terror of the Zulu arms penetrates across mountain and desert to the remote tribes of the North, Chaka paying each time the witch-doctor's price of greater and greater cruelty, murdering his own mother, whole tribes and peoples, whole regiments of his own armies, all our sympathy flies; but we read on, fascinated, until the final scene of Chaka's own murder by his brothers comes with a feeling almost of relief. It is a grim story, but it is not mere realism. Again and again the reader feels that he is obtaining, even amid the greatest horrors, a genuine insight into the mind and traditions of the African peoples as they were before the coming of the white man.

TLS. July 30, 1931, p. 596

Fekisi, the hero of [*The Traveller of the East*], a Mosuto herd boy, by courage and force of character becomes a leader among his fellows. Life among the cattle, on the pastures, at the drinking-places, at milking-time, and in the kraal at night raises questions in the mind of the boy. He gropes after the origins and meanings of things. . . . Dreams and visions impel him to seek the answers he craves. He resolves to leave the village secretly and travel to the East. His cattle alone discern his growing purpose and crowd closely round him, lowing in grief. The night-scene in which he takes leave of them, praising them in a great cattle-song, is equal in dramatic quality to the finest parts of *Chaka*. . . .

The story, though enriched by imagination, is obviously auto-biographical in part. Fekisi's quest is so broadly human that the Western reader recognizes a familiar pilgrim way, yet the whole setting is so distinctive that every step is a discovery of the African mentality. Books such as this are the literary hope of Africa: they show us the African mind at its best and should be read by those who want to see the African in his true light.

G. A. Gollock. *Africa*. Oct., 1934, pp. 510–11

The brazen foolishness of the average European (and American) is equaled only by his self-importance since he lost contact with the great primal myths of humanity. These ostentatious blind men could not be advised too strongly to read a book like *Chaka* by Thomas Mofolo, whose publication in France in 1940, if I am not mistaken, went prac-tically unnoticed. This amazing book, written by a black from southern Africa, is a mixture of several literary genres. A folk tale by its subject as well as by its precise depiction of familiar details, an epic in its structure and style, this book also aims at edification, like a moral or philosophical tale, like a cosmogony. It is a masterful challenge to those who hold the theory of the inequality of the races.

Some people will retort that the author is an educated black, taught by white colonists and therefore stamped by European culture. One need only read this book, however, to realize that its beauty and power are derived essentially from its local material and its author's heritage. In *Chaka* Mofolo uses legends and (if I can believe my friend the poet Senghor) historical facts to develop one of the fundamental themes in world literature—the will to power. . . .

Chaka is Faust, a young Faust thirsty for power, to whom Is-sanoussi-Mephistopheles, the supreme Tempter, proposes a bargain whose price is Chaka's damnation. Yet how gentle and childlike Doctor Faust seems compared to Chaka! Faust's only crime, after all, is want-ing to escape from the laws of nature and to enjoy for eternity the most precious possession—youth. Chaka, on the other hand, agrees to be-come a *monster* in order to rule. A renegade, a traitor, a perjuror, the murderer of his brothers, his mother, and his wife, he takes on the symbolic role as enemy of humanity. Because *Chaka* makes us see the numerous crimes through which all personal power is purchased, Mofolo's work is healthy and necessary. Reading it, one is reminded of the monstrous cult that still surrounds a soldier of fortune like Napoleon in France, especially in our schools.

Luc Decaunes. *PA*. No. 5, 1948, pp. 883–84†

Thomas Mofolo, having schooled himself in the traditions of his own people, as well as in the mission literature of the English (of which

Bunyan was probably the most notable example), as a writer was able to synthesize the customary notion of "doctoring" the chieftain with the folk-Christian idea of a pact with the devil. This fusion gives a strong spinal column of credibility to his Chaka story. The double necessity of a periodic magical renewal (Zulu) and of a final reckoning (Christian) ensures an accumulation rather than a mere concatenation of horrors, a regular teleology of the evil will. Each time Chaka is doctored, he becomes further involved with the diabolical sources of his strength. More and more ambitious deeds of violence are actually required of him until Chaka, sickened with visions of horror, is finally murdered by those who are nearest to him in blood. . . .

In what way is Chaka an assertion of [Mofolo's] Negritude? Perhaps in the same way that Milton's Satan is an assertion of the poet's proud, rebellious will. Senghor, like the English romantics who later made Satan the hero of the piece, has temporarily abrogated the moral framework in which Mofolo wrote. The highest tribute Mofolo's imagination could pay to the bloody hero whom his mission teachers condemned was to put him in league with the Christian devil. The horror and atrocities of his career put the great Zulu forever on the map of Africa, and any honest person who had not been exposed to modern theories of the great Immoralist, of the romantic Scourge, would have left him to the vultures in the end. That the vultures would not have him is proof of his magical invulnerability in legend, of Mofolo's deepest desire to leave him so.

> Judith Illsley Gleason. *This Africa* (Evanston, Ill.,
> Northwestern University Press, 1965), pp. 56, 65

Mofolo's skill in enlivening a situation is amply illustrated in many parts of [*Chaka*]. A good example is the scene at the river pool where Chaka is bathing at dawn, when he is visited by the King of the Deep Waters. In the calm and tranquility which reigns all around, things begin to happen suddenly, vigorously, briefly—e.g. the sudden quivering of the tuft of hair on his head and the throbbing of the skin under it; the sudden chilly wind that agitates the reeds and makes them sway madly to and fro; the sudden vigorous billowing of the water, etc.—all these things, happening one after another, begin suddenly, proceed vigorously but only briefly, and everything is normal again just as suddenly. Mofolo very skillfully uses the doubled verb and the ideophone to dramatize these happenings. He doubles his adverbs and some of his adjectives for emphasis; occasionally he draws out a vowel to achieve emphasis through syllable length.

Mofolo is a master in the creation of an atmosphere. The piece about the last days of Chaka is quite a masterpiece in itself, when Chaka is *alone*, and all his greatness and renown have turned sour in his mouth. He is alone in many senses: He is outside of the village with only a few regiments; it is night; the warriors for their part are sleeping, yet *he* is kept from sleep by his horrible dreams; the stillness of the night is pierced by the howl of a dog left alone as its owners either perished at the spear of Chaka's warriors, or ran for their lives—he is now no better than that dog; he is alone, like the orphans and the widows and widowers of those whose corpses have been devoured by the wolves, of which he is reminded by the shriek of a wolf in the tranquil night; but worst of all, he is alone in the knowledge of his guilt and its magnitude, and his gnawing conscience, striking violently at him in his state of subconsciousness, i.e., in his sleep *via* his dreams (for consciously he has suppressed any trace of conscience), reminds *him*, and *him* alone, that he has destroyed himself. . . .

Daniel P. Kunene. *The Works of Thomas Mofolo*
(Los Angeles, University of California, African
Studies Center, 1967), p. 28

While the central idea of *Chaka* is coherently and impressively Christian, it would be an oversimplification to suggest that any other types of outlook were altogether foreign to Mofolo. . . .

It is difficult to escape the impression that at [the novel's] final stage the Christian and the Sotho in Mofolo have made room for the African, who renounces, for a brief while, his tribal rancors and his new definitions of good and evil to ponder on the past greatness of his race and on its present subjugation, finding some undivulged hope, perhaps, in the notion that the white man's empire, too, will wane some day.

It may have been this final impression that, in later times, was to enable Senegal's Léopold Sédar Senghor and Mali's Seydou Badian to extol Chaka, in poetry and on the stage, as the heroic, self-denying ruler, who does not hesitate to sacrifice the tenderest passion of the heart in order to ensure the greatness and to defend the freedom of his people. Mofolo's conception of Chaka is entirely different and, as far as can be ascertained, much closer to historical fact. The Sotho author is by no means blind to his hero's inherent greatness, but he judges him and indicts him in the name of an essentially ethical view of life. Besides the technical skill and the depth of outlook which it evinces, Mofolo's novel is unique in its successful combination of traditional African and modern Christian elements.

Albert S. Gérard. *Four African Literatures*
(Berkeley, University of California Press, 1971),
pp. 125–27

[In *The Traveller of the East*] Mofolo alters the hero-quest tale in an important way; not only is there little link with nature but . . . there is an abomination of man. In addition the whole, allegorical interpretation is centered on the protagonist; it is *his* search, for *his* needs, for *his* boon. Nothing like this had existed in traditional oral literature, and perhaps Mofolo is really visualizing this as the only possibility for the new emerging individual consciousness; it should bear the consequences of egocentricity. The burden of the responsibility of the tribe could be carried by one man in the oral tales, because behind him and ahead of him there was the *wholeness* of the tribe. He had come from the tribe, and to the tribe he would return. His adventures only made him more loyal, more readily able to appreciate what he had left behind; they confirmed the superiority of the tribe. But Mofolo's hero is alienated because he has lost the ability to connect with the consciousness of the tribe, which is itself disintegrating. His death confirms his pointless vacillations and the illogicality of alienation.

By contrast Mofolo's *Pitseng* is a disappointment. All his life Mofolo had to choose between the amiable offerings of Christian camaraderie and the set diet of an uncompromising art. The difficulties of the situation were made even more emphatic, especially since he was an employee of [the mission at] Morija. Only by taking this into consideration can one accept the second novel at all; it was an attempt to pacify his teachers, employers, and publishers. . . .

To say that Mofolo's two great novels [*The Traveller of the East* and *Chaka*] belong to the genre of *Pitseng* and are mere exercises in the complacency of missionary teaching is to misunderstand them and Mofolo. They are above all the quests of befuddled individuals, catapulted from the security of tribal consciousness into the personal uncertainty of metaphysical speculation. What should concern the reader of today is not the individual inquiry but the tragic necessity for it.

> O. R. Dathorne. *The Black Mind* (Minneapolis,
> University of Minnesota Press, 1974),
> pp. 125–26, 128

MORRISON, TONI (1931–   )

UNITED STATES

I've just finished reading Toni Morrison's book, *The Bluest Eye*, and my heart hurts. It's all I can do not to lie down and cry myself into some kind of relief from the life-pain of Pecola, the central character. She is a girl born black, poor and, by majority standard, ugly. It is also an account of the people that surround her, especially Pauline, her mother, and Cholly, her father. They are the kind of people that all black people know of—or are—to varying degrees. . . .

Toni Morrison has not written a story really, but a series of painfully accurate impressions. How all of the people she talks about arrive where we meet them is what she is about with such great precision. She gives us a sense of some of the social elements of some of the people, black and white, that contribute to the erosion of innocence and beauty. To read the book, however, is to ache for remedy.

In *The Bluest Eye* she has split open the person and made us watch the heart beat. We feel faint, helpless and afraid—not knowing what to do to cover it up and keep it beating. We think of remedies past and remedies in progress to apply somehow while the thrashing heart still beats. We must think faster and work harder and hope that maybe a new breed of people, tight with God, in some dark privacy, has a plan ready to set it all—alright.

Ruby Dee. Freedomways. No. 3, 1971,
pp. 319–20

The Bluest Eye was set among unforgiving provincial black people in a small Ohio town and charted the experience of two little sisters as they watched a friend first become a pariah and then sink into madness. The book's general outline—how witnessing and understanding tragedy forces the surrender of innocence and topples wide-eyed, precocious kids into unwilling maturity—is a familiar one in American, especially Southern, fiction; but its language was unique, powerful, precise and absolutely convincing, both spare and rich at once.

Now comes *Sula*, which features another pariah, spans the years 1921 to 1965, and seems to take place in the same setting. . . . While the setting and the characters continually convince and intrigue, the novel seems somehow frozen, stylized. A more precise yet somehow icy version of *The Bluest Eye*, it refuses to invade our present in the way we want it to and stays, instead, confined to its time and place. . . .

Reading it, in spite of its richness and its thorough originality, one continually feels its narrowness, its refusal to brim over into the world outside its provincial setting.

Sara Blackburn. NYT. Dec. 30, 1973, p. 3

[In *Sula*] Morrison at first seems to combine the aims of the Black Freedom Movement and women's liberation. Sula and Nel discover when they are 11 years old "that they were neither white nor male, and that all freedom and triumph was forbidden to them." When they grow up, Nel slips on the collar of convention. She marries, has two children, becomes tied to her "nest," a slave to racism and sexism. Sula goes to the big city, gets herself an education, and returns a "liberated" woman with a strange mixture of cynicism and innocence. . . .

But the perspective Morrison gives us upon these two black women is not pure black freedom or pure women's liberation. We may wish that Nel had absorbed some of Sula's independence of mind and willingness to take risks, and had not plunged so completely into the humdrum atmosphere of conventional family life, with all its sexist and racial overtones. Yet we cannot approve the freedom that licenses Sula casually to steal Nel's husband and condemn her childhood friend to a ruined life, while she just as casually abandons him. That is not freedom but selfishness, and it is immoral, however contemptuous we may be of the pitifully conventional virtues of married life, or however much we may feel that marriage oppresses women. Besides, the freedom that Sula achieves is as much a prison as it is liberation. Totally free, she becomes obsessed with herself, unable to love, uncontained by the normal rules and boundaries we have come to associate with human beings.

Morrison does not accept—nor does she expect us to accept—the unqualified tenets of either of the two current freedom movements. There is more to both society and the individual, and she subjects each of these to a merciless analysis.

Jerry H. Bryant. *Nation.* July 6, 1974, p. 24

The ordinary spars with the extraordinary in Morrison's books. What would be a classically tragic sensibility, with its implacable move toward crisis and the extremes of pity and horror, is altered and illuminated by a thousand smaller, natural occurrences and circumstances. There is death, and violence and hubris; but young girls bicker about menstruation and complain when their mothers insist that they apply clothespins to their noses as a beauty tactic. Spring brings ants and peach pits and scratched knees; fall, cod-liver oil and brown stockings. The very ordinary restlessness of two girls on a summer day suddenly gives way to tragedy; death joins the stock of adolescent secrets they share. But teenage boys continue to strut on street corners; and errands must be run for parents. Morrison has a musician's sense of tone, texture, and emotional balance. Her themes are the stark and painful plots; her improvisations are the sounds, smells, tastes, habits, idiosyncrasies that surround them. . . .

Toni Morrison's books are filled with loss—lost friendship, lost love, lost customs, lost possibilities. And yet there is so much life in the smallest acts and gestures—Sula and Nel giggle over an old joke, the whores gossip in front of Pecola—that they are as much celebrations as elegies.

Margo Jefferson. *Ms.* Dec., 1974, pp. 34–35, 39

Sula is more fully dominated by the title character [than *The Bluest Eye*], and Sula's characterization is the more complex; in both novels, however, the protagonist is forced into premature adulthood by the *donnée* of her life. Pecola's comprehension of her world is never articulated for either the other characters or the reader; Sula, too, remains a partial enigma both in and out of her narrative. But the pain that each experiences is made vivid and plain. Taken together, the two novels can—and I think must—be read as offering different answers to a single question: What is to become of a finely attuned child who is offered no healthy outlet for her aspirations and yearnings? Pecola escapes in madness; Sula rejects society for amoral self-reliance. For both, sensitivity is a curse rather than a blessing. Morrison's second novel, though richer in many ways, is essentially a reworking of the material of the first with an alternative ending. Though her characters' problems are conditioned by the black milieu of which she writes, her concerns are broader, universal ones. Her fiction is a study of thwarted sensitivity.

Joan Bischoff. *SBL.* Fall, 1975, p. 21

MPHAHLELE, EZEKIEL (1919–   )

SOUTH AFRICA

This collection of five short stories [*Man Must Live, and Other Stories*], written by an African teacher of Johannesburg, reflects a dangerous tendency on the part of the African intelligentsia to become isolated from their people. Those who are charged with the education of the African people must inevitably superimpose upon the aboriginal raw culture in which the average pupil was nurtured, the more complex pattern of European culture and ethics. The resultant conflict between two modes of thought and life can lead either to the extinction of the weaker culture or to a fusion of cultures drawing strength equally from both sources.

Unfortunately the author of these stories has had the gods of his fathers exorcised by the missionaries. He has forgotten that he is an African. If you changed the names of the characters in his stories, they might be creatures of any race or clime. They believe in ideal love, heavenly justice, patience and the other delectable virtues; they have to struggle both with their own inherent weakness of the flesh and spirit and with the selfishness and callousness of others, just like the heroes of Victorian novels. But never once do they complain about the pass laws, the pick-up vans or the insolence of the white man, though they all live in urban locations where beer raids are the order of the day. They do not share the sufferings and the problems of the majority of their people. They are not genuine characters. . . .

The author of these stories is evidently sensitive and observant, if introspective, and he writes with great facility and precision. But the sharpest intellect cannot function in a vacuum. Art, of course, cannot be made to measure. Nor are we complaining because Mr. Mphahlele is non-political. All we do say is that he should return to his people for inspiration, otherwise his muse will wither and die.

B. P. B. *The Guardian*. Jan. 9, 1947, p. 3

"I'm the personification of the African paradox," writes Ezekiel Mphahlele in the current issue of *The Twentieth Century*, "detribalised, Westernised, but still African—minus the conflicts." His autobiography [*Down Second Avenue*] explains how he reached this point. It is valuable for several reasons. It rings true; it is the work of a new kind of self-emancipated South African; it lights up both the conditions in which he struggled to make the best of his powers, and the self that has evolved. Because the struggle was bitter and because this man of forty is truthful, his book has a partly bitter flavour: it is not the bitterness of despair or fanaticism, but the taste of the life he has known. . . .

Although he found, through white and Christian institutions and individuals, scope for his abilities, he also won it by his own brains and guts. In doing so he has come to find that formal Christianity is no longer for him, but he is able to enjoy, say, Chekhov and Vivaldi, he values his white friends too much to want to shoo them out of Africa, and he has gained, among other things, the use of the English language. If he wishes to use it, he has the talent, as this book shows, to interest and enlarge the understandings of readers whose brains are more important to them than their pigmentation. Respect for himself as a man and a writer he has already won. He is a participant in the great, non-racial effort of winning the durable from the transient.

William Plomer. *NS*. April 25, 1959, pp. 582–83

To read Ezekiel Mphahlele after a diet of West and Central African writers is like twiddling the focusing knob on a pair of glasses. His whole dilemma is so utterly different from theirs that his books help to clarify their position as much as his own. For the Negro in urban South Africa has in truth more in common with the American Negro than with his neighbours in tropical Africa. He inhabits a society which is dominated by Whites in a far grimmer and more universal sense than any tropical colony (except perhaps Angola) has ever been. And this domination is expressed, not merely in colonial ritual and pantomime, but in every department of life. His residence, his movements, his place and grade of work, his education, his sexual life are all subject to regulation, all governed by an alien mythology about the black man's place in the scheme of things. He cannot even walk down a street at certain hours or drink a glass of beer without breaking the law. An outcast in his own country, he has to scrutinize every doorway, every bench, every counter, to make sure that he has segregated himself correctly. He is on the run. . . .

[Mphahlele's] whole life has been an unrelenting struggle to achieve the way of life for which his urban upbringing and liberal education had prepared him. But to achieve that life he has had finally to become an exile. . . .

There is nothing [in *Down Second Avenue*] of Camara's poetic nostalgia, his elegy for a life full of its own dignity and significance. Mphahlele's writing is more like the taste of blood on the tongue. Yet the two men are contemporaries and perhaps not fundamentally different in temperament. What divides them is three thousand miles of Africa.

Gerald Moore. *Seven African Writers* (London,
Oxford University Press, 1962), pp. 92–94

In the past what had always put me off Ezekiel Mphahlele's writing was a certain dullness of tone, much like the ponderous speech of a dull-witted person so that it was often difficult to pursue the story to its ending. The gems were often embedded in a thick mud of cliché and lustreless writing: a succession of simple clauses, for instance, linked together by semi-colons. The texture of the prose had the feel and look of sweaty labour much like the stains of honest sweat on the cloth-cap of the toiling proletariat. . . .

The danger with this kind of writing is that it can often become a substitute for action in the story, or a substitute for a more ingenious solution to the problem of flashbacks. At his slowest it contributed to a considerable amount of dullness in Mphahlele's writing. Yet some of these problems of style were clearly attributable to external causes: the strain of maintaining an equilibrium in a dangerously melodramatic situation. If one went too far the other way in an effort to match with language the violence of the streets, the prose became strained, brittle and frayed; so that the flatness in Mphahlele's writing was sometimes due to an honourable attempt to remain "cool under fire."

It seems to me that in the latest work Mphahlele's writing has become tighter, more solid and assured as he acquires a more properly synthesised vocabulary to deal with the stresses of South African life. He has achieved greater authority and a better grip on his own particular idiom: the result is a happier fluency of tone.

Lewis Nkosi. *BO*. March, 1966, pp. 51–52

Ezekiel Mphahlele has become a spokesman for many Africans who live in South Africa. He is a gifted writer and a humane and compassionate man. His first major work was the autobiographical tale of his early life in the slums of Pretoria's Second Avenue district, *Down Second Avenue*. It has been reprinted several times, for it is a work of impressive sensitivity, with the anger and the compassion beautifully held in balance. It asks the inevitable angry question as to the injustice of such poverty—in this case rendered the sharper by the bitterness derived from colour prejudice. . . .

Exile has not been easy, as the very title of this new prize-winning novel makes clear, *The Wanderers*, with its suggestively generalized subtitle, *A Novel of Africa*. In this book with an almost painful accuracy the author describes his experiences as a wanderer with his family, as he moved across the continent seeking for those essential roots which a writer must have. The story of the novel overlaps the incidents in the brief concluding section of *Down Second Avenue* and then carries on to the writer's determination to leave East Africa for London. Yet the book is not a simple autobiography, it is a novel constructed with skill and art. Perhaps it shares something of the attitude of Arthur Miller when he wrote that powerful play *After the Fall*. You felt that you were being allowed to see more deeply than before that last deep intimacy in the sensibility of a man and an artist. If this is often painful it is because human truth is painful, and such human truth is the stuff from which derives all significant art.

[John Povey]. *AfrA*. Winter, 1969, p. 12

The language [in *The Wanderers*] adequately moves its freight—an ambitious panoramic story of wandering exiles, black and white, from South Africa. The South African episodes are the most vivid and affectionate; the polychrome peculiarities of this deplorable state, with its "colored" and Indian minorities as well as blacks, are rendered in a sharp sequence of vignettes and accents. Mr. Mphahlele, whose black characters talk a little like stage Englishmen, hears peculiar speech everywhere. . . .

When Timi Tabana, a black schoolteacher exiled for writing newspaper articles about a slave system of penal labor, travels to London, the colony of exiled South Africans there seems to him pathetic; the

"South African English accent the white spoke . . . irritated him as it had never done in his home country." And in Nigeria, after his initial exhilaration at being freed from South Africa's tyranny of passbooks and police, he is irritated by the effeminate way Nigerians slap at each other, and urges them to hit with fists, in good South African style. Prostitution and idleness are also new to him. One of the friends he makes there, in a small circle of intellectuals and mixed marriages, is named Awoonor (another is "an American historian, John Galbraith"), and, whether or not this means Kofi Awoonor, *The Wanderers* moves into the dispirited terrain of *This Earth, My Brother*... Timi's problems become those of the free: a sense of futility, elusive responsibilities, a meagre security. . . .

The Wanderers shows the English-speaking whites (but not the Afrikaners) as people who, like the blacks, are unequally matched against the vast, murderous inertia that is Africa. [Nov. 13, 1971]

John Updike. Picked-Up Pieces (New York,
Alfred A. Knopf, 1975), pp. 323–24, 326

Unlike *Down Second Avenue*, with its emotional tension, its cumulative structure, and its overwhelming sense of inevitability, *The Wanderers* might very well go any number of different ways, to any number of different conclusions. His life, Mphahlele implies in "Exile to Nigeria," had become adjusted in South Africa to the ever-present enemy, had adapted itself to a continual defensiveness, had structured itself around the negative response; in Nigeria that structure, negative as it was, exists no longer because the oppressor is no longer in his life. Mphahlele is thrown off balance by thrusting at something and expecting resistance but finding nothing there. This accounts for what he calls the "void" and also for the notable lack of tension and of energy-directing vitality, and for the virtual absence of subject in *The Wanderers*.

Another reason that *Down Second Avenue* is the better of the two books is that, paradoxically, life, as described in the earlier book, presented a necessary pattern that art, in *The Wanderers*, never comes up with. Or perhaps it would be fairer to say that Mphahlele is a finer artist as an autobiographer than he is as a novelist. Everything in *Down Second Avenue* is drawn up behind the author to show the way inevitably to exile; it is an account of the calculus of exile and as such the book achieves meaning for itself and for the life it describes. *The Wanderers*, on the other hand, is aimless, disjointed, an account of a simple, inert, mass wandering. The people are wandering into further exile, but now the exile has no goal and no meaning; it is the conclusion of nothing and a part of no pattern; it is merely moving on with neither desire nor regret—both of which were strong on departure from South Africa. . . .

Deprived by exile of his natural subject, Mphahlele fails to come up with another.

James Olney. *Tell Me Africa* (Princeton, N.J., Princeton University Press, 1973), pp. 280–81

Mphahlele's collection of short stories *The Living and the Dead, and Other Stories* marked the beginning of a new period in his creative career. The evil faced by his heroes is more concrete than in his preceding works of fiction. Simultaneously, the author's conviction is strengthened that weak human force is incapable of overcoming it. This pessimism, resulting from cruel personal experiences, is reflected in this collection, as it is in the works of the prose writers emerging at the beginning of the Sixties. It is further emphasized by Mphahlele's crudeness of expression. . . .

In his collection of short stories *In Corner B*, Mphahlele is well aware of the relationship between form and content, the necessary balance between descriptive passages and dialogue, etc. This collection shows not only the author's increasing interest in the technical aspects of fiction writing, but also his keen sense of linguistic experimentation and modern expression. Yet unlike some of his colleagues, he has never abandoned a realistic, true-to-life portrayal of reality. His latest novel *The Wanderers* is partly autobiographical. Moreover, Mphahlele is an adviser of young African authors who are about to set out into the sphere of creative writing. Mphahlele, who does not believe in magically inspired talent and who tries to be as practical as possible, feels that a writer should listen closely to his people's speech and should capture the mood, atmosphere and verbal pictures or images evoked by what a character says or does, in the character's own language.

Vladimír Klíma. In Vladimír Klíma, Karel František Růžička, and Petr Zima, *Black Africa: Literature and Language* (Dordrecht, Netherlands, D. Reidel, 1976), pp. 254–55

MQHAYI, S. E. K. (1875–1945)

SOUTH AFRICA

Reward is the title of the seventh volume recently issued in the Bantu Treasury Series edited by Professor C. M. Doke. The author, S. E. K. Mqhayi, from whose numerous Xhosa productions the present poems have been chosen, explains that the title is designed to indicate "things rare and profitable." This claim is justified by the contents because the author is without a peer among writers of Xhosa poetry, living or dead, when judged by the quantity and calibre of his output, much of which has not yet been published in book form.

The arrangement of the poems in this book is in five sections: 1. Didactic poems on subjects like Truth, Hope, Love, and so forth. 2. The passing of the old years and advents of new ones. 3. Obituary eulogia. 4. Praises of Africans who have travelled overseas. 5. Miscellaneous poems.

It is rare indeed to find other good poetry written in Xhosa on some of the subjects named, but with Mqhayi it is characteristic and it has deservedly earned him the popular appellation of *"Imbongi yesizwe"* (equivalent to Bantu Poet Laureate). Many of the poems are informative, and indeed "profitable" because informative, e.g. [a poem] in appreciation of the bi-monthly agricultural journal published at Umtata by the Bunga. The topic of the expiration of one year and the incoming of a new one is almost Mqhayi's annual exercise and monopoly, and he does it with gusto. The variety of stanza forms in this selection inevitably invites comparison with *Zulu Songs* by B. W. Vilakazi (Volume 1 in the same series) but in the Zulu language. Both authors employ forms definitely imitative of English rhymes such as the long and short metres, the sonnet and the heroic couplet. Both excel in their infinite variety of rhymes and rhythmic movement such as is also to be found in *The Orchard* by J. J. R. Jolobe (Volume 2 in the same series).

With regard to diction, Vilakazi frequently uses archaic and extraneous words imported from the neighbouring South African tongues. But Mqhayi in the pieces included in this book employs archaic words with a moderation that just obviates their getting in between the reader and the subject matter as an obstacle, and he makes very few excursions into non-Xhosa words. This moderation, however, is absent in many of Mqhayi's poems outside of this volume.

D. D. T. Jabavu. *AfrS.* 2, 3, 1943, pp. 174–75

A lover of the human race, [Mqhayi] associated himself with several progressive movements and institutions. He understood alike the illiterate and educated, and as a result, his social influence was very wide. Because of his active interest in his people, his knowledge of their history, traditional and modern, was amazing. Through the press, by public orations, and in private letters, he had a message of encouragement to give to the social leaders of his people. . . . His contribution to Southern Bantu Literature is easily the largest and most valuable that has hitherto been made by any single writer. . . .

The Case of the Twins includes fiction, history and poetry. The book owes its title to the novelette that covers its first half—the lawsuit of the twins. The plot of this novelette is suggested by Verses 28–29 of the 38th Chapter of the book of Genesis. As the author states in the preface, the purpose of the story is to give a picture of legal procedure among the Xhosa people, and to show the democratic spirit in which it is carried out. . . .

If we turn to his poetry, we find that Mqhayi, though perhaps possessing more talent, is nevertheless more limited in scope than some of the younger Nguni poets. Essentially a poet of the traditional type, for theme he is almost wholly confined to concrete subjects, usually human beings. He is confined to lyrical verse, chiefly odes and elegies. Even historical themes he was never able to put into narrative verse. . . . A sense of effort and strain is always with us when we read his rhymed verse, and very often we feel that in order to observe rhyme, the poet has sacrificed sense, virility and easy flow of language. His favourite rhyme scheme is the heroic couplet, and because he invariably writes end-stopped lines, his rhymed verse makes dull and monotonous reading.

But if we judge Mqhayi by what he has achieved instead of judging him by what he has failed to achieve, then there is no doubt that his best poetry is of a high order. . . .

Mqhayi takes the highest place in Xhosa literature. He has done more than any other writer to enrich Xhosa. In his hands it receives a fresh impress, and he has revealed all its possibilities as a powerful medium of expression of human emotion. His prose as well as his poetry contains expressions that became proverbial long before his death.

A. C. Jordan. *SAO.* Sept., 1945, pp. 135–38

[Mqhayi] eliminates all real conflict from the world created by his fancy. In *Don Jadu*, the hero passes from town to town, solving all problems overnight, and leading raw tribesmen from a primitive state to an advanced civilization in a matter of weeks. Everywhere he is acclaimed and glorified and rejoices inwardly all the while. Thus does Mqhayi allow his imagination, fostered by a repulsive hunger for self-glorification, to run riot and escape into a world of pure fancy, where probability is grossly violated and logical development of incident unknown. True, Mqhayi's imagination is colourful and productive, but it is not disciplined. His mastery of language is undoubted, but he blatantly tries to impress by playing with big words and archaisms. His glittering façade of words is unsupported and so we go away unsatisfied.

John Riordan. *AfrS.* 20, 1, 1961, p. 53

As cattle was the foundation of Xhosa economy, and therefore of Xhosa society, this was a problem of life and death for the Xhosa nation as a whole. *Don Jadu* grew out of these experiences and this realization. It was not meant as a realistic description of a situation that everyone knew anyway. It was designed as a blueprint for the future coexistence of both races in South Africa. And it was conceived in a spirit of compromise and syncretism. There are only three things that Mqhayi forcefully rejects: the South African government, the prison system, and imported hard liquor as opposed to the native home-brewed beer. His ideal state is not a preliminary study in Bandustan. It is a multi-racial society that places a high premium on education and progress, and it is a Christian society that has incorporated many of the beliefs and customs dear to African hearts. In the elaboration of this Bantu utopia, Mqhayi exhibits uncommonly powerful intellectual imagination. . . .

It was perhaps as a poet that Mqhayi was chiefly valued by the Xhosa audience, not least because he had completely mastered the form and the spirit of the traditional praise poem (*izibongo*) while adapting it

The Wanderers shows the English-speaking whites (but not the ("Poet Laureate"), and Vilakazi calls him "the Father of Xhosa poetry," because "he is responsible for a transition from the primitive bards who sang the *izibongo*." The main function of the tribal bard (*imbongi*) was to strengthen the cohesion of the group, usually by celebrating the glorious figures of the past and extolling the authority of the reigning chief. Mqhayi's volume on Hintza is an example of this, as are the obituary eulogies of local figures in *Reward*. But since the central preoccupation of the *izibongo* in its purest form is to promote the prosperity and the greatness of the group, it does not deal solely with the chiefs, but also with any public events that may be significant in that respect. . . .

If we were to believe Vilakazi, Mqhayi's attempts at innovation were not always successful. His poems dealing with nature, the Zulu critic says, are "dull," and those on religious subjects are "mere oratorical exercises" when compared with those of his successor [J. R.] Jolobe. Mqhayi "excelled in heroic poetry of the traditional type, and showed great skill in weaving his people's customs, legends, and myths into his poems."

Albert S. Gérard. *Four African Literatures*
(Berkeley, University of California Press, 1971),
pp. 58–60

Although from the onset Mqhayi tried to get away from mission-school writing, he did not involve himself with recreating the oral literature.

Instead he worked fairly closely with oral sources (in addition to in-digenous idioms, his work is full of the precision of one directed but not hamstrung by a tradition) and his story ["The Case of the Twins"] emerges as another exercise in the attempt to establish individuality. Mqhayi makes the "case" even more difficult by presenting the con-testants as twins. Who could claim to be different? His story, ostensibly about the right to rule, concerns the dubious assertion of individuality. The mere fact that they are twins not only heightens their similarity, but makes their case for separate recognition futile and ridiculous. The author asserts the predominance of the tribe, since it is an old tribal member who finally helps the court to decide. . . .

What Mqhayi did was to establish the artist's independence from the patronage of religious bodies. This does not mean that he was ahead of his time, for as late as 1942 when he published *Reward*, a collection of verse, the sections into which he divided the poems were along fairly conventional lines. For instance, the selection includes poems on "truth," "hope," and "love," on the "passing of years," on death, and perhaps, nearest to the tradition, poems of praise for Africans who had gone overseas. He imitated English rhyme as well as the sonnet and heroic couplet. But his poetic gifts were not entirely dissipated in pro-ducing conventional laudations. He expressed the new individual con-sciousness through satire and in the manner of the Sotho writer Azariel Sekese he even attacked royalty.

O. R. Dathorne. *The Black Mind*
(Minneapolis, University of Minnesota Press,
1974), pp. 132–33

NGUGI WA THIONG'O (1938–   )

KENYA

Mr. James Ngugi is, in East African terms, a prolific worker. Already he has written a full-length play [*The Black Hermit*], two novels (of which [*Weep Not, Child*] is the first published) as well as a number of articles in the *Sunday Nation* in Nairobi. Indeed, since he left Makerer, this latter work has been his means of livelihood, so that his articles have increased in quantity and expertise, as well as in the area they cover.

Of *Weep Not, Child*, the first thing to be remarked is what an important place it has, and is going to have, in the history of novel-making in East Africa. Now, after all the waiting, the first novel in English has been written here by an indigenous East African. Immediately I am reminded of Dr. [Roger] Bannister and the Magic Mile, and I feel grateful to Mr. Ngugi in knowing that, where he has broken the barrier, the rest of us will quickly follow. This is excellent. And yet this should not be allowed to blind us into empty hero-worship, to undeserved praise when the novel itself is discussed. . . .

True enough it talks about things of the greatest potential importance, but it does so unconvincingly. (I am reminded here of that old one about a house being built of bricks but a collection of bricks not necessarily being a house). Mr. Ngugi narrates the misfortunes in which people are caught, in a reporting, almost cataloguing manner which strangely enough for all its blood and thunder lacks any breath of real life. Part of the trouble lies in his characterization. I feel that all his characters are a continuation of his beliefs and desires and that he manipulates them at the end of a string throughout. It is as if his thoughts and words took human shape and became now a Ngotho, now a Njoroge and so on. And the result is a sterile and unmoving reproduction of many James Ngugis. And the result of this is that we feel not a flicker of spontaneous sympathy for his characters, whatever their misfortunes. Now this is a tragedy for the whole work, because Mr. Ngugi has staked all on his characters. . . .

Mr. Ngugi can rest assured that his first published novel is a historical landmark. And when the spark comes, what he will write after it may well be a great deal more.

John Nagenda. MakJ. Nov., 1964, pp. 69–71

In [The River Between] the hero and heroine are caught between warring factions of traditional and Christianised Kikuyus, and though the hero makes an admirable attempt to reconcile the two cultures, both within himself and in the dismally divided community, he fails because as an educated African he has begun to set great store by his own personal aspirations; also he shows the same ambiguities and equivocations of modern heroes everywhere who have submitted to the cult of self-doubt and scepticism.

This seems to me a very worthy successor to Ngugi's first novel, Weep Not, Child, which dealt with the Mau Mau conflict. Ngugi's main achievement is a series of evocative passages which are distinguished by their lack of contrivance or any striving after effect for its own sake. There is no reason to doubt that Ngugi owes a special debt to the Nigerian, Chinua Achebe, whose Things Fall Apart seems to have greatly influenced him. The main failure of Ngugi's writing so far has been his inability to allow for easy transition from one scene to another in a way that would suggest a clear progress of the novel. The action tends to jump and most of the scenes are not allowed to develop sufficiently to give the novel its accumulative power. Ngugi's advantage over [recent South African writers] stems from the fact that he has situated his characters in a community where choice can be seen to be real so that personal failure or success can be assessed in universal, human terms. Such an assessment to be possible requires certain minimum conditions of freedom.

Lewis Nkosi. NewA. May, 1965, p. 70

The River Between uses the same style and achieves the same kind of effect [as Weep Not, Child]. But in this novel there is a need for more definition and sharpness. For this is a full historical novel—a novel, that is, about contemporary society which examines certain features of that society by exploring their origin and development in the past. The obvious comparison is with Achebe's two novels about the early contacts between Africans and Europeans in his own part of Eastern Nigeria, Things Fall Apart and Arrow of God. The comparison, I think, is fair and the reason why it is unfavourable to Ngugi is that the impressionistic and personal approach used in Weep Not, Child is insufficient in a novel attempting to explore the roots of a particular problem. Such a novel must show the characters acting in a social context and under social pressures and therefore must demonstrate to us convincingly that nature of their society. Achebe's novels do this. The tribal societies he shows us are completely articulated and comprehensible and his characters act out their destinies under social pressures that are made clear to us. In *The River Between* this is not so. Although like Achebe, Ngugi has set up certain connections between his two novels—for example the school at Siriana occurs in both of them—the exact historical period of the events in *The River Between* is never revealed, at least to the reader unversed in the details of European penetration into the various regions of Kenya. The social structure of the tribe and its political organization, although the plot turns on these matters, is never demonstrated to us in such a way that we can understand their operation in the action of the novel. Hence the characters are seen in relationships only sketchily defined except in terms of emotion, and the real content of the social and political ends which they set themselves remains unspecified.

John Reed. *JCL*. Sept., 1965, p. 119

The first novel to come out of East Africa was James Ngugi's *Weep Not, Child*, written three years ago while the young Kenyan was reading English Honours at Makerere. . . . *Weep Not, Child* is a story of Kenya during the Mau Mau Emergency period. Those bloody years are recreated through the experiences of three families. . . . If we consider the story on the anagogical level . . . there is a deeper message. Ngugi is a disciple of Walt Whitman (from whose poem, "On the Beach at Night," comes the title of the novel). Ngugi believes in Whitman's concept of the brotherhood of man and remains optimistic that man can be improved. . . .

The first few pages of *Weep Not, Child*, and some latter passages are reminiscent of Alan Paton's *Cry the Beloved Country*. When Njoroge identifies himself with David and the Kikuyu with the children of Israel, it is a poor imitation of Flaubert. Ngugi commits many technical sins, probably because he is more engrossed in espousing his ideas and ideals than in adhering to artistic precepts. The novel consists of too many unrelated essays and stories; things just do not dovetail. Then, too, Ngugi explains and summarizes situations which would lend themselves to easy dramatization.

Taban lo Liyong. *AfricaR*. Dec., 1965, pp. 42–43

The non-Christian black African's view of his world, as it is presented in *The River Between*, is especially antithetical to the Calvinistic view of nature. If, at the beginning of time, God separated, forever, the good souls from the bad, then it must follow that a man's surroundings have little effect on his fixed fate. ("That's the way those people are; you can't change them.")

All this, which may seem a digression, is actually at the center of any discussion of the novel as it evolved in Middle-class Christian Europe (and later in America). If nature, environment, is of no real importance in the life of man, then neither can its role in the novel be important. And generally this is the case. Nature, in most European and American novels, is used as a backdrop, a stage-set. It is passive—just there.

But the African writer, with a different set of traditions and values, a different attitude toward his surroundings and his place in them may use those surroundings in a different way. James Ngugi does. Time and again, in *The River Between*, nature is at center stage, playing an active role, influencing a character's feelings and thoughts in a way only human beings do in most European and American novels: "He was angry with the rain. The rain carried away the soil, not only here but everywhere. That was why the land, in some parts, was becoming poor. For a time, he felt like fighting with the rain." Or: "And sometimes she would run to Honia (river) and just stay there watching the flow of the water. Then she would go home feeling at peace. So the river, especially on Sundays, was her companion." These are not simply turnings of literary phrases. They bespeak new ways of feeling and seeing.

All this is very exciting to me as a writer, because it suggests new ways of telling a story, new relationships of character and setting. More importantly, it is entirely possible that the black African writer will accomplish for the black American what his own writers have been unable to accomplish—that is, to suggest to him standards other than those of his oppressors, by which he may judge himself, his world, and his place in it.

William Melvin Kelley. *AfrF*. Winter, 1966, p. 114

Hope does exist in Ngugi's work, but it is a hope that gives little comfort. Just as men are apparently fated to fight each other—at least the empirical evidence seems to support such a view—so are they fated to desire peace. It is indeed the pattern of Ngugi's three novels that a hero who seeks to avoid conflict and violence is thrown into contact with a man who desires them. The antagonist justifies his belief in violence because of the injustices done to him and his people in the past; his solutions to these problems of injustice are an armed conflict with the oppressor and a retaliation in kind and of equal severity to the opposition. It is instructive to look at Ngugi's three published novels (he is, of course, a young writer who may take different paths in the future), because they show that no man can deny or hide his conflicts. Only the brave ones resolve them, and in this resolution lies the hope of the future for mankind. But first this hope must be shorn of its illusions.

Ngugi seems to be saying that only when people accept the present reality can they change their tomorrows. . . . It is the dream of tomorrow that makes a new day possible, but it is the illusions about tomorrow that keep it from appearing. . . .

In his ability to dramatize such insights and to provide perspective on the land about which he has chosen to devote his literary life, Ngugi is a writer who combines movement with pacifism, tradition with inventiveness. He too is trying to reconcile, to create a unity of art—a pattern to which most great writers in the world have been drawn.

Martin Tucker. Introduction to James Ngugi, Weep
Not, Child (New York, Macmillan, 1969),
pp. 10–11, 17

A Grain of Wheat, James Ngugi's latest novel, is an extremely interesting piece of work because it brings a new theme to African literature—the effects on a people of the changes brought about in themselves by the demands of a bloody and bitter struggle for independence. How fit is one for peace, when one has made revolution one's life? Set in the immediate post-Mau-Mau period the novel looks back to the personal tragedies of a number of people who were active in Mau-Mau, and examines how the experience now shapes their lives. In the uneasy peace, they have to come to terms with one another, but their relationships are determined by the experience that has put all human relationships through the test of fire—the guerilla revolution itself.

Here are the wild-looking bearded men who lived in the Aberdares for years, emerging after the revolution with almost all their instincts for normal life lost; brave men half-broken by the experience; and men accepted as brave men who must live the rest of their lives with the secret knowledge that they were traitors. Mugo, a local small farmer, is such a man. He has betrayed a fellow Gikuyu to the British; as a result of various events which enmesh him in the sense of his own guilt, he brings his own world crashing down around his head by confession, and the words of one of the Mau-Mau veterans who are his judges at a private trial sum up the light in which Ngugi presents him: "Your deeds alone will condemn you. No one will ever escape from his own actions."

It is the measure of James Ngugi's development as a writer that none of the protagonists in this novel is marred by the pseudo-nobility of some of the characters in his earlier work, and yet he succeeds in placing the so-called Mau-Mau movement in the historical, political, and sociological context of the African continental revolution. What the white world perhaps still thinks of as a reversion to primitive savagery (as opposed, no doubt, to civilized savagery in Nazi Germany) is shown to be a guerilla war in which freedom was won, and which brought with its accomplishment a high price for the people who waged it.

Nadine Gordimer. MQR. Fall, 1970, p. 226

A Grain of Wheat is Ngugi's most ambitious and successful novel to date. In the depth of its psychological penetration and the power of its characterization, in the subtlety of its narrative technique, in the density of its texture, and in the sophistication of its language, it exceeds all expectations raised by the two earlier novels, promising though they were. Its complexity of form recalls the involutions of Conrad's *Lord Jim*, on which it seems consciously to have been modelled.

Most novels, including African ones, present experience chronologically, with the story moving logically from the beginning, through various complications and problems to the resolution and conclusion. Others ignore this convention, and present experience through a series of impressions, digressions, casual anecdotes, and incidents which are not necessarily presented in chronological order. This is the method of *A Grain of Wheat*, which opens on the eve of Kenya's Independence and ends four days later. But very little in the novel actually happens during those four days; instead the reader is taken back by numerous "witnesses" to a whole series of events in the past. This is Ngugi at his most baffling and exasperating, withholding information, supplying it belatedly when he chooses, employing flashback within flashback, "reflector within reflector, point of view within point of view, cross-chronological juxtaposition of events, and impressions" [as Dorothy Van Ghent wrote of *Lord Jim*]. In no other novel of Ngugi, and possibly in no other African novel, is the reader asked to be more alert and to participate more fully. . . .

A Grain of Wheat is a profoundly satisfying work of art. Ngugi has clearly attained maturity and produced a novel which can stand unashamedly with some of the more lasting English works of fiction.

Eustace Palmer. An Introduction to the African
Novel (New York, Africana, 1972), pp. 24–25, 47

A few weeks ago (as I write these words in December 1972), Heinemann published a book of essays in London called *Homecoming* by a writer named Ngugi wa Thiong'o, and from this simple event in the publishing world, which in itself was not very important, can be drawn some implications of considerable significance for a book about African literature. The writer of *Homecoming* is not, of course, someone new on the scene but the same Gikuyu novelist whom we have encountered as James Ngugi, now writing under a name that, while different, is less new than it is old: a reversion to a traditional, as it were pre-colonial and pre-Christian, African name—Ngugi-son-of-Thiong'o. This little event, though unremarkable in itself, requires us to see, for one thing, that in African literature we are dealing with a living and changing literature and with writers who are very much alive. . . .

Besides providing this kind of salutary warning for impatient critics, Ngugi's name-change indicates that he personally intends henceforth to refuse the Western identity that is implied by a baptismal name and will choose instead to refer himself, by way of a more traditionally African identity, to his father, his family, and his ancestors. Likewise, the Marxism that Ngugi proclaims throughout his book, carrying African Socialism one step further in logical rigor to African Marxism, points to the same tendency and desire to merge individual achievement and identity with communal effort and existence. With his name-change and his Marxism, Ngugi raises a question that inevitably recurs in any discussion of African literature and that can be taken to be the basic issue, so far at least as the African writer himself is concerned, of African literature: that is, the twofold yet single question of the writer's relation to his past and to his community, which involves a definition both of his own and his community's identity.

This is not to say that Ngugi's notions are typical and that other African writers are doing or thinking the same. On the contrary, most other novelists would, to one extent or another, disagree with him in his paradoxical politics of reactionary revolution. Ngugi seems to want to make his past his future: he would revive social and cultural structures of the past as a reality of the future, and what he calls for to accomplish this is a present revolution not to achieve something new but to restore an ideal pre-colonial state that he, at least, takes to have been one of original peace, harmony, justice, and goodness.

James Olney. *Tell Me Africa* (Princeton, N.J., Princeton University Press, 1973), pp. 283–84

NZEKWU, ONUORA (1928–   )

NIGERIA

Wand of Noble Wood begins with Pete, a Lagos journalist, approaching the stage of his life when traditionally he should be thinking of marriage. He finds it hard to reconcile the marriage ideals that have grown on him during his city career with the ideals of his birthplace; and his dilemma is complicated by a pregnant mistress who as a stranger to his home town would be unacceptable there as his wife. . . .

A major criticism of this novel is the excessive amount of straight explanation of the characters' social environment and its effects on their behaviour. Nzekwu must learn to limit the filling-in of broad social background to what is strictly required for understanding the plot. He must also learn to suggest this background in the course of unravelling the plot, rather than interrupt the action with larger chunks of anthropological analysis. On the positive side, the pure though austere style is a delight to read. The conflict of ideals is vividly evoked—for instance in a brilliant passage in Chapter Four where Pete and a friend are arguing about the principles of marriage, and where both veer wildly back and forth between traditional and modern arguments. Finally, this is a powerful tragedy. The suggestion of a situation somehow too perfect to last, the succession of incidents sounding small but sinister notes through the haze of bliss, and the final disaster which seems as inevitable as it is startling—all these are beautifully managed. Nzekwu is a newcomer to novels. His faults, albeit aggravating, are those natural to a newcomer. His talents promise an exciting future.

Robin Horton. *NigM*. Sept., 1961, pp. 219, 221

Before Nigerian independence it used to be a saying in the Secretariat in Lagos that, if the Africans were to leave, tribal warfare would break out among the British administrators. The publication of Mr. Onuora Nzekwu's second novel [*Blade among the Boys*] must bring a resurgence of that partisan feeling to many a modest home in Budleigh Salterton or Torquay where retired officials from Eastern Nigeria look back with pleasure on their days among the cheerful, hardworking Ibos. The West may be richer, and the North haughtier, but in literature the East has wiped the eye of the lot of them, and the rest of West Africa as well. Cyprian Ekwensi, Chinua Achebe and Onuora Nzekwu make an unbeatable Treble Choice.

Blade among the Boys has a typically Ibo theme, a young man's education. In Iboland school-children are punished not by being given extra work but by being sent home for a day. Mr. Nzekwu's hero is desperately studious and determined to get on. His tragedy is that his (European) teachers are all tyrants, seeking unfairly for any excuse to ruin his career and succeeding at the last in expelling him for absurdly inadequate reasons. After a period in which he prospers as a railwayman he takes up again his vocation as a priest, only to be expelled once more after two years at the seminary. This time, however, the fault is with the girl his family have chosen him for a wife, who seduces him by the aid of a love potion bought from a "herbalist."

The other theme is the irresistible one of the conflict of cultures. It is sharpened by making Patrick a Roman Catholic, educated at a mission school. Mr. Nzekwu tries to hold the balance fair, but he cannot help presenting the traditional Ibo religion and culture in the more attractive light. It is this that will be the main attraction to the European reader: the masquerades, the prayers, the charms and the tribal social structure are described from within and with a luminous comprehension.

TLS. Aug. 10, 1962, p. 571

Onuora Nzekwu was born in Northern Nigeria, but his secondary schooling and teachers training took place in Onitsha (Eastern Region). He has taught both in Onitsha and in Lagos. His researches into the history of Onitsha gained him his present position as editor on *Nigeria*, a "middle-brow" (as opposed to *Black Orpheus*) magazine primarily devoted to arts, crafts, and historical and cultural affairs. Nzekwu might be taken as a kind of mean between the extremes of Ekwensi and Achebe. As an essentially popular writer, he lacks Ekwensi's ear for speech or eye for detail. This is not his interest; his is a pedagogical approach. Nor does he make use of the Western-cultural tradition, in a formative way, within the texture of his books, in the depiction of "ancestral" behavior, as Achebe does. Nzekwu's appetite for sensation can be irritating if considered as calculated to sell his books abroad, but fascinating if taken to be the genuine expression of a modern mind obsessed by the more violent aspects of immemorial practices and lore.

Nzekwu's books may be taken as illustrative of the effects of the ambiguities of British colonial practice upon a bright, highly strung, and somewhat disorganized personality. The hidden theme common to both Nzekwu's books, *Wand of Noble Wood* and *Blade among the Boys*, is that of the supernatural revenge taken by the old dispensation upon the new. The traditional society's ways have been disturbed, violated by new patterns from the West which have been planted first by Europeans and then cultivated by "emancipated" Africans themselves. The spiritual forces behind the old community manage to break through, using *their* elected human agents in retaliation. It is important to note that in Nzekwu's books these retaliatory occurrences are presented as being really supernatural in origin—another example of his uniqueness. There is absolutely *no* evidence of irony with regard to these occurrences in the books. In addition, as atavisms they have a personal rather than a communal intent and effect, which is to say that they have an emotional impact on and affect the destinies of isolated individuals only.

This is why, unlike similar mysterious and violent manifestations with a broader scope, those described by Nzekwu seem to the skeptical Western reader to be obsessional, a tumultuous inner life turned inside out.

Judith Illsley Gleason. *This Africa* (Evanston, Ill.,
Northwestern University Press, 1965), pp. 168–69

Blade among the Boys tells the story of an Ibo boy, born in Northern Nigeria, moving to the coast because of the death of his father, determined to go into the Church and finally failing to do so because of an involvement with a girl.

The standards which Nzekwu applies in this novel seem to be those of a generation ago. The boy, Patrick, fails to become a priest when he gets a girl pregnant. She is presented as a warm and intelligent person who loves Patrick. Yet their act—and it becomes this, their ACT—is seen as a grim sin. Patrick is dismissed from the seminary, and the authorities wish him "God's forgiveness and blessings." The novel finally becomes a fairly confused lecture in mission morality, a bending to what must appear to those on the outside as an unjust and totally uncomprehending authority.

The traditional Ibo way of life is generally treated patronizingly. There are exceptions, however, in the form of one or two lively scenes, such as the one in which the ancestral masks have assembled in the village square, and all women have prudently gone indoors, when suddenly an English missionary lady heaves into sight, surrounded by a lot of little schoolgirls. The lady will not budge from her course and neither will the masqueraders. They feel insulted that she will not go away, and she feels insulted that they will not. Finally, in desperation, they pursue her. The little girls flee in all directions, shrieking, and the lady drops her dignity and sprints like a gazelle. It is regrettable that Nzekwu does not more often allow his characters simply to be, as he does in this scene.

Nzekwu's third novel, *Highlife for Lizards*, concerns a woman of great spirit and independence, Agom, and it is the most successful of Nzekwu's writing. His picture of Agom is more fully drawn than anything else he has done, and local beliefs and rituals are handled with greater insight and sympathy than is shown in his previous novels.

Margaret Laurence. *Long Drums and Cannons*
(London, Macmillan, 1968), p. 192

Nzekwu's style can be terse and exact, which is in the tradition of realistic writing, and is capable of evoking a sense of place and event which gives the reader all he needs to know of the scenes and actions before him. Yet too often the narrative is marred by solid interpolations of anthropological and sociological data. It is for the most part a prose of explication rather than implication. In the third novel, *Highlife for Lizards*, he dramatises materials which he merely expounds in the earlier two novels and the result is more compelling and convincing than with the earlier books.

Within these limits, Nzekwu is a serious writer. He is concerned with issues of social, cultural, political and religious consequence at the individual and the societal levels. His novels display their concerns and conclusions through stories of personal relationships which reflect problems of belief, choice, and action, central to a generality of contemporary Nigerians. If there is none of the variety of devices which characterise, say, Achebe's or Soyinka's work—the irony, the fierce and abrasive satire, the gift for caricature, the cold assault on the failures of individuals and society—neither are there any false consolations offered. Nzekwu is a less finished artist than some of his peers; yet he is serious in exploiting the social role of the writer. Perhaps it is fair to say that Nzekwu is essentially a novelist of manners, by which we mean that he is concerned almost exclusively with the variety of problems which confront his own generation, the group of people in transition between the traditional and the modern, who are in an important sense unique since they sum up the ambiguities created by the impact of colonialism on traditional culture and make discoveries about their own natures, values and beliefs, which preclude the generation which follows them from being like them. It is not so much a difference from other cultures that distinguishes the men and women who appear in Nzekwu's novels— since the histories of all peoples comprise a continuous process of growth and modification—but rather a matter of the intensity of this difference.

G. D. Killam. *ALT*. No. 5, 1971, pp. 22–23

OKARA, GABRIEL (1921–   )

NIGERIA

The Voice is a serious and pessimistic story which reflects the post-independence mood of disillusionment which is becoming increasingly articulate among the African intellectuals. The atmosphere of the story is dense with evil, with corruption and with all sorts of manipulation among politicians and their beneficiaries. Okara as a poet-novelist steeps his story in symbolism and imagery but the most persistent symbol and the one which permeates the entire atmosphere of the story is darkness, a palpable darkness within which people grope about frantically in search of vulgar material satisfaction. It is to this darkness therefore that Okolo is attempting to introduce a spark of light that will show the people the way to a more purposeful life. His fate, grim and terrible as it appears, could overtake any would-be reformer in a social situation in which the collective traditional outlook has been sur-planted by unmitigated individualism and the attendant callousness and greed which inspires those with power to make themselves ruthlessly unassailable.

Okara's characters are not fully individuated. They stand for good or evil, virtue or vice, and are therefore ideal for exploring a moral theme. His experiment with language is even more interesting for whereas Achebe and other West African novelists are content to translate oral tradition into English by keeping as close as possible to the original meaning, Okara is the only writer who actually goes so far as to transliterate, even to the extent of reproducing syntactical forms. This gives the action of his story a peculiarly heavy-footed and tortuous movement which again seems to fit the serious moral tone and pessimistic mood of the story.

Emmanuel Obiechina. NigM. Mar., 1965, p. 62

[Okara's] is an inward concern, the "mystic inside," to use his own words. This concern with the self, the soul, runs through all his work, and it is realized by the poet in terms and images of objects and phenomena that most impinge upon his conscious. Snow-flakes, a piano, drums, social airs, an *aladura* or beachside prophet, a river, a stork, a girl too distant to possess, these are what make Okara spark. . . .

Were Okara not an undisputed artist, he could easily fall among the "pioneer" and "pilot" poets . . . The tall palm trees, the jungle drums, the innocent virgins, the mystic rhythms, the dark flesh, and the old wish not to lose face in a double sense within the alien crows and clash of so many colours washing in from outside are all well-worn wares of that otherwise respectable house. But in the gifted hands of Okara they become articles of original style and lasting worth.

John Pepper Clark. *Transition.* No. 18, 1965, p. 25

In 1964 the poet G. Okara, who is very well-known in Africa, published the novel *The Voice*, in which he portrayed the drama of a man, whose morals and principles contradict the morals of certain politicians. The bad characters representing the nascent bourgeoisie, corrupt politicians and officials have already been painted by Achebe and Ekwensi. The hero of Okara's novel, who is a seeker of truth and justice, fights such morals and behaviour. The novel is pessimistic, the hero dying in the clash with the powers that be without having found the truth he sought.

The Voice shows the development of contradictions within Nigerian society, the interests and policy of certain strata of society which come into contradiction with the interests of other social groups. The novel does not show Okara's own stand in the matter. The hero is rather conventional and nowhere does he state his position in society. Evidently, the author expressed the sentiments of a certain recently born section of the intelligentsia. He has chosen as his subject the political life in Nigeria, which he generalised in a conventional way and even presented almost as a caricature. Although the author does not display any class sympathy the conflict in the novel brings out the widely different opinions and sentiments in Nigerian society. The social import of the novel lies in the fact that it describes the morals of various social strata.

V. Vavilov. In M. A. Korostovtsev, ed., *Essays on African Culture* (Moscow, Nauka, 1966), p. 161

[The] self-conscious language [of the "questing" hero of Gabriel Okara's *The Voice*] is the device of the narcissist, a subterfuge within which the hero can contemplate his creator's navel while remaining himself impenetrable in the barrier of contrived language. *It*, the object of our hero's search, may not exist, and the hero does not himself appear to believe in it. Certainly, there is no communication of the psychic drive which sets a man on a course of single-minded enquiry into the heart of the matter or existence; it is only an occasion for the hero's narcissistic passivity. His will to motion can hardly be calculated in terms of his effect on the community. Okolo is too set a set-piece; the catalytic effect of his quest on the external world is more expected than fulfilled. Okolo has lost himself in an animism of nothingness, the ultimate self-delusion of the narcissist.

Wole Soyinka. *AfrF*. Spring, 1966, p. 62

Anne Tibble, in *African/English Literature*, compares the theme of *The Voice* to that of Dostoevski's *The Idiot*. Okolo and Myshkin do have much in common. Both need to speak the heart's truth; both are rejected by the establishment in society; both possess qualities which could be called saintly. Gabriel Okara's character has a more limited range, for Okolo is shown only in one aspect, as truth-seeker and questioner, whereas the subtly terrifying thing about Myshkin is that he really is partially idiot as well as saint, and his character fluctuates before the reader's eyes. Okolo remains constant, with no suggestion that there may be another side to his personality.

Another comparison would be with Eman in Wole Soyinka's *The Strong Breed*. Both are men of compassion and perception who are martyred by communities who fail to understand them and who therefore fear them. But Eman is a more complex character than Okolo, for in some ways he seeks his own martyrdom and his death has implications of saviourhood in it—he offers himself in order to redeem all. In terms of Christian parallels, Eman is a Christ figure, whereas Okolo could be called a Jesus figure, the difference being one of emphasis. In the case of Okolo, the emphasis is upon his teacherhood, the fact that his "spoken words" may plant some seed of truth and desire for truth. There is nothing messianic about him, nor is there any suggestion that his death will, in itself, achieve anything. It is the survival of his words and his faith which is important. He does not seek his martyrdom as Eman does, for although Okolo is drawn back to his village, it is because he feels some sense of mission there, the need to make his "teaching words" heard among his own people, rather than any need to die.

Margaret Laurence. *Long Drums and Cannons*
(London, Macmillan, 1968), p. 196

The superior quality of Okara's work seems to lie partly in its overall intensity of mood. Here is a committed poet, utterly sincere in all he brings to the poet's task and clearly anxious to persist in the cultivation of his poetic sensibility. His fellow poets are perhaps more prolific, at times more technically adventurous; but for the most part they lack the fine richness of soul, the pervading sense of an inner life and a constant preoccupation with the basic themes of life and death, which are the dominant features of Okara's work. A withdrawn melancholy figure, Okara has something of the Celtic colour of soul, with its sensitivity and large resources of sadness, yet without the Celtic sense of humour. The lyrical "I" means the collective "we" for Okara and his private experience is felt to be one that is shared by his compatriots. He is Nigeria's best example of the poet singing in solitude yet singing for his fellow men. . . .

But it is hard to be authentically African while using the poetic voice of a Welshman, and Okara had to strike out on a more independent path. A basic problem was linguistic in nature. Despite the English language's history in Africa, despite its having been "transplanted" into African societies, poets choosing to use it face a situation in which the poetic diction and imagery provided for the home tradition are at odds with the features of their own inner landscapes which have been shaped by an entirely different culture and environment. One way of bridging this gap, which means in effect the creation of a new, Africanised English idiom, is to use a device which, for want of a more accurate term, we will call transliteration. Okara decided that he would write his verse in his native Ijaw and then translate it literally into English, the second version being considered the primary work of art. . . .

[The basic aspects of Ijaw thinking] emerge by way of a device which allows the poet adequately to render authentic indigenous experience, "to put into the whirlpool of literature the African point of view, to put across how the African thinks." Through transliteration Okara has created a new idiom and found his own voice.

Adrian A. Roscoe. Mother Is Gold (Cambridge,
Cambridge University Press, 1971), pp. 28–29, 31

The most concerted attempt to preserve the mother tongue through translation is Gabriel Okara's attempt in *The Voice* to transfer Ijaw syntax and lexical rules into English. The closeness with which Okara does so can be determined by comparison with Ijaw sources, and, as one would expect, he is unable to remain consistent in his method. But the failure does not lie in this inconsistency, which would not wholly invalidate the method, or even simply in "an annoying literary squint" [Sunday O. Anozie], but in a fundamental misconception about the nature of language—that anything as complex as total meaning can be conveyed by preservation of very few of its parts. Syntax alone is not the vehicle of meaning, nor are a language's rules of collocation.

It has been remarked [by G. D. Killam] that Okara is a much better poet than novelist and that *The Voice* is most successful in short lyrical passages. Without wishing to beg the question of the incompatability of "the language of poetry" and "the language of prose," I think it quite possible that the fundamental weaknesses of meaning in *The Voice* are less apparent when subject to the firmer organization and control demanded by a verse-form. Indeed, there is a sense in which they are more acceptable, or at least accepted, there. However, the importance of Okara's work depends not on his success or failure but in the clearly conveyed realization that the artistic liberty of the African writer in English lies in the integration of expression and experience. By revealing one route to that end to be a cul-de-sac, *The Voice* remains a positive force in the development of the West African novel in English.

Peter Young. In Edgar Wright, ed., *The Critical Evaluation of African Literature* (London, Heinemann, 1973), p. 42

One of the oldest of the contemporary writers is Gabriel Okara. He was born in 1921 and so far as chronology is concerned he belongs to the generation of dedicated versifiers. But his mind is closer to the contemporary ethos. Nevertheless, he is the link between the two generations of poets, for some of his dicta sound surprisingly like Negritude. . . .

Yet his first poems do show an individual concern, although the action (and it is very correct to speak of action in an Okara poem, since the situation is intensely dramatized) tends to be converted into weak posturings. At the center of every poem is a protagonist, and the poem charts the history of his attitudes by subtly juxtaposing dissimilar images that help to emphasize his quandary. . . .

Okara achieved success not only by using symbols to illustrate certain attitudes, but by reorganizing the trite language of the public poem. "Piano and Drums" introduces technical terms at appropriate points to emphasize the cerebral nature of western culture, and it is a measure of stylistic exactitude that the harsh images associated with the piano culminate in the word "counterpoint" which later on the poet, almost naïvely, associates with "daggerpoint." Okara also reorganizes language by rendering it lyrical, and it is the ease of a songster that makes him such a satisfying poet. He adopts the techniques of songwriting by repeating whole phrases, each time with a slightly different emphasis, by beginning with dependent clauses, and by making the poem grow into a long main statement which gathers momentum as it develops.

O. R. Dathorne. *The Black Mind* (Minneapolis, University of Minnesota Press, 1974), pp. 263–65

OKIGBO, CHRISTOPHER (1932–1967)

NIGERIA

Okigbo is chiefly a poet for the ear and not for the eye. We cannot see much of his poetry. The images change quickly and he hardly ever gives us time to build up a consistent and lasting vision in our mind's eye. But we can *hear* his verse, it fills our mind like a half forgotten tune returning to memory. Everything he touches vibrates and swings and we are compelled to read on and to follow the tune of his chant, hardly worried about the fact that we understand little of what he has to say. The obscurity of Okigbo's poetry is of course deliberate. . . .

Yet, unlike some modern poets, Okigbo is not simply enjoying a private joke. One feels, on the contrary, that the mysterious names help him to throw a veil over the immediate meaning of the poem, that he is carefully creating a kind of code which he never wants us to solve completely. Because any literal allusions would detract from the song and the music, would make us pause in the middle to reflect, and this is exactly what the poet wants to avoid. He wants to carry us away on his chant—or rather on his *incantation*. For incantation is, I think, the best word one can find for Okigbo's poetry. The moment you start to read you feel you have intruded into the sacred enclosure of a secret cult. You have no right to be there, but you are too fascinated to leave. The chanting can be understood by the initiates alone, but you are receptive to its beauty. You cannot decode the meaning, but you feel it affects you physically, the incantation causes a rush of ill defined but exalted feelings in your mind. . . .

To say that in reading Okigbo's poems we are terribly conscious of the man's intellect at work does not mean at all that the poem is without feeling. Its effect on the reader is in fact *physical*, and though the language is ritualistic the effect is orgastic.

Ulli Beier. *BO*. No. 12, 1963, pp. 46–47

[Okigbo] himself says his one theme has been a combination of the processes of creation and self-purification. . . .

[The poems in *Heavensgate*] are each carefully scored out like a musical piece. Some sections in fact require playing to the flute, although to what tune the poet, like Senghor with his kora, does not say. Together, they confirm to my mind the possession by the poet of a rare gift of literary imagination. This operates by a process I will not call predatory as that employed by vampires and parasites. Rather it seizes upon what attracts it and distils therefrom, without destroying the original, a fresh artifact.

A later work, "Silences," slight as it is, presents a remarkable mosaic of world literature, music and painting. It is a stimulating game detecting within it the originals and borrowed bits. It becomes even more exciting since this is a game the poet delights playing against himself.

John Pepper Clark. Transition. No. 18, 1965, p. 25

Okigbo takes pride in acknowledging his indebtedness to the literature of Europe. The first of his "Four Canzones" he himself identifies with Virgil's First Eclogue, for example. The interesting fact is that, as it is, this particular "canzone" loses nothing as a Nigerian poem for deriving from Virgil. It is evident, of course, that the inclination to adapt and translate from other poets is something Okigbo "copied" from Ezra Pound. Yet, we can say in this case that the Virgilian experience—the experience of that eclogue of exile—is not alien to the Nigerian environment. . . .

The poetry of Okigbo is almost the poetry of echoes. . . .

In the face of [the] very obvious echoes from nontraditional poetry, what can we say of Okigbo's poetry? The first point is that Okigbo takes pride in this indebtedness. For him this is not "plagiarism," not even parasitism. When, earlier, I referred to Okigbo's "literary" imagination, I was trying, actually to find the terms of praise or censure appropriate to Okigbo's sense of his poetry. Okigbo's poetry is a poetry of the responses to pattern and organization. His poetry is also the poetry of an African, a native. Its significance derives from these two elements. On the one hand, a very strong traditional feeling (which we will come to presently), a feeling for the subject of Africa; on the other, an "individual" poet who loves to write, not as an African, but as a "prodigal"—a poet who wants to feel that his poetry belongs to the literature of the "literate generation."

M. J. C. Echeruo. NigM. June, 1966, pp. 151–53

The "difficulty" of Okigbo is such as to demand a real familiarity with his poetry, which handles a common body of symbols and turns continually upon a central pre-occupation. It is not such as to prevent his being the outstanding poet of English-speaking Africa. The familiarity he demands is no greater than that required by Eliot, by the later Yeats, by Rilke or Valéry; required, in fact, by any modern poet whose poetry rises above the occasional or the descriptive and seeks to record a whole cycle of spiritual and historical exploration.

Just how much does he owe to Eliot as a precursor in this type of poetic quest for reality? More, I believe, than is usually owed by a poet of his original talent to a single mentor. But then Eliot himself found it necessary to quote and echo other poets to an extent unprecedented in European literature. What Okigbo learnt from Eliot, and thus brought into the tradition of African poetry in English, was the art of handling complex ideas in simple language, by the constant re-arrangement of a selected group of words and symbols. Okigbo rehandles such words as laughter, dream, light, presence, voice, blood, exactly as Eliot teases out all the possible meanings of beginning, middle and end in "East Coker." Both poets use fragments of Catholic liturgy mixed with others from the classical world, paganism and magic; but where Eliot depends upon his reading of [Sir James] Frazer and Jessie Weston, Okigbo is able to draw upon a living knowledge of his forest village. It is above all the constant presence of this landscape which makes it such nonsense to dismiss Okigbo as "non-African." Obscurity itself has, in any case, a most respectable African ancestry in the poetry of oracle priests and diviners, whose concern lies close to Okigbo's own. Finally, nothing could be less like Eliot's dry world-weary tone than the lyrical, passionate voice of Okigbo with his rich, darting imagery and abundant youth. His apprenticeship was long, but the completion of his visionary sequence from *Heavensgate* to "Distances" in only three years (1961–64) is an achievement that African poetry will not easily surpass. [1969]

Gerald Moore. The Chosen Tongue (New York, Harper & Row, 1970), pp. 175–76

Okigbo's last poems, written from December 1965 to January 1966, are entitled "Path of Thunder." They were hailed as "poems prophesying war" but they are more than this; they are poems announcing Okigbo's involvement in the war as well, and all through them the ravages of war and death are described. It is clear from them which side Okigbo had chosen to support, but these are anything but partisan poems. They are an attempt to link all the earlier poems to the events in Nigeria in 1965–66. In all the poems that precede these it is sometimes hard to tell where they are set; they are certainly set in the open, in jungles or holy forests, but the symbols are universal, with the exception of some small obscure details that must be Nigerian. But "Path of Thunder" is different. The concern is Nigerian; the voice is definitely Okigbo's (these are the only poems in which he used his own name) and they are about politics and war. . . .

The cycle of poems heads towards an untimely end. Okigbo died in battle in 1967, near Nsukka. It seems clear that he was trying to control his material, all the factors that influenced his loyalties, trying to make these images fit the larger structure of his imagined poem, *Labyrinths*. And I think all of it does fit, for he conceived the poem so that it would embody all experience, and however unpoetic war is, he managed to combine this as well.

> Paul Theroux. In Bruce King, ed., *Introduction to Nigerian Literature* (London, Evans Brothers, 1971), pp. 135–36

By its theme and craft "Path of Thunder" differs from the poetry written by Christopher Okigbo up to and including the first half of December 1965. This is so because in it Okigbo makes, for the first time ever, a forthright and direct political statement which itself undisguisedly defines the poet's own revolutionary option. But genetically speaking, "Path of Thunder" cannot be separated from the earlier poetry written by Okigbo, since it directly springs from the same parent stock or source of inspiration. Its very title, "Path of Thunder," is sufficiently indicative of the point from which it has taken its off-shoot and consequently branched off into what, given life, could have become a new tree. . . .

[It has been implied] that in Okigbo's poetic sensibility there seemed to exist a genetic struggle between a romantic pursuit of art for its own sake and a constantly intrusive awareness of the social relevance of art—its function, that is, as a means of embodying significant social comments. This tendency may then explain why in the Chorus [of "Lament of the Silent Sisters"] part of the poet's central theme—the atmosphere of political and social insecurity in the country, and indeed all over Africa—should be expressed within, and as though secondary to, an overriding artistic imperative.

Another possible, and much more likely, explanation is that Okigbo in 1962 was afraid of the possible consequences of committing to his poetry statements that would have direct political connotations in the Nigerian scene. This may mean also that he had not at that time fully resolved within himself the problem of whether art should be separated from politics or a poet be free from ideological commitments. At that time, too, the conclusion he came to with himself was obviously

"Yes": refuge for the creative writer should be sought only in art and silence.

Sunday O. Anozie. *Christopher Okigbo: Creative Rhetoric* (London, Evans Brothers, 1972), pp. 174–75

[Okigbo] brought into his poetry all the heirlooms of his multiple heritage; he ranged with ease through Rome and Greece and Babylon, through the rites of Judaism and Catholicism, through European and Bengali literatures, through modern music and painting. But at least one perceptive Nigerian critic has argued that Okigbo's true voice only came to him in his last sequence of poems, "Path of Thunder," when he had finally and decisively opted for an African inspiration. This opinion may be contested, though I think it has substantial merit. The trouble is that Okigbo is such a bewitching poet, able to cast such a powerful spell that, whatever he cares to say or sing, we stand breathless at the sheer beauty and grace of his sound and imagery. Yet there is that undeniable fire in his last poems which was something new. It was as though the goddess he sought in his poetic journey through so many alien landscapes, and ultimately found at home, had given him this new thunder. Unfortunately, when he was killed in 1967 he left us only that little, tantalizing hint of the new self he had found. But perhaps he will be reincarnated in other poets and sing for us again like his sunbird whose imperishable song survived the ravages of the eagles. [1973]

Chinua Achebe. *Morning Yet on Creation Day* (Garden City, N.Y., Doubleday, 1975), pp. 44–45

All types of influences are to be found in Okigbo's verse. . . . Such imitation does not mean that Okigbo is at worst a derivative poet or at best a welder of two poetic traditions. He is much more complex than this and part of his success derives from his distinctive and private voice.

It is a voice that is not always clear; a hotchpotch of trivia makes it at times inarticulate—a solemn reference to yam tubers is based on a lewd Ibo song about the testicles of a ram—and titles of books like [Camara's] *The Gaze of the King* or of films like *Island in the Sun* are numerous in his poetry. Then there are snatches of the Bible as well as a poker-faced pidgin version of Little Bo Peep meant to look as "classical" as possible: *"etru bo pi alo a she e anando we aquandem . . ./ebili malo, ebili com com, ebili te que liquandem."* Words and allusions to a private mythological world abound—allusions to Enki, to someone named Flannagan who "preached the Pope's message," to Yunice "at the passageway." All this can be terribly misleading and can be stumbling blocks not only for eager non-African postgraduates bent on finding the "Africanness" of the work, but even for Nigerian Ibo speakers like Okigbo himself. . . .

Okigbo has himself helped to obscure the real issues relevant to an appreciation of his poetry by asserting that he does not strive toward meaning in his poetry, in the acceptable sense of the word. He has described himself to me as a "composer of sounds." . . .

Yet there is meaning in Okigbo's poetry even though it might be obscured by his anxious desire to pun or to exploit the more obvious devices of language for its tonal rather than its semantic effects. From this viewpoint "Distances" is the most pretentious and least successful of his poems. Besides the emblematic writing (which not only is out of place here but also does not succeed) there is a tendency to write nonsense; only sometimes is this redeemed by lines of beauty and meaning.

O. R. Dathorne. *The Black Mind* (Minneapolis,
University of Minnesota Press, 1974),
pp. 272–73, 276–77

Christopher Okigbo, the Nigerian poet killed in the 1967 civil war, was perhaps the most eclectic African poet of our time who wrote in English. A graduate of the University of Ibadan, he was part of the new community of African writers who did not study abroad and therefore escaped, to a large extent, the alienation and frustration of the earlier generation. Educated entirely in Africa, even though within the rigid framework of the colonial pattern, he was exposed to the best in colonial education in English and American letters. Thus the literary influences on him were varied and numerous. A few of these new writers, as illustrated earlier, also took their literary direction from the oral traditions which, given the half-hearted cultural intentions of the British, still had great influence on some of them. The important thing is that the writers were free to choose their models. . . .

The words that sum up Okigbo's poetry are ordeal, agony, and cleansing. His poetic growth came through a unified consciousness and awareness of other cultures. External sounds and internal music coalesce into bursts of poetic brilliance. He was in essence a restless, tormented soul whose poetry assumed high-pitched, prophetic resonance and clarity. In his work he combines the choral voice of Greek classical verse, the litanic cadence of the mass, and the ritualistic pattern of traditional poetry.

Kofi Awoonor. *The Breast of the Earth* (Garden
City, N.Y., Doubleday, 1975), pp. 217–18

OYONO, FERDINAND (1929–   )

CAMEROON

"Cameroon has been a country over which a curtain of phantasmagoria was drawn. The Cameroonian writer therefore must try to lift this curtain before he does anything else," asserted Ferdinand Oyono during a recent debate on black literature. He has applied himself to this effort of demythologizing, this "restoration of the truth," in his two novels: *The Life of a Houseboy* and *The Old Negro and the Medal*. . . .

Toundi the adolescent [houseboy] and Meka the old Negro initially share the same illusions about their white masters. . . . We witness the slow movement toward self-awareness on the part of two Africans facing the colonial situation. Before their bitter experiences, neither Meka nor Toundi had grasped the true, private nature of the whites. They saw the whites through a curtain of prohibitions and taboos, and they spoke with a mixture of admiration and fear about the whites' power, about their ability to shape men and objects according to their needs. Then one fine day the commanding officer asks Toundi [in *The Life of a Houseboy*] to bring him a bottle in the bathroom. The leader of the whites is "naked in his shower." And he is not even circumcised! "I feel that the commanding officer no longer frightens me," notes the houseboy. This is the first crack in the wall of white respectability. It widens decisively when Toundi discovers with amazement that his master's wife has been shamelessly sleeping with another white man in the neighborhood. There is a lot of naïveté in the adolescent's gradual discovery of the adultery of the white woman, whom he had previously seen as practically a goddess of virtue. This episode gives rise to pages full of humor and truculent descriptions that, however, avoid turning into caricature.

This same comic spirit, supported by an intense realism, is again present in *The Old Negro and the Medal*. Oyono casts harsh, ruthless light on the contradictions between the whites' sugary words and their behavior. . . .

At no time does either of these novels take on the tone of an indictment. Oyono feels no compulsion to wink at the reader in order to show him the path to take through the long commentaries. He lets the facts speak for themselves and direct the dramatic movement of the narrative. The facts themselves condemn a system in which noble sentiments exist only on the surface.

David Diop. *PA*. Dec., 1956, pp. 125–26†

In Ferdinand Oyono's *The Old Negro and the Medal*, the old Negro Meka who has lost two sons in the war and who has given his lands to the Catholic Mission is to be presented with a medal by the High Commissioner on a ceremonial visit. . . .

Meka's place between the two worlds is not an assumption of the novelist's. It is Meka's own self-dramatization as he stands there between the platform of the whites and the African crowd behind him. At the moment when he experiences his isolation, Meka is not a tragic but a comic figure. His attempts to draw strength from the thought of his ancestors looking on, and from prayer to the Christian God, are comic because of the incongruities. His shoes are hurting and he needs to relieve his bladder. Oyono's vision is a comic vision of a world where everything is taken so seriously. This does not exclude indignation— indignation at the thoughtlessness, even barbarity, of the whites in leaving an old man to wait so long under the sun, indignation at the grievousness of Meka's sacrifices. . . .

The Europeans are comic because of the shameless insincerity of their gesture of friendship, and Meka is comic because he accepts it until events have taught him better. He has made himself a fool and suffered by trying to fit himself to their ways. But he has also made the whole white administration appear fools by making his own speech at the reception and inviting the High Commissioner to dinner at his village. At the end of the novel when Meka, sadder and wiser, is back at his house with all the friends and relatives who have descended on him to celebrate and share in the great honour bestowed upon him, we have the final joke. One of the guests suggests the way Meka should have shown his contempt for their medal. He should have appeared at the ceremony wearing only a traditional *bila*, or brief slip. Then the High Commissioner would have had to bend down and pin the medal onto the slip. Oyono's reaction, like the reaction of his characters, is laughter, an ancient classical laughter at the lords of the earth caught in undignified postures and the humble trying to ape the lords.

John Reed. MakJ. No. 7, 1963, pp. 1, 7–8

Ferdinand Oyono's novels celebrate the disillusionment of the African with the white man's world. His heroes set out in a state of innocent enthusiasm; then comes the moment of truth, opening the door into a new world of bitterness or corrosive resignation. Despite the brilliance of his comic writing, this fatal *consequence* gives a kind of tragic intensity to his plots as a whole, particularly in *The Life of a Houseboy*, his first novel. He is probably the greatest master of construction among African novelists now writing. . . .

His latest novel [*The Road to Europe*] is more ambitious [than his first two works], for it depicts a situation which is in itself diffuse and hard to grasp, the situation of the young man educated beyond his fellows, but still not sufficiently so to assure him a career. Barnabas, the hero of *The Road to Europe*, has been expelled from a seminary for a supposed homosexual attachment. In his native town he finds himself at once despised and exploited; despised as a layabout who thinks himself "too good" for ordinary work; exploited as being able to write French and keep accounts. He writes to the colonial authorities for permission to study in France, and the action of the novel covers the year or so during which he waits in vain for a reply. . . .

At last Barnabas decides to act. He travels to the capital and confronts the authorities who have kept him for so long in the doldrums of frustration and idleness. But in vain. The road to Europe is still closed and the bureaucratic clown whom he confronts in the vast halls of officialdom gives him every kind of advice except to persevere in his ambition. The realist Oyono achieves a brilliant flight of fantastic comedy when Barnabas and his travelling-companion, Bendjanga-Boy, stand stupefied before the huge silent barracks of the administration buildings.

Gerald Moore. PA (English ed.). 18, 2, 1963,
pp. 61, 70–72

All the old values [Oyono] depicts still survive in spite of the new [postcolonial] era. The Houseboy always exists, even if the relations between boss and servant are governed by the social laws now in force in Africa as in Europe. The Old Negro is on the road to extinction, for he cannot be "recycled" into another sector. Nevertheless, he is a respected electoral agent. This fossillike character, although quite likable, no longer has his place in today's Africa. He suffers from being a product of colonialism; herein lies his anachronistic role. The "intellectual" [in *The Road to Europe*] is still a malignant presence, and the myth of a gracious Europe remains. The universities of Africa are not absolutely without Africans, but one might wish that they were better attended by the holders of baccalauréat [secondary school] degrees, who still prefer to live as expatriates, as in the time of Aki Barnabas. . . .

Ferdinand Oyono's originality lies not so much in having depicted the morals of an historical moment in Africa, before 1958, but in having described a situation in which mutual incomprehension is more obvious, more often operative, than unilateral rebellion.

Roger Mercier and M. and S. Battestini. Ferdinand
Oyono (Paris, Fernand Nathan, 1964), pp. 57–58†

The economy seen in Oyono's use and presentation of material is also evident in his language. Events and actions are described through the eyes of the characters; so, for much of [*The Old Negro and the Medal*], as with Toundi's diary [in *The Life of a Houseboy*], there is a conscious effort to avoid "literary" French and to use language common to everyone. The language is, therefore, simple and direct. Oyono has also reduced the dialogue and description to a minimum. Each word is chosen to give maximum effect; not only to create a precise image but to evoke associations which suggest unexpressed thoughts and details. . . .

While, in [*The Life of a Houseboy*], Oyono tries deliberately to present stereotypes to heighten the comic effect, in *The Old Negro and the Medal*, the lack of physical detail is due more to the characters' long familiarity with each other. . . . This lack of physical description is compensated by the detailed analysis of the characters' thoughts and background. In this way Oyono introduces the reader into the characters' world, not as an observer but as a participant. . . .

There is little that either [the Europeans or the Africans] can be proud of in this society. Both are corrupted and sterile. Both live behind façades which hide the insufficiency of their lives. The social criticism is cruel but Oyono shows the Africans' growing understanding of the fact that they can mock Europeans, can reject them and their social order. As yet there is no sign of a positive alternative but at least the Africans can reassert their dignity through laughter.

> A. C. Brench. *The Novelists' Inheritance in French Africa* (London, Oxford University Press, 1967),
> pp. 59–60, 63

Oyono's education meant more struggle, more isolation, more frustration than Beti's. And this has, without a doubt, contributed to the greater sadness of Oyono's satire. His irony is harsher, his laughter more nervous than Beti's. His criticism is, however, more with reference to circumstances of the colonial situation than against the system as a whole. He deals with individual personalities within the colonial setup— the new administrator, the Catholic priest, the prison director, the schoolmaster's wife—unveiling their shortcomings and their cruelty, more than he questions the colonial set-up as a whole. Neither does he, like Beti, ever refer to the implicit complicity between those who say they came to Africa "to save heathens' souls" and those whose proclaimed motive was "to civilize savages."

His satire can be said to be more destructive, more demoralizing. It does not leave the mind with much hope of a better understanding or amelioration of human relationships. At the end of Toundi's diary [in *The Life of a Houseboy*] there is no comment either by Toundi himself

or by the . . . [diary's] supposed translator. The debate is closed defin-
itively; indeed, there has not been much of a debate throughout the
novel. The same thing would be said of Oyono's *The Old Negro and the
Medal*, but not of Mongo Beti's novels.

Edris Makward. Introduction to Ferdinand Oyono,
Boy! (New York, Macmillan, 1970), pp. xv–xvi

P'BITEK, OKOT (1931-   )

UGANDA

Song of Lawino is transposed from p'Bitek's own original version in Acoli: the author accepts the term "translated," but even though in re-creating the poem in English he must, as he deprecatingly admits, have "clipped a bit of the eagle's wings and rendered the sharp edge of the warrior's sword rusty and blunt, and has also murdered rhythm and rhyme," nevertheless I think "transposed" is a juster description, since he has given us a work which stands in its own right in its new medium; we might even for once guardedly accept from the publisher's blurb the claim that the author has "almost incidentally evolved a new African form of English literature." This new "form" is a collection of thirteen related songs of some one to five hundred short, irregular lines, grouped in compact paragraphs, capturing a sinewy, fluent rhythm, with the compactness emphasized by the catching up of key words, and the tell-ing repetition of certain lines and ideas (difficult to illustrate briefly), like an unpredictable refrain. . . .

Lawino lovingly, defiantly, intimately celebrates the way of life and the way of being in her village, in order to win back her husband [Ocol], who has become brashly alienated from his own background and in all matters emulates the ways of the foreigner, above all in marrying a second, sophisticated wife. Each song concerns a different aspect of life: in the third the relationship between men and women is epitomized in the dance. . . . In each song Lawino pinpoints with sharply humorous accuracy the incongruity of the European conventions, as-sumptions and attitudes being adopted in an Acoli village, which lives according to a meaningful pattern of its own, rooted in reality. . . .

David Cook. *JCL*. Dec., 1967, pp. 12–13

I don't know what [the critic] Ali Mazrui finds in *Song of Lawino* to call it an important event. *Song of Lawino*, all considered, is an event but not the East African event. A popular event, yes. A great event? Yes. Since there is literary drought. Translation: the meaning is lost—

the meaning of deep Acoli proverbs are made very, very light by their rendition into English *word for word*, rather than *sense for sense*, or *proverb for proverb.* . . .

Too much space and energy (the little there is in this light literature) is taken up with pointing out the foibles in the Western ways of life—these foibles that are easily seen by the eyes of the simple, *unedu*, uneducated Lawino. . . .

The trouble with his method is that his discussion is conducted in a low key: it is the simple that he deals with (the girl is limited both in vocabulary and knowledge of complex things,) and he leaves the discussion of basic Christianity, basic Acoli religion (and basic many other complex things) aside—we are treated to "tribes" of "dungs" on latrine walls (Ministry of Works, please check), "red" lips—things to be seen with the eyes, things to be heard with the ears, or felt with the skin—but little to be felt with the intellect. (Lawino had lost out on intellectual development long ago.) So, Okot also suffers from the Negritudist impediment of rhythm above sense.

I had expected an epic; I got a ballad.

Taban lo Liyong. The Last Word (Nairobi, East
African Publishing House, 1969), pp. 140–42

A few critics have reacted against what they see as [Lawino's] jealousy-motivated defence of every aspect of tradition [in *Song of Lawino*]. They thus turn the fundamental opposition between two value-systems into a mere personal quarrel between Lawino and her husband. We must in fact see the class basis of her attack: Lawino is the voice of the peasantry and her ridicule and scorn is aimed at the class basis of Ocol's behaviour. The poem is an incisive critique of bourgeois mannerisms and colonial education and values. For it is Ocol's education, with the values it inculcates in him, that drives him away from the community.

With its critical realism the poem qualifies as a major contribution to African literature. Like [Frantz] Fanon on the subject of the pitfalls of national consciousness in *The Wretched of the Earth*, Lawino is asking Ocol to consciously negate and repudiate the social calling that the colonial legacy has bequeathed to the African intelligentsia. The significance of *Song of Lawino* in East Africa's literary consciousness lies not only in this ruthless exposure of the hollowness and lack of originality of a colonial middle class but also in its form. The author has borrowed from the song in the oral tradition. The African song gets its effect from an accumulation of details, statements and imagery, and in the variation of the tone and attitude of the poet-reciter to the object of praise. Lawino employs all these tactics in her disparise of Ocol.

Song of Lawino is the one poem that has mapped out new areas and new directions in East African poetry. It belongs to the soil. It is authentically East African in its tone and in its appeal. This can be seen in its reception: it is read everywhere, arousing heated debates. Some critics have even attempted a psychoanalysis of the creator of Lawino. It is the first time that a book of modern poetry has received such popular widespread acclaim. The effect on the young poets has been no less stunning, though a trifle dangerous. Many want to write like Okot p'Bitek. Unfortunately some have been taken in by its deceptive simplicity. [Sept., 1969]

Ngugi wa Thiong'o. Homecoming (New York,
Lawrence Hill, 1973), p. 75

Song of Ocol, the sequel and reply to *Song of Lawino* by the same author, is a book which has been written in the minds of many people from bus passengers to University teachers, from stalwarts of traditional African cultural values to cultural iconoclasts and schizophrenics.

This short, characteristically readable poem is a surprise not only because it has been written by p'Bitek, but also because of the way he has written it. It is a negative reply, sometimes with Socratic irony, sometimes with nostalgic sham mockery, and when the author relieves Ocol of his mock-heroic, mock-epic tone and stance, we see self-questioning, uncertainty, and even insecurity and lack of conviction.

Thematically and poetically, *Song of Ocol* is weaker than *Song of Lawino*. The artistic corollary follows that Ocol's stature is less than that of Lawino with her fire of attack, vigour of challenge, conviction of assertion and freshness of genuine self-praise abundantly lacking in Ocol. At some point one shudders at the poetic truth in Lawino's nasty remark about the effect of books on Ocol's manhood. . . .

Where Lawino convincingly and vigorously asserts the positive value of her Acoli ways, Ocol just dismisses them to defend his wounded ego without a realistically, logically or poetically sustained opposing argument. To maintain the false identity which has been imposed on him, he pathetically succumbs to self-alienation from the realities of his past and kicks against the cultural gravitation of his roots in vain. . . .

Song of Ocol, in its expansive sweep from Masailand to Ancient Mali, from the Kingdom of the Bakongo to Sudan, aspires to the status of an epic, but *Song of Lawino* in its positively intensive assertiveness remains a more accomplished work. Ocol maintains his mock-heroic stance only falteringly and in the end the author deposes him to subject the cultural foundations and socio-political values of his fellow modern men to devastating inquiry. It is evident that both poetically and thematically, p'Bitek identifies with Lawino. He denies Ocol the articu-

lation to champion his adopted values and makes him beg Lawino's
question, which detracts from the artistic finish of the poem.

R. C. Ntiru. *Mawazo*. June, 1970, pp. 60–62

As I see it, p'Bitek's power as a poet is of the kind that perpetually
raises his work above the particular emotions and experiences—necessarily very tangled in any poet, and in him probably most severely
tangled—from which it sprang. This is to be a really good poet. I don't
believe anyone could seriously think about modern Africa without trying
to weigh the meaning of *Song of Lawino* and *Song of a Prisoner*. I
believe *Song of Lawino* has an importance far beyond the boundaries of
Uganda; it is, when generalized, a poem about the situation in which we
all find ourselves, being dragged away from all our roots at an ever-
quickening rate. I believe, as I have said, that beyond the note of alarm
and anguish that it strikes as to the condition of some newly independent African countries, *Song of a Prisoner* is full of the despair and
anger, fiercely expressed, of anyone anywhere who is politically in
chains.

But having said all this, one is left with a last—and perhaps, in the
end, even more important—thing to say. And that is that Okot p'Bitek
is a marvellous poet. I wish I could read him in his own language. But in
English he has found a tone, a pattern of verse, a rhythm, that are highly
original and inventive. It would not be easy to mistake p'Bitek, in English, for anyone else. Though—and perhaps my friend Taban lo Liyong
will note this—his matter is never light, his manner often is, in a sense
that any writer must envy. I count him among the few masters I have
read of literary mischievousness. He can modulate from one mood to
another with a skill that, though startling in its effect, rarely draws
attention to itself. He is a master of writing for the human voice—and
sometimes, I suspect, for the animal or insect voice, too. Much in his
style might be made the basis of an argument for drumming, as a musical accomplishment for a poet, in much the way that one might have
said experience of the lute was a formative influence on Elizabethan
verse. And finally, Okot p'Bitek, as man and poet, is one of those
valuable souls who add manifestly to the gaiety of the nations, at the
same time that much of what he expresses is closely concerned with
their agony.

Edward Blishen. Introduction to Okot p'Bitek. *Song
of a Prisoner* (New York, Third Press, 1971),
pp. 39–40

I think perhaps the main weakness in *Song of a Prisoner*, if we compare
it to *Song of Lawino*, is the lack of individual characteristics in the

prisoner and the lack of clarification of the situation. Lawino's success springs from the fact that she is both a credible individual and a spokesman of betrayed Africa. Her individuality springs from p'Bitek's exploitation of the dramatic possibilities of the Lawino-Ocol-Clementine eternal triangle. The prisoner has individual characteristics and the reader can work out a particular situation, if he is prepared to expend the effort. But p'Bitek makes this very difficult. From a casual reading the prisoner appears to be a composite of prisoners: vagrant, murderer, dismissed bodyguard, and even disgraced minister.

Part of the explanation for this is doubtless the fact that p'Bitek wished to comment on as many areas of life as he could. But a more charitable and dramatically credible explanation is that the prisoner is suffering from hallucinations. At least once during the song the prisoner is actually tortured. Throughout the song he is suffering the ill effects of torture. His reactions obviously contain a degree of lucidity, varying from rage at his tormentors to a universalisation of his suffering, or dreams of triumphant release or peaceful escape. . . .

The prisoner is a villager in the town, whose traditional accomplishments qualify him only as bodyguard or murderer. As the leader's bodyguard he has seen the paraphernalia of wealth that the politicians enjoy, and he resents his exclusion from it. He has been denied a place "in the lift to progress," but, more fundamentally, modern Africa denies him the opportunity of expressing his own manhood. Though he is much further removed from his Acoli tradition than Lawino, the prisoner, like Lawino, is bewildered by modern African politicians who have no respect for the things which he has learnt to respect.

G. A. Heron. *EAJ.* Aug., 1971, pp. 5–6

In his preface to *The Horn of My Love*, a collection of Acoli traditional songs, Okot p'Bitek argues the case for African poetry as poetry, as an art to be enjoyed, rather than as ethnographic material to be eviscerated. The latter approach has too often predominated, even among those scholars who have actually troubled to make collections. This book, with Ulli Beier's valuable anthologies, can help to build up the stock of African poetry for enjoyment.

The Acoli (pronounced "Acholi") are a grassland people of the Uganda-Sudan borders whose songs and ceremonial dances are still remarkably alive. Not preserved, with all that this word implies of mustiness and artificiality, but continually changing; continually acquiring new words, new tunes, and in the case of the dances, new steps or instruments. Okot p'Bitek himself describes the many changes of style and title undergone by the Acoli *Orak* (Love Dance) over the past seventy years. Dances do not change in this way unless they are still in the mainstream of the people's cultural experience. . . .

[This] is a book of poetry to be handled and enjoyed, rather than a ponderous headstone placed on the living body of a popular art. It can be read with equal enjoyment, in these facing texts, by Acolis relishing the felicities of the original languages and by English readers relishing the muscularity of Okot p'Bitek's translations. Those familiar with his own poetry, especially *Song of Lawino*, will recognize here the indigenous poetic tradition in which that fine work is embedded. The bitterness of Lawino's sense of betrayal is not a personal but a cultural bitterness. And it takes on additional depth and meaning for those who understand, from these songs, why a husband who cannot show his body in the dance arena is an insult to his whole clan, not just to his deserted wife.

Gerald Moore. TLS. Feb. 21, 1975, p. 204

PETERS, LENRIE (1932–   )

GAMBIA

Lenrie Peters was born in Bathurst, Gambia, of parents who came from Sierra Leone. Educated at Trinity College, Cambridge, and University College Hospital, London, he is a poet-physician, as was the American William Carlos Williams. Peters's knowledge of medicine, like Williams's, enters his work by indirection—through empathy. But Peters's bias for opera and lieder is evident in the rhythms of his apparently "free" verse.

Peters is good at vignettes, like head- or tailpieces in a book, which shade off gradually into the background. . . . Despite certain technical uncertainties, *Poems*, by Lenrie Peters, is a unique first volume. Its author is one who will bear watching.

Melvin B. Tolson. AfrF. Winter, 1966, pp. 122–23

From Lenrie Peters, a Gambian doctor, comes one of the real disasters in African fiction brought to print by Heinemann in the last two years [*The Second Round*]. In the present scramble for African titles, it is the kind of disaster which is bound to be repeated until a well-developed cynicism by importuned readers succeeds in stemming all this chaff.

The plot of the novel—if we might call it that—is a trite one. A Sierra Leonean doctor who has been training in Britain on a government scholarship returns to Freetown already slightly changed by his sojourn in the West, truly the "man of two cultures" rendered shop-soiled by African fiction. In his fictional progress through the novel, Dr. Kawa is surrounded by a gallery of afflicted zany characters who would dance with the best cats on a hot tin roof. An important man driven out of his mind by a nymphomaniac wife, a lover dying from cancer, a raped girl who doesn't know what to feel after this brutal violation because "I have not been raped before!"—all make their ghastly melodramatic appearances before the sorely tried Dr. Kawa, perhaps already fatally softened by Western training, takes flight up-country. One wishes him well, though naturally one worries about how the doctor will make out.

I am even more worried about Dr. Lenrie Peters' future as a novelist.

Lewis Nkosi. *AfricaR.* Dec., 1966, p. 8

Satellites establishes Lenrie Peters as a major African poet writing in English. He had previously published twenty-one of these poems with Mbari [*Poems*]; this volume expands his range and solidifies his work. Born in Gambia, educated in Sierra Leone and at Cambridge, Peters is also a novelist, playwright, physician and surgeon. He speaks as a citizen of the world. Though his imagery and outlook are often African (Poem #10 on Freetown evokes the city more vividly than does all of Graham Greene's *The Heart of the Matter*), he rejects the slogans of propagandists, even in poems dealing with race, religion, and emergent African nationalism. His is an intensely personal voice expressing the "triumphant/irony of loneliness," where each individual is a satellite in his separate orbit. Engaged in "the cold war of the soul," "I will go alone darkly until I have done." There is considerable disillusionment with "love making without/transit of love," Christianity without Christ, politicians without integrity, doctors without dedication; but there remains hope for "harmony with nature/and strength in goodwill." Because of war, hypocrisy, conformity, "the path lies steeply forward," but the poet believes in passionate life, and "Life makes living true."

His verses have remarkable range in both language and content; subjects include sex, war, homecoming, surgery, the death of Churchill, the OAU, the Chinese bomb, parachute jumps, autumn, the passing of youth, the elusiveness of God, the nature of creativity, and the role of the artist. The style varies from elliptical obscurity to lucid lyricism and slashing satire; witty, learned, allusive but not pedantic, it is metaphysical verse made modern, a fusion of wit and passion, "circuitously direct like the heart" and kept at "the cutting chaotic edge of things."

Robert E. Morsberger. *BA.* Winter, 1969, pp. 151–52

Peters in his presentation of lyrical passion, his depiction of human emotions, is atypical, unlike any other African novelist—his use of the poetic to describe his characters' feelings and the episodes in his story [*The Second Round*] makes him a writer standing alone. Frequently his dialogue sounds British instead of African—an influence it was probably impossible to eradicate completely, since Peters lived in England for such a long time. Because of this, there are aspects of the writing which must surely confuse the African reader. . . .

Must we reject a novel such as this for being unaccountable to the current African situation? Is Lenrie Peters really being unfaithful to Africa by writing a story which may not appeal to the average African reader? Because he fails to incorporate oral literary materials or anthropological background into his writing should Peters' novel be excluded from the category "African writing" and placed, instead, with say, British fiction? In failing to deal with the usual African themes is Peters rejecting his African heritage and adopting that of the West? I fail to see how the attitudes that prompted these questions can have any true bearing on the significance of Peters' *The Second Round*. Certainly the history of literature is full of examples of writers who have been misunderstood or ignored by their own countrymen, and later rediscovered after having been appreciated by peoples from totally different cultures; for the history of art is, in many ways, a history of man ahead of his time, outside of his time, away from his time. I am not saying that Peters' novel will eventually be appreciated by the African reader. Rather, I am saying that the history of creative artists and writers is a history of exceptional men, and I rather suspect that African writers will in the future show a much more detailed concern with the individual in African society, as African society itself changes, for better or for worse, from a concern with the communal to a concern with the individual.

Peters' novel is not so much ahead of its time as his main character is a prophetic indication of things to come: a man (much like Clarence in Camara's *The Gaze of the King*) deeply alienated from life on all sides of him. In his depiction of the alienated African, Lenrie Peters has created a haunting story of one man's attempt to hide from the demands of the culture and the people around him, to ignore the basic foundations on which all society is based. It is a fine novel—and the fact that its appeal at the moment seems to be limited to a non-African audience certainly does not weaken its power.

Charles R. Larson. The Emergence of African Fiction
(Bloomington, Indiana University Press, 1972),
pp. 240–41

Much of *Satellites* is informed by a seriousness of purpose derived from a belief that poetry has a function, one made especially urgent by the compulsions of modern society, the "life with Figures/or chanting laws." Peters sees the intuitive life—upon which the growth of the individual largely depends—as increasingly assailed by "statistics, graphs and charts." In the face of an over-assertive intellect man suffers, *inter alia*, a retreat of the body's thinking. This weakening of links between emotion and intellect is a major theme of twentieth-century literature, one which Léopold Senghor exploited by giving prominence to claims regarding the unique nature of the African personality when he worked out the foundations of Negritude. To some extent the position Peters takes is in the tradition of Senghor's well-known stand except that he is mainly concerned with the dissociated sensibility as a contemporary problem. . . .

In *Satellites* the poems on broad African themes are underwritten. They are not undertaken with Peters's characteristic utterance and merely confirm that the subject had little power to move him. Perhaps Africa as a subject proves too large unless personalized by and engaged through elements of the kind offered by Negritude. Senghor delivers a new humanism out of the African virtues, Peters sees them as elements feeding his power as a poet. Senghor's view is perilously close to propaganda, though Senghor himself was too skilful a poet to be guilty of that. Peters, on the other hand, was never exposed in quite the same way. By making them part of his stylistic equipment, the thrusts of the African inheritance, the habit of seeing things as representational and so forth, were means to an end, rather than ends in themselves.

Edwin Thumboo. ALT. No. 6, 1973, pp. 93, 98

PLAATJE, SOL T. (1877–1932)

SOUTH AFRICA

[*Mhudi*], as the sub-title states, is an epic of South African Native life a hundred years ago, and deals principally with the Barolong tribe, the hero and heroine of the tale belonging to that people.

The story opens with a most vivid description of the big massacre of the Barolong by the warlike hordes of the Matebele. For many years afterwards descendants of the clan so butchered were taught "almost from childhood, to fear the Matebele—a fierce nation—so unreasoning in its ferocity that it will attack any individual or tribe, at sight, without the slightest provocation. Their destruction of our people, we are told, had no justification in fact or in reason; they were actuated by sheer lust for human blood."

It was by the merest accident, the writer adds, that he discovered the cause of the hatred of the Matebele. Two emissaries of King Mzilikazi of the Matebele had been sent to collect tribute from the subject Barolong tribe, but their Chief, tired of the Matebele supremacy, ordered their death. And so began the terrible massacre, for, as one of the emissaries cried while manacled and waiting the carrying out of the sentence, "A Matebele's blood never mingled with the earth without portending death and destruction."

While the opening chapters tell of the scattering of the Barolong, subsequent ones relate their re-uniting and their co-operation with a few Boers in the overthrow of Mzilikazi. Throughout the book the delightful romance of Mhudi and her husband runs like a shaft of light and relieves many a sombre page. Glimpses are given of obsolete Native customs, superstition in its absurdities and tragedies finds faithful portrayal, and the changes wrought by the advent of the Boers are full of interest. . . .

As a writer of English, Mr. Plaatje seems to hold the premier place among Bantu authors.

M. S. S. *SAO*. Dec., 1930, p. 255

Plaatje's women [in *Mhudi*] are more impressive than his men. Next to Mhudi is the stately Nandi, Mzilikazi's best loved and chief wife. For a number of years she chooses the path of an exile in order to escape the wrath of her husband who has been influenced by a jealous junior wife to kill Nandi, on the strength of some false story about the queen's unfaithfulness. When her husband has been reduced to the status of a monarch without an empire, she follows him in order to console him, knowing that he must need her. Just as the Chaka-figure excites images of heroism and fighting grit in the South African Negro, the Nandi-figure, whether in Chaka's mother or Mzilikazi's wife, is a symbol of beauty, long-suffering motherhood, gentleness and dignity. . . .

Perhaps Plaatje was too much of a historian, journalist and politician to visualize character independently of the historical events in which people were involved. But he had compassion, and this balanced the historian's detachment in him; his love for human beings was profound, and for this reason Mhudi comes alive even in the midst of epoch-making clashes, even if we consider her dialogue stilted. Somehow he sees his pathetic villain's (Mzilikazi's) fate as poetic justice, but he never gloats over it. This kind of poetic justice, the dream-like quality of the narrative, the use of the pathetic fallacy, and the weaving in of songs, are in the tradition of Bantu oral literature.

Ezekiel Mphahlele. *The African Image* (New York,
Praeger, 1962), pp. 175–76

Plaatje's novel, *Mhudi: An Epic of South African Native Life a Hundred Years Ago*, written at least ten years before its publication by Lovedale Press in South Africa in 1930, is an attempt at blending African folk material with individually realized characters in the Western novelistic tradition; the result has been both admired and denigrated by commentators.

Plaatje's story of the two Bechuana natives who survive a raid by a warring Zulu tribe, fall in love (one episode describes the admiration which the hero inspires in his female companion when he subdues a lion by wrenching its tail), and triumph over the mistreatment they endure from the Boers whom they have aided, is leavened by humor and a sense of proportion. Although the novel contains idyllic scenes of native life, the hero Ra-Thaga, and Mhudi, who becomes his wife, are not sentimental Noble Savages but peaceful citizens forced to accept the harshness of the invading white world. The political theme of Boer cruelty is present but not overwhelming; the speech by the dying, defeated Matabele warrior Mzilikazi is dramatically prophetic as he describes the coming Boer ingratitude for the aid of the Bechuana tribe. Yet Plaatje's comments on the Boer attitude are not obtrusive even when they are bitter, and they reflect a wit that bites deeper than surface humaniarianism.

Martin Tucker. *Africa in Modern Literature* (New
York, Frederick Ungar, 1967), p. 257

To the student of literature the interest of [*The Boer War Diary*] is two-fold. In terms of the development of a corpus of African literature, it must be one of the earliest works (and possibly the only diary by) a black South African. Perhaps it is the first in the English language. Plaatje, as we know, was to become a leading figure in the development of black South African literature, both in English and in the vernacular. The diary, unlike his later work, is not carefully edited by its author; it was not intended for publication and he has not attempted the literary perfection aspired to in *Native Life in South Africa, Mhudi* and his other published volumes. In this sense the personality of the author is displayed with far greater clarity here than in any of these later works. In the diary we see the humour and compassion, the determination and the faith that underlie his subsequent writing; but here it is not masked by any of the inhibitions contingent upon Plaatje's rigid perception of the rules of style, manifested so clearly later on.

The second aspect of literary significance relates to the actual use of language. Here again there arises an interdisciplinary interest—this time between literature and linguistics. Perhaps because he had no need for careful correction, Plaatje indulged freely in the use of words and phrases from Dutch, Sotho, Tswana, Xhosa and Zulu. But, as will become evident, this usage is not random. It tends to correspond, in the sociological sense, to the structure of the relationships and situations described by the author.

John L. Comaroff. Introduction to *The Boer War Diary of Sol T. Plaatje* (London, Macmillan, 1973), p. xxvii

It seems appropriate and necessary to discuss Plaatje's style. Some critics who have looked at it have rapidly dismissed it. Janheinz Jahn (in *Neo-African Literature*), for instance, derides Plaatje's "padded 'Victorian' style." And no doubt many readers have quickly rejected it for its imitative or derivative nature. This is a very superficial judgment. . . . Two examples may here suffice to show that his language use is at least interesting and not totally random and unintentional.

In his use of Biblical and epic language Plaatje does indicate he is sensitive to register. . . . He is, in other words, at an early stage, encountering the same problems which many later African writers in English have confronted: the tension between what they want to say and a language which has "foreign" and often oppressive connotations, how to translate the registers of one language into those of another language. . . . Secondly, and even more interestingly, there is Plaatje's introduction of proverbs and the fable into the novel form. This has been a frequent device of later African writers—a typical example of the fusion of African and European elements within the modern African novel. . . .

In all Plaatje's writings, the two elements of prophecy and rebuke are ever-present. And, in spite of any faults it may have, *Mhudi* must clearly be seen as one of the most interesting and significant landmarks in South African literary history.

Tim Couzens. Introduction to Sol. T. Plaatje, *Mhudi* (Johannesburg, Quagga, 1975), pp. 10–11, 15

REED, ISHMAEL (1938–   )

UNITED STATES

In *The Free-Lance Pallbearers* . . . the idea was to satirise Negro and white attitudes; Mr. Reed gives us an imaginary futuristic America, but with some clearly recognisable men and institutions. Such plot as exists is part of the satire. Mr. Reed depends on language exclusively. He is a witty with-it writer and his wisecracks are frequent and good. Yet having dispensed with the conventions of form and narrative, his novel has no means of obtaining variety and pace. The pages are all alike and although few in number, they drag with the efforts to keep up the jokiness.

David Pryce-Jones. Punch. Jan. 29, 1969, p. 179

[Reed] writes "movie books" irresistibly recalling humor columns in high-school papers. *The Free-Lance Pallbearers* features a young gentleman named Bukka Doopeyduck who wanders through a constipated country called Harry Sam; *Yellow Back Radio Broke-Down*, set in the Wild Old West, stars the Loop Garoo Kid, a black cowboy, and Drag Gibson, a bad cattleman. Testimonials from weighty sources declare Mr. Reed a comic master; he himself announces his style to be "literary neo-hoodooism"; and I can only crustily say that I read him without a guffaw, without a laugh, without a chuckle, without the shade of a smile. Packed with *Mad* Magazine silliness though his work is, Mr. Reed has one saving virtue: he is hopelessly good-natured. He may intend his books as a black variation of Jonathan Swift, but they emerge closer to the commercial cooings of Captain Kangaroo.

Irving Howe. Harper. Dec., 1969, p. 141

Yellow Back Radio Broke-Down . . . is not merely a satire on the Old West, with a black cowboy as the hero; it is not merely a parable about the contemporary black struggle vis-à-vis the white establishment; it is not merely a parody on the annexation fight between the Union and the

362

territory of Texas; it is not merely a realistic account of the slime, genocide, corruption, degeneracy and hypocrisy that infest American history and every institution and motive in our national fibre; *Yellow Back Radio Broke-Down* is ALL of these things, and more!

Ishmael Reed is a poet. Like LeRoi Jones, he has taken the American language out on a limb and whipped it to within an inch of its life. In so doing he has revitalized the American language with the nitty-gritty idioms of black people's conceptualization of what it means to live in dese new-nited states of merica. As a poet and a novelist, Reed has the imagination of a psychopath who is God, or who is Satan Himself— ghosts, voo-doo, rattlesnakes, weird rites, hoo-doo, superstitions, multiple schizophrenia, beasts, metempsychosis, demons, charms, visions, hallucinations. In fact, the novel is Reed's voo-doo doll. He once said that the novel is the worst literary form God ever visited upon mankind. Reed has risen the novel from a dead doll with pins in it into a living breathing walking talking animal. This is a thing more authentic, more difficult, more dangerous, more human than science can ever achieve. By this I mean Ishmael Reed employs the mumbo-jumbo witch-doctor experiential epistemology of the Afro-American folk heritage in combination with the psychotic semantic categories of the West to achieve a highly original, secular and existential portrait of what is going on, and has gone on, in our daily lives. Reed is not mad, he is supersane; it is America that is mad and, like the other secular existential black writers Reed depicts—no, Reed *explodes*—this madness before our very eyes.

Calvin C. Hernton. In John A. Williams and
Charles F. Harris, eds., *Amistad 1* (New York,
Random House, 1970), pp. 221–22

["Jes Grew"] is a phrase coined by James Weldon Johnson to refer to the songs that "jes' grew" up among black people, belonging to no one and everyone. Reed sees a historical significance in the phrase. It stands for the quality of natural spontaneity and joy and rhythm innate in the black spirit. . . .

Mumbo Jumbo is about the *near* success of [the] transformation from old to new in the 1920s, an "explanation" of why Jes Grew didn't reach pandemic proportions and change the face of America at that time. The reason Reed advances is as imaginative as his dissection of the Christian myth in *Yellow Back Radio Broke-Down*, and as important to the conception of black art as the work of Amiri Baraka. Jes Grew, says Reed, is an energy in search of a form, by means of which it can survive and flourish: "It must find its Speaking or strangle on its own ineloquence." The artist must provide that Speaking, the "liturgy" that is to become the voice of the ancient but heretofore mute consciousness. It is only through such a form that the sacred energy can be preserved and by which it can mutate into more forms as a testament of its inexhaustible variety. The failure of Jes Grew in the 1920s didn't result from [Woodrow] Wilson's sending the Marines to Haiti or from anything else the whites did. It failed because blacks didn't provide a Speaking equal to the power of Jes Grew. It's impossible not to see in this a reference to the Harlem Renaissance, and to read in it a suggestion that the literary art of that movement didn't provide forms that came up to those emerging from the Jes Grew musicians in New Orleans and Chicago. The total potential of black energy was not tapped.

This is an inference from the novel. We may carry it further. The trouble with the writers of the Harlem Renaissance was that they mistakenly sought to embody their energy in the liturgical forms of the white tradition, dooming their efforts from the start. The ending of *Mumbo Jumbo* suggests that the current upsurge of artistic activity among black artists is guided by an impulse more favorable to Jes Grew, the determination to reject white forms and recall black. What failed in the 1920s seems to be succeeding in the 1960s and 1970s.

Jerry H. Bryant. Nation. Sept. 25, 1972, pp. 245–46

Mumbo Jumbo isn't at all concerned with the traditional province of fiction, the registration of individual consciousness. Rather, as in his earlier books *The Free-Lance Pallbears* and *Yellow Back Radio Broke-Down*, Reed opens fictional art to the forms and mythic possibilities of popular culture, pursuing not psychological description but a perspective on history. . . .

He develops a wild and funny fantasia upon historical themes, part critique of the "Harlem Renaissance" of the 1920s, part farcical thriller about international conspiracy, part satire on blacks who yearn for "serious" (i.e., white-inspired) culture instead of trusting their own traditions and qualities, part philosophical disquisition on the destructive intentions of Faustian man. The result is something like a successful crossing of [Thomas] Pynchon, Sax Rohmer, Madame Blavatsky, and the Negritude writers of French Africa. . . .

Reed's is a quick and mocking mind, and I'm not finally sure how seriously he means his historical myth. But I'm content to read it, as I read the "systematic" works of Blake and Yeats, not primarily as analysis but as an act of continuous and powerful invention, a demonstration that the imagination, black or white, when released from conventional forms and the idea of a monolithic history, can be wonderfully entertaining and instructive, moment by moment, about the sorry narrowness of our self-understanding and our expectations about art.

Thomas R. Edwards. NYR. Oct. 5, 1972, p. 23

The satirical-grotesque distortion of American reality is the basis of Ishmael Reed's book, *The Free-Lance Pallbearers*, a potpourri of picaresque elements in its structure, and of slang in its linguistic fabric. . . .

The technique of concentrated distortion, which serves as the basis for the exaggeration or minimization of the particular, and is derived from the exploitation of slang, is the most important aspect of Reed's novel, just as it is a primary component of Ellison's novel: the similarity between the two is, however, limited to this, and to the particular way of playing with names at which the author of *Invisible Man* is a master.

Reed also produces surnames and first names that are full of allusions and irony, like Eclair Porkchop, Elijah Raven, U2 Polyglot, Nosetrouble, Rutherford Hayes, and so forth, but these names lack the symbolic density to which the entire narrative constantly contributes in *Invisible Man*; the more frequent impression is that playing with slang, for example, may too often be an end in itself. *The Free-Lance Pallbearers* is therefore a promising novel, but not quite a successful one, just as [Baraka's] *The System of Dante's Hell* is an experimental attempt worthy of attention but certainly not a complete work.

Piero Boitani. Prosatori Negri Americani del
Novecento (Rome, Edizioni di Storia e Letteratura,
1973), pp. 268, 271–72†

Ishmael Reed is a prolific writer who . . . works in more than one medium. His novels . . . have already consolidated his reputation as one of those black writers who refuse to be categorized according to the relevance of his theme. He asks no favors of any orthodoxy, but lets his imagination make its bid for the creation of new forms. Yet one cannot fail to notice the craft and discipline with which he controls the natural swing and bounce of his verse.

In his latest collection [of poems], *Conjure*, Reed's tone and rhythm derive from the militant tradition of the black underground. But his is an unusual brand of militancy; it is much concerned with the politics of language. He argues for a clean, free struggle between the liberating anarchism of the black tongue and the frozen esthetic of a conventional White Power. "May the best church win/shake hands now and come out conjuring." His verse is distinguished by a fine critical intelligence, and his stance before the wide variety of American life is supremely confident. He can evoke with poetic realism the savagery which shaped the pioneering spirit as well as crystallize the fraudulence at the heart of the "civilizing" mission.

George Lamming. *NYT*. May 6, 1973, p. 37

In his collection of poetry, *Conjure*, Reed unequivocally asserts that Neo-HooDoo, this new direction in Afro-American literature, constitutes "Our Turn," a radical severance of his destiny as a writer from the fate of his White contemporaries. . . . [Reed makes] the considerable claim that he has found a way of writing fiction unlike those decreative and self-reflexive fictive modes in which his White contemporaries seem imprisoned. Reed is careful, of course, not to establish Neo-HooDoo as a school. It is rather a characteristic stance, a mythological provenance, a behavior, a complex of attitudes, the retrieval of an idiom, but however broadly defined, Neo-HooDoo does manifest one constant and unifying refrain: Reed's fiercely professed alienation from Anglo-American literature. Ultimately, then, Neo-HooDoo is political art, as responsible as Richard Wright's *Native Son*, but without Wright's grim realism or the polemical separatism that characterizes Imamu Baraka's work. For Reed the problem is to get outside the "Euro-Am meaning world" (Baraka's term) without getting caught as an artist in a contraposed system. . . .

But where are the "original folk tales" and native idioms in Reed's fiction? How far indeed does Neo-HooDoo (both as myth and mode) take him from established literary canons? His discourse in *Yellow Back Radio Broke-Down* and *Mumbo Jumbo* curves in and around colloquial Black English, which serves him as a stylistic device, not as a language. It is withal a learned and allusive discourse as mixed in its diction as Mark Twain's. His forms are not narrative legends taken from an oral tradition, but rather the popular forms of the Western and the Gangster Novel. . . . *Yellow Back Radio Broke-Down* is a Black version of the Western [William] Burroughs has been writing in fragments and promising in full since the fifties. Not only is the content of the fiction eclectic in its composition, but Loop's performance as a *houngan* in it has a good deal of Burroughs' "Honest Bill." For the core of his narrative, Reed borrows almost intact the sociological drama Norman Mailer describes in *The White Negro*—that migration of White middle-class youth in revolt against the values of their own culture toward the counter-culture of Black America—and then weaves into this phenomenon a barely disguised account of the student uprisings at Berkeley and other campuses. . . .

Yellow Back Radio Broke-Down . . . turns into a book *about* Neo-HooDooism. And every explanation, every concealed footnote, betrays the artifice of the myth. Reed's mythopoeic lore is as arcane as the cryptic references strewn about in Burroughs' fiction. And his art, it would seem, bears as much relation to James Brown doing the "Popcorn" or Jimi Hendrix stroking his guitar as does T. S. Eliot's, whom Reed consigns in his manifesto to the graveyard of Christian culture.

Neil Schmitz. *TCL*. April, 1974, pp. 127, 132–33, 135

The plot of *The Last Days of Louisiana Red* is impossible to recount. Like Reed's last novel, *Mumbo Jumbo*, it takes the form of a hoodoo detective thriller, features the master practitioner Papa LaBas, and generally focuses upon the struggle between the upright Gumbo Workers and the dangerous advocates of "Louisiana Red." For so many story lines and themes, however, a concept as linear as "plot" seems inadequate.

Consider, for example, that one of the characters is named Chorus, a performer supposedly in his 30s who has been out of work since people started writing plays like *Antigone*. Or that Reed draws constant parallels between the Antigone myth and his own tale. Or that contemporary versions of Kingfish, Amos and Andy appear. Or that a white teacher of Afro-American literature is undone by his study of Richard Wright's *Native Son* and is captured roaming the Berkeley Hills in a chauffeur's uniform, raving in black Mississippi-Chicago dialect of the 1940s. All of this is peculiar and improbable but somehow in the context Reed creates it fits together logically and even makes sense. . . .

Reed appears deeply concerned with the relationship between the sexes, but on this topic his perspective is frighteningly distorted. Throughout *The Last Days of Louisiana Red* there is joking contempt toward women, particularly black women. When he satirizes the women's movement his originality disappears and he falls back on the tired stereotype of feminists as man-hating dykes. The method for subduing these "fierce, rough-looking women" is attack and rape.

Reed's most astounding statements occur in a confrontation between Papa LaBas and Minnie, a Moocher leader. LaBas accuses Minnie and all black women as co-conspirators with white men in keeping black men in submission. LaBas intones: "Women use our children as hostages against us. . . . The original blood-sucking vampire was a woman . . . I can't understand why you want to be liberated. Hell . . . you already liberated."

The violence and humorlessness of this diatribe, delivered by a character whom Reed respects, indicate that he wants his opinions to be taken straight. Reed's views on a difficult problem are antediluvian and for this reader they cloud the entire impact of his work. If he is so insensitive in this area, how can he be so incisive in others? (Can I laugh with a man who seems so hostile toward me?) As a critic I found *The Last*

Days of Louisiana Red brilliant. As a black woman I am not nearly so enthusiastic.

Barbara Smith. *NR*. Nov. 23, 1974, pp. 53–54

Ishmael Reed's *The Last Days of Louisiana Red* satirically attacks the forces he feels make life difficult for blacks, and for Americans in general. The unifying metaphor is "Louisiana Red," a pungent sauce symbolizing the rage causing internal fighting and dissension. Within the satirical fire the targets are numerous: the false motions of America, adversary and treacherous offerings of women, a persisting slave mentality among blacks, "moocherism" (hustling others) under various guises, the psyche of the white "liberal," criminality masked by black revolutionary pretensions, black simple-minded violence and sexual obsession, hypocrisy of an African leader, etc.

By discussions of the stories of the Greeks, involving the role of the chorus, and the plays and mythic backgrounds of *Antigone* and *The Seven against Thebes*, Reed creates a flexible frame in which disorder parallels and mirrors for the disorder in black life, and life in general. Thus Antigone's defiance of the male authority of Creon in Sophocles's play *Antigone* (and in myth) and her presumed unbounded ambitions are emblematic of the out-of-bounds modern black women. Into this disordered situation comes the conjurer or psychic detective LaBas and his assistants, who must set things aright. And there is also disorder in the world of conjurers, bearing upon the disorder in the day-to-day world. . . .

Reed's satire, as implied by statements in different parts of the book, wishes to act as a corrective. It would rescue blacks from sociological determinism and defeatism, and release energy for an individualistic march to freedom. The old virtues of self-reliance, hard work and struggle, and imagination and intuitive powers, are called into play. There would be then the correction of negative and parasitic types who "have their own boot on their own necks." . . .

Among novelists writing today, Reed ranks in the top of those commanding a brilliant set of resources and techniques. The prose is flexible, easy in its shift of gears and capacity to move on a variety of levels. The techniques of the cartoon, the caricature, the vaudevillean burlesque, the straight narrative, the detective story, are summoned at will. But his management of his resources in *The Last Days of Louisiana Red* fails to create a lasting or deep impression.

George E. Kent. *Phylon*. June, 1975, pp. 190–92

Ishmael Reed's fifth compact novel [*Flight to Canada*] should add to his reputation as one of America's most freshly—and bizarrely—imaginative satirists. He was having pointed fun with historical figures in fictional situations before E. L. Doctorow's *Ragtime* brought best-seller attention to the technique. Now he introduces an Abraham Lincoln who is neither the sainted leader of legend nor the villain pictured by political cartoonists of the time—but a kind of good-natured illiterate who gets a little tangled up in trying to explain Lincoln's actual dubious ideas for "compensatory emancipation" or sending away the slaves to colonize far parts. . . .

But it is not only white people, including one as sympathetic as Lincoln, who are shown to be victims of racial attitudes in this novel about a would-be poet fleeing a fantastic emperor of the Southland. Mr. Reed's targets include members of all races, not omitting his own black race, which his books repeatedly present as needing to resist being divided and conquered through such means as accepting others' images of blackness. In this book the slaves put down each other, if in less obvious ways than their masters do, and one of the fugitives finally discloses that he ran away not only from the slavemaster but from the slaves too.

Yet this free man has become another kind of slave, to the profits from pornography. Mr. Reed ranges from intellectual subtlety to the depths of degradation in symbolically linking self-enslavement to the impulse to enslave others. Sometimes he uses obscenities and erotic passages that raise the question whether he himself has been caught in the trap of literary fashion. Most of the time, a satirist's reforming intentions seem clear beneath prose that combines highbrow and lowbrow to provide a series of snaps, crackles, and pops commenting on our times. Yes, our times as well as Lincoln's. For in this book the assassination at Ford's Theater is callously covered by TV, for example, and Mr. Reed has blended the periods as if history existed all at once instead of in the fetters of time.

Roderick Nordell. CSM. Oct. 20, 1976, p. 25

ROUMAIN, JACQUES (1907–1944)

HAITI

Jacques Roumain is an excellent writer of prose. Although a descendant of aristocrats, he takes great pleasure in listening to the common man and proclaiming his adherence to Communism. He is interested in taking notice of the psychological difficulties that overwhelm our generation. Having been acquainted on two occasions with the "damp straw of prison cells," he nevertheless has found success with stories like *The Prey and the Darkness.*

Max Rose. *La littérature haïtienne* (Brussels, Éditions de "Conférences et Théâtres," 1938), p. 25†

Haitian-, European-, American-trained Jacques Roumain, poet, ethnologist, archeologist, and journalist, had won an enviable reputation as the militant and uncontested leader of the younger Haitian intellectuals long before his death at the age of thirty-seven. Some of his verse had been translated by Langston Hughes and others in this country, and by Nicolás Guillén in Cuba. Moreover, in Haiti he had published various prose works: *The Prey and the Darkness, The Enchanted Mountain*, and *Puppets*, all of which helped to develop the mastery that is so evident in *Masters of the Dew.* . . .

Masters of the Dew tells of one Manuel who returns after fifteen years in Cuba to find his village suffering from drought, and divided by a family feud. He discovers water, devises a means of bringing it to the village and of reconciling the two opposing groups of peasants, only to be killed by a jealous rival. As he dies, he pleads with his mother not to reveal the name of the murderer, so that the feud will not be renewed. . . .

Jacques Roumain's hero . . . realizes that injustice is by no means a purely Haitian phenomenon. . . . He describes the exploitation of the workers in the Cuban sugar fields: "They have nothing but the courage of their arms, not a handful of land, not a drop of water, except their own sweat." . . .

The style of Jacques Roumain's *Masters of the Dew* is particularly striking. He writes in French, but often obtains a Creole flavor by the mere addition of a syllable, a word, or a phrase. . . . Sometimes he employs an old French word that has been retained in the patois. . . . The result . . . is often a poetic prose, capable of being read and admired by men of good will the world over. . . .

Like Manuel, Jacques Roumain died prematurely. But he left a great Haitian novel to convince his compatriots that "Union makes strength"; to teach his fellow-authors that a novel can be at once Haitian and universal; and to enrich contemporary French literature.

Mercer Cook. *FR*. May, 1946, pp. 408–11

The son of wealthy parents . . . Jacques Roumain lived for a number of years in Zurich, where he became familiar with German culture and grew accustomed to the free expression of ideas. When he returned to Haiti, he formed a literary movement together with other writers his age, a movement sparked by the irreverence that youth so often shows toward its elders. Dismissing past achievements too lightly, the young icono-

clasts, vigorously ridiculing the Haitian literature that had been produced until then, emphatically decreed the need to create an art based
on national pride and a real knowledge of the Haitian milieu. . . .

Roumain's second novel, *Puppets*, is the urban counterpart of [his
first,] *The Enchanted Mountain*, its sociological complement; *Puppets*
is a study of the upper middle class of Port-au-Prince. Because the
bourgeoisie is defenseless against the attacks of the proletariat as well as
those of the aristocracy (and Roumain by conviction and temperament
belonged to both groups), if *Puppets* were nothing more than a list of
grievances against the unfortunate Haitian ruling class, it would have
little merit. Fortunately, while the brief novel ironically criticizes the
prejudices and sometimes pathetic triviality of the local elite, it poses a
problem of major interest: that of the new generation that refuses to
accept the comfort and respect it was born into, to submit to "hypocritical conventions" in exchange for betraying its revolutionary ideals.

Rémy Bastien. *CA.* July–Aug., 1954, pp. 244–46†

The fathers of the Haitian novel . . . left us a formula for narrative art
that does not seem to have influenced Roumain: precise, detailed, truculent, caustic description of the customs and daily activities in Haiti—in
short, Haitian critical realism. In Roumain we find a kind of symbolic
realism. For him, the novel is a great popular poem with classical outlines and almost symbolic characters. Without underestimating the immense artistic value of Roumain's form, we must bear in mind that he
did not develop or continue Haitian critical realism.

Another unusual aspect of his work deserves to be emphasized. In
this country in which tribal hatreds and jealousies and tribal customs
have not been completely eradicated, in this country in which living
conditions are so harsh and man's chances to succeed are so unfavor-
able, it is very rare to see a man take love for his fellow man as far as
Roumain does. He is the champion of a love that is so powerful; so
generous, that it surprises us in Haiti. The character of Manuel in
Masters of the Dew is unique in our milieu and our fiction. His patriotism and his basic attachments are tinged with love for his village, love
for the land, love for life, exemplary filial love, unequaled love for his
Annaïse, a cult of perfect friendship, and even total forgiveness toward
his enemies and his murderers. Could this be the book that contains
Roumain's basic message, a message that life did not permit him to
carry out in person? [1957]

Jacques-Stéphen Alexis. Preface to Jacques Roumain,
La montagne ensorcelée (Paris, Éditeurs Français
Réunis, 1972), pp. 24–25†

In [*The Enchanted Mountain*], written at the age of twenty-three, Jacques Roumain already seems in full possession of his artistic abilities. What strikes one first in this tale is its extraordinary precision: a simple story, related without digressions, with a deliberate intention to be brief; a clear, spare language that only approaches lyricism by accident; the avoidance of any complicity with the negative characters in the story or of any pity for the victims. Let me say the word that comes to my mind as a description of his novel—classical. Classical because of the clarity of its construction; classical because of the inflexible detachment that the author imposes upon himself; classical because of the moderation of its style. . . .

This somber story of love and death is related with an inexorable sobriety. Events move quickly and collide, following an implacable logic: the logic of unleashed passions; the logic of ignorance and madness; the logic of mysticism . . .

One can justly speak of [Jean] Giono's influence on Roumain, but only of the influence of *Hill*, a novel published in 1929, one year before Roumain had begun writing his novel. . . . Comparisons can be pursued in their similar mystical conception of the world. . . . Mysticism is, after all, an irrational atmosphere of misfortune. . . .

Let us not forget, however, the original, vivid contribution to Roumain's works made by our voodoo. Everything considered, Giono's influence on Roumain can only be regarded as catalytic. Haitian cultural material extends in all directions from Roumain's book and assures his literary autonomy.

> Roger Gaillard. *L'univers romanesque de Jacques Roumain* (Port-au-Prince, Henri Deschamps, 1965),
> pp. 9–12†

A writer, a diplomat, and a militant Communist, Jacques Roumain was also a great traveler. He lived, among other places, in Germany and in Belgium. But all his works are deeply rooted in his native land. His novel *Masters of the Dew* remains the most beautiful novel to come from the Caribbean. But it was even more through a few poems, the most aggressive ever written by a black poet, that he strongly influenced Césaire, Damas, and David Diop, not to mention his compatriots. . . . Even the gentle Senghor, on the rare occasions when he gets angry, spontaneously seizes Roumain's accents, rhythms, and images. Nothing is at once more violent and more humanist than the three poems in *Ebony Wood*. All the major themes of Negro revolt are condensed in a few pages: slavery, exile, forced labor, lynching, segregation, colonial oppression, nostalgia for Africa, and a gathering of the Negro diaspora under the revolutionary banner: "We shall no longer sing sad spirituals of despair."

But Roumain is not satisfied with making demands on behalf of his race. He insists on justice for all the "prisoners of hunger" and broadens his scope to include the "oppressed of all countries" beyond differences of color. What constitutes Roumain's greatness and what excuses the brutality of his language is precisely the fact that he was able to give breadth to his humanism. And his rough poetry, full of prosaic expressions drawn from political slogans, is nevertheless charged with such force and such intense emotion that it might be said that his pen brings us the very voice, the great cry, of the "wretched of the earth."

Lilyan Kesteloot. In Lilyan Kesteloot, ed., *Anthologie négro-africaine* (Verviers, Belgium, Gérard, 1967), p. 50†

Jacques Roumain . . . was a very knowledgeable ethnologist and archeologist. The love he bore for his country was tempered by a profound political understanding. The poet in him was able to communicate this knowledge and this love to us. Thus, the black peasants in *Masters of the Dew* are brothers of all the peasants in the world who seek life-giving water and fruitful land.

In this book, as in the best fiction, one can find both reality and symbolism. First, there is the problem of water (one of the major problems of farmers in many countries) linked with the problem of the monopolization of plots of land by speculators who take advantage of bankrupt peasants. Then, more generally, we find the problem of liberation and of the harvest. . . .

This theme of harvest and planting is found both in the struggle to find water and to unify the peasants and in the love between Manuel and Annaïse. Thus, the lyrical song is sustained by a powerful dramatic pulse that maintains the reader's profound interest from the first page to the last. Roumain's style should be discussed at length. He has reshaped the French language so that we can hear all the music of his people and his land.

Pierre Gamarra. *Europe*. Jan., 1971, pp. 194–95†

SEMBÈNE, OUSMANE (1923–   )

SENEGAL

The black quarter of Marseille is rather solidly depicted [in *The Black Docker*]. . . . What is odd is not, as some have said, that a black docker has written a novel but that the message, which was promised and expected, is not expressed.

A minority lives in France in conditions that are often atrocious. This minority has its problems. It is struggling in an atmosphere that comes close to creating despair. Its only support is pride; its only arms, work; its only morality, strictness. This minority of Negro workers in France spares no pains. It struggles in order to triumph over the guilty conscience of the propertied classes, supervisors, and torturers. Its message in its stammerings is one of brotherhood. This minority begs for neither pity nor favors. It proclaims its right to live. All its ideas, virtues, and "tribulations" deserve our respect if not our sympathy.

What the world was expecting from Sembène was the exact expression of this message. Therefore, this novelist would have done better if he hadn't "drowned" such a subject in additional material ranging from sexual obsessions to inferiority complexes.

A world like that of the Negro dockers in France—strange in its dignity, striking in its strictness, and eager for brotherhood—deserved a better presentation to a public that is unaware of its very existence.

Sembène did not succeed this time. Nevertheless, this novelist has something to say. Without any doubt the message that he did not know how to express in his first book will become stronger in his following works.

Lamine Diakhaté. PA. April–May, 1957, p. 154†

The novel in French West Africa has often been used as an instrument against colonialism. The great Cameroonian writers Oyono and Beti have tried to explode the myth of "France Outre Mère" in their books, but none has shown as violent hatred of the white man as Ousmane Sembène. [*Oh Country, My Beautiful People*] is about an African who has served in the French army during the great war and returns to his home in Senegal with a white wife. The book sets out to describe the difficulties the hero encounters with his own people, who object to his European wife and look with suspicion on the new way of life he is trying to introduce. It also attempts to show the conflict between the hero Faye, and the white rulers of the country, who think that he is undermining their position of prestige by living with a white woman. Faye himself is described as a rather Europeanised character. . . .

The author resolves the conflict between the progressive African and the Europeans who try to keep him down into a Wild West type of violence. In the very opening scene of the novel super-man Faye punches a white man into submission and on the next occasion he successfully fights the entire crew of a ship single handed! His sense of justice is so strong that he uses his fists whenever he sees injustice or exploitation, and needless to say, he always floors his opponent. The white victims of his fury try to retaliate at first by attempting to violate his wife. Finally they manage to hire some Africans who attack Faye in the night and kill him.

The improbability of all these scenes makes it impossible for us to accept Faye as a martyr. The author thinks of Faye as a tragic hero. Although he is killed in the end, his spirit lingers on and the work he began is continued by his people. Unfortunately this ending falls rather flat. One feels that the conflict between Faye and the colonialists would have taken a rather more subtle form—which does mean that it would have been less dangerous.

U. Beier. *BO*. Nov., 1959, pp. 56–57

Ousmane Sembène, a fervent African socialist, attempts, in *God's Bits of Wood*, to show how Africans can act independently and responsibly to achieve their freedom. This novel, set among the strikers who, in 1947, paralysed the Dakar-Niger railway, describes how the men, women and children even, come to realize their strength and dignity. The novel is the story of the way in which they are forced to face famine and poverty, to take upon themselves the responsibility for their situation and refuse to change it except on their terms. . . .

Sembène attempts to demonstrate the various ways in which [the Africans] suddenly become aware of their imposed inferiority and how they oppose their pride and will to the brute force being used against them. They begin to see their situation objectively, to analyze it dispassionately, to oppose rational, passive resistance to violence.

Their passive resistance contrasts with the violence found in [André] Malraux's *The Human Condition* which, in several respects, this novel resembles. This method of non-violent resistance, used both in

Africa and India in the struggle for independence, as well as by coloured people in America and elsewhere in the fight for civil rights, is essential for Sembène. Violence is degrading, brutish. Whenever it is used by the strikers it fails to achieve anything. It can only lead to more violence, as is shown in the efforts of the employers and administration to break the strike. . . .

Sembène has introduced entirely new concepts into the African novel in French. The characters are almost free of colonialist influence, confrontation with Europeans and European civilisation is no longer a major theme and, because of this, the presentation of African values, as in the works of Birago Diop and Laye Camara, is not an implied or explicit comparison with those of Europe.

A. C. Brench. The Novelists' Inheritance in French
Africa (London, Oxford University Press, 1967),
pp. 110, 112–13, 119

Emitaï deals not so much with characters as with a collective entity, the people—a Marxist conception of the hero. . . . The author shows Africa caught in the trap created when traditions and beliefs are confronted by Western materialism. The objective realities embodied by the soldiers and their guns are pitted against the objectivized realities of the gods. The result, Sembène shows, is the massacre of the peasants. The spiritual world is conquered by the brutal force of the weapons. The helplessness of the peasants is pathetic, "but how much time they wasted by calling upon the gods," the author seems to say. . . .

We are far from the Western world's frantic search for adulterated exoticism. There are no tom-toms, no dances, none of the authentic "primitive life" that merchandisers consider absolutely indispensable in selling Africa. In *Emitaï* folklore has been used in the English sense of the word—the collection of traditions, legends, songs, and popular customs of a country; in this case, folklore determines the very content of the film.

"Real African films will be made by Africans." All African filmmakers say so, and everyone who knows Africa's specific nature thinks so. But many others are not yet convinced. Sembène confirms the point of view of the former and will prove to the latter that they are wrong. And it will have taken him only six films to do so.

Africans feel at home with Sembène's films; they find in them their own customary reactions, reactions so habitual as to be no longer noticed. How many Europeans living in Senegal came into real contact with that country only by seeing *The Money-Order*! Thanks to Sembène, Black Africa has an identity; Africa is presented to the world not only physically but also psychologically. Sembène's films are accomplishing with the European masses the same work that Black African literature has done and is continuing to do with the elite. . . .

Paulin Soumanou Vieyra. *Ousmane Sembène,*
cinéaste (Paris, Présence Africaine, 1972),
pp. 136–37, 158–59†

Sembène's new film [*Emitaï*] has been marred by censorship but what we can see of it is a masterpiece—a new style of film, unlike the "Museum of Natural History" documentary quality that hinders *The Money-Order* stylistically, and totally different from all western manners of story-telling on film. Few films cannot be related to other films in their story or in their style; Sembène's *Emitaï* can be related to Sophocles's *Antigone* in its story, but not to any film in its style. This is true in its manner of photography—almost entirely long shots, never extracting its characters from the environment, but making the environment an integral part of the story—and in its pace. There are no flash or quick shots, the editing is never manipulated to gain speed on events, everything is made ultra-clear, as if the length of the action and the objectivity of the photography were enough to clarify not only the story but Sembène's thought processes behind the story. . . .

Here he breaks away from all the [D. W.] Griffith-inspired devices—subjective angles, cross-cutting, the speeding up of reality by progressively shorter shots, the devices of emotional story-telling—that have plagued film-makers ever since Griffith. Who has bothered to get away from the bourgeois syndrome besides [Jean-Luc] Godard (and possibly Rainer Werner Fassbinder) previously in commercial story-telling film?

Lyle Pearson. *FilmQ.* Spring, 1973, pp. 46–47

Xala, Ousmane Sembène's new novel, will probably not elicit the same emotional response as *The Money-Order*. A completely different aspect of life in Senegal and in Dakar is presented in this satirical tale, which sometimes borders on comedy or farce. But the farce, it must be stressed, is not gratuitous; it is based on the observation (which one feels is very careful) of daily life, customs, language, and social relationships.

The storyteller presents a "new greedy native bourgeoisie." El Hadji Abdou Kader Beye, the pompous, ridiculous hero of *Xala*, is a corrupt businessman, a rich tradesman. On the night of his wedding to his third wife, he discovers he is impotent: he has the *xala*. The story is about curing the *xala*. Also, and more important, it is about discovering who tied the noose on this unfortunate fifty-year-old man, who cast this particularly treacherous spell, who sought to destroy his power, in every sense of the word? Suddenly, this up-to-date bourgeois, this modern import-export businessman, whose comfortable daily life is full of the benefits of all of today's technical devices, finds himself horribly help-less. Another device, ancient and subtle [that of the *xala*], has just cracked the beautiful façade and threatens to destroy it completely. But, as the reader will see, this apparent return to the past finally uncovers the road to progress, to the future. But progress, like the story itself, sometimes skirts the straight line. . . .

The richness of social observation in this brief novel is all the more striking because it is a tale, a fable. It seems to me that in depicting contemporary customs in today's Dakar, in which the aftereffects of colonialism are still noticeable, Sembène has rediscovered the precision and the zest of the old art of storytelling. It is an African art, but also a universal art.

Pierre Gamarra. *Europe*. March, 1974, pp. 295–96†

The central theme of *Xala* is the downfall of the arrogant and insatiable new bourgeoisie of independent Africa, people "with long teeth" biting hard to control the national economy and subjugate the common man. Sembène is less worried by their existence than by the immoral way in which they make their wealth and spend it. Whether it concerns Mbaye of *The Money-Order* who robs Dieng of his money or El Hadji who goes about expropriating the poor and imprisoning them if they talk, buying cars for young girls and living a scandalously luxurious life, the story is the same: these men constitute a danger to the people and society. This is the important point that Sembène is making: wealth can only be meaningful when it is used to the advantage of society; the moment it becomes too personal and almost a cult, it corrodes man and gradually eats away the fabric of society by creating an unhealthy social life for the "have-nots." There is an Ibo proverb which says "the big tree stands because man wants it to stand," but the moment its existence is no longer in the interest of man, it is felled. This seems to be the lesson the author is trying to give in *Xala*. In fact, when the poor, the beggars and even the bankers find that El Hadji is more of a danger than an asset, they decide to pull him down. . . .

In both novels, Sembène's language is so simple that most African readers will find no difficulty in understanding what the author is saying about them. Most of the time, he translates his thoughts and those of his characters from their local dialect into French, thereby cutting down the latter to the level of the common man. His creation of images is very African and original and his satire much to the taste of the villager who would like you to say things as they are.

One might of course accuse the author of taking joy in painting a universe of misfortune and the downfall of man: Dieng is a perpetual victim; El Hadji, a one-time victimizer, is now victimized. The fact remains that, in traditional Africa, the most effective way of keeping traditional morality intact and correcting the society was to punish evildoers severely and leave good behaviour to propagate itself, since it was believed to be self-evident and self-inspiring. This seems to dictate Sembène's literary aesthetics in *The Money-Order, Xala* and even in *White Genesis*. He takes his cue from the people to create literature for the people.

A. U. Ohaegbu. *PA*. No. 91, 1974, pp. 130–31

Sembène's masterpiece is perhaps his collection of short stories *Man from Volta*. In these stories, the style of which often resembles the folk tale as told by a *griot* (teller of folk tales), Sembène avoids the dangers he had encountered in more complex narratives; each tale is a gem of concision and lyrical beauty. In his collection, Sembène is a champion of women's rights and shows a keen penetration of female psychology. In "Her Three Days," for example, he gives a touching portrayal of the suffering experienced by a neglected third wife whose husband now prefers his younger fourth wife. There could be no stronger indictment of the evils of polygamy. The story "Letters from France" is written from the point of view of a young wife, who had been forced to marry an older man. To her girlfriend she confesses the bitter unhappiness of her daily life. The young wife's disillusion and depression, when she finds that France is nothing like the country she had fantasized, are similar to the emotions experienced by Diouana, the tragic protagonist of the story "The Black Girl of...," which Sembène later adapted for the screen.

Debra Popkin. In *Encyclopedia of World Literature
in the 20th Century* (New York, Frederick Ungar,
1975), Vol. IV, p. 342

SENGHOR, LÉOPOLD SÉDAR (1906–   )

SENEGAL

Some lines [in *Songs of Darkness*] . . . seem to have been borrowed from the enumerative language dear to [Saint-John Perse]. It is possible that Senghor knows Saint-John Perse's work, and that Saint-John Perse's vast solemnity and the primitive strength of his declamation have moved the poet of *Songs of Darkness*. Nothing can evoke the dark

continent better than great elemental images coupled with constant re-
minders of the symbols that still remain from a very ancient civilization.
. . . Senghor's fondness for inversions . . . ritual images, and noble and
sacred language, and the care he takes almost to anchor his poetry in an
incantatory tone—all these things, as beautifully arranged as they are,
do not offer anything new or really creative.

The fact remains, nevertheless, that this poetry not only is very
readable but also charms and sometimes overwhelms the reader. The
images are those of a real poet, although their rhythmic garb seems
borrowed. . . . The pacing of the poems is flawless, sustained by an
inspiration with happy variations. A religious theory, in the form of a
fresco or a frieze, unfolds in many places. An incurable nostalgia for an
ancient and beloved land often overflows the somewhat stiff harmony of
the lines. We see Senghor's men live and suffer—men of the African
soil, of a thousand years of slavery, but men whose pride is never
crushed. There is anger in these lines, a sung anger that takes the form
of incantation. There is also, as in the poem "Snow over Paris," a sense
of universal human suffering.

Pierre Emmanuel. *TP*. Aug. 3, 1945, p. 3†

Under the influence of their French masters, but even more under that
of the black elite of the United States, French-speaking black intellectuals have been totally devoting themselves for the past few years to
what they rightly consider their primary obligation—the rehabilitation
and glorification of their race. Following the example of the black Americans, to whom nothing specifically Negro remains foreign for long, and
who therefore prompt them to persevere on the path they have committed themselves to, they eagerly study the past of their race, which seems
to have been destined for misfortune from the beginning of time; and in
essays that are often authoritative they record their discoveries, discoveries that have led their brothers in the United States to the most erudite
exegeses and at times the most unexpected commentaries.

Léopold Sédar Senghor would certainly never dream of minimizing
the importance of the contributions made—on the one hand to Europe
as a whole, on the other to colored Frenchmen—by the creative genius
of those whom the Yankees attack with the insulting and scornful nick-
name of Jim Crow. Senghor is moreover aware of all he owes to France
and to himself, in other words, to the race of his ancestors. Thus, he has
served both France and his race with his heart and his mind: his mind
disciplining the reasons of his heart, reasons of which reason itself is
unaware; and his heart burning his mind with the fine flame that ignites
it. His earliest writings, "What the Black Man Brings" and the ad-

mirable poems in *Songs of Darkness*, marked by a very pure musicality, are totally suffused by this double, demanding passion. . . .

Some of his teachings may seem subversive to the European, who is ordinarily sensitive only to what touches him from close by or from a great distance. Senghor, however, does not say anything that should displease Europeans. A black man, he sees himself as part of Black Africa, and feels one with the civilization of the land that witnessed his birth. Why would he behave otherwise? Did not Clemenceau accept the French Revolution and its excesses in the same way? But Senghor is carrying out a noble plan. The white race has its defects and the black race has its own. Both also have their own good points and virtues. To reconcile these differing virtues and good points, to help them form a synthesis, is this not a task worthy of a great heart? Senghor has dedicated his life to the achievement of this harmony, this reconciliation, this synthesis.

René Maran. *LetF*. Sept. 10, 1947, p. 4†

M. Senghor was the delegate from Senegal-Mauretania to the Assemblée Constituante which framed the Constitution for the Fourth Republic in 1946, and he served on the committee of the Assemblée Constituante entrusted with the job of seeing to it that the new Constitution was drawn up in impeccable French. This important political role placed M. Senghor in an excellent position to translate his ideas into action. . . .

His principle and slogan for the "new Africa" of French West Africa is: "Assimilate, don't be assimilated." He thus counsels African natives to assimilate French culture without losing their native character. . . . as for France, if the poet harbors any resentment towards the oppressors and exploiters of his Fathers, through whom he addresses France, he tactfully subdues it; and his appeal to his ancestors is clothed in characteristic Christian tolerance and patience as regards "the lord of gold and of the suburbs." He sees the hand of God in the defeat of France in 1940, and he asserts that his own participation in the war was the occasion of a "replanting of fidelity" to France. Obviously, like the Fathers whom he addresses . . . the poet has not allowed his heart to become hardened by hate, and his dream of human brotherhood fills his heart with hope. . . .

Edward Allen Jones. *FR*. May, 1948, pp. 447–48

Most notable among . . . French Africans is Senghor . . . now President of the Senegal Republic. . . . From the age of seven Senghor began an intensive study of the French language. His outstanding promise soon took him to Dakar, and at the age of twenty-two he sailed for France to continue his studies at the École Normale Supérieure in Paris. Here he was soon joined by Aimé Césaire, seven years his junior, and the two men began the long series of conversations and experiments which prepared them for the task of "giving a tongue to the black races." Another acquaintance of this period was Léon Damas of French Guiana.

None of these three men began to publish until the late thirties; they had first to master the strange status of the "assimilated" man living in a society to which he does not belong. We discover from Senghor, as later from Laye Camara, that the overwhelming impression of the star pupil from French Africa who won his way to Paris was one of isolation. Only in this new context did he discover the fallacy that had underlain his whole education. He was not and could never be a Frenchman. He had therefore to settle down and rediscover what it was to be an African. . . . The supreme irony, and perhaps the ultimate justification, of "assimilation," is that it has contributed more than anything else to this process —the rediscovery of Africa.

This search for an identity can take a form as simple as Senghor's poem "Totem." . . . It can also assume the length and complexity of Césaire's *Notebook on a Return to My Native Land* or Damas' *Black Label*. The style which Senghor made for himself actually owes little to the scornful whiplash of Césaire's poetry, or to the staccato lines and typographical tricks of Damas. But [Césaire] undoubtedly exercised a powerful influence on Senghor through his intellect and personality, an influence which Senghor has generously acknowledged in his memorable "Letter to a Poet." . . .

From Césaire [Senghor] caught something of the new literary attitude of Negritude, which demanded of its poets a strong verbal rhythm, a wealth of African allusions and a general exaltation of "the African personality." The true past of the Negro must be rediscovered beneath the layers of colonial history, his culture vindicated, and his future prepared.

Gerald Moore. *Seven African Writers* (London, Oxford University Press, 1962), pp. 2–4, 6

As a policy, cultural assimilation was only applied effectively in the Dakar region of Senegal, to the almost complete exclusion of the rest of French West Africa. Senghor is a product of this system, and Negritude and the form it takes in his poetry and thought are a reaction against it.

Senghor has completely assimilated French culture, and this has given him a great love for France, even though in politics he has so often been in opposition. His French education has given him a preference for systematized thought, of a sort particularly reminiscent of the France between the two World Wars. Many of his major political speeches, two of which can be read in his recent book, *Nationhood and the African Road to Socialism*, resemble philosophical treatises in the grand French manner. While it has provoked on one level a profound reaction against the arrogance of French culture and the way it has taken him almost by force, Senghor's education has led to his oddly ambiguous attitude to it.

One can trace the development of his drama through the various phases of his poetical works much more easily than in his essays, from the early poems of almost diffident self-discovery—*Songs of Darkness* and *Black Hosts*—to the splendid self-assertion of *Ethiopics* and the Odes of *Nocturnes*. If one only reads the prose, or if one reads the poetry superficially, one's impression will be that Senghor is making an extreme and unrealistic assertion of the supremacy, let alone the equality, of African values over those of Europe. In this context, one cannot help being puzzled by a completely unrelated and apparently illogical love of France ("Lord, among the white nations, set France at the right hand of the Father"), and one assumes it is the classic, love-hate relationship. This is to miss the point of Senghor's vision. Senghor, in actual fact, refuses to choose between Africa and Europe. After an initial hesitation, his poetry moves towards a symbiosis of the two. What he is aiming at, and what his cultural background makes him so ardently long for, is not a cultural racialism, which his philosophy of Negritude seems at times to imply, but what he has been calling recently the "Culture of the Universal," the vision of a united universe to which every culture of mankind will make its contribution, and he calls on Africa to stir itself so as not to be late at the rendez-vous of the nations.

C. H. Wake. *BA*. Spring, 1963, p. 156

The hymnic rhetoric of Léopold Sédar Senghor, unbroken by apologies, confessions, second thoughts, is the expression of a personality so firmly possessed of his Serer inheritance that he is able to evoke its atmosphere without the aid of names and phrases that are to alert the listener that he must attune himself to Africa. The names and events to which Senghor allusively refers are required by his hymnic narration like the names of the gods in Homer or Pindar or rather like the names and events the *griots* [storytellers] of Senegal were wont to weave into their songs of praise. Senghor's songs, often (ostensibly?) written for accompaniment by one or the other native instrument, are on occasion marred by a touch of preachiness and an enjoyment of verbal virtuosity for its own sake. Yet it is, as far as I can judge, Senghor and Senghor alone who has been able from his sympathetic identification with both cultures, Sérère and French, to lift an inherited art form without distorting or sugaring it, to the level of complexity which a Western audience of today requires.

Like the word of the Hebrew Prophets and the word in the universe of magic, Senghor's is more than word—it is creative power which conjures up and moulds realities. . . .

Senghor does not, and cannot, have a successor. He stands on the crest of the ridge between two cultures equally alive. Africa, to him, "is connected through the navel" with Europe, he responds equally to Seine and Sine, to the roofs of Paris in the fog and the roofs which guard his dead in Senegal.

> G. E. von Grunebaum. *French African Literature:*
> *Some Cultural Implications* (The Hague, Mouton,
> 1964), pp. 31–32

Black Hosts, most of the poems of which date from 1942 to 1944, has the appearance of a series of exercises in good citizenship, interspersed with memories. These memories are perhaps more the result of conscious choice than an irresistible impulse; they are brought in as if to justify poems that are politically committed. Looking back today, we can see that the 1940's were not the best years for this excessively didactic poetry. Nevertheless, one may grant that these poems offer a rather faithful psychological portrait of an increasingly influential person, who has chosen poetry as his field of action. It would be useless for the reader to look for any expression of personal suffering, intimate music, or excessive rage: all the poems in this collection are useful, direct, and cold, like a testimony without embellishment. . . .

Eight years elapsed between *Black Hosts* and *Ethiopics*. As a statesman, Senghor grew in stature and power, while the poet in him took the time that was needed to write texts that would have more than immediate goals. Above all, the idea of Negritude became subtler and more complex. Paying homage to Ethiopia also meant addressing a subject that excluded the relationships between the colonized and the colonizer: this work deals with permanence and duration. A sense of wisdom comes to light, as well as an ease, as if mystery were finally allowed to creep in among Senghor's excessively bare facts. The poems sometimes take on the mystique of legends; Senghor is concerned with the essence of things, profane or sacred; he is grateful to the ministrations of time, whether or not they have been understood; he catches himself dreaming of a language that might be an end in itself or might at least leave some invisible nourishment for the imagination; he plays at being difficult, and sometimes the results are fortunate. . . .

The return to obscure sources and ancestral trances is certainly a very important achievement for Senghor. For the first time, the reader feels he has been carried away by a delightful, pure delirium, something that disorients him and simultaneously plunges him into a labyrinth of noble and baffling truths, which appeal neither to his reason nor to his analytical faculties. The reader is charmed, and asks only to be charmed some more.

Alain Bosquet. NRF. Nov., 1964, pp. 882–83†

Senghor's reactions [to New York] are surprise, wonder, suspicion, and disappointment. . . .

In New York Senghor saw himself as the child of the bush, of nature, who, it seems, was uprooted from his communion with the trees, rivers, flocks, gods, and the dead; it seems that he felt ill at ease. The external beauty of this American metropolis masks an immense emptiness. Man is dehumanized. Only material life counts. The man of flesh and blood disappears in this "desert" inhabited by anguished men. It is a "desert" because it lacks the sap of human life—love. . . . How much more human, thought Senghor, was Paris, the city in which he had studied! . . .

[In Senghor's poems about New York] the influence of Arthur de Gobineau on his thought is apparent. . . . The black man, even in this overpopulated "desert," keeps his rhythm, the rhythm of life and of dancing. The consolation found in Senghor's stay in New York is the rhythmic gift of the Negro to American culture . . . The poet prefers his nights in Harlem to his days downtown. . . . The contrast between the two areas of the city is striking: the rigidity of white Manhattan and the flexibility of Harlem; the reification of the former and the feminization of the latter. Harlem is alive. . . . It seems that the black man in Harlem, despite the loss of Africa, has conserved his black heritage.

Sebastien Okechukwu Mezu. Léopold Sédar Senghor
et la défense et illustration de la civilisation noire
(Paris, Didier, 1968), pp. 124–27†

Quite apart from the lustre which attaches to his name as a statesman, and also quite apart from the halo of Negritude which hovers over his poetry, Senghor was (assuming he will not produce any more poetry) a good poet. He introduced into French poetry a shot of African images which were as original and genuine as they were interesting and profound. His was a voice with a message; a message of humanity and a concern for human values. This message could, in the socio-political climate of the post-War period, not fail to impress. He spoke in the name of a continent—presumptuous and arrogant as it might seem—which was seeking its role in the destiny of mankind, in the "Civilisation of the Universal." It was a voice which was filled with the emotions and tensions and inconsistencies and hopes and fears and frustrations of a continent seething with new ideas, and it was this voice which endeavored to induce the peoples of our [African] continent towards making an original contribution to mankind's common civilisation. . . .

Even though the narrow cult of Negritude has in fact already died a natural death its message as seen by Senghor—viz. to contribute something of lasting beauty to the world—will yet remain the guiding star of generations of African poets to come. As poet, Senghor's image will survive many a generation. . . . Quite apart from his very original poetical note, Senghor has contributed more than any other poet or writer to integrate French Africa culturally into Metropolitan France. At Strasbourg, it will be remembered, he once spoke about the emergence of a Eurafrican political community; through his poetry he has materially contributed towards the formation of a genuine cultural Eurafrican community. In so many ways a product of two continents, Senghor represents a living link between Europe and black Africa. . . .

A statesman who can write poetry with the warmth and abandon of Senghor is a phenomenon which has no peer anywhere else in the world today. No African has brought greater credit to Africa in the last two decades; long after the eccentricities and the fulminations of the Nkrumahs, the Tourés, the Kenyattas will have been relegated to oblivion, will people the world over still revel in the verse of this poet whose very name is a verse of music and whose verse is one of the closest approximations to music the spoken word has ever reached in any language at any time.

Barend van Dyk Van Niekerk. *The African Image in
the Work of Léopold Sédar Senghor* (Cape Town,
A. A. Balkema, 1970), pp. 111–12

The collection *Nocturnes* is a synthesis of Senghor's work. All of his themes appear in it: the evocation of African scenery, the role of ancestors, the bonds of blood, the relation between the visible and invisible universe. The keyword "night," found in the title of the book, binds its parts together. Daylight has always been idealized by French poets; and its apex, noon, when the sun reaches its highest point, is often invoked: "Noon the just," says Paul Valéry. "Horror was its zenith," answers Léopold Senghor and gives new meaning to black and white. The daylight is angular, cruel, the color of snow and ice. Night is plentitude, delivery from the "reasoning of the *salons*, sophistry, pirouettes and pretexts." It is black, fluid, womb-like, full of anguish yet full of hope, a mixture of possibilities. It is serene, peopled by familiar spirits of one's ancestors, yet lurking with hidden dangers. Night is delivery from the slavery of reason. Night is also the collective hour when people of the village can be reunited in rhythmic harmony to listen to the songs of the *griots*, or village story-tellers and minstrels. Night is thus Negritude. . . .

Beyond the expression of strife, differences, and new found pride, one finds in Senghor's poetry the self-examination of the individual to the sources of his inspiration, the spiritual itinerary of a poet searching for the lost "Kingdom of childhood," his haunting powers of evocation, and his luminescent images which are enduring. His is a poetry of harmony, where in fact white is not the opposite of black, but where both worlds are reconciled by a man who, at the crossroads of two cultures, is in search of awareness.

Paulette J. Trout. Introduction to Léopold Sédar
Senghor, *Nocturnes* (New York, Third Press,
1971), pp. xv–xvii

[Senghor's] use of language—typically a formal, almost Biblical tone —is quite unlike the trenchant, ironic Damas's, or the incendiary Césaire's. Unlike Damas or Césaire, Senghor has produced no single work of poetry with the far-reaching impact of *Pigments* or *Notebook on a Return to My Native Land*, which so miraculously encompass the passion and revolt of the black man in the Western world.

Senghor is essentially a poet of meditation, of nostalgia, a weaver of songs about what is closest to his heart. Stylistically, he blends a highly cultivated sensitivity to the French language and its literature with an esteem for the age-old traditions of his Serer kinfolk and their Wolof neighbors. Western critics with a background in the written literatures of Europe and America quickly see Senghor's resemblance to such French poets as Paul Claudel and Saint-John Perse—with their preference for long, flowing elegiac lines of verse—or to Walt Whitman. But anyone who has seen African poets and praise-singers perform—with all their variations of gesture, rhythm, and tone—to the accompaniment of drums and varied musical instruments—stringed ones like the kôras and khalams, or the wooden, xylophone-like balafongs—can imagine a whole other side to Senghor's poetry, derived from local traditions. This African aspect is oral. It can only be experienced in actual performance and is only suggested to the uninitiated who merely read from the printed page.

Senghor's best lyric poems are pure enchantment. Like his "Night of Sine," they operate insidiously on the reader, slowly enfolding him into a world rich with unfamiliar sights, scents, tastes, feelings. To fully appreciate much of Senghor's poetry, one has to acquire a whole new vocabulary of Senegalese allusions, to become acquainted with palaces, persons, customs, the natural and supernatural, the past and present, of another world, another culture.

Ellen Conroy Kennedy. In Ellen Conroy Kennedy, ed., *The Negritude Poets* (New York, Viking, 1975), pp. 124–25

SOYINKA, WOLE (1934–   )

NIGERIA

Some of the praise lavished recently on the tentative beginnings of a Nigerian literature in English is going to sound rather foolish twenty or even ten years from now. Wole Soyinka's *The Swamp Dwellers*, is, I like to think, his *Titus Andronicus*; indeed it is very like that play in its blend of literary allusiveness with melodrama, and also in its occasional *longueurs*. . . .

The Swamp Dwellers is not, I would submit, a play about the Niger delta; but about disappointment, frustration. . . . Now this despair may be a reprehensible state of mind; it is also a tragically common experience and thus a fit subject for tragic treatment by the dramatist who does not judge or exhort but says only: "life is like that."

For us wholly to accept that life is like that, and so be the better reconciled to it, it is necessary that the symbols of the play should have an archetypal force and that its language should carry the overtones of past usage. Wole Soyinka's play fulfils both these conditions. . . . The biblical language in which the blind beggar describes his people's struggle with the soil is . . . not used out of literary pretentiousness; it serves to link their fate with that of all who have tried to sow the desert. It is particularly effective with a Nigerian audience which may not respond so readily to the play's other overtones of language. And this may be the major short-coming of *The Swamp Dwellers*: it has an African setting, but it is written for an audience reared on Yeats and Synge. The Ibadan audience's reaction to its February performance often suggested a failure in communication, as if Mr. Soyinka, after some years out of the country, had forgotten what does and what does not move Nigerian playgoers. It may well be that there is more future for him here as a playwright in the development of the indigenous dance drama, on the lines indicated by his gay and sardonic curtain-raiser, *The Lion and the Jewel*. Or perhaps he will be able to combine the popular and indigenous with the literary and derivative, as the Elizabethans learnt to do.

M. M. Mahood. *Ibadan*. June, 1959, pp. 28–29

The first Soyinka play I encountered was *A Dance of the Forests*. I confess I found this impenetrable. After coming to know *The Lion and the Jewel*, and even more *Three Plays*, it seems probable to me that I shall one day return to *A Dance of the Forests* and gain more from it. But I have learnt that a number of my friends have allowed the difficulty of this play to deter them from reading more, so I must try to persuade such people to investigate the rest of Soyinka's published drama. . . .

I find myself anxious to investigate why I *enjoy* these plays so much. For me Soyinka's writings are linked to those of Brecht, Miller, Pinter, N. F. Simpson and sometimes Ionesco among modern playwrights by a particular kind of enjoyment that makes me want to stop immediately and read the same page more than once. The words constantly catch the rhythm of a human existence, so that one becomes aware of a character as a complete consciousness, and therefore of the complex relationship between different beings. . . .

Soyinka lets us enter into each character's private awareness, and also keeps us conscious how they appear to the outside observer: we are at once subjective and objective. We see how human beings are. We feel a spark of that outflowing towards humanity which any God worthy of man's awe must feel infinitely. A man matters to us in this context not simply because he is good, or because he does this or that, but in himself because he is himself. I think the kind of enjoyment I alluded to is related to this sense of being close to comprehending human activity at its source. A dramatist who starts at this point does not need a "plot" to keep us absorbed. He can now unfold a pattern of the way human beings sometimes behave.

Because of this approach Soyinka can, incidentally, draw us very closely into his Nigerian world; and any dramatist must bring his setting to life. The scenes are essentially Nigerian—so much so that in a lesser playwright (or for me in *A Dance of the Forests*) they might obscure the whole drama for the uninitiated. However he is never writing *about* the Nigerian background as such, but about human beings who happen to exist very fully in this particular time and place. So we see how the familiar human passions, failures, achievements, greatness or littleness of spirit, are manifested in a previously unfamiliar environment. We make contact with this society in the only meaningful way, from the inside, via what we already share in common with it.

David Cook. Transition. March–April, 1964,
pp. 38–39

The artist in Soyinka's world . . . is seen as the conscience of the nation. In *A Dance of the Forests* the Court poet is one of the few people who dares raise his voice whenever the king and his whorish queen overreach themselves. And Eman, the Christ-like figure in *The Strong Breed*, has an artist's sensitivity. He remains a stranger to the people: those who have much to give, he says, fulfil themselves in total loneliness. Certainly this is the lot of Sekoni, the civil engineer in *The Interpreters*. After completing a power station to which he has devoted much of his energy, thought, and vision, he is told by the Council that the station is not good enough, that it is not going to be used. It is not even going to be tested. We later discover that the Councillors had made an agreement with the contractors to break the contract, as this meant more money for them all. They were going to share out the loot from public funds. The shock breaks Sekoni. He turns to carving.

Confronted with the impotence of the élite, the corruption of those steering the ship of State and those looking after its organs of justice. Wole Soyinka does not know where to turn. Often the characters held up for our admiration are (apart from the artists) cynics, or sheer tribal reactionaries like Baroka [in *The Lion and the Jewel*]. The cynicism is hidden in the language (the author seems to revel in his own linguistic mastery) and in occasional flights into metaphysics. Soyinka's good man is the uncorrupted individual: his liberal humanism leads him to admire an individual's lone act of courage, and thus often he ignores the creative struggle of the masses. The ordinary people, workers and peasants, in his plays remain passive watchers on the shore or pitiful comedians on the road. [1966]

Ngugi wa Thiong'o. *Homecoming* (New York,
Lawrence Hill, 1973), p. 65

If J. P. Clark is clearly inspired by a classical ideal of austere archetypal characters and events, Wole Soyinka is of a far more romantic turn of mind: he revels in variety and diversity, alternating between farce (*The Trials of Brother Jero*), tragedy (*The Strong Breed*) and romantic mythology (*A Dance of the Forests*), changing from prose to verse within one play and employing the full panoply of the great African tradition of dance and mime. And whereas J. P. Clark's verse removes his plays into an almost timeless sphere, Soyinka's are firmly set in the present—a very recognisable independent Nigeria with its corrupting town life set against superstition and backwardness in the countryside (for example in *The Swamp Dwellers, The Lion and the Jewel*) and ambitious members of Parliament falling for the career prospects held out to them by fraudulent sectarian cultists (*The Trials of Brother Jero*). . . .

Wole Soyinka is a highly accomplished playwright. My only criticism of his dramatic technique concerns his somewhat overfree, and somewhat confusing, use of flash-back scenes. In practice the flash-back (which is largely a cinematic technique) does not work very effectively on the stage which does not possess the subtle fade-outs of the screen; so that flash-backs as a rule involve clumsy sceneshifting in the dark, loss of continuity and easy flow of the action. This is not to say that the flash-back should not be used; merely that it should be used with caution and be introduced with the utmost degree of clarity. . . . But this is a minor technical criticism of Soyinka's work. I have no doubt whatever that he is a master-craftsman of the theatre and a major dramatic poet.

Martin Esslin. *BO*. March, 1966, pp. 37, 39

Wole Soyinka's play *The Lion and the Jewel* has had various favourable reviews but one wonders why. This is a bad play. It is neither profound nor skilled technically. Soyinka has fallen into the trap of many present day African writers who dress up poor skill with exotica. . . .

Technically the play is a failure. We are given long soliloquies which are far from enhancing the dramatic quality of the play and these lines bore us with their weak prose-poetry. They lack wit, the only quality which sustains any soliloquy.

The numerous dances are thinly linked with the main action. It is difficult to understand how modern African writers fail to grasp the symbolic meaning of African dances. More often than not they depict them as sensual material, exotic entertainment but devoid of intellectual content. Scarcely do they realise that this "village exotica" contains profound intellectual experience.

The result is that, in Soyinka's play, in one episode there are several different dances, some of them quite irrelevant to the drama. This arises, one would suspect, out of a failure to understand the meaning of communal drama. By its very nature communal drama must use dramatic, symbolic expressions. The symbolic expressions are effected through bodily movement, masks, music and dance. Dance itself in the traditional drama is closely linked with the meaning and development of the story. One can understand of course how writers reared in the European form of "conversational drama" would find it difficult to infuse the techniques used in the communal symbolic drama.

Soyinka's attempt or rather his use of dancing to heighten the effect is unsuccessful precisely because all the dances are illustrative and therefore parallel to the action rather than are expressive of it. Indeed they are too many to make a successful unified image. They start and peter out before any meaning can be adduced from them. Why should dances have any meaning? Because that is the nature of drama which this play purports to convey.

The play is disappointing since Mr. Soyinka is himself a good writer. The vultures who eat up everything African will eat even a carcase but the African writer must learn to detect these birds. They are bound to be his death in the end.

Mazisi Kunene. *NewA*. March, 1967, p. 9

[In Soyinka's work] the theme of sacrifice leads into the theme of martyrdom, which for Soyinka means the *chosen* death. It can be seen in *A Dance of the Forests*, in Demoke's death wish, the one aspect of himself which he is unable fully to face, and which is symbolically expressed by the Half Child, the *abiku*, the child born with death in its soul. The same theme can be seen in *The Road*, with Professor's desire to know his own death without dying, and his inevitable death caused by his determination to know beyond the limits of human knowledge. Again, in *The Strong Breed*, Eman not only fulfills his destiny and duty, but also is drawn to a death which he himself has chosen and yielded to. Noah, in *The Interpreters*, is a man nudged falsely into the role of saintly martyr by his master Lazarus, who has messianic tendencies himself but who is compelled to fulfil them through his manipulation of someone else's life. What comes out, again and again, in all these works, is the concept of a man *giving* his own death—giving his death in order to learn its nature, in order to defeat it and in order to prove stronger than the finality.

Surrounding this central desire to control death, there are other important characteristics exhibited by Soyinka's people in their dramatic ballet-like encounters with death, encounters which are as delicately precise and as ritualistic as a bull-fight. They wish not only to conquer death by somehow anticipating it and learning it. They also desire to impose a meaning on it, a meaning which may not intrinsically be there at all. The murderer and the martyred messiah interest Soyinka for exactly the same reason—both are drawn magnetically towards death, both are fascinated with its nature, both may desire their own deaths more than anything else, even though one appears only to want to kill and the other appears only to want to save.

The murderer, the scapegoat, the messiah—none of these, in Soyinka's writing, are seen as *them*. They are, undeniably, ourselves. If there is a core to his work, it is certainly this.

Margaret Laurence. *Long Drums and Cannons*
(London, Macmillan, 1968), pp. 75–76

At the time of the writing of this review, Christopher Okigbo has already been killed fighting [in the Nigerian civil war], and Soyinka is undergoing some kind of political persecution. And these two have poetic genius. Yet to be able to admit this about them, one has to go through a series of painful admissions, as one would have to do, in order to understand the events which have so terribly eliminated Christopher and are daily grinding out Wole.

Of the published African poets in English, the only one whom Soyinka reminds us of is Christopher Okigbo himself, as much in his profundity and the frightening adroitness of his handling of English, as his obscurity to any but the few initiates or experts. However, whether Soyinka intends it or not, "Idanre" has to be understood. Because, as he has implied in the foreword to the poem and in the poem itself, it is a creation myth with nightmarish parallels to the living world. . . .

The poems [in *Idanre, and Other Poems*] are . . . interesting for the way in which together they describe another side of Soyinka himself, hitherto only glimpsed in the plays. Here, the fun-provoking satirist disappears, leaving us with only the serious and often gloomy visionary. Soaked in Yoruba mythology and obviously possessed by the grim Ogun, the poet gives us nothing for laughs now. . . .

Like [Okigbo's] *Heavensgate* and *Limits, Idanre, and Other Poems* is something good and difficult. We may have to knock our heads against it for a little while. But it should be worth it, somehow.

Ama Ata Aidoo. *WA*. Jan. 13, 1968, pp. 40–41

People who saw *Kongi's Harvest* presented at the Dakar Festival in 1966 complained of its obscurity. Since that performance and its earlier production in Nigeria (I have seen neither), the play has undergone what I understand has been major re-writing, attesting in some measure to the validity of the early criticism. In its revised form the play is still obscure, or at least somewhat unsatisfying, especially in its ending. Although I think *Kongi's Harvest* is quite a good play, in part for the kind of pomp and fanfare also found in [John Pepper Clark's] *Ozidi*, it is obviously not Soyinka's best drama to date. (That choice would be a toss-up between *The Lion and the Jewel* and *A Dance of the Forests*.) There is much of the bawdy humor Soyinka is famous for and the usual cleverly planned pieces of stage business, but reading the play two years after its earliest productions I am led to believe there are still sections that could be improved with more re-writing. . . .

I would prefer to forget the parallel with Nkrumah and Ghana which *Kongi's Harvest* is supposed to conjure up in the reader's mind, for the play is larger than that. The hunger pangs of new, unproved governments and the blind quest for power are symbolized in Kongi's and Danlola's coveting of the sacred yam. Soyinka has composed a more universal satire on power and corruption, political image-building, and at least one branch of political theory ("If the square of XQY(2bc) equals QA into the square root of X, then the progressive forces must prevail over the reactionary in the span of .32 of a single generation"—a reference to Nkrumah's *Consciencism*).

Charles R. Larson. *AfricaR*. May, 1968, pp. 56–57

Soyinka's novel, *The Interpreters*, contains some guidance about the Yoruba gods, but will be best remembered for its Joycean scatology and dashing language: the first sentence—"Metal on concrete jars my drink-lobes"—stands in my head alongside "Stately, plump Buck Mulligan." Easier to follow than [*Idanre, and Other Poems*], the novel will be of special interest to black Americans. Easier still, best of all are Soyinka's plays. I doubt if there is a better dramatic poet in English. . . .

He has written a mock-learned essay, "Salutations to the Gut," in which he argues that the god Obatala's name is a corruption of "Opapala" (hunger, I think). Anyway, he claims that "Hunger, not Sex, is the First Principle": he solemnly quotes absurd remarks in praise of food, by Dr. Johnson and John Gay. He discusses cannibalism—giving examples only from European history—while the noble and mock-heroic passages are all from Yoruba verse, some of it left untranslated. This is the taunting aspect of his tribalism. I saw him once on television, persuading a British interviewer that Nigerian babalawos, "native herbalists," can deal with mental illness at least as skillfully as European psychiatrists. The perturbed interviewer asked Soyinka if he would consider consulting a babalawo for his own mental health. He replied that he would not trust the quacks of Lagos, but might consider a good babalawo in his grandmother's village—but he seemed amazed, as if the likelihood of his going mad was too remote to be considered. He did not know then that he would be shut in a North Nigerian jail-house. . . .

This modern poet seems to belong to another century, to a world like that of Marlowe and Jonson, with great lords and private armies, high deeds and monstrous treacheries, gods, witches, and old wives' tales—poets in prison. This is the country where people are concerned, still, to make a good death.

D. A. N. Jones. *NYR*. July 31, 1969, p. 8

Writing his first novel [*The Interpreters*] Soyinka broke drastically with the unilinear plots and lone heroes which have hitherto prevailed in African fiction, whether Anglophone or Francophone. To find any work organized with comparable complexity we shall have to look back to Ousmane Sembène's great novel of the Dakar-Niger railway strike, *God's Bits of Wood*. Although the latter is a naturalistic political novel, where Soyinka's is symbolic and mystical, both writers contrive to advance the action through a number of separate figures of more or less equal importance, whose paths only cross or converge occasionally. In Sembène's work it is the purpose and situation of the strike which links all his characters and forms the real subject of the novel; in Soyinka's it is the common concern of "the interpreters" with discovering their own real natures within the total scheme of the great canvas which Kola, one of their number, is painting.

His relative inexperience in the art of fiction is revealed in the manner of Soyinka's opening, which requires the reader to assess and relate a number of widely different personalities who are all introduced, without history, in the first few pages of the novel. This helps to explain why a number of readers of this rich and fascinating work have "given up" after the first fifty pages or so. At this point the mind is congested with partial hints and obscure clues as to what is going forward, but has almost nothing tangible to work upon, either in the form of a discernible plot situated in time or in that of identifiable central characters. It is only the persevering reader who gradually discerns the pattern of self-discovery which discriminates and yet unites the little group of friends as their affairs begin to move towards crisis in the later pages of the novel.

Gerald Moore. *Wole Soyinka* (New York,
Africana, 1971), pp. 78–79

Wole Soyinka, the Nigerian patriot, poet, and political activist, was arrested on orders of the Nigerian federal government at the beginning of the Nigerian civil war. He is a Yoruba from Western Nigeria, and his offense was that of having been in touch with Biafra and with the leader of the secession, Odumegwu Ojukwu, in an effort to bring about an end to the war. . . .

The Man Died is in the main an account of Wole Soyinka's prison experience, but it is interspersed with "flash backs" about the politics of the two years leading to the Nigerian civil war. The section dealing with his actual prison experience is based partly on memory and partly on notes and jottings that he managed to make in prison on toilet paper. During his hunger strikes he was often lightheaded and near delirium, and there are long passages based on these experiences. Generally these do not work. Soyinka at his best can write very well indeed, but his weakness is still a tendency to the grandiloquent—a tendency that proves fatal to his attempt to convey the inner reality of his experience. Mostly these parts of his book come out in just a whirl of words, most of them too large and fancy to be of much service for his purpose. There are, however, moments when he seems to strike precise reality: not just what it feels like to be a prisoner but what it felt like for *him* to be a prisoner....

I find *The Man Died* on the whole a rather bad book, though bad in interesting ways. But I think Soyinka has it in him to write a great book of which *The Man Died* should have been a rejected sketch. He is potentially a notable writer, but only potentially; and those who have praised him as already a mature writer, because it sounds nice to praise African writers, have done him no service by this particular version of racism. He has lived an extraordinary, interesting life at the center of events in a crucially important period in African and world history. If he would write about this straight and plain, with no prose poetry and with his indignation there but firmly under control, he would be giving us a testimony of world importance.

Conor Cruise O'Brien. World. Feb. 13, 1973,
pp. 46, 48

It is not at all surprising that much of the creative literature which has come out of Nigeria in the past few years has been a literature fostered by the three-year Nigerian Civil War. J. P. Clark's *Casualties*, Chinua Achebe's *Girls at War* and Wole Soyinka's *Madmen and Specialists* are all powerful literary records of the devastating effects of that conflict on the country and the survivors. Soyinka's new collection of poetry, *A Shuttle in the Crypt*, is the most intensely personal of these books, though he never lapses into any self-centered sentiment about his two years of solitary confinement in a military prison. As he himself says in the Preface, "It is a map of the course trodden by the mind, not a record of the actual struggle against a vegetable existence—that belongs in another place."

Most of the poems were written in jail and in a sense can be seen as radial expansions of the two poems in the leaflet *Poems from Prison* which came out in 1969....

In places Soyinka achieves the effective liturgical rhythms of T. S. Eliot ("This death was arid/There was no groan, no sorrowing at the wake—/Only curses . . .") and elsewhere the word-twisting wit of Dylan Thomas ("The meeting is called/To odium . . ."), but comparisons with other poets fail to do Soyinka justice, for the wit, the words and the rhythms are in any final account distinctly his own. Yet for all the praise this collection deserves, it must be noted that Soyinka's tendency to be obscure is here exaggerated beyond anything he has previously written. In several of the poems the images are so personal and abstract that communication between poet and reader simply breaks down. Despite the great demands Soyinka makes of his audience, and very often because of these demands, anyone who enjoys good poetry will surely be rewarded by reading *A Shuttle in the Crypt.*

Richard Priebe. *BA.* Spring, 1973, p. 407

The news that Wole Soyinka was following up his recent spate of activity in drama, poetry and polemical prose with a second novel must have stirred expectations of another work as complex and richly textured as *The Interpreters. Season of Anomy* is not that book; it belongs, rather, with his other post-prison writings in its narrower margin of hope, its determination to face and master the dragon of terror, its more direct use of allegory and representative character. These qualities associate it in particular with his last play, *Madmen and Specialists.*

The system of *The Interpreters* was a kind of mythologized realism, which offered characters highly individuated in their daily aspects, yet drawn towards a universal harmony through the divine, eternal aspects which they shared with the gods. In *Season of Anomy* the treatment of both character and incident is allegorical throughout. The characters hardly take on individual life and there are none of the metaphysical subtleties which made his earlier novel so difficult, yet so rewarding. The rewards of *Season of Anomy* are of a kind we have come recently to expect from Mr. Soyinka—an unrelenting determination to count the cost of Nigeria's tragic years, to show us how near the human spirit came to extinction or despair. The generalized power of his allegory is all the greater because it is not precisely located in time; it has elements of the situation before, during and after the civil war.

TLS. Dec. 14, 1973, p. 1529

A Dance of the Forests, [Soyinka's] most ambitious play, attempts a fantastic unification of both the living and the dead and of men and gods, a theme which derives from the West African mythic system in which gods, men, the dead, and the living exist in a unified world. This world of the play is established, as in Tutuola's work, within the forest, the primeval landscape inhabited by all the combined forces of the universe. This forest is also a mirror of the real world, even though it also serves as the world of countless spirits. The town dwellers mingle freely with the forest dwellers who are the elemental spirits representing universal attributes. The action of the play enables a long intercourse between the town dwellers and the forest dwellers.

The effectiveness of *A Dance of the Forests* lies in its elaborate use of a significant segment of the Yoruba pantheon for the purpose of seeking a unity between men and gods and between the living and the dead. . . .

Soyinka is perhaps the most eclectic of the African writers writing in English today. His absorption of the Western idiom is complete, and at times takes over entirely his artistic direction. His freshness is in his return to his Yoruba sources, to its poetry and ideas for language and themes that dramatize his concern for fusion for the new African.

Kofi Awoonor. *The Breast of the Earth* (Garden City, N.Y., Doubleday, 1975), pp. 318, 327–28

THOBY-MARCELIN, PHILIPPE (1904–1975) and
MARCELIN, PIERRE (1908–   )

HAITI

You [Thoby-Marcelin] could write prose poems or stories dealing with the local or provincial life of your country, works in which you would have the characters speak the delightful French of the Caribbean, which seems to me to be so full of resources. John-Antoine Nau (have you read him?) tried his hand at it, but in the genre of the animated and the grotesque; there is room, alongside his works, for scenes in prose that would be both poetic and sentimental. A transplanted Frenchman cannot write those works. They have to come from your land. . . .

A danger for the poet is facility. You should be very sparing with your words; use them parsimoniously, as if they were very costly. That is half the secret; the other half is incommunicable. But reading poets, especially ancient poets, greatly helps the poetry that is within us to free itself and express itself forcefully. I believe I see the influence of the prosody of Jules Romains and Jean Cocteau in your poems; is that true? But the *personal tone*, the essence, is in the lines and stanzas that I have indicated to you, and you can be satisfied with them. [July 29, 1925]

Valery Larbaud. Quoted in *Haïti-Journal*. Dec.,
1943, pp. 5, 7†

The winner of the Second Latin American Literary Prize Competition is important for more reasons than the excellence—which is high—of its literary structure. *Canapé-Vert* is a pioneer, a pilgrim, in fact, walking among us with a story to tell and a lesson to teach. It is the first novel to appear in English giving a picture of Haitian life from the viewpoint of the Haitians themselves—it was written by two Haitians, brothers; it is a "regional" novel of native life on the Caribbean islands; it is a treatise on voodoo which gives a sensible and completely understandable picture of this over-glamorized remnant of the mystery religions. . . .

Haiti offers a study of the Negro in transition. He is freed of the negative, smothering tribal influence which made change impossible in

Africa. He is surrounded at all times with the opportunity to "progress." But the opportunity is not pressed; he can take it or leave it. Thus advancement, or change, or evolution, however you may wish to name it, proceeds naturally. And it is the natural change, this subtle development from an unself-conscious member of a group to a self-assured, self-directing individual which is illustrated in *Canapé-Vert*.

Aladin, Florina, Grande Da, Tonton Bossa, Judge Dor, Sor Cicie, all the characters of the story, believe in the pantheon of the Vodun cult. . . . They are convinced that in all matters of importance these *loas and mystères* are concerned, and that they are vitally interested and will take action within a short time. . . . The characters in *Canapé-Vert* are at the same stage as those in the Greek and Shakespearian tragedies. They determine to express their personal opinions and satisfy their desires in the face of certain anger on the part of the gods. Swiftly they are pursued and relentlessly they are punished. . . .

The story is beautifully told. The brothers who wrote it are poets, and they have written about the peasants of their country in lean, rhythmic prose that never uses ten words where one will do the trick. The picture they paint is full and detailed, but the fulness and detail are trapped in adverbial phrases and quick sentences that blossom into a dozen meanings when slowly read. The repressed and the sentimental may find the violence and simplicity of the book's action hard to take, but any mature person will thoroughly enjoy it, and find matter for contemplation when he considers that these Haitian peasants are the same people as our American Negroes, from whom we are inclined to expect a great deal of cultural advancement in return for a limited attempt to understand a basic evolutionary problem.

There have been some fine novels by and about American Negroes, but none will teach the white reader as much about the soul of his black brother as this brief, simple tragedy of Haitian peasant life.

Thomas Sugrue. *SR*. March 25, 1944, p. 13

Writing with a hard pencil in thin strokes, the Marcelin brothers of Haiti, in the third of their short novels to be published in the United States, deal in the macabre materials of illicit sex and unhappy voodoo as they eventually affect a large portion of the population of Saint-Marc. This is a charming Caribbean seacoast town which had, when I was last there, one of the loveliest flower-strewn beaches I have ever seen. Little did I suspect that this sleepy Haitian village might harbor such goings-on as are revealed in *The Pencil of God*.

The Marcelins make their tormented little tale of desire and guilt come to life in a surface kind of way, in terms of passion and conjure, without the reader ever getting to know any of the characters very well or really caring about anyone.

Though fate and the furies are leading characters, the writing has, particularly in the earlier chapters of the book, a tongue-in-cheek quality. This seems out of keeping with the kind of story being told, as though rather quaint puppets are being described instead of human beings. Like pretty scenes in a smart musical revue . . . the love affair of a middle-aged married Diogène with a 16-year-old girl is told with frequent humor and the lightness of a Ronald Firbank. . . .

The story travels fast, is never dull, but the people are almost like comic-book figures. You know *who* they are but you never know *them*, except as you might know rather exotic neighbors from occasionally seeing them out the window or gossiping about them with the servants.

Langston Hughes. *NYT*. Feb. 4, 1951, p. 5

[*The Pencil of God*] sets out to explore a problem which the Yorubas claim to have solved with *magun*. *Magun*, a magic charm, is believed to have the power of paralysing the gallant male who must carry his amorous adventures into the forbidden territory of other people's wives. . . .

The story is told in a simple direct style remarkable for its economy. The characters are boldly drawn and clear-cut. Tonton Georges, the seventy-year-old man who "had made women his principal concern in life" and still "pursued them" is probably the most amusing, the most active tale bearer in a community where gossip and tale bearing are the rule; where a small story, passing between new pairs of lips all the time, becomes distorted into terrifying proportions.

In about half the length of the normal novel, the writers have succeeded in conveying the philosophy and mode of life of a people living a type of life not unlike that of many parts of West Africa. Certainly one need not seek far among West African proverbs to find an equivalent for that which gave them the theme of their book: "The pencil of God has no eraser."

C. O. D. Ekwensi. *WAR*. July, 1952, pp. 713, 715

Canapé-Vert and *The Beast of Musseau*, void of logical action, try to imitate life in the disorder of the specific adventures that fill them. Each individual is treated with fresh interest, and each one enters the structure of the novel (especially in *Canapé-Vert*) as an important element. There are no secondary characters or elementary facts: everything receives equal weight. And in the confusion of these equivalent destinies, it is difficult to single out the novels' objective.

The main observation to be made about the writing of the Marcelins is that these works try to be precisely as meaningless and aimless as life itself. The writers take as much care as possible not to take sides or to isolate individual actions and pursue them to a logical outcome. The writers' concern seems to be to exploit facts drawn from experience and observation; and the abundance of narratives and popular tales suggests the methods of the naturalists.

How much their vision reminds me of Zola's! The Marcelins' penchant for writing about alcoholics, the mentally deficient, murderers, and women of easy virtue is not new. Moreover, there is also a dryness in their narratives and a lack of psychological analysis! Surely the truth is powerful, and the reader begins to admire the Marcelins for having simplified superstitious practices and for attempting to explain them rationally. But why, while claiming to intervene on behalf of morality, do they systematically apply arbitrary conclusions? The plot always ends, as in the theater, with the death of the protagonists.

Ghislain Gouraige. *Histoire de la littérature haïtienne* (Port-au-Prince, Imprimerie H. A. Théodore, 1960), pp. 277–78†

[After the success of *The Pencil of God*] the brothers, who had always worked together, were now to be condemned to an enforced separation. M. Philippe Thoby-Marcelin came to work in the Pan American Union in Washington and married an American wife, while his brother remained in Haiti. Eventually the two collaborators effected a partial rapprochement. Pierre arranges to spend his summers in the United States with Philippe, and they have now written another novel, which seems to me, to date, their masterpiece. It is in some ways rather different from its predecessors. It covers a good deal more ground, involving a greater variety of social types, and its tone is somewhat different. The earlier novels of the Marcelins had something of the fresh excitement of the relatively recent discovery by sophisticated city-dwellers, brought up in the Catholic religion and the tradition of French culture, of the more or less fantastic life in a kind of visionary world of the African denizens of the hinterland. Their new novel, *All Men Are Mad*, is drier and more objective. It is based on, though it does not follow literally, a real episode in Haitian history. In 1942, there was a special effort on the part of the Catholic Church to redeem the vodou worshippers for Christianity. . . .

[The material] is presented by the Marcelins in a style of unemphasized irony that belongs to the French tradition of Maupassant and Anatole France. There is almost no overt comment; the criticism is all implied. And though what happens, if viewed in an ironic light, is often extremely funny, what is suggested is also pathetic. It is sad that human beings should be living with such delusions and in such limitations; should be talking such inflated nonsense, suffering helplessly from such wretched diseases, be intimidated and dominated by such outlandish superstitions. The vodouists and the Roman Catholics are equally inept and mistaken. Here again the special plight of the Haitians is made to extend a perspective to the miseries and the futilities of the whole human race, to our bitter "ideological" conflicts and our apparently pointless ambitions. *All Men Are Mad* is a very entertaining but also a troubling book, and it is a most distinguished work of literature.

Edmund Wilson. Introduction to Philippe
Thoby-Marcelin and Pierre Marcelin, *All Men Are
Mad* (New York, Farrar, Straus & Giroux,
1970), pp. ix–xii

THURMAN, WALLACE (1902–1934)

UNITED STATES

The new Negro play, *Harlem*, written by William Jourdan Rapp and Wallace Thurman, and sub-titled "An Episode of Life in New York's Black Belt," has plenty of comedy of a distinctly low order. A few critics admitted that certain scenes needed toning down, and even intimated that the police authorities would probably attend to that aspect before the play had worn out its welcome. But none of them, so far as I know, raised a voice to protest against the particular way in which this melodrama exploits the worst features of the Negro and depends for its effects solely on the explosions of lust and sensuality. The "good" characters are hopelessly ineffectual, and all the rest are either worthless hypocrites, like the father who uses his home as a centre for debauched parties in order to pay the rent, or criminals of the worst type. Anyone given to prejudice or haphazard judgments would come away from this play with the impression that Harlem is a den of black filth where animal passions run riot and where the few Negroes with higher ideas or ideals are hopelessly snowed under by black flakes from a sodden sky. . . .

The offense to the Negro, as I see it, is not lessened by the fact that the entire cast, with the exception of one white detective, is Negro. It only doubles the irony of the exploitation. The Negro is apparently a natural-born actor, unspoiled as yet by self-consciousness. We have had enough examples of his work in the last few years to realize that, given legitimate opportunity, he is as capable at creating illusion and the feeling of deep sincerity as the best of our white actors. But to purchase his talent in order to turn it to the public degradation of his own race, to use his very powers as an actor to discredit him as a man—this, I believe, is the cheapest and most contemptible form of exploitation of which the American whites have yet been guilty.

R. Dana Skinner. Com. March 6, 1929, p. 514

Wallace Thurman, a young Negro, who has recently come out of the West, apparently has joined the ranks of the successful. And yet one wonders whether it is a success of artistic achievement or a success consummated because Mr. Thurman has become a devotee of the most fashionable of American literary cults, that dedicated to the exploitation of the vices of the Negro of the lowest stratum of society and to the mental debauching of Negroes in general.

The Blacker the Berry is a story of a girl, possessed on her mother's side of the best sort of lineage that the American Negro knows, but with a despised black skin, a legacy from a roving black father. Merely tolerated at home in Idaho among her lighter kin, she seeks a happier and fuller life at the University of Southern California where again her ambitions for comradeship are thwarted because of her ebony hue. She abandons her college work and eventually arrives in Harlem where once more color prejudice forces her downward in the social scheme of things until the end of the book leaves her economically adjusted as a school teacher but bitter, disillusioned and alone, an emotional derelict.

In spite of Emmy Lou Morgan's easy virtue and lack of fastidiousness all that the author can do fails to make her vicious. Nor does he even succeed in making her indiscretions exciting. He simply has created an incredibly stupid character. The moral that evidently is intended to adorn this tale is to the effect that young women who are black are doomed to a rather difficult existence should they aspire to anything but life in its most humdrum and sordid forms. But somehow it seems that were she as fair as a lily, a young woman, at once so dominated by the urge of sex and so stupid, would succeed in being exploited by the gentlemen of her acquaintance in one way or another.

Eunice Hunton Carter. Opportunity. May,
1929, p. 162

Wallace Thurman wanted to be a great writer, but none of his own work ever made him happy. *The Blacker the Berry*, his first book, was an important novel on a subject little dwelt upon in Negro fiction—the plight of the very dark Negro woman, who encounters in some communities a double wall of color prejudice within and without the race.

His play, *Harlem*, considerably distorted for box office purposes, was, nevertheless, a compelling study—and the only one in the theater—of the impact of Harlem on a Negro family fresh from the South. And his *Infants of the Spring*, a superb and bitter study of the bohemian fringe of Harlem's literary and artistic life, is a compelling book.

But none of these things pleased Wallace Thurman. He wanted to be a *very* great writer, like Gorki or Thomas Mann, and he felt that he was merely a journalistic writer. His critical mind, comparing his pages to the thousands of other pages he had read, by Proust, Melville, Tolstoy, Galsworthy, Dostoyevski, Henry James, Sainte-Beuve, Taine, Anatole France, found his own pages vastly wanting. So he contented himself by writing a great deal for money, laughing bitterly at his fabulously concocted "true stories," creating two bad motion pictures of the "Adults Only" type for Hollywood, drinking more and more gin, and then threatening to jump out of windows at people's parties and kill himself.

Langston Hughes. The Big Sea (New York,
Alfred A. Knopf, 1940), pp. 234–35

Perhaps the most interesting sections of *Infants of the Spring* are those containing satirical comments on the Negro Renascence. Though the so-called "New Negro" was acclaimed and patronized throughout the United States as a phenomenon in art, Thurman observes that very little "was being done to substantiate the current fad, to make it the foundation for something truly epochal." . . .

In *Infants of the Spring* Thurman had an unusual opportunity to produce a competent satire upon the young libertines of upper Manhattan and the participants in the Negro Renascence. He himself was a member of the Harlem literary coterie, and his home was a favorite meeting place for certain bohemians of black Manhattan and Greenwich Village. In practice, however, Thurman showed himself unable to master this rich literary material. *Infants of the Spring* reveals an author morbid in outlook, diffuse in thinking, and destructive in purpose. Nowhere do we find the spontaneous humor which characterizes George Schuyler's *Black No More*. Every indication suggests that Thurman had not settled in his own mind the many issues that he introduces helter-skelter in the book. More than any other novel, therefore, *Infants of the Spring* illustrates the decadence of the [Carl] Van Vechten Vogue which, like the Elizabethan tragedy and the Restoration heroic play, spent itself in excesses and exaggerations.

Hugh M. Gloster. Negro Voices in American
Fiction (Chapel Hill, University of North Carolina
Press, 1948), pp. 170–72

One might say that [Thurman], of all the Harlem literati, contained within him the paradoxes of Negro art. Robert A. Bone, whose book on the Negro novel is often faulty, is nowhere less perceptive than in his treatment of Thurman. Bone dismisses *Infants of the Spring* perfunctorily as the vehicle of Thurman's personal bitterness, self-hatred, and suicidal impulses directed to the critical destruction of the entire renaissance generation. "No one who has read *The Blacker the Berry* will doubt that the source of this self-hatred was his dark complexion." Actually, Thurman was critical of the renaissance because it was naïve, innocent, optimistic, and engaged in the promotion of art. After all the talking was over, Thurman knew that it would take a lot of hard work and skill to write good novels and short stories and poems. And he knew that little truly good art had come from that theorizing. . . .

It is on this ground that Thurman satirized the Harlem Renaissance in *Infants of the Spring*. It was not merely bohemianism which was at fault, but the very self-conscious promotion of art and culture typified by Alain Locke and the "New Negro." He knew, or at least some part of him knew, that artistic production was an extremely personal, individualistic thing, not to be turned on or off by nationalism of any kind. And as he looked over the results of a decade of Negro art, his perhaps too critical mind could find very little to applaud, his own work included. So he wrote *Infants of the Spring*, one of the best written and most readable novels of the period, to bury the renaissance once and for all.

Nathan Irvin Huggins. *Harlem Renaissance* (New York, Oxford University Press, 1971), pp. 239–41

Infants of the Spring was Thurman's second novel. In 1929, he had published *The Blacker the Berry*, a novel concerned with middle-class racial self-hatred. Although critics generally applauded his choice of subject, they panned his performance. They were quite right. Thurman could not even bring his main character to life. He was too obsessed with her hatred of her black skin to give her the human dimensions so important in skillful characterization.

Infants of the Spring was no improvement. It is warped by Thurman's bitterness over the failure of the Renaissance and, perhaps, over his own failure as an artist. Devoid of plot, the novel chronicles the aimless lives of the inhabitants of Niggeratti Manor—the Harlem intelligentsia and would-be intelligentsia who just seem to drift from party to party and drink to drink. The novel is flawed by the interminable discussions of these characters. The only two men who possess any real talent, Raymond and Paul, pontificate upon various issues of large import. They are little more than obvious mouthpieces for Thurman. In fact, Thurman is so overly concerned that each of his characters should reflect certain points of view that he never lifts them above stereotype. . . .

He never put himself at a great enough distance to look at them with some objectivity and wider perspective. One suspects that in writing of the failure of the Renaissance, he was really more concerned with his own.

James O. Young. *Black Writers of the Thirties*
(Baton Rouge, Louisiana State University Press,
1973), pp. 210, 212

TOLSON, MELVIN B. (1900–1966)

UNITED STATES

It is fitting that Dodd, Mead and Company, publishers of Dunbar's poems forty years ago, should bring out *Rendezvous with America*, a volume of poems from the pen of Melvin B. Tolson, one of the most articulate Negro poets of the present generation. Dunbar was the poet-interpreter of a people still somewhat primitive but struggling to throw off the thwarting effects of years of slavery. Tolson is the full-throated voice of a folk that feels its power surging up and that has come to demand its place in a country it helps to make great and free. Much of the promise indicated in the best of the formal English poems of Dunbar reaches its fulfillment in the poetry of Professor Tolson. . . .

Professor Tolson in his two sustained poetic efforts, "Rendezvous with America" and "Dark Symphony," catches the full and free rhythmic swing and the shifting tempo of the verses of Walt Whitman— or of the late Stephen Vincent Benét. Both poems exhibit genuine poetic feeling, facility of expression, and vividness. The title poem, which is especially strong in imagery, is so apt an interpretation of and challenge to America that it deserves a lasting place in the anthologies of American literature. . . .

Some readers will doubtless find a few of the poems difficult reading in spots, for, as a teacher of English, Tolson is fairly well saturated with literary allusions; and, occasionally, his vocabulary naturally has a tendency to be learned. But most of the poems in the present collection can be understood and enjoyed by a wide public; and they deserve a wide public. For here is poetry with pleasing melody and rhythm, maturity of expression and imagery, and personal depth and universal interest. *Rendezvous with America* establishes Tolson as a substantial American poet.

Nathaniel Tillman. *Phylon.* 5, 4, 1944, pp. 389–91

What influence [*Libretto for the Republic of Liberia*] will have upon Negro poetry in the United States one awaits with curiosity. For the first time, it seems to me, a Negro poet has assimilated completely the full poetic language of his time and, by implication, the language of the Anglo-American poetic tradition. I do not wish to be understood as saying that Negro poets have hitherto been incapable of this assimilation; there has been perhaps rather a resistance to it on the part of those Negroes who supposed that their peculiar genius lay in "folk" idiom or in the romantic creation of a "new" language within the English language. In these directions interesting and even distinguished work has been done, notably by Langston Hughes and Gwendolyn Brooks. But there are two disadvantages to this approach: first, the "folk" and "new" languages are not very different from those that White poets can write; secondly, the distinguishing Negro quality is not in the language but in the subject-matter, which is usually the plight of the Negro segregated in a White culture. The plight is real and often tragic; but I cannot think that, *from the literary point of view*, the tragic aggressiveness of the modern Negro poet offers wider poetic possibilities than the resigned pathos of Paul Laurence Dunbar, who was only a "White" *poète manqué*. Both attitudes have limited the Negro poet to a provincial mediocrity in which one's feelings about one's difficulties become more important than poetry itself.

It seems to me only common sense to assume that the main thing is the poetry, if one is a poet, whatever one's color may be. I think that Mr. Tolson has assumed this; and the assumption, I gather, has made him not less but more intensely *Negro* in his apprehension of the world than any of his contemporaries, or any that I have read. But by becoming more intensely Negro he seems to me to dismiss the entire problem, so far as poetry is concerned, by putting it in its properly subordinate place. In the end I found that I was reading *Libretto for the Republic of Liberia* not because Mr. Tolson is a Negro but because he is a poet, not because the poem has a "Negro subject" but because it is about the world of all men. And this subject is not merely asserted; it is embodied in a rich and complex language, and realized in terms of the poetic imagination.

Allen Tate. Poetry. July, 1950, pp. 217–18

Tolson's *Libretto for the Republic of Liberia*, commissioned by the first African republic, has in its American publication an introduction by Allen Tate. Mr. Tate is a Confederate of the old school who has no use for Negroes but who will salute an exception to the race. . . . But in trying to assert that Tolson has been assimilated by the Anglo-American tradition, he puts Tolson in quarantine and destroys the value of the poem—possibly this critic's conscious intention. Thus it took a Southern intellectual and poet, an anti-Negro poet, to introduce Tolson's *Libretto for the Republic of Liberia*. That was the only possible literary context for a great Negro poet ten or fifteen years ago: he must in that context be captured and returned to colonization, to that Tradition which had enslaved his ancestors, and would continue to do so if it could manage it.

The refusal to see that Tolson's significance lies in his language, Negro, and that only that language can express the poetic sensibility of the Negro at the door of freedom, is a final desperate maneuver to contain the Negro within the traditional culture. And for that it is too late. The Tradition is already antebellum.

The falsification I speak of is that of trying to assimilate Tolson into the tradition when he was doing the opposite. The fact that Tolson's *Libretto for the Republic of Liberia* is unknown by white traditionalists gives the lie to the critic's assertion that Tolson has risen above Negro experience to become an "artist." The facts are that Tolson is a dedicated revolutionist who revolutionizes modern poetry in a language of American Negritude. The forms of the *Libretto for the Republic of Liberia* and of *Harlem Gallery*, far from being "traditional," are the Negro satire upon the poetic tradition of the Eliots and Tates. The tradition cannot stand being satirized and lampooned and so tries to kick an authentic poet upstairs into the oblivion of acceptance. But the Negro artist won't stay in the attic anymore than he stayed in the cellar.

Karl Shapiro. WLB. June, 1965, p. 853

Melvin Tolson offers [*Harlem Gallery*] as preface to a comprehensive Harlem epic. Its roots are in the Twenties, but they extend to the present, and very strong here are the spirit and symbols of the African heritage the poet acknowledges and reverences. He is as skillful a language fancier as the ablest "Academician." But his language startles more, agitates more—because it is informed by the meanings of an inheritance both hellish and glorious.

You will find in this book a much embroidered concern with Art; many little scheduled and cleverly twisted echoes from known poetry ("with a wild surmise," "a Xanthippe bereft of sonnets from the Portuguese," "a mute swan not at Coole," "a paltry thing with varicose veins," etc.); a reliance on clue-things, the thing-familiar; Harlemites of various "levels" and categories; humor and wit that effectively highlight the seriousness of his communiques. . . .

Although this excellent poet's "news" certainly addresses today, it is very rich and intricate news indeed, and I believe that it will receive

410   TOLSON, MELVIN B.

the careful, painstaking attention it needs and deserves when contemporary howl and preoccupation are diminished.

Gwendolyn Brooks. *NegroD*. Sept., 1965, pp. 51–52

One admires Tolson's big-hearted mind, but his verse too obviously comes *via* Eliot and Pound in the classroom. It also comes boosted in public by a willing suspension of critical disbelief among American reviewers towards a Negro who has made the "modern" grade in poetry. Encyclopedic erudition, world-shaking utterances, sardonic epigrams fill out *Libretto for the Republic of Liberia*. What is missing is the inner world of poetry, a story and rhythm for it all. "Possibly," writes Karl Shapiro, "it is too early for the assimilation of such a poem, even by poets." And possibly it will always be so.

Tolson is at present Director of the Dust Bowl Theatre, Langston University, and Professor of Creative Literature. *Harlem Gallery* shows he knows his America well. He writes as an academic gone underground. The subterranean and gothic dimension of American life that the White Negro mind has been exploring for the past ten years is here explored once again, but this time by a real Negro mind in a kind of Menippean satire and with an overall equanimity of tone. . . .

Harlem Gallery, as a sign of its universal sweep, lists its poems "Alpha," "Beta," "Gamma," down through "Omega," and the writing simply teems with names. Fortunately, there are no notes. Even more fortunately, none are needed as the best quality of the poems is the humor with which these strange but simple people make their entrances and exits as incidents in Tolson's mind. There is a passive, droll, detached manner about this American Anti-Dream.

James Tulip. *PoetryA*. June, 1966, pp. 38–39

When Tolson had completed *Libretto for the Republic of Liberia*, he felt as if he had put the best of himself into the long ode. In only a matter of months, however, he began to think of the old manuscript of Harlem portraits which he had scrapped several years before. At first, he toyed with the problem of how to weave the characters into a story; then he conceived the idea of a great epic work which would narrate the story of the black man in America from the early 1600's to the present. He envisioned a five-volume work: *Harlem Gallery: Book I, The Curator; Book II, Egypt Land; Book III, The Red Sea; Book IV, The Wilderness;* and *Book V, The Promised Land*. This undertaking was unique and ambitious, and Tolson was an artist who refused to be hurried. He spent the next eleven years writing and polishing *Harlem Gallery: Book I, The Curator* while he was completing his teaching career at Langston University. . . . The illness which cut short Tolson's work struck without warning. . . .

In *Harlem Gallery*, he succeeded in creating, through representative types, dramatic scenes, and philosophical discussions, a community of black Americans who offer an education to all who meet them in the one hundred and seventy-three pages of their existence. In this book, his style is somewhat relaxed in comparison with *Libretto for the Republic of Liberia*—though it is also intellectually stimulating and challenging. In much of *Harlem Gallery* he employs the dramatic scene, which he enjoyed writing and wrote effectively. A former dramatist, Tolson, like Frost, had "a great love of people and of talk." Tolson ranges easily from the level of intellectual word play on down. The allusions and special learning are still there, but the sometimes strained quality of *Libretto for the Republic of Liberia* is gone. In this work, Tolson truly found his voice as he juxtaposed the literary and literal worlds in which he lived.

Joy Flasch. *Melvin B. Tolson* (New York, Twayne,
1972), pp. 38, 147

Libretto for the Republic of Liberia is not only one of the great odes in the English language, it is in many respects one of the finest poems of any kind published in the English language during the twentieth century, so far as my acquaintance goes. Allen Tate's minor caveats are meaningless to me in the presence of Tolson's afflatus and Jovian humor. I get carried away. And the "irony," which Tate comments on, that an American government has never, could never have, commissioned such an official poem to be read in Washington, only reminds me that I agree with Tolson that "these truths," of which Jefferson wrote, are bearing and will bear fruits for which white Americans must yet acquire the taste. Imagine if you can the humor of this black Pindar of a Mark Twain celebrating the dignity of the small African republic founded by American ex-slaves with a poem at once so everyday American and yet so arcane, abstruse, and allusive that even with the author's notes it flies largely over the highbrow heads, not merely in his Liberian audience but of his fellow countrymen, white or black, literati suckled on Eliot and Pound for a quarter century! . . .

It is not [Eliot's] *The Waste Land* or *Four Quartets*, I think, which limn the present or light the future with the past so well that scholars salvaging libraries of this era may someday guess what manner of men were we. Nor is it even Sandburg's *The People, Yes*, nor William Carlos Williams' *Paterson*, but Tolson's *Harlem Gallery*, rather, where the heart of blackness with the heart of whiteness lies revealed. Man, *what* do you think you are is not the white man's question but the black man's rhetorical answer to the white man's question. No poet in the English language, I think, has brought larger scope of mind to greater depth of heart than Melvin Tolson in his unfinished song to the soul of humanity.

Roy P. Basler. NewL. Spring, 1973, pp. 67, 73

TOOMER, JEAN (1894–1967)

UNITED STATES

Reading [*Cane*], I had the vision of a land, heretofore sunk in the mists of muteness, suddenly rising up into the eminence of song. Innumerable books have been written about the South; some good books have been written in the South. This book *is* the South. I do not mean that *Cane* covers the South or is the South's full voice. Merely this: a poet has arisen among our American youth who has known how to turn the essences and materials of his Southland into the essences and materials of literature. A poet has arisen in that land who writes, not as a Southerner, not as a rebel against Southerners, not as a Negro, not as apologist or priest or critic: who writes as a *poet*. The fashioning of beauty is ever foremost in his inspiration: not forcedly but simply, and because these ultimate aspects of his world are to him more real than all its specific problems. He has made songs and lovely stories of his land . . . not of its yesterday, but of its immediate life. And that has been enough.

Waldo Frank. Foreword to Jean Toomer, Cane
(New York, Boni and Liveright, 1923), p. vii

Cane does not remotely resemble any of the familiar, superficial views of the South on which we have been brought up. On the contrary, Mr. Toomer's view is unfamiliar and bafflingly subterranean, the vision of a poet far more than the account of things seen by a novelist—lyric, symbolic, oblique, seldom actual. . . .

   Cane is sharply divided into two parts. The first is a series of sketches, almost poetic in form and feeling, revolving about a character which emerges with very different degrees of clarity. The second half is a longish short story, "Kabnis," quite distinct from the sketches, and peculiarly interesting. In this Mr. Toomer shows a genuine gift for character portrayal and dialogue. In the sketches, the poet is uppermost. Many of them begin with three or four lines of verse, and end with the same lines, slightly changed. The construction here is musical, too often a little artificially so. The body of the sketch tends to poetry, and to a pattern which begins to lose its effectiveness as soon as one guesses how it is coming out. . . .

It isn't necessary to know exactly what [a passage] means in order to find pleasure in reading it. Which is one way of defining poetry. And once we begin to regard Mr. Toomer's shorter sketches as poetry, many objections to the obscurer symbolism and obliqueness of them disappear. There remains, however, a strong objection to their staccato beat. The sentences fall like small shot from a high tower. They pass from poetry into prose, and from there into Western Union.

"Kabnis," the longest piece in the book, is far the most direct and most living, perhaps because it seems to have grown so much more than been consciously made. There is no pattern in it, and very little effort at poetry. And Mr. Toomer makes his Negroes talk like very real people, almost, in spots, as if he had taken down their words as they came. A strange contrast to the lyric expressionism of the shorter pieces. A real peek into the mind of the South, which, like nearly all such genuinely intimate glimpses, leaves one puzzled, and—fortunately—unable to generalize.

Robert Littell. *NR*. Dec. 26, 1923, p. 126

The world of black folk will some day arise and point to Jean Toomer as a writer who first dared to emancipate the colored world from the conventions of sex. It is quite impossible for most Americans to realize how straight-laced and conventional thought is within the Negro World, despite the very unconventional acts of the group. Yet this contradiction is true. And Jean Toomer is the first of our writers to hurl his pen across the very face of our sex conventionality. In *Cane*, one has only to take his women characters *seriatim* to realize this: Here is Karintha, an innocent prostitute; Becky, a fallen white woman; Carma, a tender Amazon of unbridled desire; Fern, an unconscious wanton; Esther, a woman who looks age and bastardy in the face and flees in despair; Louise, with a white and a black lover; Avey, unfeeling and unmoral; and Doris, the cheap chorus girl. These are his women, painted with a frankness that is going to make his black readers shrink and criticize; and yet they are done with a certain splendid, careless truth.

Toomer does not impress me as one who knows his Georgia but he does know human beings; and, from the background which he has seen slightly and heard of all his life through the lips of others, he paints things that are true, not with Dutch exactness, but rather with an impressionist's sweep of color. He is an artist with words but a conscious artist who offends often by his apparently undue striving for effect. . . .

All of these essays and stories, even when I do not understand them, have their strange flashes of power, their numerous messages and numberless reasons for being. But still for me they are partially spoiled. Toomer strikes me as a man who has written a powerful book but who is still watching for the fullness of his strength and for that calm certainty of his art which will undoubtedly come with years.

W. E. B. Du Bois. *Crisis.* Feb., 1924, pp. 161–62

In Jean Toomer, the author of *Cane*, we come upon the very first artist of the race, who with all an artist's passion and sympathy for life, its hurts, its sympathies, its desires, its joys, its defeats and strange yearnings, can write about the Negro without the surrender or compromise of the artist's vision. So objective is it, that we feel that it is a mere accident that birth or association has thrown him into contact with the life he has written about. He would write just as well, just as poignantly, just as transmutingly, about the peasants of Russia, or the peasants of Ireland, had experience brought him in touch with their existence. *Cane* is a book of gold and bronze, of dusk and flame, of ecstasy and pain, and Jean Toomer is a bright morning star of a new day of the race in literature.

William Stanley Braithwaite. In Alain Locke, ed.,
The New Negro (New York, Albert and Charles
Boni, 1925), p. 44

In writing about Toomer, one is discussing a man who has been poetically quiet for the past eight years. His importance lies in this fact, gainsaid only by J. W. Johnson, since he neglects to include him in his *Second Book of American Negro Verse*—that whether or not he has written anything recently, he remains one of the more important Negro poets. . . .

There is ample enough poetry as poetry in his one book for him to be included in any select niche of poetical art. . . .

In *Cane* raving critics and poetasters recognized a naturalism of such a distinctive kind that the applause was deafening. This novel element in his poetry was distinctive because first of all, here was a Negro who composed not as a Negro, but as an artist, and secondly because there was not in his poetry any obsession of race. At first, the critics could not understand that a Negro could write poetry that did not reek with rebellion and propaganda. Toomer wrote as a poet, never as an apologist. Reading the turbulent and rebellious poetry of the McKay of that time, this poetry of Toomer's came upon the poetic horizon as a breath of sweet, cool air.

Eugene Holmes. *Opportunity.* Aug., 1932, p. 252

One of the most talented of the Negro writers, Jean Toomer, went to Paris to become a follower and disciple of [the Russian founder of Unitism, George] Gurdjieff's at Fontainebleau, where Katherine Mansfield died. He returned to Harlem, having achieved awareness, to impart his precepts to the literati. . . .

But the trouble with such a life-pattern in Harlem was that practically everybody had to work all day to make a living, and the cult of Gurdjieff demanded not only study and application, but a large amount of inner observation and silent concentration as well. So while some of Mr. Toomer's best disciples were sitting long hours concentrating, unaware of time, unfortunately they lost their jobs, and could no longer pay the handsome young teacher for his instructions. Others had so little time to concentrate, if they wanted to live and eat, that their advance toward cosmic consciousness was slow and their hope of achieving awareness distant indeed. So Jean Toomer shortly left his Harlem group and went downtown to drop the seeds of Gurdjieff in less dark and poverty-stricken fields. . . . From downtown New York, Toomer carried Gurdjieff to Chicago's Gold Coast—and the Negroes lost one of the most talented of all their writers—the author of the beautiful book of prose and verse, *Cane*.

The next thing Harlem heard of Jean Toomer was that he had married Margery Latimer, a talented white novelist, and maintained to the newspapers that he was no more colored than white—as certainly his complexion indicated. When the late James Weldon Johnson wrote him for permission to use some of his poems in *The Book of American Negro Poetry*, Mr. Johnson reported that the poet, who, a few years before, was "caroling softly souls of slavery" now refused to permit his poems to appear in an anthology of *Negro* verse—which put all the critics, white and colored, in a great dilemma. How should they class the author of *Cane* in their lists and summaries? With Dubose Heyward and Julia Peterkin? Or with Claude McKay and Countee Cullen? Nobody knew exactly, it being a case of black blood and white blood having met and the individual deciding, after Paris and Gurdjieff, to be merely American.

One can't blame him for that. Certainly nobody in Harlem could afford to pay for Gurdjieff. And very few there have evolved souls.

Now Mr. Toomer is married to a lady of means—his second wife —of New York and Santa Fe, and is never seen on Lenox Avenue any more. Harlem is sorry he stopped writing. He was a fine American writer.

Langston Hughes. The Big Sea (New York, Alfred A. Knopf, 1940), pp. 241–43

Jean Toomer's *Cane* is an important American novel. By far the most impressive product of the Negro Renaissance, it ranks with Richard Wright's *Native Son* and Ralph Ellison's *Invisible Man* as a measure of the Negro novelist's highest achievement. Jean Toomer belongs to that first rank of writers who use words almost as a plastic medium, shaping new meanings from an original and highly personal style. Since stylistic innovation requires great technical dexterity, Toomer displays a concern for technique which is fully two decades in advance of the period. While his contemporaries of the Harlem School were still experimenting with a crude literary realism, Toomer had progressed beyond the naturalistic novel to "the higher realism of the emotions," to symbol, and to myth. . . .

Toomer's symbols reflect the profound humanism which forms the base of his philosophical position. Man's essential goodness, he would contend, his sense of brotherhood, and his creative instincts have been crushed and buried by modern industrial society. Toomer's positive values, therefore, are associated with the soil, the cane, and the harvest; with Christian charity, and with giving oneself in love. On the other side of the equation is a series of burial or confinement symbols (houses, alleys, machines, theaters, nightclubs, newspapers) which limit man's growth and act as barriers to his soul. Words are useless in piercing this barrier; Toomer's intellectualizing males are tragic figures because they value talking above feeling. Songs, dreams, dancing, and love itself (being instinctive in nature) may afford access to "the simple beauty of another's soul." The eyes, in particular, are avenues through which we can discover "the truth that people bury in their hearts."

> Robert A. Bone. *The Negro Novel in America* (New
> Haven, Conn., Yale University Press, 1958),
> pp. 81, 84

"I am of no particular race. I am of the human race, a man at large in this human world, preparing a new race. I am of no specific region, I am of earth" [writes Toomer in *Essentials*]. Walt Whitman himself would have subscribed to this declaration of identity, which bears witness to the transcendence and sublimation of race, not to its repudiation. We will see the new race emerge in that great poetic upsurge, "Blue Meridian," which still, more than a quarter-century after publication, unfortunately remains almost unknown. In this long poem, Toomer reaches the last stage of a spiritual experiment whose point of departure was *Cane*, and which aims at the reconstruction of man. . . .

The fundamental thesis of "Blue Meridian" is the need for a regenerated America, to be achieved through the regeneration of each individual and each community composing it, of an America once more united around the spiritual dream of its founders. . . .

The ultimate driving force behind the whole body of Jean Toomer's work is his ardent longing for unity at the highest level of the spirit. Setting out from the immediate data of racial difference, he rapidly soars above them—too rapidly for the taste of those who, unable to imagine any universe not black and white, were not internally ready to join him in his pursuit of the Blue Meridian. They had expected him to be a poet of his race, but he resolved to be purely the poet of man. Did this provide sufficient reason for the accusation that he had repudiated his origins and abandoned his own people? One can scarcely believe that Jean Toomer, with a mind so tempered and with a soul so generous, could have toyed even fleetingly with the notion of treason. Quite to the contrary: it would seem that we must count him among the very great for having refused, for his own part and on behalf of his fellows, the shackles that are worn by men divided. [1963]

Jean Wagner. *Black Poets of the United States*
(Urbana, University of Illinois Press, 1973),
pp. 264, 274, 281

Now that the Jean Toomer papers have found a home at the Fisk University library it is no longer necessary to speculate as to why Toomer ceased to write after he published *Cane* in 1923. In fact, he did not cease to write. He continued to write, and write voluminously; but to no avail—he could find no publisher. The story of Toomer's literary efforts after 1923 is a story of frustration, despair and failure—this after what was surely one of the most promising beginnings in the history of American literature. Toomer's story is one of a young man caught up in the tangled skein of race relations in America. But it goes beyond even that. For a time, at least, it was the story of modern man; the story of a search for identity—for an absolute in a world that had dissolved into flux. It is a story of success—at the age of thirty-one his search for an identity-giving absolute was over. It is a story of tragedy. As long as he was searching he was a fine creative artist; when the search ended, so did his creative powers. So long as he was searching, his work was the cry of one caught in the modern human condition; it expressed modern man's lostness, his isolation. Once Toomer found an identity-giving absolute, his voice ceased to be the cry of modern man and became the voice of the schoolmaster complacently pointing out the way—his way.

S. P. Fullinwider. *Phylon*. Winter, 1966, p. 396

Jean Toomer may have considered 1933 a year of new beginnings after ten years of fruitlessness, ten years of wandering. . . .

Toomer regarded *Eight Day World* as "a revelation of the psyche of a single man or woman," an explanation of the meaning of this terrestrial and cosmic journey. He felt that for once he had expressed all the details. He was correct only that the book represented a new Toomer, with all of the flaws and few of the virtues of the old. . . .

He could not return to the style and thought of *Cane*. He refused to recognize his major limitations—inability to develop a dramatic plot, inability to write about himself effectively, and refusal to write about anyone else. He could not free his art from his dogma. To understand his work, one needed to comprehend and to believe his philosophy that the only meaningful life is a continuous growth toward Being, a process requiring the separate and total development of mind, soul, and body. Beyond that philosophy, nothing existed. Toomer could sketch, lyrically or realistically, the people whom he knew. His talent was perhaps restricted in range, but it approached genius within its limits. But the engraver wanted to paint murals and could not.

Darwin T. Turner. *In a Minor Chord: Three Afro-American Writers and Their Search for Identity* (Carbondale, Southern Illinois University Press, 1971), pp. 52–53, 56

When Jean Toomer's *Cane* was published in 1923, it was noticed by only a very few reviewers and critics, most of them black, and it sold around five hundred copies. It seemed that, as Thomas Bailey Aldrich said of an early volume of Emily Dickinson's poems, "Oblivion lingers in the immediate neighborhood." It is now known that Toomer continued to write, but after *Cane* he published only a few pieces in "little" magazines, a play *Balo*, and a privately printed collection of epigrams and aphorisms called *Essentials*. The rest was silence—and mystery. To all intents and purposes, Jean Toomer vanished. In efforts to see him, people like Allen Tate made appointments for meetings, but when the time came Toomer failed to appear. . . . At his death in 1967 he was apparently almost forgotten, and his masterwork had been out of print for nearly half a century. . . .

Finally, in 1969, two years after Toomer's death, Harper & Row brought out a new paperback edition of *Cane* in their Perennial Classic series. It found a receptive audience among both scholars and general readers, and already stories and poems by Toomer, often from *Cane* itself, are being included in anthologies of American literature.

The story of Jean Toomer and *Cane*, then, follows the archetypal pattern of birth, death, and resurrection, on a smaller scale perhaps, but similar to the stories of the reputations of Herman Melville, Henry

James, F. Scott Fitzgerald, and other American writers who have experienced oblivion and rehabilitation.

Frank Durham. Preface to Frank Durham, ed.,
The Merrill Studies in Cane (Columbus, Ohio,
Charles E. Merrill, 1971), pp. iii–iv

Toomer's answer to the quest for Negro identity [in *Cane*] is to find one's roots in the homeland, the South, and to claim it as one's own. It is to look into the fullness of the past without shame or fear. To be, and to relive the slave and the peasant and never be separated from that reality. It is to know Father John, the black, gnarled, ugly, brutalized slave. To know and to accept slavery: the horror of it, the pain of it, the humiliation of it. To absorb it all, this living and dying past, as part of blood and breath. The Negro has to embrace the slave and the dwarf in himself. He, like a son, despite all, must learn to love his father—flesh of his flesh, blood of his blood—to be a man. . . .

The real power of Jean Toomer's conception and its superiority to the romanticisms of McKay and Cullen was that *Cane*, though symbolic and mystical, dealt with the past as a palpable reality. It faced the fact of the South and slavery. The final, and perhaps supreme, irony of the primitives was that they were, in their quest for Africa, in their fancy of Timbuctoo and Alexandria, forsaking their actual past. They were in effect denying that which was immediate, personal, and discernible for something which was vague, distant, half-myth. Toomer asked to embrace the slave father, while Countee Cullen fancied "spicy grove and cinnamon tree."

Nathan Irvin Huggins. *Harlem Renaissance* (New
York, Oxford University Press, 1971),
pp. 186–87, 189

TUTUOLA, AMOS (1920–   )

NIGERIA

Technical faults notwithstanding, *The Palm-Wine Drinkard and His Dead Palm-Wine Tapster in the Deads' Town* is a valuable contribution to West African Literature, both as an exciting story told with characteristic African brevity and symbolism, and as an anthropological study.

Here may be encountered much that is familiar in the folk-lore of West Africa, and much that has never, to my knowledge, been recorded before and is peculiar to the Yorubas. Of the familiar ideas may be mentioned the impersonation of death, the conception of the spirit world, and the symbolic tale of the ever-recurring stranger (*the complete gentleman*) who seduces a maiden who has resisted the local lads, but is in reality no more than a cheap glitter of borrowed limbs. Disillusioned far away from home, the maiden is too broken hearted to think clearly of a way out and is completely helpless. We find this theme in the story of Onwuero and Ogilisi in the Ibo, and I have no doubt that other tribes record similar stories, though perhaps with slight variations.

But new are the explanations for the universal existence of death, of famine, and the impersonation of "Drum, Song, and Dance," which permit Mr. Tutuola to play delightfully upon words: "Nobody in the world could beat a drum as drum himself could beat, nobody could dance as dance himself, and nobody could sing as song himself could sing." And, in the stories of the Red men, and the man who did not know the meaning of the word "poor," one can only wonder whether a warning finger is not being pointed at the present-day Western World, and the ultimate goal to which it is drifting.

C. O. D. Ekwensi. *AA*. July, 1952, p. 258

[*The Palm-Wine Drinkard*] is the brief, thronged, grisly and bewitching story, or series of stories, written in young English by a West African, about the journey of an expert and devoted palm-wine drinkard through a nightmare of indescribable adventures, all simply and carefully described in the spirit-bristling bush. . . .

Luckily the drinkard found a fine wife on his travels, and she bore him a child from her thumb; but the child turned out to be abnormal, a pyromaniac, a smasher to death of domestic animals, and a bigger drinkard than its father, who was forced to burn it to ashes. And out of the ashes appeared a half-bodied child, talking with "a lower voice like telephone." There are many other convenient features of modern civilized life that crop up in the black and ancient midst of these fierce folk-legends, including bombs and aeroplanes, high-heel shoes, cameras, cigarettes, guns, broken bottles, policemen. There is, later, one harmonious interlude in the Faithful Mother's house, or magical, technicolour nightclub in a tree that takes photographs; and one beautiful moment of rejoicing, when Drum, Song, and Dance, three tree fellows, perform upon themselves, and the dead arise, and animals, snakes, and spirits of the bush dance together. But mostly it's hard and haunted going until the drinkard and his wife reach Deads' Town. . . .

The writing is nearly always terse and direct, strong, wry, flat and savoury; the big, and often comic, terrors are as near and understandable as the numerous small details of price, size, and number; and nothing is too prodigious or too trivial to put down in this tall, devilish story.

Dylan Thomas. Obs. July 6, 1952, p. 7

The important thing in Tutuola is his power to set down the collusion of dream and person. The startled critic will find [in *My Life in the Bush of Ghosts*] moments of *Alice in Wonderland*, Bunyan and the Bible, in the story-telling and a groping, Christian jubilation. His ghosts are apocalyptical yet local. He is carried off by a "smelling ghost" to be eaten alive by him. Obscene as a cess-pit, crawling with insects and snakes, smeared with urine and rank blood, this thing carries the child off and turns him into a horse. The story goes from one repulsive terror to another, from city after city of the dead, where river ghosts, insect ghosts, burglar ghosts, the ghosts of the Nameless town and the Hopeless town conspire to punish him or to eat him. In each episode the narrator is enslaved and beaten, in one buried alive, in another half roasted on a fire, in others crushed or bitten by snakes. . . .

This would be intolerable because preposterous reading but for two things: the dramatic idea of compulsion in an animistic culture. The boy cannot move, for example, "because the bush wanted me to be in one place"; at another point he is betrayed in his flight by "the talking land," which speaks as he runs over it and so exposes him to his enemies. These inventions are poetic and alarming. The barbarous fantasy is not free, but is ruled by the dreadful conspiracy of primitive belief and sensibility. The other strength of the story is simply its seriousness. The marvellous is domesticated. . . .

Tutuola's fancy is endless; yet it is controlled by the tribal folklore. It discernibly expresses the unconscious of a race and even moments of the nightmare element in our own unconscious. The slimy or electric movements of nightmare, its sickening logic, its hypnotising visual quality, its dreadful meaningfulness, are put down by an earnest and ingenious story-teller. One feels one has been taken back thousands of years to the first terrors of human nature. A book like this disposes at once of the illusions, so useful to settlers, that "the African is a child." Tutuola's voice is like the beginning of man on earth, man emerging, wounded and growing. He is not the specimen of the folklorist and anthropologist, but a man living out a recognisable human and moral ordeal.

V. S. Pritchett. NSN. Mar. 6, 1954, p. 291

Mr. Tutuola's work which I have seen belongs to the world of fantasy and it may seem here a little ironic to consider that the social situation of the Negro in some places belongs to the world of a fantastic and concrete brutality. It is, in a sense, a great relief to come upon *The Palm-Wine Drinkard*. And it is not only the wine that helps us. Mr. Tutuola has magic.

This novel appears to have a certain continuity which satisfies a conventional and respectable requirement of the novel; but on closer inspection, it is made up of a series of episodes which seem to be parts and even fragments of different legends. That is true. The effect of incantation on the reader is also true. But what I want to mention now, which has been passed on as a fact, is the writer's method. It has been said that these episodes were the man's recollection of his mother's or grandmother's stories, rearranged and organised to suit his purpose. If this is true, there is something of the Homeric fable in the undertaking.

The English response to this has been one of surprise, a double surprise. On one level, it is a surprise at the material itself, and on another it is the surprise at Mr. Tutuola's capacity for a certain sustained invention. This surprise may be described as the unasked question: Is it really true? And when one considers that Mr. Tutuola has always been very near, for all I know at the very centre of, what is almost wholly an oral tradition of story-telling, this surprise is understandable. And what is true of Mr. Tutuola, from the point of view of the Other's attitude would, I believe, be equally true, of Mr. Ekwensi, or any other African imaginative writer, although their methods and concerns might vary enormously.

George Lamming. *PA*. June–Nov., 1956, pp. 319–20

Tutuola published a third book, *Simbi and the Satyr of the Dark Jungle*, in 1955. Here the heroic figure is a young girl, born with great advantages of every kind, who comes to feel that these must ultimately be paid for by comparable abasement and suffering. This is a theme as universal in literature and myth as that of the deliberate quest; in reality the quest and the ordeal are simply two different ways of expressing the same life-renewing, regenerating experience. The belief that expense must somehow be balanced by equivalent earning or sacrifice, by a "storing-up," may perhaps be described as the mythic "Law of the Conservation of Energy." But in myth it is seen that *man himself*, by heroic action or sacrifice, must renew the energy of his world and keep it in equipoise. As in [*My Life in the Bush of Ghosts*], however, Tutuola seems to be only fitfully aware of this overall theme and he does not succeed in relating Simbi's adventures to it in any significant way. . . .

A much more definite decline is evident in the latest book, *The Brave African Huntress*, which was published in 1958 with illustrations by Ben Enwonwu. This is a workmanlike narrative of a young huntress who sets out for the Jungle of the Pigmies to rescue her four lost brothers. The theme is like that of a simple fairy tale, whereas *The Palm-Wine Drinkard*, a book of comparable length, displayed the close form and episodic richness of a complete heroic cycle, in which events full of terror or grotesque comedy crowded along the pages. In that book, Tutuola casts an incantatory spell over his reader with the very first page. We know at once that a whole new world of the imagination is opening before us.

Gerald Moore. Seven African Writers (London,
Oxford University Press, 1962), pp. 51, 54

[Tutuola is] a storyteller in the best Yoruba tradition, pushing the bounds of credibility higher and higher and sustaining it by sheer adroit-ness, by a juxtaposition of analogous experience from the familiar. It is typical that even the last war should spill onto *The Palm-Wine Drink-ard*. The hyperbole of the bomb and the Complete Gentleman— ". . . and if bombers saw him in a town which was to be bombed, they would not throw bombs on his presence, and if they did throw it, the bomb itself would not explode until this gentleman would leave that town, because of his beauty"—is not a rupture in the even traditionalism of Amos Tutuola. It is only writers with less confidence who scrupulously avoid such foreign bodies in their vision of the traditional back cloth. The result in Tutuola is a largeness that comes from an acceptance of life in all its manifestations; where other writers conceive of man's initiation only in terms of photographic rites, Tutuola goes through it as a major fact of a concurrent life cycle, as a progression from physical insufficiency, through the quest into the very psyche of Nature. *The Palm-Wine Drinkard*, as with [D. O.] Fagunwa's *Ogboju Ode* and uni-versal myth, is the epic of man's eternal restlessness, symbolized as always in a Search. Between the author's own exorcism and the evidence of his immediate environment, we may continue our own presumptuous search for meaning.

If however we elect to return, like Tutuola's hero, wise *only* from the stress of experience, it will not have been a totally valueless journey. For Tutuola involves us in a coordination of the spiritual and the physi-cal, and this is the truth of his people's concept of life. The accessories of day-to-day existence only become drawn into this cosmic embrace; they do not invalidate it. Questioning at the end what Tutuola's reality is, we find only a tight web enmeshing the two levels of perception. In his other books, strain becomes evident, effect for the sake of effect; the involved storyteller has yielded to the temptations of the extraneously bizarre, a dictation of his early outsider admirers who thus diffused his unified sensibility. Tutuola is not a primitive writer. With this objection removed, it is possible that the audience for which Tutuola wrote primarily (not that he thought consciously at first of any audience) would come to recognize him for what his talents offer—the contemporary imagination in a story-telling tradition.

Wole Soyinka. *ASch.* Summer, 1963, pp. 391–92

The African writer should aim to use English in a way that brings out his message best without altering the language to the extent that its value as a medium of international exchange will be lost. He should aim at fashioning out an English which is at once universal and able to carry his peculiar experience. I have in mind here the writer who has something new, something different to say. The nondescript writer has little to tell us, anyway, so he might as well tell it in conventional language and get it over with. If I may use an extravagant simile, he is like a man offering a small, nondescript routine sacrifice for which a chick, or less, will do. A serious writer must look for an animal whose blood can match the power of his offering.

In this respect Amos Tutuola is a natural. A good instinct has turned his apparent limitation in language into a weapon of great strength—a half-strange dialect that serves him perfectly in the evocation of his bizarre world. His last book, and to my mind, his finest, is proof enough that one can make even an imperfectly learned second language do amazing things. In this book, *Feather Woman of the Jungle*, Tutuola's superb storytelling is at last cast in the episodic form which he handles best instead of being painfully stretched on the rack of the novel. [1964]

Chinua Achebe. *Morning Yet on Creation Day*
(Garden City, N.Y., Doubleday, 1975), pp. 100–101

The conclusion of *The Palm-Wine Drinkard* has its sources in a Yoruba myth. In one version of the Yoruba tale it is the vulture, despised by all other birds, who volunteers to take the sacrifice to Heaven, but when he returns he finds that he is still shunned and outcast. In Tutuola's much more moving version, it is a slave who "took the sacrifice to heaven for Heaven who was senior to Land . . ." and when he returns and seeks shelter from the rain which has now begun to fall, no one will permit him into their houses lest he carry them off to Heaven as he did the sacrifice.

Gerald Moore sees the slave as a human sacrifice, and he believes that the return of the slave is really the return of a ghost. He also sees the seniority of Heaven as an indication that ". . . from henceforth the supreme deity will be the male Sky God and not the old female Earth Goddess, protectress of matriarchy" (*Seven African Writers*). Anne Tibble, in her *African/English Literature: A Survey and Anthology,* points out that this interpretation will not quite do, because Tutuola specifically refers to Land as "he," so that the deity of Heaven and the deity of Earth are both male. It is true that Tutuola does refer to Land as male; nevertheless, Moore's interpretation seems basically to be the right one. The Yoruba myth is paralleled in the myths of many cultures, for it represents a transfer of affiliation which did in fact take place in innumerable religions at one time or another—the decision that the heavenly deity was superior to the gods of earth. In many places this change took the form of a rendering of chief homage to a male deity— Our Father which art in heaven—instead of the earth mother with which most religions began, and this shift in emphasis often paralleled a similar social move away from matriarchy.

Whatever the ending contains, intentionally or unintentionally, Tutuola has completed his story not as a theologian but as an artist, with a strong sense of calm after a perilous journey.

Margaret Laurence. *Long Drums and Cannons*
(London, Macmillan, 1968), pp. 131–32

[*The Palm-Wine Drinkard*] bowled the English critics completely over. The fascination it held for Dylan Thomas can now be better understood against a background of the man's own belief in the bizarre magic and mesh of language as revealed in his poetry and recently published letters. But unlike Thomas or the much greater Joyce, Mr. Tutuola did not consciously set out to probe further into the depths of man by re-organising afresh the language he knew too well to be exhausted to accept again as an efficient tool to record, explore and extend experience. He in fact provides a concrete case of the "natural" performing in the one style known to him. Later when he grows self-conscious and avails himself of the services of a posttutorial course in English, we can see the results for what they really are as in his *Feather Woman of the Jungle*. . . .

Here is no original language as such but one to be found everywhere in Nigeria in the letters and "compositions" written among a vast group of people who for various reasons have not proceeded beyond a certain stage of school. It is a level of English considered "vulgar," half-illiterate by all sections of Nigerian society, and it is for this reason parents disapprove of their children reading Tutuola. . . .

"Naïveté," made so much of by the adulators of Mr. Tutuola and incidentally by the followers of the Onitsha market novelette, is not enough; language has to be "moulded" by the artist with skill and consciousness. Mr. Tutuola who lacks both of these qualities in his early work sacrifices something of his natural charm and power by trying to acquire them in his later works. It is as if the Onitsha market novelist were to aspire to the equipment of an Achebe. . . .

Nor is his disposition of words Yoruba as Milton's was said to be Tuscan. Rather he adheres to the practice of his adopted language, and it is because he suffers open handicaps here that his is said to be no language for others to imitate but essentially a tour de force or possibly a hoax.

J. P. Clark. *BO*. Feb., 1968, pp. 36–37

Ajaiyi and His Inherited Poverty is not different from the usual Tutuola stories. It is the story of poverty and search. The search is for wealth which, it is believed, can grant happiness to the searcher. . . .

The prose here captures the freshness and the startling originality of *The Palm-Wine Drinkard*. But Tutuola seems to have become exhausted, and the language of *Ajaiyi and His Inherited Poverty* has the tedium and pathetic boredom of almost all his later work. It seems he has begun to labour to create the old effect. And it just doesn't come off. It would perhaps be rewarding to examine the obvious "improvement" which Tutuola's language has undergone; he consults his dictionary and has begun to grasp basic English syntax. Then one gets the impression that the quaintness and the odd usage here and there are put on for effect.

Tutuola, perhaps alone among present day African writers, invites very antagonistic criticism from Africans. He is accused of illiteracy, lack of talent, and of an immensely damaging naïveté which is objectionable to the African élite and their literary spokesmen.

But Tutuola is essentially a story-teller with a remarkable genius for ordering traditional folk material into a readable form. Sadly it seems he could only do this once with *The Palm-Wine Drinkard*; his late works limp along struggling for effect and ending up as brilliant exercises in boredom. One may ask what else can he write after the ghosts, goblins, devils and the fantasy world of dreams and magic? Perhaps nothing.

George Awoonor-Williams. *WA*. April 27, 1968,
pp. 490–91

Ajaiyi and His Inherited Poverty, like Tutuola's other tales, is not traditionally Yoruba, but rather an imaginative narrative that blends tradition with contemporary life. Fantasy creatures like the Witch-Mother and Devil-Doctor live in a money economy, just as Ajaiyi and his townsmen do. As in all Tutuola's tales, both real and fantasy characters are obsessed with counting. They count their wealth in pounds, shillings and pence; they measure their fields in acres and specify the number of miles they travel; they precisely name the time of day at which action takes place; and when the wealth, distance or time exceeds the limits of imagination, it simply becomes "uncountable." . . .

Although no one would have difficulty in identifying the author of *Ajaiyi and His Inherited Poverty*, this book is different from the others. The world of fantasy which dominates *The Palm-Wine Drinkard*, *Simbi and the Satyr of the Dark Jungle*, *My Life In the Bush of Ghosts*, and *Feather Woman of the Jungle* still exists, but in *Ajaiyi and His Inherited Poverty* it is secondary. More scenes take place in the real world in *Ajaiyi and His Inherited Poverty* and human characters other than the hero are important in these scenes, especially Ajaiyi's sister Aina, and his companions, Ojo and Alabi. Ajaiyi acts in terms of contemporary values, like seeking monetary wealth for himself, and he evaluates the action of his fellow human beings, as well as the actions of the creatures of the fantasy world, in terms of the Christian ethic. . . .

The contemporary world has intruded into the composite imagery of all Tuutola's tales in many ways other than those associated with religion and the desire for large sums of money. However, Tutuola has formerly appeared to be neutral towards the cultural influences of the contemporary world. At least if he was critical of them, his criticism was sufficiently subtle or so clothed in Yoruba symbolism that it was not obvious to a non-Nigerian reader. In *Ajaiyi and His Inherited Poverty* Tutuola takes a definite stand in reference to some aspects of contemporary Nigerian life, namely, religion, kinship ties and politics.

Nancy J. Schmidt. *AT*. June–July, 1968, pp. 22–24

In Tutuola's fiction the imaginatively conceived monsters, the fanciful transformations, and other marvels of oral literature are somehow intellectually refreshing, like brainstorming sessions, utopian thinking, and the wild absurdities of *risqué* jokes. It would seem that our minds are in danger of getting petty and stuffy if we feed too regularly on commonplace reality (perhaps the "fairy tales" of science also keep minds less stodgy).

Tutuola's work is of course jampacked with monsters and marvels to give us this sort of mental fillip. What reader, no matter how badly given over to the "mimetic fallacy," could fail to be stimulated by such matters as the self-beating drum that sounds like the efforts of fifty drummers, the free-loaders' hostelry-cum-mission-hospital in the huge white tree, the exhibition of smells, the woman-hill with noisy hydra heads and fire-flashing eyes, the stumpy, weepy-eyed, ulcerous Television-handed Lady, and the concert hall of birds with a guard company of white-shoed ostriches? . . .

Even those critics and readers who do not care for Tutuola's work are likely to admit that he has one characteristic strength—his self-assurance, his literary aplomb, or composure. In spite of the junior clerk English with its distracting nonstandard syntax and vocabulary, in spite of the oddities of typography, in spite of the wildly mythical mode of fiction, Tutuola's authorial voice is magnificently composed, compellingly assured, like some oracle in the heyday of oracles, or like the passionate speech of a man speaking from lifetime convictions. . . .

Another of Tutuola's distinctive literary qualities, the memorability of his incidents, may be partly due to this verve and assurance, this sort of impetuous aplomb, and to his downright, no-nonsense style. Many of his incidents lodge fast in our consciousness; they stick like burrs in the memory. . . .

Although Tutuola is devoted to the mythical mode of thought, his works are full of graphic touches, clear and lively descriptions showing striking imaginative power, that should make the most inveterate partisans of realism lend momentary belief to his magical world.

Harold R. Collins. Amos Tutuola (New York,
Twayne, 1969), pp. 117–19

In the kaleidoscopic world of Amos Tutuola's novels, all realms flow together, all varying manifestations of reality merge and coalesce. Yoruba myths, customs, and manners synchronize with Western artifacts, bringing about a concretization of concepts and a tautness of imagery. All details are foreground, illuminated by the author's total experience. There is no inherent clash of cultures, for all cultures are his domain and from all of them he derives his material. This material is transmuted through the author's imagination, and the fusion gives to reality a sense of otherness and to myth a veracity.

Much in Tutuola is mythic and folkloric, but much springs from ordinary, everyday, lived reality. Only after being fortified by juju and prepared by sacrifice do his heroes cross over into an imaginary realm contiguous to their own real world to pursue their searches and go on their wanderings. Indeed, Tutuola's novels are the ultimate expression of return to acceptance of tradition in all its varying manifestations. All things flow together, movement away leads to movement back, return follows exile, a new day follows the agony of night.

Wilfred Cartey. In John Paden and Edward Soja,
eds., The African Experience (Evanston, Ill.,
Northwestern University Press, 1970), Vol. I, p. 590

The difficulties we face in dealing critically with Tutuola are legion. His works are as difficult to pin down as the monsters he writes about. In talking about the form of these stories, we have no label we can easily use. For convenience it is commonly referred to as the novel, but arguments have also been advanced that the form is that of the extended folktale, the prose epic, or the romance. The structure no less than the language of these works is often confusing, the characters as well as the settings are more often than not fantastic, and the situations we and the characters are presented with are always problematical. While there is a great deal of disagreement over the assessment he should be accorded, it is clear that the words, images and even the sense of what Tutuola is saying more often than not violate our prevailing notions of propriety, Western or African.

This sense of propriety being violated points to a rather significant aspect of Tutuola's work that has not yet been fully explored, namely the rhetorical stance of the author and the relationship between the authorial voice in these works and the audience. The rhetoric, of course, has been touched on by the critics who have recognized that Tutuola is more like a fireside raconteur than a conscious literary artist, but the implications have not been pursued. His rhetoric is that of a riddler; he generates confusion, transgresses propriety, and inverts our normal perceptions of the real, physical world, leaving us with the sheer joy we derive out of participating in that confusion as well as the astonishment we get on emerging from fictional chaos and finding the world reordered.

Richard Priebe. In Bernth Lindfors, ed., Critical
Perspectives on Amos Tutuola (Washington, D.C.,
Three Continents, 1975), p. 266

U TAM'SI, TCHICAYA (1931–   )

CONGO

[U Tam'si's] mind is full of images. That is his major virtue as a poet. The French educational system, the teaching of French in the teachers' training colleges, has alienated the members of our elite from their culture, to the extent that they criticize our poets for not making themselves understood, as if poetry meant understanding rather than embracing, as if it meant reasoning rather than burning with images. For the image is the only thread that leads from heart to heart, the only flame that consumes and consummates the soul. U Tam'si's mind, tongue, pen, and skin thus spout forth images as from a kaleidoscope, with the force of a geyser. Dense, changing, whirling images, filled with rhythms and colors, filled with juices and saps—*living images*. They are fireworks, an erupting volcano. . . .

Surrealism, people will say. Of course, like the poetry of Césaire, whose images explode from the heart, whose passion is lava that flows without impediment, dragging everything along, burning everything with its fervor and transforming it into pure gold. Jean-Paul Sartre said of Césaire that nothing in his work is gratuitous, nothing the result of automatic writing. There is a single passion: bearing witness to Negritude. U Tam'si, too, is a witness whose only goal is to give expression to Negritude. [1962]

Léopold Sédar Senghor. *Liberté I: Négritude et humanisme* (Paris, Éditions du Seuil, 1964), p. 367†

The Congolese poet Tchicaya U Tam'si . . . is emerging as the outstanding African poet of French expression among those who have begun publishing since the war. U Tam'si's landscape is one of forest and river, sun and moon, earth and sea, interwoven with figures drawn from Christian ritual. At the superficial level he shares with Césaire a technique which may be called surrealist, which refuses to put signposts and barriers within the poem in the form of punctuation and capital letters, leaving the dance of the words upon the page as the only interpreter

430

between the voice of the poet and our ears. More significant than this is their common ability physically to identify themselves with their land-scape, to again explore their own existence in its terms, or again explore that landscape itself with the vocabulary of their bodies.

U Tam'si draws an amazing range of effects from an apparently limited language of symbols. For example, the tree that haunts his imag-ination grows equally in the reader's mind as he progresses through the poetry, until it becomes at once the living tree of man, the crucifixion tree, the tree upon which other human sacrifices have been nailed or hung, the tree of the spirit whose branches (as in Yeats's "Byzantium") are filling with singing birds, the tree Ygdrasil which stands at the world's navel, the tree of the poet's lost identity, and, simultaneously with all these, simply a great tree of the Congo forests, its branches swarming with monkeys, butterflies, fruit and flowers.

Gerald Moore. *BO*. Aug., 1967, pp. 35–36

U Tam'si refuses to wave banners advertising Negritude; he regards poetry simultaneously as an attempt to answer the question "how to live?" and as a revival-song of a rediscovered fraternity among all men. A visionary in touch with the sources of the great tradition—Rimbaud ("He gave me the audacity to write"), Garcia Lorca, Aragon, as well as Césaire, Claudel, Chekhov—U Tam'si mixes the elements of the uni-verse to the orgiastic rhythm of the tom-tom and the dance. Elliptical and enigmatic, the images that ring forth are so many signs of the innermost self: they suggest the contours of an obsessive cosmogony: the tree, the devouring flame of the bush, rich and fertile sexuality, the sea. The poet thus invites us on a journey of initiation to the sources of the self; by rediscovering the traces of his ancestors, the poet will redis-cover himself . . .

The nostalgia of a mythical precolonial past is contrasted with the bitterness of humiliation. Cut off from his past, the mutilated poet ex-periences the cruelty of his rootlessness. . . . The consolation of Chris-tianity is offered to him, but the haunting parallels traced by U Tam'si between Christ's suffering and the suffering of black men culminate in an angry denunciation of a religion that harbors murderers.

Torn between two cultures, the poet is no longer anything but a "man who flees his own shadow." Nevertheless, even if U Tam'si's journey includes a stopover in Hell, his poetry—by contrast to that of the West—still encourages fraternal participation.

Jacques Chevrier. *Le monde*. Oct. 23, 1970, p. 20†

After the desperate outburst of *The Belly*, U Tam'si returns to a less bitter note in *Musical Arch*. Here there is hope; the man of mixed

432   U TAM'SI, TCHICAYA

culture and race is "bronze" and the hope of the world. Still at present, Europe denies the poet his "magic" as "maker" in traditional society: "It's the bow-harp/we must play in this country." He desires a stronger instrument—the license of his peers in Africa—if he is to effect change. But the "stolen fire" (the poet's knowledge) ought to be restored if he seeks peace. In other words, the truth ought not to be proclaimed too loudly. The effect is not quite as vigorous as in *The Belly*.

U Tam'si is a poet of strong conviction. His poetry is not one-sided, but explores intensively the meaning of life, very often for a Black man in a world hostile to his existence. Through rich nuances of language, through symbol and imagery, through pun and displaced syntax, he ardently describes the plight of the Congo, Africa, and all Black men. As has been noted, primary and secondary images dominate each work, but whereas [*Brush Fire*] gives only a half answer to the question of identity, *Epitome* and *The Belly* delve into the personal nature of the public manifestations of racial exploitation. U Tam'si is the greatest African poet, for not only does he side with his people, as spokesman within the African oral tradition, but he also makes alien and alienated respond to his harsh judgments. His poems move away from nice quibbles about himself to the broader concerns of his role in the history of the Black world. In this connection, his close association with the [former Belgian] Congo during 1960 was probably a turning point. After Lumumba's death, he came to realize that "the singing violin/has not burnt the wind" and that his own art had to disavow European standards in its attempt to speak for inarticulate millions. This he has certainly managed to do.

O. R. Dathorne. The Black Mind (Minneapolis,
University of Minnesota Press, 1974), pp. 384–85

In U Tam'si's work it is clear that the most persistent influences are French symbolism and surrealism, an overwhelming attachment to Catholic imagery, and a persistent return to a Congolese landscape as the ultimate focus of his inspiration. Even though aware of race, his poetry does not anchor itself in the racial memory of Negritude's atavism. It seeks what in essence is a voice to articulate an individual rather than a collective agony. In this sense, he is closer to Césaire than to Senghor, whose poetry tends to make large and expansive gestures rather than the poignant personal assertions like Césaire, locked in the purgatory of French civilization. . . .

U Tam'si's work represents one of the clearest aspects of the self-assured individual voice that contemporary poetry of Africa carries. There is nothing sentimental or insincere in the feeling, which is uniquely matched with a great passion for language. The whole world is his roving ground; history, the past, Roman Catholicism, and political events provide the feeding sources for the nourishment of the strong images of rivers, the tree, blood, and the sacrifice. Louis Aragon's "cry of the spirit that turns inward on itself" informs U Tam'si's surrealism. For him it is no frivolous exercise in verbal and imagistic agility. His Negritude retrieves itself from public affirmations and returns to a private personal agony in which a catatonic array of emotions, episodes, images, and symbols is pressed into service to explode his poetic madness and silent agony. His master is Césaire who provides the inspiration, the surrealists—Breton, Aragon—and the passion of his own poetic and musical ear supplying the unification and thrust in his verse. He may be a Negritude writer, but with an immense difference.

Kofi Awoonor. *The Breast of the Earth* (Garden City, N.Y., Doubleday, 1975), pp. 176, 184

VILAKAZI, B. W. (1906–1947)

SOUTH AFRICA

Mr. Vilakazi in the richness of his Zulu vocabulary, in the truly African flavor of his imagery and in the exuberant extravagance of some of his descriptions [in *Zulu Songs*] is a true descendant of the *imbongi* [tribal bards]. But the background of his thought is not that of the *imbongi*. He is not much concerned with warlike prowess. Aggrey [the Gold Coast scholar] is a greater hero to him than Shaka [the early-nineteenth-century Zulu chief]. The clay pot family heirloom, the song of the lark, the train that dashes by in the night, leaving him vainly waiting—all the little incidents of daily life serve as starting points for the flow of his verse. He is the human poet rather than the Zulu poet also in the attention he pays to his own emotions and those he observes in others. It is the *imbongi* come to consciousness of the abstract and of the inner self, through contact with the work of other poets and through the unconscious influence of education and European culture.

His technique also is not that of the pagan *imbongi*. He attempts rhyme, but with limited success, as Zulu syllables, invariably ending in vowels, do not present the variety of sound and tone that makes success-ful rhyming possible. Even the forms of English rhythm that he uses do not supply a perfect medium, for Zulu accents and stresses refuse to be bent into conformity with the beat of the music. But Mr. Vilakazi is an experimenter in a new field and is to be congratulated on the large measure of his success, rather than criticized for small failures. He will perhaps, as he grows surer in his art, develop a technique more in-digenous and more pliable to the Zulu words. The Zulu in which the poems are written will be the delight of the linguist and the despair of the tyro. His sensitiveness to words is remarkable and he has gathered a vocabulary which must enrich the Zulu speech. But it is when one turns to the emotional content of the poems that the real talent of the author is revealed and a new respect must be felt for the capacity of the Zulu mind and heart.

J. Dexter Taylor. *BantuS*. June, 1935, p. 164

[Vilakazi] began with fiction in a story called *For Ever*. The scene is laid at the mission station of Groutville in the days of [the Zulu king] Mpande. A girl, who as a child was a refugee from Zululand, gives a promise to a boy, who is going off to work in Durban, to wait for him "for ever." The fortunes of both are told in an interesting way. . . .

Dr. Vilakazi is the only Zulu who has attempted to write poetry on any scale, and his first collection of poems was published in the "Bantu Treasury" series under the title of *Zulu Songs*. . . . He afterwards wrote another book of poems, *Zulu Horizons*, and a novel, *Truly, Indeed*, both of which show an advance upon his previous work. The poems are concerned largely with social questions of the day as they affect the Zulu people.

D. McK. Malcolm. Africa. Jan., 1949, pp. 37–38

[Vilakazi] believed that Bantu literature would make a notable contribution to the literature of the world. He believed that his people were capable of rising high in intellectual achievement and he devoted his energies, not only to himself, but to the self-effacing and unselfish end of encouraging and advising many a budding Bantu author. . . .

By whatever standards he is judged, there can be no question that he was a poet of high merit. He revealed possibilities in the Zulu language. Even in translation his poetry has vitality and no ordinary beauty. Dr. Dexter Taylor's translation of Vilakazi's poem on the Victoria Falls ["The Victoria Falls"] came as a revelation to English readers of the powers of observation and expression which the latter possessed. He had a large vocabulary which his sensitive spirit and trained intellect used with notable dexterity.

To the African people he remains a shining example of what perseverance and pluck can accomplish, when in the charge of a disciplined mind and spirit. The early years with their remoteness from such means of culture as libraries; that unflagging determination to study by sun or candle-light; that fight with poverty which could not get him down; that refusal to be daunted however towering seemed the summit which he had to climb—these things make one of his rich legacies to his people.

R. H. W. Shepherd. Bantu Literature and Life
(Lovedale, South Africa, Lovedale Press, 1955),
p. 124

Among the Zulus Vilakazi is remembered more as a poet than as a prose writer. I think the main reason for this is that he was mainly responsible for developing poetry whose form departed radically from the traditional Izibongo (or praises). Instead of adopting the style and pattern of the Izibongo, he experimented with European forms. He divided his poems into regular stanzas. He also experimented with rhyme. Many of the poems contained in the first book of poems, *Zulu Songs*, employ rhyme. If the poems in the second book of poems entitled *Zulu Horizons* are any guide, Vilakazi was not happy with the results of his experiment because in *Zulu Horizons* he discarded rhyme almost completely. In only one poem out of a total of twenty did he employ rhyme. I am inclined to think that even in that one poem he employed rhyme because it was a sequel to a poem appearing in the first book in which he had used rhyme.

Those of you who know Zulu will realise just what it means to attempt rhyme in that language. In Zulu only five endings are possible— in the vowels, a, e, i, o, u because Zulu has open syllables. Any rhyming scheme is confined to these endings. English on the other hand uses not only open syllables but closed syllables, that is, syllables ending in consonants. The English poet is, therefore, not hampered in the same way as is a Zulu poet. A Zulu poet who attempts rhyme might have on paper something which looks like rhyme but which does not produce the desired effect on the ear. I believe that rhyme is for the ear more than for the eye. The controversy still rages as to whether or not Zulu is a suitable medium in which to attempt rhyme.

C. L. S. Nyembezi. *A Review of Zulu Literature*
(Pietermaritzburg, South Africa, University of
Natal Press, 1961), pp. 7–8

The main direction in Vilakazi's development . . . lay in ever deeper reverence for the Zulu tradition. Many of the poems in [*Zulu Horizons*] deal once more with the great events and figures of the past, the beauty of the Natal landscape, the cult of the ancestors, African respect for the wisdom of old age, or the mission of the poet in Zulu society. The writer's technique also demonstrates that he was not happy with his experiments in the earlier collection [*Zulu Songs*]. He now discards rhyme almost completely, thus rallying to the views expressed by [J. Dexter] Taylor and [Herbert I. E.] Dhlomo. . . .

Although Vilakazi did not engage actively in politics, it is clear that his experience of township life in Johannesburg, because of the contrast it offered with the sheltered seclusion of Natal mission schools and with the comparative humaneness of life in Durban, prompted him toward more explicit protest through his chosen medium. This second orientation reached its climax in what is commonly considered his best poem, "In the Gold Mines," which deals with the black laborer's life on the Rand. Vilakazi's mood and attitude are very close to those of Dhlomo in *The Valley of a Thousand Hills*. The main difference is that Dhlomo, writing in Durban, found his symbols of oppression in the "commercial dells" of the modern mercenary city, whereas Vilakazi, writing in Johannesburg, found apt emblems of man's inhumanity to man in the industrial society and in the roaring machines. . . .

Albert S. Gérard. *Four African Literatures*
(Berkeley, University of California Press, 1971),
pp. 251, 253–54

Vilakazi began his activities at the end of the 1920's when racist legislation was just starting to be applied in his country. He wrote in Zulu, and could not—and did not want to—give up his mother tongue. He wrote for his fellows with whom he had spent his youth at Groutville and during his twelve years' teaching at Mariannhill. Vilakazi felt immense respect for the culture of his nation which had been deliberately humiliated by the colonizers. As a scholar, he understood that a people's true national literature, and especially their poetry, is closely connected with the language and history of their nation.

Vilakazi's poetry is the truthful statement of a courageous man; his protest against racial oppression, it is also his emotionally expressed appeal to struggle. . . . Vilakazi sees the only path to liberation as struggle, a cruel fight which, the poet firmly believes, will be victorious. Each of Vilakazi's poems includes his central idea of the fight for freedom, stimulating and encouraging its readers and listeners. The poet admits the difficult fate of the black man and shows the need for a patient waiting for the time of victory. . . .

Vilakazi died too young. Although his life was hard in the country of racism and segregation, he succeeded in overcoming poverty and humiliation thanks to his persistence, courage, belief in his own powers and love of work. As a scholar, poet and novelist, he greatly contributed to the development of South African vernacular writing in the Bantu languages.

Karel František Růžička. In Vladimír Klíma,
Karel František Růžička, and Petr Zima,
Black Africa: Literature and Language (Dordrecht,
Netherlands, D. Reidel, 1976), pp. 236–37

WALCOTT, DEREK (1930–   )

ST. LUCIA

In a Green Night, by the West Indian poet Derek Walcott, is a striking first collection. His writing belongs to the pleasure band of the spectrum; it is full of summery melancholy, fresh and stinging colours, luscious melody and intense awareness of place—"like entering a Renoir," to quote himself. He puts all this to a purpose, however. His joyful apprehension of the immediate physical world serves to focus the other things he has to say, to give substance to conflicting loyalties. He uses a metaphysic of natural mutability and renewal—the "green yet ageing orange tree" of Marvell's Bermudas—to come to terms with the immutable historic wrongs of his people. His favourite personal symbols are of himself as a ribbed vessel, condemned to migrancy and shipwreck, and of his heart as a coal—the repository of forces stored up long ago but ready to burst into flame again.

He is an intensely and innocently literary poet—his volume hums with echoes of Villon and Dante, Catullus and the metaphysicals—but there is a kind of aptness in this, since history has made him a citizen of the world. Certainly the literariness is not a substitute for feeling, and his poems have immense freshness and verve.

P. N. Furbank. *List.* July 5, 1962, p. 33

Robert Graves notes that [Walcott] "handles English with a closer understanding of its inner magic than most (if not any) of his English-born contemporaries." Graves's favorites have always been odd; the oddest thing here is that of all the poets who have influenced Walcott (and there are many), Graves has made the slightest impact. Walcott lingers over his language like a lover; he employs orotund, mellifluously spun lines. He is, as they say, "on stage," and certainly his poems read aloud are more rewarding. In any case, these characteristics alone set him apart from his English-born contemporaries, most of whom in the manner of the Movement write wry, inelegant miniatures, the new emblem of the Welfare State.

438

But Walcott is an exotic (his descriptions are drenched with the "sea-music and sea-light" of his islands), and he is also *engagé* (factors of race and repression are the backwash beneath every breaker). His world is almost a continual surge of scenic delights and/or degradations, all of which he uses for dramatic effect, sometimes in the symbolist mode, sometimes as a sort of pictorial choreography, and sometimes as a violently-charged reverie, or as a declamation. . . .

His preoccupation with the Self, with the solitary figure against the horizon, with something vague and minatory, rings down the curtain too often, and Walcott's lush melancholy, that itch to be impressive, strikes me, after a while, as a bore. But Walcott has special gifts, which as has already been observed are not much evident in younger poets, whether English or American: his textures are musical, he has a painter's eye, his craftsmanship is adventurous, and his moral or imaginative responses aren't shabby. When these qualities triumph as they do in about a half-dozen poems, primarily "In a Green Night," "Return to D'Ennery," "Rain," and "Crusoe's Island," then the full force of his personality, the personality of *place*, the troubled beauty of his Antillean land, comes strikingly to the surface.

Robert Mazzocco. NYR. Dec. 31, 1964, pp. 18–19

Some of Derek Walcott's most quoted poems have probed aspects of regional identity. His new volume [*The Castaway*] worries the matter further, but the predicament of isolation in which he has sometimes found himself has now become more subjective, less geographical. The castaway of his recent poems may indeed wear the expression of Crusoe, with "that sun-cracked, bearded face," and his intelligence is certainly West Indian, but his confinement appears to be on an exotic island located in time. . . . It is a lonely environment compounded of approaching middle age, of lost roots ("some grill of light clanged shut on us in bondage"), of a greater ease in unburdening to the dead than to the living, and of the absence of a consoling faith or a compelling fear. . . .

A visit to New York provides no alleviation. Snow and cold are the most sensational of Northern experiences ("I thought winter would never end"), and at times they assume the proportions of a personal ice age ("since that winter I have learnt to gaze on life indifferently as through a pane of glass"). Indeed, isolation sometimes becomes a universal condition, and all men become castaways. . . .

The excitement of thought and technique is often at variance with the withdrawn mood and the absorbed self-reference. The imagery is intense and sometimes violent. Rhyme and metrical patterns are set only to be broken in a sudden racing of the poetic mechanism. The result is occasionally an inconclusiveness: images and ideas may be stranded, like unfinished remarks left hanging in conversation. But the best poems are an important and unique achievement, and of these "The Almond Trees" stands out remarkably. It accomplishes a sensitive commentary on landscape and identity, of vivid suggestion and careful structural unity.

Kevin Ireland. *JCL*. Dec., 1966, pp. 157–158

[Walcott] began as a precocious, imitative writer of great promise and has weathered successfully the sirens and becalmings apt at some stage to do in a poet's voyage through youth. His problem, as with so many writers in English-speaking, ex-English possessions, has been the provincialism of his background. He himself has stuck to the West Indies, though growing fame has given him the opportunity for travel—to England, to North and South America. The theme of his new book [*The Gulf, and Other Poems*], is the journey from and back to provincialism, and whatever crabs one may have about its details there is no doubt that he has abundantly succeeded in the difficult talk of lifting his situation on to an interesting and, indeed, universal plane. "There are homecomings without home," he says memorably, and his view of his native islands is refined and sharpened by his returning sense of significant history and life happening elsewhere. . . .

The title poem, a meditation, in an aircraft flying over the Gulf of Mexico, on racial violence, seems to me entirely successful, a poem of vision and compassion, with just the right amount of concrete detail to make effective the rhetoric and imaginative use of vocabulary that have always been Walcott's strength. In some other poems (e.g. "Mass Man") I feel that the fuss and the language is not quite justified by the donnée, and there is often an inexplicitness that seems less a studied effect than a failure to grasp. One does not expect from a poet like Walcott a directness of irony or satire but the clotted bits of this collection arise equally from a syntactical clumsiness as from the obscurity of the attitude and situation.

Roy Fuller. *London*. Nov., 1969, pp. 89–90

Derek Walcott's brooding allegorical drama, *Dream on Monkey Mountain* . . . [is] a very extended work, too long and sometimes structurally unsteady. Too many words. Yet an engrossing study, exercising its fascination upon us, designed within a lengthy framework that regularly compels. . . .

The play is rich and complex; the author's use of fable interwoven with a stark elaboration of historical evidence of oppression illuminates his work, lends it an arresting weight and texture. Walcott's characters are drawn with bold, sometimes extravagant strokes and, prodded by the author, they have an inclination to talk a bit too much. But the play also achieves a lush depiction of the many moods implicit in the ritual and realistic aspects of Caribbean Black life. . . .

Walcott is a writer who obviously loves the sound of the language he uses in his work. This affection is not always requited, the theater being an essentially visual arena. (And anyway, Walcott's ideas seem sturdy enough to reach us in a less verbally overdressed manner.) But what he has to say is extremely important at a time when, in America, Black people are regularly challenging the more basic concepts of governmental and cultural "normalcy." The thesis, as proposed in *Dream on Monkey Mountain*, is that the West cannot—nor should it—exist forever, given its deplorable record of racist exploitation and butchery throughout the world.

Clayton Riley. *NYTts*. April 4, 1971, p. 3

There is a lot in this long poem [*Another Life*] by Derek Walcott that I do not understand. It seems to me too long, too choked with people, places, and things, and there is too much foreign talk and far too much British style. Even as the poet repudiates the intrusion of European "culture" into Black West Indian life, he proves at the same time that he can write a poem in which very little that is recognizably Black West Indian survives.

Perhaps this is unfair. Perhaps there is no such thing as a Black West Indian sensibility, that quality of *difference* that, in the United States, informs the work of even the most academic black poets. I do not know. What I do know is that Walcott writes an English line that can at times rise to perfection, and that his mastery of language and expression—though occasionally rendered with a 19th century twist—is complete and beautiful to see. He is a fine, mature, often brilliant and moving poet, which makes it harder than ever to determine exactly what it is that is missing.

What it is, I think for me, is a view of Mr. Walcott's West Indies that escapes the camouflage of an essentially European interpretation. Eager to know Mr. Walcott's West Indies, *his* island, *his* people, *his* greenness, *his* sea, I am disappointed that what he chooses to tell me comes hidden behind names from Greek myths I only half remember, or written in Latin I never studied, or so sprinkled with the "glories" of English empire days that I, finally, can recognize nothing without a debilitating struggle; but must pick my way laboriously from page to page, choosing bits and pieces that speak to me and leaving the rest for the dons of Oxford.

Alice Walker. *VV*. April 11, 1974, p. 26

With the years, Walcott has evolved from the wary self-affirmation of one who "had entered the house of literature as a houseboy" to open-hearted self-evaluation. This is the honesty of the wise man who feels he has nothing to hide because he has discovered in all men the same frailty which used to make him ashamed. What appeals to me in the man as in his poetry is not so much the denseness and intensity as the kindness and frailty at the core, not the polished perdurable lines but the humanity with its doubts and loves, not the classicist but the tempered romantic. Or rather, it is the tension between the smile and the anger, the lamb and the lion.

It has been repeated that Walcott's verse is universal, that his cultural heritage makes him a "citizen of the world." Indeed, there is in his lines a high degree of universality. Such universality should not be mistaken, however, for the sort of colorless common denominator often defined by Western humanism. Walcott's universality does not lie in the so-called "ageless nature of mankind" but in his own precise, circumscribed and deeply-rooted experience, in the small-village culture of Castries [in St. Lucia] with its unique mixture of contrasting traditions. Walcott can look fruitfully on the "other life" of his childhood and youth because he is ready to accept its particulars and because he now sees himself as a native of St. Lucia first, a "citizen of the world" second.

He is thus beginning to achieve a solution to the dilemma of the Third World artist which he had described as "the natural terror of losing touch with the tribal truth and the natural ambition for universal recognition." After rendering in prose (dramatic or otherwise), in *Dream on Monkey Mountain*, the very *tone* of his people's experience, he has succeeded, in *Another Life*, in creating a poetic language which is deeply attuned with his personal growth and yet immediately universal. This is a more important achievement than restoring dialect as the only authentic alternative to classical English. It proposes an original strategy towards the development of literature as global cultural synthesis; it opens a path which is not remote from the prophetic vision that it takes another Caribbean genius, Wilson Harris, to create.

Michel Fabre. *NewL*. Fall, 1974, pp. 106–7

Derek Walcott is a poet of great verbal resources and skills engaged in a complex struggle to render his native Caribbean culture, the new world, first successor to Eden. For the past 28 years, as a poet and playwright, he has continually returned to the themes of that new world, locked in an "ancient war between obsession and responsibility," and it is one of the touchstones of his gift that he has remained attentive to the diversity and reality of the West Indies without surrendering its symbolic resonances and possibilities. Now in his sixth book of poems, *Sea Grapes*, we see him returning to his first concerns but with a new intensity, a deep, well-sharpened focus.

The 46 poems detail the sensibility of a passionate man circling an endlessly complex subject in a range of compelling voices—bitter, violent, desperate, learned, tender. . . .

The title poem marks the emotional tenor of what literature can and cannot do with a conclusive "The classics can console. But not enough."

Derek Walcott is one of the most incisive poets writing in English today. His poems do comfort and console, though, finally, as *Sea Grapes* teaches, not even the classics can rescue us from our perpetual struggle to recreate the world.

Edward Hirsch. NYT. Oct. 31, 1976, p. 38

WALKER, ALICE (1944–   )

UNITED STATES

Miss Walker's poems [in *Once*] lack little in poetic quality, in the traditional, *i.e.*, white sense. I was frequently reminded of Emily Dickinson while I read her. Miss Walker has the tight tongue, the precise wordings, the subtle, unexpected twists, the reversal of the anticipated order of words and understatements for plus emphasis, or the shifting of emotions. . . .

Her poetry is dignified, unobtrusive, almost, at times, matter-of-fact. There is a lack of celebration or affirmation that one finds so exhilarating and so often in today's black literature. Her poetry is timid thunder. Black people are explosions of love, hate, fear, joy, sorrow, *Life*. Their literature should be that way.

The reader will hear a soft hum; a lovely delicate melody will brush him and he will think, "I want to hear more." He will re-read, lean closer and strain to touch, or be pulled by the magnetic *is*ness of a lovely sound. He will wait and search and wait for the melody to break forth into some wildly glorious song which will roll and roll and roll like a chorus of thunder, under him, through him, swelling him, so that he too might burst forth, join in and sing. Though the song might be terrible, the notes our Black life's blood. But our singer does not here sing. In *Once*, she hums a haunting, poignant, yet certain, distinctive song.

Carolyn M. Rodgers. NegroD. Sept–Oct., 1968,
pp. 52, 12–13

[*The Third Life of Grange Copeland*] is an ambitious novel, for [Alice Walker's] attention is focused on a man wavering between the traditional poverty in Georgia and the glimpse of freedom that can never be his. Uprooted, he goes north, only to be disappointed by the confusing life of New York and the bitter cold. He returns to Georgia to find that his son has grown up, but little else has changed: The son, Brownfield, is satanic, methodically brutalizing his wife and children in a way which appalls even Grange, who is no angel. . . .

The violent scenes are numerous, but the arguments between husband and wife, father and son, are if anything more harrowing than the shotgun murders. It is hardly an idealized portrait of three generations of a black family, but the passions are enacted against a landscape which is carefully drawn: Baker County, the cotton fields, the ramshackle houses pitched in misery. Mrs. Walker has no lack of compassion, but has an essential detachment and so avoids being racially tendentious: She records skillfully the fakery and guilt of the cracker and the cotton picker, the awakening of Grange to his corrosive self-pity.

If the novel fails in parts it is because it attempts too much—too many years, too many characters. The movement is occasionally ponderous; elsewhere the years skip glibly by leaving the reader breathless. At times Mrs. Walker clumsily stitches episode to episode. Her strength is in her control of character rather than all the "business" that goes on in a family chronicle.

Paul Theroux. *BkWd*. Sept. 13, 1970, p. 2

Revolutionary Petunias, Alice Walker's second book of poetry, is a major achievement by a poet who deserves more critical attention than she has received. The promising seeds she planted in *Once* have blossomed into poems of extraordinary grace, wisdom, and strength.

What especially recommends this volume to readers, makers, and scholars of poetry is Miss Walker's sensitive and intelligent use of black Southern roots, the primal sources of much that gives definition and tone to Afro-American writing. Unlike poets who, in the words of Eugene Redmond, "dismiss the legacy and anger of their ancestors by practicing various forms of heresy and sacrilege," she celebrates the legacy, probes it to find practical methods for handling contemporary problems. Her preface tells us the "poems are about Revolutionaries and Lovers; and about the loss of compassion, trust, and the ability to expand in love that marks the end of hopeful strategy." Yet the poems are hopeful strategies for recapturing one's humanity. And from the gifts and lore of ethnic heritage the poet draws strength to love and to be fully human amidst the crises of twentieth-century American life. It is a sure understanding of how to apply ancestral wisdom that informs these precise, lucid and skillfully crafted poems.

Jerry W. Ward. *CLAJ*. Sept., 1973, pp. 127–28

My initial reaction to the first several stories of *In Love & Trouble* was negative. Miss Walker's search for ways to be new and different struck me as too willful and strained. I felt the same way about her earlier novel, *The Third Life of Grange Copeland*, whose style seemed too fine for the rough subject—the way two black men, a son and a father, try to degrade and destroy each other. But as I read on through these thirteen stories, I was soon absorbed by the density of reality they convey. They contain the familiar themes and situations of conventional black political and sociological fiction. There are black revolutionaries who read books and meet in small study groups, radical lady poets who read before black student audiences shouting "Right on!," and sharecroppers victimized by white landlords. But we see all these from genuinely new angles, from the point of view of the black woman or man totally absorbed in the pains of their inner life rather than the point of view of the protester or the newspaper headline.

The subtitle of the collection, *Stories of Black Women*, is probably an attempt by the publisher to exploit not only black subjects but feminine ones. There is nothing feminist about these stories, however. Neurosis and insanity, hatred and love, emptiness and indifference, violence and deceit—that is what they are about.

Jerry H. Bryant. *Nation*. Nov. 12, 1973, pp. 501–2

[*In Love & Trouble*] would be an extraordinary literary work, if its only virtue were the fact that the author sets out consciously to explore with honesty the textures and terrors of black women's lives. Attempts to penetrate the myths surrounding black women's experiences are so pitifully rare in black, feminist, or American writing that each shred of truth about these experiences constitutes a breakthrough. The fact that Walker's perceptions, style, and artistry are also consistently high makes her work a treasure, particularly for those of us whom her writing describes.

Blood and violence seem the everyday backdrop to her characters' lives—a violence all the more chilling because it is so understated. It affects the 10-year-old girl who discovered a lynched man's headless body just as surely and ruinously as it destroys the middle-aged wife trapped in a loveless marriage or the ancient black woman ousted from a white house of worship.

Even as a black woman, I found the cumulative impact of these stories devastating. I questioned the quantity of pain in these sisters' lives and also wondered why none of the men and women were able to love each other. Women love their men, but they are neither loved or understood in return. The affective relationships are between mother and child or between black woman and black woman. The only successful "romance" is in "To Hell with Dying"; it flowers between the young girl narrator and the lonely, grandfatherly Mr. Sweet.

I soon realized, however, that the reason these stories saddened me so much was because of their truthfulness. For every one of Walker's fictional women I knew or had heard of a real woman whose fate was all too similar. Harsh as these stories seem, they describe the kind of pain that can be described only by one who has shared it and has recognized its victims as real. Because Walker tells each story from the point of view of the character herself, we share the inner life of persons who have been dismissed as superdominant matriarchs or bitches by both white sociologists and together "revolutionary" brothers like.

Barbara Smith. Ms. Feb., 1974, p. 43

Meridian, Alice Walker's second novel, is the story of Meridian Hill, a young Southern black woman, from her early childhood on through her thirties. Set in the South, Meridian's story also invokes the impact of the Civil Rights movement, its major psychological and social stresses, as borne out in the lives of the three main characters, Meridian, Truman Held, a black artist and activist, and Lynne, his white wife, also a civil rights organizer.

Written in a clear, almost incandescent prose that sings and sears, there is great breadth and depth to Ms. Walker's imagination that ranges, in *Meridian*, from treatment of earlier vestiges of African and Indian life, back woods poverty, a college for black girls named Saxon (formerly a slave plantation) on to the grim confrontations of the Civil Rights era. It is an extraordinarily fine novel. . . .

In this novel as in her other works, one is aware of the very considerable size of Alice Walker's talent, the ease with which she handles language, her ability to see the essence of life in all things and take joy in it in an almost pantheistic fashion reminiscent of Tolstoy or Shakespeare.

One senses here, too, a dialectical tension between the values and practices of the black Christian tradition on the one hand and the black secular tradition of militant struggle on the other. While *Meridian* embodies one resolution of this tension, one anticipates future development of this theme, by this very talented writer, who is emerging as one of the major humanistic voices of our time.

Robert Chrisman. BlackS. April, 1976, p. [3]

WALKER, MARGARET (1915–   )

UNITED STATES

Straightforwardness, directness, reality are good things to find in a young poet. It is rarer to find them combined with a controlled intensity of emotion and a language that, at times, even when it is most modern, has something of the surge of biblical poetry. And it is obvious that Miss Walker uses that language because it comes naturally to her and is part of her inheritance. A contemporary writer, living in a contemporary world, when she speaks of and for her people older voices are mixed with hers—the voices of Methodist forebears and preachers who preached the Word, the anonymous voices of many who lived and were forgotten and yet out of bondage and hope made a lasting music. Miss Walker is not merely a sounding-board for these voices—I do not mean that. Nor do I mean that [*For My People*] is interesting and moving poetry because it was written by a Negro. It is too late in the day for that sort of meaningless patronage—and poetry must exist in its own right. These poems keep on talking to you after the book is shut because, out of deep feeling, Miss Walker has made living and passionate speech.

> Stephen Vincent Benét. Foreward to Margaret
> Walker, *For My People* (New Haven, Conn., Yale
> University Press, 1942), pp. 5–6

Miss Walker's poems [in *For My People*], though they are songs and portraits of American Negroes of today, are suffused with the prayers and hopes of the submerged and semi-submerged of all times. . . .

Miss Walker's poems for her people everywhere show that she has thought long and felt deeply about the sorrow laden past and present of the American Negro. Out of a rich experience in the lower Mississippi Valley and in Black Chicago at the head of that valley she has seen the substance of poetry in the blind struggle of her people. The Yale Series of Younger Poets, whose choice she is this year, has here launched a career indeed. Miss Walker's poems are not new to *Opportunity* readers, for several of them have appeared in these pages, but the intensity of her sustained effort may come as a surprise to those who know only her shorter pieces. Her symbols, the South, the "L," the delta, the white gods, cotton, 1619, are familiar, but her use of them is with new strength.

A full pride in the past and a healthy view of the present give her poems distinction. She is no mournful weeper wearing her pen out over the twin literary tragedies of lynching and color. Her sorrow and her pride find themselves in more tangible and commonplace symbols: the grandmothers who were strong and full of memories, the money-gods who take life away, the strange contradiction of beauty in the bitter low cotton country. Her hearty portraits of Molly Means, Stagolee, Kissie Lee . . . and of Gus the Lineman are not, fortunately, of the how-I-have-loved-thee school of feminine poets. Perhaps Miss Walker's volume marks the end of a school of Negro women poets; she is more struck by the fact that "We with/our blood have watered these fields/and they belong to us" than she is in the crenellated visions of archaic sorrow so freely indulged in by the "lady poets" in their small black and gold veined volumes. *For My People* contains some of our strongest recent verse. "Sorrow Home" is a dirge of real power.

Ulysses Lee. *Opportunity*. Dec., 1942, pp. 379–80

To appreciate the extent of innovation *Jubilee* brings to a thoroughly quarried, frequently hackneyed genre of writing, it is only necessary to recall that the Civil War novel has been the source of some of the crudest stereotypes of Negro characters in American fiction. As Robert A. Lively pointed out in *Fiction Fights the Civil War*: "the Negro is rarely a central figure in Civil War novels—he only hovers near the white heroes and heroines, to whom space and interest is given." Margaret Walker has reversed the picture completely. With a fidelity to fact and detail, she presents the little-known everyday life of the slaves, their modes of behavior, patterns and rhythms of speech, emotions, frustrations, and aspirations. Never done on such a scale before, this is the strength of her novel. As it unfolds one sees plantation life as it was seen by Negro slaves, feels the texture of American history as it was felt by Negro slaves: the Civil War with the hopes it aroused, its sordid and grim realities; the participation of the Negroes in the fight against slavery; the ugly and frustrating rise of the Ku Klux Klan; the postwar waves of terror in the South to keep the Negro down and prevent emancipation from becoming a reality.

The author is so intent on presenting her historical data as accurately as possible, on correcting the distortions which have crept into so many Civil War novels, that at times she fails to transform her raw material into accomplished literary form. There are passages of very pedestrian prose. Fortunately, the colorful and musical speech of the Negro characters in the novel transcends the stilted prose of the narrator. . . .

And there is Vyry, the heroine of the novel, who distills out of her life as a slave, and the trials of the Civil War, and the frustrated hopes of the Reconstruction years, a hard realism, a fierce spiritual force and hope. . . .

Abraham Chapman. SR. Sept. 24, 1966, pp. 43–44

[*Jubilee*] serves especially well as a response to white "nostalgia" fiction about the antebellum and Reconstruction South—especially Margaret Mitchell's poor but popular *Gone with the Wind*. One cannot read one of these novels without repeatedly contrasting it with the other. On dialect: Miss Walker's is thoroughly researched and linguistically accurate; Miss Mitchell's ranges from rather accurate to absurd. On the role of blacks: Miss Walker reveals the various levels of black mentality, as well as the devotion of some slaves to, and the intense hatred of others for, their masters; Miss Mitchell presents blacks before the Civil War as happy darkies completely devoted to "missy" and "massa." On "social controls": Miss Walker portrays vividly the savagery of white vigilante repression; Miss Mitchell portrays the Ku Klux Klan as an organization of noble and dedicated men with the highest moral objectives. In short, the novels make for an interesting and enlightening companion study—a study of painful historical reality and romanticized self-deception.

Roger Whitlow. Black American Literature (Chicago,
Nelson-Hall, 1973), pp. 138–39

After a lapse of twenty-eight years Margaret Walker has brought out a new volume of verse. Entitled *Prophets for a New Day*, it was printed by the Broadside Press. Though a very thin volume (it contains only 32 pages), the work is impressive. It is the best poetical comment to come from the civil rights movement—the movement which came to a climax with the march on Washington and which began thereafter to change into a more militant type of liberation effort.

In *Prophets for a New Day* Miss Walker, with poems like "Street Demonstration," "Girl Held without Bail," and "Sit-Ins," catches the spirit of the civil rights age, when young blacks gladly went to jail for the cause of freedom. "The Ballad of the Free," another liberation poem, treats as kindred souls Nat Turner, Gabriel Prosser, Denmark Vesey, Toussaint L'Ouverture, and John Brown. The inclusion of the last name shows that Miss Walker, though much "blacker" now in her thinking than she was in her early works, has not lost her respect for men of good will, whether black or white. Unlike most present-day Negro writers, she is willing to honor not only abolition heroes like John Brown but white martyrs of the civil rights movement as well. . . .

Arthur P. Davis. From the Dark Tower (Washington,
D.C., Howard University Press, 1974), pp. 184–85

WILLIAMS, JOHN A. (1925–   )

UNITED STATES

Though it is certainly conceivable that *Night Song* will appeal to the deep neurotic strain in a far-out section of the reading public, this reviewer is in conscience bound to report that he does not dig this novel about a mewing mess of real-gone cats whose emotions are poured from bottles and squirted from syringes, and whose brains, such as they are, are in their gonads. It's crazy, man. Real crazy! And crazy never did add up to truth. . . .

[His] characters, who are about as viable as a row of wooden dolls, meet and join on a theatrical level of action and reaction that is maudlin, morbid and mad. The Beats may be flattered by this group portrait of themselves, but they will scarcely believe the flattery.

Yet there is one matter with which a reader's sympathies may become engaged; and that matter is the author's serious intention. He wants to say something important about bi-racial love, and about the life of art and artists, and about loss and pain and grief, and one can sympathize with his desire to say important things. But the mischief of it is that a sort of sickly sentimentalism takes over, and one gets the feeling that John A. Williams is playing around with values he does not understand.

Saunders Redding. *NYHT*. Nov. 26, 1961, p. 14

John A. Williams is the author of the earlier *Night Song*, a novel about jazz. In his new work, *Sissie*, he draws in part on his authoritative knowledge of that world, but this novel is far richer and cuts deeper than most books about jazz. For *Sissie* is a chronicle of Negro life in transition, and it unites, as few novels do, the experience of the brutalized older generation of Negroes with that of the sophisticated young, who, one way or another, have made it in American life. As such, it is full of vivid contrasts, and it conveys memorably an image of the double war that Negroes wage—against their white oppressors on the one hand, and generation against generation on the other. . . .

[Sissie] may well be the authoritative portrait of the Negro mother in America, that *Machtweib* who has given the beleaguered Negro family whatever strength and stability it has. Williams depicts Sissie with stunning fidelity—her capacity to endure, her cunning, and her abiding strength, at once supportive and disabling. For what *Sissie* is really about is the effort of her children to emancipate themselves from this Big Mama who in nurturing them almost destroyed them. . . .

WILLIAMS, JOHN A.   451

Inevitably, this novel invites comparison with James Baldwin's *Another Country*. *Sissie* is by far the better work. For all his platform polemics, Baldwin does not seem to possess the grasp of the Negro *milieu* that Williams displays. And where *Another Country* is shrill and noisy, Sissie is permeated by a quiet anger that builds and builds inexorably. John A. Williams may well be a front-runner in a new surge of Negro creativity.

David Boroff. SR. March 30, 1963, p. 49

As with black music, black literature continues to grow, extend, and ceases to be invisible. Our literature now cuts and you do bleed. Mr. Williams' latest book [*The Man Who Cried I Am*] is this type of work; a blood bringer, causing you to hurt and forcing you to redefine your relationship with your surroundings. It makes you open your eyes and enables you to see much more than what is in front of you. While reading this book, we see through mirrors, across continents, into other cultures, and unconsciously we feel—that is, if we are capable of feeling. John A. Williams has written an extensively handsome and dangerous novel.

Jean-Paul Sartre said, "It is true that all art is false." He lied, or he was talking about white Western art. The book in question is a work of Art. That is, if art, among other things, is a creative effort that others can identify with, an accent on a particular life-style, communication, a bringer of knowledge, a mind wakener, movable prose which is esthetically pleasing and meaningful and, in essence, one artist's comment on life as he views it. The work is *The Man Who Cried I Am* and the artist is John A. Williams. . . .

No doubt about it, Mr. Williams can write; he proved that with *Night Song* and *Sissie*; but the Williams of this novel transcends the artist and becomes the seer, the prophet.

Don L. Lee. NegroD. March, 1968, pp. 51–52, 79

If you have an ambitious theme, you just have to go on being ambitious with it till you get to the end. Mr. Williams [in *Sons of Darkness, Sons of Light*] has the theme: the beginnings of a race war some time in the 1970s, told from everybody's point of view. The characters are treated as independent agents of history, crisscrossing like ants on separate errands, forming a pattern that none of themselves can see.

Nor does the ambition stop there. Williams has made serious overtures at understanding each of his ants in turn: the beady-eyed black businessman, the Israeli gunman who has slipped into killing out of habit, even, with a sour face, the Irish cop who starts the ball rolling by shooting a black boy.

So there we are—intricate design and compassion to burn. And there we stay. Because the author is too modest. He has decided to use his materials for a conventional fast-paced adventure yarn. The Hegelian interconnections of history, by which poisons grown in the Middle East can cause death in America, become simple plot devices, as trivial as the coincidental collisions of characters that Williams also favors. As trivial, but also as entertaining. . . .

It is a good design for a novel, and the combustible climax is not, like most such prophecies, too silly to contemplate. But a novel that winds up so many themes and characters cannot put them all to rest in 279 pages. The characters bustle about but do not grow in complexity. Nor does the background fill up: the performers always seem to be the only people in New York that day.

John Williams has a notable, attractive author's voice and an impressive range of sympathy, but this time he has been content to do a skin job.

Wilfrid Sheed. *BkWd.* June 29, 1969, p. 5

By all rights, John A. Williams's *Captain Blackman* should have been much worse than it is. Its method is documentary, its aim is consciousness raising, not the loftiest of fictional ways and goals. Williams has, apparently, gone over every inch of ground where, at any time in American history, black soldiers have fought. As he did so, he tried to imagine not only the men he knew had been there but also a binding single figure, a soldier named Abraham Blackman, who fought in all the battles, from Lexington to New Orleans to Petersburg to Fort Sill in the Indian wars, to San Juan Hill, to France, Spain, Italy, Korea, and Vietnam. As the novel opens Blackman is wounded in Vietnam trying to shield some of his company from slaughter, and the rest is his dreams and hallucinations of his role in all the earlier battles.

As a novel the book doesn't begin to count. Blackman himself may not be superhuman, but he is strictly a fantasy figure: huge, strong, brave, serious, always right, always able to speak the deeper ironies. His women, most of whom are named Mimosa Rogers, are always strong, sexy, eager, and tough-minded. The episodes, though many and varied, always carry the same message: whites are always willing to use blacks in battle, always afraid of the power blacks might have if properly rewarded for their service, always willing to find ways to ignore, degrade, or simply kill black soldiers who become a problem. So Williams has given himself practically no fictional room to move in. The coins have to keep falling exactly as Williams calls them. But, given this, *Captain Blackman* is not without merit. . . .

If Williams's fictional device is clumsy, and many of his attempts to flesh out history are vulgar, the central vision is one worth reading. It may not matter much that we learn about this or that incident that we've never heard of, but the grim joke that is our racial history does need to be told over and over, and the very sameness of the joke in each of Williams's many episodes is necessarily part of the telling, the irony, the joke.

Roger Sale. NYR. Oct. 5, 1972, p. 34

[Williams'] first two works, *The Angry Ones* and *Night Song*, apprentice works at best, are defeated by many of the structural and stylistic problems so few novice writers are able to surmount. Where they do surprise, though, is in their failure to exhibit any of those saving moments of raw talent or unmistakable power that suggest promising later careers. They suffer from a welter of extraneous details, descriptions, and asides which interrupt irreparably the narrative flow, and from a conspicuous absence of dramatic tension. Not so much shown or revealed, the novels are explained; where one expects drama, he receives the didactic, a telling and invariably fatal substitution. Unable to attract serious critical attention on their own intrinsic merits, they obtain our interest now because they contain the characters, conflicts and themes that characterize Williams' later work and because they embody in embryo form the controlling myth of his fiction. . . .

Sissie represents a considerable advance over the earlier novels, an advance that can best be appreciated perhaps by recognizing what Williams does *not* do. In *Night Song* he becomes lost in the myth of the tragic black genius. In *Sissie* the same opportunity offers itself in the figure of the dominant black matriarch. But Sissie is an individual, strong, willful, childish, destructive, bewildered. We come not so much to admire her achievement as to respect it, aware as we are every moment of all she is willing to sacrifice in order to earn her "right to live."

Ronald Walcott. CLAJ. Dec., 1972, pp. 202, 213

John A. Williams' *The Man Who Cried I Am* has attracted considerable attention among the general public not so much for its literary excellence but because in the last pages of the novel its protagonist, Max Reddick, discovers a monstrous plot—code named "King Alfred"—to eradicate the black population of the United States. The plot, similar in many ways to Nazi Germany's "final solution," employs enough facts from everyday life to give the reader an uneasy feeling that perhaps this section of the book is not pure fiction. . . .

This feature of the novel is not to be ignored. By suggesting the logical extension of America's past and present treatment of black people, the novel, hopefully, may jolt the conscience of the nation and influence its future policies. However, Williams deserves credit for the art of the novel as well as its message. The King Alfred extermination plan is only one item in a series of nightmarish elements which Williams uses to dramatize not only the psychological problems of the main character but also the frightening social conditions which foster them. Like most nightmares, these particular elements of the novel evoke emotions of fear and repugnance and often a frantic refusal to accept what is detestable or unbelievable. As in a nightmare, the seemingly impossible happens, and evil or death is manifested in peculiarly horrifying ways; perversion, savagery, and hatred may threaten one's humanity, reason, or life itself. Employing these gothic elements with considerable artistic success, Williams frees himself from the naturalistic protest format which for a time seemed the sole métier of the black novelist.

Robert E. Fleming. *CL*. Spring, 1973, pp. 186–87

After *Night Song*, Williams discovered that the writer was master of time in the novel; that time was never static but an ever-changing reality. To merge history and fiction, therefore, necessitated that the writer exercise great control over time; that he prepare to break it up—change endings into beginnings and vice versa. Flashbacks are used to accomplish this feat in *The Man Who Cried I Am* and, as a result, Reddick moves quickly and easily across three continents. In *Captain Blackman*, the manipulation of time occurs through dream sequences and stream of consciousness. Blackman, therefore, appears simultaneously as a wanderer through history and a patient on an operating table in Vietnam. Williams, however, has not completely mastered the usage of time in either novel, and, thus, both are flawed by confusion. Past and present incidents are thrust upon the reader so quickly that sometimes it is difficult to distinguish between the two. When the technique works well, however, more often in the latter than the former novel, Williams comes close to mastering the form of the historical novel.

This is no small achievement. More important is Williams' determination to explore black life realistically, to search for paradigms of the distant past, to search out images, symbols, and metaphors relevant to the present. Thus the close parallel between past and present, shown specifically in *Captain Blackman*, between characters and incidents is neither artificial nor contrived. Those who appear in Blackman's Odyssey in the sixteen hundreds, eighteen hundreds, nineteen hundreds have their mirror images in those who appear in the nineteen sixties. In other words, the men who struggled in the distant past, who met the test of manhood, differ little from those who act accordingly in the twentieth century. . . .

Addison Gayle, Jr. *The Way of the New World*
(Garden City, N.Y., Doubleday, 1975), p. 346

Obviously Williams didn't intend [*Mothersill and the Foxes*] as a serious novel, and when compared to his previous works (most notably *The Man Who Cried I Am*, a story of existential proportions about a black reporter dying of rectal cancer) it would appear that this represents an unnecessary departure for Williams. But in reading *Mothersill and the Foxes*, one gets the impression that Williams wrote it with the intention of confronting looming shadows. Unquestionably his intention was to write about sex, but more important, it appears Williams sought to break from the strictures black writers have often imposed on themselves when it comes to dealing with the whole subject of sex. In the past the choice has been either not to write about it at all, or at best, not to write too lustfully about it lest they add fuel to the prevailing myth. The myth, of course, being that of potent black male sexuality.

And though this is not to imply that Williams believes in the myth, or that he sought to dispel or even exploit it, still his characterization of Mothersill seems to have been written with a high level of consciousness. So carefully balanced between extremities, Mothersill never quite comes off as the sexual character Williams intended him to be. And this perhaps is due to a fear Williams himself has as to what the myth implies: that whether true or not, it still carries a tinge of undesirable, painful smells about it. Thus the character Odell Mothersill, a character so vulgarly successful outside the realm of sex that not only is he not the average black man, but also eons removed from those causes giving rise to the myth in the first place; he is the black man without problems who has passed through the matrix unscathed by the usual pitfalls which often hurl black men toward undesirable, self-destructive ends.

Stated quite simply, then, Mothersill is a man who loves sex and women undoubtedly for the same reason that men climb mountains, but in order to be that, and be a black man as well, Williams has deemed it necessary to shroud him with credentials and high purpose. He comes off as the proverbial over-qualified black. The subject of sex is wasted on him.

James T. Lampley. *BlackS.* Jan.–Feb., 1976,
pp. 43–44

John A. Williams is a black writer, the way the crocus is a spring flower. *The Junior Bachelor Society*, his latest novel, is the story of nine middle-aged black men and what their lives have become in the more than three decades gone by since they played ball together, and grew up together, in Central City, in upstate New York. . . .

Along with the lives of the nine principals, rendered in loving detail, Williams also fleshes out their wives, and the marital relationships, as well as the intricate crosscurrents prevailing when they all get back together. . . .

Williams not only manages it all, combines and orchestrates it all, but gives the reader (as the best novelists have always done) the sense of still *more* interconnected life out there, still *more* books out there, already written and yet to come, than what is here so brilliantly encompassed.

Ivan Gold. *NYT*. July 11, 1976, pp. 32–33

WRIGHT, RICHARD (1908–1960)

UNITED STATES

[*Uncle Tom's Children*] is a book about hatreds. Mr. Wright serves notice by his title that he speaks of people in revolt, and his stories are so grim that the Dismal Swamp of race hatred must be where they live. Not one act of understanding and sympathy comes to pass in the entire work.

But some bright new lines to remember come flashing from the author's pen. Some of his sentences have the shocking-power of a forty-four. That means that he knows his way around among words. With his facility, one wonders what he would have done had he dealt with plots that touched the broader and more fundamental phases of Negro life instead of confining himself to the spectacular. For, though he has handled himself well, numerous Negro writers, published and unpublished, have written of this same kind of incident. It is the favorite Negro theme just as how the stenographer or some other poor girl won the boss or the boss's son is the favorite white theme. What is new in the four novelettes included in Mr. Wright's book is the wish-fulfillment theme. In each story the hero suffers but he gets his man.

In the first story, "Big Boy Leaves Home," the hero, Big Boy, takes the gun away from a white soldier after he has shot two of his chums and kills the white man. . . . In the other three stories the reader sees the picture of the South that the communists have been passing around of late. A dismal, hopeless section ruled by brutish hatred and nothing else. Mr. Wright's author's solution, is the solution of the

PARTY—state responsibility for everything and individual responsibility for nothing, not even feeding one's self. And march!

Since the author himself is a Negro, his dialect is a puzzling thing. One wonders how he arrived at it. Certainly he does not write by ear unless he is tone-deaf. But aside from the broken speech of his characters, the book contains some beautiful writing. One hopes that Mr. Wright will find in Negro life a vehicle for his talents.

Zora Neale Hurston. SR. April 2, 1938, p. 32

Uncle Tom's Children has its full share of violence and brutality; violent deaths occur in three stories and the mob goes to work in all four. Violence has long been an important element in fiction about Negroes, just as it is in their life. But where Julia Peterkin in her pastorals and Roark Bradford in his levee farces show violence to be the reaction of primitives unadjusted to modern civilization, Richard Wright shows it as the way in which civilization keeps the Negro in his place. And he knows what he is writing about.

Some of the tragedies may seem too coincidentally contrived, may seem to concentrate too much upon the victims, but the book has its great importance in spite of this. The essential quality of certain phases of Negro life in the South is handled here vigorously, authentically, and with flashes of genuine poetry. Here are characters seen from the inside: Big Boy, alert, full of animal spirits, suddenly turned into a hounded fugitive; the perplexed preacher with a stake in keeping quiet and orderly, and a bitter knowledge of what his people suffer; the farmer who has labored for a home that a white man casually disrupts. In these little shacks, overburdened with poverty, the first mention of trouble with the white folks brings paralyzed fear and a conniving that is pitifully feeble. The people show a wisdom brewed of suffering, not the artless philosophy endeared to Southern mythologists. And finally there are those who are not only aware of what is being done to them but determined to do something about it, resolutely muttering: "Ah'll go ef the nex' one goes!" and "Ah ain' got but *one* time t' die." The South that Mr. Wright renders so vividly is recognizable and true, and it has not often been within the covers of a book.

Sterling A. Brown. Nation. April 16, 1938, p. 448

The skeleton of [*Native Son*] can be found in the police records of Chicago. The art of this novelist breathes upon the dead bones: they quicken, become flesh and blood, and indict our civilization. . . .

Bigger Thomas suggests Dmitry Karamazov in [Dostoyevski's] *The Brothers Karamazov* and Clyde Griffiths in [Dreiser's] *An American Tragedy*. Dmitry and Clyde and Bigger are bungled jobs from the mangled hand of Society the Potter. Wright's business with Bigger approximates a Shakespearean obsession. In his haste to get at the centrality of Bigger's reactions, he leaves the black cosmos of the South Side amorphous; minor characters, without physical differentiae and psychological entity, scarcely emerge from the shadows. Dreiser, with bedeviling assiduity, draws the details of character and environment; his story goes forward like a huge, prehistoric animal in labor. Antithetically, as Bigger moves through crescendos of violence and hysteria to a vitalizing sense of release and affirmation of life, his creator is sucked by the immediacy of the things that Bigger sees and hears and feels. Wright's is a midnight nether-world where diagnostics of character and environment gain essentiality only as they affect Bigger. From a Marxian *bema* in the lower depths Bigger's lawyer hurls nitroglycerin philippics at Society the Potter. Mr. Max plays the role of a dialectic Edgar Bergen to Bigger's fated Charlie McCarthy.

A study of the artistic styles of Hemingway and Wright reveals illuminatingly antipodal contrasts. Hemingway's characters are exteriorized; Wright's, interiorized. The works of both contain an almost Nietzschean flair for the accents of violence, "the hideous trampling march of lust and disease, brutality and death." Hemingway's uncerebral characters act; Wright's not only act but try to put together the jigsaw-puzzle reasons for their actions. Essentially, the approach of Hemingway is that of the behaviorist; that of Wright, the psycho-analyst. Thus Wright places upon himself a heavier artistic burden, since he is unwilling to let dialogue and action be the *raison d'être* of his characters. In this he is like the recent Steinbeck.

M. B. Tolson. *ModQ*. Winter, 1939, pp. 22–24

Year by year, we have been noticing the rising tide of realism, with its accompanying boon of social honesty and artistic integrity. . . . It is to Richard Wright's everlasting credit to have hung the portrait of Bigger Thomas alongside in this gallery of stark contemporary realism. There was artistic courage and integrity of the first order in his decision to ignore both the squeamishness of the Negro minority and the deprecating bias of the prejudiced majority, full knowing that one side would like to ignore the fact that there are other Negroes like Bigger and the other like to think that Bigger is the prototype of all. Eventually, of course, this must involve the clarifying recognition that there is no one type of Negro, and that Bigger's type has the right to its day in the literary calendar, not only for what it might add in its own right to Negro portraiture, but for what it could say about America.

In fact Wright's portrait of Bigger Thomas says more about America than it does about the Negro, for he is the native son of the black city ghetto, with its tensions, frustrations and resentments. The brunt of the action and the tragedy involves social forces rather than persons; it is in the first instance a Zolaesque *J'accuse* pointing to the danger symptoms of a self-frustrating democracy. Warping prejudice, short-sighted exploitation, impotent philanthropy, aggravating sympathy, inconsistent human relations, doctrinaire reform, equally impotent punishment stand behind the figures of Bigger, the Daltons, Mary, Jan and Max, as the real protagonists of the conflict. This is timely and incisive analysis of the core dilemmas of the situation of race and American democracy. Indeed in the present crisis, the social import of *Native Son*, with its bold warnings and its clear lessons, temporarily overshadows its artistic significance. Its vivid and vital revelations should be a considerable factor in awakening a social sense and conscience willing at last, after much evasion and self-deception, to face the basic issues realistically and constructively.

Alain Locke. Opportunity. Jan., 1941, pp. 4–5

The vogue of such a novel as Richard Wright's *Native Son* may suggest that the novel of "social significance" had at last entered into the thinking of the middle class, that the people who read it with bated breath or applauded it on the stage felt a deep compassion for, and even some solidarity with, the oppressed Negro masses; but that is an illusion. It is precisely because Wright himself was so passionately honest and desired to represent the sufferings of his race as forcefully as possible that the unconscious slickness of *Native Son*, its manipulation of terror in a period fascinated by terror, seems so sinister. For Wright was only the child of his generation, and his resources no different in kind from the resources of naturalism and the left-wing conception of life and literature to which, like many Negro writers, he surrendered his thinking because of the general indifference or hostility to Negroes and Negro writing. If he chose to write the story of Bigger Thomas as a grotesque crime story, it is because his own indignation and the sickness of the age combined to make him dependent on violence and shock, to astonish the reader by torrential scenes of cruelty, hunger, rape, murder, and flight and then enlighten him by crude Stalinist homilies. Bigger Thomas "found" himself in jail as Wright "found" himself, after much personal suffering and confusion, in the Communist party; what did it matter that Bigger's self-discovery was mechanical and unconvincing, or that Wright —from the highest possible motives—had written "one of those books in which everything is undertaken with seriousness except the writing" [R. P. Blackmur]?

Alfred Kazin. On Native Grounds (New York,
Harcourt, Brace, 1942), pp. 386–87

In the South the sensibilities of both blacks and whites are inhibited by the rigidly defined environment. For the Negro there is relative safety as long as the impulse toward individuality is suppressed. (Lynchings have occurred because Negroes painted their homes.) . . . The pre-individ-ualistic black community discourages individuality out of self-defense. Having learned through experience that the whole group is punished for the actions of the single member, it has worked out efficient techniques of behavior control. . . .

Within the ambit of the black family this takes the form of training the child away from curiosity and adventure, against reaching out for those activities lying beyond the borders of the black community. And when the child resists, the parent discourages him; first with the formula, "That there's for white folks. Colored can't have it," and finally with a beating.

It is not, then, the family and communal violence described by *Black Boy* that is unusual, but that Wright *recognized* and made no peace with its essential cruelty. . . .

Nowhere in America today is there social or political action based upon the solid realities of Negro life depicted in *Black Boy*; perhaps that is why, with its refusal to offer solutions, it is like the blues. Yet in it thousands of Negroes will for the first time see their destiny in public print. Freed here of fear and the threat of violence, their lives have at last been organized, scaled down to possessable proportions. And in this lies Wright's most important achievement: He has converted the Ameri-can Negro impulse toward self-annihilation and "going-under-ground" into a will to confront the world, to evaluate his experience honestly and throw his findings unashamedly into the guilty conscience of America. [Summer, 1945]

Ralph Ellison. Shadow and Act (New York,
Random House, 1964), pp. 89–91, 94

Black Boy, the story of his own youth in the South by Richard Wright, the enormously talented young Negro who also wrote *Native Son*, has been greeted by several placidly busy white reviewers and by a couple of agitated Negro reviewers as betraying too much "emotion," too much "bitterness."

Now this is the story of a colored boy who, just yesterday, found in his native community not merely that he was penalized for having the same qualities that in a white boy would have warmed his neighbors to universal praise—the qualities of courage, energy, curiosity, refusal to be subservient, the impulse to record life in words—but that he was in danger of disapproval, then of beatings, then of being killed, for these qualities, for being "uppity." Not bitterness but fear charges the book, and how this young crusader can be expected to look back only a few years to the quiet torture with anything except hatred is beyond me.

When we have a successful comedy by an ex-prisoner about the kindness and humor of the warders in a German concentration camp, then I shall expect Mr. Wright to mellow and to speak amiably of the teachers who flattened him, his colored neighbors and relatives who denounced him, the merchants who cheated him, the white fellow-mechanics who threatened him for wanting to learn their skills, and the librarian who suspected him—quite rightly—of reading that militant and bewhiskered Bolshevik, that polluter of temples and Chambers of Commerce, Comrade H. L. Mencken.

Sinclair Lewis. *Esquire*. June, 1945, p. 76

There is another book which should be taken off the book racks of the Nation; it should be removed from the book stores; its sale should be stopped. It is the recent book of the month, which has had such a great sale. Senators can understand why it has had such a sale if they will read it. It is entitled *Black Boy* by Richard Wright. Richard Wright is a Mississippian. He was born and reared near Natchez, Miss. He went from Natchez to Jackson, from Jackson to Memphis, from Memphis to Chicago, and from Chicago to Brooklyn, N.Y., where he is married to a white woman and is living happily, he says. He wrote the book *Black Boy* ostensibly as the story of his life. Actually it is a damnable lie from beginning to end. It is practically all fiction. There is just enough truth to it to enable him to build his fabulous lies about his experiences in the South and his description of the people of the South and the culture, education, and life of the southern people.

The purpose of the book is to plant the seeds of hate in every Negro in America against the white men of the South or against the white race anywhere, for that matter. That is the purpose. Its purpose is to plant the seeds of devilment and trouble-breeding in the days to come in the mind and heart of every American Negro. Read the book if you do not believe what I am telling you. It is the dirtiest, filthiest, lousiest, most obscene piece of writing that I have ever seen in print. I would hate to have a son or daughter of mine be permitted to read it; it is so filthy and so dirty. But it comes from a Negro, and you cannot expect any better from a person of his type.

Senator Theodore Bilbo [of Mississippi].
Congressional Record—Senate. June 27, 1945, p. 6808

To whom does Richard Wright address himself? Certainly not to the universal man. The essential characteristic of the notion of the universal man is that he is not involved in any particular age, and that he is no more and no less moved by the lot of the negroes of Louisiana than by that of the Roman slaves in the time of Spartacus. The universal man can think of nothing but universal values. He is a pure and abstract affirmation of the inalienable right of man. But neither can Wright think of intending his books for the white racists of Virginia or South Carolina whose minds are made up in advance and who will not open them. Nor to the black peasants of the bayous who can not read. And if he seems to be happy about the reception his books have had in Europe, still it is obvious that at the beginning he had not the slightest idea of writing for the European public. Europe is far away. Its indignation is ineffectual and hypocritical. Not much is to be expected from the nations which have enslaved the Indies, Indo-China, and negro Africa. These considerations are enough to define his readers. He is addressing himself to the cultivated negroes of the North and the white Americans of good-will (intellectuals, democrats of the left, radicals, C.I.O. workers). . . .

Each work of Wright contains what Baudelaire would have called "a double simultaneous postulation"; each word refers to two contexts; two forces are applied simultaneously to each phrase and determine the incomparable tension of his tale. Had he spoken to the whites alone, he might have turned out to be more prolix, more didactic, and more abusive; to the negroes alone, still more elliptical, more of a confederate, and more elegiac. In the first case, his work might have come close to satire; in the second, to prophetic lamentations. Jeremiah spoke only to the Jews. But Wright, a writer for a split public, has been able both to maintain and go beyond this split. He has made it the pretext for a work of art. [March, 1947]

Jean-Paul Sartre. What Is Literature? (New York,
Harper & Row, 1965), pp. 72, 74

A writer of brutal power, scornful alike of Bohemianism and finicky art, Wright still stands as the most typical as well as the most famous example of the depression-bred WPA writer. To begin with, he was angry and resentful. He was poor, kicked-around and discriminated against, and he hated it. When he was finally given a turn at a typewriter in the offices of the Illinois Writers' Project on Erie Street, he was so steamed up he immediately began turning out rugged, fighting poems and thudding, belly-punching stories between project assignments. His aim was to tear the living hearts out of his gasping readers, not even allowing them, as he later admitted, "the consolation of tears." And he came pretty close to accomplishing it. A couple of years later a group of these stories won him a prize in a competition open to all U. S. writers on WPA, led to his first book *Uncle Tom's Children* and launched the most impressive literary career yet achieved by a Negro American.

Arna Bontemps. NegroD. June, 1950, pp. 44–45

The idea of Bigger's monstrosity [in *Native Son*] can be presented without fear of contradiction, since no American has the knowledge or authority to contest it and no Negro has the voice. It is an idea, which, in the framework of the novel, is dignified by the possibility it promptly affords of presenting Bigger as the herald of disaster, the danger signal of a more bitter time to come when not Bigger alone but all his kindred will rise, in the name of the many thousands who have perished in fire and flood and by rope and torture, to demand their rightful vengeance.

But it is not quite fair, it seems to me, to exploit the national innocence in this way. The idea of Bigger as a warning boomerangs not only because it is quite beyond the limit of probability that Negroes in America will ever achieve the means of wreaking vengeance upon the state but also because it cannot be said that they have any desire to do so. . . .

Negroes are Americans and their destiny is the country's destiny. They have no other experience besides their experience on this continent and it is an experience which cannot be rejected, which yet remains to be embraced. If, as I believe, no American Negro exists who does not have his private Bigger Thomas living in the skull, then what most significantly fails to be illuminated here is the paradoxical adjustment which is perpetually made, the Negro being compelled to accept the fact that this dark and dangerous and unloved stranger is part of himself forever. [Nov.–Dec., 1951]

James Baldwin. Notes of a Native Son (Boston,
Beacon, 1955), pp. 41–42

Richard Wright's new book, *The Outsider* . . . is something very close to a Dostoevskian novel. Lonely, puzzled but constantly brooding, warm-hearted but impelled into savage hostilities, his hero lives and dies as a rebel against traditional morality, against social distinctions and divisions, against friendship and love, against organized law and organized rebellion, and against religion. His aim is to be free. He becomes an anarchic individualist. To all who love him and many who hate him he brings suffering and death; he dies alone, yet still not free, tormented by solitude and remorse. It is a moving story, for the most part expertly told. America (particularly colored America) is full of these lonesome wanderers, sad and dangerous men. Faulkner created another of them, the hero of *Light in August*; and we remember the book that opens "Call me Ishmael."

Still, the novel has one major defect. . . . His hero (when we meet him first) is a distracted, debt-ridden, heavy-drinking, lustful postal clerk, desperate to escape from the disasters his own lack of self-control has brought upon him. When the opportunity of escape is created by a terrible accident, he seizes it with astonishment and relief and goes on his way, killing and dodging like a rat caught in a henroost. We watch his agonies with understanding and even with sympathy, wishing he would sober up and straighten out; but when—only a week or two later—he emerges as a cool philosopher with his head full of Nietzsche and the answers to Lenin, we find the transition impossible to believe. It looks, in fact, as though Mr. Wright had written two different tales and then tried to blend them: one, the story of a poor incontinent man haunted by drink and desire until he would welcome any disaster as a relief; the other, an account of the adventures of a dispassionate intellectual who was educated into violence by the brutality and treachery of the Communist party until he revolted against it and became an existentialist. Both men are solitary and rebellious; the same man could have led both lives; but not in the same short space of time.

Gilbert Highet. *Harper*. May, 1953, pp. 96, 98

Wright's heavy-handed, morose approach to everything racial is the exact antithesis of his original sponsor in France, the late Gertrude Stein, who arranged with the French government officially to invite him to France, when he had trouble getting an American passport. I met the famed American author in her Paris flat several years before her death and we talked at length about Wright, who she told me was "without question the best master of English prose in America since myself. That's fairly high praise coming from me." . . .

She had never heard of Wright until her return to Paris after its liberation from the Nazis. Her books *Wars I Have Seen* was published soon after that, and among the reviews she saw was a laudatory one by Wright in *PM*. Asking a G.I. friend who this admirer of hers was, she was given a copy of *Black Boy* from the Army library.

"I was very excited and wrote for the rest of his stuff," she told me. "I found Wright was the best American writer today. Only one or two creative writers like him come along in a generation. Every time he says something it is a distinct revelation."

Ben Burns. *Reporter*. March 8, 1956, pp. 22–23

I thought of Richard Wright, with whom I had had breakfast that morning [in 1953]. This was his first visit to any part of Africa and he seemed to find it bewildering. . . .

What Wright did not understand, what his whole background and training had made difficult for him to understand, was that being black did not of itself qualify one for acceptance in tribal Africa. But how could he, when there are thousands of urban-bred Africans up and down the vast continent who do not themselves understand this? The more perceptive of the urban Africans are only now beginning to comprehend, but slowly. . . .

Richard Wright was surprised that even educated Africans, racially conscious literate people, had not heard of him and were skeptical of a grown man earning his living by writing. They could not understand what kind of writing brought a man enough money to support a family. Wright really wanted to understand the African, but—"I found the African an oblique, a hard-to-know man."

My sympathies were all with Wright.

Peter Abrahams. *Holiday.* April, 1959, p. 75

When I saw Richard Wright at his apartment in Paris three days before he died, he did not look ill. He looked perfectly all right—except that it appeared he was freshly laid out for dead. I had not seen Wright for many years. When I rang his doorbell, his charming teen-age daughter, Julia, said, "Daddy is in the bedroom," and she escorted me there. The foot of the bed faced the door. Fully clothed in a gray suit and tie, but two-thirds covered by a quilt, Wright lay all dressed up flat on his back on the bed. The effect was startling—as if he were on a bier. I stopped short in the door. Without thinking, my words came out even before I greeted him. "Man," I said, "you look like you are ready to go to glory!"

We both laughed as Wright, while we shook hands, explained to me he was waiting for a car to come at any moment to take him to the hospital, that was why he already had his jacket and tie on. Periodically, he said, he needed routine treatments for an old stomach ailment he had picked up in Africa. He felt fine, he told me as he offered me a cigarette, except that he had been unable to eat anything much for three days. The medicine he had taken, he grinned, upset him worse than the ailment. As he talked, he seemed and looked very much like the young Dick Wright I had known in Chicago before he became famous—vigorous, questioning, very much alive, and with a big warm smile. He wanted to know the happenings in the states. "How is Harlem these days? I'd like to see it again." . . .

Three days later in London, I learned that Richard Wright was dead. I was his last visitor at home.

Langston Hughes. *Ebony*. Feb., 1961, p. 94

In *Native Son* Richard Wright jolted the American literary scene with Bigger Thomas, a hapless, bitter, damned, ignorant, brutal, ghetto-condemned black Negro, who would have whipped half to death any one of Hemingway's soldiers and he-men on a southside Chicago street corner. Bigger was not romantic like Queequeg in *Moby Dick*, nor was he legendary like John Henry. He was no Stepin Fetchit or Mantan Moreland. He was none of the shadow, soft and unobtrusive, mysterious, that we find in our literature. He was a Negro that few white people ever believed they would meet face to face, and yet, they faced him every day. He was real.

If Theodore Dreiser took his place in American literature by telling us of the damned relationship between American love and the American dollar in *An American Tragedy*; if Upton Sinclair and Frank Norris achieved their positions by giving us the first full-blown stink of the bottomside of capitalism in *The Jungle* and *The Pit*; if Sinclair Lewis could name the emptiness of America *Babbit*; then Richard Wright deserves a place beside them because he gave us a stunning view of the economic and spiritual poverty of millions of people. He deserves to be included among the American authors college students find in their literature books because he brought an entirely new dimension to American letters—a dimension that we have come to accept, after so long a time, as real.

John A. Williams. Introduction to Richard Wright,
White Man, Listen! (Garden City, N.Y.,
Doubleday, 1964), pp. x–xi

Of all black American novelists, and indeed of all American novelists of any hue, Richard Wright reigns supreme for his profound political, economic, and social reference. Wright had the ability, like Dreiser, of harnessing the gigantic, overwhelming environmental forces and focusing them, with pinpoint sharpness, on individuals and their acts as they are caught up in the whirlwind of the savage, anarchistic sweep of life, love, death, and hate, pain, hope, pleasure, and despair across the face of a nation and the world. . . . Wright's forte, it seems to me, was in reflecting the intricate mechanisms of a social orgnization, its functioning as a unit. [1967]

Eldridge Cleaver. *Soul on Ice* (New York,
McGraw-Hill, 1968), pp. 108–9

Richard differed from the [French] existentialists in that they understood modern life through philosophical contemplation. In the black American fear led to dread, then anger, then self-hatred and ended in a sense of emptiness and meaninglessness—the ennui and malaise of Sartre's characters. But it was more than philosophy to the black man; it was life itself. He knew that his own unbearable times of futility arose when he was confronted by the abysmal ignorance and stupidity of the white man who could not understand what a Negro was saying. And his preoccupation with self-hate and anguish was an examination of a reality, not philosophy. . . .

The Outsider despaired that white Americans could liberate themselves from their fears, panic and terror when they confronted black men striving for liberation from irrational ties. Cross Damon, an intellectual black man, awakened in a society which could not contain such a giant. In an immoral society, a man conditioned, shaped and molded by that society attempted to form his own morality and failed.

Perhaps we should define freedom negatively, by showing what it is not, Richard had told Jean-Paul Sartre. And the anti-hero of *The Outsider*, a rebel without a set of values, finds an uncreative freedom because it is in a vacuum. Richard used elements from existentialist thought, picked up the philosophy as if it were a dark coat, plucked out the threads he needed and then threw it aside. Just like the French existentialists Richard knew, Damon was driven by an emotional compulsion, religious in its intensity, to feel and weigh the worth of himself. He longed for an experience deeply felt enough to remove or transform his eternal sense of dread. But at the edge of doom Damon drew back and repudiated a dead-end philosophy. Struggling to still an exploding ball of fire that leaped white-hot in his chest, he warned: the search cannot be done alone; never alone; alone a man was nothing. A bridge between man and man had to be made. Tell others not to come down this road, he forced through dying lips.

Constance Webb. *Richard Wright: A Biography*
(New York, G. P. Putnam's Sons, 1968),
pp. 280, 310

Lawd Today, Richard Wright's first novel (published posthumously in 1963), is in some ways more sophisticated than his second, the more sensational *Native Son,* which established his popularity, and to a large extent his reputation. It is ironic that this should be so in view of the fact that *Native Son* has subsequently come to be regarded as a brilliant but erratic work by an author who was perhaps ignorant of modern experimental techniques in prose fiction. For had *Lawd Today* been published when Wright completed it, such an impression might never have gained acceptance.

If the novel reveals anything about its author, it indicates that Wright had learned his Joyce, his Dos Passos, his James T. Farrell, his Gertrude Stein only too well. It is not that *Lawd Today* is a hodgepodge of the styles of the above authors—actually, Wright is usually in good control of his material—but that Wright here appears as much interested in craftsmanship, form and technique, as he is in making explicit social comment. Indeed, social comment derives from the way Wright structures the novel—twenty-four hours in the life of a Negro postal worker—and the theme does not confine itself to Negro oppression but says something about the very quality of life in urban America. Moreover, Wright uses here for the first time a Negro anti-hero: Jake Jackson is a loutish, heavy-handed, narrow, frustrated, and prejudiced petit bourgeois who, though unable to cope with his environment, refuses to reject it—and is incapable of dreaming of a life different from the kind he knows. Yet, for all his limitations, Wright invests him with a sense of life that simmers just below the surface of his dreary existence.

Here then lies the crux of Wright's success, for despite the huge indebtedness to other modern authors, the book is distinctly Wright's and the life and times he evokes are as immediate and as crushingly felt as his more popular radical fiction.

Edward Margolies. *The Art of Richard Wright*
(Carbondale, Southern Illinois University Press,
1969), pp. 90–91

There was a brief, wonderful trip to Paris in 1946, a return to New York in November, and in the following July the Wrights returned to Paris for good. . . .

The native son, the black boy from Mississippi, spent the rest of his life as an adopted citizen of France. And the work in exile, book after book, was voluminous. But as he sent these new books back across the seas, critics began to feel that the serenity he had chosen for himself had severely damaged his writing. While the man was surviving in peace, the tight hard center of the talent was getting unwound. If there are no second acts in the dramas of American writers' lives, the work of Richard Wright in France seemed to prove the rule in his case. Reviewing *The Long Dream* for the New York *Times* (October 26, 1958), Saunders Redding would speak of Wright as if he were already dead, calling (rather cruelly) in the last line: "Come back, Dick Wright, to life again!" . . .

Robert A. Bone has said that the last novel in exile, *The Long Dream*, is "a still more disastrous performance" than *The Outsider*. It is a strange verdict; while *The Long Dream* is a retreat to old ground, it is ground Wright knows well and can cover with considerable authority. . . .

The novel is a *Bildungsroman,* the story of a black boy's gradual discovery of what the Southern community means and the illness that it endures. If that is its strength, it was essentially the same strength of *Black Boy. The Long Dream* does not really take us into any new territory; it re-establishes Wright's claim to the old. . . .

The trouble with the new version was that it was not so cleanly written a book as was *Black Boy,* nor is it so consistently alert in its moral attention; Fishbelly's story is overlong, full of speeches, infected with Wright's late tendency to insert pat Freudian symbols, where too often the characters suddenly blurt into spokesmen for the author's message. Where it is good, *The Long Dream* is very good, conveying the harsh dirty world of the South as a surrealistic nightmare, yet Wright is not altogether sure of himself, and pads the narrative, falls into old errors.

Dan McCall. *The Example of Richard Wright*
(New York, Harcourt Brace Jovanovich, 1969),
pp. 138, 140, 155, 159–60

During the first week in June, 1938, I received in rapid succession two airmail special delivery letters. I answered one at once but before he could receive my answer he wrote again in great excitement. He said, "I have just learned of a case in Chicago that has broken there and is exactly like the story I am starting to write. See if you can get the newspaper clippings and send them to me." The case was that of a young black boy named Nixon who had been accused of rape, and when the police captured him they forced a confession of five major crimes, of which rape was only one.

I went at once to the offices of the five daily Chicago newspapers to get all the back issues; and I began what lasted a year, sending Wright every clipping published in the newspapers on the Nixon case. Frankly, there were times when the clippings were so lurid I recoiled from the headlines, and the details in the stories were worse. They called Nixon a big black baboon. When I went into news offices or bought papers on the stands, I listened to jeers and ugly insults about all black people. . . .

[In November] Wright explained a little about the new book and told about the clippings. He said he had enough to spread all over his nine by twelve bedroom floor and he was using them in the same way Dreiser had done in *An American Tragedy.* He would spread them all out and read them over and over again and then take off from there in his own imagination. The major portion of *Native Son* is built on information and action of those clippings. . . .

    We went to the Library and checked out on my library card two books we found on the Loeb-Leopold case and on Clarence Darrow, their lawyer. The lawyer's defense of Bigger in *Native Son* was modeled after Darrow's defense. Wright was so long sending those books back that I wrote him a hot letter reminding him that I had not borrowed those books permanently! He finished the book early in the Spring of 1939 and he wrote that he had never worked so hard before in all his life.

Margaret Walker Alexander. In David Ray and
Robert M. Farnsworth, eds., Richard Wright:
Impressions and Perspectives (Ann Arbor, University
of Michigan Press, 1973), pp. 58–61

Like the period 1947–52, the last years of Wright's life could have merely corresponded to a pessimistic phase. His close friends and relatives all testify that he did not at the time suffer from even the slightest mental illness, and his work is certainly confirmation of this. The evidence, in fact, betrays nothing more than intense physical exhaustion due to recurring disease, combined with a nervous reaction to the numerous "slings and arrows of outrageous fortune." Wright's heart attack, then, can be characterized as an indirect consequence of the tensions which he suffered throughout his life, as well as the more immediate result of his recent illness and anxiety, and was not hastened or heralded by any sort of mental derangement.

    Answering this last question is important in evaluating Wright's literary career because it enables us to consider whether, as some American critics claim, Wright's death may be interpreted as the natural conclusion to a period of artistic decline due to his living abroad, or, rather, as the abrupt interruption of a cyclic process of development. Even admitting that the best of Wright's fiction was written in the early forties, I am in favor of the second interpretation and would rather say that death caught him in a period of evolution. . . .

    It seems unfair, therefore, to limit Wright's literary achievements to two books just because critics are right in hailing them as his best. *Black Boy* and *Native Son* do not represent the extent of Wright's accomplishment and critics should beware of claiming that Wright could never find literary salvation outside of the Old South and the ghetto.

Michel Fabre. The Unfinished Quest of Richard
Wright (New York, William Morrow, 1973),
pp. 525, 527

WORKS MENTIONED

Listed here, author by author, are all works mentioned in the critical selections. Each writer's works are arranged alphabetically, and the year of first publication is given. The language of writers not publishing in English is given after their names, and their works are arranged alphabetically by the literal translation used uniformly throughout this book. Following each literal translation in parentheses are the original title and the date of first publication. If a published translation of a full-length work exists, its title and year of first publication is given after a colon. Collections of an author's work in English translation that do not correspond to a collection in the original language are listed at the end of the author's works.

ABRAHAMS, PETER

Dark Testament, 1942
Mine Boy, 1946
A Night of Their Own, 1965
The Path of Thunder, 1948
Song of the City, 1945
Tell Freedom, 1954
This Island Now, 1966
Wild Conquest, 1950
A Wreath for Udomo, 1956

ACHEBE, CHINUA

Arrow of God, 1964
Girls at War, and Other Stories, 1972
A Man of the People, 1966
Morning Yet on Creation Day, 1975
No Longer At Ease, 1960
"Onitsha, Gift of the Niger," 1975
Things Fall Apart, 1958

AIDOO, AMA ATA

Anowa, 1970
The Dilemma of a Ghost, 1965
"No Sweetness Here," 1963
No Sweetness Here, 1970

ALEXIS, JACQUES-STÉPHEN (French)

Comrade General Sun (*Compère Général Soleil*, 1955)
In the Blink of an Eye (*L'espace d'un cillement*, 1959)
The Musical Trees (*Les arbres musiciens*, 1957)
Romancero in the Stars (*Romancero aux étoiles*, 1960)

ALUKO, T. M.

Chief the Honourable Minister, 1970
His Worshipful Majesty, 1973
Kinsman and Foreman, 1966
One Man, One Matchet, 1964
One Man, One Wife, 1959

AMADI, ELECHI

The Concubine, 1966
The Great Ponds, 1969

ANTHONY, MICHAEL

"Cricket in the Road," 1973
Cricket in the Road, 1973
The Games Were Coming, 1963
Green Days by the River, 1967
"The Valley of Cocoa," 1961
The Year in San Fernando, 1965

ARMAH, AYI KWEI

The Beautyful Ones Are Not Yet Born, 1967
Fragments, 1970
Two Thousand Seasons, 1973
Why Are We So Blest?, 1972

ATTAWAY, WILLIAM

Blood on the Forge, 1941
Let Me Breathe Thunder, 1939

AWOONOR, KOFI

"Lament of the Silent Sister," 1971
Night of My Blood, 1971
Rediscovery, 1964
This Earth, My Brother..., 1971

BALDWIN, JAMES

The Amen Corner, 1968
Another Country, 1962
Blues for Mister Charlie, 1964
The Fire Next Time, 1963
Giovanni's Room, 1956
Go Tell It on the Mountain, 1953
If Beale Street Could Talk, 1974
Nobody Knows My Name, 1961
Notes of a Native Son, 1955
Tell Me How Long the Train's Been Gone, 1968

BARAKA, AMIRI

Blues People: Negro Music in White America, 1963
"The Clearing," 1961
The Dead Lecturer, 1964
Dutchman, 1964
"Notes for a Speech," 1961
Preface to a Twenty Volume Suicide Note, 1961
The Slave, 1964
Slave Ship, 1967
The System of Dante's Hell, 1965
The Toilet, 1967
"The Turncoat," 1961

BETI, MONGO (French)

African Unity ("L'unité africaine," 1960)
Cruel Town (*Ville cruelle*, 1954)
The King Miraculously Healed (*Le roi miraculé*, 1958): *King Lazarus*, 1960
Mission Accomplished (*Mission terminée*, 1957): *Mission to Kala*, 1958
Perpétue and the Habit of Unhappiness (*Perpétue et l'habitude de malheur*, 1974)
Plunder of Cameroon (*Main basse sur le Cameroun*, 1972)
The Poor Christ of Bomba (*Le pauvre Christ de Bomba*, 1956): *The Poor Christ of Bomba*, 1971
Tumultuous Cameroon ("Tumultueux Cameroun," 1959)
Without Hate, without Love ("Sans haine et sans amour," 1953)

BHÊLY-QUÉNUM, OLYMPE (French)

An Endless Trap (*Un piège sans fin*, 1960)
The Song of the Lake (*Le chant du lac*, 1965)

BONTEMPS, ARNA

Black Thunder, 1936
Drums at Dusk, 1939
God Sends Sunday, 1931
Personals, 1963

BRATHWAITE, EDWARD

The Arrivants: A New World Trilogy, 1973
  Rights of Passage, 1967
  Masks, 1968
  Islands, 1969

BROOKS, GWENDOLYN

"The Anniad," 1949
Annie Allen, 1949
"The Ballad of Rudolph Reed," 1960
"The Bean Eaters," 1960
The Bean Eaters, 1960
Beckonings, 1975
"A Black Wedding Song," 1975
"Five Men against the Theme 'My Name Is Red Hot. Yo Name Ain
    Doodley Squat,'" 1975
In the Mecca, 1968
Maud Martha, 1953
Report from Part One, 1972
"Sammy Chester Leaves 'Godspell' and Visits *Upward Bound* on a
    Lake Forest Lawn, Bringing West Afrika," 1975
A Street in Bronzeville, 1945

BROWN, STERLING A.

"Children of the Mississippi," 1932
"The Last Ride of Wild Bill," 1975
The Last Ride of Wild Bill, and Eleven Narrative Poems, 1975
Southern Road, 1932

BRUTUS, DENNIS

China Poems, 1975
Letters to Martha, and Other Poems from a South African Prison, 1968
Poems from Algiers, 1970
Sirens, Knuckles, Boots, 1963
Thoughts Abroad, 1970

BULLINS, ED

Clara's Ole Man, 1968
The Duplex, 1971
The Electronic Nigger, 1969
The Fabulous Miss Marie, 1972
The Gentleman Caller, 1968
Goin' A Buffalo, 1969
The Hungered One, 1971
In New England Winter, 1969
In the Wine Time, 1969
The Pig Pen, 1971
The Reluctant Rapist, 1973
The Taking of Miss Janie, unpublished

CAMARA, LAYE (French)

The Black Child (*L'enfant noir*, 1953): *The Dark Child*, 1954
Dramouss (*Dramouss*, 1966): *A Dream of Africa*, 1968
The Gaze of the King (*Le regard du roi*, 1954): *The Radiance of the King*, 1956

CÉSAIRE, AIMÉ (French)

And the Dogs Were Silent (*Et les chiens se taisaient*, 1956)
Discourse on Colonialism (*Discours sur le colonialisme*, 1950): *Discourse on Colonialism*, 1972
Notebook on a Return to My Native Land (*Cahier d'un retour au pays natal*, 1939): *Return to My Native Land*, 1969
A Season in the Congo (*Une saison au Congo*, 1966): *A Season in the Congo*, 1969
A Tempest (*Une tempête*, 1969)
The Tragedy of King Christophe (*La tragédie du roi Christophe*, 1963): *The Tragedy of King Christophe*, 1970

CHESNUTT, CHARLES W.

The Conjure Woman, 1899
The Colonel's Dream, 1905

The House behind the Cedars, 1900
The Marrow of Tradition, 1901
"Mars Jeems's Nightmare," 1899
"A Matter of Principle," 1899
"Po' Sandy," 1899
"The Wife of His Youth," 1898
The Wife of His Youth, and Other Stories of the Color Line, 1899

CLARK, JOHN PEPPER

America, Their America, 1964
Casualties: Poems 1966–68, 1970
The Masquerade, 1964
Ozidi, 1966
Poems, 1962
The Raft, 1964
A Reed in the Tide, 1965
Song of a Goat, 1961

CULLEN, COUNTEE

The Ballad of the Brown Girl, 1927
"The Black Christ," 1929
The Black Christ, and Other Poems, 1929
Caroling Dusk, 1927
Color, 1925
Copper Sun, 1927
"Heritage," 1925
The Lost Zoo, 1940
The Medea, 1935
One Way to Heaven, 1932
"The Shroud of Color," 1925
"Uncle Jim," 1927

DADIÉ, BERNARD BINLIN (French)

The Black Skirt (*Le pagne noir*, 1955)
Boss of New York (*Patron de New York*, 1964)
The Circle of Days (*La ronde des jours*, 1956)
Climbié (*Climbié*, 1956): *Climbié*, 1971
A Negro in Paris (*Un Nègre à Paris*, 1959)

DAMAS, LÉON-GONTRAN (French)

Black Label (*Black-Label*, 1956)
Et Cetera ("Et cætera," 1937)

Graffiti (*Graffiti*, 1952)
Limbed ("Limbé," 1937)
Pigments (*Pigments*, 1937)
Reality ("Réalité," 1937)

African Songs of Love, War, Grief, and Abuse, 1963

DEMBY, WILLIAM

Beetlecreek, 1950
The Catacombs, 1965

DIOP, BIRAGO (French)

The Bone ("L'os," 1958)
Breaths ("Souffles," 1960)
An Errand ("Une commission," 1947)
The Excuse ("Le prétexte," 1958)
The Inheritance ("L'héritage," 1947)
Little-Husband ("Petit-mari," 1947)
Lures and Lights (*Leurres et lueurs*, 1960)
New Tales of Amadou Koumba (*Les nouveaux contes d'Amadou Koumba*, 1958)
Tales of Amadou Koumba (*Les contes d'Amadou Koumba*, 1947)

Tales of Amadou Koumba (selections from both *Les contes* and *Les nouveaux contes*), 1966

DIOP, DAVID (French)

Hammer Blows (*Coups de pilon, 1956*): *Hammer Blows* in *Hammer Blows, and Other Writings*, 1973
Negro Tramp ("Nègre clochard," 1956)
To a Black Child ("À un enfant noir," 1956)
The Vultures ("Les vautours," 1956)

DUNBAR, PAUL LAURENCE

"At Shaft 11," 1898
The Fanatics, 1901
Folks from Dixie, 1898
"The Ingrate," 1899
"Keep a-Pluggin' Away," 1893
"Little Brown Baby," 1897

The Love of Landry, 1900
Majors and Minors, 1895
"A Negro Love Song," 1895
"One Man's Fortunes," 1900
"The Poet," 1902
"Preparation," 1895
"Silas Jackson," 1900
The Sport of the Gods, 1902
"The Strength of Gideon," 1899
"Sympathy," 1899
"The Trustfulness of Polly," 1900
The Uncalled, 1898
"We Wear the Mask," 1896
"When de Co'n Pone's Hot," 1895
"When Malindy Sings," 1895

EKWENSI, CYPRIAN

Beautiful Feathers, 1963
Burning Grass, 1962
Iska, 1966
Jagua Nana, 1961
People of the City, 1954
When Love Whispers, 1947

ELLISON, RALPH

Invisible Man, 1952
Shadow and Act, 1964

GAINES, ERNEST J.

The Autobiography of Miss Jane Pittman, 1971
Bloodline, 1968
Catherine Carmier, 1964
Of Love and Dust, 1967

HANSBERRY, LORRAINE

Les Blancs, 1972
The Drinking Gourd, 1972
A Raisin in the Sun, 1960
The Sign in Sidney Brustein's Window, 1965

HARRIS, WILSON

Ascent to Omai, 1970
Black Marsden, 1972
Companions of the Day and Night, 1975
Eternity to Season, 1960
The Eye of the Scarecrow, 1965
The Far Journey of Oudin, 1961
Palace of the Peacock, 1960
The Secret Ladder, 1963
Tumatumari, 1968
The Waiting Room, 1967
The Whole Armour, 1962

HAYDEN, ROBERT

Angle of Ascent, 1975
"The Diver," 1966
"Frederick Douglass," 1962
Heart-Shape in the Dust, 1940
the lion and the archer, 1948
"Middle Passage," 1962
"Ole Jim Crow," 1940
Selected Poems, 1966
"These Are My People," 1940

HIMES, CHESTER

All Shot Up, 1960
The Big Gold Dream, 1960
Cast the First Stone, 1952
The Crazy Kill, 1959
Cotton Comes to Harlem, 1965
For Love of Imabelle, 1957
If He Hollers Let Him Go, 1945
Lonely Crusade, 1947
The Primitive, 1955
The Quality of Hurt, 1972
The Real Cool Killers, 1959
The Third Generation, 1954

HUGHES, LANGSTON

Ask Your Mama, 1961
The Big Sea, 1940
"Crowns and Garlands," 1967

"Dinner Guest: Me," 1967
"Final Call," 1967
Fine Clothes to the Jew, 1927
Five Plays, 1963
"Justice," 1967
Laughing to Keep from Crying, 1952
Little Ham, 1963
Montage of a Dream Deferred, 1951
"Northern Liberal," 1967
Not without Laughter, 1930
One-Way Ticket, 1949
The Panther and the Lash, 1967
Selected Poems, 1959
Simply Heavenly, 1958
Soul Gone Home, 1937
Tambourines to Glory, 1958 (novel)
Tambourines to Glory, 1958 (play)
The Ways of White Folks, 1934
The Weary Blues, 1926

HURSTON, ZORA NEALE

Dust Tracks on a Road, 1942
Jonah's Gourd Vine, 1934
Moses, Man of the Mountain, 1939
Mules and Men, 1935
Seraph on the Suwanee, 1948
Tell My Horse, 1938
Their Eyes Were Watching God, 1937

JOHNSON, JAMES WELDON

Along This Way: The Autobiography of James Weldon Johnson, 1933
The Autobiography of an Ex-Colored Man, 1912 (reprinted 1927 with
    spelling "Ex-Coloured")
The Book of American Negro Poetry, 1922 (editor)
"The Creation," 1920
"Fifty Years," 1913
Fifty Years, and Other Poems, 1917
God's Trombones: Seven Negro Sermons in Verse, 1927
"O Black and Unknown Bards," 1908

JORDAN, A. C. (Xhosa and English)

Tales from Southern Africa, 1973
Towards an African Literature, 1973
The Wrath of the Ancestors (*Ingqumbo yeminyanya*, 1940)

KANE, CHEIKH HAMIDOU (French)

Ambiguous Adventure (*L'aventure ambiguë*, 1961): *Ambiguous Adventure*, 1963

KELLEY, WILLIAM MELVIN

Dancers on the Shore, 1964
dem, 1967
A Different Drummer, 1962
A Drop of Patience, 1965
Dunfords Travels Everywheres, 1970

KILLENS, JOHN OLIVER

And Then We Heard the Thunder, 1963
The Cotillion, 1971
'Sippi, 1967
Youngblood, 1954

KUNENE, MAZISI

"Anthem of Decades," 1970
"Europe," 1970
"Exile," 1970
Zulu Poems, 1970

LA GUMA, ALEX

And a Threefold Cord, 1964
In the Fog of the Season's End, 1972
The Stone Country, 1967
A Walk in the Night, 1962

LAMMING, GEORGE

The Emigrants, 1954
In the Castle of My Skin, 1953
Natives of My Person, 1972
Of Age and Innocence, 1958
The Pleasures of Exile, 1960
Season of Adventure, 1960
Water with Berries, 1971

MARAN, RENÉ (French)

Batouala (*Batouala*, 1921): *Batouala*, 1922
The Book of the Bush (*Le livre de la brousse*, 1934)

MCKAY, CLAUDE

Banana Bottom, 1933
Banjo, 1929
"Enslaved," 1921
"Flame-Heart," 1920
Gingertown, 1932
"The Harlem Dancer," 1917
"Harlem Shadows," 1922
Harlem Shadows, 1922
Home to Harlem, 1928
"If We Must Die," 1919
A Long Way from Home, 1927
"Outcast," 1922
"Spring in New Hampshire," 1919
"To the White Fiends," 1919

MITTELHOLZER, EDGAR

Children of Kaywana, 1952
Corentyne Thunder, 1941
The Harrowing of Hubertus, 1954
Kaywana Blood, 1958
A Morning at the Office, 1950

MOFOLO, THOMAS (Sotho)

Chaka (*Chaka*, 1925): *Chaka*, 1931
The Traveller of the East (*Moeti oa bochabela*, 1907): *The Traveller of the East*, 1934
Pitseng (*Pitseng*, 1910)

MORRISON, TONI

The Bluest Eye, 1970
Sula, 1974

MPHAHLELE, EZEKIEL

Down Second Avenue, 1959
In Corner B, 1967
The Living and the Dead, and Other Stories, 1961
Man Must Live, and Other Stories, 1946
The Wanderers, 1971

MQHAYI, S E. K. (Xhosa)

The Case of the Twins ("Ityala lama-wele," 1914): "The Case of the
    Twins" in *The New African*, Jan.–April, 1966
The Case of the Twins (*Ityala lama-wele*, 1914)
Don Jadu (*U-Don Jadu*, 1929)
Reward (*I-nzuzo*, 1942)

NGUGI WA THIONG'O

The Black Hermit, 1968
A Grain of Wheat, 1967
*Homecoming: Essays on African and Caribbean Literature, Culture and
    Politics*, 1972
The River Between, 1965
Weep Not, Child, 1964

NZEKWU, ONUORA

Blade among the Boys, 1962
Highlife for Lizards, 1965
Wand of Noble Wood, 1961

OKARA, GABRIEL

"Piano and Drums," 1959
The Voice, 1964

OKIGBO, CHRISTOPHER

"Distances," 1964
"Four Canzones," 1962
Heavensgate, 1962
Labryinths, with Path of Thunder, 1971
"Lament of the Silent Sisters," 1962
Limits, 1964
"Path of Thunder," 1968
"Silences," 1962, 1965

OYONO, FERDINAND (French)

The Life of a Houseboy (*Une vie de boy*, 1956): *Houseboy*, 1966
The Old Negro and the Medal (*Le vieux nègre et la médaille*, 1956):
    The Old Man and the Medal, 1967
The Road to Europe (*Chemin d'Europe*, 1960)

P'BITEK, OKOT

The Horn of My Love, 1974
Song of Lawino, 1966
Song of Ocol, 1970
Song of a Prisoner, 1971

PETERS, LENRIE

Poems, 1964
Satellites, 1967
The Second Round, 1965

PLAATJE, SOL T.

The Boer War Diary of Sol T. Plaatje, 1973
Mhudi, 1930
Native Life in South Africa, 1916

REED, ISHMAEL

Conjure, 1972
Flight to Canada, 1976
The Free-Lance Pallbearers, 1967
The Last Days of Louisiana Red, 1974
Mumbo Jumbo, 1972
Yellow Back Radio Broke-Down, 1969

ROUMAIN, JACQUES (French)

Ebony Wood (*Bois-d'ébène*, 1945): *Ebony Wood*, 1972
The Enchanted Mountain (*La montagne ensorcelée*, 1931)
Masters of the Dew (*Gouverneurs de la rosée*, 1944): *Masters of the
    Dew*, 1947
The Prey and the Darkness (*La proie et l'ombre*, 1930)
Puppets (*Les fantoches*, 1931)

SEMBÈNE, OUSMANE (French)

The Black Docker (*Le docker noir*, 1956)
The Black Girl of... ("La noire de...," 1962)
Emitaï (*Emitaï*, unpublished screenplay)
God's Bits of Wood (*Les bouts de bois de Dieu*, 1960): *God's Bits of Wood*, 1962
Her Three Days ("Ses trois jours," 1962)
Letters from France ("Lettres de France," 1962)
Man from Volta (*Voltaïque*, 1962): *Tribal Scars, and Other Stories*, 1975
The Money-Order [novel] (*Le mandat* in *Véhi-Ciosane ou Blanche-Genèse, suivi du Mandat*, 1965): *The Money-Order* in *The Money-Order, with White Genesis*, 1972
The Money-Order [film] (*Le Mandat*, unpublished screenplay)
Oh Country, My Beautiful People (*Oh pays, mon beau peuple*, 1957)
White Genesis (*Véhi-Ciosane ou Blanche-Genèse* in *Véhi-Ciosane ou Blanche-Genèse, suivi du Mandat*, 1965): *White Genesis* in *The Money-Order, with White Genesis*, 1972
Xala (*Xala*, 1973): *Xala*, 1976

SENGHOR, LEÓPOLD SÉDAR (French)

Black Hosts (*Hosties noires*, 1948)
Ethiopics (*Éthiopiques*, 1956)
Letter to a Poet ("Lettre à un poète," 1945)
Nationhood and the African Road to Socialism (*Nation et la voie africaine du socialisme*, 1961): *On African Socialism*, 1964
Night of Sine ("Nuit de Sine," 1945)
Nocturnes (*Nocturnes*, 1961): *Nocturnes*, 1971
Snow over Paris ("Neige sur Paris," 1945)
Songs of Darkness (*Chants d'ombre*, 1945)
Totem ("Le totem," 1945)
What the Black Man Brings ("Ce que l'homme noir apporte," 1939)

Selected Poems (New York, 1964)

SOYINKA, WOLE

A Dance of the Forests, 1963
"Idanre," 1967
Idanre, and Other Poems, 1967
The Interpreters, 1965
Kongi's Harvest, 1967
The Lion and the Jewel, 1963
Madmen and Specialists, 1971
The Man Died, 1972
Poems from Prison, 1969

The Road, 1965
"Salutations to the Gut," 1962
Season of Anomy, 1973
A Shuttle in the Crypt, 1972
The Strong Breed, 1963
The Swamp Dwellers, 1963
Three Plays, 1963
The Trials of Brother Jero, 1963

THOBY-MARCELIN, PHILIPPE and
MARCELIN, PIERRE (French)

All Men Are Mad (*Tous les hommes sont fous*, 1970): *All Men Are Mad*, 1970
The Beast of Musseau (*La bête de Musseau*, 1946): *The Beast of the Haitian Hills*, 1946
Canapé-Vert (*Canapé-Vert*, 1944): *Canapé-Vert*, 1944
The Pencil of God (*Le crayon de Dieu*, 1951): *The Pencil of God*, 1951

THURMAN, WALLACE

The Blacker the Berry, 1929
Harlem, unpublished (with William Jourdan Rapp)
Infants of the Spring, 1932

TOLSON, MELVIN B.

"Dark Symphony," 1941
Harlem Gallery, 1965
Libretto for the Republic of Liberia, 1953
"Rendezvous with America," 1942
Rendezvous with America, 1944

TOOMER, JEAN

Balo, 1927
"Blue Meridian," 1936
Cane, 1923
Eight Day World, unpublished
Essentials: Definitions and Aphorisms, 1931

TUTUOLA, AMOS

Ajaiyi and His Inherited Poverty, 1967
The Brave African Huntress, 1958

Feather Woman of the Jungle, 1962
My Life in the Bush of Ghosts, 1954
*The Palm-Wine Drinkard and His Dead Palm-Wine Tapster in the
    Deads' Town*, 1952
Simbi and the Satyr of the Dark Jungle, 1955

U TAM'SI, TCHICAYA (French)

The Belly (*Le ventre*, 1964)
Brush Fire (*Feu de brousse*, 1957): *Brush Fire*, 1964
Epitome (*Épitomé*, 1962)
Musical Arch (*Arc musical*, 1970)

Selected Poems, 1970

VILAKAZI, B. W. (Zulu)

For Ever (*Noma Nini*, 1935)
In the Gold Mines ("Ezinkomponi," 1945)
Truly, Indeed (*Nje Nempela*, 1949)
The Victoria Falls ("Impophoma yeVictoria," 1935)
Zulu Horizons (*Amal'ezulu*, 1945): *Zulu Horizons*, 1962
Zulu Songs (*Inkondlo kaZulu*, 1935): *Zulu Songs* in *Zulu Horizons*,
    1962

WALCOTT, DEREK

"The Almond Trees," 1965
Another Life, 1973
The Castaway, 1965
"Crusoe's Island," 1965
Dream on Monkey Mountain, 1970
"The Gulf," 1969
The Gulf, and Other Poems, 1969
In a Green Night, 1962
"In a Green Night," 1962
"Mass Man," 1969
"Return to D'Ennery, Rain," 1962
"Sea Grapes," 1976
Sea Grapes, 1976

WALKER, ALICE

In Love & Trouble: Stories of Black Women, 1973
Meridian, 1976
Once: Poems, 1968

Revolutionary Petunias, and Other Poems, 1973
The Third Life of Grange Copeland, 1970
"To Hell with Dying," 1973

WALKER, MARGARET

"The Ballad of the Free," 1970
For My People, 1942
"Girl Held without Bail," 1970
Jubilee, 1966
Prophets for a New Day, 1970
"Sit-Ins," 1970
"Sorrow Home," 1942
"Street Demonstration," 1970

WILLIAMS, JOHN A.

The Angry Ones, 1960
Captain Blackman, 1972
The Junior Bachelor Society, 1976
The Man Who Cried I Am, 1967
Mothersill and the Foxes, 1975
Night Song, 1961
Sissie, 1963
Sons of Darkness, Sons of Light, 1969

WRIGHT, RICHARD

"Big Boy Leaves Home," 1936
Black Boy, 1945
Black Power, 1954
Lawd Today, 1963
The Long Dream, 1958
Native Son, 1940
The Outsider, 1953
Uncle Tom's Children, 1938

COPYRIGHT ACKNOWLEDGMENTS

489

THE AMERICAN SCHOLAR. For excerpts from "From a Common Back Cloth: A Reassessment of the African Literary Image" by Wole Soyinka. Reprinted from *The American Scholar*, Volume 32, Number 3, Summer, 1963. Copyright © 1963 by the United Chapters of Phi Beta Kappa. By permission of the publishers (Achebe, Beti, Camara, Tutuola); "Charles W. Chesnutt: The Marrow of Tradition" by John Wideman. Reprinted from *The American Scholar*, Volume 42, Number 1, Winter, 1972–73. Copyright © 1972 by the United Chapters of Phi Beta Kappa. By permission of the publisher.

ASSOCIATION POUR LA DIFFUSION DE LA PENSÉE FRANÇAISE. For excerpts from article by Roger Mercier on Maran in *Tendances*.

THE ATLANTIC MONTHLY. For excerpt from article by Peter Davison on Brooks.

ÉDITIONS AUBIER-MONTAIGNE. For excerpts from Sunday O. Anozie, *Sociologie du roman africain* (Bhêly-Quénum, Kane).

HOUSTON A. BAKER, JR. For excerpt from article on Johnson in *The Virginia Quarterly Review*.

BEACON PRESS. For excerpt from James Baldwin, *Notes of a Native Son*. Copyright © 1951, 1955 by James Baldwin. Reprinted by permission of Beacon Press (Wright).

OLYMPE BHÊLY-QUÉNUM. For excerpt from article on Camara in *L'Afrique actuelle* 28, Avenue Émile Zola, 78300 Poissy, France.

BIM. For excerpts from articles by Edward Brathwaite on Harris, Lamming.

BLACK AMERICAN LITERATURE FORUM. For excerpt from article by Robert J. Willis on Hansberry in *Negro American Literature Forum*.

BLACK ORPHEUS. For excerpts from articles by Akanji on Camara; Ulli Beier on Clark, Okigbo, Sembène; J. P. Clark on Tutuola; Martin Esslin on Soyinka; Gerald Moore on U Tam'si; Lewis Nkosi on La Guma, Mphahlele; Paul Theroux on Awoonor, Brutus.

THE BLACK SCHOLAR. For excerpts from articles by Robert Chrisman on A. Walker; James T. Lampley on Williams.

THE BOBBS-MERRILL COMPANY, INC. For excerpt from Nikki Giovanni, *Gemini* (Chesnutt).

GEORGES BORCHARDT, INC. For excerpts from Franck Jotterand, *Le nouveau théâtre américain* (Bullins). Léopold Sédar Senghor, *Liberte I: Négritude et humanisme* (Abrahams, Camara, Césaire, U Tam'si).

ANTHONY BOXILL. For excerpt from article on Lamming in *World Literature Written in English*.

EDWARD BRATHWAITE. For excerpts from articles on Harris, Lamming in *Bim*.

1964 by The Modern Poetry Association; Laurence Lieberman on Hughes, copyright © 1968 by The Modern Poetry Association; Allen Tate on Tolson, copyright 1950 by The Modern Poetry Association; Amos N. Wilder on Brooks, copyright 1945 by The Modern Poetry Association. Reprinted by permission of the Editor of *Poetry*.

POETRY AUSTRALIA. For excerpt from article by James Tulip on Tolson.

JOHN POVEY. For excerpt from article on Brutus in *Journal of the New African Literature and the Arts*.

PRAEGER PUBLISHERS, INC. For excerpts from Margaret Laurence, *Long Drums and Cannons* (Aluko, Amadi, Nzekwu, Okara, Soyinka, Tutuola); Ezekiel Mphahlele, *The African Image* (Kunene, Plaatje).

PRÉSENCE AFRICAINE. For excerpts from Hubert Juin, *Aimé Césaire, poète noir*; Thomas Melone, *Mongo Béti: l'homme et le destin*; C. Quillateau, *Bernard Binlin Dadié: L'homme et l'œuvre*; Léopold Sédar Senghor's Preface to *Les nouveaux contes d'Amadou Koumba* by Birago Diop; Léopold Sédar Senghor's essay in *Hommage à René Maran*; Paulin Soumanou Vieyra, *Ousmane Sembène, cinéaste*; from articles by Olympe Bhêly-Quénum on B. Diop; Joseph Miezan Bognini on Dadié; Andrée Clair on Bhêly-Quénum; Gerald Moore on Oyono; anon. on D. Diop in *Présence africaine* (English edition); Mongo Beti on Camara; Maryse Conde on Amadi; Luc Decaunes on Mofolo; René Depestre on Dadié, D. Diop; Lamine Diakhaté on Sembène; David Diop on Beti, Oyono; Nicolás Guillen on Hughes; Barthélemy Kotchy on Maran; Georges Lamming on Tutuola; A. U. Ohaegbu on Sembène; Magdeleine Paz on B. Diop in *Présence africaine*.

PRINCETON UNIVERSITY PRESS. For excerpts from James Olney, *Tell Me Africa: An Approach to African Literature* (copyright © 1973 by Princeton University Press), pp. 126–127, 202–203, 280–281, and 283–284. Reprinted by permission of Princeton University Press (Achebe, Camara, Mphahlele, Ngugi).

THE PROGRESSIVE. For excerpt from article by Nora Sayre on Bullins. Reprinted by permission from *The Progressive*, 408 W. Gorham St., Madison, Wisc. 53703. Copyright © 1969, The Progressive, Inc.

G. P. PUTNAM'S SONS. For excerpts from Norman Mailer, *Advertisements for Myself* (Ellison); Constance Webb, *Richard Wright: A Biography*.

QUAGGA PRESS. For excerpt from Tim Couzens's Introduction to *Mhudi* by Sol. T. Plaatje.

RANDOM HOUSE, INC. For excerpts from Wilfred Cartey, *Whispers from a Continent* (Ekwensi); Ralph Ellison, *Shadow and Act*. Copyright © 1945 by Ralph Ellison. Reprinted by permission of Random House, Inc. (Baraka, Wright); John Simon, *Uneasy Stages* (Bullins); John Updike, *Picked-Up Pieces*. Copyright © 1971, 1974 by John Updike. Reprinted by permission of Alfred A. Knopf, Inc. Originally appeared in *The New Yorker* (Amadi,

Awoonor, La Guma, Mphahlele); Carl Van Vechten's Introduction to *The Autobiography of an Ex-Coloured Man* by James Weldon Johnson.

ARTHUR RAVENSCROFT. For excerpt from *Chinua Achebe*.

C. J. REA. For excerpt from article on Aidoo in *African Forum*.

J. SAUNDERS REDDING. For excerpts from articles on Achebe, Killens in *African Forum*; on Baldwin, Williams in *New York Herald Tribune Book Section*.

PAUL R. REYNOLDS, INC. For excerpts from John A. Williams's Introduction to *White Man, Listen!* by Richard Wright; Richard Wright's Introduction to *In the Castle of My Skin* by George Lamming; from articles by Richard Wright on Bontemps in *Partisan Review and Anvil*; on Himes in *PM*.

ALFRED RICE. For excerpt from article by Ernest M. Hemingway on Maran in *Toronto Star Weekly*.

HOWARD ROSENSTONE. For excerpt by Ed Bullins in *New Plays from the Black Theatre*, Ed Bullins, ed. (Baraka).

ROTHCO CARTOONS INC. For excerpt from article by David Pryce-Jones on Reed in *Punch*.

RUSSELL & VOLKENING, INC. For excerpts from articles by Nadine Gordimer on Abrahams, Achebe in *TLS*; on La Guma, Ngugi in *The Michigan Quarterly Review*. Reprinted by permission of Nadine Gordimer. Copyright © 1961, 1970, 1975 by Nadine Gordimer.

SATURDAY REVIEW. For excerpts from articles by John W. Aldridge on Baldwin; Arna Bontemps on Cullen, Hughes; David Boroff on Williams; Abraham Chapman on M. Walker; John Howard Griffin on Killens; Zora Neale Hurston on Wright; Alain Locke on Hughes; Charles Miller on Armah; Thomas Sugrue on Thoby-Marcelin and Marcelin in *Saturday Review*; Conor Cruise O'Brien on Soyinka in *World*. Copyright © 1927, 1938, 1944, 1952, 1963, 1966, 1968, 1973, 1974 by The Saturday Review, Inc.

THE SCARECROW PRESS, INC. For excerpt from Jacqueline Covo, *The Blinking Eye* (Ellison).

SCHOCKEN BOOKS INC. For excerpt from Wayne F. Cooper's Introduction to *The Passion of Claude McKay*. Copyright © 1973 by Wayne F. Cooper and Hope McKay Virtue.

MARTIN SECKER & WARBURG LIMITED. For excerpt from Alfred Kazin, *Contemporaries* (Baldwin).

ÉDITIONS SEGHERS. For excerpts from François Dodat, *Langston Hughes*; Lilyan Kesteloot, *Aimé Césaire*.

A. J. SEYMOUR. For excerpt from *Edgar Mittelholzer: The Man and His Work*.

KARL SHAPIRO. For excerpt from article on Tolson in *Wilson Library Bulletin*.

THE SHOE STRING PRESS, INC. For excerpts from Donald C. Dickinson, *A Bio-Bibliography of Langston Hughes, 1902–1967*; J. Noel Heermance, *Charles W. Chesnutt: America's First Great Black Novelist*. Reprinted by permission of Archon Books, The Shoe String Press, Inc., Hamden, Connecticut.

SOUTH AFRICAN OUTLOOK. For excerpts from articles by A. C. Jordan on Mqhayi; I. Oldjohn on Jordan; M. S. S. on Plaatje.

SOUTHERN ILLINOIS UNIVERSITY PRESS. For excerpts from *The Art of Richard Wright* by Edward Margolies. Copyright © 1969 by Southern Illinois University Press. Reprinted by permission of Southern Illinois University Press; *In a Minor Chord* by Darwin T. Turner. Copyright © 1971 by Southern Illinois University Press. Reprinted by permission of Southern Illinois University Press (Cullen, Hurston, Toomer).

SOUTHWEST REVIEW. For excerpt from article by James Presley on Hughes.

WOLE SOYINKA. For excerpt from article on Okara in *African Forum*.

THE SPECTATOR. For excerpts from articles by Anthony Burgess on Harris; Peter Cohen on Anthony; Geoffrey Grigson on Lamming; Auberon Waugh on Achebe.

STEPHEN SPENDER. For excerpt from article on Baldwin in *Partisan Review*; on Ellison in *The Listener*.

STANDPUNTE. For excerpt from article by R. H. W. Shepherd on Jordan.

STUDIES IN BLACK LITERATURE. For excerpts from articles by Joan Bischoff on Morrison; Donald Bayer Burness on Aidoo.

GUNTHER STUHLMANN. For excerpts from Edward Margolies, *Native Sons* (Attaway, Demby, Himes).

ROSLYN TARG LITERARY AGENCY. For excerpts from Chester Himes, *The Quality of Hurt* (Baldwin); William Targ, *Indecent Pleasures* (Himes).

ELLEN TARRY. For excerpt from *The Third Door* (McKay).

ALLEN TATE. For excerpt from article on Tolson in *Poetry*.

THREE CONTINENTS PRESS. For excerpt from Richard Priebe's essay in *Critical Perspectives on Amos Tutuola*, Bernth Lindfors, ed.

EDWIN THUMBOO. For excerpts from articles on Brutus in *Joliso*; on Peters in *African Literature Today*.

TIMES NEWSPAPERS LIMITED. For excerpts from articles by C. P. Snow on Abrahams in *The Sunday Times*; anon. on Abrahams, Himes, Mittelholzer, Mofolo, Nzekwu, Soyinka in *The Times Literary Supplement*.

RUTH S. TOLSON. For excerpts from articles by Melvin B. Tolson on Peters in *African Forum*; on Wright in *The Modern Quarterly*.

TRANSITION. For excerpts from articles by Daniel Abasiekong on Brutus; Chinua Achebe on Awoonor; John Pepper Clark on Okara, Okigbo; David Cook on Soyinka; David Rubadiri on Abrahams; Austin J. Shelton on Achebe.

TWAYNE PUBLISHERS, INC. For excerpts from Harold E. Collins, *Amos Tutuola*; Joy Flasch, *Melvin B. Tolson*.

TWENTIETH CENTURY LITERATURE. For excerpt from article by Neil Schmitz on Reed.

UNIVERSITY OF CALIFORNIA PRESS. For excerpts from Albert S. Gérard, *Four African Literatures: Xhosa, Sotho, Zulu, Amharic*. Copyright © 1971 by Regents of the University of California. Reprinted by permission of the University of California Press (Jordan, Mofolo, Mqhayi, Vilakazi); from article by Lyle Pearson on Sembène in *Film Quarterly*.

THE UNIVERSITY OF CHICAGO MAGAZINE. For excerpt from article by Ralph Ellison on Baldwin. Reprinted with permission from the April, 1962 *University of Chicago Magazine*.

THE UNIVERSITY OF CHICAGO PRESS. For excerpt from Eugene Levy, *James Weldon Johnson: Black Leader, Black Voice*. Copyright © 1973 by The University of Chicago Press.

THE UNIVERSITY OF MICHIGAN PRESS. For excerpt from Robert M. Farnsworth's Introduction to *The Conjure Woman* by Charles W. Chesnutt.

THE UNIVERSITY OF MINNESOTA PRESS. For excerpts from O. R. Dathorne, *The Black Mind* (Aluko, Damas, Mofolo, Mqhayi, Okara, Okigbo, U Tam'si).

UNIVERSITY OF NATAL PRESS. For excerpt from C. L. S. Nyembezi, *A Review of Zulu Literature* (Vilakazi).

THE UNIVERSITY OF NORTH CAROLINA PRESS. For excerpts from Benjamin Brawley, *Paul Lawrence Dunbar*; Hugh Gloster, *Negro Voices in American Fiction* (Bontemps, Chesnutt, Dunbar, Johnson, Thurman); J. Saunders Redding, *To Make a Poet Black* (Chesnutt, Cullen, Dunbar).

UNIVERSITY OF OKLAHOMA PRESS. For excerpts from articles by Martin Banham on La Guma; David Dorsey on Brutus; Robert E. Morsberger on Peters; C. E. Nelson on Damas; Richard Priebe on Aluko, Armah, Soyinka; Edwin Thumboo on Clark; C. H. Wake on Senghor in *Books Abroad* (now *World Literature Today*).

THE UNIVERSITY OF WISCONSIN PRESS. For excerpt from Robert E. Fleming, "The Nightmare Level of *The Man Who Cried I Am*," in *Contemporary Literature*, © 1973 by the Regents of the University of Wisconsin (Williams).

THE VIKING PRESS INC. For excerpts from Eric Bentley, *Theatre of War*, copyright © 1972 by Eric Bentley (Baraka); Ellen Conroy Kennedy in *The Negritude Poets*, Ellen Conroy Kennedy, ed., copyright © 1975 by Ellen Conroy Kennedy (Senghor); David Littlejohn, *Black on White*, copyright © 1966 by David Littlejohn, reprinted by permission of Grossman Publishers (Dunbar, Killens).

THE VILLAGE VOICE. For excerpt from article by Alice Walker on Walcott. Reprinted by permission of *The Village Voice*. Copyright © The Village Voice, Inc., 1974.

THE VIRGINIA QUARTERLY REVIEW. For excerpts from articles by Houston A. Baker, Jr., on Johnson; Raymond Nelson on Himes.

HOPE MCKAY VIRTUE. For excerpt from Claude McKay, *Harlem: Negro Metropolis* (Johnson).

JEAN WAGNER. For excerpts from *Black Poets of the United States* (Brown, Cullen, Dunbar, Johnson, McKay, Toomer).

A. P. WATT & SON. For excerpts from Margaret Laurence, *Long Drums and Cannons* (Aluko, Amadi, Nzekwu, Okara, Soyinka, Tutuola).

WEST AFRICA. For excerpts from articles by Ama Ata Aidoo on Brathwaite, Soyinka; George Awoonor-Williams on Tutuola; D. B. on Amadi; K. W. on Aidoo.

AMOS N. WILDER. For excerpt from article on Brooks in *Poetry*.

WITWATERSRAND UNIVERSITY PRESS. For excerpts from D. D. T. Jabavu's review of *Inzuzo* by S. E. K. Mqhayi (2, 3, 1943); John Riordan, "The Wrath of the Ancestral Spirits" (20, 1, 1961) (Jordan, Mqhayi) in *African Studies*; J. Dexter Taylor, "*Ikondlo ka Zulu:* An Appreciation" (9, 2, 1935) in *Bantu Studies* (Vilakazi).

WORLD LITERATURE WRITTEN IN ENGLISH. For excerpts from articles by Anthony Boxill on Lamming; Harold R. Collins on Armah; R. Langenkamp on Clark.

THE YALE REVIEW. For excerpts from articles by Louis O. Coxe on Abrahams; Babette Deutsch on Brooks. Copyright © 1950, 1955 by Yale University.

YALE UNIVERSITY LIBRARY. For excerpt from article by Fannie Hurst on Hurston in *The Yale University Library Gazette*.

YALE UNIVERSITY PRESS. For excerpts from Stephen Vincent Benét's Foreword to *For My People* by Margaret Walker; Kimberly W. Benston, *Baraka: The Renegade and the Mask*; Robert A. Bone, *The Negro Novel in America* (Attaway, Bontemps, Demby, Himes, Hughes, Hurston, McKay, Toomer).

ZAÏRE-AFRIQUE. For excerpt from article by Christophe Gudijiga on Camara in *Congo-Afrique*.

INDEX TO CRITICS

Names of critics are cited on the pages given.